The Game Is Afoot

PARODIES, PASTICHES AND
PONDERINGS OF SHERLOCK HOLMES

The Game Is
Afoot

PARODIES, PASTICHES AND
PONDERINGS OF
Sherlock Holmes

Edited by Marvin Kaye

ST. MARTIN'S PRESS NEW YORK

To
the memory of
Arthur Conan Doyle
and
Basil Rathbone

Production Editor: David Stanford Burr
Design: Judith A. Stagnitto

Library of Congress Cataloging-in-Publication Data

The Game is afoot / Marvin Kaye, editor.
        p.   cm.
      ISBN 0-312-10468-5
      1. Detective and mystery stories, English—Parodies, imitations,
etc.   2. Holmes, Sherlock (Fictitious character)—Fiction.
3. Detective and mystery stories, American.   4. Holmes, Sherlock
(Fictitious character)   I. Kaye, Marvin.
PR1309.H55G35   1994
823.008'0351—dc20
                                       93-44057
                                         CIP

First Edition: April 1994

10 9 8 7 6 5 4 3 2 1

Contents

SIX CLASSIC PASTICHES

SCHOLARLY PONDERINGS

PARODIES ABSURDES ET CRUELLES

NEW ADVENTURES OF SHERLOCK HOLMES

PIECES PROBLEMATICAL

Acknowledgments

"A Study in Scarlet" (p. xiv) and "The Adventure of the Retired Colourman" (p. 514) copyright © 1978 Isaac Asimov, from *Asimov's Sherlockian Limericks,* published by permission of the Estate of Isaac Asimov, c/o Ralph Vicinanza, Ltd.

"The Adventure of the Circular Room" by August Derleth copyright © 1946, 1951 April R. Derleth and Walden W. Derleth, reprinted by permission of Arkham House Publishers, Inc.

"The Adventure of the Marked Man" by Stuart Palmer copyright © 1944 The American Mercury, Inc. for *Ellery Queen's Mystery Magazine,* July 1944, reprinted by permission of Scott Meredith Literary Agency, Inc.

"The Enchanted Garden" copyright © 1949 H. F. Heard, renewed 1977 by Gerald Heard, reprinted by permission of Russell and Volkening, Inc., as agents for the author.

"But Our Hero Was Not Dead" by Manly Wade Wellman, copyright © 1941 *Argosy Magazine,* reprinted by permission of The Pimlico Agency.

"In the Island of Uffa" copyright © 1965 Poul Anderson, reprinted by permission of the author.

"The Tibetan Adventures of Sherlock Holmes" copyright © 1982 Amanda Russell, reprinted by permission of the author.

"The Histrionic Holmes" copyright © 1971, 1994 Marvin Kaye. All rights reserved.

"How Holmes Came to Play the Violin" copyright © 1951 Jacques Barzun, reprinted by permission of the author.

"The Really Final Solution" copyright © 1994 Nick Pollotta, published by permission of the author.

"A Letter from Mycroft Holmes" copyright © 1968 Jon White, reprinted by permission of the author.

"The Murder of Conan Doyle" copyright © 1955 Ray Russell, reprinted from *Playboy* by permission of the author.

"The Adventure of the Conk-Singleton Papers" by John Dickson

Carr, copyright © 1949 Unicorn Mystery Book Club, Inc., reprinted by permission of Harold Ober Associates, Inc.

"Journal of a Ghurka Physician" copyright © 1994 Daniel M. Pinkwater, published with the permission of the author.

"The Struldbrugg Reaction" by John Sutherland, copyright © 1964 Mercury Press, Inc., for *The Magazine of Fantasy and Science Fiction,* July 1964. Reprinted by permission of the author.

"The Moriarty Gambit" copyright © 1962 Fritz Leiber, from *Chess Review,* V. 30 # 2, reprinted by permission of the Richard Curtis literary agency.

"The Adventure of the Missing Countess" copyright © 1994 Jon Koons, published by permission of the author.

"The Gibraltar Letter" copyright © 1990 Sam Benady, reprinted by permission of Gibraltar Books, Ltd.

"The Strange Case of the Tongue-Tied Tenor" copyright © 1994 Carole Buggé, published by permission of the author.

"Our American Cousins" copyright © 1994 Roberta Rogow, published by permission of the author.

"Sussex Interview" by P. M. Stone, copyright © 1940, 1969 Vincent Starrett, reprinted by permission of Biblo & Tannen, Inc.

"The Adventure of the Bogle-Wolf" copyright © 1949 Anthony Boucher, from *Illustrious Client's Second Case-Book* edited by J. N. Williamson, reprinted by permission of Curtis Brown, Ltd.

"Sherlock Holmes in Oz" copyright © 1994 Ruth Berman, reprinted by permission of the author.

"The Sinister Cheesecake" copyright © 1994 Craig Shaw Gardner, published by permission of the author.

"The Adventure of the Death-Fetch" copyright © 1994 Darrell Schweitzer, published by permission of the author.

"The Theft of the Persian Slipper" copyright © 1976 Edward D. Hoch, first published in *Ellery Queen's Mystery Magazine,* February 1977, reprinted by permission of the author.

"The Dynamics of an Asteroid" copyright © 1953 Robert Bloch, reprinted by permission of The Pimlico Agency.

"Daydream" by Basil Rathbone, copyright © 1984 Rodion Rathbone, permission granted by Héloïse Rathbone and Richard Rodion Rathbone.

In Search of Sherlock Holmes

Just as the Sons of the Desert—an international organization loosely patterned on the Baker Street Irregulars—insists its members are not Laurel and Hardy "fans," but *aficionados,* so scholars devoted to the "canon" of fifty-six short stories and four novels about the world's greatest consulting detective prefer to be called Holmesians (Hol-MEE-sians), not Sherlockians.

Nowadays Sherlockians far outnumber Holmesians. It is not necessary to embrace the Talmudic hairsplitting many Holmes scholars (myself included) indulge in to consider it unfortunate that film, TV and theatrical versions of Sherlock Holmes and Dr. Watson have distorted the Arthur Conan Doyle originals in the popular imagination.

The following "pop" quiz will demonstrate my point.

QUESTION: In how many tales did Professor Moriarty appear?
ANSWER: So many film, stage and TV actors have played Moriarty that one might expect him to figure in many stories, but though he is referred to in "The Adventure of the Empty House" and *The Valley of Fear,* he only appears in person in ONE story, "The Final Problem."

QUESTION: Name the only woman Holmes ever regarded romantically.
ANSWER: This is a trick question. Dramatists sometimes try to provide Holmes with a love interest, usually Irene Adler because "A Scandal in Bohemia" begins with the statement, "To Sherlock Holmes she is always *the* woman." But a few sentences later, Dr. Watson elaborates:

> It was not that he felt any emotion akin to love for Irene Adler. All emotions, and that one particularly, were abhorrent to his cold, precise, but admirably balanced mind. He was, I take it, the most perfect reasoning and observing machine that the world has seen: but, as a lover, he would have placed himself in a false position. He never spoke of the softer passions, save with a gibe and a sneer.

QUESTION: Describe Dr. Watson's most embarrassing gaffe.

ANSWER: Reread the above passage. Does it sound like the words of a bumbler? Watson's dimwitted reputation stems mainly from the way Nigel Bruce played him in the Universal films (but see Appendix II).

QUESTION: What was the street address of Holmes's home and office?

ANSWER: Most films show Mrs. Hudson's front door with "221B" prominently displayed, which makes as much sense as my landlord inscribing "12E," the number of my twelfth-floor apartment, on the street-level facade of his building. Holmes lives and works one flight up in *apartment B*. The correct street address is *221*, period.

QUESTION: In which case does Holmes say, "Quick, Watson, the needle!", shortly before taking a seven percent solution of cocaine?

ANSWER: "This is, without doubt, one of the most revolting phrases in the English language," writes C. B. H. Vaill in Volume I, Number 4, of *The Baker Street Journal,* adding that "It is a cheap and vulgar attempt at characterization which has no basis in fact, aimed at the mentality, say, of a studio audience. . . . Sherlock Holmes never uttered this bleat. . . . Holmes never could have uttered it." The only time Holmes is ever shown "shooting up" is in *The Sign of the Four,* his second recorded case; after that, Watson mentions his friend's drug habit as a thing of the past. Holmes's employment of cocaine was desultory and comparatively mild. As William S. Baring Gould points out in *Sherlock Holmes of Baker Street,* ". . . a seven-per-cent solution is *not* an extraordinarily heavy dosage of cocaine. In 1898, British pharmacology officially established the strength of *injectio cocainae hypodermica* at *ten* per cent."

QUESTION: How many times did Holmes say, "The game is afoot?"★

ANSWER: Though Watson alludes to this often-quoted expression in "The Adventure of Wisteria Lodge," the only time Holmes ever says it directly is in "The Adventure of the Abbey Grange" in what is surely the most dramatic opening scene of all Sherlock Holmes adventures—

It was on a bitterly cold night and frosty morning, towards the end of the winter of '97, that I was awakened by a tugging at my shoulder. It was Holmes. The candle in his hand shone upon his eager, stooping face, and told me at a glance that something was amiss.

"Come, Watson, come!" he cried. "The game is afoot. Not a word! Into your clothes and come!"

★For the origin of the phrase, see chapter two of my study, *The Histrionic Holmes,* included in this collection.

My own initial exposure to the Holmesian canon was through the media: the Basil Rathbone/Nigel Bruce films mentioned above, the same acting duo on radio, and an early Classics Comics rendering of *A Study in Scarlet* and *The Hound of the Baskervilles*. By 1969, I'd sought out and read the originals. I have one of the world's worst memories, but I remember that was the year because at that time I was completing research for my first published book, *The Histrionic Holmes,* a study of The Great Detective's acting and makeup skills.

That project coincided with an even more important event in my life. Across the street from Gracie Mansion, home of the mayor of New York, is a medical center that tour guides once pointed out as the only hospital ever to lose its liquor license. Late on the evening of November 3, 1970, I sat in one of its waiting rooms trying without much success to read the galleys of *The Histrionic Holmes* while my wife Saralee gave birth to our daughter, Terry Ellen. *The Game Is Afoot* thus represents a kind of cyclical return for me, and I have taken advantage of the fact by including my first book as part of the package, along with a sampling of other quasi-scholarly Holmesian "ponderings." Most of this collection, however, is devoted to pastiches and parodies of The Master Sleuth, the latter ranging from affectionate and good-natured lampoons to a smattering of meaner-spirited spoofs too clever to ignore. As for the pastiches—sincere attempts to recreate the tone and texture of Doyle's ratiocinative prose—the passion of an aficionado has governed my selection. I have included a generous assortment of classics, and also commissioned several brand-new Sherlock Holmes adventures for *The Game Is Afoot*.

Tracking down obscure pieces, especially when they are by well-known authors, is one of my passions as an anthologist, but the sleuthing I had to do for *The Game Is Afoot* was more than usually difficult. I am deeply grateful to a number of individuals whose aid, cooperation and suggestions proved invaluable, including Poul and Karen Anderson, Jill Bauman, Peter E. Blau, April Derleth, Henry Enberg, Edward Ferman, Jon Koons, Barry Malzberg, Kay McCauley, Philip Moser, Otto Penzler, Héloïse and Richard Rodion Rathbone, William B. R. Reiss, Susan Rice, Ray Russell, Tom Schantz, Darrell Schweitzer, Craig Tenney, Patty Tobias, Jon White and the staff of the copyright search office of the Library of Congress. But the lion's share of thanks goes to my editor, Keith Kahla, a genius in the art of making the crooked straight and rough places plain . . . as well as being a Holmesian before whom I feel like the veriest Sherlockian.

Now it is time to bundle up warm and brave the London fog. We have an appointment in Baker Street . . . at Number *221!*

—MARVIN KAYE
New York, 1993

Meet the quick mind that restlessly combs
Through the smallest of clues as it roams
    From initial confusion
    To triumphant conclusion.
My friends, here we have Sherlock Holmes.

—Isaac Asimov

Preliminary
Ponderings

*H*olmes buffs will argue who was the definitive Holmesian artist, Sidney Edward Paget, who first illustrated the series in England, or the American artist F R E D E R I C D O R R S T E E L E (1874–1944), who modeled his Holmes on the actor William Gillette. In 1929, when Gillette began a round of farewell appearances of his own play, Sherlock Holmes, Steele was tapped to write the following article for the commemorative program. Subtitled "A Little History of the World's Most Famous Fictional Character," this rare essay provides a good overview of the subject, although Steele disregards The Valley of Fear, claiming it "is not a detective story," which is erroneous.

Sherlock Holmes: A Little History of the World's Most Famous Fictional Character

F R E D E R I C D O R R S T E E L E

W H A T D O Y L E T H I N K S O F S H E R L O C K H O L M E S

Sir Conan Doyle's own attitude toward his best known character has always been deprecatory. He is somewhat impatient with a public which insists on thinking of him first as the author of Sherlock Holmes and only afterward as the author of his novels, of his *History of the War in South Africa* (for which he was honored with knighthood), and of his later works dealing with occult science. In his *Memories and Adventures* he says: "Yet it was still the Sherlock Holmes stories for which the public clamored . . . I saw that I was in danger of being entirely identified with what I regarded as a lower stratum of literary achievement." In the preface to *The Case Book* he writes: "He may perhaps have stood a little in the way of recognition of my more serious literary work."

It is possible to sympathize with this attitude when we remember that he wrote such splendid historical novels as *Sir Nigel* and that he created such magnificent characters as Rodney Stone and Brigadier Gerard. But no man can control the lightning of his own fame. The fact is indisputable that Doyle's Sherlock Holmes is known to more people living today than any other imaginary character, (unless we except the quaint figure of Charlie

Chaplin which overleaps the barriers of language.) No character in written fiction—not Hamlet, nor Don Quixote, nor Pickwick—is now so widely known as Sherlock Holmes.

WHAT WAS THE FIRST SHERLOCK HOLMES STORY?

The first appearance of Sherlock Holmes was made in *A Study in Scarlet* which Dr. Doyle wrote in 1886 during his leisure time as a practicing physician. After numerous rejections, it was finally sold for twenty-five pounds to the publishers of *Beeton's Christmas Annual,* and was published the following year. Dr. Doyle did not take Sherlock Holmes very seriously—he was much more interested in writing historical novels—but after he had finished *Micah Clarke,* and had found the publishers apathetic, he turned again to Sherlock Holmes and wrote the second story, *The Sign of the Four.* This was followed by another historical novel, *The White Company.* Then came the memorable volumes, *The Adventures* and the *Memoirs.* In the last story of this collection, Dr. Watson recorded the end of his hero in a hand-to-hand fight with his archenemy Moriarty, both going over an Alpine cliff in a death grapple.

WHY DID DOYLE KILL SHERLOCK HOLMES?

We have it on the word of Dr. Doyle himself that he had feared the public might tire of his great detective, and since he himself preferred to write of other things, he "did the deed." A few years later appeared *The Hound of the Baskervilles,* the longest, and one of the best, of the Sherlock Holmes tales. This, however, was an account of earlier events. Dr. Doyle of course might have continued this method indefinitely, but he felt that the public resented Holmes' death. There were constant complaints in all walks of life. In Richard Harding Davis' story *In the Fog* (1901) one of the characters, a British cabinet minister, laments: (I quote from memory) "What would I not give if just for a night Sherlock Holmes could come back to life and give us one more story!" So at last appeared (in 1903) the series called *The Return of Sherlock Holmes.*

HOW SHERLOCK CAME BACK

In the first story of that series, *The Empty House,* Doyle cheerfully explained that Sherlock Holmes never had died at all: he had escaped with his life from his encounter with Moriarty, and, fearing the vengeance of the latter's accomplices, had remained hidden for some years, even from Watson himself. These stories were published in *Collier's Weekly* between September 1903 and January 1905, and ended with *The Second Stain* in which Dr. Watson announced the unwillingness of Holmes that any more reminiscences should be published—"since he has definitely retired from London and betaken himself to study and bee-farming on the Sussex Downs."

THE LATER STORIES

Nevertheless, two more volumes were to follow:—*His Last Bow* (8 stories, 1918) and *The Case Book of Sherlock Holmes* (12 stories, 1927). These were printed individually in *Collier's, American, Hearst's International* and *Liberty.* They describe occurrences at various dates, both before and after the "retirement." In *The Veiled Lodger* Dr. Watson writes:—"When one considers that Sherlock Holmes was in active practice for twenty-three years, and that during seventeen of these I was allowed to co-operate with him and to keep notes of his doings, it will be clear that I have a mass of material at my command."

The latest story in time of supposed occurrence was *His Last Bow,* which tells of the war service of Sherlock Holmes on the 3rd of August, 1914,—"the most terrible August in the history of the world." This story appeared in *Collier's* for September 22, 1917, and is the final story in the collection to which it gives its name.

A Study in Scarlet 1887
The Sign of the Four. 1889
The Adventures of Sherlock Holmes (12 stories) 1891
Memoirs of Sherlock Holmes (11 stories). 1893
The Hound of the Baskervilles 1902
The Return of Sherlock Holmes (13 stories) 1905
Sherlock Holmes: His Last Bow (8 stories) 1918
The Case Book of Sherlock Holmes (12 stories) 1927

One story, *The Cardboard Box,* published in the *Strand Magazine* as one of the series, *The Adventures,* was suppressed by the author and did not appear in book form until 1918, when it was included in *His Last Bow.* One or two titles were changed, to the confusion of the bibliographer: as *The Singular Experience of Mr. J. Scott Eccles,* which became *Wisteria Lodge* in the same book. It may be noted also that Sherlock Holmes appeared as a character in a novel of adventure entitled *The Valley of Fear;* but since that was not a detective story, it is properly omitted from this list. The total number of Sherlock Holmes stories is fifty-nine—(or, including *The Valley of Fear,* sixty). Of the thirty-two stories written since 1903, I have had the pleasure of illustrating twenty-nine.

One must be on guard against the author's trick of referring by name to stories which never had been told. Mr. Arthur Bartlett Maurice long ago compiled a list of twenty-two of these purely imaginary titles. Who knows how many have since been added? Mr. Maurice, an ardent Sherlockian, prepared an exhaustive article for a "Sherlock Holmes Number" of *Collier's Weekly,* August 15, 1908, giving in great detail all the facts and legends that had accumulated up to that time.

THE ORIGIN OF SHERLOCK HOLMES

Dr. Doyle long since told us that the character of Sherlock Holmes was based on his memory of Dr. Joseph Bell, Surgeon in the Infirmary at the University of Edinburgh. Not only were Dr. Bell's physical traits described—his hawk-like features, his tall, angular figure—but also many of his habits and his methods of deduction. But it is an interesting fact that the character of Holmes underwent a marked evolution during the first few years of its existence. Beginning as a self-disciplined thinking machine who rigidly excluded from his mind all information not pertinent to the case at hand, knowing or caring nothing for the arts, Holmes developed within a few years into a veritable encyclopedia of such knowledge.

DID DR. WATSON TELL ALL THE STORIES?

In almost every instance the Sherlock Holmes tale is told in the first person by the faithful Watson, but there are a few exceptions in the latest volume. *The Adventure of the Mazarin Stone* is told by an abstract narrator, both Holmes and Watson being referred to in the third person. In *The Adventure of the Blanched Soldier* and *The Adventure of the Lion's Mane* the story is written by Holmes himself, Watson being referred to, but having no part in the events.

BAKER STREET

In the second chapter of *A Study in Scarlet,* Dr. Watson tells how, in 1878, he and Sherlock Holmes engaged rooms at "221B Baker Street." These lodgings have become for thousands of readers almost a hallowed spot—like The Old Curiosity Shop or Ann Hathaway's cottage. Pilgrimages have been made to it. Poems have been written about it: witness Miss Carolyn Wells' well remembered *Ballade of Baker Street.* Numerous attempts have been made to prove a particular house to be the one described by the author. Mr. Maurice speaks of the locality as "Upper Baker Street," and prints a photograph of the street, but without designating the house.

No better instance of the keen interest aroused in readers of the tales can be cited than the researches a few years ago of Dr. Gray C. Briggs of St. Louis, a devoted Sherlockian, who spent part of a summer vacation in London, mapped Baker Street with great care, fixed the place as No. 111, by an analysis of the story, *The Empty House,* and took his findings to Sir Conan Doyle. In a letter to me he reported in part as follows:—

> It may interest you to know that I mapped Baker Street, checking every house. In *The Adventure of the Empty House* the description of this old pile is definite. It is approached by turning into a narrow alley or passage, going thru a wooden gate, thru a yard, thru a straight hall which extends to a front door of solid wood but having a fan-shaped glass transom. This house Doyle refers to in this way: 'We are in Camden House which stands opposite our own old quarters.' There is only one house on the whole of Baker Street which answers this description. It has a rear entrance of wood leading into a blind alley. I saw the long straight hall extending clear thru the house. And when I told Sir Arthur that the sign 'Camden House' was over the door he was amazed. He told me, in such seriousness that I could not doubt him, that he did not believe he had ever been on Baker Street in his life, and, if he had, it had been many years ago—so long that he had forgotten! There is something spooky about Doyle anyway.

ILLUSTRATIONS FOR SHERLOCK

Many of the earlier stories made their first appearances in the *Strand Magazine,* London, with illustrations by Sidney Paget. In America some of the early stories appeared serially in *Harper's Weekly,* with pen-and-ink illustrations by W. H. Hyde. A glance at a reprint of one of these, here reproduced,* shows a marked unlikeness to our present conception of the character. That conception was entirely created by Mr. Gillette.

This is a good place to answer the question so often asked, "which came first, Gillette's play or Steele's pictures?" The play first saw the calcium in 1899, but *The Return of Sherlock Holmes,* with my pictures, was not published until four years later. Everybody agreed that Mr. Gillette was the ideal Sherlock Holmes, and it was inevitable that I should copy him. So I made my models look like him, and even in two or three instances used photographs of him in my drawings. But while the actor was seen by thousands, the maga-

---

*In the illustrated program this article first appeared in.—MK

zines and books were seen by millions; so after a score of years had gone by, few could remember which "did it first." Even so well informed a historian as Mr. Clayton Hamilton has tried to give me credit which belongs entirely to Mr. Gillette. I did not see the play until a later revival, some time after my first series of drawings was completed. Mr. Gillette was good enough to ask me back to his dressing room and to chat with me about our mutual friend. After the lapse of twenty-four years, it was a rare pleasure, last month, to see him again and to draw him, for the first time, from life.

MR. GILLETTE'S PLAY

The best realization of the character—indeed we may say the best realization of a book ever made on the stage—was the absurd and delightful melodrama concocted by William Gillette. It is an outright invention of Mr. Gillette, using the characters of Holmes, Watson, and Moriarty. It fits together with great skill a dozen scenes and incidents of the well remembered stories, and it remains not a dramatization of any one story but a satisfying synthesis of all.

The play opened at the Garrick in New York on November 6, 1899, with the following original cast:

SHERLOCK HOLMES	*William Gillette*
DOCTOR WATSON	*Bruce McRae*
JOHN FORMAN	*Ruben Fax*
SIR EDWARD LEIGHTON	*Harold Heaton*
COUNT VON STAHLBURG	*Alfred Howard*
PROFESSOR MORIARTY	*George Wessells*
JAMES LARRABEE	*Ralph Delmore*
SIDNEY PRINCE	*George Honey*
ALFRED BASSICK	*Henry Herrman*
JIM CRAIGIN	*Thomas McGrath*
THOMAS LEARY	*Elwyn Eaton*
LIGHTFOOT McTAGUE	*Julius Weyms*
JOHN	*Henry S. Chandler*
PARSONS	*Soldene Powell*
BILLY	*Henry McArdle*

ALICE FAULKNER	*Katherine Florence*
MRS. FAULKNER	*Jane Thomas*
MADGE LARRABEE	*Judith Berolde*
THERESE	*Hilda Englund*
MRS. SMEEDLEY	*Kate Ten Eyck*

After its long run in America Mr. Gillette took it to London and played it for a triumphant season in Sir Henry Irving's *Lyceum Theatre.* The whole-hearted acceptance by the English of the American actor in a character so utterly British is an interesting phenomenon. But on analysis it is not surprising. Mr. Gillette represented to them an admirable American type, the lean, silent and sardonic New Englander—another Connecticut Yankee at King Arthur's Court; and they relished his savor as, a generation earlier, they had relished the California types of Bret Harte.

It was during this engagement that Mr. Gillette "discovered" Charlie Chaplin, an orphan boy as yet unknown to cinema fame. He needed a youthful actor for the part of Billy the office boy, and selected Chaplin from among a group of aspirants for the part. A year or two later, when he played *Clarice* in London, he used a curtain-raiser of his own entitled *A Strange Predicament,*★ and in this Chaplin again played a part.

SHERLOCK HOLMES AS PUBLIC PROPERTY

During 1907–8 a Sherlock Holmes play, copied, with many alterations, from the Gillette play, was given in Paris, with M. Gemier in the title role. It had an entirely new last act, based on the capture of Captain Moran in *The Empty House,* but it was Moriarty (instead of Moran) who shot at the dummy of Holmes across the street and was caught in the act.

Countless imitations and parodies of Sherlock Holmes have been written. Perhaps the most interesting of these was a parody called *The Adventures of the Two Collaborators,* which was written for Dr. Doyle by James M. Barrie to commemorate their partnership as joint librettists of a light opera which met with dismal failure at the Savoy. This delightful bit of nonsense may be found in *Memories and Adventures.*

Advertisers have seized upon Holmes for their own purposes. He has been put on the stage many times; Weber and Fields burlesqued him; Montgomery and Stone did a Holmes and Watson scene in *The Red Mill.* Not only Mr. Gillette's supremely successful play, but several other attempts have been made on the stage, and later in the movies. John Barrymore is credited with an admirable film rendering of the great detective. A play based on *The Sign of the Four* met with some success in America. Sherlock Holmes plays have been produced in Germany, France and Spain.

There is a sheaf of index cards, perhaps an inch thick, pertaining to Sherlock Holmes, under "Doyle, A. Conan" in the Public Library. You may

★Better known as *The Painful Predicament of Sherlock Holmes.*—MK

see, if you wish, stories and plays translated into several European tongues; you may read, if you can, *The Sign of the Four in the advanced style of Pitman's Shorthand;* you may feast your eyes on *The Police King;* or *The Adventures of Sherlock Holmes, translated into Arabic, Beirut,* 1911; you will find three or four Spanish plays, one of which bears the resounding title *La Captura de Raffles, or El Triunfo de Sherlok Holmes, Melodrama Moderno, by Luis Millá y Gacio, Barcelona,* 1912.

"NOT LIKE THE OLD ONES"

It is a singular fact that many readers confess lack of zest in reading the later stories as compared with the stories of thirty years ago. The same thing has happened to no less a literary figure than Rudyard Kipling. Perhaps the change has come more in the reader than in the thing read. To those who say "They're not like the old stories" one can reply "you are growing old." Or one can direct the malcontent to read *The Sussex Vampire,* a tale that compares favorably with the earliest, not only in characterization and "color," but also in ingenuity of plot.

Certainly Sir Conan himself is not one to admit any such shortcomings. In an article, *The Truth About Sherlock Holmes,* are these words: "I would not write a Holmes story without a worthy plot and without a problem which interested my own mind, for that is the first requisite before you can interest anyone else. If I have been able to sustain this character for a long time, and if the public find, as they will find, that the last story is as good as the first, it is entirely due to the fact that I never, or hardly ever, forced a story."

TECHNIQUE

We can imagine Sherlock Holmes smiling tolerantly on his critics; his general acceptance as the emperor of detectives makes any inquiry into his qualifications superfluous. The reader is at liberty to study out for himself the indebtedness of Doyle to Poe, Gaboriau, and other writers of this type of fiction.

In a lucid paper called *The Technique of the Detective Story,* Brander Matthews once laid down principles and ethics for the game the author plays—or should play—with his reader. Briefly summarized, the triumph of the author consists in his laying before the reader clearly and fairly all the clues (including, of course, false clues) which are available to the detective, who then solves the problem. Such is the formula for the true detective story. Analyzed on this highly technical theory, the Sherlock Holmes stories sometimes fall short. In some, accident, rather than deduction, plays a part in the solution; in a few there is no solution at all (as in *The Veiled Lodger*). But where Doyle never fails is in the atmosphere with which he surrounds the adventures, the racy picturesqueness of the persons and events which, while often fantastic, are made believable to us by their matter-of-fact, homely narration. Half the battle was won when he had invented the inimitable Watson: no detective could hope to compete with Sherlock if presented by any other than precisely that delightful person. Thanks to Watson we do not merely wonder and admire, but are admitted to a discreet degree of personal friendship with the greatest detective of all time.

A CONFESSION

A fondness for detective stories is almost universal. I know few people who will not confess, when pressed, their addiction to this form of narcotic. I myself am happily—or unhappily—immune. I have never been able to read Gaboriau, nor "Arsène Lupin," nor Oppenheim, nor Van Dine. But Sherlock Holmes is another matter. He is the supreme anodyne. In the hands of honest Dr. Watson, I am ready, when he gives the word, to lie back, relax, and "breathe deep."★

★[POSTSCRIPT: Since the foregoing lines were written Sir Arthur Conan Doyle has passed over to that other world which had so often occupied his thoughts.—F. D. S.]

Several of the earliest stories of ARTHUR CONAN DOYLE (1859–1930) prefigure elements of the Sherlock Holmes tales, but the following obscure narrative is an especially interesting "five-finger exercise" because its narrator, like Doyle himself and Watson, is a physician, and also because it refers indirectly to Dr. Joseph Bell, the Edinburgh professor on whom Doyle patterned Sherlock Holmes. Though "The Recollections of Captain Wilkie" first appeared in print in 1895 in the Edinburgh periodical, Chamber's Journal, a footnote at the end states that he wrote it several years earlier. There is some reason to believe it might actually be Doyle's first work of fiction.

The Recollections of Captain Wilkie

ARTHUR CONAN DOYLE

I

"Who can he be?" thought I, as I watched my companion in the second-class carriage of the London and Dover Railway.

I had been so full of the fact that my long-expected holiday had come at last, and that for a few days at least the gaieties of Paris were about to supersede the dull routine of the hospital wards, that we were well out of London before I observed that I was not alone in the compartment. In these days we have all pretty well agreed that "Three is company and two is none" upon the railway. At the time I write of, however, people were not so morbidly sensitive about their travelling companions. It was rather an agreeable surprise to me to find that there was some chance of whiling away the hours of a tedious journey. I therefore pulled my cap down over my eyes, took a good look from beneath it at my vis-à-vis, and repeated to myself, "Who can he be?"

I used rather to pride myself on being able to spot a man's trade or profession by a good look at his exterior. I had the advantage of studying under a Professor at Edinburgh who was a master of the art, and used to electrify both his patients and his clinical classes by long shots, sometimes at the most unlikely of pursuits, and never very far from the mark. "Well, my man," I have heard him say, "I can see by your fingers that you play some musical instrument for your livelihood, but it is a rather curious one—something quite out of my line." The man afterwards informed us that he earned a few coppers by blowing *Rule Britannia* on a coffee-pot, the spout of which was pierced to form a rough flute. Though a novice in the art compared to the shrewd Professor, I was still able to astonish my ward companions on occasion, and I never lost an opportunity of practising myself. It was not mere curiosity, then, which led me to lean back on the cushions and analyse the quiet middle-aged man in front of me.

I used to do the thing systematically, and my train of reflections ran somewhat in this wise: "General appearance vulgar, fairly opulent, and extremely self-possessed—looks like a man who could outchaff a bargee, and yet be at his ease in the best middle-class society. Eyes well set together, and nose rather prominent—would be a good long-range marksman. Cheeks flabby, but the softness of expression redeemed by a square-cut jaw and a well-set lower lip. On the whole, a powerful type. Now for the hands— rather disappointed there. Thought he was a self-made man by the look of him, but there is no callus in the palm, and no thickening at the joints. Has never been engaged in any real physical work, I should think. No tanning on the backs of the hands; on the contrary, they are very white, with blue projecting veins and long delicate fingers. Couldn't be an artist with that face, and yet he has the hands of a man engaged in delicate manipulations. No red acid spots upon his clothes, no ink-stains, no nitrate-of-silver marks upon the hands (this helps to negative my half-formed opinion that he was a photographer). Clothes not worn in any particular part. Coat made of tweed, and fairly old; but the left elbow, as far as I can see it, has as much of the fluff left on as the right, which is seldom the case with men who do much writing. Might be a commercial traveller, but the little pocket-book in the waistcoat is wanting, nor has he any of those handy valises suggestive of samples."

I give these brief headings of my ideas merely to demonstrate my method of arriving at a conclusion. As yet I had obtained nothing but negative results; but now, to use a chemical metaphor, I was in a position to pour off this solution of dissolved possibilities and examine the residue. I found myself reduced to a very limited number of occupations. He was neither a lawyer nor a clergyman, in spite of a soft felt hat, and a somewhat clerical cut about the necktie. I was wavering now between pawnbroker and horse-dealer; but there was too much character about his face for the former; and he lacked that extraordinary equine atmosphere which hangs over the latter even in his hours of relaxation; so I formed a provisional diagnosis of betting man of methodistical proclivities, the latter clause being inserted in deference to his hat and necktie.

Pray, do not think that I reasoned it out like this in my own mind. It is only now, sitting down with pen and paper, that I can see the successive steps.

As it was, I had formed my conclusion within sixty seconds of the time when I drew my hat down over my eyes and uttered the mental ejaculation with which my narrative begins.

I did not feel quite satisfied even then with my deductions. However, as a leading question would—to pursue my chemical analogy—act as my litmus paper, I determined to try one. There was a *Times* lying by my companion, and I thought the opportunity too good to be neglected.

"Do you mind my looking at your paper?" I asked.

"Certainly, sir, certainly," said he most urbanely, handing it across.

I glanced down its columns until my eye rested upon the list of the latest betting.

"Hullo!" I said, "they are laying odds upon the favourite for the Cambridgeshire.—But perhaps," I added, looking up, "you are not interested in these matters?"

"Snares, sir!" said he violently, "wiles of the enemy! Mortals are but given a few years to live; how can they squander them so!—They have not even an eye to their poor worldly interests," he added in a quieter tone, "or they would never back a single horse at such short odds with a field of thirty."

There was something in this speech of his which tickled me immensely. I suppose it was the odd way in which he blended religious intolerance with worldly wisdom. I laid the *Times* aside with the conviction that I should be able to spend the next two hours to better purpose than in its perusal.

"You speak as if you understood the matter, at any rate," I remarked.

"Yes, sir," he answered; "few men in England understood these things better in the old days before I changed my profession. But that is all over now."

"Changed your profession?" said I interrogatively.

"Yes; I changed my name too."

"Indeed?" said I.

"Yes; you see, a man wants a real fresh start when his eyes become opened, so he has a new deal all round, so to speak. Then he gets a fair chance."

There was a short pause here, as I seemed to be on delicate ground in touching on my companion's antecedents, and he did not volunteer any information. I broke the silence by offering him a cheroot.

"No; thanks," said he; "I have given up tobacco. It was the hardest wrench of all, was that. It does me good to smell the whiff of your weed.— Tell me," he added suddenly, looking hard at me with his shrewd grey eyes, "why did you take stock of me so carefully before you spoke?"

"It is a habit of mine," said I. "I am a medical man, and observation is everything in my profession. I had no idea you were looking."

"I can see without looking," he answered. "I thought you were a detective, at first; but I couldn't recall your face at the time I knew the force."

"Were you a detective, then?" said I.

"No," he answered with a laugh; "I was the other thing—the detected, you know. Old scores are wiped out now, and the law cannot touch me, so I don't mind confessing to a gentleman like yourself what a scoundrel I have been in my time."

"We are none of us perfect," said I.

"No; but I was a real out-and-outer. A 'fake,' you know, to start with, and afterwards a 'cracksman.' It is easy to talk of these things now, for I've changed my spirit. It's as if I was talking of some other man, you see."

"Exactly so," said I. Being a medical man I had none of that shrinking from crime and criminals which many men possess. I could make all allowances for congenital influence and the force of circumstances. No company, therefore, could have been more acceptable to me than that of the old malefactor; and as I sat puffing at my cigar, I was delighted to observe that my air of interest was gradually loosening his tongue.

"Yes; I'm a changed man now," he continued, "and of course I am a happier man for that. And yet," he added wistfully, "there are times when I long for the old trade again, and fancy myself strolling out on a cloudy night with my jemmy in my pocket. I left a name behind me in my profession, sir. I was one of the old school, you know. It was very seldom that we bungled a job. We used to begin at the foot of the ladder, in my younger days, and then work our way up through the successive grades, so that we were what you might call good men all round."

"I see," said I.

"I was always reckoned a hard-working, conscientious man, and had talent too—the very cleverest of them allowed that. I began as a blacksmith, and then did a little engineering and carpentering, and then I took to sleight-of-hand tricks, and then to picking pockets. I remember, when I was home on a visit, how my poor old father used to wonder why I was always hovering around him. He little knew that I used to clear everything out of his pockets a dozen times a day, and then replace them, just to keep my hand in. He believes to this day that I am in an office in the City. There are few of them could touch me in that particular line of business, though."

"I suppose it is a matter of practice?" I remarked.

"To a great extent. Still, a man never quite loses it, if he has once been an adept.—Excuse me; you have dropped some cigar ash on your coat," and he waved his hand politely in front of my breast, as if to brush it off.—"There," he said, handing me my gold scarf pin, "You see I have not forgot my old cunning yet."

He had done it so quickly that I hardly saw the hand whisk over my bosom, nor did I feel his fingers touch me, and yet there was the pin glittering in his hand. "It is wonderful!" I said as I fixed it again in its place.

"Oh, that's nothing! But I have been in some really smart jobs. I was in the gang that picked the new patent safe. You remember the case. It was guaranteed to resist anything; and we managed to open the first that was ever issued, within a week of its appearance. It was done with graduated wedges, sir, the first so small that you could hardly see it against the light, and the last strong enough to prise it open. It was a cleverly managed affair."

"I remember it," said I. "But surely someone was convicted for that?"

"Yes, one was nabbed. But he didn't split, nor even let on how it was done. It would have been as much as his life was worth.—Perhaps I am boring you, talking about these old wicked days of mine?"

"On the contrary," I said, "you interest me extremely."

"I like to get a listener I can trust. It's a sort of blow-off, you know, and I feel lighter after it. When I am among my new and highly respectable acquaintances, I dare hardly think of what has gone before.—Now, I'll tell you about another job I was in. To this day, I cannot think about it without laughing."

I lit another cigar, and composed myself to listen.

"It was when I was a youngster," said he. "There was a big City man in those days who was known to have a very valuable gold watch. I followed him about for several days before I could get a chance; but when I did get one, you may be sure I did not throw it away. He found, to his disgust, when he got home that day, that there was nothing in his fob. I hurried off with my prize, and got it stowed away in safety, intending to have it melted down next day. Now, it happened that this watch possessed a special value in the owner's eyes because it was a sort of ancestral possession—presented to his father on coming of age, or something of that sort. I remember there was a long inscription on the back. He was determined not to lose it if he could help it, and accordingly he put an advertisement in an evening paper offering thirty pounds reward for its return, and promising that no questions should be asked. He gave the address of his house, 31 Caroline Square, at the end of the advertisement. The thing sounded good enough, so I set off for Caroline Square, leaving the watch in a parcel at a public-house which I passed on the way. When I got there, the gentleman was at dinner; but he came out quick enough when he heard that a young man wanted to see him. I suppose he guessed who the young man would prove to be. He was a genial-looking old fellow, and he led me away with him into his study.

" 'Well, my lad,' said he, 'what is it?'

" 'I've come about that watch of yours,' said I. 'I think I can lay my hands on it.'

" 'Oh, it was you that took it!' said he.

" 'No,' I answered; 'I know nothing whatever about how you lost it. I have been sent by another party to see you about it. Even if you have me arrested, you will not find out anything.'

" 'Well,' he said, 'I don't want to be hard on you. Hand it over, and here is my cheque for the amount.'

" 'Cheques won't do,' said I; 'I must have it in gold.'

" 'It will take me an hour or so to collect it in gold,' said he.

" 'That will just suit,' I answered, 'for I have not got the watch with me. I'll go back and fetch it, while you raise the money.'

"I started off, and got the watch where I had left it. When I came back, the old gentleman was sitting behind his study table, with the little heap of gold in front of him.

" 'Here is your money,' he said, and pushed it over.

" 'Here is your watch,' said I.

"He was evidently delighted to get it back; and after examining it care-fully, and assuring himself that it was none the worse, he put it into the watch-pocket of his coat with a grunt of satisfaction.

" 'Now, my lad,' he said, 'I know it was you that took the watch. Tell me how you did it, and I don't mind giving you an extra five-pound note.'

" 'I wouldn't tell you in any case,' said I; 'but especially I wouldn't tell you when you have a witness hid behind that curtain.' You see, I had all my wits about me, and it didn't escape me that the curtain was drawn tighter than it had been before.

" 'You are too sharp for us,' said he good-humouredly. 'Well, you have got your money, and that's an end of it. I'll take precious good care you don't get hold of my watch again in a hurry.—Good-night.—No; not that door,' he added as I marched towards a cupboard. 'This is the door,' and he stood up and opened it. I brushed past him, opened the hall door, and was round the corner of the square in no time. I don't know how long the old gentleman took to find it out, but in passing him at the door, I managed to pick his pocket for the second time, and next morning the family heirloom was in the melting-pot after all.—That wasn't bad, was it?"

The old war-horse was evidently getting his blood up now. There was a tone of triumph in the conclusion of his anecdote which showed that, sometimes at least, his pride in his smartness surpassed his repentance of his misdeeds. He seemed pleased at the astonishment and amusement I expressed at his adroitness.

"Yes," he continued with a laugh, "it was a capital joke. But some-times the fun lies all the other way. Even the sharpest of us comes to grief at times. There was one rather curious incident which occurred in my career. You may possibly have seen the anecdote, for it got into print at the time."

"Pray, let me hear it," said I.

II

"Well, it is hard lines telling stories against one's self, but this was how it happened. I had made a rather good haul, and invested some of the swag in buying a very fine diamond ring. I thought it would be something to fall back upon when all the ready was gone and times were hard. I had just purchased it, and was going back to my lodgings in the omnibus, when, as luck would have it, a very stylishly dressed young lady came in and took her seat beside me. I didn't pay much attention to her at first; but after a time something hard in her dress knocked up against my hand, which my experienced touch soon made out to be a purse. It struck me that I could not pass the time more profitably or agreeably than by making this purse my own. I had to do it very carefully; but I managed at last to wriggle my hand into her rather tight pocket, and I thought the job was over. Just at this moment she rose abruptly to leave the 'bus, and I had hardly time to get my hand with the purse in it out of her pocket without detection. It was not until she had been gone some time that I found out that, in drawing out my hand in that hurried manner, the new and ill-fitting ring I wore had slipped over my finger and remained in the young lady's pocket. I sprang out, and ran in the direction in which she had gone, with the intention of picking her pocket once again. She had disappeared, however; and from that day till this I have never set eyes on her. To make the matter worse, there was only four-pence-halfpenny in coppers inside the purse. Serve me right for trying to rob such a pretty girl; still, if I had that two hundred quid now, I should not be reduced to—Good heavens, forgive me! What am I saying?"

He seemed inclined to relapse into silence after this; but I was determined to draw him out a little more, if I could possibly manage it. "There is less personal risk in the branch you have been talking of," I remarked, "than there is in burglary."

"Ah!" he said, warming to his subject once again, "it is the higher game which is best worth aiming at.—Talk about sport, sir, talk about fishing or hunting! why, it is tame in comparison! Think of the great country-house with its men-servants and its dogs and its fire-arms, and you with only your jemmy and your centre-bit, and your mother-wit, which is best of all. It is the triumph of intellect over brute-force, sir, as represented by bolts and bars."

"People generally look upon it as quite the reverse," I remarked.

"I was never one of those blundering life-preserver fellows," said my companion. "I did try my hand at garrotting once; but it was against my principles, and I gave it up. I have tried everything. I have been a bedridden widow with three young children; but I do object to physical force."

"You have been what?" said I.

"A bedridden widow. Advertising, you know, and getting subscriptions. I have tried them all.—You seem interested in these experiences," he continued; "so I will tell you another anecdote. It was the narrowest escape for penal servitude that ever I had in my life. A pal and I had gone down on a country beat—it doesn't signify where it was—and taken up our headquarters in a little provincial town. Somehow it got noised abroad that we were there, and householders were warned to be careful, as suspicious characters had been seen in the neighbourhood. We should have changed our plans when we saw the game was up; but my chum was a plucky fellow, and wouldn't consent to back down. Poor little Jim! He was only thirty-four round the chest, and about twelve at the biceps; but there is not a measuring tape in England could have given the size of his heart. He said we were in for it, and we must stick to it; so I agreed to stay, and we chose Morley Hall, the country-house of a certain Colonel Morley, to begin with.

"Now, this Colonel Morley was about the last man in the world that we should have meddled with. He was a shrewd, cool-headed fellow, who had knocked about and seen the world, and it seems that he took a special pride in the detection of criminals. However, we knew nothing of all this at that time; so we set forth hopefully to have a try at the house.

"The reason that made us pick him out among the rest was that he had a good-for-nothing groom, who was a tool in our hands. This fellow had drawn up a rough plan of the premises for us. The place was pretty well locked up and guarded, and the only weak point we could see was a certain trap-door, the padlock of which was broken, and which opened from the roof into one of the lumber-rooms. If we could only find any method of reaching the roof, we might force a way securely from above. We both thought the plan rather a good one, and it had a spice of originality about it which pleased us. It is not the mere jewels or plate, you know, that a good cracksman thinks about. The neatness of the job, and his reputation for smartness, are almost as important in his eyes.

"We had been very quiet for a day or two, just to let suspicion die away. Then we set out one dark night, Jim and I, and got over the avenue railings and up to the house without meeting a soul. It was blowing hard, I remember, and the clouds hurrying across the sky. We had a good look at the front of the house, and then Jim went round to the garden side. He came running back in a minute or two in a great state of delight. 'Why, Bill,' he said, gripping me by the arm, 'there never was such a bit of luck! They've been repairing the roof or something, and they've left the ladder standing.' We went round together, and there, sure enough, was the ladder towering above our heads, and one or two labourers' hods lying about, which showed that some work had been going on during the day. We had a good look round, to see that everything was quiet, and then we climbed up, Jim first, and I after him. We got to the top, and were sitting on the slates, having a bit of a breather, before beginning business, when you can fancy our feelings to see the ladder that we came up by suddenly stand straight up in the air, and then slowly descend until it rested in the garden below! At first, we hoped it might have slipped, though that was bad enough; but we soon had that idea put out of our head.

" 'Hullo, up there!' cried a voice from below.

"We craned our heads over the edge, and there was a man, dressed, as far as we could make out, in evening dress, and standing in the middle of the grass plot. We kept quiet.

" 'Hullo!' he shouted again. 'How do you feel yourselves? Pretty comfortable, eh? Ha! ha! You London rogues thought we were green in the country. What's your opinion now?"

"We both lay still, though feeling pretty considerably small, as you may imagine.

" 'It's all right; I see you,' he continued. 'Why, I have been waiting behind that lilac bush every night for the last week, expecting to see you. I knew you couldn't resist going up that ladder, when you found the windows were too much for you.—Joe! Joe!'

" 'Yes, sir,' said a voice, and another man came from among the bushes.

" 'Just you keep your eye on the roof, will you, while I ride down to the station and fetch up a couple of constables?—*Au revoir,* gentlemen! You don't mind waiting, I suppose?' And Colonel Morley—for it was the owner of the house himself—strode off; and in a few minutes we heard the rattle of his horse's hoofs going down the avenue.

"Well, sir, we felt precious silly, as you may imagine. It wasn't so much having been nabbed that bothered us, as the feeling of being caught in such a simple trap. We looked at each other in blank disgust, and then, to save our lives, we couldn't help bursting into laughter at our own fix. However, it was no laughing matter; so we set to work going round the roof, and seeing if there was a likely waterpipe or anything that might give us a chance of escape. We had to give it up as a bad job; so we sat down again, and made up our minds to the worst. Suddenly an idea flashed into my head, and I groped my way over the roof until I felt wood under my feet. I bent down, and found that the Colonel had actually forgotten to secure the padlock! You will often notice, as you go through life, that it is the shrewdest and most cunning man who falls into the most absurd mistakes; and this was an example of it. You may guess that we did not lose much time, for we expected to hear the constables every moment. We dropped through into the lumber-room, slipped down-stairs, tore open the library shutters, and were out and away before the astonished groom could make out what had happened. There wasn't time enough to take any little souvenir with us, worse luck. I should have liked to have seen the Colonel's face when he came back with the constables and found that the birds were flown."

"Did you ever come across the Colonel again?" I asked.

"Yes; we skinned him of every bit of plate he had, down to the salt-spoons, a few years later. It was partly out of revenge, you see, that we did it. It was a very well-managed and daring thing, one of the best I ever saw, and all done in open daylight too."

"How in the world did you do it?" I asked.

"Well, there were three of us in it—Jim was one; and we set about it in this way. We wanted to begin by getting the Colonel out of the way, so I wrote him a note purporting to come from Squire Brotherwick, who lived about ten miles away, and was not always on the best of terms with the master of Morley Hall. I dressed myself up as a groom and delivered the note myself. It was to the effect that the Squire thought he was able to lay his hands on the scoundrels who had escaped from the Colonel a couple of years before, and that if the Colonel would ride over, they would have little difficulty in securing them. I was sure that this would have the desired effect; so, after handing it in, and remarking that I was the Squire's groom, I walked off again, as if on the way back to my master's.

"After getting out of sight of the house, I crouched down behind a hedge; and, as I expected, in less than a quarter of an hour the Colonel came swinging past me on his chestnut mare. Now, there is another accomplishment I possess which I have not mentioned to you yet, and that is, that I can copy any handwriting that I see. It is a very easy trick to pick up, if you only give your mind to it. I happened to have come across one of Colonel Morley's letters some days before, and I can write so that even now I defy an expert to detect a difference between the hands. This was a great assistance to me now, for I tore a leaf out of my pocket-book and wrote something to this effect:

" 'As Squire Brotherwick has seen some suspicious characters about, and the house may be attempted again, I have sent down to the bank, and ordered them to send up their bank-cart to convey the whole of the plate to a place of safety. It will save us a good deal of anxiety to know that it is in absolute security. Have it packed up and ready, and give the bearer a glass of beer.'

"Having composed this precious epistle, I addressed it to the butler, and carried it back to the Hall, saying that their master had overtaken me on the way and asked me to deliver it. I was taken in and made much of downstairs; while a great packing-case was dragged into the hall, and the plate stowed away among cotton-wool and stuffing. It was nearly ready, when I heard the sound of wheels upon the gravel, and sauntered round just in time to see a business-like closed car drive up to the door. One of my pals was sitting very demurely on the box; while Jim, with an official-looking hat, sprang out and bustled into the hall.

" 'Now, then,' I heard him say, 'look sharp! What's for the bank? Come on!'

" 'Wait a minute, sir,' said the butler.

" 'Can't wait. There's a panic all over the country, and they are clamouring for us everywhere. Must drive on to Lord Blackbury's place, unless you are ready.'

" 'Don't go, sir!' pleaded the butler. 'There's only this one rope to tie.—There; it is ready now. You'll look after it, won't you?"

" 'That we will. You'll never have any more trouble with it now,' said Jim, helping to push the great case into the car.

" 'I think I had better go with you and see it stowed away in the bank,' said the butler.

" 'All right!' said Jim, nothing abashed. 'You can't come in the car, though, for Lord Blackbury's box will take up all the spare room—Let's see—it's twelve o'clock now. Well, you be waiting at the bank door at half-past one, and you will just catch us.'

" 'All right—half-past one,' said the butler.

" 'Good-day!' cried my chum; and away went the car, while I made a bit of a short cut and caught it round a turn of the road. We drove right off into the next county, got a down-train to London; and before midnight, the Colonel's silver was fused into a solid lump."

I could not help laughing at the versatility of the old scoundrel. "It was a daring game to play," I said.

"It is always the daring game which succeeds best," he answered.

At this point the train began to show symptoms of slowing down, and my companion put on his overcoat and gave other signs of being near the end of his journey. "You are going on to Dover?" he said.

"Yes."

"For the Continent?"

"Yes."

"How long do you intend to travel?"

"Only for a week or so."

"Well, I must leave you here. You will remember my name, won't you? John Wilkie, I am pleased to have met you.—Is my umbrella behind you?" he added, stretching across.—"No; I beg your pardon. Here it is in the corner;" and with an affable smile, the ex-cracksman stepped out, bowed, and disappeared among the crowd upon the platform.

I lit another cigar, laughed as I thought of my late companion, and lifted up the *Times* which he had left behind him. The bell had rung, the wheels were already revolving, when, to my astonishment, a pallid face looked in at me through the window. It was so contorted and agitated, that I hardly recognised the features which I had been gazing upon during the last couple of hours. "Here, take it," he said—"take it. It's hardly worth my while to rob you of seven pounds four shillings; but I couldn't resist once more trying my hand;" and he flung something into the carriage and disappeared.

It was my old leather purse, with my return ticket, and the whole of my travelling expenses. How he had taken it he knows best himself; I suppose it was while he was bending over in search of an imaginary umbrella. His newly re-awakened conscience had then pricked him, so that he had been driven to instant restitution.

*D*R. HAROLD EMERY JONES *was a fellow student of Arthur Conan Doyle's at the Edinburgh Royal Infirmary, where they studied under Dr. Joseph Bell, whose surgical demonstrations of observation and deduction were so remarkable that they provided the kernel of inspiration for the world's greatest consulting detective.*

The Original of Sherlock Holmes

DR. HAROLD EMERY JONES

When it was known that Dr. Conan Doyle had decided on bringing Sherlock Holmes back to the land of the living, a number of his admirers were fearful lest the author wreck his own reputation and destroy the interesting and unique character of Sherlock Holmes, by attempting what was seemingly an impossibility or, at any rate, an absurdity. Conan Doyle's friends, however, had supreme confidence in his ability to revivify Sherlock Holmes in an artistic and natural manner. After "The Adventure of the Empty House," admirers and friends could not but exclaim in unison: "How simple! How plausible! How clever!"

The great mystery, which has as yet never been cleared up, is whether Holmes ever really existed. Is Holmes merely the creation of Doyle's ingenious brain? Or is there really an individual who is the living embodiment of Sherlock Holmes?

Conan Doyle is essentially an Edinburgh product. He was born there. His medical studies were pursued in that ancient city of medical lore. His father was a well-known artist. He himself was the nephew of the famous Dicky Doyle, and his grandfather was the celebrated caricaturist John Doyle, known to the public as H. B. So the author had, to say the least, a heritage of promise. His first literary venture was as editor of a school magazine in Germany, where he was sent to receive his early education. Prior to that he had attended a private school in England. Leaving Germany, he returned to Edinburgh, where he entered the University for the purpose of studying medicine.

To a man of Doyle's alertness, memory, and imagination, this training was invaluable. It was in the infirmary wards at Edinburgh, in the dispensaries, and in the out-patient department that he first encountered that subtle and wonderful character who is now world-renowned, the original of the great detective, Sherlock Holmes.

All Edinburgh medical students remember Joseph Bell—Joe Bell—as they called him. Always alert, always up and doing, nothing ever escaped that keen eye of his. He read both patients and students like so many open books. His diagnosis was almost never at fault.

One would never dream, by looking through "Who's Who" (in England), that the person described as follows is the original of the great detective, Sherlock Holmes:

"Joseph Bell, M.D., F.R.C.S., Edinburgh; consulting Surgeon to the Royal Infirmary and Royal Hospital for Sick Children. Member of University Court, Edinburgh University; born in Edinburgh in the year 1837. The eldest son of Benjamin Bell, Surgeon, and of Cecilia Craigie. Married to Edith Katherine, daughter of the Honorable James Erskine Murray. Went through the ordinary course of a Hospital Surgeon at Edinburgh Royal Infirmary, from Dresser to Senior Surgeon and Consulting Surgeon. Twenty-three years (1873–96) editor of the 'Edinburgh Medical Journal.' "

Yet he is the original Sherlock Holmes—the Edinburgh medical students' ideal—who could tell patients their habits, their occupations, nationality, and often their names, and who rarely, if ever, made a mistake. Oftentimes he would call upon one of the students to diagnose the cases for him. Telling the House Surgeon to usher in a new patient, he delighted in putting the deductive powers of the student to the test, with results generally amusing, except to the poor student victim himself.

This is Conan Doyle's description of Joseph Bell: "He would sit in the patients' waiting-room, with a face like a Red Indian, and diagnose the people as they came in, before even they opened their mouths. He would tell them their symptoms, and would even give them details of their past life, and he would hardly ever make a mistake."

What Edinburgh student of Conan Doyle's student years can fail to recognize in the stoic-faced professor, Joe Bell, the "king of deduction"?

"What is the matter with this man, sir?" he suddenly inquired of a trembling student. "Come down, sir, and look at him! No! You mustn't touch him. Use your eyes, sir! Use your ears, use your brain, your bump of perception, and use your powers of deduction."

After looking at the patient, the embryonic Holmes blurted out: "Hip-joint disease, sir!"

"Hip-nothing!" Bell retorted. "The man's limp is not from his hip, but from his foot, or rather from his feet. Were you to observe closely, you would see that there are slits, cut by a knife, in those parts of the shoes where the pressure of the shoe is greatest against the foot. The man is a sufferer from corns, gentlemen, and has no hip trouble at all. He has not come here to be treated for corns, gentlemen. We are not chiropodists. His trouble is of a much more serious nature. This is a case of chronic alcoholism, gentlemen. The rubicund nose, the puffed, bloated face, the bloodshot eyes, the tremulous hands and twitching face muscles, with the quick, pulsating temporal arteries, all show this. These deductions, gentlemen, must, however, be confirmed by absolute and concrete evidence. In this instance my diagnosis is confirmed by the fact of my seeing the neck of a whiskey-bottle protruding from the patient's right-hand coat pocket.

"From close observation and deduction, gentlemen, you can make a correct diagnosis of any and every case. However, never neglect to ratify your deductions, to substantiate your diagnosis with the stethoscope, and by other recognized and every-day methods of diagnosis."

Of another patient he would say: "Gentlemen, we have here a man who is either a cork-cutter or a slater. If you will only use your eyes a moment you will be able to define a slight hardening—a regular callous, gentlemen—on one side of his forefinger, and a thickening on the outside of his thumb, a sure sign that he follows the one occupation or the other."

Or again: "Gentlemen, a fisherman! You will notice that, though this is a very hot summer's day, the patient is wearing top-boots. When he sat on the chair they were plainly visible. No one but a sailor would wear top-boots at this season of the year. The shade of tan on his face shows him to be a coast-sailor, and not a deep-sea sailor—a sailor who makes foreign lands. His tan is that produced by one climate, a 'local tan,' so to speak. A knife scabbard shows beneath his coat, the kind used by fishermen in this part of the world. He is concealing a quid of tobacco in the furthest corner of his mouth and manages it very adroitly indeed, gentlemen. The summary of these deductions shows that this man is a fisherman. Further, to prove the correctness of these deductions, I notice several fish-scales adhering to his clothes and hands, while the odor of fish announced his arrival in a most marked and striking manner."

On one occasion he called upon a student to diagnose a case. The student made a miserable failure of it.

"Get out your notebook, man," said Bell, "and see whether you can't express your thoughts that way." Then, turning to the class, the Professor continued: "The gentleman has ears and he hears not, eyes and he sees not! You come from Wales, don't you, sir?"—again turning to the poor victim—"I thought so! A man who says 'silling' for shilling, who rattles his R's, who has a peculiar, rough, broad accent like yours, sir, is not a Scotchman. You are not an Irishman! You are not an Englishman! Your speech 'smacks of Wales.' And to clinch the matter, gentlemen"—once more addressing the class—"when I asked Mr. Edward Jones—that is his name, gentlemen—to transfer his thoughts to paper, he nervously pulled out his notebook, and, to his chagrin, with it a letter. Mr. Jones endeavored to palm the letter, gentlemen; but he is evidently a little out of training at present, as he blundered most beautifully. The postmark shows that the letter was posted yesterday morning at Cardiff. The address was written by a female—undoubtedly Mr. Jones's sweetheart—for the very sight of it caused our friend to blush furiously. It was addressed to Mr. Edward Jones! Now, gentlemen! Cardiff is in South Wales, and the name Jones proclaims our friend a Welshman."

According to Doyle, Bell's faculty of deduction was at times highly dramatic. "Ah," he would say to one of the patients, "you are a soldier, and a non-commissioned officer at that. You have served in Bermuda. Now how do I know that, gentlemen? Because he came into the room without even taking his hat off, as he would go into an orderly room. He was a soldier. A slight, authoritative air, combined with his age, shows that he was a non-commissioned officer. A rash on his forehead tells me he was in Bermuda and subject to a certain rash known only there."

Bell was as full of dry humor and satire, and he was as jealous of his reputation, as the detective Sherlock Holmes ever thought of being.

One day, in the lecture theatre, he gave the students a long talk on the necessity for the members of the medical profession cultivating their senses— sight, smell, taste, and hearing. Before him on a table stood a large tumbler filled with a dark, amber-colored liquid.

"This, gentlemen," announced the Professor, "contains a very potent drug. To the taste it is intensely bitter. It is most offensive to the sense of smell. Yet, as far as the sense of sight is concerned—that is, in color—it is no different from dozens of other liquids.

"Now I want to see how many of you gentlemen have educated your powers of perception. Of course, we might easily analyze this chemically, and find out what it is. But I want you to test it by smell and taste; and, as I don't ask anything of my students which I wouldn't be willing to do myself, I will taste it before passing it round."

Here he dipped his finger in the liquid, and placed it in his mouth. The tumbler was passed round. With wry and sour faces the students followed the Professor's lead. One after another tasted the vile decoction; varied and amusing were the grimaces made. The tumbler, having gone the round, was returned to the Professor.

"Gentlemen," said he, with a laugh, "I am deeply grieved to find that not one of you has developed this power of perception, which I so often speak about; for if you had watched me closely, you would have found that, while I placed my forefinger in the medicine, it was the middle finger which found its way into my mouth."

These methods of Bell impressed Doyle greatly at the time. The impression made was a lasting one.

But, while Joseph Bell is the original Sherlock Holmes, another Edinburgh professor "had a finger in the pie," so to speak.

While Joseph Bell gave Doyle the idea of the character Holmes, the man who, unknowingly perhaps, influenced Doyle in adapting that character to the detection of crime, was Sir Henry Littlejohn.

"Little-John," as the students called him, was the Police Surgeon and the Medical Officer of Health to the City of Edinburgh. He was also Lecturer on Forensic Medicine and Public Health at the Royal College of Surgeons.

No teacher ever took a greater interest in his students than did Sir Henry. He not only lectured to "his boys"—as he always spoke of them—in the lecture-room, but he took them to the city slaughter-houses, and to the reservoirs which supply Edinburgh with water. Here he would explain the why and the wherefore of hygiene. As Police Surgeon he had unlimited liberties and unequaled facilities for the study of crime and criminals. It was a common but interesting sight to see the dapper Sir Henry Littlejohn, little both in stature and name, walking along the street with a crowd of medical students trailing along behind. His lectures on crime and criminals were always entertaining and instructive, as they were generally straightforward statements of personal experiences.

While Bell was lecturing deduction and perception into Doyle's receptive and imaginative brain, Sir Henry Littlejohn was giving Doyle material for his detective stories.

Whenever a mysterious or suspected murder was perpetrated, Sir Henry loved to ferret out the criminals and clear up the crime. He always gave expert medical evidence in the law courts, and, being Police Surgeon, of necessity testified for the Crown on behalf of the prosecution.

It was a red-letter day for Edinburgh medical students when Sir Henry was due in the witness-box. How they flocked around the courthouse, and how they fought to gain an entrance! Even standing-room was at a premium on these occasions; one and all were anxious to hear their "Littlejohn" testify. For Sir Henry never got the worst of the argument. He was never entrapped by the smartest of lawyers, and never disconcerted by the severest of cross-examinations.

One case, out of hundreds of a similar kind, will exemplify his knowledge of criminals and crime, and show his readiness of repartee.

A woman was charged with the poisoning of her husband. Arsenic had been found in the stomach of the dead man. The prosecution failed, however, to prove that the woman had purchased arsenic. As the law in the British Isles is very explicit and severe in its restriction of the sale of poisons, and at all times is strictly enforced, the defence made much of the failure of the prosecution to prove the purchasing of the arsenic. No poison in class A—in which class arsenic is placed—can be bought at any chemist's shop unless the sale is entered in the Government Poison Book—a book kept specially for that purpose. The signatures of vender, buyer, and a witness, known to both parties, must be attached. No record of the sale of arsenic could be found in any of the city druggists' establishments. Sir Henry's attention was called to this fact by the attorney for the defence.

"So you found arsenic in the stomach of the deceased?" inquired the lawyer.

"I did," answered Sir Henry, in his usual quick and decided manner.

"But where could the arsenic have been procured?" questioned the attorney. "We have no record of the sale!"

"Why," retorted Littlejohn scornfully, "there is enough arsenic in the room where the man slept to poison a small army, right at hand, on the very walls of the room itself. The green wall-paper, with which the walls of the room are covered, is saturated with arsenic."

"True, perhaps," replied the man of law, "but surely the defendant is not sufficiently versed in chemistry—she is certainly not well enough educated—to understand the very difficult and complicated process of extracting arsenic from wall-paper, even if the wall-paper contains arsenic—which is very, very doubtful."

"Some women's intuition is greater than certain men's knowledge," answered Sir Henry, pointedly and dryly.

The cross-examining lawyer immediately ceased his questioning. The woman later admitted her crime, and Little-John again scored.

The University, with its associations, with its antiquity, with the respect and affection shown professors by students, with the unlimited trouble taken by professors with the students, and the general atmosphere and environments of both the University and Edinburgh itself, had undoubtedly an influence upon Conan Doyle's literary work, and a potent influence at that.

The British publisher Ward, Lock & Co. issued an 1892 edition of the first Sherlock Holmes adventure, A Study in Scarlet, *with the following introduction by* DR. JO-SEPH BELL *(1837–1911), the surgeon and teacher who was Doyle's model for Sherlock Holmes. An Edinburgh native, Dr. Bell was affiliated with "Auld Reekie" (the University) and consulting surgeon to the Royal Infirmary and the Royal Hospital for Sick Children. According to Doyle's biographer John Dickson Carr, after mystifying students with canny observations about his patients, Dr. Bell would regard his pupils with a Sherlockian stare and proclaim, "The trained eye! A simple matter."*

Mr. Sherlock Holmes

DR. JOSEPH BELL

It is not entirely a bad sign of this weary, worn-out century that in this, its last decade, even the petty street-bred people are beginning, as the nurses say, to take notice. An insatiable and generally prurient curiosity as to the doings of the class immediately above us is pandered to by the society journals, and encouraged even by the daily newspapers. Such information is valueless intellectually, and tends to moral degradation; it exercises none of the senses, and pauperises the imagination. Celebrities at home, illustrated interviews, society scandal on all levels merely titillate the itching ear of the gossip. Memoirs, recollections, anecdotes of the Bar or of the Academy are much more interesting, and may be valuable as throwing sidelights on history, but still only amuse and help to kill the time of which we forget the value. But in the last few years there has been a distinct demand for books which, to a certain poor extent, encourage thought and stimulate observation. The whole "Gamekeeper at Home" series and its imitations opened the eyes of town dwellers, who had forgotten or never known White of Selborne, to the delightful sights and sounds that were the harvest of the open eye and ear. Something of the same interest is given to the "crowded city's horrible street" by the suggestions of crime and romance, of curiosity and its gratification, which we find written with more or less cleverness in the enormous mass of so-called detective literature under which the press groans. Every bookstall has its shilling shocker, and every magazine which aims at a circulation must have its mystery of robbery or murder. Most of these are poor enough stuff; complicated plots, which can be discounted in the first chapter, extraordinary coincidences, preternaturally gifted detectives, who make discoveries more or less useless by flashes of insight which no one else can understand, become wearisome in their sameness, and the interest, such as it is, centres only in the results and not in the methods. We may admire Lecoq, but we do not see ourselves in his shoes. Dr. Conan Doyle has made a well-deserved success for his detective stories, and made the name of his hero beloved by the boys of this country by the marvellous cleverness of his method. He shows how easy it is, if only you can observe, to find out a great deal as to the works and ways of your innocent and unconscious friends, and, by an extension of the same method, to baffle the criminal and lay bare the manner of his crime. There is nothing new under the sun. Voltaire taught us the method of Zadig, and every good teacher of medicine or surgery exemplifies every day in his teaching and practice the method and its results. The precise and intelligent recognition and appreciation of minor differences is the real essential factor in all successful medical diagnosis. Carried into ordinary life, granted the presence of an insatiable curiosity and fairly acute senses, you have Sherlock Holmes as he astonishes his somewhat dense friend Watson; carried out in a specialised training, you have Sherlock Holmes the skilled detective.

Dr. Conan Doyle's education as a student of medicine taught him how to observe, and his practice, both as a general practitioner and a specialist, has been a splendid training for a man such as he is, gifted with eyes, memory, and imagination. Eyes and ears which can see and hear, memory to record at once and to recall at pleasure the impressions of the senses, and an imagination capable of weaving a theory or piecing together a broken chain or unravelling a tangled clue, such are implements of his trade to a successful diagnostician. If in addition the doctor is also a born story-teller, then it is a mere matter of choice whether he writes detective stories or keeps his strength for a great historical romance as is the "White Company." Syme, one of the greatest teachers of surgical diagnosis that ever lived, had a favourite illustration which, as a tradition of his school, has made a mark on Dr. Conan Doyle's method, "Try to learn the features of a disease or injury as precisely as you know the features, the gait, the tricks of manner of your most intimate friend." Him, even in a crowd, you can recognise at once; it may be a crowd of men dressed alike, and each having his complement of eyes, nose, hair, and limbs; in every essential they resemble each other, only in trifles do they differ; and yet, by knowing these trifles well, you make your diagnosis or recognition with ease. So it is with disease of mind or body or morals. Racial peculiarities, hereditary tricks of manner, accent, occupation or the want of it, education, environment of all kinds, by their little trivial impressions gradually mould or curve the individual, and leave finger marks or chisel scores which the expert can recognise. The great broad characteristics which at a glance can be recognised as indicative of heart disease or consumption, chronic drunkenness or long-continued loss of blood, are the common property of the veriest tyro in medicine, while to masters of their art there are myriads of signs eloquent and instructive, but which need the educated eye to detect. A fair-sized and valuable book has lately been written on the one symptom, the pulse; to any one but a trained physician it seems as much an absurdity as is Sherlock Holmes' immortal treatise on the one hundred and fourteen varieties of tobacco ash. The greatest stride that has been made of late years in preventive and diagnostic medicine consists in the recognition and differentiation by bacteriological research of those minute organisms which disseminate cholera and fever, tubercle and anthrax. The importance of the infinitely little is incalculable. Poison a well at Mecca with the cholera bacillus, and the holy water which the pilgrims carry off in their bottles will infect a continent, and the rags of the victims of the plague will terrify every seaport in Christendom.

Trained as he has been to notice and appreciate minute detail, Dr. Doyle saw how he could interest his intelligent readers by taking them into his confidence, and showing his mode of working. He created a shrewd, quick-sighted, inquisitive man, half doctor, half virtuoso, with plenty of spare time, a retentive memory, and perhaps with the best gift of all—the power of unloading the mind of all the burden of trying to remember unnecessary details. Holmes tells Watson: "A man should keep his little brain-attic stocked with all the furniture that he is likely to use, as the rest he can put away in the lumber-room of his library, where he can get it if he wants it." But to him the petty results of environment, the sign-manuals of labour, the stains of trade, the incidents of travel, have living interest, as they tend to satisfy an insatiable, almost inhuman, because impersonal curiosity. He puts the man in the position of an amateur, and therefore irresponsible, detective, who is consulted in all sorts of cases, and then he lets us see how he works. He makes him explain to the good Watson the trivial, or apparently trivial, links in his chain of evidence. These are at once so obvious, when explained, and so easy, once you know them, that the ingenuous reader at once feels, and says to himself, I also could do this; life is not so dull after all; I will keep my eyes open, and find out things. The gold watch, with its scratched keyhole and pawn-brokers' marks, told such an easy tale about Watson's brother. The dusty old billycock hat revealed that its master had taken to drinking some years ago, and had got his hair cut yesterday. The tiny thorn-prick and fearsome footmark of the thing that was neither a child nor a monkey enabled Holmes to identify and capture the Andaman Islander. Yet, after all, you say, there is nothing wonderful; we could all do the same.

The experienced physician and the trained surgeon every day, in their examinations of the humblest patient, have to go through a similar process of reasoning, quick or slow according to the personal equations of each, almost automatic in the experienced man, laboured and often erratic in the tyro, yet requiring just the same simple requisites, senses to notice facts, and education and intelligence to apply them. Mere acuteness of the senses is not enough. Your Indian tracker will tell you that the footprint on the leaves was not a redskin's, but a paleface's, because it marked a shoe-print, but it needs an expert in shoe-leather to tell where that shoe was made. A sharp-eyed detective may notice the thumb-mark of a grimy or bloody hand on the velvet or the mirror, but it needs all the scientific knowledge of a Galton to render the ridges and furrows of the stain visible and permanent, and then to identify by their sign-manual the suspected thief or murderer. Sherlock Holmes has acute senses, and the special education and information that make these valuable; and he can afford to let us into the secrets of his method. But in addition to the creation of his hero, Dr. Conan Doyle in this remarkable series of stories has proved himself a born story-teller. He has had the wit to devise excellent plots, interesting complications; he tells them in honest Saxon-English with directness and pith; and, above all his other merits, his stories are absolutely free from padding. He knows how delicious brevity is, how everything tends to be too long, and he has given us stories that we can read at a sitting between dinner and coffee, and we have not a chance to forget the beginning before we reach the end. The ordinary detective story, from Gaboriau or Boisgobey down to the latest shocker, really needs an effort of memory quite misplaced to keep the circumstances of the crimes and all the wrong scents of the various meddlers before the wearied reader. Dr. Doyle never gives you a chance to forget an incident or miss a point.

Early Parodies
—Con Amore

The Singular Adventure of the Unexpected Doorscraper

KENNETH GRAHAME

"What's up, Ratty?" asked the Mole.

"*Snow* is up," replied the Rat briefly; "or rather, *down*. It's snowing hard."

The Mole came and crouched beside him, and, looking out, saw the wood that had been so dreadful to him in quite a changed aspect. Holes, hollows, pools, pitfalls, and other black menaces to the wayfarer were vanishing fast, and a gleaming carpet of faery was springing up everywhere, that looked too delicate to be trodden upon by rough feet. A fine powder filled the air and caressed the cheek with a tingle in its touch, and the black boles of the trees showed up in a light that seemed to come from below.

"Well, well, it can't be helped," said the Rat, after pondering. "We must make a start, and take our chance, I suppose. The worst of it is, I don't exactly know where we are. And now this snow makes everything look so very different."

It did indeed. The Mole would not have known that it was the same wood. However, they set out bravely, and took the line that seemed most promising, holding on to each other and pretending with invincible cheerfulness that they recognized an old friend in every fresh tree that grimly and silently greeted them, or saw openings, gaps, or paths with a familiar turn in them, in the monotony of white space and black tree-trunks that refused to vary.

An hour or two later—they had lost all count of time—they pulled up, dispirited, weary, and hopelessly at sea, and sat down on a fallen tree-trunk to recover their breath and consider what was to be done. They were aching with fatigue and bruised with tumbles; they had fallen into several holes and got wet through; the snow was getting so deep that they could hardly drag their little legs through it, and the trees were thicker and more like each other than ever. There seemed to be no end to this wood, and no beginning, and no difference in it, and, worst of all, no way out.

"We can't sit here very long," said the Rat. "We shall have to make another push for it, and do something or other. The cold is too awful for anything, and the snow will soon be too deep for us to wade through." He peered about him and considered. "Look here," he went on, "this is what occurs to me. There's a sort of dell down there in front of us, where the ground seems all hilly and humpy and hummocky. We'll make our way down into that, and try and find some sort of shelter, a cave or hole with a dry floor to it, out of the snow and the wind, and there we'll have a good rest before we try again, for we're both of us pretty dead beat. Besides, the snow may leave off, or something may turn up."

So once more they got on their feet, and struggled down into the dell, where they hunted about for a cave or some corner that was dry and a protection from the keen wind and the whirling snow. They were investigating one of the hummocky bits the Rat had spoken of, when suddenly the Mole tripped up and fell forward on his face with a squeal.

"O, my leg!" he cried. "O, my poor shin!" and he sat up on the snow and nursed his leg in both his front paws.

"Poor old Mole!" said the Rat kindly. "You don't seem to be having much luck to-day, do you? Let's have a look at the leg. Yes," he went on, going down on his knees to look, "you've cut your shin, sure enough. Wait till I get at my handkerchief, and I'll tie it up for you."

"I must have tripped over a hidden branch or a stump," said the Mole miserably. "O my! O my!"

"It's a very clear cut," said the Rat, examining it again attentively. "That was never done by a branch or a stump. Looks as if it was made by a sharp edge of something in metal. Funny!" He pondered awhile, and examined the humps and slopes that surrounded them.

"Well, never mind what done it," said the Mole, forgetting his grammar in his pain. "It hurts just the same, whatever done it."

But the Rat, after carefully tying up the leg with his handkerchief, had left him and was busy scraping in the snow. He scratched and shovelled and explored, all four legs working busily, while the Mole waited impatiently, remarking át intervals, "O, *come* on, Rat!"

Suddenly the Rat cried "Hooray!" and then "Hooray-oo-ray-oo-ray-oo-ray!" and fell to executing a feeble jig in the snow.

"What *have* you found, Ratty?" asked the Mole, still nursing his leg.

"Come and see!" said the delighted Rat, as he jigged on.

The Mole hobbled up to the spot and had a good look.

"Well," he said at last, slowly, "I *see* it right enough. Seen the same sort of thing before, lots of times. Familiar object, I call it. A door-scraper! Well, what of it? Why dance jigs round a door-scraper?"

"But don't you see what it *means, you*—you dull-witted animal?" cried the Rat impatiently.

"Of course I see what it means," replied the Mole. "It simply means that some *very* careless and forgetful person has left his door-scraper lying about in the middle of the Wild Wood, *just* where it's *sure* to trip *everybody* up. Very thoughtless of him, I call it. When I get home I shall go and complain about it to—to somebody or other, see if I don't!"

"O dear! O dear!" cried the Rat, in despair at his obtuseness. "Here, stop arguing and come and scrape!" And he set to work again and made the snow fly in all directions around him.

After some further toil his efforts were rewarded, and a very shabby door-mat lay exposed to view.

"There, what did I tell you?" exclaimed the Rat, in great triumph.

"Absolutely nothing whatever," replied the Mole, with perfect truthfulness. "Well now," he went on, "you seem to have found another piece of domestic litter, done for and thrown away, and I suppose you're perfectly happy. Better go ahead and dance your jig round that if you've got to, and get it over, and then perhaps we can go on and not waste any more time over rubbish-heaps. Can we *eat* a door-mat? Or sleep under the door-mat? Or sit on a door-mat and sledge home over the snow on it, you exasperating rodent?"

"Do—you—mean—to—say," cried the excited Rat, "that this door-mat doesn't *tell* you anything?"

"Really, Rat," said the Mole quite pettishly, "I think we'd had enough of this folly. Who ever heard of a door-mat *telling* any one anything? They simply don't do it. They are not that sort at all. Door-mats know their place."

"Now look here, you—you thick-headed beast," replied the Rat, really angry, "this must stop. Not another word, but scrape—scrape and scratch and dig and hunt around, especially on the sides of the hummocks, if you want to sleep dry and warm to-night, for it's our last chance!"

The Rat attacked a snow-bank beside them with ardour, probing with his cudgel everywhere and then digging with fury; and the Mole scraped busily too, more to oblige the Rat than for any other reason, for his opinion was that his friend was getting light-headed.

Some ten minutes' hard work, and the point of the Rat's cudgel struck something that sounded hollow. He worked till he could get a paw through and feel; then called the Mole to come and help him. Hard at it went the two animals, till at last the result of their labours stood full in view of the astonished and hitherto incredulous Mole.

In the side of what had seemed to be a snow-bank stood a solid-looking little door, painted a dark green. An iron bell-pull hung by the side, and below it, on a small brass plate, neatly engraved in square capital letters, they could read by the aid of moonlight:—

MR. BADGER.

The Mole fell backwards on the snow from sheer surprise and delight. "Rat!" he cried in penitence, "you're a wonder! A real wonder, that's what you are. I see it all now! You argued it out, step by step, in that wise head of yours, from the very moment that I fell and cut my shin, and you looked at the cut, and at once your majestic mind said to itself, 'Door-scraper!' And then you turned to and found the very door-scraper that done it! Did you stop there? No. Some people would have been quite satisfied; but not you. Your intellect went on working. 'Let me only just find a door-mat,' says you to yourself, 'and my theory is proved!' And of course you found your door-mat. You're so clever, I believe you could find anything you liked. 'Now,' says you, 'that door exists, as plain as if I saw it. There's nothing else remains to be done but to find it!' Well, I've read about that sort of thing in books, but I've never come across it before in real life. You ought to go where you'll be properly appreciated. You're simply wasted here, among us fellows. If I only had your head, Ratty——"

"But as you haven't," interrupted the Rat rather unkindly, "I suppose you're going to sit on the snow all night and *talk*? Get up at once and hang on to that bell-pull you see there, and ring hard, as hard as you can, while I hammer!"

While the Rat attacked the door with his stick, the Mole sprang up at the bell-pull, clutched it and swung there, both feet well off the ground, and from quite a long way off they could faintly hear a deep-toned bell respond.

In 1893, Richard D'Oyly Carte, the original producer in London of the Gilbert and Sullivan operettas, mounted a production of Jane Annie, *a musical comedy written by two illustrious collaborators, Arthur Conan Doyle and* JAMES M. BARRIE *(1860–1937), the beloved playwright-novelist who created* Peter Pan. *The show was not a success (for details, see Appendix I), but at least whimsical Barrie capitalized on the failure by scribbling the following Sherlock Holmes spoof on the flyleaf of one of his books and sending it off to his erstwhile partner. Doyle declared it the best of all Holmes parodies he'd ever seen, and included it in his own autobiography,* Memories and Adventures. *(How could he resist calling it* Memoirs and Adventures?!*)*

The Adventure of the Two Collaborators

JAMES M. BARRIE

In bringing to a close the adventures of my friend Sherlock Holmes I am perforce reminded that he never, save on the occasion which, as you will now hear, brought his singular career to an end, consented to act in any mystery which was concerned with persons who made a livelihood by their pen. "I am not particular about the people I mix among for business purposes," he would say, "but at literary characters I draw the line."

We were in our rooms in Baker Street one evening. I was (I remember) by the centre table writing out *The Adventure of the Man without a Cork Leg* (which had so puzzled the Royal Society and all the other scientific bodies of Europe), and Holmes was amusing himself with a little revolver practice. It was his custom of a summer evening to fire round my head, just shaving my face, until he had made a photograph of me on the opposite wall, and it is a slight proof of his skill that many of these portraits in pistol shots are considered admirable likenesses.

I happened to look out of the window, and perceiving two gentlemen advancing rapidly along Baker Street asked him who they were. He immediately lit his pipe, and, twisting himself on a chair into the figure 8, replied:

"They are two collaborators in comic opera, and their play has not been a triumph."

I sprang from my chair to the ceiling in amazement, and he then explained:

"My dear Watson, they are obviously men who follow some low calling. That much even you should be able to read in their faces. Those little pieces of blue paper which they fling angrily from them are Durrant's Press Notices. Of these they have obviously hundreds about their person (see how their pockets bulge). They would not dance on them if they were pleasant reading."

I again sprang to the ceiling (which is much dented), and shouted: "Amazing! But they may be mere authors."

"No," said Holmes, "for mere authors only get one press notice a week. Only criminals, dramatists and actors get them by the hundred."

"Then they may be actors."

"No, actors would come in a carriage."

"Can you tell me anything else about them?"

"A great deal. From the mud on the boots of the tall one I perceive that he comes from South Norwood. The other is as obviously a Scotch author."

"How can you tell that?"

"He is carrying in his pocket a book called (I clearly see) *Auld Licht Something*.* Would anyone but the author be likely to carry about a book with such a title?"

I had to confess that this was improbable.

It was now evident that the two men (if such they can be called) were seeking our lodgings. I have said (often) that my friend Holmes seldom gave way to emotion of any kind, but he now turned livid with passion. Presently this gave place to a strange look of triumph.

"Watson," he said, "that big fellow has for years taken the credit for my most remarkable doings, but at last I have him—at last!"

Up I went to the ceiling, and when I returned the strangers were in the room.

"I perceive, gentlemen," said Mr. Sherlock Holmes, "that you are at present afflicted by an extraordinary novelty."

The handsomer of our visitors asked in amazement how he knew this, but the big one only scowled.

"You forget that you wear a ring on your fourth finger," replied Mr. Holmes calmly.

I was about to jump to the ceiling when the big brute interposed.

"That tommy-rot is all very well for the public, Holmes," said he, "but you can drop it before me. And, Watson, if you go up to the ceiling again I shall make you stay there."

Auld Licht Idylls (1888) was one of Barrie's first books.—MK

Here I observed a curious phenomenon. My friend Sherlock Holmes *shrank*. He became small before my eyes. I looked longingly at the ceiling, but dared not.

"Let us cut the first four pages," said the big man, "and proceed to business. I want to know why—"

"Allow me," said Mr. Holmes, with some of his old courage. "You want to know why the public does not go to your opera."

"Exactly," said the other ironically, "as you perceive by my shirt stud." He added more gravely, "And as you can only find out in one way I must insist on your witnessing an entire performance of the piece."

It was an anxious moment for me. I shuddered, for I knew that if Holmes went I should have to go with him. But my friend had a heart of gold.

"Never," he cried fiercely, "I will do anything for you save that."

"Your continued existence depends on it," said the big man menacingly.

"I would rather melt into air," replied Holmes, proudly taking another chair. "But I can tell you why the public don't go to your piece without sitting the thing out myself."

"Why?"

"Because," replied Holmes calmly, "they prefer to stay away."

A dead silence followed that extraordinary remark. For a moment the two intruders gazed with awe upon the man who had unravelled their mystery so wonderfully. Then drawing their knives—

Holmes grew less and less, until nothing was left save a ring of smoke which slowly circled to the ceiling.

The last words of great men are often noteworthy. These were the last words of Sherlock Holmes: "Fool, fool! I have kept you in luxury for years. By my help you have ridden extensively in cabs, where no author was ever seen before. *Henceforth you will ride in buses!*"

The brute sunk into a chair aghast.

The other author did not turn a hair.

> *To A. Conan Doyle*
> *from his friend*
> *J. M. Barrie*

The Mystery of Pinkham's Diamond Stud

JOHN KENDRICK BANGS

"It is the little things that tell in detective work, my dear Watson," said Sherlock Holmes as we sat over our walnuts and coffee one bitter winter night shortly before his unfortunate departure to Switzerland, whence he never returned.

"I suppose that is so," said I, pulling away upon the very excellent stogie which mine host had provided—one made in Pittsburgh in 1885, and purchased by Holmes, whose fine taste in tobacco had induced him to lay a thousand of these down in his cigar-cellar for three years, and then keep them in a refrigerator, overlaid with a cloth soaked in Château Yquem wine for ten. The result may be better imagined than described. Suffice it to say that my head did not recover for three days, and the ash had to be cut off the stogie with a knife. "I suppose so, my dear Holmes," I repeated, taking my knife and cutting three inches of the stogie off and casting it aside, furtively, lest he should think I did not appreciate the excellence of the tobacco, "but it is not given to all of us to see the little things. Is it, now?"

"Yes," he said, rising and picking up the rejected portion of the stogie. "We all see everything that goes on, but we don't all know it. We all hear everything that goes on, but we are not conscious of the fact. For instance, at this present moment there is somewhere in this world a man being set upon by assassins and yelling lustily for help. Now his yells create a certain atmospheric disturbance. Sound is merely vibration, and once set going, these vibrations will run on and on and on in ripples into the infinite—that is, they will never stop, and sooner or later these vibrations must reach our ears. We may not know it when they do, but they will do so none the less. If the man is in the next room, we will hear the yells almost simultaneously—not quite, but almost—with their utterance. If the man is in Timbuctoo, the vibrations may not reach us for a little time, according to the speed with which they travel. So with sight. Sight seems limited, but in reality it is not. *Vox populi, vox Dei.* If *vox,* why not *oculus*? It is a simple proposition, then, that the eye of the people being the eye of God, the eye of God being all-seeing, therefore the eye of the people is all-seeing—Q. E. D."

I gasped, and Holmes, cracking a walnut, gazed into the fire for a moment.

"It all comes down, then," I said, "to the question, who are the people?"

Holmes smiled grimly. "All men," he replied, shortly; "and when I say all men, I mean all creatures who can reason."

"Does that include women?" I asked.

"Certainly," he said. "Indubitably. The fact that women *don't* reason does not prove that they can't. I *can* go up in a balloon if I wish to, but I *don't.* I *can* read an American newspaper comic supplement, but I *don't.* So it is with women. Women can reason, and therefore they have a right to be included in the classification whether they do or don't."

"Quite so," was all I could think of to say at the moment. The extraordinary logic of the man staggered me, and I again began to believe that the famous mathematician who said that if Sherlock Holmes attempted to prove that five apples plus three peaches made four pears, he would not venture to dispute his conclusions, was wise. (This was the famous Professor Zoggenhoffer, of the Leipsic School of Moral Philosophy and Stenography.—ED.)

"Now you agree, my dear Watson," he said, "that I have proved that we see everything?"

"Well—" I began.

"Whether we are conscious of it or not?" he added, lighting the gas-log, for the cold was becoming intense.

"From that point of view, I suppose so—yes," I replied, desperately.

"Well, then, this being granted, consciousness is all that is needed to make us fully informed on any point."

"No," I said, with some positiveness. "The American people are very conscious, but I can't say that generally they are well-informed."

I had an idea this would knock him out, as the Bostonians say, but counted without my host. He merely laughed.

"The American is only self-conscious. Therefore he is well-informed only as to self," he said.

"You've proved your point, Sherlock," I said. "Go on. What else have you proved?"

"That it is the little things that tell," he replied. "Which all men would realize in a moment if they could see the little things—and when I say 'if they could see,' I of course mean if they could be conscious of them."

"Very true," said I.

"And I have the gift of consciousness," he added.

I thought he had, and I said so. "But," I added, "give me a concrete example." It had been some weeks since I had listened to any of his detective stories, and I was athirst for another.

He rose up and walked over to his pigeon-holes, each labelled with a letter, in alphabetical sequence.

"I have only to refer to any of these to do so," he said. "Choose your letter."

"Really, Holmes," said I, "I don't need to do that. I'll believe all you say. In fact, I'll write it up and *sign my name* to any statement you choose to make."

"Choose your letter, Watson," he retorted. "You and I are on terms that make flattery impossible. Is it F, J, P, Q, or Z?"

He fixed his eye penetratingly upon me. It seemed for the moment as if I were hypnotized, and as his gaze fairly stabbed me with its intensity, through my mind there ran the suggestion "Choose J, choose J, choose J." To choose J became an obsession. To relieve my mind, I turned my eye from his and looked at the fire. Each flame took on the form of the letter J. I left my chair and walked to the window and looked out. The lamp-posts were twisted into the shape of the letter J. I returned, sat down, gulped down my brandy-and-soda, and looked up at the portraits of Holmes's ancestors on the wall. They were all J's. But I was resolved never to yield, and I gasped out, desperately,

"Z!"

"Thanks," he said, calmly. "Z be it. I thought you would. Reflex hypnotism, my dear Watson, is my forte. If I wish a man to choose Q, B takes hold upon him. If I wish him to choose K, A fills his mind. Have you ever observed how the mind of man repels a suggestion and flees to something else, merely that it may demonstrate its independence of another mind? Now I have been suggesting J to you, and you have chosen Z—"

"You misunderstood me," I cried, desperately. "I did not say Z; I said P."

"Quite so," said he, with an inward chuckle. "P was the letter I wished you to choose. If you had insisted upon Z, I should really have been embarrassed. See!" he added. He removed the green-ended box that rested in the pigeon-hole marked Z, and, opening it, disclosed an emptiness.

"I've never had a Z case. But P," he observed, quietly, "is another thing altogether."

Here he took out the box marked P from the pigeon-hole, and, opening it, removed the contents—a single paper which was carefully endorsed, in his own handwriting, "The Mystery of Pinkham's Diamond Stud."

"You could not have selected a better case, Watson," he said, as he unfolded the paper and scanned it closely. "One would almost think you had some prevision of the fact."

"I am not aware," said I, "that you ever told the story of Pinkham's diamond stud. Who was Pinkham, and what kind of a diamond stud was it—first-water or Rhine?"

"Pinkham," Holmes rejoined, "was an American millionaire, living during business hours at Allegheny City, Pennsylvania, where he had to wear a brilliant stud to light him on his way through the streets, which are so dark and sooty that an ordinary search-light would not suffice. In his leisure hours, however, he lived at the Hotel Walledup-Hysteria, in New York, where he likewise had to wear the same diamond stud to keep him from being a marked man. Have you ever visited New York, Watson?"

"No," said I.

"Well, when you do, spend a little of your time at the Walledup-Hysteria. It is a hotel with a population larger than that of most cities, with streets running to and from all points of the compass; where men and women eat under conditions that Lucullus knew nothing of; where there is a carpeted boulevard on which walk all sorts and conditions of men; where one pays one's bill to the dulcet strains of a string orchestra that woo him into a blissful forgetfulness of its size; and where, by pressing a button in the wall, you may summon a grand opera, or a porter who on request will lend you enough money to enable you and your family to live the balance of your days in comfort. In America men have been known to toil for years to amass a fortune for the one cherished object of spending a week in this Olympian spot, and then to be content to return to their toil and begin life anew, rich only in the memory of its luxuries. It was here that I spent my time when, some years ago, I went to the United States to solve the now famous Piano Case. You will remember how sneak thieves stole a grand piano from the residence of one of New York's first families, while the family was dining in the adjoining room. While in the city, and indeed at the very hotel in which I stopped, and which I have described, Pinkham's diamond stud disappeared, and, hearing that I was a guest at the Walledup-Hysteria, the owner appealed to me to recover it for him. I immediately took the case in hand. Drastic questioning of Pinkham showed that beyond all question he had lost the stud in his own apartment. He had gone down to dinner, leaving it on the centre-table, following the usual course of most millionaires, to whom diamonds are of no particular importance. Pinkham wanted this one only because of its associations. Its value, $80,000, was a mere bagatelle in his eyes.

"Now of course, if he positively left it on the table, it must have been taken by some one who had entered the room. Investigation proved that the maid, a valet, a fellow-millionaire from Chicago, and Pinkham's children had been the only ones to do this. The maid and the valet were above suspicion. Their fees from guests were large enough to place them beyond the reach of temptation. I questioned them closely, and they convinced me at once of their innocence by conducting me through the apartments of other guests wherein tiaras of diamonds and necklaces of pearls—ropes in very truth—rubies, turquoise, and emerald ornaments of priceless value, were scattered about in reckless profusion.

" 'D' yez t'ink oi'd waste me toime on an eighty-t'ousand-dollar shtood, wid all dhis in soight and moine for the thrubble uv swipin' ut?' said the French maid.

"I acquitted her at once, and the valet similarly proved his innocence, only with less of an accent, for he was supposed to be English, and not French, as was the maid, although they both came from Dublin. This narrowed the suspects down to Mr. Jedediah Wattles, of Chicago, and the children. Naturally I turned my attention to Wattles. A six-year-old boy and a four-year-old girl could hardly be suspected of stealing a diamond stud. So drawing on Pinkham for five thousand dollars to pay expenses, I hired a room in a tenement-house in Rivington Street—a squalid place it was—disguised myself with an oily, black, burglarious mustache, and dressed like a comic-paper gambler. Then I wrote a note to Wattles, asking him to call, saying that I could tell him something to his advantage. He came, and I greeted him like a pal. 'Wattles,' said I, 'you've been working this game for a long time, and I know all about you. You are an ornament to the profession, but we diamond-thieves have got to combine. Understand?' 'No, I don't,' said he. 'Well, I'll tell you,' said I. 'You're a man of good appearance, and I ain't, but I know where the diamonds are. If we work together, there's millions in it. I'll spot the diamonds, and you lift 'em, eh? You can do it,' I added, as he began to get mad. 'The ease with which you got away with old Pinky's stud, that I've been trying to pull for myself for years, shows me that.' "

"I was not allowed to go further. Wattles's indignation was great enough to prove that it was not he who had done the deed, and after he had thrashed me out of my disguise, I pulled myself together and said, 'Mr. Wattles, I am convinced that you are innocent.' As soon as he recognized me and realized my object in sending for him, he forgave me, and, I must say, treated me with great consideration.

"But my last clew was gone. The maid, the valet, and Wattles were proved innocent. The children alone remained, but I could not suspect them.

Nevertheless, on my way back to the hotel I bought some rock-candy, and, after reporting to Pinkham, I asked casually after the children.

" 'They're pretty well,' said Pinkham. 'Billie's complaining a little, and the doctor fears appendicitis, but Polly's all right. I guess Billie's all right too. The seventeen-course dinners they serve in the children's dining-room here aren't calculated to agree with Billie's digestion, I reckon.'

" 'I'd like to see 'em,' said I. 'I'm very fond of children.'

"Pinkham immediately called the youngsters in from the nursery. 'Guess what I've got,' I said, opening the package of rock-candy. 'Gee!' cried Billie, as it caught his eye. 'Gimme some!' 'Who gets first piece?' said I. 'Me!' cried both. 'Anybody ever had any before?' I asked. 'He has,' said Polly, pointing to Billie. The boy immediately flushed up. ' 'Ain't, neither!' he retorted. 'Yes you did, too,' said Polly. *'You swallered that piece pop left on the centre-table the other night!'* 'Well, anyhow, it was only a little piece,' said Billie. 'An' it tasted like glass,' he added. Handing the candy to Polly, I picked Billie up and carried him to his father.

" 'Mr. Pinkham,' said I, handing the boy over, 'here is your diamond. It has not been stolen; it has merely been swallowed.' 'What?' he cried. And I explained. The stud mystery was explained. Mr. Pinkham's boy had eaten it."

Holmes paused.

"Well, I don't see how that proves your point," said I. "You said that it was the little things that told—"

"So it was," said Holmes. "If Polly hadn't told—"

"Enough," I cried; "it's on me, old man. We will go down to Willis's and have some Russian caviare and a bottle of Burgundy."

Holmes put on his hat and we went out together. It is to get the money to pay Willis's bill that I have written this story of "The Mystery of Pinkham's Diamond Stud."

A *ccording to Ellery Queen in* The Misadventures of Sherlock Holmes, *the follow-ing amusing selection first appeared in the November 4th, 1893, issue of* Punch *under the delightful editorial byline Cunnin Toil and was published with seven other Holmesian travesties as* The Adventures of Picklock Holes, Together with a Perversion and a Burlesque *(Bradbury, Agnew & Co., London, 1901).* R U D O L F   C H A M B E R S L E H M A N N *was a liberal Member of Parliament and the father of novelist Rosamond and poet-editor-publisher John Lehmann.*

The Umbrosa Burglary

R .   C .   L E H M A N N

During one of my short summer holidays I happened to be spending a few days at the delightful riverside residence of my friend James Silver, the extent of whose hospitality is only to be measured by the excellence of the fare that he sets before his guests, or by the varied amusements that he provides for them. The beauties of Umbrosa (for that is the attractive name of his house) are known to all those who during the summer months pass up (or down) the winding reaches of the Upper Thames. It was there that I witnessed a series of startling events which threw the whole county into a temporary turmoil. Had it not been for the unparalleled coolness and sagacity of Picklock Holes the results might have been fraught with disaster to many distinguished fami-lies, but the acumen of Holes saved the situation and the family plate, and restored the peace of mind of one of the best fellows in the world.

The party at Umbrosa consisted of the various members of the Silver family, including, besides Mr. and Mrs. Silver, three high-spirited and un-married youths and two charming girls. Picklock Holes was of course one of the guests. In fact, it had long since come to be an understood thing that wherever I went Holes should accompany me in the character of a profes-sional detective on the lookout for business; and James Silver, though he may have at first resented the calm unmuscularity of my marvellous friend's im-movable face, would have been the last man in the world to spoil any chance of sport or excitement by refraining from offering a cordial invitation to

Holes. The party was completed by Peter Bowman, a lad of eighteen, who to an extraordinary capacity for mischief added an imperturbable cheerfulness of manner. He was generally known as Shockheaded Peter, in allusion to the brush-like appearance of his delicate auburn hair, but his intimate friends sometimes addressed him as Venus, a nickname which he thoroughly deserved by the almost classic irregularity of his Saxon features.

We were all sitting, I remember, on the riverbank, watching the countless craft go past, and enjoying that pleasant industrious indolence which is one of the chief charms of life on the Thames. A punt had just skimmed by, propelled by an athletic young fellow in boating costume. Suddenly Holes spoke.

"It is strange," he said, "that the man should be still at large."

"What man? Where? How?" we all exclaimed breathlessly.

"The young puntsman," said Holes, with an almost aggravating coolness. "He is a bigamist, and has murdered his great aunt."

"It cannot be," said Mr. Silver, with evident distress. "I know the lad well, and a better fellow never breathed."

"I speak the truth," said Holes, unemotionally. "The induction is perfect. He is wearing a red tie. That tie was not always red. It was, therefore, stained by something. Blood is red. It was, therefore, stained by blood. Now it is well known that the blood of great aunts is of a lighter shade, and the colour of that tie has a lighter shade. The blood that stained it was, therefore, the blood of his great aunt. As for the bigamy, you will have noticed that as he passed he blew two rings of cigarette smoke, and they both floated in the air *at the same time.* A ring is a symbol of matrimony. Two rings together mean bigamy. He is, therefore, a bigamist."

For a moment we were silent, struck with horror at this dreadful, this convincing revelation of criminal infamy. Then I broke out:

"Holes," I said, "you deserve the thanks of the whole community. You will of course communicate with the police."

"No," said Holes, "they are fools, and I do not care to mix myself up with them. Besides, I have other fish to fry."

Saying this, he led me to a secluded part of the grounds, and whispered in my ear.

"Not a word of what I am about to tell you. There will be a burglary here to-night."

"But Holes," I said, startled in spite of myself at the calm omniscience of my friend, "had we not better do something; arm the servants, warn the police, bolt the doors and bar the windows, and sit up with blunderbusses— anything would be better than this state of dreadful expectancy. May I not tell Mr. Silver?"

"Potson, you are amiable, but you will never learn my methods." And with that enigmatic reply I had to be content in the meantime.

The evening had passed as pleasantly as evenings at Umbrosa always pass. There had been music; the Umbrosa choir, composed of members of the family and guests, had performed in the drawing-room, and Peter had drawn tears from the eyes of every one by his touching rendering of the well-known songs of "The Dutiful Son" and "The Cartridge-bearer." Shortly afterwards, the ladies retired to bed, and the gentlemen, after the customary interval in the smoking-room, followed. We were in high good-humour, and had made many plans for the morrow. Only Holes seemed preoccupied.

I had been sleeping for about an hour, when I was suddenly awakened with a start. In the passage outside I heard the voices of the youngest Silver boy and of Peter.

"Peter, old chap," said Johnny Silver, "I believe there's burglars in the house. Isn't it a lark?"

"Ripping," said Peter. "Have you told your people?"

"Oh, it's no use waking the governor and the mater; we'll do the job ourselves. I told the girls, and they've all locked themselves in and got under their beds, so they're safe. Are you ready?"

"Yes."

"Come on then."

With that they went along the passage and down the stairs. My mind was made up, and my trousers and boots were on in less time than it takes to tell it. I went to Holes's room and entered. He was lying on his bed, fully awake, dressed in his best detective suit, with his fingers meditatively extended, and touching one another.

"They're here," I said.

"Who?"

"The burglars."

"As I thought," said Holes, selecting his best basket-hilted life-preserver from a heap in the middle of the room. "Follow me silently."

I did so. No sooner had we reached the landing, however, than the silence was broken by a series of blood-curdling screams.

"Good heavens!" was all I could say.

"Hush," said Holes. I obeyed him. The screams subsided, and I heard the voices of my two young friends, evidently in great triumph.

"Lie still, you brute," said Peter, "or I'll punch your blooming head. Give the rope another twist, Johnny. That's it. Now you cut and tell your governor and old Holes that we've nabbed the beggar."

By this time the household was thoroughly roused. Agitated females and inquisitive males streamed downstairs. Lights were lit, and a remarkable sight met our eyes. In the middle of the drawing-room lay an undersized burglar, securely bound, with Peter sitting on his head.

"Johnny and I collared the beggar," said Peter, "and bowled him over. Thanks, I think I could do a ginger-beer."

The man was of course tried and convicted, and Holes received the thanks of the County Council.

"That fellow," said the great detective to me, "was the best and cleverest of my tame team of country-house burglars. Through him and his associates I have fostered and foiled more thefts than I care to count. Those infernal boys nearly spoilt everything. Potson, take my advice, never attempt a master-stroke in a houseful of boys. They can't understand scientific induction. Had they not interfered I should have caught the fellow myself. He had wired to tell me where I should find him."

Sherlock Holmes does not even appear in the next selection, yet CHARLES BAT-TELL LOOMIS *manages to hit him with a cleverly-aimed barb. One of the earliest and rarest of all American caricatures, "A La Sherlock Holmes" is the sixth chapter from* The Four-Masted Catboat *and* Other Truthful Tales, *published in 1899 by The Century Co., New York.*

A La Sherlock Holmes

CHARLES LOOMIS

Jones and I recently had occasion to take a drive of four or five miles in upper Connecticut. We were met at the station by Farmer Phelps, who soon had us snugly wrapped in robes and speeding over the frozen highway in a sleigh. It was bitter cold weather—the thermometer reading 3° above zero. We had come up from Philadelphia, and to us such extreme cold was a novelty, which is all we could say for it.

As we rode along, Jones fell to talking about Conan Doyle's detective stories, of which we were both great admirers—the more so as Doyle has declared Philadelphia to be the greatest American city. It turned out that Mr. Phelps was familiar with the " 'Meemoirs' of Sherlock Holmes," and he thought there was some "pretty slick reasonin' " in it. "My girl," said he, "got the book out er the library an' read it aout laoud to my woman an' me. But of course this Doyle had it all cut an' dried afore he writ it. He worked backwards an' kivered up his tracks, an' then started afresh, an' it seems more wonderful to the reader than it reely is."

"I don't know," said Jones; "I've done a little in the observation line since I began to read him, and it's astonishing how much a man can learn from inanimate objects, if he uses his eyes and his brain to good purpose. I rarely make a mistake."

Just then we drove past an outbuilding. The door of it was shut. In front of it, in a straight row and equidistant from each other, lay seven cakes of ice, thawed out of a water-pan.

"There," said Jones; "what do we gather from those seven cakes of ice and that closed door?"

I gave it up.

Mr. Phelps said nothing.

Jones waited impressively a moment, and then said quite glibly: "The man who lives there keeps a flock of twelve hens—not Leghorns, but probably Plymouth Rocks or some Asiatic variety. He attends to them himself, and has good success with them, although this is the seventh day of extremely cold weather."

I gazed at him in admiration.

Mr. Phelps said nothing.

"How do you make it all out, Jones?" said I.

"Well, those cakes of ice were evidently formed in a hens' drinking-pan. They are solid. The water froze a little all day long, and froze solid in the night. It was thawed out in the morning and left lying there, and the pan was refilled. There are seven cakes of ice; therefore there has been a week of very cold weather. They are side by side: from this we gather that it was a methodical man who attended to them; evidently no hireling, but the goodman himself. Methodical in little things, methodical in greater ones; and method spells success with hens. The thickness of the ice also proves that comparatively little water was drunk; consequently he keeps a small flock. Twelve is the model number among advanced poultrymen, and he is evidently one. Then, the clearness of the ice shows that the hens are not excitable Leghorns, but fowl of a more sluggish kind, although whether Plymouth Rocks or Brahmas or Langshans, I can't say. Leghorns are so wild that they are apt to stampede through the water and roil it. The closed door shows he has the good sense to keep them shut up in cold weather.

"To sum up, then, this wide-awake poultryman has had wonderful success, in spite of a week of exceptionally cold weather, from his flock of a dozen hens of some large breed. How 's that, Mr. Phelps? Isn't it almost equal to Doyle?"

"Yes; but not accordin' to Hoyle, ez ye might say," said he. "Your reasonin' is good, but it ain't quite borne aout by the fac's. In the fust place, this is the fust reel cold day we 've hed this winter. Secon'ly, they ain't no boss to the place, fer she 's a woman. Thirdly, my haouse is the nex' one to this, an' my boy an' hers hez be'n makin' those ice-cakes fer fun in some old cream-pans. Don't take long to freeze solid in this weather. An', las'ly, it ain't a hen-haouse, but an ice-haouse."

The sun rode with unusual quietness through the heavens. We heard no song of bird. The winds were whist. All nature was silent.

So was Jones.

*T*his obscure lampoon, with its wonderful titular echo of The Sign of the Four, was first published as "The Sign of the '400': Being a Continuation of the Adventures of Sherlock Holmes," by Conan Doyle "per R. K. M." It appeared in the October 24, 1894, issue of the American humor magazine, Puck.

The Sign of the "400"

R. K. MUNKITTRICK

For the nonce, Holmes was slighting his cocaine and was joyously jabbing himself with morphine—his favorite 70 per cent solution—when a knock came at the door; it was our landlady with a telegram. Holmes opened it and read it carelessly.

"H'm!" he said. "What do you think of this, Watson?"

I picked it up. "COME AT ONCE. WE NEED YOU. SEVENTY-TWO CHINCH-BUGGE PLACE, S.W.," I read.

"Why, it's from Athelney Jones," I remarked.

"Just so," said Holmes; "call a cab."

We were soon at the address given, 72 Chinchbugge Place being the town house of the Dowager Countess of Coldslaw. It was an old-fashioned mansion, somewhat weather-beaten. The old hat stuffed in the broken pane in the drawing room gave the place an air of unstudied artistic negligence, which we both remarked at the time.

Athelney Jones met us at the door. He wore a troubled expression. "Here's a pretty go, gentlemen!" was his greeting. "A forcible entrance has been made to Lady Coldslaw's boudoir, and the famous Coldslaw diamonds are stolen."

Without a word Holmes drew out his pocket lens and examined the atmosphere. "The whole thing wears an air of mystery," he said, quietly.

We then entered the house. Lady Coldslaw was completely prostrated and could not be seen. We went at once to the scene of the robbery. There was no sign of anything unusual in the boudoir, except that the windows and furniture had been smashed and the pictures had been removed from the walls. An attempt had been made by the thief to steal the wallpaper, also. However, he had not succeeded. It had rained the night before and muddy footprints led up to the escritoire from which the jewels had been taken. A heavy smell of stale cigar smoke hung over the room. Aside from these hardly noticeable details, the despoiler had left no trace of his presence.

In an instant Sherlock Holmes was down on his knees examining the footprints with a stethoscope. "H'm!" he said; "so you can make nothing out of this, Jones?"

"No, sir," answered the detective; "but I hope to; there's a big reward."

"It's all very simple, my good fellow," said Holmes. "The robbery was committed at three o'clock this morning by a short, stout, middle-aged, hen-pecked man with a cast in his eye. His name is Smythe, and he lives at 239 Toff Terrace."

Jones fairly gasped. "What! Major Smythe, one of the highest thought-of and richest men in the city?" he said.

"The same."

In half an hour we were at Smythe's bedside. Despite his protestations, he was pinioned and driven to prison.

"For heaven's sake, Holmes," said I, when we returned to our rooms, "how did you solve that problem so quickly?"

"Oh, it was easy, dead easy!" said he. "As soon as we entered the room, I noticed the cigar smoke. It was cigar smoke from a cigar that had been given a husband by his wife. I could tell that, for I have made a study of cigar smoke. Any other but a hen-pecked man throws such cigars away. Then I could tell by the footprints that the man had had appendicitis. Now, no one but members of the '400' have that. Who then was hen-pecked in the '400,' and had had appendicitis recently? Why, Major Smythe, of course! He is middle-aged, stout, and has a cast in his eye."

I could not help but admire my companion's reasoning, and told him so. "Well," he said, "it is very simple if you know how."

Thus ended the Coldslaw robbery, so far as we were concerned.

It may be as well to add, however, that Jones's arrant jealousy caused him to resort to the lowest trickery to throw discredit upon the discovery of my gifted friend. He allowed Major Smythe to prove a most conclusive alibi, and then meanly arrested a notorious burglar as the thief, on the flimsiest proof, and convicted him. This burglar had been caught while trying to pawn some diamonds that *seemed* to be a portion of the plunder taken from 72 Chinchbugge Place.

Of course, Jones got all the credit. I showed the newspaper accounts to Holmes. He only laughed, and said: "You see how it is, Watson; Scotland Yard, as usual, gets the glory." As I perceived he was going to play "Sweet Marie" on his violin, I reached for the morphine, myself.

This parody from the May 1915 issue of The Century *is by* CAROLYN WELLS *(1869–1942), who was an anthologist, essayist and one of America's most prolific mystery/suspense authors. Her numerous works include* The Doorstep Murders, The Fourteenth Key, The Luminous Face, The Room with the Tassels *and* Spooky Hollow.

The Adventure of the Clothes-line

CAROLYN WELLS

The members of the Society of Infallible Detectives were just sitting around and being socially infallible, in their rooms in Fakir Street, when President Holmes strode in. He was much saturniner than usual, and the others at once deduced there was something toward.

"And it's this," said Holmes, perceiving that they had perceived it. "A reward is offered for the solution of a great mystery—so great, my colleagues, that I fear none of you will be able to solve it, or even to help me in the marvelous work I shall do when ferreting it out."

"Humph!" grunted the Thinking Machine, riveting his steel-blue eyes upon the speaker.

"He voices all our sentiments," said Raffles, with his winning smile. "Fire away, Holmes. What's the prob?"

"To explain a most mysterious proceeding down on the East Side."

Though a tall man, Holmes spoke shortly, for he was peeved at the inattentive attitude of his collection of colleagues. But of course he still had his Watson, so he put up with the indifference of the rest of the cold world.

"Aren't all proceedings down on the East Side mysterious?" asked Arsène Lupin, with an aristocratic look.

Holmes passed his brow wearily under his hand.

"Inspector Spyer," he said, "was riding on the Elevated Road—one of the small numbered Avenues—when, as he passed a tenement-house district, he saw a clothes-line strung from one high window to another across a court-yard."

"Was it Monday?" asked the Thinking Machine, who for the moment was thinking he was a washing machine.

"That doesn't matter. About the middle of the line was suspended—"

"By clothes-pins?" asked two or three of the Infallibles at once.

"Was suspended a beautiful woman."

"Hanged?"

"No. *Do listen!* She hung by her hands, and was evidently trying to cross from one house to the other. By her exhausted and agonized face, the inspector feared she could not hold on much longer. He sprang from his seat to rush to her assistance, but the train had already started, and he was too late to get off."

"What was she doing there?" "Did she fall?" "What did she look like?" and various similar nonsensical queries fell from the lips of the great detectives.

"Be silent, and I will tell you all the known facts. She was a society woman, it is clear, for she was robed in a chiffon evening gown, one of those roll-top things. She wore rich jewelry and dainty slippers with jeweled buckles. Her hair, unloosed from its moorings, hung in heavy masses far down her back."

"How extraordinary! What does it all mean?" asked M. Dupin, ever straightforward of speech.

"I don't know yet," answered Holmes, honestly. "I've studied the matter only a few months. But I will find out, if I have to raze the whole tenement block. There *must* be a clue somewhere."

"Marvelous! Holmes, marvelous!" said a phonograph in the corner, which Watson had fixed up, as he had to go out.

"The police have asked us to take up the case and have offered a reward for its solution. Find out who was the lady, what she was doing, and why she did it."

"Are there any clues?" asked M. Vidocq, while M. Lecoq said simultaneously, "Any footprints?"

"There is one footprint; no other clue."

"Where is the footprint?"

"On the ground, right under where the lady was hanging."

"But you said the rope was high from the ground."

"More than a hundred feet."

"And she stepped down and made a single footprint. Strange! Quite strange!" and the Thinking Machine shook his yellow old head.

"She did nothing of the sort," said Holmes, petulantly. "If you fellows would listen, you might hear something. The occupants of the tenement houses have been questioned. But, as it turns out, none of them chanced to be at home at the time of the occurrence. There was a parade in the next street, and they had all gone to see it."

"Had a light snow fallen the night before?" asked Lecoq, eagerly.

"Yes, of course," answered Holmes. "How could we know anything, else? Well, the lady had dropped her slipper, and although the slipper was not found, it having been annexed by the tenement people who came home first, I had a chance to study the footprint. The slipper was a two and a half D. It was too small for her."

"How do you know?"

"Women always wear slippers too small for them."

"Then how did she come to drop it off?" This from Raffles, triumphantly.

Holmes looked at him pityingly.

"She kicked it off because it was too tight. Women always kick off their slippers when playing bridge or in an opera box or at a dinner."

"And always when they're crossing a clothes-line?" This in Lupin's most sarcastic vein.

"Naturally," said Holmes, with a taciturnine frown. "The footprint clearly denotes a lady of wealth and fashion, somewhat short of stature, and weighing about one hundred and sixty. She was of an animated nature—"

"Suspended animation," put in Luther Trant, wittily, and Scientific Sprague added, "Like the Coffin of Damocles, or whoever it was."

But Holmes frowned on their light-headedness.

"We must find out what it all means," he said in his gloomiest way. "I have a tracing of the footprint."

"I wonder if my seismospygmograph would work on it," mused Trant.

"I am the Prince of Footprints," declared Lecoq, pompously. "I will solve the mystery."

"Do your best, all of you," said their illustrious president. "I fear you can do little; these things are unintelligible to the unintelligent. But study on it, and meet here again one week from tonight, with your answers neatly typewritten on one side of the paper."

*T*he Infallible Detectives started off, each affecting a jaunty sanguineness of demeanor, which did not in the least impress their president, who was used to sanguinary impressions.

They spent their allotted seven days in the study of the problem; and a lot of the seven nights, too, for they wanted to delve into the baffling secret by sun or candlelight, as dear Mrs. Browning so poetically puts it.

And when the week had fled, the Infallibles again gathered in the Fakir Street sanctum, each face wearing the smug smirk and smile of one who had quested a successful quest and was about to accept his just reward.

"And now," said President Holmes, "as nothing can be hid from the Infallible Detectives, I assume we have all discovered *why* the lady hung from the clothes-line above that deep and dangerous chasm of a tenement court-yard."

"We have," replied his colleagues, in varying tones of pride, conceit, and mock modesty.

"I cannot think," went on the hawk-like voice, "that you have, any of you, stumbled upon the real solution of the mystery; but I will listen to your amateur attempts."

"As the oldest member of our organization, I will tell my solution first," said Vidocq, calmly. "I have not been able to find the lady, but I am convinced that she was merely an expert trapezist or tightrope walker, prac-tising a new trick to amaze her Coney Island audiences."

"Nonsense!" cried Holmes. "In that case the lady would have worn tights or fleshings. We are told she was in full evening dress of the smartest set."

Arsène Lupin spoke next.

"It's too easy," he said boredly; "she was a typist or stenographer who had been annoyed by attentions from her employer, and was trying to escape from the brute."

"Again I call your attention to her costume," said Holmes, with a look of intolerance on his finely cold-chiseled face.

"That's all right," returned Lupin, easily. "Those girls dress every old way! I've seen 'em. They don't think anything of evening clothes at their work."

"Humph!" said the Thinking Machine, and the others all agreed with him.

"Next," said Holmes, sternly.

"I'm next," said Lecoq. "I submit that the lady escaped from a near-by lunatic asylum. She had the illusion that she was an old overcoat and the moths had got at her. So of course she hung herself on the clothes-line. This theory of lunacy also accounts for the fact that the lady's hair was down—like *Ophelia's,* you know."

"It would have been easier for her to swallow a few good moth balls," said Holmes, looking at Lecoq in stormy silence. "Mr. Gryce, you are an experienced deducer; what did *you* conclude?"

Mr. Gryce glued his eyes to his right boot toe, after his celebrated habit. "I make out she was a-slumming. You know, all the best ladies are keen about it. And I feel that she belonged to the Cult for the Betterment of Clothes-lines. She was by way of being a tester. She had to go across them hand over hand, and if they bore her weight, they were passed by the cen-sor."

"And if they didn't?"

"Apparently that predicament had not occurred at the time of our problem, and so cannot be considered."

"I think Gryce is right about the slumming," remarked Luther Trant, "but the reason for the lady hanging from the clothes-line is the imperative necessity she felt for a thorough airing, after her tenemental visitations; there is a certain tenement scent, if I may express it, that requires ozone in quantities."

"You're too material," said the Thinking Machine, with a faraway look in his weak, blue eyes. "This lady was a disciple of New Thought. She had to go into the silence, or concentrate, or whatever they call it. And they always choose strange places for these thinking spells. They have to have solitude, and, as I understand it, the clothes-line was not crowded?"

Rouletabille laughed right out.

"You're way off, Thinky," he said. "What ailed that dame was just that she wanted to reduce. I've read about it in the women's journals. They all want to reduce. They take all sorts of crazy exercises, and this crossing clothes-lines hand over hand is the latest. I'll bet it took off twenty of those avoirdupois with which old Sherly credited her."

"Pish and a few tushes!" remarked Raffles, in his smart society jargon. "You don't fool me. That clever little bear was making up a new dance to thrill society next winter. You'll see. Sunday-paper headlines: STUNNING NEW DANCE! THE CLOTHES-LINE CLING! CAUGHT ON LIKE WILDFIRE! *That's* what it's all about. What do you know, eh?"

"Go take a walk, Raffles," said Holmes, not unkindly; "you're sleepy yet. Scientific Sprague, you sometimes put over an abstruse theory, what do you say?"

"I didn't need science," said Sprague, carelessly. "As soon as I heard she had her hair down, I jumped to the correct conclusion. She had been washing her hair, and was drying it. My sister always sticks her head out of the skylight; but this lady's plan is, I should judge, a more all-round success."

As they had now all voiced their theories, President Holmes rose to give them the inestimable benefit of his own views.

"Your ideas are not without some merit," he conceded, "but you have overlooked the eternal-feminine element in the problem. As soon as I tell you the real solution, you will each wonder why it escaped your notice. The lady thought she heard a mouse, so she scrambled out of the window, preferring to risk her life on the perilous clothes-line rather than stay in the dwelling where the mouse was also. It is all very simple. She was doing her hair, threw her head over forward to twist it, as they always do, and so espied the mouse sitting in the corner."

"Marvelous! Holmes, marvelous!" exclaimed Watson, who had just come back from his errand.

Even as they were all pondering on Holmes's superior wisdom, the telephone bell rang.

"Are you there?" said President Holmes, for he was ever English of speech.

"Yes, yes," returned the impatient voice of the chief of police. "Call off your detective workers. We have discovered who the lady was who crossed the clothes-line, and why she did it."

"I can't imagine you really know," said Holmes into the transmitter; "but tell me what you think."

"A-r-r-rh! Of course I know! It was just one of those confounded moving-picture stunts!"

"Indeed! And why did the lady kick off her slipper?"

"A-r-r-r-h! It was part of the fool plot. She's Miss Flossy Flicker of the Flim-Flam Film Company, doin' the six-reel thriller, 'At the End of Her Rope.' "

"Ah," said Holmes, suavely, "my compliments to Miss Flicker on her good work."

"Marvelous, Holmes, marvelous!" said Watson.

*S*herlock Holmes *always enjoyed a cordial relationship with Americans (cf. subsequent selections by H. F. Heard, Roberta Rogow and Craig Shaw Gardner), and this is certainly evident on the remarkable day when he settled fair and square for the Knockers and the Pickle Eaters. This droll slice of Americana appeared in the Sunday edition of the* Seattle Post-Intelligencer *on February 25, 1906.*

Sherlock Holmes Umpires Baseball

ANONYMOUS

A bunch of old-time fans were sitting in the rear of a downtown cigar stand the other day, talking over the good old times of the past, when baseball was the real goods and everybody would turn out to witness an exhibition of the national sport, without too much regard to the quality of the article.

The discussion finally wandered into the umpire line, when one old-timer, that looked like a reproduction of the character of the fat man portrayed by Gibson in his famous cartoon, "Three Strikes and Out," broke into the conversational game.

"Did any of you ever hear of the time Sherlock Holmes umpired a baseball game?"

No one had, and so he continued:

"I was playing on a nine in a small town in Iowa one summer and was mixed up in a way in the first and only exhibition ever given by Sherlock Holmes of the correct way to umpire.

"We were playing a series of games with another town about thirty miles distant, and the feeling between the two teams and their following was at a high pitch. Hardly a game passed without ending in a free-for-all fight or mobbing the umpire.

"There were two twins playing on our team that looked so much alike that even the players that worked with them every day were unable to tell them apart, except by looking at their feet. One of the twins had a very slight deformity to his right foot, so slight that it would never be noticed by a casual observer.

"In order to keep the records straight on the batting order we named one of the twins 'Leftfoot' and the other 'Rightfoot.'

" 'Rightfoot' had been batting like a fiend ever since the opening of the season, while 'Leftfoot' was somewhat weak with the stick, but the best fielder on the team. 'Leftfoot' played center field and 'Rightfoot' covered the right garden.

"Whenever it looked as if we were in a pinch it was the custom to ring in 'Rightfoot' in place of 'Leftfoot' occasionally to even up matters. He was always good in a pinch, and many a time had won the game by taking the place of 'Leftfoot' at the bat.

"We called our team the Knockers and the other bunch with which we were playing the series answered to the name of the Pickle Eaters.

"The Pickle Eaters had grown suspicious that we were working a smooth game on the batting order and were getting very particular about the selection of an umpire.

"We had a game scheduled at home one Sunday afternoon and were looking for a large bunch of trouble when the Pickle Eaters entered a protest against the regular umpire acting and refused to start the game until some one else was selected.

"Just as the controversy had reached the stage when it looked as if it would be necessary to dish back the money to the crowd, a tall, cadaverous-looking man, leading a dog that looked like a cross between a bloodhound and an Irish setter, stepped from the bleachers and volunteered to take charge of the ceremonies.

"Without even waiting for an answer the tall stranger walked out to the position back of the pitcher's box and called the game. The assurance of the man won the point, and both teams went into the game without further argument.

"Talk about science in umpiring a ball game, that guy certainly had everything skinned that ever came over the pike. He could outrun any man on either team and was always at the spot when it looked as if the decision would be close. There was no disputing his decision, because he was always in the proper position to hand out the right dope.

"It was in the last inning that the real sensational decision of the game occurred, which marked the stranger as the greatest exponent of the baseball umpiring art and assisted in revealing his identity.

"We were up for the last crack at the ball, with the Pickle Eaters two runs in the lead. There were two out and all of the bases full when the scorer called 'Leftfoot' to the bat. It was a tight hole and the captain decided to take a chance on ringing in 'Rightfoot.' He gave the signal and the chief willow swisher went to the plate. He swatted the first one that came over squarely on the nose and landed it over the center field fence, and went trailing around the bases, bringing in all of the men ahead of him.

"Almost as soon as 'Rightfoot' landed on the ball the head guy of the Pickle Eaters was out with the big protest, claiming that it was the wrong man up. The lanky one listened to his tale of woe and was at the bench to meet 'Rightfoot' when he wandered in from his little canter. Before the startled player had time to draw his breath the umpire had grabbed his foot with one hand and sliced a piece off the heel of his shoe with a sharp knife that he was carrying in the other hand. He performed a similar operation on 'Leftfoot' and then started for the outfield like a shot.

"When he reached the spot where 'Rightfoot' was accustomed to stand in the right garden he went down on his knees and examined the ground for several minutes with a microscope, then made for the center pasture, where he repeated the performance. Without saying a word he rushed back to the bleachers' stand, where his dog was fastened, and after releasing the queer-looking animal rubbed the piece of leather that he had clipped from 'Rightfoot's' shoe over his nose and ordered the dog to 'go find him.' The hound went around the bases at a modest canter, almost perfectly imitating the gait of 'Rightfoot,' and wound up at the players' bench by taking a firm hold on the surplus bottom of 'Rightfoot's' trousers.

" ' "Rightfoot" out for batting out of his turn,' shouted the umpire. 'Side out and the Pickle Eaters win.'

"Not even a protest was entered to the decision. It was all done so quick and in such an amazing manner that no one thought of disputing the decision.

"The players gathered in a crowd to discuss the strange proceedings, but when they looked for the stranger both he and the dog had disappeared. No one had noticed them leave the grounds, and just how he got away is a mystery that is still being discussed by the old-timers back in the little village.

"We were asking each other who the man could possibly be when the town constable came forward and volunteered the information that the erstwhile umpire was Sherlock Holmes, who had been investigating a strange murder case in an adjoining hamlet."

Six Classic
Pastiches

The Adventure of the Circular Room

AUGUST DERLETH

It was a wild, windy night in April of a year in the early nineties when the diabolic affair of the circular room was brought to the attention of Sherlock Holmes. I had been engaged in compiling my notes from which these narratives of my friend's experiences are fashioned in an effort to elucidate his extraordinary methods, and this task had taken all the leisure moments of that day, for my medical practise had not yet grown to such a degree that I had no free time during the afternoon. Holmes was at work on his since-published commentary, designed as a companion piece for Dr. Hans Gross's remarkable *Criminal Investigation.* He had just put his notes aside, and had reached for his violin upon the mantel, when he heard the sound of hoofbeats on the road beyond our lodgings in Baker Street.

"Who could be seeking our lodgings on such a night as this?" I asked, hoping I had correctly interpreted the slowing-up of the hoofbeats.

Holmes had already stepped to the window and drawn aside the curtain, to look down to where the street-lamp shone before the building.

"A young woman of great determination, to dare such weather. Wind and rain, Watson—Oh, to be in England now that April's here!—But she is coming up the steps, and her brougham waits."

Our bell pealed insistently.

Holmes stood with his head cocked a little to one side, listening. He had permitted the curtain to fall back over the window, and stood with his hands in the pockets of his dressing-gown. "Ah, Mrs. Hudson has not yet gone to bed. She has not long since put on her bedroom slippers and her robe. There she is at the door."

In a moment Mrs. Hudson's heavy footsteps came creaking up the stairs, followed by lighter steps, which, however, came with no less assurance. Mrs. Hudson knocked on our door, tried it, and opened it apologetically.

"A young lady to see you, Mr. Holmes."

"Show her in, by all means, Mrs. Hudson."

Mrs. Hudson stepped back, and there walked into our quarters a firm-eyed young woman whose dark hair was molded severely about her head under a small toque of an inexpensive fur. She paused just past the threshold, her waterproof thrown back over her shoulders.

"Do sit down, Miss . . . ?"

"Manahan."

"Miss Manahan. I trust nothing has happened to your patient?"

"So do I." She gasped. Then she smiled, and her rather severe face broke out into most attractive features. "I have heard of your methods, Mr. Holmes. That is why I came to you."

"It is evident that you are a trained nurse, for your cuffs show under your jacket, and there is a small iodine stain on your finger, though there is no wound there. You have come to consult me about your patient?"

Miss Manahan sat down, having given me her waterproof to hang up. She clasped her hands, bit her lip, and looked faintly uneasy.

"I do hope I am not doing the wrong thing, Mr. Holmes, but I have such a strong feeling about this that I could not put it off any longer."

"I assure you, I have every respect for a woman's intuition."

"Thank you. You make me feel more right about coming here, though I am sure I do not know what Mr. and Mrs. Davies would think if they knew."

"They need not know. But pray let us hear your story, Miss Manahan."

Thus urged, our attractive visitor composed herself, sat thinking for a moment as if to choose a point of departure, and then began. "Mr. Holmes, I have been out of work for some time, and quite by accident I chanced upon an advertisement in the *News of the World* a fortnight ago. I have it here." She took it from a little bag she carried in her pocket, and handed it to Holmes, who spread it on the table so that I, too, could read it.

Wanted: A capable young woman with professional nursing knowledge to serve as companion for elderly lady. Applicant

should be prepared against distressing circumstances. Good remuneration. Please apply to Mr. Wellman Davies, in care of this
paper.

Holmes handed it back without a word.

"I made application, and three days later I received a letter asking me to
call at a house in Richmond, just out of London along the upper reaches of
the Thames. I found the house to be of recent construction, very pleasant and
rather modern, set on the shore of the river in commodious surroundings,
and occupied by Mr. and Mrs. Wellman Davies, who had in their care Mr.
Davies' elderly aunt, a Mrs. Lydia Thornton, who had only recently been
released from an institution for mental health, and was still in an uncertain
state to the extent of needing a companion with some knowledge of professional nursing.

"Mrs. Thornton proved to be a genteel lady approaching sixty years of
age. She had been confined, she confided, for seven years, during which time
her nephew had very kindly managed her affairs, and finally, when her condition had improved, she had been released, so that she might come to live in
the house the Davies had built for her with funds which the executor of her
late husband's estate allowed them at her request. My patient was very unsure
of herself, still; following her husband's death, she had gone through a mental
breakdown not uncommon to people of middle age; she was difficult at
night, but by day, generally, she was so normal that it was hard to believe in
her mental state."

"It is often so," I put in.

"Yes, and I soon discovered that she was the victim of alarming hallucinations. She was convinced, for instance, that her late husband called to her
to come to him. She heard his voice in the night, and told me about it quite
matter-of-factly, as if it were nothing at all strange. That, I believe, is common enough in such cases."

"Is it, Watson?" Holmes looked at me.

"Yes, indeed. The woman has plainly come to accept it as a part of her
existence."

"Pray go on, Miss Manahan. I fancy you have something more to tell
us."

"The hallucination which seems to me the strangest of the lot is one
which so profoundly disturbs my patient that I fear for her mind, and I am
sure she will eventually need to return to confinement. I discovered it on the
second morning after I came, though I was not wholly unprepared for it;
both Mr. and Mrs. Davies had very considerately and delicately told me that
Mrs. Thornton might 'break out' at any time, and I must not be too distressed
or alarmed, for her 'seizures' did not last long. Nevertheless, I was alarmed at
Mrs. Thornton's initial 'seizure.'

"I occupy the adjoining room to Mrs. Thornton's, which is a lovely, circular room at one corner of the house, constructed to afford a view of the grounds, the summer-house and the Thames there. On the morning in question, I had not yet risen, when I heard my patient scream; then my door was flung open, and she came into my room wide-eyed with fear, and trembling, laboring under the amazing hallucination that her room had been changed, that she was being preyed upon by outside forces—for she had gone to sleep with her bed facing the windows, as usual, and had awakened to find herself and her bed facing my room.

"I persuaded her to return to her room with me, and we found it just as I had last seen it when I left her on the previous night. I thought this a most amazing hallucination, and I found it recurrent—sometimes nightly for a while, and then not occurring for two or three days at a time. I could understand her auditory hallucination about her dead husband's calling to her, since I could believe in the psychological basis for this; but the more I considered this hallucination of hers about her room, the more puzzled I became.

"At the same time, I began to be aware of something strange in the house. I cannot describe it, Mr. Holmes, but it was an impression that grew upon me. I cannot understand it, either, for I have been very well treated, not only by my patient, but also by Mr. and Mrs. Davies and their single servant, a woman who comes by the day from the vicinity. As my patient's hallucination persisted, my own impression about the strangeness of the house grew, and several times I found myself being regarded with something akin to alarm by Mr. Davies, who looked away when I saw him looking at me. This has been going on for approximately a fortnight; I am unable to put my finger on anything *wrong*, Mr. Holmes, yet I know there *is* something wrong there."

She was still, expecting Holmes's questions. Holmes sat touching the lobe of one ear with his long, bony fingers for a few moments in silence; then he asked whether our client had correlated any facts in the matter. "Did the occurrence of your patient's outbreaks or 'seizures,' as you call them, coincide with any household event apart from them?"

"I think not. It is only that on the day before her first seizure, she was visited by her sister-in-law, who said something which upset her very badly. In the early dawn of the next day she had her first outbreak."

"Ah! Has her sister-in-law visited her since then?"

"Three times, Mr. Holmes."

"And afterward?"

"She had those outbreaks."

"According to your narrative, however, she also had such outbreaks on mornings which did not follow visits by her sister-in-law."

"Yes, Mr. Holmes."

"Neither Mr. nor Mrs. Davies offered any explanation of these seizures?"

"No, Mr. Holmes. They were very much distressed by them, and hoped that I would not mind too much, for they had looked forward to bringing Mrs. Thornton back to a normal existence, and wanted, at all costs, to avoid the necessity of sending their aunt back to the asylum."

"Do you know what form her insanity took?"

"I believe it was manic depression which came as a result of her husband's sudden and rather shocking death; this took place during her delayed climacteric. The situation is not uncommon."

Holmes flashed a glance at me.

"Yes, that is right. Those years are very difficult, and any untoward shock may bring about disastrous mental breakdowns."

Holmes touched his fingertips together in a characteristic gesture, and closed his eyes. "With what does Mrs. Thornton occupy herself during the day?"

"She reads, or I read to her. She plays solitaire; sometimes I play with her. Once or twice she has evinced a desire to play chess, but she always tires and is unable to finish a game."

"How does she strike you as a chess player?"

Miss Manahan was somewhat startled by the abruptness of Holmes's question. "She is not a good player."

"I fancy that is in part due to her mental instability, wouldn't you say so, Watson?"

I agreed.

Holmes's eyes flashed open and fixed upon Miss Manahan in a long, keen stare. "Have you yourself sought any explanation of why your patient should labor under the extraordinary delusion that her room and bed, as well as her own person, are at the mercy of malefic forces?"

"No, Mr. Holmes, I have been unable to do so. My knowledge of mental cases is limited."

"What would you say of this, Watson?" asked Holmes.

"It is highly unusual. In most such cases there is usually a well-hidden source for all hallucinations and illusions, and once it is discovered and exposed to the patient, the cure is often forthcoming. Mrs. Thornton's illusion is most extraordinary."

"Surely, Miss Manahan, you have your patient's case history from the institution where she was confined?"

"Certainly, Mr. Holmes."

"You have studied it?"

"Of course."

"Very well. What then of her previous record?"

"In what respect?"

"Manifestly in regard to the particular hallucination to which you refer."

"There was no previous record of its occurrence."

"Ha!" exclaimed Holmes, sitting upright in his chair and regarding Miss Manahan with that peculiarly benevolent expression which he always bestowed upon his clients when his interest was aroused. "Surely even insanity has a pattern, Miss Manahan?"

"There are many kinds, Mr. Holmes."

"Yes, yes—but you yourself have grave doubts, is it not so?"

"Yes, it is. But, Mr. Holmes, Mrs. Thornton is very convincing in her agitation. She struggles so hard *not* to believe in her hallucination, and each time we return to the room to find it as it was before, she breaks down in tears; that sorrow is genuine, Mr. Holmes, and it is most terribly distressing. I am appalled by it; I was impelled to come here by it; I cannot understand what is happening; I admit I have had little experience with mental cases— but, Mr. Holmes, if ever I saw a woman who is fighting very bravely and very hard to escape her mental prison, that woman is my patient. I admire her very much, I admire her courage, and it is heartbreaking to endure her horror and terror and her final grief, as each time she is brought to face the room unchanged in every respect."

"You have come here on your own account, then?"

"Entirely. I want so to help her, if I can, and if somehow her sister-in-law is responsible for the pattern of events, I want to know what to do to prevent my patient's being so dreadfully upset."

"What do you suggest?"

"Mr. Holmes, it is Thursday, my day off. Tomorrow night Mr. and Mrs. Davies are leaving to visit some relatives in Edinburgh. If it is possible, could you come out to the house at 23 Linley Road and yourself speak to Mrs. Thornton?"

"At what time are your employers leaving?"

"They are planning to take the seven o'clock from Victoria."

"Very well. We shall be at the house at approximately that hour, or as soon thereafter as possible."

Miss Manahan rose. "Thank you, Mr. Holmes."

I brought her waterproof, helped her into it, and showed her to the door.

Holmes was sitting in an attitude of deep contemplation when I returned.

"What did you think of the young lady, Watson?"

"Most capable and conscientious."

"With spirit, imagination, and levelheadedness, moreover. Miss Manahan clearly suspects a nasty business, and I have no doubt she is correct. Is that not a most curious hallucination of Mrs. Thornton's?"

"I have never had any clinical experience with anything even remotely similar."

Holmes chuckled. "Allowing for the fact that your clinical experience is somewhat limited, I fancy that states the case well enough. What explanation could you, as a medical man, have to offer?"

"I have not seen the patient, Holmes."

"Come, come—do not stand on ceremony. I am not asking you to prescribe."

"Well, then. I should say that some sudden dislocation in time or space could account for it."

"If, for instance, the sister-in-law had imparted to the patient a piece of very shocking information?"

"Possibly."

Holmes closed his eyes. "And what did you make of her dead husband's voice calling to her?"

"Very common in such cases. The relation between the shock of his death and her initial collapse is very clear."

"Dear me! How insistent we all are upon simplifying even the most remote aspects of human experience! It has been well said that perhaps it is we who are insane, and the so-called insane who are sane. What a proposition!— eh, Watson? And yet, how dreadfully logical! The case of Mrs. Thornton fascinates me out of all proportion to its importance, for its evidence of the depths of depravity and despair of which the human mind is capable."

" 'Depravity' is not the word."

"I beg your pardon, Watson. Let us just settle on 'decay,' then. I fear poor Mrs. Thornton is close to the brink, and our client is rightfully loath to see the poor lady go over it again. Would that more young ladies in the nursing profession were possessed of such conscience!"

The house in Richmond was indeed an attractive one, viewed as we saw it in the early twilight of the following evening. It was a building of one storey, low and rambling, with a quaint round corner crowned by a colorful turret; clearly it had been built by someone of imagination with a good sense of harmony, for even its trim in white and blue was pleasing to the eye. It was set, moreover, on a gentle slope toward the Thames, in spacious grounds which had been landscaped, and the summer- or tea-house Miss Manahan had described was set in the midst of a scant grove halfway between the house and the river.

Mrs. Thornton was plainly the most genteel of ladies. She was dressed in a white dress, with a few frills, and wore a velvet band about her neck to support a cameo. Her eyes were bird-like, and her appearance elfin. Holmes and I were introduced to her as friends of Miss Manahan's, and the old lady seemed quite pleased to meet someone new.

For a little while Holmes talked generalities in his most garrulous vein. Both Miss Manahan and Mrs. Thornton easily fell into his mood, and it was with something of a grave change in manner that Holmes introduced the subject of the late Mr. Thornton.

"I understand you have lost your husband, Mrs. Thornton?"

She seemed somewhat startled, but responded readily enough. "Yes, that was eight years ago—no, nine it is now, I think. It was sudden."

"Quite a shock to you?"

"Yes, a severe shock." She smiled. "It took me some time to get over it. I am afraid we poor women are not as strong mentally as we are physically."

It was Miss Manahan who next undertook to change the subject, by making mention of her patient's sister-in-law.

"I am afraid Miss Lavinia is not very kind," said Mrs. Thornton hesitantly. "If she could only know Wellman and Pauline as I know them."

"They are very kind to you, Mrs. Thornton?"

"If it had not been for them, I would still be—I would still be in the asylum." She said this bravely, though with obvious effort. "When it seemed that I was improving my condition, Wellman was notified, and he would not rest until he had secured my release. He had my authority to build this little house for me, and we are all living here very cozily together. I do not know where I should be without Wellman; he has always managed my affairs, and it is distressing that my sister-in-law should say the things she does." She looked toward the window suddenly and, with an expression of dismay, cried out, "Oh, it is coming up fog!"

"We'll draw the curtains, never mind, Mrs. Thornton," said Miss Manahan reassuringly. Then she turned to Holmes and asked casually whether he would like to see the house before Mrs. Thornton retired.

"If Mrs. Thornton would not mind."

"By no means, Mr. Holmes. I am quite proud of it. I worked over every detail of it with Wellman when it was under construction, and it is almost like my own creation! Do you go, too, Dr. Watson; I can keep quite well by myself for so short a time!"

Thus urged, I followed Holmes, whose interest, of course, was Mrs. Thornton's bedroom, the spacious chamber in the rounded corner of the house. This was, as Miss Manahan had said, a singularly attractive room, with a small bed set almost in the center, and facing toward the windows which opened upon the lawns sloping toward the river. A dressing-table stood over against the wall to the left, and to the right, immediately next to the door leading into Miss Manahan's room, stood a little case filled with books. A comfortable rocking-chair of recent manufacture, a little table, and several other chairs were distributed about the room, into which opened three doors—one to a bath jointly shared by Mrs. Thornton and Mr. and Mrs. Davies, on the left, one to Miss Manahan's room, and one into the hall that ran along the building there, separating the bedrooms from the drawing-room, dining-room, and kitchen on the side of the house facing the road.

Holmes stood for a few moments in silence, gazing about the room. "This is the way the room has always been?"

"Yes, Mr. Holmes."

"And when Mrs. Thornton has her seizures?"

"She describes it in various ways. She says she has awakened to find herself facing the door to the hall, with the book-case over against the windows; or again, facing the Davies' room, with the dressing-table against the windows."

"You have never observed anything which might give her cause or reason for such hallucinations?"

"No, Mr. Holmes."

"Have the Davies offered any explanation?"

"Yes. They felt that perhaps the fact that the room was unusual in that it was circular was at the bottom of her hallucination, and they offered to exchange rooms with her; but she would not hear of it."

"Ah! Why not?"

"Because she felt she must fight this out by herself."

Holmes looked at me with a strange gleam in his eyes. "Surely that is remarkable insanity, is it not, Watson?"

"Most remarkable."

He smiled and began to move around the room; he looked casually at the dressing-table, the book-case; he examined the windows and opened the door to the bath, muttering to himself as he went along. "Hm! Bath in pale green. Very neat. . . . They have certainly given her the best view of the river," adding over his shoulder to Miss Manahan, "You will have to draw the curtains all the way, for the fog is growing thicker every minute. I can hardly make out the summer-house." Then he got down on his knees and examined the bed and the floor, crawling around in a manner which puzzled and amused our client, for he was careless, as always, of his clothing, and he picked up all manner of lint, hairs, and the like, for only a few small rugs were laid on the floor, and the rest of it was bare, though not highly polished. He was occupied at this for some time before he rose to his feet, dusted himself, and confessed himself finished.

"There are then two bedrooms beside this, and two baths?" he asked.

"Yes, Mr. Holmes."

"A drawing-room, a kitchen, a dining-room—and what else?"

"A little room for storage, and two closets, with a pantry. That is all."

"No basement?"

"Only a small cellar for fruit directly under the kitchen."

"Ah, well, I shall just look around."

So he did, much to my amazement, even descending into the small, square concrete cellar under the kitchen. When he came up again he looked extremely thoughtful and somewhat perplexed.

"We can return to Mrs. Thornton now," he said.

Upon our return, darkness having fallen, Mrs. Thornton bade us good-night and retired to her room, accompanied by Miss Manahan. Holmes lit his pipe and sat with his long legs stretched out before him, looking quizzically over at me with his keen eyes.

"Did not Mrs. Thornton strike you as a most unusual mental case?"

"Indeed she did."

"I watched you with some interest, Watson. The expressions of your features are informative. I submit you did not believe Mrs. Thornton at all deranged."

"Well, it is true her entire manner is that of one who has recovered from a mental lapse."

"Is it not, indeed! I fancy very few patients would have the courage to speak so openly and frankly of their troubles."

"Oh, some of them do nothing else."

"Ah, yes, the hypochondriacs. But you did not think Mrs. Thornton one."

"No."

"You felt that her conduct was inconsistent with her seizures? Come, is it not so?"

"Well, yes, I admit I did. But of course, the trouble with such mental cases is that the patient always seems perfectly normal, and it is difficult to tell which is the real psyche, to put it in those terms—the woman we saw or the woman she is overnight. I thought her comments about the sister-in-law most indicative."

"That it was Miss Lavinia Thornton who was at the bottom of her trouble?"

"I think there can be no doubt of it. I believe we should pay the lady a call and hear what she has to say."

"Oh, I fancy we can avoid doing so," said Holmes with assurance. "I know what the lady has to say."

"Surely you have not seen her already?"

"I have had no occasion to do so. Mrs. Thornton told us."

He left me to puzzle this out for myself, and went back into reflective silence, puffing at his pipe from time to time, and crossing and re-crossing his legs. He got up presently and suggested that, in view of Miss Manahan's present occupation, we might just walk about the grounds a bit.

We left the house and found that the fog had indeed grown thick. It was evident, however, that Holmes wished to see the summer-house before we returned to our lodgings, for it was directly there that he walked, with an uncanny instinct for its direction from the house. It was, like the house, of wood, but with a little stone terrace around it, and a stone floor; it was not locked—indeed, it seemed to have no lock—and Holmes made his way inside. Like most structures of its kind, it was obviously designed chiefly for use at lawn or garden parties, or for reposing on a summer's day, made up, as it was, of a single large room, with quaint, rustic benches and a table to match. Holmes used his lantern to examine the walls and floor.

"Are those not large stone blocks, Watson?" he inquired thoughtfully.

"Yes. Though I have seen larger."

"It is a substantial floor."

I agreed that it was.

"Hm! It does not seem to you that there is anything noteworthy about it?"

"Nothing beyond the fact that it is a very workmanlike job. If ever I decide to leave Baker Street, I shall have to look up Mr. Davies' builder."

"Well, there is surely no time like the present. Perhaps Miss Manahan can find it out for us."

We returned to the house, where we found our client awaiting us amid some wonderment as to where we had gone. Holmes explained that we had walked on the grounds, and then asked whether Mrs. Thornton had gone to sleep.

"Not yet, Mr. Holmes."

"Ah! Would you be so good as to ask her two questions for me? Whether, if she knows the name of the builder of this house, she might be kind enough to let my friend Watson here have it? And whether her late husband's executor can easily be reached by telephone?"

Miss Manahan looked at him somewhat strangely, but immediately departed to do as he requested. She came back in a few moments with both questions answered; the builder lived in London, not very far, as it turned out, from Baker Street; and, as for the executor, he was no longer active, since her husband's estate had naturally now been turned over to her, and her nephew was taking care of it for her.

"Now there is just one more thing," said Holmes. He produced from his pocket a piece of ordinary chalk. "After your patient has gone to sleep, let us just try an experiment. Take this chalk and draw a small line down any portion of the wall, across the narrow molding between wall and floor, and out onto the floor, constructing a line of approximately a foot in length, as inconspicuously as possible."

She took the chalk with an absurd expression of bafflement on her attractive features. "I am afraid your methods are quite beyond me, Mr. Holmes."

"Oh, there is nothing at all mysterious about my methods, Miss Manahan, believe me. They are all too simple. We have been proceeding all along on the theory that Mrs. Thornton's tale is a fabrication born of hallucination out of her mental condition. Let us just now proceed from the opposite pole. Mrs. Thornton's tale is either true or not true; that is simple logic. We shall have to discover the answer to the riddle ourselves, for plainly she cannot help us."

I could not help adding a question of my own. "Would it not be appropriate to learn whether or not Mrs. Thornton's sister-in-law has visited her recently?"

Miss Manahan responded at once. "It is strange that you should ask, Doctor. Miss Lavinia called this morning."

"Ah, and I fancy the result of her call was the same as before?" put in Holmes.

"Yes. Mrs. Thornton was left much distressed."

"Well, I daresay we can do no more here. How long, by the way, are Mr. and Mrs. Davies planning to be gone?"

"They expect to return Sunday night."

"Capital! That will give us every opportunity of solving this little mystery. I trust your night will not be too difficult a one, Miss Manahan, but if any trouble should arise, pray do not hesitate to call on us, no matter what the hour. In any case, I hope you will send us a wire in the morning and inform us how Mrs. Thornton spent the night."

"I will do so, Mr. Holmes."

We bade our client good night and made our way back to the nearest conveyance into the city. Holmes was singularly silent, with a foreboding frown on his forehead, and he walked hunched up, his chin sunk into the folds of his coat.

"What do you make of it?" I asked.

"A devilish business, Watson. It goes against my grain."

"Ah, you have a theory, then?"

"On the contrary, I have the solution."

"Impossible!" I cried. "I have been with you every moment."

"Ah, yes, physically. Nothing is ever impossible with quite your vehemence, my dear fellow."

More than that he would not say.

In the morning Miss Manahan, instead of using the telegraph, came to see us in person.

She had a sorry tale to tell, for Mrs. Thornton had suffered a most difficult night. It had begun, as on other occasions, with the conviction that she heard her husband's voice calling to her, but last night there was an additional note in that the poor distraught lady had fancied her husband had begged her to leave this earthly plane and join him, and this had kept her awake for more than an hour at approximately midnight. In the early hours, everything had gone as usual: Mrs. Thornton had come into Miss Manahan's room crying that "they" had changed things again, "they" were after her, as always. When they had returned, the room had been just as it should be.

I listened attentively to Miss Manahan's recital, and when she had finished I could not prevent myself from identifying the poor woman's type of delusion. "Paranoidal delusions," I said, shaking my head. "I'm afraid it is all up with her. She will get progressively worse."

"And the chalk mark, Miss Manahan?"

"I believe it was just as I made it."

Holmes chuckled delightedly. "Aha! I detect a note of hesitation in your voice, Miss Manahan. Come, come—what is it?"

"Well," she laughed nervously. "I'm afraid I am beginning to have hallucinations, too, Mr. Holmes. I did think the mark was a little off kilter, but I guess I must have drawn it crookedly; I did it in a hurry, and did not want to wake my patient; but when I first saw it this morning, I did get somewhat of a surprise."

"Ah, no doubt. I fancy we shall be over in your direction tonight, Miss Manahan. Can you put us up?"

"Why—I think so."

"Expect us then. We shall arrive directly after dinner." He turned to me when she had left. "It is as I thought, Watson. We shall have to lose no time putting an end to this diabolic game."

Fog rose again, as on the previous night, when we set out for Richmond, and Holmes made no secret of his elation, saying that he preferred not to be seen in the vicinity of 23 Linley Road, and generally acting in a most mysterious manner, which he said nothing whatever to explain. Nor did he volunteer any explanation to Miss Manahan; he asked at once to see her patient, the gentle Mrs. Thornton, and when the old lady came, he sat down next to her, took one of her frail hands in his, and spoke most cajolingly.

"Do you know, Mrs. Thornton, I have become most interested in your trouble. Unlike Miss Manahan, I am beginning to believe that your room actually is changed, just as you described it to Miss Manahan to be."

I thought that this blunt approach might be harmful to the patient, and was hard pressed to interfere; but I knew better, and Mrs. Thornton's reaction was one of bewildered interest, as if at first she had not understood that Miss Manahan had spoken to us of her hallucinations, and secondly, as if she were pleasantly surprised to discover someone who did not dismiss her hallucinations for what they were.

"Will you give Dr. Watson and me an opportunity to look into the matter?"

"Why, certainly, Mr. Holmes." She looked hesitantly at Miss Manahan, and was reassured by the young woman's confident smile.

"Then for tonight only I want you to share Miss Manahan's room, and permit Dr. Watson and myself to occupy your own. I assure you we shall look into the matter with fairness and impartiality."

For only a moment the old lady hesitated. Then she began to tremble, biting her lip, her emotions aroused. "I am afraid—I—it's no use. It is nothing anyone else sees, or hears—nothing. Oh, Mr. Holmes, if only you could!"

"Let us just see," replied Holmes calmly. "Surely there is no harm in trying."

In the end, Mrs. Thornton gave in. Thereupon, Holmes and I retired at once to the patient's room, though not before abjuring both the ladies to carry on for the remainder of the evening as if they were quite alone in the house.

Once in the room, Holmes drew the curtains and turned up the light. He took a magnifying glass from his pocket, found the chalk mark Miss Manahan had made, and came to his knees to examine it.

"Ah, our Miss Manahan is not perfect in observation. Look here, Watson."

I took the glass and held it over the angle of the chalk line.

"I submit that Miss Manahan could not have drawn that line in such a fashion. There is a clear, if fractional break, between the wall and the floor. Or let us say, rather, between the edge of the molding and the floor."

"Yes, that is all very true," I conceded, "but what is the explanation?"

"Ah, it is the obvious one, surely." He pocketed his glass, took out his pen-knife, opened it, and slipped its blade beneath the molding; he moved it freely about. "Does not that suggest anything to you?"

"The molding appears to be attached to the wall rather than the floor."

"Ah, well, that is very often done." He moved along the wall five feet and again passed his knife-blade between the molding and the floor. "I fancy that is the rule." He got up. "Hm! Now let us see. We shall not go to bed, of course, but let us rig up some sort of dummy to occupy Mrs. Thornton's place. I fancy we shall want to be out of sight of that bathroom door, for, unless I am greatly mistaken, it plays its own small part in this mystery."

I looked at the door. "I am in the woods, Holmes. How can you possibly make such an assertion?" I strode over, opened the door, and looked into the bathroom.

Holmes observed me with manifest patience. "Let us say that you make yourself comfortable on the floor behind the door as it opens. I myself will find a place behind the bed." As he spoke, he began to arrange Mrs. Thornton's bed with a roll of blanket and a pillow to simulate someone sleeping there. Having finished this, he turned out the light, crossed to the windows, and threw up the shades, together with the central window, which was the largest; this, despite the fog, he opened half way. In the adjoining room, meanwhile, the ladies were preparing for bed.

"Now, then, Watson—not a sound. Whatever you hear, say nothing; whatever happens, do nothing until I give you the word."

"If you would give me a hint, Holmes . . ."

"We shall see devil's work tonight, Watson, unless I am much mistaken."

He said no more; so I composed myself to snatch as much sleep as possible.

Some two hours passed in absolute silence, when there came to my ears the faint sound of a whispered voice. It seemed to rise from somewhere in my immediate vicinity, and, as I listened, it increased in volume. "Lydia! Lydia!" it cried. "Come to me. Come over. All is pain where you are. Only here will it end in joy again. Lydia! Lydia!"

A man's voice—or was it a man's voice? It had a hollow, funereal sound, and I felt my skin prickle, as if something of the fog flowing into the room through the open window had penetrated my flesh. It was horrible, it was grotesque, it was damnable.

Then I heard Holmes stir, and in a moment he raised his own voice in a remarkable quavering cry that might have been Mrs. Thornton herself replying. "Frank? Frank? Where are you, Frank?"

"Come over to me, Lydia. Come. It does not matter how you do it, only come. We can be happy again over here." Then the voice faded as it had come, diminishing altogether in a last whispered, "Lydia!" urgent and compelling.

Holmes waited a few moments before coming quietly to my side and whispering into my ear. "I fancy that is somewhat more than an auditory illusion, is it not, Watson?"

"Good God! I begin to understand!" I answered. "It is damnable. But why—why?"

"Wait yet a little. It is far from over."

In two hours time, everything happened as before, I had dozed off and was awakened by the voice calling once again. This time Holmes did not come to my side, though a low clucking sound he made after the voice had ceased assured me he had heard.

Then all was silence again, and so it remained until dawn.

It was then that I became conscious of a tremor in the floor of the room where I sat. I was about to call out to Holmes when his cluck of warning stopped me. And then the entire floor began to move, slowly, almost imperceptibly. I had hardly time to assimilate this before Holmes's urgent whisper reached me. "Keep behind the bathroom door." I crept backward along that weirdly moving floor, revolving slowly, soundlessly, until the dressing-table was indeed before the windows lining the east wall of that room, and the book-case over before one door. There was now light enough in the room to see it as Mrs. Thornton must have seen it, and it took no imagination to understand how horrified and terrified the poor, stricken lady must have been at this sight, and how much more to come back into the room and find it as it should be.

As soon as the movement stopped, Holmes twitched the folded blanket and pillow from the bed, gave vent to a low sobbing moan, and, hastening across the floor to the door leading into Miss Manahan's room, he opened it and slammed it shut. This accomplished, he raced silently around the room to where I crouched, one hand warningly grasping my shoulder.

On the instant, the door to the bath-room was cautiously opened, someone looked into the room, and then immediately the door was drawn noiselessly shut once more.

"So!" whispered Holmes. "That is dastardly work indeed, Watson. And one alone could not do it, no!" He peered around one edge of the window nearest us. "Ha! there is the signal. Come along."

He darted to the open window, crawled out, dropped to the ground, and ran off into the now rising fog. I followed close upon his heels. Without hesitation, he ran to the summer-house and entered it.

The rustic table had been moved aside, and in the center of the floor gaped an opening through which light flowed upward. Holmes walked cat-like to the edge of the opening and looked down. I peered over his shoulder.

There below was an extraordinary sight. A man was bent at some kind of great instrument, whose shafts passed into a tunnel leading in the direction of the house we had just left, and before him, attached in some fashion to the machine at which he worked with such quiet persistence, was a perfect mini-ature, walls and floor, of the room we had just quitted, and, as he worked, the miniature floor slowly shifted its position, righting itself.

"Good morning, Mr. Wellman Davies," said Holmes in a scornful voice. "I fancy you will have no further occasion to carry on your devil's work."

At the sound of Holmes's voice, Davies whipped around. His hand reached out for a spanner which lay nearby, but Holmes's hand was quicker; he showed his revolver, and Davies, a short, benevolent-looking man with pale grey eyes and a clipped moustache, whose nose showed signs of eye-glasses having been worn, hesitated, and glared at us in baffled rage.

"Come up, come up, Mr. Davies. We have yet to take your wife. How did you find your friends in Scotland?"

"In reality," said Holmes in the brougham on our way back to Baker Street through the first morning sun to penetrate the night's dense yellow fog, "the problem offered of no other solution. Indeed, Mrs. Thornton, poor unsuspecting soul, told us all herself. What had Miss Lavinia, her sister-in-law, to say that would upset her? Why, could it be other than criticism of, and warnings about Mr. and Mrs. Davies? Surely not, for Mrs. Thornton said, you remember, 'If she could only know Wellman and Pauline as I know them.' Alas! poor woman!

"The fundamental problem was, of course, that of the circular room. Either it was changed, as Mrs. Thornton said, or it was not. Miss Manahan and Mrs. Thornton herself were convinced that it could be nothing but an hallucination. On the contrary, I proceeded from the assumption that something *was* wrong with that room, and I sought for evidence that it was so. Obviously, the walls were fixed, but the floor did not seem to be. When the space between the molding along the wall at the floor and the floor itself was manifest, it was clear that in some fashion the floor was constructed on a large turntable. I thought there might be a clue in the basement; but there was no basement beyond that concrete-walled cellar. Hence I sought the summer-house, and it was immediately apparent to my eye that the large stone blocks concealed a trapdoor. The assumption was obvious that that diabolic business was carried on from there. An accomplice was clearly indicated, and who else but Mrs. Davies? It was she who made sure that Mrs. Thornton had fled her room, and signalled her husband in the summer-house so that he could return the room to its normal appearance, which he was enabled to do by means of that small-scale model geared to the original.

"It was Davies, of course, who imitated her dead husband's voice from the bathroom. Obviously, they did not go to Scotland, but crept back to the house to carry on their fell game, and the reason for that blind seemed inherent in Miss Manahan's story; she told us, you will remember, that Mr. Davies had begun to look at her with apprehension, as if he feared she might leave them; it was just the opposite; he realized that Miss Manahan was not obtuse, and might begin to suspect their involvement in the matter; so he and his wife absented themselves, for the purpose of establishing to Miss Manahan's knowledge that things occurred in their absence, never dreaming that Miss Manahan had already consulted us.

"And the motive for this horrible plot to drive that poor lady into hopeless insanity was surely obvious, too; Davies had control of his aunt's money, and he did not want to relinquish that control. She was wealthy; he was not. He had already squandered some of her money on this house, and if he could succeed in so breaking down the poor lady's mental health that she could be confined once more, or in driving her to suicide by that bogus haunting of her with her husband's voice, his squandering might never be uncovered, and he would remain permanently in control of her late husband's estate, for it had been placed in her hands, and she had given it over to Davies to manage. A callous, diabolic business, long premeditated. I shall see to it that Mr. and Mrs. Wellman Davies get their just deserts."

In 1944, the pseudonymous Ellery Queen commissioned two superb Sherlock Holmes pastiches from S T U A R T P A L M E R (1905–1968), creator of the delightful Hildegarde Withers mysteries and past president of the Mystery Writers of America. Palmer, who also penned articles and poems about the immortal sleuth, wrote "The Adventure of the Remarkable Worm" for the now-scarce anthology, The Misadventures of Sherlock Holmes. *"The Adventure of the Marked Man" was first published in the July 1944 issue of* Ellery Queen's Mystery Magazine.

The Adventure of the Marked Man

S T U A R T P A L M E R

It was on a blustery afternoon late in April of the year '95, and I had just returned to our Baker Street lodgings to find Sherlock Holmes as I had left him at noon, stretched out on the sofa with his eyes half-closed, the fumes of black shag tobacco rising to the ceiling.

Busy with my own thoughts, I removed the litter of chemical apparatus which had overflowed into the easy chair, and settled back with a perturbed sigh. Without realizing it, I must have fallen into a brown study. Suddenly Holmes's voice brought me back to myself with a start.

"So you have decided, Watson," said he, "that not even this difference should be a real barrier to your future happiness?"

"Exactly," I retorted. "After all, we cannot—" I stopped short. "My dear fellow!" I cried, "this is not at all like you!"

"Come, come, Watson. You know my methods."

"I had not known," said I stiffly, "that they embraced having your spies and eavesdroppers dog the footsteps of an old friend, simply because he chose a brisk spring afternoon for a walk with a certain lady."

"A thousand apologies! I had not realized that my little demonstration of a mental exercise might cause you pain," murmured Holmes in a deprecating voice. He sat up, smiling. "Of course, my dear fellow, I should have allowed for the temporary mental aberration known as falling in love."

"Really, Holmes!" I retorted sharply. "You should be the last person to speak of psycho-pathology—a man who is practically a walking case history of manic-depressive tendencies—"

He bowed. "A touch, a distinct touch! But Watson, in one respect you do me an injustice. I was aware of your plans to meet a lady only because of the excessive pains you took with your toilet before going out. The lovely Emilia, was it not? I shall always remember her courage in the affair of the Gorgiano murder in Mrs. Warren's otherwise respectable rooming house. And indeed, why not romance? There has been a very decent interval since the passing of your late wife, and the widow Lucca is a most captivating person."

"That is still beside the point. I do not see—"

"None so blind, Watson, none so blind," retorted Holmes, stuffing navy-cut into his cherrywood pipe, a sure sign that he was in one of his most argumentative moods. "It is really most simple, my dear fellow. It was not difficult for me to deduce that your appointment, on an afternoon as pleasantly gusty as this, was in the park. The remnants of peanut shell upon your best waistcoat speak all too plainly of the fact that you have been amusing yourself by feeding the monkeys. And your return at such an early hour, obviously having failed to ask the lady to dine with you, indicates most clearly that you have had some sort of disagreement while observing the antics of the hairy primates."

"Granted, Holmes, for the moment. But pray continue."

"With pleasure. As a good medical man, you cannot fail to have certain deep convictions as to the truth contained in the recent controversial publications of Mr. Charles Darwin. What is more likely than that in the warmth of Indian Summer romance you were unwise enough to start a discussion of Darwin's theories with the Signora Lucca, who like most of her countrywomen is no doubt deeply religious? Of course she prefers the Garden of Eden account of humanity's beginning. Hence your first quarrel and your hasty return home, where you threw yourself into a chair and permitted your pipe to go out while you threshed through the entire situation in your mind."

"That is simple enough, now that you explain it," I admitted grudgingly. "But how could you possibly know the conclusion which I had just reached?"

"Elementary, Watson, most elementary. You returned with your normally placid face contorted into a pout, the lower lip protruding most angrily. Your glance turned to the mantelpiece, where lies a copy of 'The Origin of Species' and you looked even more belligerent than before. But then after a moment the flickering flames of the fireplace caught your eye, and I could not fail to see how that domestic symbol reminded you of the connubial felicity which you once enjoyed. You pictured yourself and the lovely Italian seated before such a fire, and your expression softened. A distinctly fatuous smile crossed your face, and I knew that you had decided that no theory should be permitted to come between you and the lady you plan to make the second Mrs. Watson." He tapped out the cherrywood pipe into the grate. "Can you deny that my deductions are substantially correct?"

"Of course not," I retorted, somewhat abashed. "But Holmes, in a less enlightened reign than this our Victoria's, you would be in grave danger of being burned as a witch."

"A wizard, pray," he corrected. "But enough of mental exercises. Unless I am mistaken, the persistent ringing of the doorbell presages a client. If so, it is a serious case and one which may absorb all my faculties. Nothing trivial would bring out an Englishman during the hour sacred to afternoon tea."

There was barely time for Holmes to turn the reading lamp so that it fell upon the empty chair, and then there were quick steps on the stair and an impatient knocking at the door. "Come in!" cried Holmes.

The man who entered was still young, some eight and thirty at the outside, well-groomed and neatly if not fashionably attired, with something of professorial dignity in his bearing. He put his bowler and his sturdy malacca stick on the table, and then turned toward us, looking questioningly from one to the other. I could see that his normally ruddy complexion was of an unhealthy pallor. Obviously our caller was close to the breaking point.

"My name is Allen Pendarvis," he blurted forth, accepting the chair to which Holmes was pointing. "I must apologize for bursting in upon you like this."

"Not in the least," said Holmes. "Pray help yourself to tobacco, which is there in the Persian slipper. You have just come up from Cornwall, I see."

"Yes, from Mousehole, near Penzance. But how—?"

"Apart from your name—'By the prefix Tre-, Pol-, Pen- ye shall know the Cornishmen'—you are wearing a raincoat, and angry storm clouds have filled the southwest sky most of the day. I see also that you are in great haste, as the Royal Cornishman pulled into Paddington but a few moments ago, and you have lost no time in coming here."

"*You*, then, are Mr. Holmes!" decided Pendarvis. "I appeal to you, sir. No other man can give me the help I require."

"Help is not easy to refuse, and not always easy to give," Holmes replied. "But pray continue. This is Dr. Watson. You may speak freely in his presence, as he has been my collaborator on some of my most difficult cases."

"No one of your cases," cried Pendarvis, "can be more difficult than mine! I am about to be murdered, Mr. Holmes. And yet—and yet I have not an enemy in the world! Not one person, living or dead, could have a reason to wish me in my coffin. All the same, my life has been thrice threatened, and once attempted, in the last fortnight!"

"Most interesting," said Holmes calmly. "And have you any idea of the identity of your enemy?"

"None whatever. I shall begin at the beginning, and hold nothing back. You see, gentlemen, my home is in a little fishing village which has not changed materially in hundreds of years. As a matter of fact, the harbor quay of Mousehole, which lies just beyond my windows, was laid down by the Phoenicians in the time of Uther Pendragon, the father of King Arthur, when they came trading for Cornish tin . . ."

"I think in this matter we must look closer home than the Phoenicians," said Holmes dryly.

"Of course. You see, Mr. Holmes, I live a very quiet life. A small income left to me by a deceased aunt makes it possible for me to devote my time to the avocation of bird photography." Pendarvis smiled with modest pride. "A few of my photographs of terns on the nest have been printed in ornithology magazines. Only the other day—"

"Nor do I suspect the terns," Holmes interrupted. "And yet someone seeks your life, or your death. By the way, Mr. Pendarvis, does your wife inherit your estate in the unhappy event of your demise?"

Pendarvis looked blank. "Sir? But I have never married. I live alone with my brother Donal. Bit of a gay dog, Donal. Romantic enough for us both. All of the scented missives in the morning mail are addressed to him."

"Ah," said Holmes. "We need not apply the old rule of *cherchez la femme,* then? That eliminates a great deal. You say that your brother is your heir?"

"I suppose so. There is not much to inherit, really. The income stops at my death, and who would want my ornithological specimens?"

"That puts a different light on it, most certainly. But let us set aside the problem of *cui bono,* at least for the moment. What was the first intimation that someone had designs upon your life?"

"The first threat was in the form of a note, roughly printed upon brown butcher's-paper and shoved beneath the door last Thursday week. It read: 'Mr. Allen Pendarvis, you have but a short while to live'."

"You have that note?"

"Unfortunately, no. I destroyed it, thinking it to be but the work of a stupid practical joker." Pendarvis sighed. "Three days later came the second."

"Which you kept, and brought with you?"

Pendarvis smiled wryly. "That would be impossible. It was chalked upon the garden wall, repeating the first warning. And the third was marked in the mud of the harbor outside my bedroom window, visible on last Sunday morning at low tide, but speedily erased. It said 'Ready to die yet, Mr. Allen Pendarvis?' "

"These warnings were of course reported to the police?"

"Of course. But they did not take them seriously."

Holmes gave me a look, and nodded. "We understand that official attitude, do we not, Watson?"

"Then you can also understand, Mr. Sherlock Holmes, why I have come to you. I am not used to being pooh-poohed by a local sub-inspector! And so, when it finally happened last night—" Pendarvis shuddered.

"Now," interrupted Holmes, as he applied the flame of a wax vesta to his clay pipe, "we progress. Just what did happen?"

"It was late," the ornithologist began. "Almost midnight, as a matter of fact, when I was awakened by the persistent ringing of the doorbell. My housekeeper, poor soul, is hard of hearing, and so I arose and answered the door myself. Imagine my surprise to find no one there. Without all was Stygian blackness, the intense gloomy stillness of a Cornish village at that late hour. I stood there for a moment, shivering, holding my candle and peering into the darkness. And then a bullet screamed past me, missing my heart by a narrow margin and extinguishing the candle in my hand!"

Holmes clasped his lean hands together, smiling. "Really! A pretty problem, eh, Watson? What do you make of it?"

"Mr. Pendarvis is lucky in that his assailant is such a poor shot," I replied. "He must have presented a very clear target, holding a light in the doorway."

"A clear target indeed," Holmes agreed. "And why, Mr. Pendarvis, did not your brother answer the door?"

"Donal was in Penzance," Pendarvis answered. "For years it has been his invariable custom to attend the Friday night boxing matches there. Afterwards he usually joins some of his cronies at the Capstan and Anchor."

"Returning in the wee sma' hours? Of course, of course. And now, Mr. Pendarvis, I believe I have all that I need. Return to your home. You shall hear from us shortly." Holmes waved a languid hand at the door. "A very good evening to you, sir."

Pendarvis caught up his hat and stick, and stood dubiously in the doorway. "I must confess, Mr. Holmes, that I had been led to expect more of you."

"More?" said Holmes. "Oh, yes. My little bill. It shall be mailed to you on the first of the month. Good-night, sir."

The door closed upon our dissatisfied client, and Holmes, who had been leaning back on the sofa in what appeared to be the depths of dejection, abruptly rose and turned toward me. "Well, Watson, the solution seems disappointingly easy, does it not?"

"Perhaps so," said I stiffly. "But you are skating upon rather thin ice, are you not? You may have sent that poor man to his death."

"To his death? No, my dear Watson. I give you my word on that.

Excuse me, I must write a note to our friend Gregson of the Yard. It is most important that an arrest be made at once."

"An arrest? But of whom?"

"Who else but Mr. Donal Pendarvis? A telegram to the authorities of Penzance should suffice."

"The brother?" I cried. "Then you believe that he was not actually attending the boxing matches at the time of the attempted murder of our client?"

"I am positive," said Sherlock Holmes, "that he was engaged in quite other activities." I waited, but evidently he preferred not to take me further into his confidence. Holmes took quill and paper, and did not look up again until he had finished his note and dispatched it by messenger. "That," he said, "should take care of the situation for the time being." Whereupon he rang for Mrs. Hudson, requesting a copious dinner.

My friend maintained his uncommunicative silence during the meal, and devoted the rest of the evening to his violin. It was not until we were at the breakfast table next morning that there was any reference whatever to the case of the Cornish ornithologist.

The doorbell rang sharply, and Holmes brightened. "Ah, at last!" he cried. "An answer from Gregson. No, it is the man himself, and in a hurry, too." The steps on the stairs came to our door, and in a moment Tobias Gregson, tall, pale, flaxen-haired as ever, entered.

Smartest and sharpest of the Scotland Yard Inspectors, Holmes had always called him. But Gregson was in a bad frame of mind at the moment.

"You have had us for fair, Mr. Holmes," he began. "I felt in my bones that I should not have obeyed your unusual request, but remembering the assistance you have given us in the past, I followed out your suggestion. Bad business, Mr. Holmes, bad business!"

"Really?" said Holmes.

"Quite. It's this man Pendarvis, Donal Pendarvis, that you wanted arrested."

"No confession?"

"Certainly not. And moreover, the fellow is no doubt instituting a suit at law this very minute, for false arrest."

Holmes almost dropped his cup. "You mean he is no longer in custody?"

"I mean exactly that. He was arrested last night and held in Penzance gaol, but he made such a fuss about it that Owens, the sub-inspector there, was forced to let him go free."

Sherlock Holmes drew himself up to his full height, throwing aside his napkin. "I agree, sir. Bad business it is." He stood in deep thought for a moment. "And the other request I made? Have they located a man of that description?"

"No, Mr. Holmes. Sub-inspector Owens has lived in Penzance all his life, and he swears that no such person exists."

"Impossible, quite impossible," said Holmes. "He must be mistaken!"

Gregson rose. "We all have our successes and our failures," he said comfortingly. "Good morning, Mr. Holmes. Good morning, doctor."

As the door closed behind him, Holmes turned suddenly to me. "And why, Watson, are you not already packing? Do you not choose to accompany me to Cornwall?"

"To Cornwall? But I understood . . ."

"You have heard everything, and understood nothing. I shall have to demonstrate to you, and to the sub-inspector, on the scene. But enough of this. The game is afoot. You had best bring your service revolver and a stout ash, for there may be rough work before this little problem is solved." He consulted his watch. "Ah, we have just half an hour to catch the ten o'clock train from Paddington."

We boarded it with but a moment or two to spare, and when we were rolling southwest through the outskirts of London my friend began a dissertation upon hereditary tendencies in fingerprint groupings, a subject upon which he was planning a monograph. I kept my impatience to myself as long as I could, and finally interrupted him. "I have but one question, Holmes. Why are we going to Cornwall?"

"The spring flowers, Watson, are at the height of their season. The perfume will be pleasant after the fogs of London. Meanwhile, I intend to have a nap. You might occupy yourself with considering the unusual nature of the warning notes received by Mr. Allen Pendarvis."

"Unusual? But they seemed clear enough to me. They were definitely intended to let Mr. Pendarvis know that he was a marked man."

"Brilliantly put, Watson!" said Sherlock Holmes, and placidly settled down to sleep.

He did not awaken until we were past Plymouth, and the expanse of Mount's Bay was outside our window. There were whitecaps rolling in from the sea, and a gusty wind. "I fancy there will be more rain by dusk," said Holmes pleasantly. "An excellent night for the type of hunting we expect to engage in."

We had hardly alighted at Penzance when a broad man in a heavy tweed ulster approached us. He must have stood fifteen stone of solid brawn and muscle, and his face was grave. An apple-cheeked young police constable followed him.

"Mr. Holmes?" said the elder man. "I am Sub-inspector Owens. We were advised that you might be coming down. And high time it is. A sorry muddle you have got us into."

"Indeed?" said Holmes coolly. "It has happened, then?"

"It has," replied Sub-inspector Owens seriously. "At two o'clock this afternoon." The constable nodded in affirmation, very grave.

"I trust," Holmes said, "that you have not moved the body?"

"The body?" The two local policemen looked at each other, and the constable guffawed. "I was referring," Owens went on, "to the suit for false arrest. A writ was served upon me in my office."

My companion hesitated only a moment. "I should not, if I were you, lose any sleep over the forthcoming trial of the case. And now before going any farther, Dr. Watson and I have just had a long train journey and are in need of sustenance. Can you direct us to the Capstan and Anchor, inspector?"

Owens scowled, then turned to his assistant. "Tredennis, will you be good enough to show these gentlemen to the place?" He turned back to Holmes. "I shall expect you at the police station in an hour, sir. This affair is not yet settled to my satisfaction."

"Nor to mine, sir," said Holmes, and we set off after the constable. That strapping young man led us at a fast pace to the sign of the Capstan and Anchor. "Into the saloon bar with you, Watson," my companion said to me in a low voice. He lingered a moment at the door, and then turned and joined me. "Just as I thought. Constable Tredennis has taken up his post in a doorway across the street. We are not trusted by the local authorities."

He ordered a plate of kidneys and bacon, but left them to cool while he chatted with the barmaid, a singularly ordinary young woman from all that was apparent to me. But Holmes returned to the table smiling. "She confesses to knowing Mr. Donal Pendarvis, at least to the point of giggling when his name is mentioned. But she says that he has not been frequenting the public house in recent weeks. By the way, Watson, suppose I asked you for a description of our antagonist? What sort of game are we hunting, should you say?"

"Mr. Donal Pendarvis?"

Holmes frowned. "That gentleman resembles his extraordinarily dull brother, from best accounts. No, Watson, dig deeper than that. Look back upon the history of the case, the warning messages—"

"Very well," said I. "The intended murderer is a poor shot with a rifle. He is a person who holds a grudge a long time—even a fancied grudge, for Mr. Allen Pendarvis does not even have an idea of the identity of his assailant. He is a man of primitive mentality, or else he would not have stooped to the savagery of torturing his intended victim with warning messages. He is a newcomer to the town, a stranger . . ."

"Hold, Watson!" interrupted Holmes, with an odd smile. "You have reasoned amazingly. Yet I hear the patter of rain against the panes, and we must not keep our constable waiting in the doorway."

A brisk walk uphill, with the rain in our faces, brought us at last to the steps of the police station, but there I found that the way was barred, at least to me. Sub-inspector Owens, it appeared, wished to speak to Mr. Holmes alone.

"And so it shall be," replied Holmes pleasantly, to the burly constable in the door. He turned to me. "Watson, I stand in need of your help. Would you be good enough to occupy the next hour or so in a call on one or two of your local colleagues? You might represent yourself as in search of a casual patient whose name has escaped you. But you have, of course, some important reason for locating him. A wrong prescription, I fancy . . ."

"Really, Holmes!"

"Be as vague as you can about age and appearance, Watson, but specify that the man you seek is a crack shot, he is very conversant with the locality, of unimpeachable respectability and—most important of all—he has a young and beautiful wife."

"But Holmes! You imply that is the description of our murderer? It is the exact opposite of what I had imagined."

"The reverse of the coin, Watson. But you must excuse me. Be good enough to meet me here in—shall we say—two hours? Off with you now, I must not keep the sub-inspector cooling his heels."

He passed on inside and I turned away into the rain-swept street, shaking my head dubiously. How I wished, at that moment, for the warmth and comfort of my fireside, any fireside! But well I knew that Holmes had some method in his madness. With difficulty I managed to secure a hansom cab, and for a long time rattled about the steep streets of the ancient town of Penzance, in search of the ruby lamp outside the door which would signify the residence of a medical man.

My heart was not in the task, and it was no surprise to me that, in spite of the professional courtesy with which I was greeted by my medical colleagues, they were unable to help me by so much as one iota. Owens, for all his pomposity, had been correct when he reported that of all the citizenry of Penzance, no such person as Holmes sought had ever existed. Or if he had, he was not among their patients.

I returned to the police station to find Holmes waiting for me. "Aha, Watson!" he cried genially. "What luck? Very little, I suppose, else you should not wear the hangdog look of a retriever who has failed to locate the fallen bird. No matter. If we cannot go to our man, he shall come to us. I have to some extent regained the confidence of the sub-inspector, Watson. You see, I have given my word that before noon tomorrow Mr. Donal Pendarvis shall have withdrawn his suit for false arrest. In return we are to have the support of a stalwart P. C. for this night's work."

In a few moments there appeared down the street the figure of a uniformed man astride a bicycle. It turned out to be our friend Tredennis, who apologized for his delay. This was to have been his evening off duty, and it had been necessary to hurry home and explain matters to his better half.

"Maudie she worries if I'm not reporting in by nine o'clock," he said, his pink cheeks pinker than ever with the exertion of his ride. "But I told her that any man would be glad to volunteer for a tour of duty with Mister Holmes, the celebrated detective from England."

"From *England*?" I put in wonderingly. "And where are we now?"

"In Cornwall," said Holmes, nudging me gently with his elbow. "Ah, Watson, I see that your hansom has been kept waiting. Any moment now and we shall be setting our trap, somewhere near the home of Mr. Pendarvis."

"It's a good three miles, sir," said Constable Tredennis. "By the road, that is. Along the shore it's a good bit less, but it's coming high tide and no easy going at any season."

"We shall take the road," Holmes decided. Soon we were rattling along a cobbled street that wound up and down dale, past looming ranks of fisherman's houses, with the wind blowing ever wet and fresh against our cheeks. "A land to make a man cherish his hearth, eh, Watson?"

We rode on in silence for some time, and then the constable stopped the cab at the head of a steep sloping street that wound down toward the shore. There was a strong odor of herring about the place, mingled with that of tar and salt seaweed. I observed that as we went down the sloping street Holmes gave a most searching glance to right and left, and that at every subsequent street corner he took the utmost pains to see that we were not followed.

Frankly, I knew not what near-human game we were hoping to entrap in this rain-swept, forgotten corner of a forgotten seaside town, but I was well assured, from the manner in which Holmes held himself, that the adventure was a grave one, and nearing its climax. I felt the reassuring weight of the revolver in my coat pocket, and then suddenly the constable caught my arm.

"In here," he whispered. We turned into a narrow passage near the foot of the street, passed through what appeared to be in the dimness a network of mews and stables, and came at last to a narrow door in the wall, which Holmes unlocked with a key affixed to a block of wood. We entered it together, and closed it behind us.

The place was black as ink, but I felt that it was an empty house. The planking beneath my feet was old and bare, and my outstretched hand touched a stone wall wet with slime. Then we came to an empty window with a broken shutter, through which the dank night air came chilly.

"We are in what was once the Grey Mouse Inn," whispered the young constable. "Yonder, Mr. Holmes, is the house."

We peered across a narrow street and through the open, unshaded window panes of a library, brilliantly lighted by two oil lamps. I could see a line of bookcases, a table, and a mantelpiece in the background. For a long while there was nothing more to see except the dark street, the darker doorway of the house, and that one lighted window.

"There is no other entrance?" demanded Holmes in a whisper.

"None," said the constable. "The other windows give out onto the harbor, and at this hour the tide is passing high."

"Good," said Holmes. "If our man comes, he must come this way. And we shall be ready for him."

"More than ready," said young Tredennis stoutly. He hesitated. "Mr. Holmes, I wonder if you would be willing to give a younger man a word of advice. What, do you think, are the opportunities for an ambitious policeman up London way? I have often thought of trying to better myself . . ."

"Listen!" cried Holmes sharply. There had come a sharp screaming sound, like the shriek of a rusty gate. It came again, and I recognized it as the cry of a gull.

The silence crept back again. From far away came the barking of a dog, suddenly silenced. Then suddenly appeared in the room across the way, a man in a wine-colored dressing gown who entered the library, turned down the lamps, and blew them out. It could be none other than our client, Mr. Allen Pendarvis.

"As usual he keeps early hours," said Holmes dryly. We waited until one might have counted a hundred, and then another light showed in the room. The man returned, bearing a lamp—but mysteriously, in the few minutes that had passed, he had changed his apparel. Mr. Pendarvis now wore a dinner coat with the collar and tie askew. He crossed to the bookcase, removed a volume, and from the recess took out a small flask, which he placed in his pocket. Then he put back the book and left the room.

"A lightning-change artist!" I cried.

Holmes, gripping my arm, said, "Not quite, Watson. That is the brother. They are very alike, from this distance."

We waited in silence, for what seemed an interminable length of time. But no light reappeared. Finally Holmes turned to me. "Watson," he said, "we have drawn another blank. I should have sworn that the murderer would have struck tonight. I dislike to turn back . . ."

"My orders, sir, are to remain here until sunrise," put in the constable. "If you wish to return to the town, rest assured that I shall keep my eyes open."

"I am sure of it," said Holmes. "Come, Watson. The game is too wary. We have no more to do here."

He led me back across the sagging floor, through the door into the mews, and finally brought me out into the street again. But once there, instead of heading up the slope toward where our hansom was waiting, he suddenly drew me into the shadows of an alleyway. I would have spoken, but

I felt his bony fingers across my lips. "Shh, Watson. Wait here—and never take your eyes off that doorway."

We waited, for what seemed an eternity. I stared with all my might at the doorway of the Pendarvis house. But I saw nothing, not even when Holmes gripped my arm.

"Now! Watson," he whispered, and started out in that direction, I tardily at his heels.

As we came closer I saw that a man was standing with his finger pressed against the Pendarvis doorbell. Holmes and I flung ourselves upon him, but he was a wiry customer, and we for all our superior strength and numbers were flung back and forth like hounds attacking a bear. And then the door was opened suddenly from within, and we all tumbled into a hallway lighted only by a candle held aloft in the hand of the surprised householder.

Our captive suddenly ceased his struggles, and Holmes and I drew back to see that we had succeeded in overcoming none other than Constable Tredennis himself. He held in his right hand an extremely businesslike revolver, which fell to the carpet with a dull thump.

"Mr. Pendarvis," said Holmes, "Mr. Donal Pendarvis, permit me to introduce you to your intended murderer."

No one spoke. But the apple-cheeked constable now had a face the color of the under side of a flounder. All thought of resistance was gone. "You are uncanny, Mr. Holmes," the young man muttered. "How could you know?"

"How could I fail to know?" said Holmes, arranging his disheveled clothing. "It was fairly evident that since there was no citizen in Penzance who possessed both an ability as a marksman, a knowledge of the tides, and an attractive young wife, our man must be a member of the profession where marksmanship is encouraged." He turned toward the man who still held the candle, though with trembling fingers. "It was also evident that your brother, who still sleeps soundly upstairs, was never intended as a victim at all. Else the murderer would hardly have bothered with warning messages. It was you, Mr. Donal Pendarvis, who was the bull's-eye of the target."

"I—I do not understand," said the man with the candle, backing away. I kept a close grip upon the unresisting form of the prisoner, and watched Holmes as he quietly produced his cherrywood pipe and lighted it.

"There was an excellent motive for Constable Tredennis to murder you, sir," said Holmes to our unwilling host. "No man cares to have his garden plucked by a stranger. Your death would have begun an inquiry which would have led straight to the husband of the lady you see on Friday nights . . ."

"That is a black lie!" shouted Tredennis, and then subsided.

"Unless," Holmes continued quietly, "it was obvious to all the world that Donal Pendarvis was killed by accident, that he met his death at the hands of a madman with an unexplained grudge against his brother Allen. That is why the warning notes so unnecessarily stressed the name of *Allen* Pendarvis. That is why the murderer-to-be carefully missed his supposed victim and shot out the candle. I did my best, Mr. Pendarvis, to assure your safety by having you taken into custody. That subterfuge failed, and so I was forced to this extreme means."

Tredennis twisted out of my grasp. "Very well, make an end of it!" he cried. "I admit it all, Mr. Holmes, and shall gladly leave it to a jury of my peers—"

"You had best leave it to me, at the moment," advised Holmes. "Mr. Pendarvis, you do not know me, but I have saved your life. May I ask a favor in return?"

Donal Pendarvis hesitated. "I am listening," he said. "You understand, I admit nothing . . ."

"Of course. I venture to suggest that, instead of remaining here in the household of your brother and amusing yourself with dangerous dalliance, you betake yourself to fields which offer a greater opportunity for the use of your time and energy. The wheat fields of Canada, perhaps, or the veldt of South Africa . . ."

"And if I refuse?"

"The alternative," said Holmes, "is an exceedingly unpleasant scandal, involving a lady's name. Your lawsuit for false arrest will present the yellow press with unusual opportunities, will it not, when they learn that it all arose from an honest attempt upon my part to save your neck from a just punishment?"

Mr. Donal Pendarvis lowered the candle, and a slow smile spread across his handsome face. "I give you my word, Mr. Holmes. I shall leave by the first packet."

He extended his hand, and Holmes grasped it. And then we turned back into the night, our prisoner between us. We went up the cobbled street in silence, the young constable striding forward as to the gallows.

We found the hansom still waiting, and set off at once for Penzance. But it was Holmes who called on the driver to stop as we pulled into the outskirts of the town.

"Can we drop you off at your dwelling, constable?" he asked.

The young man looked up, his eyes haunted. "Do not make sport of me, Mr. Holmes. You copped me for fair and I am ready to—"

Holmes half-shoved him out of the hansom. "Be off with you, my young friend. You must leave it to me to satisfy your sub-inspector with a story which Doctor Watson and I shall contrive out of moonbeams. For your part, you must make up your own mind as to your tactics in dealing with your Maudie. After all, the immediate problem is removed, and if you wish to transfer to some other duty with less night work, here is my card. I shall be glad to say a word in your behalf to the powers at Scotland Yard."

The hansom, at Holmes's signal, rolled onward again, cutting short the incoherent thanks of the chastened young constable.

"I am quite aware of what is in your mind," said Holmes to me as we approached our destination. "But you are wrong. The ends of justice will be better served by sending our young culprit back to his Maudie instead of by publicly disgracing him . . ."

"It is of no use, Holmes," said I firmly. "Nothing that you can say will change my decision. Upon our return to London I shall ask Emilia to become my wife."

Sherlock Holmes let his hand fall on my shoulder, in a comradely gesture. "So be it. Marry her and keep her. One of these days I shall return to the country and the keeping of bees. We shall see who suffers the sharpest stings."

The Strange Case of the Megatherium Thefts

S.C. ROBERTS

I have already had occasion, in the course of these reminiscences of my friend Sherlock Holmes, to refer to his liking for the Diogenes Club, the club which contained the most unsociable men in London and forbade talking save in the Strangers' Room. So far as I am aware, this was the only club to which Holmes was attracted, and it struck me as not a little curious that he should have been called upon to solve the extraordinary mystery of the Megatherium Thefts.

It was a dull afternoon in November and Holmes, turning wearily from the cross-indexing of some old newspaper-cuttings, drew his chair near to mine and took out his watch.

"How slow life has become, my dear Watson," he said, "since the successful conclusion of that little episode in a lonely west-country village. Here we are back amongst London's millions and nobody wants us."

He crossed to the window, opened it a little, and peered through the November gloom into Baker Street.

"No, Watson, I'm wrong. I believe we are to have a visitor."

"Is there someone at the door?"

"Not yet. But a hansom has stopped opposite to it. The passenger has alighted and there is a heated discussion in progress concerning the fare. I cannot hear the argument in detail, but it is a lively one."

A few minutes later the visitor was shown into the sitting-room—a tall, stooping figure with a straggling white beard, shabbily dressed and generally unkempt. He spoke with a slight stutter.

"M-Mr. Sherlock Holmes?" he inquired.

"That is my name," replied Holmes, "and this is my friend, Dr. Watson."

The visitor bowed jerkily and Holmes continued: "And whom have I the honour of addressing?"

"My n-name is Wiskerton—Professor Wiskerton—and I have ventured to call upon you in connexion with a most remarkable and puzzling affair."

"We are familiar with puzzles in this room, Professor."

"Ah, but not with any like this one. You see, apart from my p-professorial standing, I am one of the oldest members of——"

"The Megatherium?"

"My dear sir, how did you know?"

"Oh, there was no puzzle about that. I happened to hear some reference in your talk with the cabman to your journey having begun at Waterloo Place. Clearly you had travelled from one of two clubs and somehow I should not associate you with the United States."

"You're p-perfectly right, of course. The driver of that cab was a rapacious scoundrel. It's s-scandalous that——"

"But you have not come to consult me about an extortionate cab-driver?"

"No, no. Of course not. It's about——"

"The Megatherium?"

"Exactly. You see, I am one of the oldest m-members and have been on the Committee for some years. I need hardly tell you the kind of standing which the Megatherium has in the world of learning, Mr. Holmes."

"Dr. Watson, I have no doubt, regards the institution with veneration. For myself, I prefer the soothing atmosphere of the Diogenes."

"The w-what?"

"The Diogenes Club."

"N-never heard of it."

"Precisely. It is a club of which people are not meant to hear—but I beg your pardon for this digression. You were going to say?"

"I was g-going to say that the most distressing thing has happened. I should explain in the first place that in addition to the n-noble collection of books in the Megatherium library, a collection which is one of our most valuable assets, we have available at any one time a number of books from one of the circulating libraries and——"

"And you are losing them?"

"Well—yes, in fact we are. But how did you know?"

"I didn't know—I merely made a deduction. When a client begins to describe his possessions to me, it is generally because some misfortune has occurred in connexion with them."

"But this is m-more than a m-misfortune, Mr. Holmes. It is a disgrace, an outrage, a—"

"But what, in fact, has happened?"

"Ah, I was c-coming to that. But perhaps it would be simpler if I showed you this document and let it speak for itself. P-personally, I think it was a mistake to circulate it, but the Committee over-ruled me and now the story will be all over London and we shall still be no nearer a solution."

Professor Wiskerton fumbled in his pocket and produced a printed document marked *Private and Confidential* in bold red type.

"What do you m-make of it, Mr. Holmes? Isn't it extraordinary? Here is a club whose members are selected from among the most distinguished representatives of the arts and sciences and this is the way they treat the c-club property."

Holmes paid no attention to the Professor's rambling commentary and continued his reading of the document.

"You have brought me quite an interesting case, Professor," he said, at length.

"But it is more than interesting, Mr. Holmes. It is astonishing. It is inexplicable."

"If it were capable of easy explanation, it would cease to be interesting and, furthermore, you would not have spent the money on a cab-fare to visit me."

"That, I suppose, is true. But what do you advise, Mr. Holmes?"

"You must give me a little time, Professor. Perhaps you will be good enough to answer one or two questions first?"

"Willingly."

"This document states that your Committee is satisfied that no member of the staff is implicated. You are satisfied yourself on that point?"

"I am not s-satisfied about anything, Mr. Holmes. As one who has s-spent a great part of his life amongst books and libraries, the whole subject of the maltreatment of books is repugnant to me. Books are my life-blood, Mr. Holmes. But perhaps I have not your s-sympathy?"

"On the contrary, Professor, I have a genuine interest in such matters. For myself, however, I travel in those byways of bibliophily which are associated with my own profession."

Holmes moved across to a shelf and took out a volume with which I had long been familiar.

"Here, Professor," he continued, "if I may rid myself of false modesty for the moment, is a little monograph of mine *Upon the Distinction Between the Ashes of the Various Tobaccos.*"

"Ah, most interesting, Mr. Holmes. Not being a smoker myself, I cannot pretend to appraise your work from the point of view of scholarship, but as a bibliophile and especially as a c-collector of out-of-the-way monographs, may I ask whether the work is still available?"

"That is a spare copy, Professor; you are welcome to it."

The Professor's eyes gleamed with voracious pleasure.

"But, Mr. Holmes, this is m-most generous of you. May I b-beg that you will inscribe it? I derive a special delight from what are called 'association copies'."

"Certainly," said Holmes, with a smile, as he moved to the writing-table.

"Thank you, thank you," murmured the Professor, "but I fear I have distracted you from the main issue."

"Not at all."

"But what is your p-plan, Mr. Holmes? Perhaps you would like to have a look round the Megatherium? Would you care, for instance, to have luncheon to-morrow—but no, I fear I am engaged at that time. What about a c-cup of tea at 4 o'clock?"

"With pleasure. I trust I may bring Dr. Watson, whose co-operation in such cases has frequently been of great value?"

"Oh-er-yes, certainly."

But it did not seem to me that there was much cordiality in his assent.

"Very well, then," said Holmes. "The document which you have left with me gives the facts and I will study them with great care."

"Thank you, thank you. To-morrow, then, at 4 o'clock," said the Professor, as he shook hands, "and I shall t-treasure this volume, Mr. Holmes."

He slipped the monograph into a pocket and left us.

"Well, Watson," said Holmes, as he filled his pipe, "what do you make of this curious little case?"

"Very little, at present. I haven't had a chance to examine the *data.*"

"Quite right, Watson. I will reveal them to you." Holmes took up the sheet which the Professor had left.

"This is a confidential letter circulated to members of the Megatherium and dated November 1889. I'll read you a few extracts:

'In a recent report the Committee drew attention to the serious loss and inconvenience caused by the removal from the Club of books from the circulating library. The practice has continued. . . . At the end of June, the Club paid for no less than 22 missing volumes. By the end of September 15 more were missing. . . . The Committee was disposed to ascribe these malpractices to some undetected individual member, but they have regretfully come to the conclusion that more members than one are involved. They are fully satisfied that no member of the staff is in any way implicated. . . . If the offenders can be identified, the Committee will not hesitate to apply the Rule which empowers expulsion.'

There, Watson, what do you think of that?"

"Most extraordinary, Holmes—at the Megatherium, of all clubs."

"Corruptio optimi pessima, my dear Watson."

"D'you think the Committee is right about the servants?"

"I'm not interested in the Committee's opinions, Watson, even though they be the opinions of Bishops and Judges and Fellows of the Royal Society. I am concerned only with the facts."

"But the facts are simple, Holmes. Books are being stolen in considerable quantities from the club and the thief, or thieves, have not been traced."

"Admirably succinct, my dear Watson. And the motive?"

"The thief's usual motive, I suppose—the lure of illicit gain."

"But what gain, Watson? If you took half a dozen books, with the mark of a circulating library on them, to a secondhand bookseller, how much would you expect to get for them?"

"Very little, certainly, Holmes."

"Yes, and that is why the Committee is probably right in ruling out the servants—not that I believe in ruling out anybody or anything on *a priori* grounds. But the motive of gain won't do. You must try again, Watson."

"Well, of course, people are careless about books, especially when they belong to someone else. Isn't it possible that members take these books away from the club, intending to return them, and then leave them in the train or mislay them at home?"

"Not bad, my dear Watson, and a perfectly reasonable solution if we were dealing with a loss of three or four volumes. In that event our Professor would probably not have troubled to enlist my humble services. But look at the figures, Watson—twenty-two books missing in June, fifteen more in September. There's something more than casual forgetfulness in that."

"That's true, Holmes, and I suppose we can't discover much before we keep our appointment at the Megatherium tomorrow."

"On the contrary, my dear Watson, I hope to pursue a little independent investigation this evening."

"I should be delighted to accompany you, Holmes."

"I am sure you would, Watson, but if you will forgive me for saying so, the little inquiry I have to make is of a personal nature and I think it might be more fruitful if I were alone."

"Oh, very well," I replied, a little nettled at Holmes's superior manner, "I can employ myself very profitably in reading this new work on surgical technique which has just come to hand."

I saw little of Holmes on the following morning. He made no reference to the Megatherium case at breakfast and disappeared shortly afterwards. At luncheon he was in high spirits. There was a gleam in his eye which showed me that he was happily on the trail.

"Holmes," I said, "you have discovered something."

"My dear Watson," he replied, "your acuteness does you credit. I have discovered that after an active morning I am extremely hungry."

But I was not to be put off.

"Come, Holmes, I am too old a campaigner to be bluffed in that way. How far have you penetrated into the Megatherium mystery?"

"Far enough to make me look forward to our tea-party with a lively interest."

Being familiar with my friend's bantering manner, I recognized that it was no good pressing him with further questions for the moment.

Shortly after 4 o'clock Holmes and I presented ourselves at the portals of the Megatherium. The head porter received us very courteously and seemed, I thought, almost to recognize Sherlock Holmes. He conducted us to a seat in the entrance-hall and, as soon as our host appeared, we made our way up the noble staircase to the long drawing-room on the first floor.

"Now let me order some tea," said the Professor. "Do you like anything to eat with it, Mr. Holmes?"

"Just a biscuit for me, Professor, but my friend Watson has an enormous appetite."

"Really, Holmes——" I began.

"No, no. Just a little pleasantry of mine," said Holmes, quickly. I thought I observed an expression of relief on the Professor's face.

"Well, now, about our p-problem, Mr. Holmes. Is there any further information that I can give you?"

"I should like to have a list of the titles of the books which have most recently disappeared."

"Certainly, Mr. Holmes, I can get that for you at once."

The Professor left us for a few minutes and returned with a paper in his hand. I looked over Holmes's shoulder while he read and recognized several well-known books that had been recently published, such as *Robbery under Arms, Troy Town, The Economic Interpretation of History, The Wrong Box,* and *Three Men in a Boat.*

"Do you make any particular deductions from the titles, Mr. Holmes?" the Professor asked.

"I think not," Holmes replied; "there are, of course, certain very popular works of fiction, some other books of more general interest and a few titles of minor importance. I do not think one could draw any conclusion about the culprit's special sphere of interest."

"You think not? Well, I agree, Mr. Holmes. It is all very b-baffling."

"Ah," said Holmes suddenly, "this title reminds me of something."

"What is that, Mr. Holmes?"

"I see that one of the missing books is *Plain Tales from the Hills.* It happens that I saw an exceptionally interesting copy of that book not long ago. It was an advance copy, specially bound and inscribed for presentation to the author's godson who was sailing for India before the date of publication."

"Really, Mr. Holmes, really? That is of the greatest interest to me."

"Your own collection, Professor, is, I suspect, rich in items of such a kind?"

"Well, well, it is not for me to b-boast, Mr. Holmes, but I certainly have one or two volumes of unique association value on my shelves. I am a poor man and do not aspire to first folios, but the p-pride of my collection is that it could not have been assembled through the ordinary channels of trade. . . . But to return to our problem, is there anything else in the Club which you would like to investigate?"

"I think not," said Holmes, "but I must confess that the description of your collection has whetted my own bibliographical appetite."

The Professor flushed with pride.

"Well, Mr. Holmes, if you and your friend would really care to see my few t-treasures, I should be honoured. My rooms are not f-far from here."

"Then let us go," said Holmes, with decision.

I confess that I was somewhat puzzled by my friend's behaviour. He seemed to have forgotten the misfortunes of the Megatherium and to be taking a wholly disproportionate interest in the eccentricities of the Wiskerton collection.

When we reached the Professor's rooms I had a further surprise. I had expected not luxury, of course, but at least some measure of elegance and comfort. Instead, the chairs and tables, the carpets and curtains, everything, in fact, seemed to be of the cheapest quality; even the bookshelves were of plain deal and roughly put together. The books themselves were another matter. They were classified like no other library I had ever seen. In one section were presentation copies from authors; in another were proof-copies bound in what is known as "binder's cloth"; in another were review copies; in another were pamphlets, monographs, and off-prints of all kinds.

"There you are, Mr. Holmes," said the Professor, with all the pride of ownership. "You may think it is a c-collection of oddities, but for me every one of those volumes has a p-personal and s-separate association—including the item which came into my hands yesterday afternoon."

"Quite so," said Holmes, thoughtfully, "and yet they all have a common characteristic."

"I don't understand you."

"No? But I am waiting to see the remainder of your collection, Professor. When I have seen the whole of your library, I shall perhaps be able to explain myself more clearly."

The Professor flushed with annoyance.

"Really, Mr. Holmes, I had been warned of some of your p-peculiarities of manner; but I am entirely at a loss to know what you are d-driving at."

"In that case, Professor, I will thank you for your hospitality and will beg leave to return to the Megatherium for consultation with the Secretary."

"To tell him that you can't f-find the missing books?"

Sherlock Holmes said nothing for a moment. Then he looked straight into the Professor's face and said, very slowly:

"On the contrary, Professor Wiskerton, I shall tell the Secretary that I can direct him to the precise address at which the books may be found."

There was silence. Then an extraordinary thing happened.

The Professor turned away and literally crumpled into a chair; then he looked up at Holmes with the expression of a terrified child:

"Don't do it, Mr. Holmes. Don't do it, I b-b-beseech you. I'll t-tell you everything."

"Where are the books?" asked Holmes, sternly.

"Come with me and I'll show you."

The Professor shuffled out and led us into a dismal bedroom. With a trembling hand he felt in his pocket for his keys and opened a cupboard alongside the wall. Several rows of books were revealed and I quickly recognized one or two titles that I had seen on the Megatherium list.

"Oh, what m-must you think of me, Mr. Holmes?" the Professor began, whimpering.

"My opinion is irrelevant," said Sherlock Holmes, sharply. "Have you any packing-cases?"

"No, but I d-daresay my landlord might be able to find some."

"Send for him."

In a few minutes the landlord appeared. Yes, he thought he could find a sufficient number of cases to take the books in the cupboard.

"Professor Wiskerton," said Holmes, "is anxious to have all these books packed at once and sent to the Megatherium, Pall Mall. The matter is urgent."

"Very good, sir. Any letter or message to go with them?"

"No," said Holmes, curtly, "but yes—stop a minute."

He took a pencil and a visiting-card from his pocket and wrote "With the compliments of" above the name.

"See that this card is firmly attached to the first of the packing-cases. Is that clear?"

"Quite correct, sir, if that's what the Professor wants."

"That is what the Professor most particularly wants. Is it not, Professor?" said Holmes, with great emphasis.

"Yes, yes, I suppose so. But c-come back with me into the other room and l-let me explain."

We returned to the sitting-room and the Professor began:

"Doubtless I seem to you either ridiculous or despicable or both. I have had two p-passions in my life—a passion for s-saving money and a passion for acquiring b-books. As a result of an unfortunate dispute with the Dean of my faculty at the University, I retired at a c-comparatively early age and on a very small p-pension. I was determined to amass a collection of books; I was equally determined not to s-spend my precious savings on them. The idea came to me that my library should be unique, in that all the books in it should be acquired by some means other than p-purchase. I had friends amongst authors, printers, and publishers, and I did pretty well, but there were many recently published books that I wanted and saw no m-means of getting until—well, until I absent-mindedly brought home one of the circulating library books from the Megatherium. I meant to return it, of course. But I didn't. Instead, I b-brought home another one. . . ."

"*Facilis descensus* . . .," murmured Holmes.

"Exactly, Mr. Holmes, exactly. Then, when the Committee began to notice that books were disappearing, I was in a quandary. But I remembered hearing someone say in another connexion that the b-best defence was attack and I thought that if I were the first to go to you, I should be the last to be s-suspected."

"I see," said Holmes. "Thank you, Professor Wiskerton."

"And now what are you going to do?"

"First," replied Holmes, "I am going to make certain that your landlord has those cases ready for despatch. After that, Dr. Watson and I have an engagement at St. James's Hall."

"*A* trivial little case, Watson, but not wholly without interest," said Holmes, when we returned from the concert hall to Baker Street.

"A most contemptible case, in my opinion. Did you guess from the first that Wiskerton himself was the thief?"

"Not quite, Watson. I never guess. I endeavour to observe. And the first thing I observed about Professor Wiskerton was that he was a miser—the altercation with the cabman, the shabby clothes, the unwillingness to invite us to lunch. That he was an enthusiastic bibliophile was, of course, obvious. At first I was not quite certain how to fit these two characteristics properly together, but after yesterday's interview I remembered that the head porter of the Megatherium had been a useful ally of mine in his earlier days as a Commissionaire and I thought a private talk with him might be useful. His brief characterization put me on the right track at once—'Always here reading', he said, 'but never takes a square meal in the club.' After that, and after a little hasty research this morning into the Professor's academic career, I had little doubt."

"But don't you still think it extraordinary, in spite of what he said, that he should have taken the risk of coming to consult you?"

"Of course it's extraordinary, Watson. Wiskerton's an extraordinary man. If, as I hope, he has the decency to resign from the Megatherium, I shall suggest to Mycroft that he puts him up for the Diogenes."

The prolific and well-beloved Canadian-American essayist VINCENT STARRETT *(1886–1974) taught writing at Northwestern University, wrote the popular "Books Alive" column for the* Chicago Tribune *and in 1934 cofounded the Baker Street Irregulars with Christopher Morley. According to Holmes scholar Edgar W. Smith, the best book ever written about the great sleuth is Starrett's biography and appreciation,* The Private Life of Sherlock Holmes. *"The Adventure of the Unique Hamlet," from that volume, has been anthologized so often I debated whether to include it in* The Game Is Afoot, *but too many Holmes buffs regard it as the finest ever written to leave it out.*

The Adventure of the Unique Hamlet

VINCENT STARRETT

"Holmes," said I, one morning as I stood in our bay window, looking idly into the street, "surely here comes a madman. Someone has incautiously left the door open and the poor fellow has slipped out. What a pity!"

It was a glorious morning in the spring, with a fresh breeze and inviting sunlight, but as it was early few persons were as yet astir. Birds twittered under the neighboring eaves, and from the far end of the thoroughfare came faintly the droning cry of an umbrella-repair man; a lean cat slunk across the cobbles and disappeared into a courtway; but for the most part the street was deserted save for the eccentric individual who had called forth my exclamation.

My friend rose lazily from the chair in which he had been lounging, and came to my side, standing with long legs spread and hands in the pockets of his dressing gown. He smiled as he saw the singular personage coming along; and a personage indeed he seemed to be, despite his curious actions, for he was tall and portly, with elderly whiskers of the variety called mutton-chop, and eminently respectable. He was loping curiously, like a tired hound, lifting his knees high as he ran, and a heavy double watch-chain bounced against and rebounded from the plump line of his figured waistcoat. With one hand he clutched despairingly at his silk, two-gallon hat, while with the other he made strange gestures in the air in an emotion bordering upon distraction. We could almost see the spasmodic workings of his countenance.

"What under heaven can ail him?" I cried. "See how he glances at the houses as he passes."

"He is looking at the numbers," responded Sherlock Holmes, with dancing eyes, "and I fancy it is ours that will bring him the greatest happiness. His profession, of course, is obvious."

"A banker, I should imagine, or at least a person of affluence," I ventured, wondering what curious bit of minutiae had betrayed the man's vocation to my remarkable companion, in a single glance.

"Affluent, yes," said Holmes, with a mischievous twinkle, "but not exactly a banker, Watson. Notice the sagging pockets, despite the excellence of his clothing, and the rather exaggerated madness of his eye. He is a collector, or I am very much mistaken."

"My dear fellow!" I exclaimed. "At his age and in his station! And why should he be seeking us? When we settled that last bill—"

"Of books," said my friend, severely. "He is a book collector. His line is Caxtons, Elzevirs, and Gutenberg Bibles; not the sordid reminders of unpaid grocery accounts. See, he is turning in, as I expected, and in a moment he will stand upon our hearthrug and tell the harrowing tale of an unique volume and its extraordinary disappearance."

His eyes gleamed and he rubbed his hands together in satisfaction. I could not but hope that his conjecture was correct, for he had had little recently to occupy his mind, and I lived in constant fear that he would seek that stimulation his active brain required in the long-tabooed cocaine bottle.

As Holmes finished speaking the doorbell echoed through the house; then hurried feet were sounding on the stairs, while the wailing voice of Mrs. Hudson, raised in protest, could only have been occasioned by frustration of her coveted privilege of bearing up our caller's card. Then the door burst violently inward and the object of our analysis staggered to the center of the room and, without announcing his intention by word or sign, pitched headforemost to our center rug. There he lay, a magnificent ruin, with his head on the fringed border and his feet in the coal scuttle; and sealed within his lifeless lips was the amazing story he had come to tell—for that it was amazing we could not doubt in the light of our client's extraordinary behavior.

Sherlock Holmes ran quickly for the brandy bottle, while I knelt beside the stricken man and loosened his wilted neckband. He was not dead, and when we had forced the nozzle of the flask between his teeth he sat up in groggy fashion, passing a dazed hand across his eyes. Then he scrambled to his feet with an embarrassed apology for his weakness, and fell into the chair which Holmes invitingly held towards him.

"That is right, Mr. Harrington Edwards," said my companion, soothingly. "Be quite calm, my dear sir, and when you have recovered your composure you will find us ready to listen."

"You know me then?" cried our visitor. There was pride in his voice and he lifted his eyebrows in surprise.

"I had never heard of you until this moment; but if you wish to conceal your identity it would be well," said Sherlock Holmes, "for you to leave your bookplates at home." As Holmes spoke he returned a little package of folded paper slips, which he had picked from the floor. "They fell from your hat when you had the misfortune to collapse," he added whimsically.

"Yes, yes," cried the collector, a deep blush spreading across his features. "I remember now; my hat was a little large and I folded a number of them and placed them beneath the sweatband. I had forgotten."

"Rather shabby usage for a handsome etched plate," smiled my companion; "but that is your affair. And now, sir, if you are quite at ease, let us hear what it is that has brought you, a collector of books, from Poke Stogis Manor—the name is on the plate—to the office of Mr. Sherlock Holmes, consulting expert in crime. Surely nothing but the theft of Mahomet's own copy of the Koran can have affected you so strongly."

Mr. Harrington Edwards smiled feebly at the jest, then sighed. "Alas," he murmured, "if that were all! But I shall begin at the beginning.

"You must know, then, that I am the greatest Shakespearean commentator in the world. My collection of *ana* is unrivaled and much of the world's collection (and consequently its knowledge of the veritable Shakespeare) has emanated from my pen. One book I did not possess: it was unique, in the correct sense of that abused word; the greatest Shakespeare rarity in the world. Few knew that it existed, for its existence was kept a profound secret among a chosen few. Had it become known that this book was in England—any place, indeed—its owner would have been hounded to his grave by wealthy Americans.

"It was in the possession of my friend—I tell you this in strictest confidence—of my friend, Sir Nathaniel Brooke-Bannerman, whose place at Walton-on-Walton is next to my own. A scant two hundred yards separate our dwellings; so intimate has been our friendship that a few years ago the fence between our estates was removed, and each roamed or loitered at will in the other's preserves.

"For some years now, I have been at work upon my greatest book— my *magnum opus*. It was to be my last book also, embodying the results of a lifetime of study and research. Sir, I know Elizabethan London better than any man alive; better than any man who ever lived, I think—" He burst suddenly into tears.

"There, there," said Sherlock Holmes, gently. "Do not be distressed. Pray continue with your interesting narrative. What was this book—which, I take it, in some manner has disappeared? You borrowed it from your friend?"

"That is what I am coming to," said Mr. Harrington Edwards, drying his tears, "but as for help, Mr. Holmes, I fear that is beyond even you. As you surmise, I needed this book. Knowing its value, which could not be fixed, for the book is priceless, and knowing Sir Nathaniel's idolatry of it, I hesitated before asking for the loan of it. But I had to have it, for without it my work could not have been completed, and at length I made my request. I suggested that I visit him in his home and go through the volume under his eyes, he sitting at my side throughout my entire examination, and servants stationed at every door and window, with fowling pieces in their hands.

"You can imagine my astonishment when Sir Nathaniel laughed at my precautions. 'My dear Edwards,' he said, 'that would be all very well were you Arthur Bambidge or Sir Homer Nantes (mentioning the two great men of the British Museum), or were you Mr. Henry Hutterson, the American railway magnate; but you are my friend Harrington Edwards, and you shall take the book home with you for as long as you like.' I protested vigorously, I can assure you; but he would have it so, and as I was touched by this mark of his esteem, at length I permitted him to have his way. My God! If I had remained adamant! If I had only . . ."

He broke off and for a moment stared blindly into space. His eyes were directed at the Persian slipper on the wall, in the toe of which Holmes kept his tobacco, but we could see that his thoughts were far away.

"Come, Mr. Edwards," said Holmes, firmly. "You are agitating yourself unduly. And you are unreasonably prolonging our curiosity. You have not yet told us what this book is."

Mr. Harrington Edwards gripped the arm of the chair in which he sat. Then he spoke, and his voice was low and thrilling:

"The book was a *Hamlet* quarto, dated 1602, presented by Shakespeare to his friend Drayton, with an inscription four lines in length, written and signed by the Master, himself!"

"My dear sir!" I exclaimed. Holmes blew a long, slow whistle of astonishment.

"It is true," cried the collector. "That is the book I borrowed, and that is the book I lost! The long-sought quarto of 1602, actually inscribed in Shakespeare's own hand! His greatest drama, in an edition dated a year earlier than any that is known; a perfect copy, and with four lines in his own handwriting! Unique! Extraordinary! Amazing! Astounding! Colossal! Incredible! Un—"

He seemed wound up to continue indefinitely; but Holmes, who had sat quite still at first, shocked by the importance of the loss, interrupted the flow of adjectives.

"I appreciate your emotion, Mr. Edwards," he said, "and the book is indeed all that you say it is. Indeed, it is so important that we must at once attack the problem of rediscovering it. Compose yourself, my dear sir, and tell us of the loss. The book, I take it, is readily identifiable?"

"Mr. Holmes," said our client, earnestly, "it would be impossible to hide it. It is so important a volume that, upon coming into its possession, Sir Nathaniel Brooke-Bannerman called a consultation of the great binders of the Empire, at which were present Mr. Rivière, Messrs. Sangorski and Sutcliffe, Mr. Zaehnsdorf, and certain others. They and myself, with two others, alone know of the book's existence. When I tell you that it is bound in brown levant morocco, with leather joints and brown levant doublures and fly-leaves, the whole elaborately gold-tooled, inlaid with seven hundred and fifty separate pieces of various colored leathers, and enriched by the insertion of eighty-seven precious stones, I need not add that it is a design that never will be duplicated, and I mention only a few of its glories. The binding was personally done by Messrs. Rivière, Sangorski, Sutcliffe, and Zaehnsdorf, working alternately, and is a work of such enchantment that any man might gladly die a thousand deaths for the privilege of owning it for twenty minutes."

"Dear me," quoth Sherlock Holmes, "it must indeed be a handsome volume, and from your description, together with a realization of importance by reason of its association, I gather that it is something beyond what might be termed a valuable book."

"Priceless!" cried Mr. Harrington Edwards. "The combined wealth of India, Mexico, and Wall Street would be all too little for its purchase."

"You are anxious to recover this book?" asked Sherlock Holmes, looking at him keenly.

"My God!" shrieked the collector, rolling up his eyes and clawing at the air with his hands. "Do you suppose——"

"Tut, tut!" Holmes interrupted. "I was only testing you. It is a book that might move even you, Mr. Harrington Edwards, to theft—but we may put aside that notion. Your emotion is too sincere, and besides you know too well the difficulties of hiding such a volume as you describe. Indeed, only a very daring man would purloin it and keep it long in his possession. Pray tell us how you came to lose it."

Mr. Harrington Edwards seized the brandy flask, which stood at his elbow, and drained it at a gulp. With the renewed strength thus obtained, he continued his story:

"As I have said, Sir Nathaniel forced me to accept the loan of the book, much against my wishes. On the evening that I called for it, he told me that two of his servants, heavily armed, would accompany me across the grounds to my home. 'There is no danger,' he said, 'but you will feel better'; and I heartily agreed with him. How shall I tell you what happened? Mr. Holmes, it was those very servants who assailed me and robbed me of my priceless borrowing!"

Sherlock Holmes rubbed his lean hands with satisfaction. "Splendid!" he murmured. "This is a case after my own heart. Watson, these are deep waters in which we are adventuring. But you are rather lengthy about this, Mr. Edwards. Perhaps it will help matters if I ask you a few questions. By what road did you go to your home?"

"By the main road, a good highway which lies in front of our estates. I preferred it to the shadows of the wood."

"And there were some two hundred yards between your doors. At what point did the assault occur?"

"Almost midway between the two entrance drives, I should say."

"There was no light?"

"That of the moon only."

"Did you know these servants who accompanied you?"

"One I knew slightly; the other I had not seen before."

"Describe them to me, please."

"The man who is known to me is called Miles. He is clean-shaven, short and powerful, although somewhat elderly. He was known, I believe, as Sir Nathaniel's most trusted servant; he had been with Sir Nathaniel for years. I cannot describe him minutely for, of course, I never paid much attention to him. The other was tall and thickset, and wore a heavy beard. He was a silent fellow; I do not believe he spoke a word during the journey."

"Miles was more communicative?"

"Oh yes—even garrulous, perhaps. He talked about the weather and the moon, and I forget what all."

"Never about books?"

"There was no mention of books between any of us."

"Just how did the attack occur?"

"It was very sudden. We had reached, as I say, about the halfway point, when the big man seized me by the throat—to prevent outcry, I suppose—and on the instant, Miles snatched the volume from my grasp and was off. In a moment his companion followed him. I had been half throttled and could not immediately cry out; but when I could articulate, I made the countryside ring with my cries. I ran after them, but failed even to catch another sight of them. They had disappeared completely."

"Did you all leave the house together?"

"Miles and I left together; the second man joined us at the porter's lodge. He had been attending to some of his duties."

"And Sir Nathaniel—where was he?"

"He said good night on the threshold."

"What has he had to say about all this?"

"I have not told him."

"You have not told him!" echoed Sherlock Holmes, in astonishment.

"I have not dared," confessed our client miserably. "It will kill him. That book was the breath of his life."

"When did all this occur?" I put in, with a glance at Holmes.

"Excellent, Watson," said my friend, answering my glance. "I was about to ask the same question."

"Just last night," was Mr. Harrington Edwards's reply. "I was crazy most of the night, and didn't sleep a wink. I came to you the first thing this morning. Indeed, I tried to raise you on the telephone, last night, but could not establish a connection."

"Yes," said Holmes, reminiscently, "we were attending Mme. Trentini's first night. You remember, Watson, we dined later at Albani's."

"Oh, Mr. Holmes, do you think you can help me?" cried the abject collector.

"I trust so," answered my friend, cheerfully. "Indeed, I am certain I can. Such a book, as you remark, is not easily hidden. What say you, Watson, to a run down to Walton-on-Walton?"

"There is a train in half an hour," said Mr. Harrington Edwards, looking at his watch. "Will you return with me?"

"No, no," laughed Holmes, "that would never do. We must not be seen together just yet, Mr. Edwards. Go back yourself on the first train, by all means, unless you have further business in London. My friend and I will go together. There is another train this morning?"

"An hour later."

"Excellent. Until we meet, then!"

*W*e took the train from Paddington Station an hour later, as we had promised, and began our journey to Walton-on-Walton, a pleasant, aristocratic little village and the scene of the curious accident to our friend of Poke Stogis Manor. Sherlock Holmes, lying back in his seat, blew earnest smoke rings at the ceiling of our compartment, which fortunately was empty, while I devoted myself to the morning paper. After a bit I tired of this occupation and turned to Holmes to find him looking out of the window, wreathed in smiles, and quoting Horace softly under his breath.

"You have a theory?" I asked, in surprise.

"It is a capital mistake to theorize in advance of the evidence," he replied. "Still, I have given some thought to the interesting problem of our friend Mr. Harrington Edwards, and there are several indications which can point to only one conclusion."

"And whom do you believe to be the thief?"

"My dear fellow," said Sherlock Holmes, "you forget we already know the thief. Edwards has testified quite clearly that it was Miles who snatched the volume."

"True," I admitted, abashed. "I had forgotten. All we must do, then, is to find Miles."

"And a motive," added my friend, chuckling. "What would you say, Watson, was the motive in this case?"

"Jealousy," I replied.

"You surprise me!"

"Miles had been bribed by a rival collector, who in some manner had learned about this remarkable volume. You remember Edwards told us this second man joined them at the lodge. That would give an excellent opportunity for the substitution of a man other than the servant intended by Sir Nathaniel. Is not that good reasoning?"

"You surpass yourself, my dear Watson," murmured Holmes. "It is excellently reasoned, and, as you justly observe, the opportunity for a substitution was perfect."

"Do you not agree with me?"

"Hardly, Watson. A rival collector, in order to accomplish this remarkable coup, first would have to have known of the volume, as you suggest, but also he must have known upon what night Mr. Harrington Edwards would go to Sir Nathaniel's to get it, which would point to collaboration on the part of our client. As a matter of fact, however, Mr. Edwards's decision to accept the loan, was, I believe, sudden and without previous determination."

"I do not recall his saying so."

"He did not say so, but it is a simple deduction. A book collector is mad enough to begin with, Watson; but tempt him with some such bait as this Shakespeare quarto and he is bereft of all sanity. Mr. Edwards would not have been able to wait. It was just the night before that Sir Nathaniel promised him the book, and it was just last night that he flew to accept the offer—flying, incidentally, to disaster also. The miracle is that he was able to wait an entire day."

"Wonderful!" I cried.

"Elementary," said Holmes. "If you are interested, you will do well to read Harley Graham on *Transcendental Emotion;* while I have myself been guilty of a small brochure in which I catalogue some twelve hundred professions and the emotional effect upon their members of unusual tidings, good and bad."

We were the only passengers to alight at Walton-on-Walton, but rapid inquiry developed that Mr. Harrington Edwards had returned on the previous train. Holmes, who had disguised himself before leaving the coach, did all the talking. He wore his cap peak backwards, carried a pencil behind his ear, and had turned up the bottoms of his trousers; while from one pocket dangled the end of a linen tape measure. He was a municipal surveyor to the life, and I could not but think that, meeting him suddenly in the highway, I should not myself have known him. At his suggestion, I dented the crown of my hat and turned my jacket inside out. Then he gave me an end of the tape measure, while he, carrying the other, went on ahead. In this fashion, stopping from time to time to kneel in the dust and ostensibly to measure sections of the roadway, we proceeded toward Poke Stogis Manor. The occasional villagers whom we encountered on their way to the station bar paid us no more attention than if we had been rabbits.

Shortly we came in sight of our friend's dwelling, a picturesque and rambling abode, sitting far back in its own grounds and bordered by a square of sentinel oaks. A gravel pathway led from the roadway to the house entrance and, as we passed, the sunlight struck fire from an antique brass knocker on the door. The whole picture, with its background of gleaming countryside, was one of rural calm and comfort; we could with difficulty believe it the scene of the sinister tragedy we were come to investigate.

"We shall not enter yet," said Sherlock Holmes, passing the gate leading into our client's acreage; "but we shall endeavor to be back in time for luncheon."

From this point the road progressed downward in a gentle incline and the trees were thicker on either side of the road. Sherlock Holmes kept his eyes stolidly on the path before us, and when we had covered about one hundred yards he stopped. "Here," he said, pointing, "the assault occurred."

I looked closely at the earth, but could see no sign of struggle.

"You recall it was midway between the two houses that it happened," he continued. "No, there are few signs; there was no violent tussle. Fortunately, however, we had our proverbial fall of rain last evening and the earth has retained impressions nicely." He indicated the faint imprint of a foot, then another, and still another. Kneeling down, I was able to see that, indeed, many feet had passed along the road.

Holmes flung himself at full length in the dirt and wriggled swiftly about, his nose to the earth, muttering rapidly in French. Then he whipped out a glass, the better to examine something that had caught his eye; but in a moment he shook his head in disappointment and continued with his exploration. I was irresistibly reminded of a noble hound, at fault, sniffing in circles in an effort to re-establish a lost scent. In a moment, however, he had it, for with a little cry of pleasure he rose to his feet, zigzagged curiously across the road and paused before a hedge, a lean finger pointing accusingly at a break in the thicket.

"No wonder they disappeared," he smiled as I came up. "Edwards thought they continued up the road, but here is where they broke through." Then stepping back a little distance, he ran forward lightly and cleared the hedge at a bound, alighting on his hands on the other side.

"Follow me carefully," he warned, "for we must not allow our own footprints to confuse us." I fell more heavily than my companion, but in a moment he had me by the heels and helped me to steady myself. "See," he cried, lowering his face to the earth; and deep in the mud and grass I saw the prints of two pairs of feet.

"The small man broke through," said Sherlock Holmes, exultantly, "but the larger rascal leaped over the hedge. See how deeply his prints are marked; he landed heavily here in the soft ooze. It is significant, Watson, that they came this way. Does it suggest nothing to you?"

"That they were men who knew Edwards's grounds as well as the Brooke-Bannerman estate," I answered; and thrilled with pleasure at my friend's nod of approbation.

He lowered himself to his stomach, without further conversation, and for some moments we crawled painfully across the grass. Then a shocking thought occurred to me.

"Holmes," I whispered in horror, "do you see where these footprints tend? They are directed toward the home of our client, Mr. Harrington Edwards!"

He nodded his head slowly, and his lips were tight and thin. The double line of impressions ended abruptly at the back door of Poke Stogis Manor!

Sherlock Holmes rose to his feet and looked at his watch.

"We are just in time for luncheon," he announced, and brushed off his garments. Then, deliberately, he knocked upon the door. In a few moments we were in the presence of our client.

"We have been roaming about the neighborhood," apologized the detective, "and took the liberty of coming to your rear door."

"You have a clue?" asked Mr. Harrington Edwards, eagerly.

A queer smile of triumph sat upon Holmes's lips.

"Indeed," he said, quietly, "I believe I have solved your little problem, Mr. Harrington Edwards."

"My dear Holmes!" I cried, and "My dear sir!" cried our client.

"I have yet to establish a motive," confessed my friend; "but as to the main facts there can be no question."

Mr. Harrington Edwards fell into a chair; he was white and shaking.

"The book," he croaked. "Tell me!"

"Patience, my good sir," counseled Holmes, kindly. "We have had nothing to eat since sunup, and we are famished. All in good time. Let us first dine and then all shall be made clear. Meanwhile, I should like to telephone to Sir Nathaniel Brooke-Bannerman, for I wish him also to hear what I have to say."

Our client's pleas were in vain. Holmes would have his little joke and his luncheon. In the end, Mr. Harrington Edwards staggered away to the kitchen to order a repast, and Sherlock Holmes talked rapidly and unintelligibly into the telephone and came back with a smile on his face. But I asked no questions; in good time this extraordinary man would tell his story in his own way. I had heard all that he had heard, and had seen all that he had seen; yet I was completely at sea. Still, our host's ghastly smile hung heavily in my mind, and come what would I felt sorry for him. In a little time we were seated at table. Our client, haggard and nervous, ate slowly and with apparent discomfort; his eyes were never long absent from Holmes's inscrutable face. I was little better off, but Sherlock Holmes ate with gusto, relating meanwhile a number of his earlier adventures—which I may someday give to the world, if I am able to read my illegible notes made on the occasion.

When the sorry meal had been concluded we went into the library, where Sherlock Holmes took possession of the easiest chair with an air of proprietorship that would have been amusing in other circumstances. He screwed together his long pipe and lighted it with almost malicious lack of haste, while Mr. Harrington Edwards perspired against the mantel in an agony of apprehension.

"Why must you keep us waiting, Mr. Holmes?" he whispered. "Tell us, at once, please, who—who—" His voice trailed off into a moan.

"The criminal," said Sherlock Holmes, smoothly, "is—"

"Sir Nathaniel Brooke-Bannerman!" said a maid, suddenly, putting her head in at the door; and on the heels of her announcement stalked the handsome baronet, whose priceless volume had caused all this commotion and unhappiness.

Sir Nathaniel was white, and he appeared ill. He burst at once into talk.

"I have been much upset by your call," he said, looking meanwhile at our client. "You say you have something to tell me about the quarto. Don't say—that—anything—has happened—to it!" He clutched nervously at the wall to steady himself, and I felt deep pity for the unhappy man.

Mr. Harrington Edwards looked at Sherlock Holmes. "Oh, Mr. Holmes," he cried, pathetically, "why did you send for him?"

"Because," said my friend, "I wish him to hear the truth about the Shakespeare quarto. Sir Nathaniel, I believe you have not been told as yet that Mr. Edwards was robbed, last night, of your precious volume—robbed by the trusted servants whom you sent with him to protect it."

"*What!*" screamed the titled collector. He staggered and fumbled madly at his heart, then collapsed into a chair. "My God!" he muttered, and then again: "My God!"

"I should have thought you would have been suspicious of evil when your servants did not return," pursued the detective.

"I have not seen them," whispered Sir Nathaniel. "I do not mingle with my servants. I did not know they had failed to return. Tell me—tell me all!"

"Mr. Edwards," said Sherlock Holmes, turning to our client, "will you repeat your story, please?"

Mr. Harrington Edwards, thus adjured, told the unhappy tale again, ending with a heartbroken cry of "Oh, Nathaniel, can you ever forgive me?"

"I do not know that it was entirely your fault," observed Holmes, cheerfully. "Sir Nathaniel's own servants are the guilty ones, and surely he sent them with you."

"But you said you had solved the case, Mr. Holmes," cried our client, in a frenzy of despair.

"Yes," agreed Holmes, "it is solved. You have had the clue in your own hands ever since the occurrence, but you did not know how to use it. It all turns upon the curious actions of the taller servant, prior to the assault."

"The actions of—" stammered Mr. Harrington Edwards. "Why, he did nothing—said nothing!"

"That is the curious circumstance," said Sherlock Holmes.

Sir Nathaniel got to his feet with difficulty.

"Mr. Holmes," he said, "this has upset me more than I can tell you. Spare no pains to recover the book and to bring to justice the scoundrels who stole it. But I must go away and think—think—"

"Stay," said my friend. "I have already caught one of them."

"What! Where?" cried the two collectors together.

"Here," said Sherlock Holmes, and stepping forward he laid a hand on the baronet's shoulder. "You, Sir Nathaniel, were the taller servant; you were one of the thieves who throttled Mr. Harrington Edwards and took from him your own book. And now, sir, will you tell us why you did it?"

Sir Nathaniel Brooke-Bannerman toppled and would have fallen had not I rushed forward and supported him. I placed him in a chair. As we looked at him we saw confession in his eyes; guilt was written in his haggard face.

"Come, come," said Holmes, impatiently. "Or will it make it easier for you if I tell the story as it occurred? Let it be so, then. You parted with Mr. Harrington Edwards on your doorsill, Sir Nathaniel, bidding your best friend good night with a smile on your lips and evil in your heart. And as soon as you had closed the door, you slipped into an enveloping raincoat, turned up your collar, and hastened by a shorter road to the porter's lodge, where you joined Mr. Edwards and Miles as one of your own servants. You spoke no word at any time, because you feared to speak. You were afraid Mr. Edwards would recognize your voice, while your beard, hastily assumed, protected your face and in the darkness your figure passed unnoticed.

"Having strangled and robbed your best friend, then, of your own book, you and your scoundrelly assistant fled across Mr. Edwards's fields to his own back door, thinking that, if investigation followed, I would be called in, and would trace those footprints and fix the crime upon Mr. Harrington Edwards—as part of a criminal plan, prearranged with your rascally servants, who would be supposed to be in the pay of Mr. Edwards and the ringleaders in a counterfeit assault upon his person. Your mistake, sir, was in ending your trail abruptly at Mr. Edwards's back door. Had you left another trail, then, leading back to your own domicile, I should unhesitatingly have arrested Mr. Harrington Edwards for the theft.

"Surely you must know that in criminal cases handled by me, it is never the obvious solution that is the correct one. The mere fact that the finger of suspicion is made to point at a certain individual is sufficient to absolve that individual from guilt. Had you read the little works of my friend and colleague, Dr. Watson, you would not have made such a mistake. Yet you claim to be a bookman!"

A low moan from the unhappy baronet was his only answer.

"To continue, however: there at Mr. Edwards's own back door you ended your trail, entering his house—his own house—and spending the night under his roof, while his cries and ravings over his loss filled the night and brought joy to your unspeakable soul. And in the morning, when he had gone forth to consult me, you quietly left—you and Miles—and returned to your own place by the beaten highway."

"Mercy!" cried the defeated wretch, cowering in his chair. "If it is made public, I am ruined. I was driven to it. I could not let Mr. Edwards examine the book, for that way exposure would follow; yet I could not refuse him—my best friend—when he asked its loan."

"Your words tell me all that I did not know," said Sherlock Holmes, sternly. "The motive now is only too plain. The work, sir, was a forgery, and knowing that your erudite friend would discover it, you chose to blacken his name to save your own. Was the book insured?"

"Insured for £100,000, he told me," interrupted Mr. Harrington Edwards, excitedly.

"So that he planned at once to dispose of this dangerous and dubious item, and to reap a golden reward," commented Holmes. "Come, sir, tell us about it. How much of it was forgery? Merely the inscription?"

"I will tell you," said the baronet, suddenly, "and throw myself upon the mercy of my friend, Mr. Edwards. The whole book, in effect, was a forgery. It was originally made up of two imperfect copies of the 1604 quarto. Out of the pair I made one perfect volume, and a skillful workman, now dead, changed the date for me so cleverly that only an expert of the first water could have detected it. Such an expert, however, is Mr. Harrington Edwards—the one man in the world who could have unmasked me."

"Thank you, Nathaniel," said Mr. Harrington Edwards, gratefully.

"The inscription, of course, also was forged," continued the baronet. "You may as well know everything."

"And the book?" asked Holmes. "Where did you destroy it?"

A grim smile settled on Sir Nathaniel's features. "It is even now burning in Mr. Edward's own furnace," he said.

"Then it cannot yet be consumed," cried Holmes, and dashed into the cellar. He was absent for some time and we heard the clinking of bottles and, finally, the clang of a great metal door. He emerged, some moments later, in high spirits, carrying a charred leaf of paper in his hand.

"It is a pity," he cried, "a pity! In spite of its questionable authenticity, it was a noble specimen. It is only half consumed; but let it burn away. I have preserved one leaf as a souvenir of the occasion." He folded it carefully and placed it in his wallet. "Mr. Harrington Edwards, I fancy the decision in this matter is for you to announce. Sir Nathaniel, of course, must make no effort to collect the insurance."

"Let us forget it, then," said Mr. Harrington Edwards, with a sigh. "Let it be a sealed chapter in the history of bibliomania." He looked at Sir Nathaniel Brooke-Bannerman for a long moment, then held out his hand. "I forgive you, Nathaniel," he said, simply.

Their hands met; tears stood in the baronet's eyes. Powerfully moved, Holmes and I turned from the affecting scene and crept to the door unnoticed. In a moment the free air was blowing on our temples, and we were coughing the dust of the library from our lungs.

They are a strange people, these book collectors," mused Sherlock Holmes, as we rattled back to town.

"My only regret is that I shall be unable to publish my notes on this interesting case," I responded.

"Wait a bit, my dear Doctor," counseled Holmes, "and it will be possible. In time both of them will come to look upon it as a hugely diverting episode, and will tell it upon themselves. Then your notes shall be brought forth and the history of another of Mr. Sherlock Holmes's little problems shall be given to the world."

"It will always be a reflection upon Sir Nathaniel," I demurred.

"He will glory in it," prophesied Sherlock Holmes. "He will go down in bookish chronicle with Chatterton, and Ireland, and Payne Collier. Mark my words, he is not blind even now to the chance this gives him for a sinister immortality. He will be the first to tell it." (And so, indeed, it proved, as this narrative suggests.)

"But why did you preserve the leaf from *Hamlet?*" I inquired. "Why not a jewel from the binding?"

Sherlock Holmes laughed heartily. Then he slowly unfolded the leaf in question, and directed a humorous finger to a spot upon the page.

"A fancy," he responded, "to preserve so accurate a characterization of either of our friends. The line is a real jewel. See, the good Polonius says: 'That he is mad, 'tis true: 'tis true 'tis pittie; and pittie it is true.' There is as much sense in Master Will as in Hafiz or Confucius, and a greater felicity of expression . . . Here is London, and now, my dear Watson, if we hasten we shall be just in time for Zabriski's matinee!"

A catalog of every actor who impersonated Sherlock Holmes on stage and screen would be long and full of surprises, including John Barrymore, Ronald Howard (son of Leslie), Raymond Massey, Joseph Bell (!), O. P. Heggie, best remembered as the blind man in the 1935 film The Bride of Frankenstein . . . and Boris Karloff, who played a retired beekeeper with the telltale name of Mr. Mycroft in A Sting of Death, a 1955 TV adaptation of A Taste for Honey (see Appendix I) by science-fantasy writer H. F. HEARD (1889–1971). In September, 1945, with editorial fanfare, a Mr. Mycroft short story was published by Ellery Queen's Mystery Magazine, but oddly, when "The Enchanted Garden" appeared in March, 1949, the normally exegetical "Queens" did not offer a single prefatory word about this eerie late Holmesian adventure.

The Enchanted Garden

H . F . H E A R D

" 'Nature's a queer one,' said Mr. Squeers," I remarked.

"I know what moves you to misquote Dickens," was Mr. Mycroft's reply.

Here was a double provocation: first, there was the injury of being told that the subject on which one was going to inform someone was already known to him, and secondly, there was the insult that the happy literary quotation with which the information was to be introduced was dismissed as inaccurate. Still it's no use getting irritated with Mr. Mycroft. The only hope was to lure his pride onto the brink of ignorance.

"Then tell me," I remarked demurely, "what I have just been reading?"

"The sad, and it is to be feared, fatal accident that befell Miss Hetty Hess who is said to be extremely rich, and a 'colorful personality' and 'young for her years'—the evidence for these last two statements being a color photograph in the photogravure section of the paper which establishes that her frock made up for its brevity only by the intense viridity of its green color."

I am seldom untruthful deliberately, even when considerably nonplussed; besides it was no use: Mr. Mycroft was as usual one move ahead. He filled in the silence with: "I should have countered that naturalists are the queer ones."

I had had a moment to recover, and felt that I could retrieve at least a portion of my lost initiative. "But there's no reason to link the accident with the death. The notice only mentions that she had had a fall a few weeks previously. The cause of death was 'intestinal stasis'."

"Cause!" said Mr. Mycroft. He looked and sounded so like an old raven as he put his head on one side and uttered "caws," that I couldn't help laughing.

"Murder's no laughing matter!" he remonstrated.

"But surely, *cher maître,* you sometimes are unwilling to allow that death can ever be through natural causes!"

"Cause? There's sufficient cause here."

"Post hoc, propter hoc," I was glad to get off one of my few classic tags. "Because a lady of uncertain years dies considerably *after* a fall from which her doctor vouched there were no immediate ill effects, you would surely not maintain that it was *on account* of the fall that the rhythm of her secondary nervous system struck and stopped for good? And even if it was, who's to blame?"

"Cause." At this third quothing of the Raven I let my only comment be a rather longer laugh—and waited for my lecture. Mr. Mycroft did not fail me. He went on: "I'll own I know nothing about causality in the outer world, for I believe no one does really. But I have spent my life, not unprofitably, in tracing human causality. As you're fond of Dickens, I'll illustrate from Copperfield's Mr. Dick. The *causes* of King Charles's head coming off may have been due to four inches of iron going through his neck. I feel on safer ground when I say it was due to his failing to get on with his parliament. You say Miss Hess died naturally—that is to say (1) her death, (2) her accident a fortnight before, and (3) the place where that accident took place, all have only a chance connection. Maybe your case would stand were I not watching *another* line of causality."

"You mean a motive?"

"Naturally."

"But motives aren't proof! Or every natural death would be followed by a number of unnatural ones—to wit, executions of executors and legatees!"

"I don't know whether I agree with your rather severe view of human nature. What I do know is that when a death proves to be far too happy an accident for someone who survives, then we old sleuths start with a trail which often ends with our holding proofs that not even a jury can fail to see."

"Still," I said, "suspicion can't always be right!"

What had been no more than an after-lunch sparring-match suddenly loomed up as active service with Mr. Mycroft's, "Well, the police agree with you in thinking that there's no proof, and with me in suspecting it *is* murder. That's why I'm going this afternoon to view the scene of the accident, unaccompanied—unless, of course, you would care to accompany me?"

I may sometimes seem vain but I know my uses. So often I get a ringside seat because, as Mr. Mycroft has often remarked, my appearance disarms suspicion.

"We are headed," Mr. Mycroft resumed as we bowled along in our taxi, "for what I am creditably informed is in both senses of the word a gem of a sanctuary—gem, because it is both small and jewelled."

We had been swaying and sweeping up one of those narrow rather desolate canyons in southern California through which the famous "Thirteen suburbs in search of a city" have thrust corkscrew concrete highways. The lots became more stately and secluded, the houses more embowered and enwalled, until the ride, the road, and the canyon itself all ended in a portico of such Hispano-Moorish impressiveness that it might have been the entrance to a veritable Arabian Nights Entertainments. There was no one else about, but remarking, "This is Visitors' Day," Mr. Mycroft alit, told our driver to wait, and strolled up to the heavily grilled gate. One of the large gilt nails which bossed the gate's carved timbers had etched round it in elongated English so as to pretend to be Kufic or at least ordinary Arabic the word PRESS. And certainly it was as good as its word. For not only did the stud sink into the gate, the gate followed suit and sank into the arch, and we strolled over the threshold into as charming an enclosure as I have ever seen. The gate closed softly behind us. Indeed, there was nothing to suggest that we weren't in an enchanted garden. The ground must have risen steeply on either hand. But you didn't see any ground—all manner of hanging vines and flowering shrubs rose in festoons, hanging in garlands, swinging in delicate sprays. The crowds of blossom against the vivid blue sky, shot through by the sun, made the place intensely vivid. And in this web of color, like quick bobbins, the shuttling flight of humming-birds was everywhere. The place was, in fact, alive with birds. But not a single human being could I see.

Birds are really stupid creatures and their noises, in spite of all the poetry that has been written about them, always seem to me tiring. Their strong point is, of course, plumage. I turned to Mr. Mycroft and remarked that I wished the Polynesian art of making cloaks of birds' feathers had not died out. He said he preferred them alive but that he believed copies of the famous plumage-mantles could now be purchased for those who liked to appear in borrowed plumes.

"This, I understand," continued Mr. Mycroft, "is supposed to be the smallest and choicest of all the world's bird sanctuaries. It is largely reserved for species of that mysterious living automaton, the hummingbird," and as was the way with the old bird himself, in a moment he seemed to forget why we were there. First, he scanned the whole place. The steep slopes came down till only a curb-path of marble divided the banks of flowers from a floor of water. At the farther end of this was a beautiful little statue holding high a lance, all of a lovely, almost peacock-green hue. And from this lance rose a spray of water, a miniature fountain. This little piece of art seemed to absorb him and as he couldn't walk on the water and examine it, he took binoculars from his pocket and scanned it with loving care. Then his mind shifted and slipping the glasses back in his pocket, he gave the same interest to the birds. His whole attention now seemed to be involved with these odd little bird-pellets. Hummingbirds are certainly odd. To insist on flying all the time you are drinking nectar from the deep flask of a flower always seems to me a kind of *tour de force* of pointless energy. In fact, it really fatigues me a little even to watch them. But the general plan of the place was beautiful and restful: there was just this narrow path of marble framing the sheet of water and this wall of flowers and foliage. The path curved round making an oval and at the upper end, balancing the fine Moorish arch through which we had entered, there rose a similar horseshoe arch, charmingly reflected in the water above which it rose. It made a bridge over which one could pass to reach the marble curb on the other side of the water.

"A bower," remarked Mr. Mycroft. He loitered along, cricking back his neck farther and farther to watch the birds perched on sprays right against the sky. He had now taken a pen from his pocket and was jotting down some ornithological observation. Poor old dear, he never could enjoy but must always be making some blot of comment on the bright mirror of—well, what I mean is that I was really taking it in and he was already busy manufacturing it into some sort of dreary information. And poor Miss Hess, she too must wait till he came back to her actual problem, if indeed there was one.

I watched him as he stepped back to the very edge of the marble curb so that he might better view a spray of deep purple bougainvillea at which a hummingbird was flashing its gorget. Yes, it would have been a pretty enough bit of color contrast, had one had a color camera to snap it, but I had seen a sign on the gate outside asking visitors not to take photographs. So I watched my master. And having my wits about me I suddenly broke the silence. "Take care!" I shouted. But too late. Mr. Mycroft had in his effort to see what was too high above him stepped back too far. The actual edge of the marble curb must have been slippery from the lapping of the ripples. His foot skidded. He made a remarkable effort to recover. I am not hard-hearted but I could not help tittering as I saw him—more raven-like than ever—flap his arms to regain his balance. And the comic maneuver served perfectly—I mean it still gave me my joke and yet saved him from anything more serious than a loss of gravity. His arms whirled. Pen and paper scrap flew from his hands to join some hummingbirds but the Mycroft frame, under whose over-arching shadow so many great criminals had cowered, collapsed not grace-fully but quite safely just short of the water.

I always carry a cane. It gives poise. The piece of paper and even the pen—which was one of those new "light-as-a-feather" plastic things—were bobbing about on the surface. Of course, Mr. Mycroft who was a little crest-fallen at such an absent-minded slip, wouldn't let me help him up. In fact he was up before I could have offered. My only chance of collecting a "Thank-you" was to salvage the flotsam that he had so spontaneously "cast upon the waters." I fished in both the sopped sheet and the pen, and noticed that Mr. Mycroft had evidently not had time to record the precious natural-history fact that he had gleaned before his lack of hindsight attention parted the great mind and the small sheet. Nor when I handed him back his salvaged apparatus did he do so; instead he actually put both pen and sopped sheet into his pocket. "Shaken," I said to myself; "there's one more disadvantage of being so high up in the clouds of speculation."

As we continued on our way along the curb and were approaching the horseshoe Moorish arch-bridge, Mr. Mycroft began to limp. My real fond-ness for him made me ask, "Have you strained anything?"

Mr. Mycroft most uncharacteristically answered, "I think I will rest for a moment."

We had reached the place where the level marble curb, sweeping round the end of the pond, rose into the first steps of the flight of stairs that ran up the back of the arch. These stairs had a low, fretted rail. It seemed to me that it might have been higher for safety's sake, but I suppose that would have spoiled the beauty of the arch, making it look too heavy and thick. It certainly was a beautiful piece of work and finished off the garden with charming effectiveness. The steps served Mr. Mycroft's immediate need well enough, just because they were so steep. He bent down and holding the balustrade with his left hand, lowered himself until he was seated. So he was in a kind of stone chair, his back comfortably against the edge of the step above that one on which he sat. And as soon as he was settled down, the dizziness seemed to pass, and his spirits obviously returned to their old bent. He started once more to peek about him. The irrelevant vitality of being interested in anything mounted once again to its usual unusual intensity.

After he had for a few moments been swinging his head about in the way that led to his fall—the way a new-born baby will loll, roll, and goggle at the sky—he actually condescended to draw me into the rather pointless ap-preciations he was enjoying. "You see, Mr. Silchester, one of their breeding boxes." He pointed up into the foliage, which here rose so high that it reared a number of feet above the highest pitch of the arch.

"Surely," I asked, for certainly it is always safer with Mr. Mycroft to offer information armored in question form, "surely breeding boxes are no new invention?"

Mr. Mycroft's reply was simply, "No, of course not," and then he became vague.

I thought: Now he'll start making notes again. But no, poor old pride-in-perception was evidently more shaken by his fall than I'd thought. I felt a real sympathy for him, as I stood at a little distance keeping him under observation but pretending to glance at the scene which, though undoubtedly pretty, soon began to pall for really it had no more sense or story about it than a kaleidoscope. Poor old thing, I repeated to myself, as out of the corner of my eye, I saw him let that big cranium hang idly. But the restless, nervous energy still fretted him. Though his eyes were brooding out of focus, those long fingers remained symptomatic of his need always to be fiddling and raveling with something. How important it is, I reflected, to learn young how to idle well. Now, poor old dear, he just can't rest. Yes, Britain can still teach America something; a mellow culture knows how to meander; streams nearer their source burst and rush and tumble.

The Mycroft fingers were running to and fro along the curb of the step against which he was resting his back. I thought I ought to rouse him. He must be getting his fingernails into a horrid condition as they aimlessly scraped along under that ledge and the very thought even of someone rasping and soiling his nails sets my teeth on edge.

My diagnosis that the dear old fellow was badly shaken was confirmed when I suggested, "Shall we be getting on?" and he answered, "Certainly." And I must say that I was trebly pleased when, first, Mr. Mycroft took my extended hand to pull him to his feet, then accepted my arm as we went up the bridge and down its other side, and once we were outside the gate let me hold the door of the cab open for him. At that moment from an alcove in the gate-arch popped a small man with a book. Would we care to purchase any of the colored photographs he had for sale, and would we sign the visitors' book? I bought a couple and said to Mr. Mycroft, "May I sign Mr. Silchester and friend?"—for this was a ready way for him to preserve his anonymity, when he remarked, "I will sign," and in that large stately hand the most famous signature was placed on the page.

As we swirled down the canyon, Mr. Mycroft gave his attention to our new surroundings. Suddenly he exclaimed, "Stop!" The cab bumped to a standstill. The spot he had chosen was certainly a contrast to our last stop. Of course, once outside the houses of the rich, this countryside is pretty untidy. We had just swished round one of those hairpin curves all these canyon roads make as they wiggle down the central cleft. The cleft itself was in slow process of being filled by the cans and crocks that fall from the rich man's kitchen. Something, disconcerting to a sane eye even at this distance, had caught Mr. Mycroft's vulture gaze. Even before the cab was quite still, he was out and went straight for the garbage heap. I need not say that not only did I stay where I was, I turned away. For that kind of autopsy always makes me feel a little nauseated. Mr. Mycroft knows my reasonable limits. He had not asked me to go with him and when he came back he spared me by not displaying his trophy, whatever it might be. I caught sight of him stuffing a piece of some gaudy colored wrapping-paper into his pocket as he climbed into the seat beside me, but I was certainly more anxious not to notice than he to conceal.

Nor, when we reached home, did Mr. Mycroft become any more communicative. Indeed, he went straight to his study and there, no doubt, unloaded his quarry. He did not, as a matter of fact, put in an appearance till dinner. Nor did the dinner rouse him. I can hardly blame him for that. For I, too, was a little abstracted and so have to confess that I had ordered a very conventional repast, the kind of meal that you can't remember five minutes after you have ordered it or five minutes after it has been cleared away—a dinner so lacking in art that it can arouse neither expectation nor recollection.

Truth to tell, I was not a little disconcerted at the tameness of our "adventure." Mr. M. had as good as told me that he would disclose a plot and a pretty ugly one, but all we had seen was a charming enough stage, set for comedy rather than tragedy. And not a soul in view, far less a body.

The only incident, and surely that was tamely comic and I had to enjoy even that by myself, was Mr. Mycroft's skid. Indeed, as we sat on in silence I was beginning to think I might say something—perhaps a little pointed—about pointless suspicion. But on looking across at Mr. M. who was sitting dead still at the other side of the table, I thought the old fellow looked more than a little tired. So I contented myself with the feeling that his fall had shaken him considerably more than he chose to allow.

But as I rose to retire, after reading my half-chapter of Jane Austen—for me an unfailing sedative—the old fellow roused himself.

"Thank you for your company, Mr. Silchester. Quite a fruitful day." Perhaps he saw I was already "registering surprise." For he added, "I believe we sowed and not only reaped this afternoon but if you will again give me your company, we will go tomorrow to gather the harvest."

"But I thought today was Visitors' Day?"

"Oh," he carelessly remarked, "I expect the proprietor will be glad of callers even the day after. The place was quite deserted, wasn't it? Maybe he's thinking of closing it. And that would be a pity before we had seen all that it may have to offer."

Well, I had enjoyed the little place and was not averse to having one more stroll round it. So, as it was certain we should go anyhow, I agreed with the proviso, "I must tell you that though I agree the place is worth a second visit for its beauty, nevertheless I am still convinced that to throw a cloud of suspicion over its innocent brightness might almost be called professional obsessionalism."

I was rather pleased at that heavy technical-sounding ending and even hoped it might rouse the old man to spar back. But he only replied, "Excellent, excellent. That's what I hoped you'd think and say. For that, of course, is the reaction I trust would be awakened in any untrained—I mean, normal mind."

The next afternoon found us again in the garden, I enjoying what was there and Mr. M. really liking it as much as I did but having to spin all over its brightness the gossamer threads of his suspicions and speculations. The water was flashing in the sun, the small spray-fountain playing, birds dancing—yes, the place was the nicest *mis-en-scène* for a meditation on murder that anyone could ask. Again we had the place to ourselves. Indeed, I had just remarked on the fact to Mr. M. and he had been gracious enough to protrude from his mystery mist and reply that perhaps people felt there might still be a shadow over the place, when a single other visitor did enter. He entered from the other end. I hadn't thought there was a way in from that direction but evidently behind the bridge and the thicket there must have been. He strolled down the same side of the small lake as we were advancing up. But I didn't have much chance to study him for he kept on turning round and looking at the bridge and the fountain. I do remember thinking what a dull and ugly patch his dreary store suit made against the vivid living tapestries all around us. The one attempt he made to be in tune was rather futile: he had stuck a bright red hibiscus flower in his button-hole. And then that thought was put out of my mind by an even juster judgment. Mr. M. was loitering behind— sometimes I think that I really do take things in rather more quickly than he—at least, when what is to be seen is what is meant to be seen. He pores and reflects too much even on the obvious. So it was I who saw what was going forward and being of a simple forthright nature took the necessary steps at once. After all, I did not feel that I had any right to be suspicious of our host who was certainly generous and as certainly had been put in a very unpleasant limelight by police and press. My duty was to see that what he offered so freely to us should not be abused or trespassed on. As the man ahead turned round again to study the fountain and the arch I saw what he was doing. He had a small color camera pressed against him and was going to take a photo of the fountain and the bridge. Now, as we knew, visitors were asked expressly not to do this. So I stepped forward and tapped him on the shoulder, remarking that as guests of a public generosity we should observe the simple rule requested of us. He swung round at my tap. My feelings had not been cordial at first sight, his action had alienated them further, and now a close-up clinched the matter. His hat was now pushed back and showed a head of billiard-baldness; his eyes were weak and narrowed-up at me through glasses, rimless glasses that like some colorless fly perched on his nose—that hideous sight-aid called rightly a *pince-nez*.

Suddenly his face relaxed. It actually smiled, and he said, "That is really very kind of you. It is a pity when the rule is not kept for it does deprive the pension house for pets of a little income—almost all that one can spare for that excellent work. I am grateful, grateful." I was taken aback, even more so with the explanation. "I have the responsibility for this place. Owing to a very ungenerous press campaign we are not getting the visitors we used to. So I thought I would take a few more photos for the sales-rack at the gate. Yes, I am the owner of this little place, or as I prefer to say, the trustee of it in the joint interests of the public and philanthropy. May I introduce myself?—I am Hiram Hess, Jr."

After my *faux pas* I stumbled out some kind of apology.

"Please don't make any excuse. I only wish all my guests felt the same way in our common responsibility," he replied. "Indeed, now that you have done me one kindness, you embolden me to ask for another. I believe that the public has been scared away and this seems a heaven-sent opportunity."

All this left me somewhat in the dark. I am not averse to being treated as an honored guest and murmured something about being willing to oblige. Then I remembered Mr. M. and that I was actually taking the leading part in a scene and with the "mystery character" to whom he had in fact introduced me. I turned round and found Mr. M. at my heels. I think I made the introduction well and certainly the two of them showed no signs of not wishing to play the parts in which I was now the master of ceremonies. Mr. Hess spoke first: "I was just about to ask your friend . . ."—"Mr. Silchester," I prompted—"whether he would add another kindness. I was told only yesterday by a friend that natural history photos sell better if they can be combined with human interest of some sort. Of course when I was told that, I saw at once he was right. It must be, mustn't it?" Mr. M. made a "Lord Burleigh nod." "I am glad you agree. So I suggested that I might ask a movie star to pose. But my friend said No, I should get a handsome young man whose face has not been made wearisome to the public and that would give a kind of mystery element to the photo. People would ask, 'In what movie did that face appear?' " I own that at this personal reference—I am a Britisher, you know—I felt a little inclined to blush. "And," hurried on Mr. Hess, "now, the very day after I am told what to do, I am offered the means to do it!"

Frankness has always been my forte. Like many distinguished and good-looking people, I like being photographed and these new colored ones are really most interesting. "I would be most happy to oblige," I said, and turned to see how Mr. M. would react to my taking the play out of his hands. Of course this odd little man couldn't be a murderer. I'm not a profound student of men but that was now perfectly clear to me. Mr. M. merely treated us to another of his "Lord Burleigh nods" and then, "While you are posing Mr. Silchester, may I walk about?"

"Please look upon the place as your own," left Mr. M. free to stroll away and he seemed quite content to use his fieldglasses looking at the birds and blooms.

"Now," said Mr. Hess, all vivacity and I must confess, getting more likable every moment, "my idea is that we put the human interest, if I may so describe my collaborator, right in the middle of the scene. You will be the focus round which the garden is, as it were, draped." Then he paused and exclaimed, "Why, of course, that's the very word—why didn't I think of it before? I wonder whether you would be kind enough to agree—it would make the picture really wonderful."

Again I was a little at a loss, but the small man's enthusiasm was quite infectious. "How can I help further?" I asked.

"Well, it was the word drape that shot the idea into my head, darting like one of these sweet birdkins. Don't you think, Mr. Silchester, that men's clothes rather spoil the effect here?"

He looked down on his own little store suit and smiled. It was true enough but a sudden qualm shook my mind. The thought of stripping and posing, with Mr. Mycroft in the offing—well, I felt that awkward blush again flowing all over me. Whether my little host guessed my confusion or not, his next words put me at ease. "Do you think that you'd consent to wear just for the photo a robe I have?"

My relief that I was not to be asked to disrobe but to robe made me say, "Of course, of course," and without giving me any further chance to qualify my consent, off hurried little Hess. He was not gone more than a couple of minutes—not enough time for me to go back to where Mr. Mycroft was loitering near the gate at the other end of the pool—before once again he appeared, but nearly hidden even when he faced me. For what he was hold-ing in his arms and over his shoulder was one of those Polynesian feather cloaks of which I had remarked to Mr. Mycroft that I thought they were one of the finest of all dresses ever made by man.

"Of course," Hess said, "this isn't one of the pieces that go to mu-seums. I always hoped that somehow I would make a picture of this place in which this cloak would play the leading part."

All the while he said this he was holding out the lovely wrap for me to examine and as he finished he lightly flung the robe over my shoulder. "Oh, that's it, that's it!" he said, standing back with his head on one side like a bird. And looking down, I could not help thinking that I too was now like a bird and, to be truthful, a very handsome one.

So, without even casting a look behind me to see if Mr. Mycroft was watching and perhaps smiling, I followed Mr. Hess as he led the way, saying over his shoulder, heaped with the Polynesian robe, "I said right in the centre and I mean to keep my word." It was clear what he meant, for already he was mounted on the steps of the horseshoe-arch bridge and was going up them. Yes, I was to be the *clou* of the whole composition. When we reached the very apex of the arch, he held out the cloak to me, remarking, "You will find it hangs better if you'll just slip off your coat." I agreed and obeyed. I had already laid aside my cane. He was evidently quite an artist and was deter-mined to pose me to best possible effect. He tried a number of poses and none seemed to him good enough. "I have it!" he finally clicked out. "Oh, the thing gets better and better! Why you aren't in the movies . . . But of course after this . . . photogenic—why, it's a mild word! I'm not asking for anything theatrical—only an accent, as it were—just the natural inevitable drama, one might say. The cloak itself sets the gesture. You see, the sun is high above and you are the centre of this pool of flowers and birds. And so we would get perfect action, perfect face lighting, and perfect hang of drapery if you would just stretch up your arms to the sun and let the light pour on your face. You stand here, with your back to the garden—its high-priest offering all its life to the sun."

While the little man had been saying this, he had been arranging the robe to make it hang well, tucking it in at my feet. "The shoes mustn't show, you know," he said, as he stooped like a little bootblack and arranged my train; then he shifted my stance until he had me close to the balustrade, for only there could he get the light falling full on my upturned face. One couldn't help falling in with his fancy—it was infectious. I rolled up my sleeves so that now, as I stood looking into the sun, I confess I could not help feeling the part. I forgot all about my old spider, Mr. Mycroft. I was one with nature, transformed by the robe which covered every sign of the civilized man on me, and by my setting. Mr. Hess darted back to the other side of the arch, up which we had come, and began—I could see out of the corner of my upturned eye—to focus his camera.

And then he seemed to spoil it all. After some delay he became uncertain. Finally, he came back up to me. "It's magnificent. I've never had the chance to take such a photo. But that's what so often happens with really great opportunities and insights into art and high beauty, isn't it?"

I was more than a little dashed. "Do you mean that you have decided not to take the photo?" I asked. Perhaps there was a touch of resentment in my voice. After all, I had been to a great deal of inconvenience; I had lent myself to a very unusual amount of free model work and laid myself open to Mr. Mycroft's wry humor which would be all the more pointed if the photo was never taken.

"No—Oh, of course not!" But the tone had so much reservation in it that I was not in the slightest reassured, and even less so when he showed his hand, for then I was certain he had just thought up a none-too-unclever way of getting out of the whole business. "But as I've said, and as I know you know, whenever one glimpses a true summit of beauty one catches sight of something even more remarkable beyond."

I snapped out, "Am I to presume that on reconsideration you would prefer not a high light but a foil, not myself but my old sober friend down by the gate?"

I had been growing quite resentful. But my resentment changed to outrage at the absurdity of his answer. It was a simple "Yes." Then seeing me flush, he hurriedly added, "I do believe that majestic old figure would make a perfect foil to yours."

Of course, this was an amend of sorts, but of a very silly sort. For could the man be such a fool as to think that while I might be generous and accommodating to a fault, my old friend would fall in with this charade?

"I think," I said with considerable dignity, beginning to draw the robe away from my shoulders, "that when you want models, Mr. Hess, you had better pay for them."

But my arm got no further than halfway down the coat-sleeve. For my eyes were held. Looking up at the sun makes you a little dizzy and your sight blotchy, but there was no doubt what I was seeing. That silly little Hess had run along the curb and as I watched was buttonholing Mr. Mycroft. I didn't wait to struggle into my jacket but running down the steps went to where they stood together by the exit. I couldn't hear what was being said but was sure I guessed. Yet, in a moment, I was again at a loss. For instead of Mr. Mycroft turning down the grotesque offer, beckoning to me, and going out of the gate, Mr. M. was coming toward me, and he and Hess were talking quite amicably. Of course, I could only conclude that Hess had been spinning some new kind of yarn but all I could do was to go right up to them and say, "Perhaps you will be good enough to tell me what you have arranged!"

I was still further bewildered when it was Mr. M. who answered, "I think Mr. Hess's idea is excellent. If the picture is to be the success which he hopes, it should have contrast and, if I may put it in that way, significance—a picture with a story. Wasn't that your telling phrase, Mr. Hess?"

Hess beamed: "Precisely, precisely! Mr. Mycroft is so instantly intuitive." And the little fellow looked Mr. M. up and down with a mixture of surprise and complacency that I found very comic and sedative to my rightly ruffled feelings. Still I was quite in the dark as to what had happened to make the three of us so suddenly and so unexpectedly a happy family with—of all people—Mr. M. as the matchmaker. Hess, however, was bubbling over to tell me:

"Do forgive me, rushing off like that. So impulsive. But that's the way I am—'stung with the sudden splendor of a thought.' You see, that was the way I was with you, wasn't I? And I know you're an artist too and so you must know that when one idea comes, generally an even brighter one comes rushing on its heels," he tittered. "I was also a bit frightened, I must confess," he ran on. "What if Mr. Mycroft had refused? I knew if I asked you, you'd say he would; and of course you'd have been right. So I just rushed on to my fate, risked losing the whole picture—the best so often risks the good, doesn't it?"

While the little fellow had been pouring out this excited rigmarole, he had been leading us back to the bridge and as Mr. M. followed without any kind of unwillingness, I fell in too. After all, it looked as though we were going to get the photo. As we reached the steps it was Mr. M. who forestalled Hess just as Hess was about to give us some directions. "You would like us, wouldn't you, to pose on the other side of the bridge-top?"

"Yes, that's it—just where I had Mr. Silchester."

I took up my position, picking up the robe, putting down my jacket. Hess arranged the fall of the robe as before. I must admit he was neat at that sort of thing. He moved me to exactly the spot I had held, asked me once more to raise my bared arms to the sun and throw back my head—"Just like a priest of Apollo," was his phrase, a phrase which I didn't quite like Mr. M. hearing. And even when Hess remarked to Mr. Mycroft, "with Mr. Silchester it's an inevitable piece of casting, isn't it?"—Mr. M. replied only, "Yes, quite a pretty piece of casting." I could only imagine that now Mr. Mycroft saw that the little fellow was obviously as harmless as a hummingbird—and about as brainless.

But Hess couldn't stay content with one triumph; he must try to crown it with another. "And you, Mr. Mycroft, you too are going to be perfectly cast," and he chuckled.

"I am ready to fall in with any of your plans for philanthropy," was Mr. Mycroft's answer. The pomposity might have been expected but the agreeability was certainly one more shock of surprise.

"Now," and the little man had put down his camera and was fussing like a modiste round a marchioness client whom she was fitting for a ball dress, "now, Mr. Silchester is set and ready. You, Mr. Mycroft, would you please just sit here, just behind him, on the balustrade. You see, my idea has about it something of what great artists call inevitability! The group casts itself—it's a great piece of moving sculpture. Here is Mr. Silchester gazing with stretched-out arms at the glorious orb of day, his face flooded with its splendor, the very symbol of youth accepting life—life direct, warm, pulsing, torrential . . ." As he ran on like this I began to have a slight crick in my neck, and with one's head thrown back my head began to throb a little and my eyes got quite dizzy with the sunlight. "Now, please, Mr. Silchester," said the voice at my feet, "hold the pose for just a moment more while I place Mr. Mycroft," and I heard our little artist in *tableau vivant* cooing to Mr. Mycroft. "And you, you see, are the wisdom of age, grey, wise, reflective, a perfect contrast, looking down into the deep waters of contemplation."

Evidently Mr. Mycroft fell in with all this, even to having himself shifted until he was right behind me. I remember I was a little amused at the thought of Mr. Mycroft being actually put at my feet and, more, that there I stood with the leading role and with my back to him—he who was so used to being looked up to. Perhaps it was this thought that gave one more stretch to the tiring elastic of my patience. And in a moment more evidently Mr. Mycroft's cooperation had been so full that Hess was content. The little fellow ran back down the steps of the other side of the bridge and I could just see from the corner of my rather swimming eyes that he had picked up his camera and was going to shoot us. But again he was taken with a fussy doubt. He ran back to us. We were still too far apart. He pushed us closer till my calves were actually against Mr. Mycroft's shoulder blades.

"The composition is perfect in line and mass," murmured Hess, "it is a spot of high-lighting color that's wanted and right near the central interest, the upturned, sun-flooded face. Mr. Silchester, please don't move an inch. I have the very thing here."

I squinted down and saw the little fellow flick out from his button-hole the hibiscus blossom which he was wearing. I saw what was coming. The beautiful Samoans did always at their feasts wear a scarlet hibiscus set behind the ear so that the blossom glowed alongside their eye. In silence I submitted as Hess fitted the flower behind my left ear and arranged the long trumpet of the blossom so that it rested on my cheek bone. Then at last he was content, skipped back to his camera, raised it on high, focussed. . . . There was a click—I am sure I heard that. And I'm equally sure there was a buss, or twang. And then involuntarily I clapped my hands to my face and staggered back to avoid something that was dashing at my eye. I stumbled heavily backwards against Mr. Mycroft, felt my balance go completely, the cloak swept over my head and I plunged backwards and downwards into the dark.

My next sensation was that I was being held. I hadn't hit anything. But I was in as much pain as though I had. For one of my legs was caught in some kind of grip and by this I was hanging upside down. For suddenly the bell-like extinguisher in which I was pending dropped away—as when they unveil statues—and I was exposed. Indeed I could now see myself in the water below like a grotesque narcissus, a painfully ludicrous pendant.

How had I managed to make such a grotesque stumble? I could only suppose that the long gazing at the sun had made me dizzy and then some dragon-fly or other buzzing insect had darted at me—probably at that idiotic flower—which in spite of my fall still stuck behind my ear. That had made me start and I had overturned. For though the flower held its place, the cloak was gone and now lay mantling the surface of the pond some six feet below me.

These observations, however, were checked by another dose of even more severe pain. I was being hauled up to the balustrade above me by my leg and the grip that paid me in foot by foot was Mr. Mycroft's sinewy hands. When my face came up far enough for me to see his, his was quite without expression. He did have the kindness to say, "Sun dizziness, of course," and then over his shoulder where I next caught sight of the anxious face of little Hess, "Don't be alarmed. I caught him just in time. I fear, however, that your valuable cloak will not be the better for a wetting."

The little fellow was full of apologies. While this went on Mr. Mycroft had helped me into my jacket, given me my cane and led me, still shaken, to the gate, accompanied all the way by a very apologetic Hess. When we were there Mr. Mycroft closed the incident quietly. "Don't apologize, Mr. Hess. It was a brilliant idea, if the execution fell a little below expectation," and then putting his hand up to my ear, "I am sure you would like this flower as a souvenir of an eventful day. I hope the picture-with-a-meaning will develop."

As we swirled away in a taxi, every sway of the car made me nearly sick. When we were home Mr. Mycroft broke the silence: "I have a call to make and one or two small things to arrange."

Mr. Mycroft didn't come back till dinner was actually being put on the table and he too looked as fresh as snow, after a hot shower and a clean change of linen, I felt. He was kind, too, about the meal. The avocado-and-chive paste served on hot crackers he praised by the little joke that the paste showed symbolically how well my suavity and his pungency really blended. The Pacific lobster is a creature of parts but it needs skill to make it behave really *à la Thermidor,* and I was pleased that the chef and I had made my old master confess that he would not know that it was not a Parisian *langouste.* The chicken *à la King* he smilingly said had something quite regal about it while the *bananes flambées* he particularly complimented because I had made them out of a locally grown banana which, because it is more succulent than the standard varieties, lends itself to better blending with alcohol. Indeed, he was so pleased that while the coffee was before us he asked whether I'd like to hear the end of the story in which I had played so important a part. Of course I admitted that nothing would give me more pleasure. But I was more than usually piqued when he said quietly, "Let me begin at the end. As we parted I said I was going to make a call. It has been answered as I wished. Do not fear that we shall have to visit the bird sanctuary again. It is closed—permanently. Now for my story. It seemed for both of us to be marked by a series of silly little misadventures. First, it was my turn to fall and you kindly helped me. Then, on our second call, it was your turn to endure the humiliation of an upset. But each served its purpose."

"But what did you gain from skidding on our first visit?" I asked.

"This," said Mr. Mycroft, rising and taking from the mantelshelf, where I had seen him place his fountain pen when he sat down to dinner, the little tube.

"That was only a recovery, not a gain," I said.

"No," he replied, "it garnered something when it fell. To misquote— as both of us like doing—'Cast your pen upon the waters and in a few moments it may pick up more copy than if you'd written for a week with it!' "

My "What do you mean?" was checked as he carefully unscrewed the top.

"See those little holes," he said, pointing to small openings just under the shoulder of the nib; then he drew out the small inner tube. It wasn't of rubber—it was of glass and was full of fairly clear water.

"This is water—water from the pond in the bird sanctuary. It looks like ordinary pond-water. As a matter of fact, it contains an unusually interesting form of life in it."

I began to feel a faint uneasiness.

"Oh, don't be alarmed. It is safely under screw and stopper now and is only being kept as Exhibit A—or, if you like it better, a stage-property in a forthcoming dramatic performance which will be Act Three of the mystery play in which you starred in Act Two, Scene Two."

"But I don't quite see . . ." was met by Mr. Mycroft more graciously than usual with, "There's really no reason why you should. I couldn't quite see myself, at the beginning. Yes, I do indeed admire such richness of double-dyed thoroughness when I come across it. It is rare for murderers to give one such entertainment, so elaborate and meticulous. They usually shoot off their arrows almost as soon as it enters their heads that they can bring down their bird and without a thought of how it may strike a more meditative mind afterwards. But this man provided himself with a second string of rather better weave than his first."

Well, when Mr. Mycroft gets into that kind of strain it is no use saying anything. So I swallowed the I.D.S. formula that was again rising in my throat and waited.

"You remember, when you helped me to my feet and the pen had been salvaged, that with your aid we completed the round of the little lake. But when we had gone no farther than the beginning of the high-backed bridge, I felt I must rest. Do you recall what I did then?"

Could I recall! Naturally, for that was the very incident that had confirmed my suspicion that Mr. Mycroft was really shaken. I answered brightly:

"You sat, I can see it now, and for a moment you appeared to be dazed. And while you rested, as the beautiful old song, *The Lost Chord,* expresses it, your 'fingers idly wandered.' But I noticed that they must be getting dirty, because, whether you knew it or not, they were feeling along under the jutting edge of the slab that made the step against which your back was resting."

"Admirable. And the quotation is happy, for my fingers were idly wandering (to go on with the old song) over the 'keys'!"

Mr. Mycroft cocked his old head at me and went on gaily, "And may I add that I am not less pleased that you thought the old man was so shaken that he really didn't know what he was doing! For that is precisely the impression that I had to give to another pair of eyes watching us from nearby cover. Well, after that little rest and glance about at those sentimental birdy-homes, the breeding boxes, I told you we could go home. And now may I ask you three questions?" I drew myself up and tried to sharpen my wits. "First," said my examiner, "did you observe anything about the garden generally?"

"Well," I replied, "I remember you called my attention to the little Nereid who held a spear from which the jet of the small fountain sprang?"

"Yes, that's true and indeed in every sense of the word, to the point. But did you notice something about—I will give you a clue—the flowers?"

"There were a lot of them!"

"Well, I won't hold you to that longer. I couldn't make out myself whether it had any significance. Then in the end I saw the light—yes, the light of the danger signal! Does that help you?"

"No," I said, "I remain as blind as a bat to your clue."

"Then, secondly, if the flowers failed to awake your curiosity, what about the birds?"

"Again, a lot of them and I did like that mynah bird with its charmingly anaemic hostess voice."

"No, that was off the trail. I'll give you another clue—what about the breeding boxes?"

"Well, they're common enough little things, aren't they?"

"All right," he replied with cheerful patience, "now for my last question. When we were coming back do you remember any special incident?"

Then I did perk up. "Yes, of course—the contrast stuck in my mind. After being bathed in all that beauty we passed a dump corner and you got out and hunted for curios in the garbage."

"And brought back quite a trophy," said the old hunter as he pulled something out of his pocket, remarking "Exhibit B."

And then, do you know, my mind suddenly gave a dart—I do things like that every now and then. The thing he had pulled out and placed on the table was only a piece of cellophane or celluloid. It was also of a very crude and common red. It was the color that made my mind take its hop, a hop backwards. "I don't know what that dirty piece of road-side flotsam means but I now recall something about the garden—there wasn't a single red flower in it!"

Mr. Mycroft positively beamed. His uttered compliment was of course the "left-handed" sort he generally dealt me. "Mr. Silchester, I have always known it. It is laziness, just simple laziness, that keeps you from being a first-rate observer. You can't deny that puzzles interest you, but you can't be bothered to put out your hand and pluck the fruit of insight crossed with foresight."

I waved the tribute aside by asking what the red transparency might signify.

"Well," he said, "it put an idea into your head by what we may call a negative proof. Now, go one better and tell me something about it, itself, from its shape."

"Well, it's sickle-shaped, rather like a crescent moon. No," I paused, "no, you know I never can do anything if I strain. I have to wait for these flashes."

"All right," he said, "we will humor your delicate genius. But I will just say that it is a beautiful link. The color and the shape—yes, the moment I saw it lying there like a petal cast aside, my mind suddenly took wings like yours." He stopped and then remarked, "Well, the time has come for straight narrative. We have all the pieces of the board, yourself being actually the queen. It only remains to show you how the game was played. First, a tribute to Mr. Hess not as a man but as a murderer—an artist, without any doubt. Here are the steps by which he moved to his first check and how after the first queen had been taken—I refer to his aunt and her death—he was himself checkmated.

"You have noted that the garden has no red flowers and I have also suggested that the breeding box by the bridge interested me. About the water from the pond I have been frank and will shortly be franker. So we come to our second visit. It was then that our antagonist played boldly. How often have I had occasion to remind you that murderers love living over again the deaths they dealt, repeating a kill. That was Mr. Hess's wish. Of course, it wasn't pure love of art—he certainly knew something about me." Mr. Mycroft sighed, "I know you don't believe it, but I don't think you can imagine how often and how strongly a detective wishes to be unknown. To recognize you must remain unrecognized." He smiled again.

"Now note: You go up to him and ask him not to take photos. He shows first a startled resentment at your impudence, then a generous courtesy as proprietor for your interference on his behalf. Next, a sudden happy thought—how well you would look as part of the picture he was planning. He dresses you up, taking care to place you in a position in which you'll trip and fall. Now he has the middle link in his chain. But you were merely a link. You see, his real plan is to get me down too. He could, you will admit, hardly have hoped to lure me to act as model for a sun worshipper. But put you in that role and then he might persuade me to get into the picture also. Then, when you went over backwards, you would pull me into the pond as well."

"But," I said, "we should have had no more than a bad wetting."

"I see you are going to call for all my proofs before you will yield to the fact that we were really in the hands of a man as sane as all careful murderers are. You remember that charming little statuette which so took my fancy when we first visited the garden? It was of bronze. Not one of those cheap cement objects that people buy at the road-side and put in their gardens. It is a work of art, a museum-piece."

"It had patinated very nicely," I remarked, just to show I could talk *objet d' art* gossip as well as the master.

"I'm glad you observed that," he replied. "Yes, bronze is a remarkable material and worthy of having a whole Age named after it. More remarkable, indeed, than iron, for though iron has a better edge, it won't keep if constantly watered."

"What are you driving at?" For now I was getting completely lost in the old spider's spinning.

"That pretty little sham spear from which the water sprayed wasn't sham at all. It was a real spear, or shall we say, a giant hollow-needle. Because it was bronze it would keep its point unrusted. The only effect the water would have—and that would add to its lethal efficacy—would be to give it a patina. Further, I feel sure from the long close look I was able to give when we were being posed for our plunge, the blade of the spear had been touched up with a little acetic acid. That would no doubt corrode the fine edge a little but would make it highly poisonous—though not to the life in the pool."

"Why are you so interested in the pond-life?" I asked.

Mr. Mycroft picked up the small tube which he had removed from the fountain pen and which was now standing on a small side-table. "You'll remember, I said this pippet contains an interesting form of life—a very powerful form, if not itself poisoned. So powerful that, like most power-types, it tends to destroy others, yes, far higher types. This is really a remarkably fecund culture of a particularly virulent strain of typhoid bacillus."

I drew back. I don't like things like that near where I eat.

"Oh, it is safe enough so long as you don't drink it." I gasped. "So, you see, that was his plan. But, thoughtful man that he was, it was only his second string. He was a very thorough worker and had two concealed tools. If you fall over a bridge headlong and just underneath you is a Nereid holding a charming little wand, there is a good chance that you will fall, like the heroic Roman suicides, on your spear and so end yourself; and if the spear has round its socket some poison, the wound is very likely to give you blood-poisoning. But of course you may miss the point. People falling through the air are apt to writhe which may alter quite considerably the point at which they make their landing, or in this case, their watering. Well, thoughtful Mr. Hess realized how much human nature will struggle against gravitational fate—so he provided himself with a wider net. For when people fall headlong over a bridge, the natural reaction of panic is to open the mouth. So when they strike the water, they inevitably swallow a mouthful. And a little of this brew goes a long way."

"Now, now," I broke in, "I don't think any jury will send the nephew to join the aunt on that evidence."

"Why not?" was Mr. Mycroft's unexpectedly quiet rejoinder.

"First," I said, picking off the points on my fingers just as Mr. Mycroft sometimes does when closing a case, "granted this tube does contain typhoid germs, they may have been in this water from natural pollution. Proof that Hess poisoned the water cannot be sustained. Secondly, let me call the attention of judge and jury to the fact that when Miss Hess died a fortnight after her slight ducking, she did not die of typhoid. The cause of death was 'intestinal stasis.' Typhoid kills by a form of dysentery. Emphatically, that condition is polar to stasis."

"You are quite right," rejoined Mr. Mycroft, "the old-fashioned typhoid used to kill as you have described. But, would you believe it, the typhus germ has had the cunning to reverse his tactics completely. I remember a friend of mine telling me some years ago of this, and he had it from the late Sir Walter Fletcher, an eminent student of Medical Research in Britain. It stuck in my mind: the typhoid victim can now die with such entirely different symptoms that the ordinary doctor, unless he has quite other reasons to detect the presence of the disease, does not even suspect that his patient has died of typhoid, and with the best faith in the world fills in the death certificate never suggesting the true cause. "Yes," he went on meditatively, "I have more than once noticed that when a piece of information of that sort sticks in my mind, it may be prophetic. Certainly in this case it was."

I felt I might have to own defeat on that odd point when Mr. Mycroft remarked, "Well, let's leave Miss Hess and the medical side alone for a moment. Let's go back to the garden. I referred to you as the middle link. I have to be personal and even perhaps put myself forward. Mr. Hess was not averse to murdering you—if that was the only way of murdering me. We see how he maneuvered you to pose and then having got you in place, he set out to get me. You would stagger back, knock me off my perch, and both of us would plunge into the poisonous water, and one might be caught on the poisonous point. It was beautifully simple, really."

"You have got to explain how he would know that I would suddenly get dizzy, that a dragonfly or something would buzz right into my eyes and make me stagger."

"Quite easy—I was just coming to that. That was the first link in the chain. Now we can bring everything together and be finished with that really grim garden. Please recall the thing you noticed."

"No red flowers," I said dutifully and he bowed his acknowledgment.

"Next, the two things which you couldn't be expected to puzzle over. The breeding box which you did see but did not understand, and the under-curb of the step which even I didn't see but felt with my hand. That breeding box had the usual little doorway or round opening for the nesting bird to enter by, but to my surprise the doorway had a door and the door was closed. Now, that's going too far in pet-love sentimentality and although very cruel people are often very kind to animals, that kind of soapy gesture to bird-mother comfort seemed to me strange—until I noticed, on the under-side of the next box, a small wheel. When I felt under the jamb of the step, I found two more such wheels—flanged wheels, and running along from one to the other, a black thread. Then when I knew what to look for, I could see the same black thread running up to the wheel fixed in the bird-box. I couldn't doubt my deduction any longer. That little door could be opened if someone raised his foot slightly and trod on the black thread that ran under the step curb.

"Now, one doesn't have to be a bird fancier to know that birds don't want to breed in boxes where you shut them up with a trap-door. What then could this box be for? You do, however, have to be something of a bird specialist to know about hawking and hummingbirds. The main technique of the former is the hood. When the bird is hooded it will stay quietly for long times on its perch. Cut off light and it seems to have its nervous reactions all arrested. Could that box be a hood not merely for the head of a bird but for *an entire bird?* Now we must switch back, as swoopingly as a hummingbird, to Miss Hess. You remember the description?"

It was my turn to be ready. I reached round to the paper rack and picked out the sheet that had started the whole adventure. I read out, "The late Miss Hess, whose huge fortune has gone to a very quiet recluse nephew whose one interest is birds, was herself a most colorful person and wonderfully young for her years." I added, "There's a colored photo of the colorful lady. She's wearing a vivid green dress. Perhaps that's to show she thought herself still in her salad days?"

"A good suggestion," replied Mr. Mycroft generously, "but I think we can drive our deductions even nearer home. Of course, I needed first-hand information for that. But I had my suspicions before I called."

"Called where?"

"On the doctor of the late lady. He was willing to see me when I could persuade him that his suspicions were right and that his patroness had really been removed by foul means. Then he told me quite a lot about the very odd person she was. She was shrewd in her way. She kept her own doctor and she paid him handsomely and took the complementary precaution of not remembering him in her will. Yes, he had every reason for keeping her going and being angry at her being gone. She was keen on staying here and not only that but on keeping young. But her colorfulness in dress was something more, he told me, than simply 'mutton dressing itself up to look like lamb.' She was color-blind and like that sort—the red-green colorblindness—she was very loath to admit it. That bright green dress of the photo pretty certainly seemed to her bright red."

I was still at a loss and let the old man see it.

"Now comes Hess' third neat piece of work. Note these facts: the aunt is persuaded to come to the garden—just to show that the nephew has turned over a new page and is being the busy little bird lover—sure way to keep in the maiden lady's good graces. He takes her round." Suddenly Mr. Mycroft stopped and picked up the celluloid red crescent. "Many color-blind persons have eyes that do not like a glare. The thoughtful nephew, having led auntie round the garden, takes her up the bridge to view the dear little birdie's home. She has to gaze up at it and he has thoughtfully provided her with an eye-shade—green to her, red to him, and red to something else. Certain species of hummingbirds are particularly sensitive to red—all animals, of course, prefer red to any other color. When young these particular hummingbirds have been known to dash straight at any object that is red and thrust their long bill toward it, thinking no doubt it is a flower. They will dart at a tomato held in your hand. Well, the aunt is gazing up to see the birdie's home; she's at the top of the bridge, just where you stood. Nephew has gone on, sure that aunt is going to follow. He is, in fact, now down by that lower step. He just treads on the concealed black thread. The door flies open, the little feathered bullet which had been brooding in the dark sees a flash of light and in it a blob of red. The reflex acts also like a flash. It dashes out right at Miss Hess' face. Again a reflex. This time it is the human one. She staggers back, hands to face—not knowing what has swooped at her—the flight of some of these small birds is too quick for the human eye. Of course she falls, takes her sup of the water, goes home shaken, no doubt not feeling pleased with nephew but not suspicious. After a fortnight we have a condition of stasis. The sound, but naturally not very progressive doctor, sees no connection. The police and public are also content. Nevertheless, she dies."

"And then?" I said, for I was on tiptoe of interest now.

"Well, Hess couldn't put a red eye-hood over your eyes, hoping you'd think it green and so make you a mark for his bird-bullet. So he put an hibiscus behind your ear. Each fish must be caught with its own bait, though the hook is the same. His effort with us was even more elaborate than with his aunt. What a pity that artists can't be content with a good performance but must always be trying to better it! Well, the bird sanctuary is closed and with it the sanctuary of a most resourceful murderer."

*During World War I, Sherlock Holmes took "His Last Bow," emerging from retire-
ment to battle German espionage agents. During World War II, the Basil Rathbone films
were updated to permit Holmes to fight Nazis. Truer to Conan Doyle's time-frame is the
following story (also known as "The Man Who Was Not Dead") from the August 9,
1941, issue of* Argosy. M A N L Y   W A D E   W E L L M A N *(1903–1986), prolific con-
tributor to* Weird Tales, The Magazine of Fantasy and Science Fiction *and other
periodicals, won the World Fantasy Award, the Mystery Writers of America's "Edgar" for
fact-crime and was a Pulitzer Prize nominee.* Sherlock Holmes of Baker Street, W. S.
Baring-Gould's *"official" biography, pays Wellman a handsome compliment by incor-
porating "But Our Hero Was Not Dead" into the chronology of the detective's life.*

But Our Hero Was Not Dead

M A N L Y   W A D E   W E L L M A N

Out of the black sky plummeted Boling, toward the black earth. He knew
nothing of the ground toward which he fell, save that it was five miles inland
from the Sussex coast and, according to Dr. Goebbels's best information,
sparsely settled.

The night air hummed in his parachute rigging, and he seemed to drop
faster than ten feet a second, but to think of that was unworthy of a trusted
agent of the German Intelligence. Though the pilot above had not dared
drop him a light, Boling could land without much mishap . . . Even as he told
himself that, land he did. He struck heavily on hands and knees, and around
him settled the limp folds of the parachute.

At once he threw off the harness, wadded the fabric and thrust it out of
sight between a boulder and a bush. Standing up, he took stock of himself.
The left leg of his trousers was torn, and the knee skinned—that was all. He
remembered that William the Conquerer had also gone sprawling when he
landed at Hastings, not so far from here. The omen was good. Boling
stooped, like Duke William, and clutched a handful of pebbles.

"Thus do I seize the land!" he quoted aloud, for he was at heart theatrical.

His name was not really Boling, though he had prospered under that and other aliases. Nor, though he wore the uniform of a British private, was he British. Born in Chicago late in 1917, of unsavory parents, he had matured to a notable career of imposture and theft. He had entered the employment of the Third Reich, not for love of its cause or thirst for adventure, but for the very high rate of pay. Boling was practical as well as gifted. He had gladly accepted the present difficult and dangerous mission, which might well be the making of his fortune.

Now the early gray dawn came and peered over his shoulder. Boling saw that he was on a grassy slope, with an ill-used gravel road below it. Just across that road showed lighted windows—a house with early risers. He walked toward those lights.

Which way was Eastbourne, was his first problem. He had never seen the town; he had only the name and telephone number there of one Philip Davis who, if addressed by him as "Uncle," would know that the time had arrived to muster fifteen others.

They, in turn, would gather waiting comrades from the surrounding community, picked, hard men who whole years ago had taken lodging and stored arms thereabouts. These would organize and operate as a crack infantry battalion. After that, the well-tested routine that had helped to conquer Norway, Holland, Belgium, France—seizure of communications, blowing up of rails and roads, capture of airdromes.

Reinforcements would drop in parachutes from overhead, as he, Boling, had done. At dusk this would be done. In the night, Eastbourne would be firmly held, with a picked invasion corps landing from barges.

Crossing the road toward the house, Boling considered the matter as good as accomplished. He needed only a word from the house-dwellers to set him on his way.

*H*e found the opening in the chin-high hedge of brambles and flowering bushes, and in the strengthening light he trod warily up the flagged path. The house, now visible, was only a one-story cottage of white plaster, with a roof of dark tiling. Gaining the doorstep, Boling swung the tarnished knocker against the stout oak panel.

Silence. Then heavy steps and a mumbling voice. The door creaked open. A woman in shawl and cap, plump and very old—past ninety, it seemed to Boling—put out a face like a cheerful walnut.

"Good morning," she said. "Yes, who is that?" Her ancient eyes blinked behind small, thick lenses like bottle bottoms. "Soldier, ain't you?"

"Right you are," he responded in his most English manner, smiling to charm her. This crone had a London accent, and looked simple and good-humored. "I'm tramping down to Eastbourne to visit my uncle," he went on plausibly, "and lost my way on the downs in the dark. Can you direct me on?"

Before the old woman could reply, a dry voice had spoken from behind her: "Ask the young man to step inside, Mrs. Hudson."

The old woman drew the door more widely open. Boling entered one of those living rooms that have survived their era. In the light of a hanging oil lamp he could see walls papered in blue with yellow flowers, above gray-painted wainscoting. On a center table lay some old books, guarded by a pudgy china dog. At the rear, next a dark inner doorway, blazed a small but cheerful fire, and from a chair beside it rose the man who had spoken.

"If you have walked all night, you will be tired," he said to Boling. "Stop and rest. We're about to have some tea. Won't you join us?"

"Thank you, sir," accepted Boling heartily. This was another Londoner, very tall and as gaunt as a musket. He could not be many years younger than the woman called Mrs. Hudson, but he still had vigor and presence.

He stood quite straight in his shabbiest of blue dressing gowns. The lamplight revealed a long hooked nose and a long lean chin, with bright eyes of blue under a thatch of thistledown hair. Boling thought of Dr. Punch grown old, dignified and courteous. The right hand seemed loosely clenched inside a pocket of the dressing gown. The left, lean and fine, held a blackened old briar with a curved stem.

"I see," said this old gentleman, his eyes studying Boling's insignia, "that you're a Fusilier—Northumberland."

"Yes, sir, Fifth Northumberland Fusiliers," rejoined Boling, who had naturally chosen for his disguise the badges of a regiment lying far from Sussex. "As I told your good housekeeper, I'm going to Eastbourne. If you can direct me, or let me use your telephone—"

"I am sorry, we have no telephone," the other informed him.

Mrs. Hudson gulped and goggled at that, but the old blue eyes barely flickered a message at her. Again the gaunt old man spoke: "There is a telephone, however, in the house just behind us—the house of Constable Timmons."

Boling had no taste for visiting a policeman, especially an officious country one, and so he avoided comment on the last suggestion. Instead he thanked his host for the invitation to refreshment. The old woman brought in a tray with dishes and a steaming kettle, and a moment later they were joined by another ancient man.

This one was plump and tweedy, with a drooping gray mustache and wide eyes full of childish innocence. Boling set him down as a doctor, and felt a glow of pride in his own acumen when the newcomer was so introduced. So pleased was Boling with himself, indeed, that he did not bother to catch the doctor's surname.

"This young man is of your old regiment, I think," the lean man informed the fat one. "Fifth Northumberland Fusiliers."

"Oh, really? Quite so, quite so," chirruped the doctor, in a katydid fashion that impelled Boling to classify him as a simpleton. "Quite. I was with the old Fifth—but that would be well before your time, young man. I served in the Afghan War." This last with a proud protruding of the big eyes. For a moment Boling dreaded a torrent of reminiscence; but the Punch-faced man had just finished relighting his curved briar, and now called attention to the tea which Mrs. Hudson was pouring.

The three men sipped gratefully. Boling permitted himself a moment of ironic meditation on how snug it was, so shortly before bombs and bayonets would engulf this and all other houses in the neighborhood of Eastbourne.

Mrs. Hudson waddled to his elbow with toasted muffins. "Poor lad," she said maternally, "you've torn them lovely trousers."

From the other side of the fire bright blue eyes gazed through the smoke of strong shag. "Oh, yes," said the dry voice, "you walked over the downs at night, I think I heard you say when you came. And you fell?"

"Yes, sir," replied Boling, and thrust his skinned knee into view through the rip. "No great injury, however, except to my uniform. The King will give me a new one, what?"

"I daresay," agreed the doctor, lifting his mustache from his teacup. "Nothing too good for the old regiment."

That led to discussion of the glorious past of the Fifth Northumberland Fusiliers, and the probable triumphant future. Boling made the most guarded of statements, lest the pudgy old veteran find something of which to be suspicious; but, to bolster his pose, he fished forth a wad of painstakingly forged papers—pay-book, billet assignment, pass through lines, and so on. The gaunt man in blue studied them with polite interest.

"And now," said the doctor, "how is my old friend Major Amidon?"

"Major Amidon?" repeated Boling to gain time, and glanced as sharply as he dared at his interrogator. Such a question might well be a trap, simple and dangerous, the more so because his research concerning the Fifth Northumberland Fusiliers had not supplied him with any such name among the officers.

But then he took stock once more of the plump, mild, guileless face. Boling, cunning and criminal, knew a man incapable of lying or deception when he saw one. The doctor was setting no trap whatever; in fact, his next words provided a valuable cue to take up.

"Yes, of course—he must be acting chief of brigade by now. Tall, red-faced, monocle—"

"Oh, Major Amidon!" cried Boling, as if remembering. "I know him only by sight, naturally. As you say, he's acting chief of battalion; probably he'll get a promotion soon. He's quite well, and very much liked by the men."

The thin old man passed back Boling's papers and inquired courteously after the uncle in Eastbourne. Boling readily named Philip Davis, who would have been at pains to make for himself a good reputation. It developed that both of Boling's entertainers knew Mr. Davis slightly—proprietor of the Royal Oak, a fine old public house. Public houses, amplified the doctor, weren't what they had been in the eighties, but the Royal Oak was a happy survival from that golden age. And so on.

With relish Boling drained his last drop of tea, ate his last crumb of muffin. His eyes roamed about the room, which he already regarded as an ideal headquarters. Even his momentary nervousness about the constable in the house behind had left him. He reflected that the very closeness of an official would eliminate any prying or searching by the enemy. He'd get on to Eastbourne, have Davis set the machinery going, and then pop back here to wait in comfort for the ripe moment when, the chief dangers of conquest gone by, he could step forth . . .

He rose with actual regret that he must get about his business. "I thank you all so much," he said. "And now it's quite light—I really must be on my way."

"Private Boling," said the old man with the blue gown, "before you go, I have a confession to make."

"Confession?" spluttered the doctor, and Mrs. Hudson stared in amazement.

"Exactly." Two fine, gaunt old hands rose and placed their finger tips together. "When you came here I couldn't be sure about you, things being as they are these days."

"Quite so, quite so," interjected the doctor. "Alien enemies and all that. You understand, young man."

"Of course," Boling smiled winningly.

"And so," continued his host, "I was guilty of a lie. But now that I've had a look at you, I am sure of what you are. And let me say that I do have a telephone, after all. You are quite free to use it. Through the door there."

Boling felt his heart warm with self-satisfaction. He had always considered himself a prince of deceivers; this admission on the part of the scrawny dotard was altogether pleasant. Thankfully he entered a dark little hallway from the wall of which sprouted the telephone. He lifted the receiver and called the number he had memorized.

"Hello," he greeted the man who made guarded answer. "Is that Mr. Philip Davis? . . . Your nephew, Amos Boling, here. I'm coming to town at once. I'll meet you and the others wherever you say . . . What's the name of your pub again? . . . The Royal Oak? Very good, we'll meet there at nine o'clock."

"That will do," said the dry voice of his host behind his very shoulder. "Hang up, Mr. Boling. At once."

Boling spun around, his heart somersaulting with sudden terror. The gaunt figure stepped back very smoothly and rapidly for so aged a man. The right hand dropped again into the pocket of the old blue dressing gown. It brought out a small, broad-muzzled pistol, which the man held leveled at Boling's belly.

"I asked you to telephone, Mr. Boling, in hopes that you would some-how reveal your fellow agents. We know that they'll be at the Royal Oak at nine. A party of police will appear to take them in charge. As for you—Mrs. Hudson, please step across the back yard and ask Constable Timmons to come at once."

Boling glared. His right hand moved, as stealthily as a snake, toward his hip.

"None of that," barked the doctor from the other side of the sitting room. He, too, was on his feet, jerking open a drawer in the center table. From it he took a big service revolver, of antiquated make but uncommonly well kept. The plump old hand hefted the weapon knowingly. "Lift your arms, sir, and at once."

Fuming, Boling obeyed. The blue dressing gown glided toward him, the left hand snatched away the flat automatic in his hip pocket.

"I observed that bulge in your otherwise neat uniform," commented the lean old man, "and pondered that pocket pistols are not regulation for infantry privates. It was one of several inconsistencies that branded you as an enemy agent. Will you take the armchair, Mr. Boling? I will explain."

There was nothing to do, under the muzzles of those guns, but to sit and listen.

"The apparition of a British soldier trying hard to disguise an American accent intrigued me, but did not condemn you at first. However, the knee of your trousers—I always look first at the trouser knee of a stranger—was so violently torn as to suggest a heavy fall somewhere. The rest of your kit was disarranged as well. But your boots—I always look at boots second—were innocent of scuff or even much wear. I knew at once that your story of a long night's tramp, with trippings and tumblings, was a lie."

Boling summoned all his assurance. "See here," he cried harshly, "I don't mind a little joke or whatever, but this has gone far enough. I'm a soldier and as such a defender of the realm. If you offer me violence—"

"There will be no violence unless you bring it on yourself. Suffer me to continue: You caused me even more suspicion when, calling yourself a private of the Fifth Northumberland Fusiliers, you yet patently failed to recognize the name of my old friend here. He, too, was of the Fifth, and in civilian life has won such fame as few Fusiliers can boast. The whole world reads his writings—"

"Please, please," murmured the doctor gently.

"I do not seek to embarrass you, my dear fellow," assured the lean host, "only to taunt this sorry deceiver with his own clumsiness. After that, Mr. Boling, your anxiety to show your credentials to me, who had not asked for them and had no authority to examine them; your talk about the service, plainly committed to memory from a book; and, finally, your glib talk about one Major Amidon who does not exist—these were sufficient proof."

"Does not exist?" almost barked the doctor. "What do you mean? Of course Major Amidon exists. He and I served together . . ."

Then he broke off abruptly, and his eyes bulged foolishly. He coughed and snickered in embarrassed apology.

"Dear me, now I know that I'm doddering," he said more gently. "You're right, my dear fellow—Major Amidon exists no longer. He retired in 1910, and you yourself pointed out his death notice to me five years ago. Odd how old memories cling on and deceive us—good psychological point there somewhere . . ."

His voice trailed off, and his comrade triumphantly resumed the indictment of Boling:

"My mind returned to the problem of your disordered kit and well-kept shoes. By deductive reasoning I considered and eliminated one possibility after another. It was increasingly plain that you had fallen from a height, but had not walked far to get here. Had you traveled in a motor? But this is the only road hereabouts, and a bad one, running to a dead end two miles up the downs. We have been awake for hours, and would have heard a machine. A horse, then? Possible, even in these mechanized times, but your trousers bear no trace of sitting astride a saddle. Bicycle? But you would have worn a clip on the ankle next the sprocket, and that clip would have creased your trouser cuff. What does this leave?"

"What?" asked the fat doctor, as eagerly as a child hearing a story.

"What, indeed, but an airplane and a parachute? And what does a parachute signify in these days but German invasion—which has come to our humble door in the presence of Mr. Boling?" The white head bowed, like an actor's taking a curtain call, then turned toward the front door. "Ah, here returns Mrs. Hudson, with Constable Timmons. Constable, we have a German spy for you to take in charge."

Boling came to his feet, almost ready to brave the two pistols that covered him. "You're a devil!" he raged at his discoverer.

The blue eyes twinkled. "Not at all. I am an old man who has retained the use of his brains, even after long and restful idleness."

The sturdy constable approached Boling, a pair of gleaming manacles in his hands. "Will you come along quietly?" he asked formally, and Boling held out his wrists. He was beaten.

The old doctor dropped his revolver back into its drawer, and tramped across to his friend.

"Amazing!" he almost bellowed. "I thought I was past wondering at you, but—amazing, that's all I can say!"

A blue-sleeved arm lifted, the fine lean hand patted the doctor's tweed shoulder affectionately. And even before the words were spoken, as they must have been spoken so often in past years, Boling suddenly knew what they would be:

"Elementary, my dear Watson," said old Mr. Sherlock Holmes.

Scholarly
Ponderings

*T*hough hardly as extensive as the annals of Conan Doyle scholarship, there is a considerable body of literary research devoted to Charles Dickens's unfinished final novel, The Mystery of Edwin Drood. It was inevitable that Sherlock Holmes would be enlisted to apply his methods to the grim puzzle of the Christmas Eve disappearance of choirmaster John Jasper's nephew Edwin from the cathedral village of Cloisterham. At least nine such attempts have been penned (for details, see Appendix I). One of the earliest is E D M U N D P E A R S O N's theory, which appeared in the April 2, 1913, issue of the Boston Evening Transcript.

Sherlock Holmes and the Drood Mystery

E D M U N D   P E A R S O N

"Watson," said Sherlock Holmes, beaming at me across the breakfast table, "can you decipher character from handwriting?"

He held an envelope toward me as he spoke. I took the envelope and glanced at the superscription. It was addressed to Holmes at our lodging in Baker Street. I tried to remember something of an article I had read on the subject of handwriting.

"The writer of this," I said, "was a modest, self-effacing person, and one of wide knowledge, and considerable ability. He—"

"Excellent, Watson, excellent! Really, you outdo yourself. Your reading is quite Watsonian, in fact. I fear, however, you are a bit astray as to his modesty, knowledge, and so on. As a matter of fact, this letter is from Mr. Thomas Sapsea."

"The famous Mayor of Cloisterham?"

"Quite so. And for pomposity, egregious conceit coupled with downright ignorance, he has not his peer in England. So you did not score a bull's-eye there, my dear fellow."

"But what does he want of you?" I asked, willing to change the subject. "He isn't going to engage you to solve the mystery of Edwin Drood?"

"That is precisely what he is doing. He is all at sea in the matter. Come, what do you say to a run down to Cloisterham? We can look into this matter to oblige the mayor, and take a ramble through the cathedral. I'm told they have some very fine gargoyles."

An hour later, we were seated in a train for Cloisterham. Holmes had been looking through the morning papers. Now he threw them aside, and turned to me.

"Have you followed this Drood case?" he asked.

I replied that I had read many of the accounts and some of the speculations on the subject.

"I have not followed it as attentively as I should have liked," he returned; "the recent little affair of Colonel Raspopoff and the Czarina's rubies has occupied me thoroughly of late. Suppose you go over the chief facts—it will help clear my mind."

"The facts are these," I said. "Edwin Drood, a young engineer about to leave for Egypt, had two attractions in Cloisterham. One was his affianced wife—a young schoolgirl, named Miss Rosa Bud. The other was his devoted uncle and guardian, Mr. John Jasper. The latter is choirmaster of the cathedral. There were, it seems, two clouds over his happiness. One of these was the fact that his betrothal to Miss Bud—an arrangement made by their respective parents while Edwin and Rosa were small children—was not wholly to the liking of either of the principals. They had, indeed, come to an agreement, only a few days before Edwin Drood's disappearance, to terminate the engagement. They parted, it is believed, on friendly, if not affectionate terms.

"The other difficulty lay in the presence, in Cloisterham, of one Neville Landless—a young student from Ceylon. Landless has, it seems, a strain of Oriental blood in his nature—he is of dark complexion and fiery temper. Actual quarrels had occurred between the two, with some violence on Landless's part. To restore them to friendship, however, Mr. Jasper, the uncle of Edwin, arranged for a dinner in his rooms on Christmas Eve, at which they were to be the only guests. The dinner took place, everything passed off amicably, and the two left together, late in the evening, to walk to the river, and view the great storm which was raging. After that they parted—according to Landless—and Drood has never been seen again. His uncle raised the alarm next morning, Landless was detained, and questioned, while a thorough search was made for the body of Drood. Beyond the discovery of his watch and pin in the weir, nothing has been found. Landless had to be released for lack of evidence, but the feeling in Cloisterham was so strong against him that he had to leave. He is thought to be in London."

"H'm," remarked Holmes, "who found the watch and pin?"

"A Mr. Crisparkle, minor canon of the cathedral. Landless was living in his house, and reading with him. I may add that Landless has a sister—Miss Helena—who has also come to London."

"H'm," said Holmes. "Well, here we are at Cloisterham. We can now pursue our investigations on the spot. We will go to see Mr. Sapsea, the mayor."

Mr. Sapsea proved to be exactly the pompous Tory jackass that Holmes had described. He had never been out of Cloisterham, and his firm conviction of the hopeless inferiority of all the world outside England was so thoroughly provincial that I suspected him of some connection with the "Saturday Review." He was strong in his belief that young Neville Landless had murdered Drood and thrown his body into the river. And his strongest reason for this belief lay in the complexion of Landless.

"It is un-English, Mr. Holmes," said he, "it's un-English and when I see a face that is un-English, I know what to suspect of that face."

"Quite so," said Holmes; "I suppose that everything was done to find the body?"

"Everything, Mr. Holmes, everything that my—er—knowledge of the world could possibly suggest. Mr. Jasper was unwearied in his efforts. In fact, he was worn out by his exertions."

"No doubt his grief at the disappearance of his nephew had something to do with that, as well."

"No doubt of it at all."

"Landless, I hear, is in London?"

"So I understand, sir, so I understand. But Mr. Crisparkle, his former tutor, has given me—in my capacity as magistrate—assurances that he can be produced at any moment. At present he can be found by applying to Mr. Grewgious, at Staple Inn. Mr. Grewgious is a guardian of the young lady to whom Edwin Drood was betrothed."

Holmes made a note of Mr. Grewgious's name and address on his shirt-cuff. We then rose to depart.

"I see," said the mayor, "that you are thinking of paying a call on this un-English person in London. That is where you will find a solution of the mystery, I can assure you."

"It is probable that I shall have occasion to run up to London this evening," said Holmes, "though I believe that Dr. Watson and I will stroll about Cloisterham a bit, first. I want to inspect your gargoyles."

When we were outside, Holmes's earliest remark was, "But I think we had better have a little chat with Mr. John Jasper."

We were directed to Mr. Jasper's rooms, in the gatehouse, by a singularly obnoxious boy, whom we found in the street, flinging stones at the passers-by.

"That's Jarsper's," said he, pointing for an instant toward the arch, and then proceeding with his malevolent pastime.

"Thanks," said Holmes, shortly, giving the imp sixpence, "here's something for you. And here," he continued, reversing the boy over his knee, and giving him a sound spanking, "here is something else for you."

On inquiry it appeared that Mr. Jasper was at home. He would see us, said the landlady, but she added that "the poor gentleman was not well."

"Indeed?" said Holmes. "What's the matter?"

"He do be in a sort of daze, I think."

"Well, well, this gentleman is a doctor—perhaps he can prescribe."

And with that we went up to Mr. Jasper's room. That gentleman had recovered, apparently, from his daze, for we heard him chanting choir music, as we stood outside the door. Holmes, whose love for music is very keen, was enraptured, and insisted on standing for several moments, while the low and sweet tones of the choirmaster's voice, accompanied by the notes of a piano, floated out to us. At last we knocked and the singer admitted us.

Mr. Jasper was a dark-whiskered gentleman who dwelt in a gloomy sort of room. He had, himself, a gloomy and reserved manner. Holmes introduced us both, and informed Mr. Jasper that he was in Cloisterham at the request of the mayor, Mr. Sapsea, to look up some points in connection with the disappearance of Edwin Drood.

"Meaning his murder?" inquired Mr. Jasper.

"The word I used," said Holmes, "was disappearance."

"The word I used," returned the other, "was murder. But I must beg to be excused from all discussion of the death of my dear boy. I have taken a vow to discuss it with no one, until the assassin is brought to justice."

"I hope," said Holmes, "that if there is an assassin, I may have the good fortune—"

"I hope so, too. Meanwhile—" and Mr. Jasper moved toward the door, as if to usher us out. Holmes tried to question him about the events of Christmas Eve, prior to the young man's disappearance, but Mr. Jasper said that he had made his statement before the mayor, and had nothing to add.

"Surely," said Holmes, "I have seen you before, Mr. Jasper?"

Mr. Jasper thought not.

"I feel almost positive," said my friend; "in London, now—you come to London at times, I take it?"

Perhaps. But he had never had the pleasure of meeting Mr. Holmes. He was quite sure. Quite.

We departed, and as we strolled down the High Street, Holmes asked me if I would object to spending the night in Cloisterham.

"I shall rejoin you tomorrow," he added.

"But are you going away?"

"Yes, to London. I am going to follow Mr. Sapsea's advice," he added with a smile.

"I thought you wanted to see the gargoyles," I objected.

"So I did. And do you know, my dear fellow, I believe I have seen one of the most interesting of them all."

Holmes's remark was entirely enigmatic to me, and while I was still puzzling over it, he waved his hand and entered the omnibus for the station. Left thus alone in Cloisterham, I went to the Crozier, where I secured a room for the night. In passing the gatehouse I noticed a curious looking man with his hat in his hand, looking attentively at Mr. Jasper's window. He had, I observed, white hair, which streamed in the wind. Later in the afternoon, having dropped in at the cathedral to hear the vesper service, I saw the same man. He was watching the choirmaster, Mr. Jasper, with profound scrutiny. This made me uneasy. How did I know but what another plot, like that which had been hatched against the nephew, was on foot against the uncle? Seated in the bar at the Crozier, after dinner, I found him again. He willingly entered into conversation with me, and announced himself as one Mr. Datchery—"an idle buffer, living on his means." He was interested in the Drood case and very willing to talk about it. I drew him out as much as I could, and then retired to my room to think it over.

That he wore a disguise seemed clear to me. His hair looked like a wig. If he was in disguise, who could he be? I thought over all the persons in any way connected with the case, when suddenly the name of Miss Helena Landless occurred to me. Instantly I was convinced that it must be she. The very improbability of the idea fascinated me from the start. What more unlikely than that a young Ceylonese girl should pass herself off for an elderly English man, sitting in bars and drinking elderly English drinks? The improbable is usually true, I remembered. Then I recalled that I had heard that Miss Landless, as a child, used to dress up as a boy. I was now positive about the matter.

I was on hand to meet Holmes when he returned the next day. He had two men with him and he introduced them as Mr. Tartar and Mr. Neville Landless. I looked with interest at the suspected man, and then tried to have speech with Holmes. But he drew me apart.

"These gentlemen," said he, "are going at once to Mr. Crisparkle's. They will remain there until tonight, when I expect to have need of them. You and I will return to your hotel."

On the way I told him about Mr. Datchery, and my suspicions about that person. He listened eagerly, and said that he must have speech with Datchery without delay. When I told him of my belief that Datchery was the sister of Landless, in disguise, Holmes clapped me on the back, and exclaimed:

"Excellent, Watson, excellent! Quite in your old vein!"

I flushed with pride at this high praise from the great detective. He left me at the Crozier, while he went forth to find Datchery, and also, he said, to have a word with Mr. Jasper. I supposed that he was about to warn the choirmaster of the fact that he was watched.

Holmes returned to the inn in capital spirits.

"We shall have our work cut out for us, tonight, Watson," said he, "and perhaps we will have another look at the gargoyles."

During dinner he would talk of nothing except bee-keeping. He conversed on this topic, indeed, until long after we had finished our meal, and while we sat smoking in the bar. About eleven, an ancient man, called Durdles, came in, looking for Mister Holmes.

"Mr. Jarsper he's a-comin' down the stair, sir," said he.

"Good!" exclaimed Holmes, "come, Watson, we must make haste. This may be a serious business. Now, Durdles!"

The man called Durdles led us rapidly, and by back ways, to the churchyard. Here he showed us where we could stand, hidden behind a wall, and overlooking the tombs and gravestones. I could not imagine the object of his nocturnal visit. Holmes gave our guide some money, and he made off. While I stood there, looking fearfully about, I thought I saw the figures of two men behind a tomb, at some little distance. I whispered to Holmes, but he motioned for silence.

"Hush!" he whispered, "Look there!"

I looked where he indicated, and saw another figure enter the churchyard. He carried some object, which I soon guessed to be a lantern, swathed in a dark wrapping. He unfolded a part of this wrapping, when he reached one of the tombs, and I recognized by the light the dark features of Mr. Jasper. What could he be doing here at this hour? He commenced to fumble in his pockets, and presently produced a key with which he approached the door of the tomb. Soon it swung open, and Mr. Jasper seemed about to step inside. But he paused for an instant, and then fell back, with a fearful scream of terror. Once, twice, did that awful cry ring through the silent churchyard. At its second repetition a man stepped from the tomb. Then Jasper turned, and ran frantically toward the cathedral.

The two men whom I had previously noticed sprang from behind a monument and pursued him.

"Quick!" said Holmes, "after him!"

We both ran in the same direction as fast as we could. Hindered by the darkness and by our unfamiliarity with the ground, however, we made poor progress. The fleeing choirmaster and his two strange pursuers had already vanished into the gloom of the cathedral. When at last we entered the building the sound of hurrying footsteps far above us was all we could hear. Then, as we paused, for an instant at fault, there came another dreadful cry, and then silence.

Men with lights burst into the cathedral and led us up the staircase toward the tower. The twisting ascent was a long business, and I knew from

Holmes's face that he dreaded what we might find at the top. When we reached the top there lay the choirmaster, Jasper, overpowered and bound by Mr. Tartar. The latter, then, had been one of the men I had seen behind the monument.

"Where is Neville?" said Holmes quickly.

Tartar shook his head and pointed below.

"This man," said he, indicating Jasper, "fought with him, and now I fear he really has a murder to answer for."

One of the men in the group which had followed us to the top stepped forward and looked down toward Jasper. It was the man whom we had seen step out of the tomb. I started when I saw that, except for the wig and a few changes in his costume, it was the same man who had called himself "Datchery."

Jasper gazed up at him and his face was distorted with fear.

"Ned! Ned!" he cried, and hid his face on the stone floor.

"Yes, yer may hide yer face," said old Durdles, trembling with rage, "yer thought yer had murdered him,—murdered Mr. Edwin Drood, yer own nephew. Yer hocussed him with liquor fixed with pizen, same's yer tried to hocus Durdles, an' tried to burn him up with quicklime in the tomb. But Durdles found him, Durdles did."

He advanced and would have ground the head of the prostrate choirmaster under his heel, if some men had not held him back.

"Of course," said Holmes to me on the train back to London next morning, "no one in Cloisterham thought of suspecting the eminently respectable Mr. Jasper. They started with the presumption of his innocence. He was a possible object of suspicion to me from the first. This was because he was one of the two men who last saw Edwin Drood. When we had our interview with him—Jasper, I mean—I recognized him as the frequenter of a disreputable opium den near the docks. You may remember that I have had occasion to look into such places in one other little problem we studied together. He was, then, leading a double life. That was as far as I had gone when I returned to London last night. But while there I had a talk with Mr. Grewgious, as well as with poor young Landless and his sister. From them I learned that Jasper was in love with his nephew's betrothed, and had, indeed, been persecuting her with his attentions, both before and after Edwin's disappearance. From Mr. Grewgious's manner I became convinced that he, at any rate, viewed Jasper with profound suspicion. But he was a lawyer, and very cautious; he evidently had no certain proof. Other hints which were dropped led me to suspect that he was not mourning the death of young Drood.

"This was a curious thing—the whole crux to the mystery lay in it. I sat up all night, Watson, and consumed about four ounces of tobacco. It needed some thinking. Why, if Jasper had plotted murder, had he failed to carry it out? The opium, the opium, Watson—you know, yourself, that a confirmed opium-smoker is apt to fail, is almost sure to fail, in any great enterprise. He tries to nerve himself before the deed, and ten to one he merely stupefies himself, and the plot miscarries. This morning I saw Mr. Grewgious again, and charged him in so many words with keeping secret the fact that Drood was alive. He admitted it, and told me that Drood was in Cloisterham masquerading as Datchery."

"But why should he do that?" I asked, "why did he let Neville rest under suspicion of murder?"

"Because he had no certain proof of Jasper's guilt," said Holmes, "and he was trying to collect evidence against him. He was himself drugged when the attempt was made upon his life, he was rescued on that occasion by Durdles, and his disappearance was connived at by Mr. Grewgious. The lawyer further told me of the ring which Edwin Drood carried with him, and which the would-be murderer overlooked when he took the watch and pin. Then, it was only necessary for me to drop a hint to Jasper about the ring. That sent him back to the tomb, into which he supposed he had flung Drood's body to be consumed by quicklime. There he found the living, and not the dead Edwin Drood, as you saw. But the opium was really the clew to the whole thing—I went to see the old hag who keeps the den he frequented, and learned from her that he babbled endlessly about the murder in his dreams. He had arrived at a point where he could not distinguish between the real attempt at murder and a vision. He acted as in a vision when he tried to commit the deed, and so it failed.

"As for your theory about Miss Landless being Datchery—well, my dear fellow, I am glad for the sake of that proper, clerical gentleman, Mr. Crisparkle, that his intended wife has not been masquerading in trousers at the Cloisterham inns. Poor Landless—I shall never forgive myself for his death. His murderer will meet the fate he richly deserves, without a doubt.

"And now, Watson, we were discussing bees. Have you ever heard of planting buckwheat near the hives? I am told that they do wonderfully on buckwheat."

*I*n *"The Problem of Thor Bridge," Watson reveals that "in the vaults of the bank of Cox & Co., at Charing Cross, there is a travel-worn and battered tin dispatch-box . . . crammed with papers, nearly all of which are records of cases to illustrate the curious problems which Mr. Sherlock Holmes had at various times to examine." One of the most puzzling of these cases-to-be-told is "the singular adventures of the Grice-Patersons in the island of Uffa," which, according to Watson in "The Five Orange Pips," happened in 1887—but* where? *Uffa cannot be found on any map. This is the problem that the Holmesian scholar* POUL ANDERSON, *Hugo-winning author of such superb science-fantasy novels as* The Devil's Game, The High Crusade, Queen of Air and Darkness *and* Three Hearts and Three Lions, *assiduously investigates.*

In the Island of Uffa

POUL ANDERSON

To travel hopefully, they say, is better than to arrive. So perhaps I am not merely indulging a sour grapes attitude when I suggest this heresy: that it is, after all, for the best that we will never read the untold adventures of Sherlock Holmes. Of course, if by some magic we could throw a distracting sop to whatever Cerberus guards the vaults of the bank of Cox & Co. at Charing Cross—if we could burst open that travel-worn and battered tin dispatch-box with the name John H. Watson, M.D., Late Indian Army, painted upon the lid—ah, keep your paradise, complete with houris, for we have better places to go!

And yet . . . consider . . . once we had really learned what happened to Mr. James Phillimore, who, stepping back into his own home to get his umbrella, was never more seen in this world; once we had shuddered at the repulsive story of the red leech and the terrible death of Crosby the banker; once we had followed the Master on his grim course in the tracking and arrest of Huret, the Boulevard assassin—well, what *would* we do for an encore?

As it is, the glamour of unfulfillment is left us. Our dreams can be unlimited. Many and many a long dark evening, when the storms grow louder and louder, and the wind cries and sobs like a child in the chimney, we can sit on our respective sides of the fireplace, wondering, pondering, arguing, even thinking our efforts have yielded us a glimpse of the truth itself. Is this not a deeper sharing of Watson's life and Watson's hero than passive readership can ever be?

In this spirit my wife and I have considered one of the most tantalizing passages in the entire Canon. I quote from *The Five Orange Pips*: "The year '87 furnished us with a long series of cases of greater or less interest, of which I retain the records. Among my headings under this one twelve months, I find an account of the adventure of the Paradol Chamber, of the Amateur Mendicant Society, who held a luxurious club in the lower vault of a furniture warehouse, of the facts connected with the loss of the British barque Sophy Anderson, of the singular adventures of the Grice Pattersons in the island of Uffa, and finally of the Camberwell poisoning case." Indeed there were giants in those days!

The Camberwell affair has been brilliantly reconstructed by Stillman Drake. But I have seen no satisfactory treatment of any of the others. The late Fletcher Pratt did suggest once—in conversation with me; I have not been able to find his paper on the subject—that the island of Uffa was Denmark. I suppose he was led to this conclusion by the fact that there is a legendary person of that name, whose story is told in the 13th century Gesta Danorum of Saxo Grammaticus. And a rousing good yarn it is, exactly the kind which would appeal to a man like Pratt, with one lone hero defending the land against a horde of enemy invaders.

Nevertheless, I am afraid the idea will not bear closer examination. Though the kingdom of Denmark contains many islands, it is not one itself. And in fact the Danish Uffa's stamping grounds were in Jutland, which is a peninsula. Besides, while we know that Holmes visited Scandinavia at least once and probably oftener, nearly all his work was done in England.

Watson's language gives us still more reason to look for an English setting. He speaks of "the adventure of the Paradol Chamber" and, elliptically, "the adventure of the Amateur Mendicant Society." This implies events which concerned Holmes and himself directly: they went somewhere, visited a scene, encountered the principals. On the other hand, he speaks "of the facts connected with the loss of the British barque *Sophy Anderson*"— which indicates that while Holmes interpreted facts laid before him, and perhaps gathered certain clues himself, he was not so actively involved. He entered as an advisor after the event had happened. And getting back to the subject of the present inquiry, Watson speaks "of the singular adventures of the Grice Pattersons in the island of Uffa." Not "the adventure of the island of Uffa" or "our adventures in the island of Uffa"—no, he specifically states that the business happened to the Grice Pattersons.

Therefore it seems pretty clear that they came to Holmes afterward, sorely puzzled. The bulk of the Watson manuscript no doubt consists of their first person narrative. At the end, Holmes cuts through the fog of their bewilderment, seizes upon the crucial clue which they had and did not recognize, and explains everything.

This pattern, not infrequent in the Canon, best fits an English setting. If the Grice Pattersons had had their strange experiences in some foreign country like Denmark, the trail might seem hopelessly cold to them by the time they got back to London. They would most likely not have gone to Holmes at all.

Admittedly, the foregoing argument is a logical *non sequitur.* Holmes did occasionally have cases brought to him whose origins were remote in both space and time. But if we can find a consistent explanation of Watson's enigmatic remark, one which does involve a place in England, the argument will gain considerable strength.

Turning to the source of all knowledge and wisdom, the eleventh edition of the *Encyclopaedia Britannica,* we discover no island of Uffa as such. However, we do come upon mention of a chieftain named Uffa, who led the Teutonic invaders of what is now East Anglia in the 6th century A.D. Tradition has it that he made a fortification in Norwich about 570. He established his capital at Thetford, in southern Norfolk, about 575, and it is generally accepted that he raised those earthworks called Castle Hill. You might call him the Norfolk builder.

This entire region is flat, seamed with watercourses and studded with small lakes. Not far north of Thetford lie those wide, shallow, reedy meres known as the Norfolk Broads, which are still rich country for the fisherman and the wildfowl hunter, and must have been even more so in early days.

(In this connection, though it is utterly irrelevant, I cannot forbear to quote a book review which my brother, who is a geologist, called to my attention. It appeared in the staid *Geological Times* for Jan.–Feb. 1961:

"THE MAKING OF THE BROADS, J. M. Lambert et al, Royal Geographical Society, London, 1960, 153 pp., ills., 25 shillings.

"This work fills a need in an interdisciplinary field of which all too many geologists are ignorant. Assuredly it could never have been written in the United States. The authors demonstrate how original natural processes have been modified by man over a period of some seven centuries. Refined techniques of dating are introduced, and the critical features of beds clearly illustrated.

"Though technical in detail, this book will prove particularly edifying to the lay reader.—R.G.")

But to return to our muttons. Even closer to Thetford lies the edge of the Fen country, wide, wild, and wet, a land of brackish marsh and tangled growth where civilization was long held at bay. Here, at a later date, fled Hereward the Wake, the last warrior of that Anglo-Saxon England of which Uffa was among the first. Surely in the days of the Teutonic invasion, many a Romano-Briton, Pict, or outlawed Angle found refuge there. A menace to the peace of Uffa's new kingdom, these savage skulkers and raiders had to be kept in check. He must have established more than one strongpoint in the wilderness, each garrisoned under the leadership of some reliable man.

There are numerous islands in the Fen country. As early as the 7th century, a mere hundred years after Uffa, Cistercian monks began to colonize them. Could one of these be the place we seek? Perhaps. And yet we hark back to Watson and see that he does not speak of the Grice Pattersons having their singular adventures on the island of Uffa. No, it is *in* the island.

This is an important distinction. An island has to get very big before you can properly say you are in it. Otherwise you are on it. You may live in Borneo, but you live on the Isle of Wight. Since the island of Uffa is obviously quite small—there being no large ones in the English interior—you can only be in it if you are inside it. In other words, you find a tunnel, or dig one. This suggests archeological excavation. That is the more reasonable when we recall that archeology had begun to boom in Europe in 1887. Schliemann had completed his excavation of Troy only five years before. A fever of excitement swept the Western world. People were digging everywhere. In addition, the Romantic movement had gotten northern Europeans interested in their own pre-Christian ancestors. What more natural, then, than that a wealthy dilettante, hearing about an island of Uffa in the Fens, should go there to see what he could find?

Watson's phrase "the Grice Pattersons" strongly suggests dilettantism. Serious husband-and-wife teams were still unheard of in any field as rugged as archeology. If Grice Patterson had meant business, he would not have cluttered himself up with a woman, out in the fogs and reeds, digging through mud and chalk beds. Nevertheless his wife was interested enough to come along and submit herself to just those hardships. So I see them as an independently wealthy couple, still fairly young, he a bit of an intellectual as well as a sportsman, she quite a bit of a bluestocking. Norfolk was hardly a place where such people would choose to live. They probably maintained a flat in London and a weekend cottage somewhere in the Home Counties. Flitting from enthusiasm to enthusiasm—folk dancing, the Upanishads, Wagner, Ibsen, philately, butterfly collecting—they came at last upon archeology. In 1887, one way or another, they learned that up in the Fens was an island said to be Uffa's. At once they packed pick, shovel, mackintosh, boots, and evening clothes, and with a servant or two caught the 11:43 from Paddington.

We can deduce what they found. Uffa's wooden fort had long moldered away, but a burial mound from about that time still stood. This is the only work that could have endured so many centuries and also invite digging. The island itself being very small, the mound practically *was* the island. I say the island was small because then the surrounding shallow water would make it easily defensible. On the other hand, the barrow must have been large, or the Grice Pattersons could not have gotten inside it.

Possibly the Anglian garrison had all perished in an outlaw attack, and were buried by King Uffa at the site they had so bravely defended for him. That would account for the name. Incidentally, such a grave, full of vengeful ghosts, would be even more effective than a fortress of live men in keeping the Fen runners at a distance. Gruesome legends would be handed down among the local peasantry for more than a thousand years. Woe unto him who ventured into the island of Uffa!

Of course, by the 19th century it no longer lay far out in the wilderness. The Fens had been largely drained. Settlement had encroached. No doubt there was a sizeable village within walking distance. However, if superstitious fears clustered about the island—and we have just shown that this was probably the case—then it was avoided. It stood by itself in a reed-grown pool, dark and ominous.

Dire warnings must have been croaked to the Grice Pattersons. But they laughed. Full of beans and enlightenment, they splashed across to the island of Uffa and began digging. Though the damp soil yielded readily enough, they would scarcely have riddled it with tunnels. Yet Watson says they had adventures in the island. Accordingly, I think they must have come upon a central chamber. The heathen Teutonic custom was, indeed, to erect a wooden room about a dead chieftain and then heap dirt on it. Oak timbers could well last 1300 years in the earth; they have done better than this in Denmark.

However, since the Grice Pattersons had more than one adventure in the island, they must not have been able to clean out the relics they found in a single day. Probably part of the chamber had caved in. They found just enough rusty remnants of weapons and the like to convince them that a real hoard, with golden treasures, lay in the section which had collapsed. So day after day, by flickering lantern light, Grice Patterson, the few local men he had been able to engage, and even his wife toiled to clear out the rest of the tumulus. And that was when the singular adventures began.

We can readily conjecture what sort of adventures—exactly the ghostly manifestations that the yokels had warned about. Runic curses drawn in blood; weird, threatening cries as twilight closed in; the day's work undone during the night when they returned to the village inn; perhaps even the lantern blown out by a gust from the entry shaft, just after sunset, and a great shape storming in through the dark, seizing Mrs. Grice Patterson by the throat and nearly choking her unconscious before it was forced to flee.

Grice Patterson himself would not have fallen prey to the unreasoning dread that gripped his hirelings. He must have felt sure that mortal man was at work. Someone else wanted that ancient gold, now that he had shown the possibility of its being there. But who? His thoughts turned to the villagers. For the most part they were simple rustics, but some had shown him black hostility. He set up camp on the island and mounted guard with a revolver each night.

But then his terrified laborers quit. I am certain that the Grice Pattersons did not. In the bulldog English spirit, they went to Norwich to recruit new navvies. This would take a few days. Meanwhile they had browbeaten a local constable into keeping watch on the site. But when they returned, they found the poor man had been frightened away one night and the barrow ransacked. Someone had dug ahead of them. Without being able to prove it, I feel intuitively that they found a tiny fragment of gold left behind. At least, this would convince them that a treasure had indeed been stolen. Unable to get effective help from the local police, the Grice Pattersons returned to London and laid the case in Sherlock Holmes' lap.

We decided near the beginning of this inquiry that, in all probability, Holmes did not go to Norfolk but solved the problem where he sat, in 221B Baker Street. Now he would not have done this if he thought an ancient hoard really had been looted. That would have been a major crime, theft of Crown property, not to mention a disaster to that early English historiography in which we know he was interested. Therefore the testimony of the Grice Pattersons convinced him that something less rare was involved.

We can almost hear the dialogue. The clients' description of the villagers, including one man who had been strange and surly since his business partner disappeared; a description of the hole which the intruder dug; the bit of dropped gold. There must have been something like that piece of gold, to provide Holmes with his key clue. At once the puzzle clicked together for him.

Where could a murder victim better be hidden than in the feared and shunned island of Uffa? How aghast must the murderer not have been when outsiders arrived and began to dig ever closer to the body? How hard must he not have tried to frighten them away? In the end, of course, during their temporary departure, he stole in, dug up the skeleton which had joined the bones of Uffa's warriors so few years ago, and carried it elsewhere—but unbeknownst to him, a modern tooth filling dropped out.

And thus the curse was fulfilled on him who disturbed the sleep of the ancients. Holmes needed only send a telegram to Norwich, or better yet to Scotland Yard. Given this much of a lead, the police would not have been slow to apprehend the killer and prove his guilt. Disappointed in their hope of coming upon a Fafnir's heap of gold, the Grice Pattersons took up woman suffrage. And once again Mr. Sherlock Holmes was free to devote his life to examining those interesting little problems which the complex life of London so plentifully presents.

*A*fter Holmes almost tumbled into Reichenbach Falls, he "traveled for two years in Tibet . . . visiting Lhassa and spending some days with the head lama." Asian scholars have racked their brains over problems in Holmes's explanation. The following article, researched "on the scene," was published in India in the August 1982 issue of Tibetan Review. Specialist in travel accident insurance, A M A N D A R U S S E L L has studied law, fine art and graphic design, and is a choral singer and writer. Her poem "The Orchid Nursery" appeared in the anthology Masques III. She lives in southern California near her father, Ray Russell, whose own selection appears later this volume.

The Tibetan Adventures of Sherlock Holmes

A M A N D A R U S S E L L

Sherlock Holmes, that fictional detective who is more well-known than are many real historical personages, spent two years in Tibet—if a purely imaginary character can be said truly to have spent any time anywhere.

The Tibetan journey was referred to by Holmes in two sentences of Sir Arthur Conan Doyle's story, "The Adventure of the Empty House," first published in 1903. Since then, it has been a challenge to devotees of Sir Arthur's writings to speculate on what the Great Detective might have done in the Land of Snows. It may seem odd to some to speculate on the activities of a character of fiction; yet, many scholars have spent a great deal of time and effort doing just that in the case of Sherlock Holmes. Their dedication is proof of how "real" Holmes is in the minds of many readers. This article is not meant to be a complete summary of everything ever written on Holmes's Tibetan adventures; rather, it is a comparison of two of the more interesting accounts.

Conan Doyle was a writer of wide-ranging talent who did not consider the Holmes stories to be his finest works. By 1893, he had tired of his most famous creation and wanted to kill off the sleuth. He proceeded to do this in the story "The Final Problem," in which Holmes disappears, apparently pushed over a cliff into Switzerland's Reichenbach Falls by his archenemy, Professor Moriarty.

There was a great public outcry at the loss of Holmes, so a decade later Conan Doyle revived him in "The Adventure of the Empty House." In this story, Holmes speaks the following words to his relieved friend and biographer, Dr. Watson:

> The course of events in London did not run so well as I had hoped, for the trial of the Moriarty gang left two of its most dangerous members, my own most vindictive enemies, at liberty. I travelled for two years in Tibet, therefore, and amused myself by visiting Lhassa, and spending some days with the head lama. You may have read of the remarkable explorations of a Norwegian named Sigerson, but I am sure that it never occurred to you that you were receiving news of your friend.

These "remarkable explorations" apparently took place between late 1891 and September of 1893. It will be useful, then, to recall something of the political situation in the real Tibet of 1891. The Thirteenth Dalai Lama was still a minor of 15, so the country was ruled by the Regent, Demo Trinley Rabgyas. (Sherlockians have disagreed on whether or not the Regent was the "head lama" Holmes spoke of—but more on this later.) Tibet was trying to remain isolated from international politics, but this was becoming increasingly difficult. The surrounding powers—Russia, China, and the British in India—were all interested in Tibet's trade potential; Britain had chosen to accept the Chinese claim of "suzerainty" over Tibet. So the Tibetan Government at this time was justifiably wary of foreigners, particularly the British.

With this historical background in mind, let us turn to the account of the detective's journey given by William S. Baring-Gould in his book, *Sherlock Holmes of Baker Street: A Life of the World's First Consulting Detective* (Clarkson Potter, 1962). Baring-Gould, a noted Holmes scholar, relies heavily in the Tibetan section of his book on A. Carson Simpson's four-volume *Sherlock Holmes's Wanderjahre* (International Printing Company, 1953, 1954, 1955, 1956).

This fanciful account has Holmes, as Sigerson, visiting Tibet on behalf of the British Government, at the behest of his brother Mycroft. In Conan Doyle's stories, Mycroft worked for the Government, and had made himself so indispensable by his vast knowledge that it could be said he *was* the British Government. Baring-Gould writes, "Then, as in more recent years, Russian intrigue on the northern borders of India was continuous, and a source of great concern to Britain. Tibet was being infiltrated by Mongols and Buriats, acting as agents for Russia. Mycroft, *as* the British Government, would be delighted to have a trained observer, versed in the ways of international espionage, on the ground, to give him a true report on conditions in that vital but inaccessible border country." Who else but brother Sherlock?

Having reached India, Holmes went to Darjeeling to make prepara-
tions for the journey, buying provisions and recruiting and outfitting the men
and animals who would make up the caravan. Here he also "received the
permit necessary to enter and travel in Tibet—an imposing document, dated
in the Year of the Iron Female Hare, signed by the Head Lama, Regent
during the minority of the Dalai Lama . . ."

The trek begins. Battling leeches in the Teesta Valley and in the forests
of Sikkim, Holmes presses on, climbing towards the Tibetan frontier. He
crosses the Jelep La and descends into the Chumbi Valley. Passing through
Gyantse, Holmes continues toward Lhasa, on the way crossing the Tsangpo
by the famous iron-chain suspension bridge. Arriving in Lhasa, his first act is
to call on the head lama, presenting him with the traditional white scarf.

"We know that Holmes visited Tibet on behalf of the British Government, but this still leaves a question unanswered. Why did the regent, the
head lama, take the unprecedented course of inviting Holmes to come to
Lhasa to see him?" The answer, as offered by both Simpson and Baring-
Gould, is that the head lama had learned the detective's true identity and
wanted him to find out the truth about the legendary Abominable Snowman.
Simpson reasons that as this creature's only traces were footprints in the snow,
and Holmes was the world's greatest expert on footprints, what could be
more natural? Furthermore, the head lama had a good reason for wanting to
know more about the Snowman. Since, according to legend, the Tibetan
people are descended from a monkey (an incarnation of Chenresig), it was
possible that the Snowman was somehow related to the present-day Tibetans.

The account continues to say that Holmes even climbed Mt. Everest in
pursuit of the creature, but what he finally reported to the head lama remains
a mystery. As well as searching for the Snowman, Holmes also took the opportunity while in Tibet to study Buddhism, taking instruction from the head
lama.

This version of Holmes's Tibetan odyssey, while colourful, must be
criticized on several counts. First of all, it is doubtful that Holmes would have
been welcomed into Tibet if it were known he represented the British Government. During this period, as mentioned earlier, the Chinese had convinced Britain that China exercised "suzerainty" over Tibet. As a result, Britain signed several treaties with China (in 1876, 1886, and 1890) giving
Britain the "right" to send missions of exploration into Tibet. These treaties
were always repudiated by the Tibetans, who refused to let such missions into
the country. Therefore, it is more likely that Holmes went to Tibet as a
private citizen, disguising his nationality by posing as a Norwegian. It is also
likely that no one discovered his real identity. The head lama would not have
been pleased to learn that his distinguished guest was a spy who had entered
the country under false pretenses. Yet, this account has the lama rewarding

Holmes for his mendacity by becoming a client, and by giving him Buddhist teachings!

The theory of Holmes searching for the Abominable Snowman at the head lama's request is also rather far-fetched. It is obvious that the Tibetan Government had more pressing problems to deal with at the time than tracking down a legendary monster. It is possible that "Sigerson," as an explorer, might have searched for traces of the creature, but only to satisfy his own curiosity.

Another view of Holmes's Tibetan adventures is offered by Winifred M. Christie in her article, "On the remarkable explorations of Sigerson" (*Sherlock Holmes Journal,* September 1952). Christie's account differs from Baring-Gould's in several respects, the first being that in her opinion, Holmes did not visit Tibet as an agent of the British Government.

Quoting from Holmes's own brief description of his journey, she writes, "Listen to that airiness—'I amused myself by visiting Lhassa'—and you, who know his methods, will instantly perceive that he is just masking his pride in a tremendous adventure, perhaps the supreme adventure of his life. Now, nobody visits Tibet by chance. There is far too much to be planned. I am convinced that Mr. Holmes had long felt Tibet drawing him like a magnet." She continues, citing references from Holmes stories to show that the detective had deep and firsthand knowledge of the Buddhism of Ceylon. "We may surmise that from then onwards he felt urgently impelled to make an equally exhaustive study of Buddhism in Tibet." In other words, it was not the wishes of his brother Mycroft, but his own intellectual and spiritual curiosity that brought Holmes to Tibet. It was the Reichenbach incident and the need to disappear that created the perfect opportunity.

Christie then takes up the question of why Holmes posed as a Norwegian. "Well, here we must, I fear, plunge into very deep waters indeed—the political maelstrom of Tibet in 1891. In the 80's and 90's the English were in bad odour in Tibet. Few Europeans and, I venture to think, no Englishmen, would risk trying to get in either by the overland route from Europe or by the roads from China." The route through Sikkim, by then a British protectorate, would have been the safest choice, especially for a subject of a neutral state.

"It is easy to see why he chose Norway and became Sigerson. First of all, Norwegians are really rather like ourselves [the British]. They are quiet in manner and gesture. There are tall and short ones, dark and fair. Even aquiline-Sherlockian-types may be seen any day in Oslo." Another reason for choosing Norway, Christie points out, is that Holmes had helped Scandinavian royalty more than once in the past, and with these connections, could easily obtain the necessary travel documents.

The journey under way, we see Holmes, a gifted linguist, immediately tackling the Tibetan language. He visits "tiny wayside lamaseries" where the monks are impressed by his courtesy and by his "permits to visit their priestly rulers."

Once in Lhasa, "Sigerson" meets the mysterious head lama. Christie's identification of this figure is different from Baring-Gould's: "Properly speaking, the term 'head lama' doesn't exist. To which of Tibet's august rulers can this phrase refer? As we know, there are actually two Grand Lamas, the Dalai Lama and the Pan-chen Lama. In 1891 the young Dalai Lama, enthroned as the spiritual ruler but not yet the temporal head of Tibet, lived in some seclusion. Mr. Holmes's study of Buddhism . . . would fit him for an audience with this wonderful youth, but I doubt whether he was Mr. Holmes's host. Nor do I think this 'head lama' was the Regent. Far more probably it was the Pan-chen Lama—the Teshai Lama, as he is usually called by Europeans—who cared for the distinguished stranger. He had crowds of disciples, was a power on the Council, and made many contacts."

"Sigerson" spends the next two years exploring the country, discovering such natural wonders as the blue Himalayan poppy. At this point, Christie briefly mentions the Abominable Snowman as another possible discovery, about which the whole truth has not yet been revealed.

What was it that made Holmes leave Tibet and return home? Christie suggests that "he must have relied on an Inner Voice," and waited for a Sign: "and here it was. Fingering the famous Treasury of Sa-skya Pandita, I fancy he found these two ancient Tibetan aphorisms, startlingly close together:

> *If a clear-sighted man walks discreetly, will he not avoid the Precipice?*

and

> *If we do to others what is agreeable to us, others also, in the same manner, will honour us with a pleasing Return.*

With this remarkable juxtaposition, the account concludes. It is a more believable one than Baring-Gould's for two reasons—first, that Holmes was not in Tibet as a British agent, and second, that the Abominable Snowman isn't given as much emphasis. As for the identity of the head lama, the Pan-chen Lama theory is as plausible as the Regent theory. This is one mystery that may never be solved.

One question never asked by either Baring-Gould or Christie is, how did Holmes reconcile his false identity as Sigerson with his alleged Buddhist beliefs?

Was his interest in Buddhism merely intellectual? Or was he a sincere believer who considered the temporary identity a "skillful means" necessary to enter the Tibet of his dreams? Sherlockians have disagreed on the question of Holmes's Buddhism. Some make the case for the detective's conversion while in Tibet, citing changes for the better in his behaviour after his return. In any case, Holmes's religious beliefs (or lack of them) is too complex a subject to explore further in this article.

These are two of the more interesting theories read by this writer. There are many others—including James Nelson's notion that Holmes found the Abominable Snow*woman* (!) and T. F. Foss's assertion that Holmes was not in Tibet at all, but in India spying on the Russians. Most lovers of the Great Detective, however, would rather believe his own account. So the fact of Sherlock Holmes's Tibetan adventure will always remain—in the land of the imagination.

In 1969, I asked Luther Norris, a publisher of Holmesiana, why no one had ever written a major study of Holmes's acting. Was Sherlock really an accomplished thespian? Surely, Victorian theatrical makeup was too primitive for his more complicated disguises . . . ? Luther invited me to write such a book. Flattered, yet skeptical, I reread Watson and soon realized that Holmes was indeed a fine actor. More important was my discovery that greasepaint was available significantly earlier than the Encyclopaedia Britannica *claimed. The Histrionic Holmes was published in 1971 in an edition of 300 copies that sold out swiftly and received generous ''press'' notices by Holmesians, especially John Dickinson Carr in* Ellery Queen's Mystery Magazine. *Space limitations forced Luther to cut part of the second chapter. This material has been restored, making this the first complete edition of* The Histrionic Holmes.

The Histrionic Holmes

MARVIN KAYE

CHAPTER ONE

An Actor Prepares

> Gwendolyn: Of course I suppose you're the real one!—Detectives have
> so many disguises and things that it might be you were only pretending
> —but still, why should you?

—FROM WILLIAM GILLETTE'S
The Harrowing Predicament
of Sherlock Holmes

Popular culture has fostered the notion that a great actor must be a gregarious extrovert possessed of a mystical kind of innate "talent" that catapults him, sans training, to the apex of his profession.

But those more intimately acquainted with the psychology of the accomplished thespian find that very nearly the opposite is often true. The veteran actor, skilled in a wide variety of roles, is a devoted acolyte of his art with long years of patient practice and study behind him. And, rather than being a "life of the party"—however much he may affect that role as his public image—he frequently harbors an introverted personality whose anti-gregariousness and paradoxically complementary loneliness *drive* him to the world of the theatre as a means of self-expression and way of life.

So, the making of a great actor is not so much a matter of "talent"—a mystique that has wasted the lives of many an adolescent—but the presence of a psychological *need* so powerful that the would-be Roscian surmounts all obstacles, internal and external, in his quest for establishing a purpose to his existence.

Only in the light of this conception of the performing artist may we begin to approach the evolution of the Histrionic Holmes.[1]

"The factors that shape the personality of the actor, as is the case of every individual, are to be found in his early environment," states Yoti Lane in her study, *The Psychology of the Actor* (Secker & Warburg, London, 1959). And this is certainly true in the case of Sherlock Holmes, whose formative years, emotional as well as professional, are chiefly chronicled in his earliest cases. With the exception of a few latter clues to his family and personality, Sherlock gives us most of the evidence needed for unriddling what drove him to study thespianic technique in *Gloria Scott, The Musgrave Ritual,* and, to lesser extent, *A Study in Scarlet.*

Outside the Canon, the scholar also is able to find some helpful biographical information in William S. Baring-Gould's *Sherlock Holmes of Baker Street,* the "official life" of the great detective.

Of the embryonic actor, Miss Lane tells us that "some psychic discomfort . . . forces him to reject the world accepted by the majority of people for a smaller world of painted canvas and artificial light . . ." Oftentimes, this spiritual malaise strikes an only child—or one whose family position places him in a situation analogous to that of an only child—when he discovers that the favored place he has held is in no way respected by the macrocosm into which he must eventually venture.

This realization, Miss Lane tells us, may result in withdrawal into the family's bosom and correspondent retreat from the world, or the child "may

---

[1] That there are other springs for the acting motivation is, of course, not denied, and there are even examples of professionals who have attained the pinnacle of success, financial and artistic, without having the internal insecurity cited—the late David Burns was one such actor. But, in Holmes' case, we must embrace the psychological-necessity theory, as all evidence points that way.

use his intelligence to try and attract as much attention and favor in the larger world as he enjoys at home."

But the latter course of action, which may lead to an acting career and its opportunities for public fulfillment, also tends to widen the gap between the individual and the society he is attempting to please, inasmuch as actors are generally regarded as strange phenomena by the solid middle-class public. When this occurs, the young artist finds his unease with society *en masse* considerably aggravated, and he becomes further introverted, meeting the public only across the footlights or behind the mask his publicity agent chooses to forge.

It is the contention of the author that the early life of Sherlock Holmes fostered in the Master a personality that naturally would seek the theatrical life, at least for a time. For many of the great detective's character traits are precisely the sort that we have described.

We know he is manic-depressive; his periods of energy alternate with fits of black gloom during which, in his earlier days, he takes dosages of narcotic—far from "normal" behavior.

We know Holmes has no great liking for formal visits or society, a point repeatedly made by Watson.[2] Yet, in his early years, though he is a lonely college student, his desire for applause and fame—which never wholly left him[3]—drove him to entertain his school acquaints with displays of his deductive powers. ". . . Young Trevor began to talk about those habits of observation and inference which I had already formed into a system . . ." occurs in *Gloria Scott*. In *Musgrave Ritual*: ". . . I understand, Holmes, that you are turning to practical ends those powers with which you used to amaze us."

It is also evident that the early Holmes is already a somewhat perceptive young man . . . possessed of a sensitivity that might, under the proper circumstances, lead him to try his hand at acting. His view of the allegedly prideful Reginald Musgrave as one really trying to cover natural shyness with a haughty mask is remarkable for showing more charity and compassion than his fellows. It also suggests that diffidence may have been a familiar thing to Sherlock, whose supposed emotionlessness has already been postulated (by other Holmesian scholars) as being *his* mask or protective shell.[4] One who

---

[2] In *A Scandal in Bohemia, The Engineer's Thumb, The Noble Bachelor* and *The Greek Interpreter.*
[3] Examples abound. One occurs early in *Valley of Fear:* " 'Talk away, Mr. Holmes. I'm just loving it. It's fine!' Holmes smiled. He was always warmed by genuine admiration—the characteristic of the real artist."
[4] It is apparent from his later behavior that, at some time, Holmes came to realize he is not meant to be a gregarious animal. The mature detective came to enjoy his solitariness, and in this, he is repeating the pattern of many actors and other artists who learn that attempting to conform to the crowd's way is not worth it.

suffers from loneliness and alienation from his peers is likely to be quick to perceive similar feelings in others.

It is of prime importance to note the single friendship Holmes did form in his academic days: Trevor, ". . . a hearty, full-blooded fellow, full of spirit and energy, the very opposite to me in most respects . . ." The personality contrast itself must have been attractive to Holmes, but note what follows: ". . . it was a bond of union when I learned that he was as friendless as I." Clearly, Holmes is no willing social exile; the pain of loneliness leads him to a kindred soul.

What have we learned thus far about Sherlock's early personality? As a student, he was a moody, lonely, practically friendless individual. He apparently hid behind a mask of indifference, yet his desire to entertain his schoolmates with his powers of deduction points to an inner self eager to obtain the approval of his peer group.

In other words, he exhibits a kind of spiritual malaise (in the words of Yoti Lane) capable of rendering him ripe for turning his thoughts to a career as an actor.

Now it is a significant fact that Sherlock Holmes did indeed occupy the probably-pampered position of an only child—one of the important factors often present in the shaping of the actor. Baring-Gould gives the ages of his older brothers Sherrinford and Mycroft as nine and seven, respectively, at Sherlock's birth.

It is likely that he was the object of an undue transference of affection from his mother, whose artistic antecedents must also have provided the child with ample fodder for growth of imagination. We can imagine Mrs. Holmes cradling the child Sherlock in her arms and telling him tales of his illustrious relatives, as well as fancy-stirring fables and narratives.

But Sherlock's father was another matter. An ex-military man, according to Baring-Gould, he was a member of a line of country squires (as noted in *The Greek Interpreter*): the double tradition of landed gentry/military discipline must have boded ill for young Sherlock, whose fantasy world was being richly nourished by his mother.

In fact, the author strongly doubts that the marriage of Sherlock's parents was as happy as Baring-Gould describes. The contrast in their backgrounds points to a growing estrangement, with Sherlock eventually becoming the battleground for their clash of will.

There is psychological support for this hypothesis. Miss Lane tells us a woman disappointed with her husband often provides the primal cause for a child becoming an actor, through excess rechannelling of affection.

Such a woman would be doubly spurred if her husband were a product of long traditions, for it is rare that an actor comes from a home where the father is a military man. "Concerning this," Miss Lane continues, ". . . In a large number of cases, the actor comes from a home where the father has not played a dominant role, or has been absent for long periods. Freed from the necessity of emulating the father, the desire to create . . . has an opportunity to develop."

Since Siger Holmes' influence would likely stifle Sherlock's imagination, it seems probable to infer some physical separation between father and son during the formative years. Now Baring-Gould tells us the Holmes family took long trips abroad, living like gypsies, when Sherlock was a child. When they finally returned to England, Father Holmes decided Sherlock should become an engineer, first sending the boy to board school. "A man of strong character," Baring-Gould describes Siger, noting that the elder Holmes had a "hostility to imagination. It had to be suppressed, because he disapproved of it."

It should now be apparent what actually happened to Sherlock. Given a generous heritage of imagination by his mother, the young lad must have encountered paternal hostility. Rather than let her baby be crushed by the dictatorial Siger (the way her eldest must have been, at least in her eyes, since he became the next country squire in his manhood), Mrs. Holmes stole away with young Sherlock, and possibly also Mycroft, and made her home in various parts of Europe.

So the itinerant years were actually times of pursuit, and when Siger finally found his family and brought them back to England, Sherlock, at least, was already formed in character and unlikely to be content with an engineer's lot. Board school was doubtless an unsuccessful attempt to "straighten the boy out."

Now this was unfortunate for the sheltered youth. Long used to being the center of maternal attention, Sherlock's imagination had been developed to the exclusion of his social tutoring. Travel abroad, while enriching his fantasy-life, must have kept him from the companionship of other children, at least to the extent of forming close friendships. So he was doubly unsuited to entering a board school, and if it were not for his early proficiency in boxing, those years might have been more miserable than they probably were. It is here that we must look for the beginnings of Holmes' later acedia.

Siger Holmes' action, far from straightening Sherlock out, only solidified the boy's position as an actor-in-the-making. All he needed to embrace the art of theatre as ersatz mother was exposure to it at its best.

Such exposure probably occurred at college, where he may have witnessed a professional production during one of the holidays—much in the same way that Conan Doyle (Watson's agent) did in his student period.[5]

The young Holmes likely confided his interest in histrionics to his parents, and must have met with paternal opprobrium. By this time, Sherlock

---

[5]Vide John Dickson Carr's *The Life of Arthur Conan Doyle.*

was in his teens, and this stifling of his interests must at last have bred defiance against Siger's authority.

According to Baring-Gould, Sherlock's decision to follow his own bent in giving up engineering for studies more useful to a detective led to his being disinherited. But it seems more probable that estrangement resulted in more flamboyant a fashion. It is the author's belief that Sherlock simply declared, in the best adolescent tradition, that he was going to quit school to become an actor!

That there was an estrangement is corroborated by two pieces of evidence from the Canon: (1) Holmes had great financial difficulty establishing himself at Montague Street, suggesting a cutting-off of funds; (2) he spent the whole of a long vacation with the Trevor family, an indication that he was *persona non grata* at home . . . certainly torturous to a lonely youth with strong maternal affectional ties.

The sequence of events would appear to be thus: attending college, where he met Reginald Musgrave, Sherlock became interested in acting; he encountered paternal disapproval, which forced Holmes to "make a stand" by quitting school for a theatrical life; disinheritance followed.

After a season of striving and putting in some repertory appearances, Sherlock returned to academic life, apparently with whatever funds he managed to save from his acting salary. Spending a lonely summer by himself, he received the invitation to visit the Trevors; while there, the elder of that name made his famous suggestion that Sherlock capitalize on his observational and deductive gifts.

Baring-Gould suggests the season in repertory came after Sherlock had been trying, for some time, to establish himself at Montague Street, but to leave on a sabbatical when trying to build up a business would be madness. Any fledgling actor knows he must be omnipresent at all the casting offices for many weary months before any work comes his way.

It remains to consider, in brief, the early professional acting of Holmes. Baring-Gould suggests he traveled with a Shakespearean acting company, and this is sound, for the Bard demands an excellence of style and facility with makeup (at least for character roles, which Holmes, by stature and physiognomy, would have been well suited for). Such technique and makeup knowhow is amply chronicled by Watson.

But some of the roles attributed to Sherlock by Baring-Gould are unlikely—Mercutio, Macbeth, Malvolio, Shylock, Mephistopheles in Goethe's *Faust*, etc.—for any of three possible reasons. First, he is physically unsuited for certain of these roles. Second, he was too young for some roles; even if his technique was sufficient to convincingly portray old age, it is rare for a theatrical manager to permit a younger company member to do so when there are veteran actors available for casting. Third, some of the roles attributed to Holmes are such "plums" that a new repertory company member would never be allowed a crack at them; they are reserved for those actors whose company seniority (and acting skill) has earned them the right to play them.

Roles which Holmes probably *did* play—if we adopt Baring-Gould's suggestions for works Holmes appeared in, as well as the detective's own Canonical allusions (see next chapter)—may have included Horatio; Valentine in *Faust;* Tybalt; the Duke of Venice; Ross in *Macbeth;* Andrew Aguecheek; Gloster in *Henry VI;* Don John in *Much Ado About Nothing* and perhaps Caesar in *Antony and Cleopatra.*

One question remains concerning the early Histrionic Holmes: why did he leave the repertory company and return to school? One can only speculate. His salary may have been incommensurate with his needs. He may have been impatient to play better roles. Or he may have encountered unexpected professional jealousy which may have made advancement even more difficult than normal.[6]

But more likely, his excellent mind was already outgrowing his youthful need for acting as a means of self-expression. We will return to this point at the conclusion of this essay.

CHAPTER TWO

Preliminary Catalog of Canonical Impersonations, Theatric Quotations, Paraphrases and Allusions

As the principal purpose of this study is to investigate the histrionic artistry and technique of Sherlock Holmes, it is fitting that a playbill be included of the great detective's chief recorded performances. The present chapter is meant to serve that aim.

But the same purpose—as well as space limitations—dictates the exclusion of an exhaustive compendium of Canonical impersonations, roleplaying, improvisatory charades and deceptions. Such a comprehensive catalog would be composed of upwards of 150 items.

A word of explanation is in order, since the latter assertion may surprise some Sherlockian scholars who, familiar with earlier articles on Holmesian thespianism, would have put the tally at a modest fifteen or twenty instances. The issue is a matter of definition: precisely what qualifies as an acting performance?

---

[6]For further discussion, see Chapter 3.

To begin with, a purist-completist (such as the author) will feel compelled to include more than just the instances wherein the Master assumes another identity (with or without makeup and/or costume).

For instance, there are "charades" such as the orange-and-water accident in *The Reigate Squires* or the more elaborately produced mock conflagration in *A Scandal in Bohemia*. Or the bogus botany hunts in *Wisteria Lodge*.

Then there are simple "impromptus"; for example, Holmes' hiding of his suspicion of Stapleton in Chapter 12 of *The Hound of the Baskervilles;* or, in *A Study in Scarlet,* the scene outside Lauriston Gardens #3, in which Sherlock lounges up and down the pavement, and so on "with an air of nonchalance which, under the circumstances, seemed . . . to border upon affectation . . ." (Chapter 3).

There are also kinds of performances that might be termed "feignings", as, for instance, a pretended limp in *Priory School* and a fainting spell in *Reigate Squires*—moments similar to the above "impromptus"—but requiring more technique to execute.

In our hypothetical comprehensive catalog, some of the examples cited might appear to be nothing more than deceptions, lies, or mere subterfuges. But to an accomplished actor, any embroidery upon whatever absolute Truth one cares to recognize is a kind of histrionic challenge—an opportunity to perfect that which a lesser "decipient" would fail to bring off.

To elucidate: even so slight a deception as, for example, the pretended knowledge of one Lysander Starr of Topeka (in *The Three Garridebs*) dictates a momentary *self-belief* by Holmes in the falsehood. His acting method could have allowed him to do no less; and this, in the author's eyes, would warrant inclusion in a full listing of the Master's Roscian endeavors.

Another consideration: while the principal interest of the Sherlockian student naturally revolves round the histrionic triumphs of the detective himself, there are many other personages in the sixty tales who indulge in disguise and role-taking. In the fifth chapter of *A Study in Scarlet* alone, Jefferson Hope pretends to be drunk in order to allay suspicion—a more difficult task than the layman conceives, involving problems of balance, optical focus, gait, etc. (I imagine Hope going limp against the railings, caterwauling and caroling in a poor imitation of a stage drunk. A constable remarks, "He was an *uncommon* drunk sort of man.") In the same chapter, an "old crone" visits Holmes on Jefferson Hope's prompting. Later, the murderer refuses to divulge his accomplice's identity and Holmes says, "Old woman be damned! . . . It must have been a young man, and an active one, too, besides being an incomparable actor." And what about "props," so to speak, that take on alternate personality? Such as the monstrous canine impersonating the hellish hound of the Baskerville legend? Or the dummies that portray Holmes? The true completist simply doesn't know where to stop!!!

Obviously, a complete enumeration of all villainous charades would take up too much space, but before examining Sherlock Holmes's impersonatory career, let us at least take a moment to consider John H. Watson's. After all, the good doctor is so honest, open and straightforward[1] that his entire histrionic catalog encompasses only half-a-dozen instances.

Dr. Watson's Six ''Performances''

1. In *The Sign of the Four,* Watson overacts, by his own admission, when he presents the alleged Agra treasure to Mary Morstan, who must have "detected a hollow ring" in his congratulations.
2. In *A Scandal in Bohemia,* a very slight, human attempt at deception occurs when the doctor tries to trim Holmes's estimate of his postmarital weight by half-a-pound . . .

   "Wedlock suits you . . . I think, Watson, that you have put on seven and a half pounds since I saw you."

   "Seven!" I answered.

   "Indeed, I should have thought a little more. Just a trifle more, I fancy, Watson."
3. In *The Hound of the Baskervilles,* Watson and Holmes conceal their suspicion of the villain when they encounter him on the moor.
4. In *The Adventure of the Dancing Men,* I think that Watson deliberately pulls Holmes's leg when he cries "How absurdly simple" after the Great Man explains a deduction concerning South African securities. Watson is fully capable of twitting Holmes. Cf. *The Valley of Fear:*

   ". . . You have heard me speak of Professor Moriarty?"

   "The famous scientific criminal, as famous among crooks as—"

   "My blushes, Watson," Holmes murmured, in a deprecating voice.

   "I was about to say 'as he is unknown to the public.' "

   "A touch—a distinct touch!" cried Holmes. "You are developing a certain unexpected vein of pawky humour, Watson, against which I must learn to guard myself."
5. Watson's most difficult assignment occurs in *The Adventure of the Illustrious Client* when Holmes asks him to portray Dr. Hill Barton, of Half Moon Street. This singular performance demonstrates how unsuited Watson is to the theatrical profession. Once his "cover" is "blown," his facility for improvisation proves grossly inadequate. (One wonders why he did not *at least* bone up on Baron Gruner's own text). At the same time, this adventure shows how well Holmes knew how to deploy his forces. He accu-

---

[1] Also untutored. He once mistook "Eumenides" for "amenities."

rately gauged Watson's limitations, but used him this once as an actor, anyway, because Holmes only needed a short time to accomplish his purposes.

6. Watson's last bow appropriately occurs during *His Last Bow* when, on the night of August 2, 1914, he accepts the role of a chauffeur. At the climax of such a dangerous assignment, Holmes only trusted his friend in a non-speaking role. (In this regard, Martha Hudson clearly had to be the superior thespian since she served "on the scene" as a British spy.)

THE EIGHTEEN[2] MAJOR PERFORMANCES OF SHERLOCK HOLMES

The first line of each entry records the role played and the place of occurrence. The technical notes list costume and makeup specifications within the Watsonian text. The remarks encapsulate some of the present author's thinking and opinions on the calibre and technique of the various portrayals.

1. A SEAMAN. *Sign of the Four* (Chapter 9).
   Notes: Rude sailor dress. Pea jacket. Coarse red scarf.
   Remarks: Ruddy coloration. Change of gait. Accent?
2. AGED MAN IN SEAFARING GARB. *Sign of the Four* (Chapter 9).
   Notes: Old pea-jacket, buttoned to throat. Bowed back, shaky knees, asthmatic; colored scarf; bushy white brows; long gray side-whiskers.
   Remarks: Convincing old age study, well described in text. A separate role, or a completion of Role #1?
3. DRUNKEN-LOOKING GROOM. *A Scandal in Bohemia.*
   Notes: Ill-kempt; side-whiskered. Face inflamed; clothes disreputable.
   Remarks: Unsteady gait and probable lack of coordination. Dirty face, hands?
4. AN AMIABLE AND SIMPLE-MINDED NON-CONFORMIST CLERGYMAN. *A Scandal in Bohemia.*
   Notes: Broad black hat, baggy trousers, white tie, sympathetic smile; general look of peering and benevolent curiosity.
   Remarks: The clothes practically make the man. A narrow stance, weight distributed towards heels. Glasses?

---

[2]Four cases cited in earlier articles on Holmes' acting are rejected: (1) The botany hunt in *Wisteria Lodge,* merely a charade, as is (2) the fishing pretext in *Shoscombe Old Place* . . . neither requiring special acting technique; (3) Holmes' dress-up as a burglar in *Milverton,* most inappropriate, since that is precisely what he is in that story; and (4) on the moor "like any other tourist" in the *Hound* . . . no acting attempt, but rather an effort to stay *offstage.*

5. A TALL, THIN OLD MAN. *The Man with the Twisted Lip.*
   Notes: Wrinkled, bent with age; doddering, loose-lipped senility.
   Remarks: A masterpiece of makeup and acting combined, although few
   eyes had to be deceived. Subtle use of shadows and highlights, lines,
   some sort of hair touchup.

6. A COMMON LOAFER. *Adventure of the Beryl Coronet.*
   Notes: Collar turned up; shiny, seedy coat; red cravat; worn boots.
   Remarks: Unshaven? Or perhaps a dark color rubbed into the beard
   grain to appear dirty.

7. MR. HARRIS, AN ACCOUNTANT. *The Stock-Broker's Clerk.*
   Remarks: A simple role assumption, requiring no technical preparation
   and little acting virtuosity (even Watson was permitted to participate).

8. A REGISTRATION AGENT. *The Crooked Man.*
   Remarks: Again a simple role assumption, requiring no technical preparation and little acting virtuosity.

9. A VENERABLE ITALIAN PRIEST. *The Final Problem.*
   Notes: Decrepit; uses broken English; wrinkled; nose hangs down near
   chin; protruding lower lip; dull eyes; drooping figure; black cassock,
   hat.
   Remarks: Brilliant performance (no less would do!) starting with the
   psychological anonymity of the cloth; adding liner, shadows and
   highlights, probably nose putty; culminating with facial distortion and
   change of internal rhythm, stance . . . every acting device imaginable.

10. STRANGE OLD BOOK COLLECTOR. *Adventure of the Empty
    House.*
    Notes: Elderly, deformed; curved back; white side-whiskers; wizened
    face.
    Remarks: Holmes' most excruciating performance (self-confessed)—
    change of gait; leading center probably the forehead; side-whiskers
    probably grown and colored, rather than built.

11. SIGERSON. *Adventure of the Empty House.*
    Remarks: Sherlock's alias while abroad. (But see Chapter Five.)

12. CAPTAIN BASIL. *Adventure of Black Peter.*
    Remarks: One of the detective's apparently many aliases. Nautical garb,
    though absent in tale, is inferable?

13. ESCOTT, A PLUMBER. *Adventure of Charles Augustus Milverton.*
    Notes: Rakish young workman; goatee beard and a swagger.
    Remarks: Clothing and a ruder manner of speech important; the inci-
    dental wooing took real acting technique (cf. Nero Wolfe necking in
    "In the Best Families"; like father, like son?) The goatee is suspect.

14. APPROACHING DISSOLUTION (a "feigning", but so elaborate as
    to rank it with his most memorable performances). *Adventure of the Dying
    Detective.*

Notes: Gaunt, wasted face; eyes shining as if feverish; cheeks flushed; dark crusts on lips.

Remarks: A technical triumph that any actor would be proud of—an intensive study of "the part" coupled with a resourceful employment of unfamiliar makeup materials (relics, perhaps, of a less sophisticated era of makeup, or else evidence of an early dating of the adventure).

15. FRENCH OUVRIER. *Disappearance of Lady Frances Carfax.*

Notes: Unshaven; blue blouse; carries cudgel.

Remarks: Simple performance, utilizing workman's clothes, temporary abstinence from shaving.

16. ALTAMONT. *His Last Bow.*

Notes: Irish-American character, with taste for Yankee dialect. Clear-cut features; small goatee, like caricature of Uncle Sam.

Remarks: Simply his greatest performance, not because of the appearance (a mere matter of sprouting a goatee) or the manner of speech, but for the prolonged role portrayal, which probably could not be relaxed much—if at all—during the whole two years the operation covered.

17. A WORKMAN LOOKING FOR A JOB (also referred to as AN OLD SPORTING MAN). *Adventure of the Mazarin Stone.*

Remarks: An off-stage performance with no particulars. But we may assume the reliable old clothes and stubbly-face (or dirty-face) effect.

18. AN OLD WOMAN. *Adventure of the Mazarin Stone.*

Notes: A very baggy parasol carried as part of the ensemble.

Remarks: Another off-stage performance, but with one detail reported: Sherlock's dropping of the parasol and its retrieval by Count Sylvius. An alteration of carriage is necessary here (no theories that Sherlock studied Kabuki?). Otherwise, clothes make the woman.

REMARKS ON THEATRICAL QUOTATIONS,
PARAPHRASALS, ALLUSIONS AND REFERENCES
UTTERED BY SHERLOCK HOLMES

The Canon abounds with all sorts of Holmesian literary allusions, quotes and paraphrasals, including a wide range of authors from the Bible and Hafiz through Carlyle, Darwin and Rochefoucauld, to name but a few.

Among these references are several derived from dramatic literature and the language of the theatre, almost all of which are directly uttered by the Master himself.

While the references to theatricalism are only of passing interest,[3] those quotations and paraphrases of dramatic literature are of keen importance to the student of Sherlockian acting technique. Assuming (along with Baring-Gould) that Holmes must have acted professionally in his youth, the natural desire is to want to learn which roles he took, which plays he preferred, etc.

Those plays which an actor recalls well enough to quote or allude to (even subconsciously) tend to be (a) ones in which he excelled, or thought he excelled, or (b) ones with a part or parts he would like to play. In Sherlock Holmes' case, of course, this is no infallible guide, since the great detective reached an emotional maturity and mental loftiness which might well account for a familiarity with less popular theatrical compositions.

Most of Holmes' references to dramatic literature are Shakespearean, which supports the Baring-Gould hypothesis that Sherlock toured with a repertory company devoted to the Bard.

Four non-Shakespearean references are also made (three for certain; the fourth is open to some dispute). One is a direct quote from Goethe's *Faust*, Part One; it has been documented by other Canonical students, and it occurs in Chapter 6 of *The Sign of the Four*.

Two paraphrasals are from Roman drama. Considering Holmes' familiarity with antique authors, it is likely he was well acquainted with these sources on a reading basis, if not as an actor. In *A Study in Scarlet*, he remarks, "There is nothing new under the sun," (in Chapter 3) which is generally attributed to those words in Ecclesiastes I, 9. But perhaps he also knew the prologue to Terence's *Eunuchus:* "In fine, nothing is said now that has not been said before."

And in *The Adventure of the Empty House*, the Master consoles Watson with, "Work is the best antidote to sorrow," a close paraphrase of Plautus' "Patience is the best antidote for every trouble." (*Rudens*, Act II, Scene 5).

There is one more non-Shakespearean reference. In *The Adventure of the Three Gables*, Holmes warns, "You can't play with edged tools forever without cutting those dainty hands." Compare "There is no jesting with edge tools" (Beaumont & Fletcher, *The Little French Lawyer*, Act I, Scene 2) and "It is no jesting with edge tools" (*The True Tragedy of Richard III*, 1594).

As for the Shakespearean references, they are derived from *All's Well That Ends Well*, *Antony and Cleopatra*, *Hamlet*, possibly *Henry IV*, Part One, *Henry V*, *Henry VI*, Part Two, *Much Ado About Nothing*, *Romeo and Juliet* (arguable), and *Twelfth Night*. Baring-Gould states that the latter must have been Sherlock's favorite play, since it is the only one he quotes on two sepa-

---

[3]Such expressions as "the plot thickens" (*A Study in Scarlet*) or "disappear from the scene" (*Dying Detective*) prove little, since they are in the speech of any amateur theatregoer.

rate occasions. This is erroneous, since he quotes either *Henry IV* or *Henry V* (probably the latter) at least twice, and if the latter, then three times. There is also a case to be made for *Hamlet,* which may have been alluded to three times as well.[4]

A complete listing of Shakespearean references and/or allusions made by Sherlock Holmes follows. The play title, Shakespeare's original line, and its place of occurrence are followed by Holmes' version of the line.

HAMLET. "What a piece of work is a man!" (and cf. second choral interlude of Sophocles' *Antigone*) Act II, Scene 2.

HOLMES: "A strange enigma is man!" *The Sign of the Four* (Chapter 10).

HAMLET. "How weary, stale, flat, and unprofitable,/Seem to me all the uses of this world!" Act I, Scene 2.

HOLMES: ". . . it would make all fiction with its conventionalities and foreseen conclusions most stale and unprofitable." *A Case of Identity*.

HAMLET. "What's Hecuba to him or he to Hecuba,/That he should weep for her?" Act II, Scene 2.

HOLMES: "Who is Cadogan West, and what is he to Mycroft?" *Bruce-Partington Plans*.

TWELFTH NIGHT. "Journeys end in lovers meeting". Song, Act II, Scene 3.

HOLMES: "Journeys end in lovers' meetings." *Empty House*. And "Journeys end with lovers' meetings." *Red Circle*.

HENRY V. " 'a babbled of green fields." (Probably the best scholarly rendering of a difficult line.) Act II, Scene 2.

HOLMES: ". . . and the landlady babbled of green peas." *Three Students*.

HENRY V. "The game's afoot." Act III, Scene 1. Or HENRY IV, Part 1. "Before the game is afoot thou still let'st slip." Act I, Scene 3.

HOLMES: "Come, Watson, come! The game is afoot." *Abbey Grange*. (Also: a Watsonian reference to this line occurs in *Wisteria Lodge*.)

ALL'S WELL THAT ENDS WELL. Title.

HOLMES: "All is well that ends well." *Sign of the Four* (Chapter 11).

ROMEO AND JULIET. "These violent delights have violent ends." Act II, Scene 6.

HOLMES: "Violence does, in truth, recoil upon the violent . . ." *Speckled Band.*

---

[4]Perhaps *Twelfth Night* was Watson's favorite play. If he saw fit to put it in Sherlock's mouth twice, perhaps it is because the old song, "O Mistress Mine," held some sentimental meaning for him. It is, indeed, a poignant bit of poesy. Another consideration: if Watson authored the second part of *The Valley of Fear*, it should be noted that another phrase from *Twelfth Night* slips in there: "as one who did not wish to have greatness thrust upon him" (Chapter 3)—an echo of Malvolio's famous letter. (ACT II, Scene 5)

ANTONY AND CLEOPATRA. "Age cannot wither her, nor custom stale/Her
   infinite variety." Act II, Scene 2.
HOLMES: "I trust that age doth not wither nor custom stale my infinite vari-
   ety." *Empty House.*
HENRY VI. PART 2. "Thrice is he arm'd that hath his quarrel just." Act III,
   Scene 2.
HOLMES: "Thrice is he armed who hath his quarrel just." *Lady Frances Carfax.*
MUCH ADO ABOUT NOTHING. "O that I had been writ down an ass!" Act IV,
   Scene 2.
HOLMES: "You can write me down an ass this time, Watson." *Bruce-Parting-
   ton Plans.*

A final note: Holmes' knowledge of dramatic literature also extends to
the Miracle Plays of the Middle Ages . . . he discusses them, Watson tells us,
during the *Sign of the Four* investigation (Chapter 10).

CHAPTER THREE

The Histrionic Holmes

Those who delve into the literature of contemporaneous theatrical criticism
are often amused to discover that one particular formula seems to crop up in
varying guise from generation to generation. Its form bears the following
outline:

> Never has the stage brought forth a third murderer the likes of
> Mr. Bainsworthy's! The terrors he implies in his thundertones
> soon make the happy spectator realize he is privileged to be wit-
> nessing a new, apotheosized art of acting. Mr. Bainsworthy so
> modernizes the histrionic method that he, in truth, "holds the
> mirror up to nature"—far outstripping that declamatory false fire
> with which an earlier gaggle of Herods bludgeoned a suffering
> public . . .

Fine sentiments, these—except for their regular recurrence. If every breed of
actor constitutes a refinement over the "hammery" of its predecessors, what
must Terence have had to work with?
   But acting styles *do* change from one era to another—even though the
literature of criticism has, in most cases, been woefully inadequate to appraise
them (except, perhaps, in retrospect). At any rate, from what we are able to

reconstruct of the dramatic technique of Sherlock Holmes, it seems apposite to say the theatre of his time stood as a foil to his premonitory skill.

Before examining some of his methods of creating a role, let us briefly catalog those facilities his contemporaries-in-greasepaint probably developed in the young apprentice.

The prevalent school of emoting at the time of Holmes' introduction to repertory was founded on physical skills and their perfection. In fact, some of our older limelighters may still speak of 'the English method' of building a character, i.e., from the outside, giving attention to physical appearance and mannerisms and letting the internal pattern form itself instinctually.[1]

This so-called physical system, with its books of plates depicting Mrs. Siddons' facial expressions for showing emotion and with its turgid literature of Nineteenth Century barn-stormer melodramas to illuminate, consisted of a wide range of bodily and vocal exercises aimed at making the actor comfortable and sure of himself on stage. Several of these are evidenced by Holmes in his later years and were probably perfected in his formative days in repertory.

The power of concentration, for example, is one of the first faculties any actor must develop. The ability to stay "in character" and pay attention to what is happening on stage, even after the fiftieth performance, is basic to the professional, and Holmes shows a rare intensity of concentration several times in the Canon. (For instance: his undisturbed engrossment in Chapter Four of *A Study in Scarlet,* when he peers and probes and crawls about the room for twenty minutes despite the slightly hostile glares of Gregson and Lestrade.)

Concentration, too, is used by the actor-in-training in practicing mime—for the imaginary re-creation in space of physical reality is one of the most difficult of acting tasks, and a kind of mental "tunnel-vision" must be nurtured to improve one's capacities. Holmes continually demonstrates his excellence in this department by his skill in recalling physical details of people and objects. One such moment occurs in *A Case of Identity,* when Sherlock invites Watson to try his hand at bringing Miss Sutherland's physical accoutrements to mind.

The latter point leads into the next principal skill Holmes could be expected to study in repertory: observation. Actors of all schools generally

---

[1]None of the ensuing discussion should be construed as endorsement or condemnation of any approach to acting. The author, schooled in the external school, the early Stanislavski approach *and* the later Stanislavski "method of physical objectives" sees value in all of them and believes the truly skilled performer approaches his art eclectically, having all techniques ready to hand and using those appropriate to the specific character, depending on the time available for rehearsal.

agree there is no substitute for looking at people's faces, hands, walks, etc., so that a "morgue" of the tools of impersonation can be built up in the artist's mind. Some go so far as to clip pictures of interesting faces and other features from magazines and books and keep them in scrapbooks.

Holmes' genius at observation is, of course, everywhere chronicled, the earliest instance occurring in *Gloria Scott* and the most formal statement appearing in the Master's own article, *The Book of Life*. His attention to types of hands is amply shown in *The Sign of the Four* where he alludes to a monograph he has written on the influences of diverse trades on the shape and condition of the metacarpals. And his skill in analyzing facial types—important in the execution of character makeup—is underscored in *The Hound of the Baskervilles* when he boasts that, "My eyes have been trained to examine faces and not their trimmings. It is the first quality of a criminal investigator that he should see through a disguise."

In addition to concentration and observation, Holmes had to develop an artistic sense that could enable him to look at the character he was creating and adjust it as the variables of performance would warrant it. This skill— whether we call it "superobjective" or the "puppet/puppeteer" relationship—is also at the Master's fingertips: "It is of first importance . . . not to allow your judgment to be biased by personal qualities . . . The emotional qualities are antagonistic . . ." *(Sign of the Four)*. Rather than showing lack of feeling, this indicates a deliberate repression of personal propensities . . . so necessary to artistic shaping and revision.

What other skills can we assume for Holmes as a result of studying and practising acting? Sureness of movement, certainly, since learning to walk gracefully on stage is one of the classic physical drills for the fledgling actor. Vocal development is also to be assumed—we know Holmes possesses a keen, incisive voice, probably due to long hours spent reciting sonorous doggerel calculated to improve diction, strengthen the diaphragm and enable the performer to "project".

Baring-Gould notes Holmes' skill with languages, and this points to facility with foreign accents, another basic study of the novitiate actor.

The great detective also apparently learned facility in the area of makeup and probably developed, in his early years, that love of costuming which he carried into his bloodhound days. (Doubtless, it was at this time that he realized the particular power of the costume to transfigure the actor into a new personality without the need of additional reinforcement from makeup and histrionics.)

Holmes also must have learned such technical feats as how to break the fall so a "faint" can be duplicated without injury; how to weave about, slur the voice and unfocus the eyes so as to show apparent inebriation; and—most important in later years—how to simulate old age simply by affecting a tremor, redistributing the weight onto the heels and standing "with a narrow base"—that is, with feet close together—to project a sense of weakness, enfeeblement.

Skill in fencing has also been noted by Watson, and since that sport is vital in Elizabethan drama, we may assume Holmes either learned it at this time, or at least again indulged in it and developed further proficiency with the foil.

Now it must be noted that some of the skills cited were already natural abilities of Holmes, to greater or lesser degree, as statements in his earliest recorded cases lead one to infer.

His power of observation, in particular, as well as his ability for intense concentration, must have been the envy of many a veteran member of the company . . . not to mention Sherlock's proficiency with languages, or those unusually acute senses[2] which would enable him to project subtle nuances of experience in his theatrical work.

A certain amount of professional jealousy was inevitable . . . comparable, in fact, to that which he would encounter later as a detective. But if he had only been blessed with well-developed natural faculties, Holmes might have advanced more swiftly within his repertory company.

Unfortunately for him (though happily for us) he probably committed the one unpardonable sin in the rigid hierarchy of the fifth-rate repertory troupe: he dared to be relevantly innovative.

For instance, the example cited above from *A Case of Identity* indicates that Holmes was familiar with the form of the "object exercise" used in modern New York acting schools. In this exercise the student studies a physical object minutely for some time, then attempts to describe to the instructor the exact size, weight, look and feel of the object—down to the minutest detail. This, of course, is practically what Holmes asks Watson to do, and one can imagine how unpopular he might have been had he suggested such a problem to one of his maturer histrionic compatriots.

We may also infer that Holmes, in his characteristically thorough fashion, made something of a science of physical movement on stage. His skill with varying gaits and walks at the time of his detectival impersonations point to a studied analysis of the internal rhythms of various types and ages of people, and the way they differ. Linked with this was, very likely, a rudimentary formulation of a concept called "leading center," a term which refers to a point upon the body from which an imaginary string might pull the character along while walking.

The theory to the "leading center" conception is that people will walk in different manners depending on their backgrounds, upbringing, psychological origins; the job of the actor is to find the "center" from which the

---

[2]See *The Blanched Soldier*.

imaginary force emanates.[3] Having found it, the actor then uses it to distinguish the gait and stride of the character in a psychologically meaningful manner.

The unusual shuffling gait that we can imagine the old bookseller counterfeiting in *Empty House* or the mincing steps of the old woman in *Mazarin Stone* point to Holmes' conscious alteration of walk. And this deliberate alteration prefigures the concepts of "leading center" and internal rhythm.

And yet, these essentially superficial accomplishments pale before Sherlock's experiments in psychological technique . . . experiments which foreshadow Stanislavski and place the Master years ahead of his limelit contemporaries.

Who can fail to note the family resemblance between Holmes' careful reconstructions of details he has observed (especially, in the passage noted above in *Case of Identity*) and the emotional "recall"?

The "recall" is an exercise in which the performer attempts to relive, in his imagination, some past event. The recreation, to be valid, must be so vivid that the actor can reconstruct the exact order of events, no matter how long past, and (what is more) move through the rehearsal area as if it were the locality in question.

The important thing to note is that most "recalls" begin by reconstruction of physical detail, sometimes one sense at a time . . . which brings to mind Holmes' remarkable faculty for observing and remembering articles of dress, condition of hands, and so on. But the most strikingly advanced acting method of Sherlock Holmes is his employment of improvisatory identification in his solution of (apparently) a great number of cases. It is a technique which he himself recommends several times in the Canon, and it clearly points to the manner in which he must have approached his more difficult impersonations.

The earliest, and most complete reference occurs in *The Musgrave Ritual:* "You know my methods in such cases, Watson. I put myself in the man's place, and, having first gauged his intelligence, I try to imagine how I should myself have proceeded under the same circumstances. In this case the matter was simplified by Brunton's intelligence being quite first-rate, so that it was unnecessary to make any allowance for the personal equation . . ."

Another example crops up in *Sign of the Four:* "I then put myself in the

---

[3]Thus, an introspective, cerebral individual might "lead" with the forehead; a prostitute may be impelled from the hips; an athlete, from the center of the chest (the most pleasing "center" for normal walking). In *Marat/Sade,* one member of the Royal Shakespeare Company seemed to use a shifting "center"—the shoulder, then the head, the chest, etc.— indicating lack of coordination and internal turmoil, as well as mental disorder.

place of Small and looked at it as a man of his capacity would . . . I wondered what I should do myself if I were in his shoes."

In *Dying Detective,* Holmes adds a dimension to the technique by assuring Culverton Smith that "The best way of successfully acting a part is to be it . . . I give you my word that for three days I have tasted neither food nor drink . . ."

And, in *The Retired Colourman,* the great detective extends himself far enough to recommend his method: "You'll get results, Inspector, by always putting yourself in the other fellow's place, and thinking what you would do yourself. It takes some imagination, but it pays."

Now the thoughtful reader may, at this juncture, point out that these examples merely point to logical police procedure, not acting styles. However, this form of improvisatory identification is so basic to the latter-day actor, it seems impossible not to allow that Holmes used a similar formula in his creation of artificial characters. In such wise, he would not have stopped with the thought processes of the individual to be counterfeited, but would have added the complete spectrum of physio-psychological impersonation.

However, this dichotomy between acting technique and detectival process is well noted, and a moment should be taken to consider the ways in which Sherlock's dramatic proclivities manifested themselves in quotidian routine.

The most important single phenomenon is that which the author chooses to label the Holmesian "dramatic sense," examples of which abound so frequently as to almost warrant a book in itself—everything from retrieved articles turning up in crockery and coats down to the mere (convenient) withholding of information to render denouements more exciting. Holmes himself sums up this trait (or fault, if you will) in *Valley of Fear:* "Watson insists that I am the dramatist in real life . . . *Some touch of the artist wells up within me, and calls insistently for a well-staged performance.* Surely our profession . . . would be a drab and sordid one if we did not sometimes set the scene so as to glorify our results. The blunt accusation, the brutal tap upon the shoulder—what can one make of such a 'denouement'?"

The emphasis, of course, is mine, yet it should be apparent that this passage is probably the most telling one in the entire Canon concerning the Master's dramaturgic disposition.

This tendency to dramatize is closely linked with Holmes' love of work for its own rewards—art for art's sake, a maxim that necessarily governs most actors (inasmuch as tangible rewards are so seldom). Here again, examples are abundant, and one must represent the many: "As to reward, my profession is its own reward; but you are at liberty to defray whatever expenses I may be put to, at the time which suits you best." *(Speckled Band.)*

A more practical use for the Holmesian dramatic sense is indicated by the detective in *The Blanched Soldier:* "It is my habit to sit with my back to the window and to place my visitors in the opposite chair, where the light falls full upon them.[4] Mr. James M. Dodd seemed somewhat at a loss how to begin the interview. I did not attempt to help him, for his silence gave me more time for observation. I have found it wise to impress clients with a sense of power, and so I gave him some of my conclusions." Note the dramatic pause, followed by the oracular revelations; it is not improbable that Holmes could also have made a more than capable director, so instinctive is his sense of timing.

Two other left-overs from his acting days are noteworthy in Holmes' work habits as a consulting detective: his need, on occasion, to "rehearse" in private (" 'It would be as well if you could make it convenient not to return before evening . . .' I knew that seclusion and solitude were very necessary for my friend in those hours of intense mental concentration . . ."),[5] and his crucial need to keep himself at the level an actor, or other performer would call "concert pitch". (". . . here at last there was a fitting object for those remarkable powers which, like all special gifts, become irksome to their owner when they are not in use. That razor brain blunted and rusted with inaction.")[6]

*L*et us now turn our attention to those eighteen "performances" recorded by Watson in the Sacred Writings. What can we tell about them in light of what has already been observed? And which demanded the most technique from the great detective? (That is, from the sole standpoint of acting. In general, the more difficult characterizations also involved more complicated makeups—but this issue will be delayed until the ensuing chapter.)

The usual mode of criticism is to analyze technical proficiency as it is displayed during performance, but there is an important extra factor to consider in reviewing Holmes' histrionic accomplishments: a factor that does not apply to the work of the ordinary thespian. For the latter performer practices his art before spectators fully aware that they are witnessing an artificiality. Not so with the spy or the detective.

Whenever Sherlock dons disguise, it is to escape notice in his own person and, in some cases, to convince some party or parties that he is, *in fact*, the person he pretends to be.

Thus, a meaningful evaluation of the Master's impersonatory forays must reflect the degree of risk he is incurring.

In general, we may say that Holmes acts before three types of specta-

---

[4]Like a spotlight?
[5]From *The Hound of the Baskervilles*.
[6]From *The Valley of Fear*.

tors: those not at all looking to be fooled; those not expecting an impersonation, but capable of becoming aware of Sherlock incognito;—and, most dangerous, those fully anticipating the use of disguise.

In the first category may be included the two (or is it one?) seamen in
Sign of the Four, the accountant in *Stock-Broker's Clerk,* the registration agent
in *The Crooked Man,* Captain Basil (a borderline case between this and the
second classification) in *Black Peter,* and the workman in *Disappearance of Lady
Frances Carfax.*

Also includable under this heading would be the diaphonous Sigerson,
except that the author cannot bring himself to accept this personage as anything but apocryphal. The very name seems suspect, for Holmes allegedly
was traveling in lands where he might safely pass unidentified in his own
person, and, to quote the Master in another context *(A Study in Scarlet):*
"There was no reason to suppose that he was going under an assumed name.
Why should he change his name in a country where no one knew his original
one?"

The impersonations of Mr. Harris, the accountant; and that of the registration agent both were "performed" for persons very unlikely to note anything amiss in the false Sherlock. Since he would be dealing with strangers,
Holmes knew there was no need whatever for physical disguise or changes in
personality. Only two things need be done: a little advance "boning up" in
the professions he was assuming, just in case some basic question were asked
of him; and selection of an alias, since Watson's accounts of his activities were
already bringing him a degree of renown.

The French *ouvrier* in the Carfax case required little more in the way of
disguise, so Holmes brought off the job with a change of clothes, and by
letting his beard grow. But since he was posing as a laborer, it seems probable
that he also altered his stride to a more heavy, plodding tread (probably dis-
tributing his weight at the center of the foot; i.e., walking flatfooted to give a
sense of ponderousness, perhaps even clumsiness). His familiarity with the
French language (a maternal heritage, no doubt) here stood him in good
stead.

Captain Basil is a bit problematic. We are told Holmes used this alias in
other cases, but during the *Black Peter* affair, one might argue that Patrick
Cairns could have sensed something amiss with the Master's ultimate charade. Yet, even granting the point, one must hair-split and stress that the
harpooner would only have tripped to the deception, not to Holmes' actual
identity.

So, the case remains within the border of our first classification, for
Holmes still had but to convince a stranger that he (Holmes) was someone
else.

While specific details on Captain Basil's costuming and makeup are not
supplied in Watson's text, we may reasonably assume that the detective af-

fected some sort of nautical manner in speech, perhaps a "rolling" gait, as well as proper costume and makeup.

There is great probability to the theory that the first seaman described in *Sign of the Four* is merely a way-station towards construction of the elderly naval man who appears later in the same chapter. This old tar is a far more elaborate effort of Holmes' than Captain Basil, yet there seems to be no urgent reason in the text for the sleuth to have adopted such a demanding disguise. It almost appears to be a mere Holmesian indulgence—a whimsical display of dramatic pyrotechnics for the sole purpose of dazzling his colleagues. If so, it is successful; Watson and Athelney Jones are completely taken in by it.

And no wonder! The student of Sherlockian acting must afford this portrayal a place of honor in the roster of the Master's performances. The various techniques he employs are masterfully executed: "A heavy step was heard ascending the stair, with a great wheezing and rattling as from a man who was sorely put to it for breath . . . His back was bowed, his knees were shaky, and his breathing was painfully asthmatic." All these details show great attention to internal rhythm, distribution of weight in walking and, of course, labored respiration. But the most masterful stroke is the added fillip Holmes gives to his entrance: as he mounts the stairs, "Once or twice he stopped, as though the climb were too much for him . . ."

It appears that the Master here anticipated yet another Stanislavskian discovery: the off-stage beat—the mental preparation by the actor of where he has been, where he is going, what his physio-mental-psychological state is just prior to entrance. Something of a complement to the golfer's "follow-through," the off-stage beat enables the actor to enter "in character."

This is precisely what Holmes does, and the extra color contributed by the pauses on the stairway is of brilliant hue. Surely, Watson and Jones are convinced long before the seaman appears!

Turning to the second type of impersonation—in which the deceived is capable of penetrating Holmes' disguise—we would list the two dissimulations in *Scandal in Bohemia;* the tall, thin man in *Twisted Lip;* the common loafer in *Beryl Coronet;* the workman and the old woman in *Mazarin Stone* and Escott, the plumber who appears in *Charles Augustus Milverton.*

There is little to be said about the loafer searching for the coronet piece: Holmes disguises himself in disreputable clothing and alters his appearance and, probably, speech to "take in" a servant or two; the only danger lies in being spotted by a family member, which is easily avoided by the masquerade.

A similar problem is met in the Escott characterization; the servant wench Holmes must impose upon is hardly a threat, but the danger always looms that Milverton himself might spy the detective. So Holmes affects a swaggering gait, disguises himself (but more of that in the next chapter) and surely adopts a ruder mode of speech, together with lower-class idiom and thought patterns. Here, too, he must have done some quick brush-up research on the plumbing profession, just in case a sticky question was asked.

We do not know precisely how much danger Holmes is in of being recognized in *Twisted Lip,* but it must be fairly acute to cause him to adopt such a difficult characterization. Here we have another study in old age, with its palsied joints, trembling fingers, bent (and painful) posture. In addition, we are told the old man he portrays is in doddering, loose-lipped senility. So we can infer general waggling and shaking of the head, a pendulous lower lip, and perhaps disjointed mumblings . . . all doubly difficult when we remember that the Master must also concentrate on the real business of his visit to the opium den!

The risk run in the Irene Adler affair is poignantly keen, and it is fine evidence of the sleuth's talents that he so ably brings it off. Holmes might feel he failed in this venture, but it is greatly to his credit that he could completely hoodwink a professional performer (in the guise of the drunken-seeming groom) and then turn right around and successfully reintroduce himself in a completely different character (that of the amiable, simple-minded non-conformist clergyman).

The groom took little acting skill, merely a slightly unsteady gait—if the seeming drunkenness were to be stressed, which seems doubtful. But the selection of the clergyman as the successive role was an excellent choice of Holmes'. Irene was recently married, and who more amiable and sympathetic to her sight than a man of the cloth? Too, what individual would appear least like the rather disreputable individual the incipient Nortons hauled in off the street?

Much of the effectiveness of a clerical disguise must rest on that anonymity and tacit role-acceptance which any uniform bestows upon the deceiver. In addition, we are told that Holmes affects a somewhat vacuous smile and a kind of peering stare. (The latter is no small matter; it is through the eyes, Cyrano tells us, that our souls are mirrored, and anyone who saw Alec Guinness portray Dylan Thomas may remember how the "aliveness" of the actor's eyes alone was capable of dominating a stage full of milling supporting players.) In keeping with the meekness of this role, we can also assume Sherlock stood narrow-based (feet close together) with his weight on his heels—a technical stage trick for giving the impression of weakness.

The greatest risks that Holmes incurred in this second class of impersonations took place in the *Mazarin Stone* investigation. Indeed, one is tempted to advance the two roles cited—an old woman, and a workman looking for a job—to the third category . . . except for the fact that Holmes' adversary, Count Sylvius, is not astute enough to penetrate either costume to the inner man, even though he is well aware that the "two" have been following him.

Now the workman out of a job (or "an old sporting man," as the Count describes him), must have shared a strong resemblance to the common loafer in *Beryl Coronet,* but the old woman must have been extremely difficult and painful for Holmes to execute effectively, and it is likely he might have avoided it if Sylvius weren't such a dangerous opponent. Perhaps two days as the workman seemed too chancy to Sherlock, not so much for the possibility of having his illusion penetrated, but rather because of the likelihood of some frontal attack. So he dressed in woman's garb, added old age makeup, then went through the torturous business of compounding a mincing feminine walk with the hesitation of old age and the need to take several inches off his height (more about this later).

This "old woman" must be ranked with the aged seaman and the tall, thin old man as pinnacles of Holmesian dramatics—as must the four remaining major impersonations (which also comprise the third variety of performance the Master encountered).

The full spectrum of histrionic skills in the Master's command had to be employed in this final quartet of characters: the venerable Italian priest in *The Final Problem;* the strange old book collector in *Adventure of the Empty House;* the elaborate feigning in *The Dying Detective* and—of course—Sherlock's "last bow," Altamont.

In each of these cases, the antagonists to be deceived were of such stature that the great sleuth was taxed to employ every acting trick possible in deceiving them. Total psychological immersion in character was paramount in importance ("The best way of successfully acting a part is to be it."), as well as artistic selection of technical methods to build up impressions of veracity.

Of course, the feigned disease in *Dying Detective* is done in Holmes' own character, yet it must surely be included in our third category of criticism: in which those to be fooled were fully expecting the detective to attempt some variety of subterfuge. In this memorable case, the test is especially hard, since the villain is completely familiar with the symptoms of the ailment Holmes counterfeits.

Much of the genius of this impersonation is due to skillful makeup, but we cannot ignore the increasing debility the detective affects, due in part, no doubt, to his avoiding sustenance for days. Too, the wandering mind adds to the effectiveness of the performance, meretricious though Holmes' babblings may appear to any actor attempting an "in depth" portrayal of a diseased mind. (But the latter trick is used only for Watson's benefit, and may be excused.) The real power of this performance lies in the off-stage beat Holmes prepares: a full-fledged improvisation involving days of personal psychological conditioning, as well as the masterful employment, against their knowledge, of Mrs. Hudson and Watson as part of the *mise en scène.*

Not quite so severe a test is put to Holmes in the case of the Italian priest or the aged bookseller, except insofar as Moriarty and Moran, respectively, are formidable opponents who fully expect Sherlock to assume disguise.

The character of the priest is a desperate event in the Master's career, and he combines acting, costume and makeup to great effect: the anonymity of the cloth; alteration of internal rhythm to indicate the slower tempo of advanced age; a change in gait, (probably with leading center emanating from the top of the lowered head and the knees); again, a protruding lip (so specified in the text); adoption of the Italian tongue for further camouflage; squinting of the eyes to give a leaden, dull-eyed effect (in conjunction with the makeup). It is likely that Holmes also redistributed his weight to the heels for a more shuffling walk, and may have reinforced the general dullness of the characterization (not meant pejoratively) by giving the appearance of stoutness.[7]

The bookseller of the *Empty House* foray is in considerable contrast to the former role. Here we have crooked, angular old age, which, considering Holmes' stature, might appear at first to be simpler to execute than venerable corpulence. Not so; this portrayal must be counted as Holmes' most excruciating one, in terms of physical discomfort—the more so since he had to keep it up for protracted periods of time.

It is far easier to walk in the position needed to mimic stoutness, due to the even weight distribution. The bookseller, on the other hand, is deformed, with a curved back that necessitates Holmes' taking off several inches of his six-foot height for hours at a time. In this case, the legs would have to be foreshortened by bending at the knees and affecting a shuffling gait with leading center from the forehead. Watson tells us that Holmes wore the seedy frockcoat of a book merchant. The garment probably was tailored with generous "bag" at the knees to minimize the bend. To the other techniques of old age portrayal we may also assume affectation of myopia, since the character Holmes plays appears to be a voracious reader—as well as seller—of books. (This would add further physical discomfort to the role; the way to imitate near-sightedness is to peer with a deliberate unfocusing of the eyes.)

*I*t is paradoxical that Sherlock Holmes' greatest performance in the Canon should also be his simplest, so far as external technique is concerned. For the

---

[7]Nowadays, actors tend to adopt prosthetic devices for such an effect, but a veteran player would probably walk on his heels on a rather wide base (feet far apart), pull the arms back so as to foreshorten them, droop the chin on the breast to create fat folds, then protrude the stomach (easier to do for a diaphragm-breather, such as trained actors generally are), simultaneously hollowing the back. The latter telltale is covered by the drape of whatever material is worn. A cassock would be ideal for the purpose.

double agent Altamont only requires the growth of a beard and the affectation of a "Yankee" mode of speech.

The reason it is such a great performance is the extended psychological deception it entails, not just of Von Bork and others of the German intelligence system (not to mention the constabulary and underworld of Chicago, Buffalo and Skibbareen), but of Holmes himself. The best way to act a role, the Master has told us, is to be it, and here he must fool himself and others for two solid years!

The psychological strain involved here cannot be too boldly underscored; the line between reality and fantasy is *de facto* blurred by the improvisational form.[8] And with the mounting risk of protracted undercover work, the human tendency is to want to relax occasionally from the play-acting . . .

What does Holmes say on the subject? In speaking of Hollis (whom Von Bork characterizes as mad), Holmes remarks:

> "Well, he went a bit woozy towards the end. It's enough to make a man bug-house when he has to play a part from morning to night with a hundred guys all ready to set the coppers wise to him."

Now, the stuff of improvisation is often derived from the actor's internal life, and here it appears to be a veiled echo of the hidden stresses which Holmes must master to successfully create the role of Altamont afresh each day of the long portrayal.

That he could never relax—and did not—is what makes his final bow so worthy of critical acclaim.

CHAPTER FOUR

Technical Notes on the Mechanics of Makeup with Some Observations on the Maintenance of Dressing Rooms

What song the Syrens sang or what name Achilles assumed when he hid himself among women—or what tools Sherlock employed in fashioning disguises—although puzzling questions, are not beyond *all* conjecture . . .

---

[8]A theme well-developed in much contemporary espionage fiction. See especially, Thomas Hinde's terrifying *The Day the Call Came.*

Our rude authorial insertion is no mere conceit—the theatrical scholar who attempts to reconstruct the Master's more elaborate characterizations finds himself *vis à vis* with one of the great unsolved mysteries of the Canon. Surprisingly enough, it is an area almost unexplored in Holmesian scholarship.

There are two reasons for the existence of the technical puzzle: (a) Holmes himself gives us few glimpses into his disguise tricks of the trade, and (b) the art of theatrical makeup, although it was undergoing profound changes in the Nineteenth Century, is poorly documented.

The first consideration is not insurmountable, although the student eagerly awaits the publication of *The Whole Art of Detection* for the glimpses it will undoubtedly contain of Sherlock's makeup technique. And it is fervently hoped that one of the chapters of that long-delayed volume will be entitled "On Malingering."

The historical consideration is of greater pith, yet even here there is ample room for some sound speculation.

First of all, though, it may be wise to note those particulars of which we *can* be certain: dressing-room facilities and available costumery.

Two textual remarks show us that Holmes maintained at least six "disguise parlors" in various parts of London. In *Scandal in Bohemia* Sherlock returns in the role of a drunken-looking groom and retires to his bedroom before rejoining Watson in mufti. Inference: he maintained a dressing-room off the bedroom. It could, of course, have been in the bedroom itself, but this might have proved inordinately messy even for someone as leisurely as Holmes. A character actor's makeup table is a veritable catch-all of grease, powder and mucilage. More likely, he would have had a separate chamber, or at least a partitioned alcove, for his paraphernalia.

In *Black Peter,* Watson observes that his friend "had at least five small refuges in different parts of London, in which he was able to change his personality."

Now each of these dressing-rooms would have a few indispensables: a chest-high makeup table (probably some four feet wide by a foot deep, to keep all materials within arm's reach); a stool or chair; a mirror—contemporary sources recommend sixteen by twelve—on the wall behind the table; ample illumination, and one or two racks for hanging costumes.

The kinds of costumery kept in various parts of town is not easy to answer, but it is probable that some duplication of clothing and uniforms was deliberately instituted by Sherlock. For instance, when he embarks on his first recorded disguise in *Sign of the Four,* Sherlock affects to be a seaman of his own age and physique. When he returns at the close of the day, he has grown aged and feeble, and his nautical garb has been subtly altered.

More than likely, the Master subscribed to a modified kind of "basics-and-separates" costume philosophy. This theatrical method consists of dressing the actor in a *basic* clothing ensemble, such as leotards, black shirt-and-tights, or perhaps nondescript shirt and pants . . . and then adding *separates* such as capes, caps, jackets, sashes, pantaloons, etc., etc. Holmes probably had several varieties of jackets, vests, trousers, and accessories, and varied the effect by varying the match.

In addition, certain complete-and-correct uniforms had to be part of the Holmesian wardrobe . . . priestly garb; military uniforms, perhaps; certainly correct nautical gear. And on at least one occasion, Sherlock donned petticoats and dress . . . perhaps a wardrobe addition suggested by Irene Adler's changes of sex.[1]

Whether Sherlock maintained these several "quick-change establishments" for the bulk of his detectival career, or whether they are a latter-day addition, is open to speculation.

Despite Baring-Gould's dating of *Black Peter* as taking place in 1895— six years earlier than his dating of *The Priory School*—it cannot be forgotten that the order of *The Return of Sherlock Holmes* puts *Black Peter* directly after the latter tale.

This means that, scarcely has the reader finished learning about Holmes' pocketing of ducal monies in *The Priory School,* than he is hearing Watson relate how the detective keeps at least five refuges around London! Cause-and-effect, perhaps???

There is one objection to this theory: the already-cited scene from *Sign of Four* in which Sherlock leaves the house in one makeup, only to return in a much-altered guise. Since this novel is commonly agreed to take place early in the detective's career (1888, according to Baring-Gould), it seems probable that Holmes had *at least one refuge* that early, equipped with ample costuming and makeup materials.

While the author finds it hard to imagine Holmes allowing anyone else to tamper with his disguises (a thing many character actors tend to rebel against), it should be noted that he *might* have gone to a professional makeup parlor at the time of *The Sign of the Four.* (Perhaps he merely rented space at one?) One C. H. Fox, a London wig-maker of the period,[2] advertised the following in *The Art of Making Up,* a pamphlet he published for one shilling a copy in 189?:

---

[1] For details on textually-specific costumery, consult chapter two.

[2] Situated at 27 Wellington Street, Strand, WC.

DISGUISES FOR DETECTIVE BUSINESS

Persons wishing to be disguised can be made up so that their most intimate friends and relatives would not know them.

For this service, Fox charged 10s. 6d., which included the cost of makeup materials used. He also gave advice on the proper accompanying costume for no extra charge. (Who knows? Perhaps Sherlock moonlighted in his more impecunious days, giving lessons at Fox' for dressing-room and makeup privileges?)

Neither technique nor materials of making up differs appreciably today from the last years of the Nineteenth Century. To be sure, today's thespian has a few more miracle substances available which Sherlock would have revelled in . . . especially, liquid latex, which would have been of inestimable aid to him in old age disguises. But there are more similarities than differences.

However, a little earlier in the Nineteenth Century, there were indeed profound differences in available makeup substances, for grease paint is a comparative latecomer on the theatrical scene.

The problem is that existing makeup histories fail to pinpoint the advent of grease paint, and because of this, it is difficult to analyze the contents of the Holmesian makeup box.

Yet the problem is far from unsolvable.

The history of theatrical makeup, to begin with, is a progress upward from crude substances to materials of greater refinement. The ancient Roman players are said to have stained their faces with dyes made from certain kinds of leaves. Later, a few simple dry substances were relied upon for the most necessary hues—red, white and black—that a strolling player might desire. A little carmine, some burnt paper, and a bit of chalk provided the means.

The invention of grease paint revolutionized the art of makeup. According to some sources, a C. Herbert, of Berlin, is credited with first making these convenient sticks of coloring pigment; others attribute the discovery to a German character actor, Carl Baudius.

But the date of invention and, more crucial, of general usage, stands in doubt. Maurice Hageman, in a text entitled *Hageman's Make-Up Book* (The Dramatic Publishing Co., Chicago, 1898), states that dry materials and powders preceded the use of grease paint, but does not note the date of discovery.

However, Hageman *does* say this: "Stage lighting has been greatly modified and a makeup that was sufficient five years ago would leave the face expressionless today." This would seem to place the commercial availability of grease paint somewhere between 1893 and 1898, a supposition apparently borne out by a statement in the Encyclopaedia Britannica that the introduction of electric lighting in theatres necessitated the improvement of makeup. By 1890, says the encyclopedia, this demand for stage makeup warranted the commercial-scale manufacture of grease paint.

If we go by these sources, Sherlock Holmes would have had to rely on makeup materials for many of his roles that were hardly subtle enough for close work. Of the eighteen key impersonations recorded in the Canon, only one occurs in the year 1890 (Baring-Gould reckoning), while a mere four take place after that year.

But the author is of the opinion that the introduction of grease paint came several years earlier than either the encyclopedia or Hageman would have us believe.

This view is based on two facts. First, if the installation of electricity in theatre buildings hastened the marketing of grease paint, it should be remembered that Richard D'Oyly Carte opened the then-brand-new Savoy Theatre in the Strand—with full electrical facilities—way back in October of 1881. Hageman's half-decade estimate would then put the introduction of grease paint into commercial channels somewhere about 1886, two years earlier than Sherlock's first recorded acting-on-a-case.

The second fact turned up after searching fruitlessly for several weeks for a contemporary makeup text that predated 1881, the year the Savoy lit up *Patience*. Such a text was finally found . . . the only one listed in the New York Public Library card catalog as having been published prior to the 1890's. Its quaint title page has a charm which warrants partial inclusion:

HOW TO "MAKE-UP"

A Practical Guide
to the
Art of "Making-Up,"
For Amateurs, & c.

Shewing, by a series of *Novel Illustrations,*
the manner in which the face may be "Made-Up"
to represent the different stages of life,
Vis.: Youth, Manhood, Maturity, Old Age, etc.
by
"Haresfoot and Rouge."

This booklet, which sold for two shillings, was printed by the venerable theatrical firm of Samuel French, and bears a copyright of *1877* . . . four years before the commercial theatrical use of electricity.

Most of it treats of the art of makeup in the older manner: dry powders for pigmentation (including prepared fuller's earth, possibly mined within ten miles of Reading?); Crayons d'Italie, specially-prepared pencils for drawing old-age veins; Indian Ink for drawing clown's brows, etc.

But the last chapter of *How to "Make-Up"* is entitled "Grease Paints" and begins thus: "By the introduction of grease paints, the art of making up has been very much simplified, and rendered more effective, compared with the old method. These paints impart a clearer and more lifelike appearance to the skin, the lights and shades in 'making-up' for old men and character parts being more easily graduated.

"A further important advantage is, that being of a greasy nature, they are to a great extent, impervious to perspiration. This is, in itself, sufficient to recommend their use, *especially for any very arduous character* (italics mine), as it enables the actor to go through his part without fear of his make-up being affected by his exertions . . ."

Following this descriptive chapter, the French company touts a line of eleven shades of grease paint for commercial sale, price 15¢ each stick.

Again adopting the dating in *The Annotated Sherlock Holmes,* we see one of the Master's earliest cases, *The Musgrave Ritual,* set in the year 1879, at least two years after improved makeup was apparently on the market. (And if Sherlock had spent some time before that as a touring actor, he must have been aware of the condition of the makeup industry and how it was changing). At any rate, both the French booklet and the introduction of electricity precede the year 1888 when a certain seaman stalked up the stairs.

A reconstruction of the Holmesian makeup kit(s) and how the great detective used his supplies is now possible. The material, its use(s), and its cost (prices as of 1898, Hageman) are listed.

Probable Contents of Holmes' Kit

Makeup kit—Storage of materials—$2.50

Assorted grease paints—Basic coloration—$1.35 for nine colors

Blending powders to match grease paints—Setting grease paints and preventing sweat from "running" it—$3.15 for nine boxes

Mascaro (sic)—To color brows, cheeks, hair stuff—35¢

Camel's hair brush—For applying mascaro—10¢

Eye liner (Blue, carmine)—Lining of eyes, also shadows, scars—60¢ for two sticks

Stomps (several)—Paper pencils for applying eye liner—10¢ each

Clown white—For highlighting shadows, lines—30¢

Cocoa butter or Cold cream—For coating pores prior to putting on makeup, and for removing makeup—30¢ a cake or 60¢ a can

Eyebrow pencils, black and brown—For subtle aging lines—50¢ for two

Hare's foot—To apply rouge—30¢
Lip rouge—For healthy lip or cheek coloration—35¢ a tube
Powder puff (large)—For applying setting powder—30¢
Burnt cork—For unshaven look, dirty face (laborer)—30¢
Assortment of wigs, beards—Quick changes or heavily disguised
    roles—Range: wigs, $1.25 to 4.50; beards, $1.25 to 2.50
Crepe hair—Building beards, mustaches, whiskers, false eyebrows,
    etc.—40¢ a yard
Spirit gum—Adhesion of hair stuff to face—35¢ a bottle
Blue lining sticks (like Crayons d'Italie?)—Especially recommended for
    tattoos, as in seafaring disguises—20¢ a stick

Other items were also necessary in each dressing room: towels, tissues or the equivalent, scissors for fashioning false beards, etc., and alcohol for removing spirit gum.

Holmes might also have had a substance for blacking out teeth, but whether it was Cobbler's Wax or the more expensive Email Noir (a liquid) is anyone's guess, since both were available.

A more important question is when nose putty first found its way into the Master's makeup box. It was on the market in 1898, for Hageman sold sticks of it for 35¢, but there is no mention of it in the Samuel French pamphlet, so it evidently made a late debut in the world of drama.

Nose putty would have been indispensable to Holmes in fashioning false noses, cheeks, scars, changing the shape of his ears, and so on. Earlier, such effects were accomplished by the crude method of gumming down some linen or wool to the portion of the face involved, then painting and powdering the wool to match the skin tone. Such a method would have been of small use to Holmes, since it would hardly bear close inspection, and it is interesting to observe that we have record of only one impersonation that probably required nose putty: the venerable Italian priest in *The Final Problem* whose nose hung down near the chin. This adventure, of course, did not take place until 1891, which may provide a clue to the introduction of nose putty on the commercial market.[3]

The rather peculiar materials utilized in *The Dying Detective* are not commonplaces of the makeup box, and have been deliberately postponed for later discussion.

---

[3]It has been argued that the much-maligned Watson may merely have failed to accurately describe this Holmesian manifestation. But it should be remembered that the doctor's literary agent, Arthur Conan Doyle, was himself a theatrical producer; certainly he would have offered pertinent advice to the doctor on what could or could not be accomplished with makeup.

It now remains to analyze the eighteen principal characterizations enumerated in Chapter Two, from the point of view of makeup technique . . . the first step being elimination of Mr. Harris, the accountant of *The Stock-Broker's Clerk,* and the unnamed registration agent of *The Crooked Man,* neither of which required any special makeup or costuming. Also being eliminated: the phantom Sigerson, an apocryphal guise.

"Every actor," says Hageman, "who has been in the theatrical profession gradually, and of his own accord, follows a certain routine and uses different expedients to reach a successful result (in building makeup) . . . the art of making-up is largely one of personal intuition and natural aptitude."

Certainly this must be true of Sherlock Holmes, whose makeup prowess was equal to any veteran character actor. (Of course, it must be remembered that acting technique accounted for much of the effectiveness of his disguises, but this also speaks well for the technical execution—for character actors know that a good makeup helps to put them "in character.")

Because Holmes must be considered a master of makeup, and said masters are markedly individual in their methods, it is impossible to reconstruct a precise routining of the great detective's dressing room procedures, but certain steps are so basic it is probable they were always followed:

1. Cleaning of the face, and donning of "work clothes."
2. An initial coating of cold cream or cocoa butter, immediately removed.
3. If hair stuff was to be part of the makeup, it would be put on next. Strands of hair would be applied in whichever pattern the effect called for; once the spirit gum was dry, the hair would be trimmed with scissors.
4. Basic color would be applied to the face, and blended in, taking great care not to stain it on the beard line, or mustache (if any).
5. If the character was to be young, florid coloration might be added to the cheeks. If older, lines around the eyes and other wrinkle spots would be drawn. Possibly shadowing would be put in the cheek hollows.
6. Highlighting would then be put on, over the dark lines and hollows previously drawn. (The theory is that for every dark spot, where the light does not strike, there must be a prominence which does reflect the light. Thus shadow on the sides of the nose, and highlight—for example, white grease paint—on the bridge, would emphasize the beakiness of the feature. Reversal of the two substances would give a broader, flatter look.)
7. Powder would be brushed on and off to "set" the makeup.
8. Hands and other skin surfaces showing would be coated with the base color.
9. If a wig or bald pate were to be used, it would be added and adjusted, especially at the line of jointure.
10. Finally, the costume would be donned.

Even in these simple steps, the Master might have made some variations. Some character actors prefer building hair pieces after everything else is on, first wiping away the makeup from the needed skin surfaces so the spirit gum will "take".

An important point to note in the consideration of Holmesian makeup is that Sherlock had the perfect face for character work. The author, as a former makeup teacher and crew manager, knows how frustrating it is to attempt to "age" a round, youthful face. Healthy apple cheeks resist shadow-and-light effects, especially at close quarters. But Sherlock Holmes' craggy, angular features lend themselves marvelously to the powder-and-paintman's craft. The hard lines of his jaw and nose are superb for both highlighting and toning down, and the almost emaciated cheeks pictured in some Canonical portraiture lend themselves to aging.

Many of the Holmesian performances, of course, required little in the way of complex preparation. The seaman *(Sign of the Four)* and Captain Basil—assuming he affected more than the non-disguise of "Black Peter"—probably needed nothing more elaborate than a coating of Hageman's #7 grease paint (healthy sunburn) and a dusting of a matching powder.

Likewise, the drunken-looking groom *(Scandal in Bohemia),* the common loafer *(Beryl Coronet),* the French worker *(Lady Frances Carfax),* and the workman looking for a job *(Mazarin Stone)* must have all shared a family resemblance. Probably #7 coloring would also be used (with the possible exception of the out-of-work laborer; he is alternatively described as an "old sporting man" so #11 [ruddy, old] may have been used on him). A dirty, unshaven effect could be gained by a light rubbing of the beard with powdered blue, an older dry makeup material; by rubbing in a light quantity of cigarette ash into the beard (which substance Holmes would have in ample supply), or, if there were time, by simply letting the beard grow—the superior method, of course.

In addition, the groom got side-whiskers pasted on and probably carmine on the ball of the nose, for an inebriated look (possibly also on the cheek hollows to add to the flushed appearance).

The plumber, Escott, in *Charles Augustus Milverton,* might seem to be a similar case to the above quartet of roles, but it is not. The former impersonations were for short periods of time and were meant to be seen at some distance. Not so with Escott: here Holmes had to play a part at close quarters, in proximity to a villain who would recognize him. It also meant getting on intimate terms with a young lady who would be expected to note any marked variation in facial configuration from day to day.

The author recently had occasion to interview Frank Nallan, the New York Police Department's fabled "actor cop," who played many roles in his career and was responsible for hundreds of arrests. Nallan made the same point: any role requiring repeat appearances before the same people must be effected without much, if any, makeup. A false mustache or beard would be distinctly inadvisable, due to the unlikelihood of making an exact match from one day to another . . . this in a day when these items can be executed with much greater sophistication than was possible in the time of C.A. Milverton.

Hence, the goatee beard described in the text is most suspect, and it is doubtful that Holmes could have grown one in time for the occasion. If he did indeed wear one, it could have only been with painstaking inspection each day to see that it was exactly the same, an almost impossible task for even the finest makeup expert.★

Holmes tacitly acknowledges this point in *His Last Bow,* in which he remarks that he will be glad to get rid of his Uncle Sam-like goatee after suffering with it for two years. In this "epilogue" of the Master, it is evident that Holmes did not dare use a lick of makeup. Everything had to be genuine, including the beardlet. (Although Steele must have been unsure, since his September 22, 1917, cover of *Collier's* shows Holmes with hand covering the telltale hairpiece.)

The actual appearance of Escott must remain an unsolved mystery, although the Irregular seems to have four choices: (a) accept the Canon, without question; (b) attribute the error to either Watson or, less likely, Conan Doyle, as an attempt to make the piece even more colorful; (c) assume that Holmes wore some other disguise, or (d) believe that the Master was so spartan that he would leave the same goatee pasted on for days.†

To proceed with our analysis, the amiable and simple-minded clergyman in *Scandal in Bohemia* presents few makeup demands: likely, a coating of #8 grease paint (sallow, young men) and matching powder is all the makeup needed. To this, the clerical dress and clear-glass spectacles are inferable. (The character had a certain peering look, so glasses seem called for, possibly on a string?) If Holmes were very concerned about Irene recognizing him, he might also have touched up his cheeks with some rosy coloring, but the anonymity inherent in any kind of uniform seems to render extra frills unnecessary.

Some similarity of technique may have been utilized in the tall, thin old man *(Twisted Lip)* and the strange old bookman *(Empty House)* Holmes played, because both had to pass more than casual inspection. Extremely careful work with eye shadow, lines about the eye corners and forehead, graying of the hair is imaginable. Much of both performances, of course, depends on acting ability—as is evidenced by Holmes' lightning-quick

---

★In 1968, if memory serves.—MK
†Unlikely—it would start to look matted.—MK

change to recognizability in the latter tale—but the makeup had to be carefully executed, nonetheless. In the case of the old man in the opium den, at least, Sherlock had the benefit of dim, flickering lights which would seem to shift about the contours of his face and take advantage of the hollows and prominences, first lighting one area, then outlining another, so that the overall effect (and obfuscation) of the makeup was considerably heightened by the atmospherics.

In the first story of the "Return" series, though, Sherlock had to go abroad in daylight with his makeup, so that the blending of shadows and highlight had to be artistically perfect . . . a key testimony to Holmes' surpassing skill. Here, too, he is reported to use hair stuff—white sidewhiskers—over a protracted period of time. But in this case, it is less likely that he would be observed at close quarters day after day by any single personage. Yet, considering Holmes' healthy respect for Moriarty's successors, it is probable he showed enough foresight to grow sidewhiskers during his hiatus, after which it would be no great matter to whiten them.

More latitude could be exercised in building sidewhiskers in *Sign of the Four,* when he is only out for a few hours in the guise of an aged seaman. Here, he must have stripped off the coloration he put on earlier in the day and—considering the decrepitude of his characterization—repainted himself with #10 (sallow, old). The addition of some touches of color on his cheeks and the whiskers practically completes the disguise, although he surely must have grayed his hair as well, and his eyebrows. The text specifies that he affects bushy white brows, but it is not likely that Holmes gave himself false brows; his own were bushy enough (a detail noted in the first chapter of *The Valley of Fear.*) The genius of this characterization may be noted in the fact that he effectively imitated old age while only thirty-four![4]

Probably Sherlock's most audacious masquerade is as an old woman in *Mazarin Stone* . . . which indicates that in his later period (Baring-Gould dates this adventure in 1903) Holmes' makeup kit may also have contained an assortment of exonia paste, a distaff substitute for grease paint, more delicately colored, that came in china jars, 75¢ each. The pigments were limited, and he must have chosen a mixture of pink and brunette, or possibly brunette and white, which he could have blended in his hand or in a saucer. Otherwise, a woman's gray wig, perhaps spectacles, and dress would complete the disguise—drag being a kind of uniform for the male, with automatic "psychological masking potential".

We have now reached the two makeups that the author regards as the

---

[4]Baring-Gould dating.

pinnacle of Sherlock Holmes' technical skill: the venerable Italian priest *(Final Problem)* and the simulation of a rare disease *(The Dying Detective)*.

The former makeup only had to pass inspection briefly, but the eyes it had to deceive were the keenest in the world of crime. Thus every possible trick of Holmes' must have been utilized: we have the psychological advantage of the clerical garb again; we have old age shadows and lines, since Watson makes special mention of wrinkles. The nose dangling to the lower lip speaks of the presence of nose putty, which probably had reached the market by '91. The protruding lower lip probably was acting rather than makeup (an effect that could be brought off for a short period). This lip detail and the hanging nose also seems to indicate some fullness, bulbosity or obesity to this character—in which case, the highlights would go on the cheeks and fleshy portions of the face to round them out. Indeed, Sherlock may have even built up his cheeks in layers of linen and nose putty to give real texture to his pudginess.

What if nose putty were not on the market by then? Hageman points out that a serviceable substitute could be found in diachylum or diachylon, a material well-known to magicians and also used by apothecaries in making plasters.

Would Holmes have thought of this expedient? Very probably he would, because a good character actor will doubtlessly experiment with materials beyond the usual substances found in a makeup box.

Which brings us to the greatest triumph of makeup application in the Canon, that of the disease in *Dying Detective*. Here, Sherlock simulates the symptoms of the fatal illness so well that Watson's medical expertise is deceived and Culverton Smith (who has had firsthand knowledge of the progress of the malady) is totally taken in. And Holmes accomplishes it with the most unorthodox of makeup: vaseline, belladonna, and beeswax—rouge being the only conventional substance (doubtless for a flushed, feverish appearance, since it is applied to Holmes' cheeks).

The economy of the Master's methods is astonishing. The vaseline is an admirable choice for giving the forehead a glistening, sweat-soaked look, while nothing more loathsome can be imagined by the author than the beeswax crusts about Holmes' lips to simulate the semi-mucous excrescences of a long convalescence. While Holmes does not mention it, it is at least possible that some highlighting was also added to the cheekbones and nasal bridge, inasmuch as Mrs. Hudson tells Watson she could see "his bones sticking out of his face."

The most amazing touch is the belladonna drops Holmes puts in his eyes. Watson says, "His eyes had the brightness of fever"—and little wonder, since the effect of that drug in the eyes is to dilate the pupils!

CHAPTER FIVE

His Greatest Impersonation?

That wise old observation about Sherlock Holmes never being quite the same after falling into the Reichenbach cataract has only one thing wrong with it. Lest we forget, *he was never in it* in the first place.

That Sherlock Holmes himself returned to active practice a few years later has never been doubted by the author, despite ingenious attempts to prove the later Holmes is actually his brother Sherrinford[1], his arch-enemy Moriarty[2], or a figment of Watson's imagination.[3]

But, though the author is willing enough to accept the reappearance of Holmes in *The Adventure of the Empty House,* he is far less able to credit the wild and wooly tale Holmes relates to Watson concerning that period which Edgar W. Smith so aptly named "the Great Hiatus." Especially suspect is that part of the hiatus apparently spent in Tibet, including the Sigerson masquerade.

It is the contention of the author that Holmes was actually involved in an entirely different impersonation at the time, one which must rank with his greatest performances.

The objections and fallacies connected with what Holmes tells Watson of his travels post-Reichenbach have been amply treated by several other authors. Especially see Chapter 48 of *The Annotated Sherlock Holmes.*

Suffice it to say that the author is most strongly persuaded against accepting the Tibetan tale because of (a) the considerations advanced by Edgar W. Smith to the effect that Englishmen would hardly have been welcome in Tibet, Persia and other trouble spots at the time Holmes purportedly visited them, and (b) the fact that when the Master was supposedly in Asia, a letter appeared in the *Daily Gazette,* obviously of Holmesian authorship. Its text, quoted in *The Man With the Watches,* was carried in a spring edition, 1892, of that London newspaper.[4]

The evidence points to Holmes returning to London after Reichenbach. But what did he then do? It seems improbable that he would have

---

[1]Anthony Boucher, "Was the Later Holmes an Imposter?" in *Profile by Gaslight.*

[2]Many sources, e.g., letter of May 2, 1968, to *The New York Times,* from Edward Case, referring to Reichenbach as a "cunning charade."

[3]Several sources, notably Ronald A. Knox, *Studies in the Literature of Sherlock Holmes.*

[4]For a discussion *in extenšio,* vide *The Sherlockian Doyle,* published by Luther Norris in an edition uniform to this volume. But the author rejects the theory in that volume that Holmes astrally projected himself to London to write the missive in question!!!

risked disguise in that city for nearly three years, considering the ferocious tenacity of Col. Moran.

Perhaps he returned to the city just long enough to reorder his life and slip out once more in disguise. After a lengthy absence, he might then chance a quiet return so that he could begin setting up new nets for Moriarty's henchmen.

Since the letter in the *Gazette* appeared in 1892, and Holmes battled at the falls on May 4, 1891, it appears that he stayed away from London for some months before returning and drafting the letter—for whatever psychological purpose he thought meet. Perhaps he intended to slip out a second time (to the south of France?) and wanted to put Moran on a false scent with the implication that Sherlock was still in London?[5]

It is the first absence we are here concerned with—where might Holmes have gone for several months? To the United States? That theory has been advanced, not without claim to merit.

But there is an even more attractive possibility, one which can be supported with some textual evidence . . . if one widens one's literary horizons to include more than just Dr. Watson's reports. For it is a fact that his agent, Arthur Conan Doyle, also handled another manuscript of more than passing interest to the Holmesian scholar.

Think a moment—what world-shaking scientific event took place at the turn of the century?

Surely there was no more profound adventure in that age than the discovery in South America of sentient prehistoric life—an expedition chronicled by a reporter, Edward Dunn Malone, who worked for the same *Daily Gazette* that carried Holmes' letter.

This tale, sold by the Doyle agency under the fanciful title of *The Lost World,* centered around the brilliant, if fiery-tempered, Professor George Edward Challenger—who, it must be remembered, was no less than Sherlock Holmes' first cousin on his father's side![6]

Consider Challenger's position at the time of that history-making adventure . . . forced to confront a scientific body hostile to his discoveries, and reasonably certain that one of his colleagues would accept a mission to visit the tropical plateau to prove or disprove Challenger's claims. The professor would never let the expedition take place without him, yet he knew the

---

[5]What of Watson? And the public? Would they not marvel at the letter from a man they thought dead? But here is a theory: the letter may have been signed "Sherlock Holmes," with the quotation marks perhaps giving the impression of a joke in questionable taste (to all but Moran).

[6]For details, see the standard biography of Holmes, *Sherlock Holmes of Baker Street,* by W. S. Baring-Gould.

place's dangers. He had a pretty good idea, it is likely, who his travelling companions would be—the acidulous, scrawny Summerlee, and (albeit, at the last moment) the adolescent, foolhardy Malone.

Who more desirable on such a dangerous trek than his fearless, athletic cousin, Sherlock?—one of the few men whose intellects were as fully developed as the professor's—and, consequently, one of the only persons Challenger could tolerate for very long at a time.

But Sherlock had his own problem at the moment—a nearly final one, in fact—and Challenger's invitation, while fortuitous, must have proved vexatious to both men, since it would depend on whether Holmes survived Reichenbach or no. As it evolved, with Moran out of the law's clutches, Sherlock could only accompany his cousin on the exciting new adventure to South America if it could be arranged without danger to the detective or the rest of the party.

Disguise was the only answer, and there is only one role that Sherlock could have assumed: that of Lord John Roxton, huntsman and explorer—the last of the Challenger expedition as named in Malone's account.

This assertion, naturally, entails the answering of several vital questions before it may be accepted as a valid hypothesis. The first question is that of the dates.

While *The Lost World* was published in 1912 and has been believed by some students to have taken place in 1906, there is no evidence in the notes of Malone to determine the year. On the other hand, the months that elapse during the trek are well documented. The party of explorers leaves England in late spring, probably in mid-June, and returns nearly half-a-year later, on November 5th.

So, if we take the adventure to have occurred in the year 1891, Holmes had ample time to return from Switzerland—at least a month-and-a-half—assume the disguise of Lord John Roxton, pop up at the scientific meeting chronicled by Malone, volunteer to go on the expedition, and leave shortly thereafter for a period of almost six months . . . until the "heat had died down."

Returning, as described by Malone, still in the role of Roxton, Sherlock stayed in London for some months—at least five—wrote the letter to the *Gazette* (possibly giving it "as Roxton" to Malone to ensure its being printed) and then set sail once more.

The second principal question the Roxton/Holmes hypothesis gives rise to is whether Sherlock could have physically portrayed the sportsman. That he could and did is evident by a comparison of the well-known Holmes physiognomy to that of Roxton, as well as of their respective physiques.

Holmes, as we know, is about six feet tall and extremely thin. Roxton is "a tall, thin man." Holmes has an angular face with strong, aquiline features. Roxton is possessed of a "strongly-curved nose . . . hollow, worn cheeks . . ." Holmes has bushy eyebrows; Roxton: "His eyebrows were tufted and overhanging, which gave those naturally *cold eyes* an almost ferocious aspect . . ." (Emphasis mine.) In this passage, Malone also adds this detail on his height—"a little over six feet, but he seemed shorter on account of a *peculiar rounding of the shoulders.*" (Again, the emphasis is mine, this time because the detail is so reminiscent of the way Sherlock takes a few inches off his height when portraying the old bookseller.)

Of course, there are a few differences between the two: Roxton has skin "of a rich flower-pot red from sun and wind," as well as "crisp, virile mustaches" and a "small, aggressive tuft upon his projecting chin." But the skin tone is a simple matter of grease paint coloration, easily replaced by actual sunburn on the trek, while the hair piece is characteristic of Holmes, who used a goatee on several other occasions. Likely enough, he grew what hair he could prior to appearing as Lord John in public; after a time, he completely replaced any false hairstuff with his own—as the expedition proceeded.

In the matter of physical appearance, Holmes was in luck, since Roxton had been out of the country some time before the night of Challenger's scientific discussion. The professor, of course, was in on the deception from the first, while Summerlee—his vision narrowed to scientific circles—would not be difficult to fool. But Malone was another matter: as a reporter, it would be likely he'd be familiar with Roxton, at least by reputation—and indeed, on his first close view of the disguised detective, Malone compares him mentally with photos of the explorer that he'd seen in his newspaper's morgue.

Holmes could take no chances. Moran was on the lookout for him, and the chance of a reporter scooping the world with the story of Sherlock's reappearance was too dangerous to be ignored. So Holmes tested Malone (Chapter Six of *The Lost World*) by inviting him to his apartment (the real Roxton's, of course) and trying out his impersonation at leisure.[7]

It may be objected that while Holmes might fool Malone for the duration of the trip, the truth would eventually have to come out, with ensuing exposure—a thing that never happened. But Malone moved in different circles than either Holmes or Roxton, and despite the pact between the reporter and the huntsman (at the end of *Lost World*) to go back to the Amazon, no further chronicle exists of any major adventure between the two. (*The Poison Belt* is a fictional exploit [probably of Malone's authoring], as is clearly stated in *The Land of Mist:* "The great Professor Challenger has been very improp-

---

[7]It is interesting to observe that one of the expressions he repeatedly puts in Roxton's mouth: "Here's a pretty business," appears as early as 1888, when he says it during the *Sign of the Four* case.

erly and imperfectly used in fiction. A daring author placed him in impossible and romantic situations in order to see how he would react to them." As for *The Land of Mist,* in which Roxton reappears, it is dated much later, 1926, a time distant enough so that Malone may have been taken in by the real Roxton. But it is more likely that *Land of Mist* is also apocryphal: a tract on spiritualism most likely penned by Watson's agent.)

Though it is only of tangential concern here, the reader doubtless wants to know who the real Roxton was. It obviously had to be someone of whom Holmes had considerable knowledge (a simple matter, with the Master's huge files) and it must have been a personage familiar enough in manner and appearance (through being often described in print) so that the detective could make a valid decision whether or not to impersonate him.

There is one likely candidate in the Canon, a man with a "huge body . . . craggy and deeply seamed face with . . . fierce eyes and hawklike nose . . . ," a man who is also a world-famous explorer and huntsman—and a man who, like Roxton, calls himself a law unto himself.

The considerate Watson, of course, alters his name, to Sterndale, but the resemblance is apparent. And it is somewhat suggestive that Holmes favorably judges this fierce hunter's case in *The Devil's Foot* and allows him to escape the penalties of the law. Perhaps Holmes owed him a favor that dated back to 1891?

Of course, the entire Roxton/Holmes hypothesis would be nothing more than an interesting theory if it were only based on coincidence of dating and accidents of physical resemblance.

But there are far more telling clues in the text of *The Lost World.* Despite the masterful physical miming of the Master, despite the colorful alteration in speech pattern, Holmes reveals himself to the careful reader time after time in the things he does and says—signal clues to his own mental activity and idiom. Here are some of the more obvious points:

(1) Challenger sends the three men "under sealed orders" to Manaos. The "orders" turn out to be a blank sheet of paper. Malone suggests it has been written on in invisible ink. "I don't think!" said Lord John Roxton, holding the paper to the light. ". . . nothing has ever been written upon this paper."

(2) When the party comes on the old camp of Maple White, it is Roxton/ Holmes whose keen habit of observation finds the crude signpost left by the discoverer of the plateau. A moment later they run across an impaled skeleton, and it is "Roxton" who immediately deduces the exact manner of death: "He has fallen or been chucked from the top (of the plateau), and so been impaled. How else could he come by his broken bones, and how could he have been stuck through by these canes with their points so high above our heads?" There speaks the Master!

(3) Inside the "Lost World," it is again Roxton who discovers the first foot-print of prehistoric life. Again, Holmes lets slip his automatic habit of observation: ". . . the track is a fresh one. The creature has not passed ten minutes. Look how the water is still oozing into that deeper print!"

(4) Twice Holmes reveals how familiar he is with soils and minerals. Gazing at a herd of iguanodon through a field-glass, he is able to identify patches on the creatures as asphalt. At another time, he notes a nesting place (where the pterodactyls roost) and recognizes it as a volcanic pit, with blue clay around the edges . . . a clue to the existence of diamonds, which he later rigs up a scheme for obtaining.

(5) The most telling point, however, comes in the penultimate chapter of the tale. Trapped on the plateau, the party befriends one of the natives who gives them a chart containing some peculiar lines. It puzzles the scientific men . . . but Roxton/Holmes almost immediately deciphers its significance as a map and leads the party back to safety. It may be a little surprising that the crude chart, a little reminiscent of the "dancing men", is so quickly solved by Holmes, while the latter takes so long. But perhaps the remembrance of the "Lost World" chart involved Holmes in a slight case of psychological "set" in 1898, when the "dancing men" case occurred.

One matter remains to be considered concerning this impersonation of the Master's: why did he keep it a secret from Watson (and, consequently, from the world)?

No positive answer can be given, but perhaps the delayed publication of Malone's manuscript in book form provides a clue.[8]

It is probable that Holmes was aware that Watson would be extremely hurt to learn he'd been excluded from Holmes' greatest adventure. (Perhaps *His Last Bow* was a belated affair-of-conscience on Holmes' part?) Even worse, Sherlock knew Watson might be distressed to find himself temporarily replaced by Malone as official Holmesian historian.

Now the newspaper recounting of the Amazon expedition did not worry the detective. It appeared when Watson presumed Holmes to be dead, and newspapers are rarely saved for long periods of time. But a book edition of the Malone manuscript was another matter—it would enable Watson to review the whole affair in the light of subsequent knowledge, and it might possibly motivate him to take a more critical look at Holmes' Tibetan fable.

So Holmes did the only thing possible: in the guise of Roxton, he recommended Arthur Conan Doyle's literary agency to Malone. Working

---

[8]Initially, of course, Holmes needed to ensure the safety of the adventurers from the revenge of Moran—and he rarely trusted Watson's ability to dissemble.

behind the scenes with Doyle, Holmes made sure that the *Lost World* manuscript was kept out of hard-back circulation as long as possible.

The story finally appeared in cloth covers in 1912, so this means that Doyle kept Malone "on the hook" for nearly twenty years! This will, of course, appear exceedingly improbable to the layman—but anyone who attempts to market a manuscript through a New York theatrical agency will doubtlessly concede the point . . .

CURTAIN SPEECH

It has been the burthen of this study to reemphasize the propriety of Watson's valuation that "the stage lost a fine actor" when Sherlock Holmes became a criminal specialist.

If the author's hypothesis is granted, the Histrionic Holmes was first driven to acting by deep-seated needs within himself, longings and perceptions clamoring to be expressed.

The mystery that piques the imagination, then, is what made Holmes turn from the mimic pursuit to a career of ratiocination . . .

Perhaps, like other performers antique and contemporary, Sherlock discovered that the rewards of Creative Art are richer, more satisfying than those of Interpretive Art. And all acting, except for pure improvisation, is interpretation of another's thesis, however lower-case creative the individual actor may be.

Furthermore, the mature Holmes hardly could be expected to be content in a profession where the chief activity—in the higher view—is essentially a passive imitation and exegesis of the dynamics of life and the pain of becoming. We all know, of course, what Sherlock's course was: direct involvement with the immediate experience of criminous improvisation, with the unfolding dramas of actual, not mimetic performers.

In the following quote of Bernard Shaw's ("On Cutting Shakespear," *Fortnightly Review,* August 1919), we hear an echo of the Master's developing intellect—which eventually carried him even beyond detection and into more rarified strata of perception:

> Can men whose intellectual standards have been screwed up to Goethe's *Faust,* Wagner's *Ring,* and "deep revolving" Ibsen soul histories, be expected to sit and listen to such penny-reading twaddle as *The Seven Ages of Man,* or even Hamlet's soliloquy on suicide?

If this is so for spectators and critics—ultimate receptacles of dramaturgic and histrionic art—how much more likely is it to be true of the performer outstripping his emotional springs?

So, in Holmes' case, once the great detective attained an intellectual depth capable of riddling Goethe's *Faust,* it is likely that he grew dissatisfied with his well-mastered ability to interpret his comprehension plastically.

In fine, Holmes became one of the few actors in history capable of rendering an intellectually faithful Faust. But in the process, he lost his *need* to play the role.

In the scope of his investigations, though, he had ample opportunity to indulge that need whenever it rearose in vestigial form.

And his reward for this has been the claque-less applause of the generations . . .

THE REST IS SILENCE

*M*ember of the Legion of Honor, Fellow of the Royal Society of Arts, Fellow of Churchill College, Cambridge University, and Professor Emeritus of Columbia University, JACQUES BARZUN is a distinguished cultural historian, philosopher and author of Berlioz and the Romantic Century, The Use and Abuse of Art, and other books and articles on educational theory, theatre and genre literature, including essays and speeches on both Sherlock Holmes and Nero Wolfe. "How Holmes Came to Play the Violin," from the July 1951 issue of The Baker Street Journal, is a splendid bit of theorizing that puckishly punctures its own pretensions and, by extension, all Holmesian scholarship.

How Holmes Came to Play the Violin

JACQUES BARZUN

In her entertaining *Labours of Hercules,* the creator of Hercule Poirot hints that she may be the first to have speculated about the mother of Sherlock Holmes. She then goes on to sketch for us a truly appalling scene: "Your mother and the late Mrs. Holmes, sitting sewing little garments or knitting— 'Achille, Hercule, Sherlock, Mycroft . . .' "

This supposition is, on the one hand, demonstrably unfair to the great band of Holmes scholars, who by definition have speculated about everything; and, on the other, it is depressing in its insistence that Holmes came into the world in the regular middle-class way. So unconventional a mind cannot have been prenatally nurtured at any knitting party. It consequently occurred to me that with a little effort of research and imagination it should be possible to find some *ir*regularity, of the sort that always attends the birth of the great.

I began by pondering the singular incident of Mrs. Holmes's appearance in the canon: she does not appear. We somehow feel that Holmes was silent from some deep cause. His was a studied silence, and Watson knew nothing about either Mycroft or Holmes's forebears until circumstances betrayed Sherlock into giving him a few scraps of information. Yet from these we learn that Holmes was extraordinarily proud of his heredity, and for a most un-English reason: because it was artistic. In fact, he claimed a connection with Vernet, the French painter.

We may think that here we hold a firm clue. Alas! it is an illusion. Vernet is the name, not of one, but of a whole tribe of French painters, none of whom settled in England or acknowledged offshoots there. This line of investigation is blocked—at least to step-by-step research. It leads, so to speak, to a barrel of creosote. We are forced to make a jump (a long shot, Watson!) and hope it lands us closer to the heart of truth.

But it need not be a cast at random. We know that Holmes revered art. He loved music especially—witness his neglect of tantalizing questions in Watson's mind so that he might hear Sarasate or Norman Neruda. It is not contrary evidence that Holmes is reported as waving his hands in time with the soloist; some few musical people have been known to do it, and the habit may easily be a Watsonism projected on the Master. Neither does it prove him tone-deaf that he turned musicologist and wrote on the polyphonic motets of Lassus. Finally, as everyone knows, Holmes played the violin with uncommon skill. Indeed, his technique was so uncommon that he frequently played with the instrument "thrown across his knee."

Pursuing the stream of associations and asking ourselves what the word "knee" irresistibly suggests, I think we may safely answer: "at the mother's knee." But do not hasten to the next association and conclude that Holmes's mother was a housemaid. Consider rather the musical point in relation to the mother. Historically, a number of violin-like instruments have been bowed across the player's lap; but so played a modern violin can only give "open" notes; the strings cannot readily be "stopped" to produce any but their fundamental tone. All this suggests the beginner on the instrument, and if to this is added Watson's testimony that Holmes was of a wild melancholy when he inflicted those meaningless wails on his friend, I believe we have the makings of a hypothesis. At those moments, I submit, Holmes was thinking of his childhood and his mother; he was reproducing something of the atmosphere he had known when he first began to show an interest in music—childish scrapings across the strings of his mother's fiddle, doubtless when she herself had finished practicing.

The next question is obvious: why was the adult Holmes melancholy and unable to disburden himself in words? The answer is no less plain: something painful and (preferably) shameful must be associated in his mind with his early years. This guess is reenforced by the negative truth that Holmes never mentioned who taught him to play. It is normal to confide, "Old Bogenbrecher gave me my first lessons," or "My mother taught me." But this would have led to embarrassing inquiries from Watson: What sort of player was your mother? Where. . . . ? etc., etc.

Arrived at this point we may profitably make the required jump, and after the first shock of horror and surprise, see where we stand. Holmes was obviously brought up in a retired way by his mother *alone*. She was a Vernet, and unmarried.

Now of the Vernets eligible for the high honor of having borne Sherlock Holmes, there is, I am glad to say, only one that fits our case; and as it happens, information about her early life at least is abundant. She was Louise, daughter of Horace Vernet (1789–1863) the painter of Napoleonic scenes, whom the Emperor had decorated with his own hand in 1814 after the young artist had fought in his behalf on the Paris barricades of that year. His daughter Louise must by then have been two or three years old, for we find her aged 18 or 19 when we hear of her in the *Memoirs* and letters of the composer Berlioz. She figures there (in 1830–31) as the accomplished, musical daughter of the Director of the French Academy at Rome—a post to which Vernet had been elevated in 1828.

Through Berlioz's descriptions, we see her at the piano, singing the songs which he and other musicians in Rome wrote for her or brought her from abroad. Mendelssohn was then in the Eternal City; so was Glinka, and so for a short time were many other young artists destined to fame. Most of them naturally found their way to the Academy, which on Thursdays held open house for youth and intellect. When a ball was planned, Mlle. Louise led the frolic. She was known for her well-bred abandon and would dance the wild Roman *saltarello*—for propriety's sake with her grandfather, Carle Vernet. All the Vernets were musical. Horace, his son, would paint in a studio cluttered with musical instruments, and Louise certainly did not feign the passion she felt for music and dance.

These circumstances must be firmly grasped if they are to tide us over the lacuna which follows. It is definitely ascertainable that Berlioz, when he left Rome in 1831, was not betrothed to Louise Vernet. Nor did he ever marry her. No more did Mendelssohn or Glinka. Gounod, who came along shortly thereafter, was altogether too young and too timid to propose. It took no prophet—a woman's intuition was enough—to recognize that the supply of first-rate musicians in Rome was running out. Bizet was not due for another 18 years and Debussy would not arrive until 27 more. But all the while Louise was languishing for a musical mate. Does it not seem plausible that, abandoning caution, and at the same time lowering her sights, she may one evening have danced the *saltarello* with a visiting Englishman named Holmes? That he was musical is self-evident; but why he did not honorably carry off Louise as his bride can only be conjectured.

Religion, or some insurmountable difference of opinion with the girl's father over concert pitch, may have precluded marriage and forced an unsanctified elopement. In any case the *liaison* was no frivolous short-lived affair: it lasted at the very least the twenty years necessary to bring into the world Mycroft, Sherlock, and that "Dr. Verner" whom Holmes alluded to as his cousin when he bought Watson's practice, but who was, I am convinced, a third brother. Holmes, born in 1854, was the youngest, therefore doubly in the great tradition which assigns genius most often to illegitimate and youngest sons.

There remains the problem of Holmes's father. It would be tempting to select Edward Holmes, a friend of Keats and an accomplished music critic who wrote one of the earliest and best biographies of Mozart. But I fear he was indomitably conventional and married the granddaughter of a gentleman who was utterly well-known. Indeed, this Holmes left two legal daughters so respectable that in translating Berlioz' *Memoirs* into English they found themselves expurgating the text by reflex action.

The alternative would be to see in the father of the celebrated woman composer, Augusta Holmes, the putative father of Sherlock and Mycroft. But we must not stretch musical genealogy too far. Augusta was born in France in 1847 and it taxes credulity to envision a peripatetic Holmes, Sr., whose love of music made him set up households close to so many conservatories—instead of the more usual other way round.

No, Holmes Senior escapes scrutiny, defies identification, vanishes into legend. We infer that he existed and that he was a true artist only because Sherlock on reaching maturity assumed the patronymic. This proves the son an artist too, for it would be hard to imagine a worse-sounding name for a public figure than "Sherlock Vernet." Rhythm required a final monosyllable; ease of retention called for a simple but not too common English name; and the note of anguish and pleading in the distressed made it imperative that they should call for help on an aspirate. All these profoundly musical requisites were met in that marvelous name *Holmes,* to find which, all that the heaven-born Sherlock had to do was to ask his mother.

We now know how Holmes came to play the violin, not only in the first, second and third positions, but also in that of *dorsal decubitus* (the violin's, that is), which remains the greatest contribution to the art since Paganini's double stops.

There is only one thing to be urged against the hypothesis which has led to so satisfactory a result, and that is, that we know all about poor Louise Vernet's life after 1831. She married a promising young painter named Paul Delaroche (the same who did a fine portrait of the beautiful prima donna Henrietta Sonntag) and died young, to the permanent beclouding of her husband's happiness.

That is final, as someone remarked: and Holmes echoed: "It is final!" with peculiar merriment. Let his ringing derision attend all Norwood Builders who erect false systems with paltry clues of their own contriving, and let some soberer scholar, unmoved by Mrs. Agatha Christie's provocation, inquire whether the link between Holmes and Vernet is not the latter's Napoleonic scenes, which so captivated that Emperor-worshipper, Sir Arthur Conan Doyle.

Parodies Absurdes Et Cruelles

NICHOLAS POLLOTTA *describes himself as "a thirty-eight-year-old Republican with Virgo rising, although the political affiliation of my moustache has yet to be clearly determined." A retired stand-up comic from Manhattan and ex-security courier, he is the author of numerous genre novels, including* Illegal Aliens, Bureau 13, Doomsday Exam, Full Moonsters, Satellite Night Live, Satellite Night Special, Satellite Night Fever *and the forthcoming* American Knights. *A specialist in non-English editions of the Holmesian Canon, Mr. Pollotta is a member of two Sherlockian societies, The Master's Class of Philadelphia and The Baker Street Slightly-Irregulars of Baltimore— unless they blackball him for writing "The Really Final Solution."*

The Really Final Solution

NICK POLLOTTA

Sherlock Holmes and Rupert Jameson, the mad Kensington bricklayer, stared hatefully at each other across the swirling pool of acid in the basement of the old Hofnagel Mansion.

"So," cackled the burly mason, cracking the scarred knuckles of his massive hands. "You entered my deathtrap, innocent as a newborn!"

In return, Holmes merely sneered in disdain. "Not a bit of it," he replied stoutly. "I was fully aware that the blind bookstore owner was from Belgium, and thus could have no possible knowledge of the gray-striped cat, or the woman with the scarf."

Breath hissed through tobacco-stained clenched teeth. "But when the bank telegram arrived, you had Lestrade pour the bucket of water out the window!"

"Into another empty bucket waiting on the ground," stated the sleuth triumphantly. "Held and guarded by my close friend and companion, Doctor John Watson!"

And from out of the basement shadows stepped a powerful bulldog of a man, sporting a full Queen's regimental moustache and a small medical bag.

The murderer gasped in astonishment. "But if he caught the water, then you knew—"

"Everything about the blueprints!"

"But then, when the little blonde girl asked for more—"

"We already had the mastiff tied and helpless!"

"So, the carriage ride to the boathouse—"

"Was a sham! And therefore—"

"ENOUGH!" bellowed an exasperated Watson. Drawing the Adams .32 pistol from the pocket of his great coat, the physician emptied the weapon into the criminal genius.

Jameson staggered backwards from the brutal impact of the soft-lead bullets, his bald head smacking against the stonework wall with an audible crack. Limply, the man slid to the floor, toppled over and fell into the boiling vat. With a sizzling hiss, his muscular form vanished into the swirling chemicals.

Stepping away from the billowing clouds of fumes, Watson poured a small open bottle of poison into the vat, staining the concoction a vicious mottled green and then tossed in his bullseye lantern. With a loud whoof, the chemicals burst into flames; a roaring inferno that filled the cellar with hellish heat and pungent smoke.

"I say Watson, was that really quite necessary?" demanded Holmes as they closed and locked the cellar door behind them. Flickering lights played upon their shoes from under the jamb. "I was about to make him admit to stealing the gold bullion from the one-legged Russian."

In proper military fashion, Watson cracked apart his revolver, pocketed the spent shells and reloaded. "Irrelevant, old man. After that incredible debacle with Prof. Moriarty, did you actually believe that I would ever again allow you to play dice with these master criminals?"

"But Watson, it is for the intellectual conflict that I play this dangerous game!"

"Not justice?"

Throwing open the front door and allowing his associate to exit first, the consulting detective sullenly admitted that justice was a consideration in the matter. At least to some small degree. Holmes pouted as Dr. Watson knelt by an elderberry bush and retrieved a small wooden box. Meticulously, the physician attached two bare end wires to the screws atop the coal miner's tool and pulled the plunger fully upwards.

"Never again will we face a lunatic genius twice."

Holmes gasped. Watson flamboyantly rammed the plunger downward. In a chemical thunderclap, the house erupted with strident flame. The windows disintegrated into twinkling shards. The burning building began to collapse inward upon itself to the sound of ancient splintering wood.

"Finito!" sighed the doctor, painfully straightening from his work and dusting off his hands. Ouch. His old wound was acting up again. Bedamn that

Jezail bullet! The war in India had been much safer than his chronic romances.

With the dancing light of the conflagration illuminating the English countryside, the great detective blinked in somber thought. Then slowly, ever so slowly, Holmes turned to stare at his old friend with new-found respect shining in his eyes. "Indeed," murmured Sherlock Holmes softly, an excited smile playing on his lips, "it has just occurred to me this very night, what a truly excellent opponent you would make."

"Eh? What was that?" Dr. Watson gasped.

"Out of curiosity, John, you don't have any secrets in your past in which Scotland Yard would be interested, have you? A crime of passion, perhaps? Exactly from whom, and under what circumstances, did you receive your bullet wound? And precisely what happened to the person or persons who gave it to you?"

Seeing that infamous hunting expression on the thin man's face, the physician swung up his Adams for protection. But Holmes knocked it from his hands with an ebony walking stick. Watson rushed for the hansom, but Holmes tackled him. The two men grappled as they fell wrestling to the hard ground.

This, each man thought, struggling for supremacy, could be the end of a beautiful friendship.

The confusion of a literary character's opinions with that of his author's views is a common failing of critics. Arthur Conan Doyle freely expressed his admiration for Edgar Allan Poe's seminal literary sleuth C. Auguste Dupin, but Sherlock Holmes did not. Protests cropped up, which is why Dr. Harold Emery Jones wrote "The Original of Sherlock Holmes" (elsewhere in this volume) in 1904 so that "the absurd fiction that Conan Doyle drew upon Poe for his ideas (will be) silenced forever." But the February 1905 issue of The Critic *still ran the following egregious parody.*

The Unmasking of Sherlock Holmes

ARTHUR CHAPMAN

In all my career as Boswell to the Johnson of Sherlock Holmes, I have seen the great detective agitated only once. We had been quietly smoking and talking over the theory of thumbprints, when the landlady brought in a little square of pasteboard at which Holmes glanced casually and then let drop on the floor. I picked up the card, and as I did so I saw that Holmes was trembling, evidently too agitated either to tell the landlady to show the visitor in or to send him away. On the card I read the name:

> MONSIEUR C. AUGUSTE DUPIN,
> *Paris.*

While I was wondering what there could be in that name to strike terror to the heart of Sherlock Holmes, M. Dupin himself entered the room. He was a young man, slight of build and unmistakably French of feature. He bowed as he stood in the doorway, but I observed that Sherlock Holmes was too amazed or too frightened to return the bow. My idol stood in the middle of the room, looking at the little Frenchman on the threshold as if M. Dupin had been a ghost. Finally, pulling himself together with an effort, Sherlock Holmes motioned the visitor to a seat, and, as M. Dupin sunk into the chair, my friend tumbled into another and wiped his brow feverishly.

"Pardon my unceremonious entrance, Mr. Holmes," said the visitor, drawing out a meerschaum pipe, filling it, and then smoking in long, deliberate puffs. "I was afraid, however, that you would not care to see me, so I came in before you had an opportunity of telling your landlady to send me away."

To my surprise Sherlock Holmes did not annihilate the man with one of those keen, searching glances for which he has become famous in literature and the drama. Instead he continued to mop his brow and finally mumbled, weakly:

"But—but—I thought y-y-you were dead, M. Dupin."

"And people thought you were dead, too, Mr. Sherlock Holmes," said the visitor, in his high, deliberate voice. "But if you can be brought to life after being hurled from a cliff in the Alps, why can't I come out of a respectable grave just to have a chat with you? You know my originator, Mr. Edgar Allan Poe, was very fond of bringing people out of their graves."

"Yes, yes, I'll admit that I have read that fellow, Poe," said Sherlock Holmes testily. "Clever writer in some things. Some of his detective stories about you are not half bad, either."

"No, not half bad," said M. Dupin, rather sarcastically, I thought. "Do you remember that little story of 'The Purloined Letter,' for instance? What a little gem of a story that is! When I get to reading it over I forget all about you and your feeble imitations. There is nothing forced there. Everything is as sure as fate itself—not a false note—not a thing dragged in by the heels. And the solution of it all is so simple that it makes most of your artifices seem clumsy in comparison."

"But if Poe had such a good thing in you, M. Dupin, why didn't he make more of you?" snapped Sherlock Holmes.

"Ah, that's where Mr. Poe proved himself a real literary artist," said M. Dupin, puffing away at his eternal meerschaum. "When he had a good thing he knew enough not to ruin his reputation by running it into the ground. Suppose, after writing 'The Murders of the Rue Morgue' around me as the central character, he had written two or three books of short stories in which I figured. Then suppose he had let them dramatize me and further parade me before the public. Likewise suppose, after he had decently killed me off and had announced that he would write no more detective stories, he had yielded to the blandishments of his publishers and had brought out another interminable lot of tales about me? Why, naturally, most of the stuff would have been worse than mediocre, and people would have forgotten all about that masterpiece, 'The Murders of the Rue Morgue,' and also about 'The Purloined Letter,' so covered would those gems be in a mass of trash."

"Oh, I'll admit that my string has been overplayed," sighed Sherlock Holmes moodily, reaching for the hypodermic syringe, which I slid out of his reach. "But maybe Poe would have overplayed you if he could have drawn down a dollar a word for all he could write about you."

"Poor Edgar—poor misunderstood Edgar!—maybe he would," said Dupin, thoughtfully. "Few enough dollars he had in his stormy life. But at the same time, no matter what his rewards, I think he was versatile genius enough to have found something new at the right time. At any rate he would not have filched the product of another's brain and palmed it off as his own."

"But great Scott, man!" cried Sherlock Holmes, "you don't mean to say that no one else but Poe has a right to utilize the theory of analysis in a detective story, do you?"

"No, but see how closely you follow me in all other particulars. I am out of sorts with fortune and so are you. I am always smoking when thinking out my plans of attack, and so are you. I have an admiring friend to set down everything I say and do, and so have you. I am always dazzling the chief of police with much better theories than he can ever work out, and so are you."

"I know, I know," said Sherlock Holmes, beginning to mop his forehead again. "It looks like a bad case against me. I've drawn pretty freely upon you, M. Dupin, and the quotation marks haven't always been used as they should have been where credit was due. But after all I am not the most slavish imitation my author has produced. Have you ever read his book, 'The White Company' and compared it with 'The Cloister and the Hearth'? No? Well do so, if you want to get what might be termed 'transplanted atmosphere.' "

"Well, it seems to be a great age for the piratical appropriating of other men's ideas," said M. Dupin, resignedly. "As for myself, I don't care a rap about your stealing of my thunder, Sherlock Holmes. In fact, you're a pretty decent sort of a chap, even though you are trying my patience with your continual refusal to retire; and besides you only make me shine the brighter in comparison. I don't even hold that 'Dancing Men' story against you, in which you made use of a cryptogram that instantly brought up thoughts of 'The Gold-Bug.' "

"But you did not figure in 'The Gold-Bug,' " said Sherlock Holmes with the air of one who had won a point.

"No, and that merely emphasizes what I have been telling you—that people admire Poe as a literary artist owing to the fact that he did not overwork any of his creations. Bear that in mind, my boy, and remember, when you make your next farewell, to see that it is not one of the Patti kind, with a string to it. The patience of even the American reading public is not exhaustless, and you cannot always be among the 'six best-selling books' of the day."

And with these words, M. Dupin, pipe, and all, vanished in the tobacco-laden atmosphere of the room, leaving the great detective, Sherlock Holmes, looking at me as shamefacedly as a schoolboy who had been caught with stolen apples in his possession.

*P*arodists delight in coining such absurd variations on Sherlock Holmes's name as Picklock Holes, Thinlock Bones, Padlock Homes, Holmlock Shears and WILLIAM B. KAHN's Oilock Combs, who was featured in a series of spoofs in The Smart Set magazine. "The Succored Beauty" first appeared in October 1905.

The Succored Beauty

WILLIAM B. KAHN

One night, as I was returning from a case of acute indigestion—it was immediately after my divorce and I was obliged to return to the practice of my profession in order to support myself—it chanced that my way homeward lay through Fakir street. As I reached the house where Combs and I had spent so many hours together, where I had composed so many of his adventures, an irresistible longing seized me to go once more upstairs and grasp my friend by the hand, for, if the truth must be told, Combs and I had had a tiff. I really did not like the way in which he had procured evidence for my wife when she sought the separation, and I took the liberty of telling Combs so, but he had said to me: "My dear fellow, it is my business, is it not?" and though I knew he was not acting properly I was forced to be placated. However, the incident left a little breach between us which I determined on this night to bridge.

As I entered the room I saw Combs nervously drinking a glass of soda water. Since I succeeded in breaking him of the morphine habit he had been slyly looking about for some other stimulant and at last he had found it. I sighed to see him thus employed.

"Good evening, Combs," said I, extending my hand.

"Hello, Spotson," cried he, ignoring my proffered digits. "You are well, I see. It really is too bad, though, that you have no servant again. You seem to have quite some trouble with your help." And he chuckled as he sipped the soda water.

Familiar as I was with my friend's powers, this extraordinary exhibition of them really startled me.

"Why, Oilock," said I, calling him, in my excitement, by his prænomen, "how did you know it?"

"Perfectly obvious, Spotson, perfectly obvious. Merely observation," answered Combs as he took out his harmonica and began playing a tune thereon.

"But how?" persisted I.

"Well, if you really wish to know," he replied, as he ceased playing, "I suppose I will be obliged to tell you. I see you have a small piece of court-plaster upon the index finger of your left hand. Naturally, a cut. But the plaster is so small that the cut must be very minute. 'What could have done it?' I ask myself. The obvious response is a tack, a pin or a needle. On a chance I eliminate the tack proposition. I take another chance and eliminate the pin. Therefore, it must have been the needle. 'Why a needle?' query I of myself. And glancing at your coat I see the answer. There you have five buttons, four of which are hanging on rather loosely while the fifth one is tightly sewn to the cloth. It had recently been sewn. The connection is now clear. You punctured your finger with the needle while sewing on the button. But," he continued musingly and speaking, it seemed, more to himself than to me, "I never saw nor heard of the man who would sew unless he was compelled to. Spotson always keeps a servant; why did she not sew the button on for him? The reply is childishly easy: his servant left him."

I followed his explanation with rapt attention. My friend's powers were, I was happy to see, as marvelous as they were when I lived with him.

"Wonderful, Combs, wonderful," I cried.

"Merely observation," he replied. "Some day I think that I shall write a monograph on the subject of buttons. It is a very interesting subject and the book ought to sell well. But, hello, what is this?"

The sound of a cab halting before the door caused Combs's remark. Even as he spoke there was a pull at the bell, then the sound of hasty footsteps on the stairs. A sharp knock sounded upon the door. Combs dropped into his armchair, stuck out his legs in his familiar way and then said: "Come in."

The door opened and there entered, in great perturbation, a young lady, twenty-three years of age, having on a blue tailor-made suit, patent-leather shoes and a hat with a black pompon ornamenting it. She wore some other things, but these were all that I noticed. Not so Combs. I could see by the penetrating glance he threw at her that her secret was already known to that astute mind.

"Thank heaven," she cried, turning to me, "that I have found you in!"

"Are you ill, madam?" I began; but suddenly realizing that I was not in my office but in Combs's consultation room, I drew myself up stiffly and said: "That is Mr. Combs."

The young lady turned to him. Then, lifting her handkerchief to her beautiful eyes she burst into tears as she said: "Help me, help me, Mr. Combs."

The great man did not reply. An answer to such a remark he would have regarded as too trivial. The lady took down her handkerchief and, after glancing dubiously at me, said to Mr. Combs: "Can I see you privately?"

Once, and once only did I ever before or, indeed, since, see such a look of rage on Combs's face. That was when Professor O'Flaherty and he had that altercation in Switzerland. (See "Memoirs of Oilock Combs." Arper & Co. $1.50.)

"Madam," said he in frigid tones, "whatever you desire to say to me you may say before Dr. Spotson. How under the sun, woman," he cried, losing control of himself for a moment, "would the public know of my adventures if he were not here to write them?"

I threw Combs a grateful look while he reached for the soda water. The visitor was momentarily crushed. At last, however, she recovered her equanimity.

"Well, then," she said, "I will tell you my story."

"Pray, begin," said Combs rather testily.

"My name is Ysabelle, Duchess of Swabia," the visitor commenced.

"One moment; please," interrupted Combs. "Spotson, kindly look up that name in my index."

I took down the book referred to, in which Combs had made thousands of notes of people and events of interest, and found between "Yponomeutidæ" and "yttrium" the following item, which I read aloud:

> "Ysabelle, Duchess of Swabia; Countess of Steinheim-bach; Countess of Riesendorf, etc., etc. Born at Schloss Ochsen-fuss, February 29, 1876. Her mother was the Duchess Olga, of Zwiefelfeld, and her father was Hugo, Duke of Kaffeeküchen. At three years of age she could say 'ha, ha!' in German, French, English, Italian and Spanish. Between the ages of five and fifteen she was instructed by Professor Grosskopf, the eminent philosopher of the University of Kleinplatz. By sixteen her wisdom teeth had all appeared. A very remarkable woman!"

As I read this last sentence, the duchess again burst into tears.

"Pray, pray, compose yourself, duchess," said Combs, taking a pipe from the table and filling it with some tobacco which he absent-mindedly took from my coat-pocket.

The duchess succeeded in calming herself. Then, rising majestically and gazing at Combs with those wonderful eyes which had played havoc with so many royal hearts, she said, in solemn tones:

"I am lost!"

The manner in which she made this statement as well as the declaration itself seemed to make a deep impression upon Combs. Without uttering one word he sat there for fully four minutes. The way in which he puffed nervously at the pipe showed me that he was thinking. Suddenly, with an exclamation of delight, he dashed out of the room and down the stairs, leaving the amazed duchess and myself in his apartments. But not for long. In forty-three seconds he was again in the room and, dropping into his chair thoroughly exhausted, he triumphantly cried:

"I have it!"

Never had I seen my friend wear such a look of victory. The achievement which merited such an expression upon his countenance must have been remarkable. By and by he recovered from his fatigue. Then he spoke.

"Madam," he said, "I have the answer."

The duchess sobbed in ecstasy.

Combs continued:

"The moment that you said you were lost," he began, "an idea came to me. You must have noticed, Spotson, how preoccupied I seemed before. Well, that is the sign of an idea coming to me. Before it had time to vanish I dashed down the steps, into the vestibule, looked at the number of this house and jotted it down. Madam," he cried, drawing out a book and looking at one of the pages, "madam, you are saved! You are no longer lost! This is No. 62 Fakir street. You are found!"

During this entire recital the duchess had not said a word. When Combs had finished she stood for a moment as if she did not understand and then, realizing the fact that she was rescued, she wept once more.

"My savior," she cried as she prepared to leave the room, "how can I ever thank you?" And she pressed into Combs's outstretched hand a large gold-mesh, diamond-studded purse.

The door closed, the carriage rolled away and the Duchess of Swabia was gone.

"Spotson," said Combs to me, "don't forget to write this one down. It has a duchess in it and will sell well to cooks and chambermaids. By the way, I wonder what she gave me."

He opened the purse and there, neatly folded, lay two hundred pounds in bills.

"Bah!" cried Combs contemptuously, "how ungrateful these royal personages always are."

*I*ired of "agenting" new installments of Sherlock Holmes's exploits for the readers of *The Strand Magazine, Arthur Conan Doyle arranged to have him pushed off Reichenbach Falls. But a few years later, he offered Watson's memorable "reminiscence,"* The Hound of the Baskervilles, *and that paved the way for the sleuth's ultimate resurrection. The generally accepted theory for Conan Doyle's change of heart is that he acceded to widespread public demand. But* L U K E S H A R P *propounded a less charitable notion in the following sinister tale. Luke Sharp was the pseudonym of Robert Barr (1850–1912), a* Detroit Free Press *journalist who wrote what is believed to be the first Sherlockian parody, "The Adventures of Sherlaw Kombs," in 1892.*

The Adventure of the Second Swag

L U K E   S H A R P

The time was Christmas Eve, 1904. The place was an ancient, secluded manor house, built so far back in the last century as 1896. It stood at the head of a profound valley; a valley clothed in ferns waist deep, and sombrely guarded by ancient trees, the remnants of a primeval forest. From this mansion no other human habitation could be seen. The descending road which connected the king's highway with the stronghold was so sinuous and precipitate that more than once the grim baronet who owned it had upset his automobile in trying to negotiate the dangerous curves. The isolated situation and gloomy architecture of this venerable mansion must have impressed the most casual observer with the thought that here was the spot for the perpetration of dark deeds, were it not for the fact that the place was brilliantly illumined with electricity, while the silence was emphasised rather than disturbed by the monotonous, regular thud of an accumulator pumping the subtle fluid into a receptive dynamo situated in an outhouse to the east.

The night was gloomy and lowering after a day of rain, but the very sombreness of the scene made the brilliant stained glass windows stand out like the radiant covers of a Christmas number. Such was the appearance presented by "Undershaw," the home of Sir Arthur Conan Doyle, situated among the wilds of Hindhead, some forty or fifty miles from London. Is it any wonder that at a spot so remote from civilisation law should be set at defiance, and that the one lone policeman who perambulates the district should tremble as he passed the sinister gates of "Undershaw"?

In a large room of this manor house, furnished with a luxuriant elegance one would not have expected in a region so far from humanising influences, sat two men. One was a giant in stature, whose broad brow and smoothly shaven strong chin gave a look of determination to his countenance, which was further enhanced by the heavy black moustache which covered his upper lip. There was something of the dragoon in his upright and independent bearing. He had, in fact, taken part in more than one fiercely-fought battle, and was a member of several military clubs; but it was plain to be seen that his ancestors had used war clubs, and had transmitted to him the physique of a Hercules. One did not need to glance at the Christmas number of the Strand, which he held in his hand, nor read the name printed there in large letters, to know that he was face to face with Sir Arthur Conan Doyle.

His guest, an older man, yet still in the prime of life, whose beard was tinged with grey, was of less warlike bearing than the celebrated novelist, belonging, as he evidently did, to the civil and not the military section of life. He had about him the air of a prosperous man of affairs, shrewd, good-natured, conciliatory, and these two strongly contrasting personages are types of the men to whom England owes her greatness. The reader of the Christmas number will very probably feel disappointed when he finds, as he supposes, merely two old friends sitting amicably in a country house after dinner. There seems, to his jaded taste, no element of tragedy in such a situation. These two men appear comfortable enough, and respectable enough. It is true that there is whisky and soda at hand, and the box of cigars is open, yet there are latent possibilities of passion under the most placid natures, revealed only to writers of fiction in our halfpenny Press. Let the reader wait, therefore, till he sees these two men tried as by fire under a great temptation, and then let him say whether even the probity of Sir George Newnes comes scatheless from the ordeal.

"Have you brought the swag, Sir George?" asked the novelist, with some trace of anxiety in his voice.

"Yes," replied the great publisher; "but before proceeding to the count would it not be wise to give orders that will insure our being left undisturbed?"

"You are right," replied Doyle, pressing an electric button.

When the servant appeared he said: "I am not at home to anyone. No matter who calls, or what excuse is given, you must permit none to approach this room."

When the servant had withdrawn, Doyle took the further precaution of thrusting in place one of the huge bolts which ornamented the massive door studded with iron knobs. Sir George withdrew from the tail pocket of his dress coat two canvas bags, and, untying the strings, poured the rich red gold on the smooth table.

"I think you will find that right," he said; "six thousand pounds in all."

The writer dragged his heavy chair nearer the table, and began to count the coins two by two, withdrawing each pair from the pile with his extended forefingers in the manner of one accustomed to deal with great treasure. For a time the silence was unbroken, save by the chink of gold, when suddenly a high-keyed voice outside penetrated even the stout oak of the huge door. The shrill exclamation seemed to touch a chord of remembrance in the mind of Sir George Newnes. Nervously he grasped the arms of his chair, sitting very bolt upright, muttering:—

"Can it be he, of all persons, at this time, of all times?"

Doyle glanced up with an expression of annoyance on his face, murmuring, to keep his memory green:—

"A hundred and ten, a hundred and ten, a hundred and ten."

"Not at home?" cried the vibrant voice. "Nonsense! Everybody is at home on Christmas Eve!"

"You don't seem to be," he heard the servant reply.

"Me? Oh, I have no home, merely rooms in Baker Street. I must see your master, and at once."

"Master left in his motor car half an hour ago to attend the county ball, given tonight, at the Royal Huts Hotel, seven miles away," answered the servant, with that glib mastery of fiction which unconsciously comes to those who are members, even in a humble capacity, of a household devoted to the production of imaginative art.

"Nonsense, I say again," came the strident voice. "It is true that the tracks of an automobile are on the ground in front of your door, but if you will notice the markings of the puncture-proof belt, you will see that the automobile is returning and not departing. It went to the station before the last shower to bring back a visitor, and since its arrival there has been no rain. That suit of armour in the hall spattered with mud shows it to be the casing the visitor wore. The blazonry upon it of a pair of scissors above an open book resting upon a printing press, indicates that the wearer is first of all an editor; second, a publisher; and third, a printer. The only baronet in England whose occupation corresponds with his heraldic device is Sir George Newnes."

"You forget Sir Alfred Harmsworth," said the servant, whose hand held a copy of Answers.

If the insistent visitor was taken aback by this unlooked-for rejoinder, his manner showed no trace of embarrassment, and he went on unabashed.

"As the last shower began at ten minutes to six, Sir George must have arrived at Haslemere station on the 6.19 from Waterloo. He has had dinner, and at this moment is sitting comfortably with Sir Arthur Conan Doyle, doubtless in the front room, which I see is so brilliantly lighted. Now, if you will kindly take in my card—"

"But I tell you," persisted the perplexed servant, "that the master left in his motor car for the county ball at the Royal—"

"Oh, I know, I know. There stands his suit of armour, too, newly black-leaded, whose coat of arms is a couchant typewriter on an automobile rampant."

"Great heavens!" cried Sir George, his eyes brightening with the light of unholy desire, "you have material enough there, Doyle, for a story in our January number. What do you say?"

A deep frown marred the smoothness of the novelist's brow.

"I say," he replied sternly, "that this man has been sending threatening letters to me. I have had enough of his menaces."

"Then triply bolt the door," advised Newnes, with a sigh of disappointment, leaning back in his chair.

"Do you take me for a man who bolts when his enemy appears?" asked Doyle fiercely, rising to his feet. "No, I will unbolt. He shall meet the Douglas in his hall!"

"Better have him in the drawing-room, where it's warm," suggested Sir George, with a smile, diplomatically desiring to pour oil on the troubled waters.

The novelist, without reply, spread a copy of that evening's Westminster Gazette over the pile of gold, strode to the door, threw it open, and said coldly:—

"Show the gentleman in, please."

There entered to them a tall, self-possessed, calm man, with clean-shaven face, eagle eye, and inquisitive nose.

Although the visit was most embarrassing at that particular juncture, the natural courtesy of the novelist restrained him from giving utterance to his resentment of the intrusion, and he proceeded to introduce the bidden to the unbidden guest as if each were equally welcome.

"Mr. Sherlock Holmes, permit me to present to you Sir George—"

"It is quite superfluous," said the newcomer, in an even voice of exasperating tenor, "for I perceive at once that one who wears a green waistcoat must be a Liberal of strong Home Rule opinions, or the editor of several publications wearing covers of emerald hue. The shamrock necktie, in addition to the waistcoat, indicates that the gentleman before me is both, and so I take it for granted that this is Sir George Newnes. How is your circulation, Sir George?"

"Rapidly rising," replied the editor.

"I am glad of that," asserted the intruder, suavely, "and can assure you that the temperature outside is as rapidly falling."

The great detective spread his hands before the glowing electric fire, and rubbed them vigorously together.

"I perceive through that evening paper the sum of six thousand pounds in gold."

Doyle interrupted him with some impatience.

"You didn't see it through the paper; you saw it in the paper. Goodness knows, it's been mentioned in enough of the sheets."

"As I was about to remark," went on Sherlock Holmes imperturbably, "I am amazed that a man whose time is so valuable should waste it in counting the money. You are surely aware that a golden sovereign weighs 123.44 grains, therefore, if I were you, I should have up the kitchen scales, dump in the metal, and figure out the amount with a lead pencil. You brought the gold in two canvas bags, did you not, Sir George?"

"In the name of all that's wonderful, how do you know that?" asked the astonished publisher.

Sherlock Holmes, with a superior smile, casually waved his hand toward the two bags which still lay on the polished table.

"Oh, I'm tired of this sort of thing," said Doyle wearily, sitting down in the first chair that presented itself. "Can't you be honest, even on Christmas Eve? You know the oracles of old did not try it on with each other."

"That is true," said Sherlock Holmes. "The fact is, I followed Sir George Newnes into the Capital and Counties Bank this afternoon, where he demanded six thousand pounds in gold; but when he learned this would weigh ninety-six pounds seven ounces avoirdupois weight, and that even troy weight would make the sum no lighter, he took two small bags of gold and the rest in Bank of England notes. I came from London on the same train with him, but he was off in the automobile before I could make myself known, and so I had to walk up. I was further delayed by taking the wrong turning on the top and finding myself at that charming spot in the neighbourhood where a sailor was murdered by two ruffians a century or so ago."

There was a note of warning in Doyle's voice when he said:—

"Did that incident teach you no lesson? Did you not realise that you are in a dangerous locality?"

"And likely to fall in with two ruffians?" asked Holmes, slightly elevating his eyebrows, while the same sweet smile hovered round his thin lips. "No; the remembrance of the incident encouraged me. It was the man who had the money that was murdered. I brought no coin with me, although I expect to bear many away."

"Would you mind telling us, without further circumlocation, what brings you here so late at night?"

Sherlock Holmes heaved a sigh, and mournfully shook his head very slowly.

"After all the teaching I have bestowed upon you, Doyle, is it possible that you cannot deduce even so simple a thing as that? Why am I here? Because Sir George made a mistake about those bags. He was quite right in taking one of them to "Undershaw," but he should have left the other at 221B, Baker Street. I call this little trip 'The Adventure of the Second Swag.' Here is the second swag on the table. The first swag you received long ago, and all I had for my share was some honeyed words of compliment in the stories you wrote. Now, it is truly said that soft words butter no parsnips, and, in this instance, they do not even turn away wrath. So far as the second swag is concerned, I have come to demand half of it."

"I am not so poor at deduction as you seem to imagine," said Doyle, apparently nettled at the other's slighting reference to his powers. "I was well aware, when you came in, what your errand was. I deduced further that if you saw Sir George withdraw gold from the bank, you also followed him to Waterloo station."

"Quite right."

"When he purchased his ticket for Haslemere, you did the same."

"I did."

"When you arrived at Haslemere, you sent a telegram to your friend, Dr. Watson, telling him of your whereabouts."

"You are wrong there; I ran after the motor car."

"You certainly sent a telegram from somewhere, to someone, or at least dropped a note in the post-box. There are signs, which I need not mention, that point irrevocably to such a conclusion."

The doomed man, ruined by his own self-complacency, merely smiled in his superior manner, not noticing the eager look with which Doyle awaited his answer.

"Wrong entirely. I neither wrote any telegram, nor spoke any message, since I left London."

"Ah, no," cried Doyle. "I see where I went astray. You merely inquired the way to my house."

"I needed to make no inquiries. I followed the rear light of the automobile part way up the hill and, when that disappeared, I turned to the right instead of to the left, as there was no one out on such a night from whom I could make inquiry."

"My deductions, then, are beside the mark," said Doyle hoarsely, in an accent which sent cold chills up and down the spine of his invited guest, but conveyed no intimation of his fate to the self-satisfied later arrival.

"Of course they were," said Holmes, with exasperating self-assurance.

"Am I also wrong in deducing that you have had nothing to eat since you left London?"

"No, you are quite right there."

"Well, oblige me by pressing that electric button."

Holmes did so with much eagerness, but, although the trio waited some minutes in silence, there was no response.

"I deduce from that," said Doyle, "that the servants have gone to bed. After I have satisfied all your claims in the way of hunger for food and gold, I shall take you back in my motor car, unless you prefer to stay here the night."

"You are very kind," said Sherlock Holmes.

"Not at all," replied Doyle. "Just take that chair, draw it up to the table and we will divide the second swag."

The chair indicated differed from all others in the room. It was straight-backed, and its oaken arms were covered by two plates, apparently of German silver. When Holmes clutched it by the arms to drag it forward, he gave one half articulate gasp, and plunged headlong to the floor, quivering. Sir George Newnes sprang up standing with a cry of alarm. Sir Arthur Conan Doyle remained seated, a seraphic smile of infinite satisfaction playing about his lips.

"Has he fainted?" cried Sir George.

"No, merely electrocuted. A simple device the Sheriff of New York taught me when I was over there last."

"Merciful heavens! Cannot he be resuscitated?"

"My dear Newnes," said Doyle, with the air of one from whose shoulders a great weight is lifted, "a man may fall into the chasm at the foot of the Reichenbach Fall and escape to record his adventures later, but when two thousand volts pass through the human frame, the person who owns that frame is dead."

"You don't mean to say you've murdered him?" asked Sir George, in an awed whisper.

"Well, the term you use is harsh, still it rather accurately sums up the situation. To speak candidly, Sir George, I don't think they can indite us for anything more than manslaughter. You see, this is a little invention for the reception of burglars. Every night before the servants go to bed, they switch on the current to this chair. That's why I asked Holmes to press the button. I place a small table beside the chair, and put on it a bottle of wine, whisky and soda, and cigars. Then, if any burglar comes in, he invariably sits down in the chair to enjoy himself, and so you see, that piece of furniture is an effective method of reducing crime. The number of burglars I have turned over to the parish to be buried will prove that this taking off of Holmes was not premeditated by me. This incident, strictly speaking, is not murder, but manslaughter. We shouldn't get more than fourteen years apiece, and probably that would be cut down to seven on the ground that we had performed an act for the public benefit."

"Apiece!" cried Sir George. "But what have I had to do with it?"

"Everything, my dear sir, everything. As that babbling fool talked, I saw in your eye the gleam which betokens avarice for copy. Indeed, I think you mentioned the January number. You were therefore accessory before the fact. I simply had to slaughter the poor wretch."

Sir George sank back in his chair well nigh breathless with horror. Publishers are humane men who rarely commit crimes; authors, however, are a hardened set who usually perpetrate a felony every time they issue a book. Doyle laughed easily.

"I'm used to this sort of thing," he said. "Remember how I killed off the people in 'The White Company.' Now, if you will help me to get rid of the body, all may yet be well. You see, I learned from the misguided simpleton himself that nobody knows where he is to-day. He often disappears for weeks at a time, so there really is slight danger of detection. Will you lend a hand?"

"I suppose I must," cried the conscience-stricken man.

Doyle at once threw off the lassitude which the coming of Sherlock Holmes had caused, and acted now with an energy which was characteristic of him. Going to an outhouse, he brought the motor car to the front door, then, picking up Holmes and followed by his trembling guest, he went outside and flung the body into the tonneau behind. He then threw a spade and a pick into the car, and covered everything up with a waterproof spread. Lighting the lamps, he bade his silent guest get up beside him, and so they started on their fateful journey, taking the road past the spot where the sailor had been murdered, and dashing down the long hill at fearful speed toward London.

"Why do you take this direction?" asked Sir George. "Wouldn't it be more advisable to go further into the country?"

Doyle laughed harshly.

"Haven't you a place on Wimbledon Common? Why not bury him in your garden?"

"Merciful motors!" cried the horrified man. "How can you propose such a thing? Talking of gardens, why not have him buried in your own, which was infinitely safer than going forward at this pace."

"Have no fear," said Doyle reassuringly, "we shall find him a suitable sepulchre without disturbing either of our gardens. I'll be in the centre of London within two hours."

Sir George stared in affright at the demon driver. The man had evidently gone mad. To London, of all places in the world. Surely that was the one spot on earth to avoid.

"Stop the motor and let me off," he cried. "I'm going to wake up the nearest magistrate and confess."

"You'll do nothing of the sort," said Doyle. "Don't you see that no person on earth would suspect two criminals of making for London when they have the whole country before them? Haven't you read my stories? The moment a man commits a crime he tries to get as far away from London as possible. Every policeman knows that, therefore, two men coming into London are innocent strangers, according to Scotland Yard."

"But then we may be taken up for fast driving, and think of the terrible burden we carry."

"We're safe on the country roads, and I'll slow down when we reach the suburbs."

It was approaching three o'clock in the morning when a huge motor car turned out of Trafalgar Square, and went eastward along the Strand. The northern side of the Strand was up, as it usually is, and the motor, skilfully driven, glided past the piles of wood-paving blocks, great sombre kettles holding tar, and the general debris of a repaving convulsion. Opposite Southampton Street, at the very spot so graphically illustrated by George C. Haite on the cover of the *Strand Magazine,* Sir Arthur Conan Doyle stopped his motor. The Strand was deserted. He threw pick and shovel into the excavation, and curtly ordered his companion to take his choice of weapons. Sir George selected the pick, and Doyle vigorously plied the spade. In almost less time than it takes to tell, a very respectable hole had been dug, and in it was placed the body of the popular private detective. Just as the last spadeful was shovelled in place the stern voice of a policeman awoke the silence, and caused Sir George to drop his pick from nerveless hands.

"What are you two doing down there?"

"That's all right, officer," said Doyle glibly, as one who had foreseen every emergency. "My friend here is controller of the Strand. When the Strand is up he is responsible, and it has the largest circulation in the—I mean it's up oftener than any other street in the world. We cannot inspect the work satisfactorily while traffic is on, and so we have been examining it in the night-time. I am his secretary; I do the writing, you know."

"Oh, I see," replied the constable. "Well, gentlemen, good morning to you, and merry Christmas."

"The same to you, constable. Just lend a hand, will you?"

The officer of the law helped each of the men up to the level of the road.

As Doyle drove away from the ill-omened spot he said:—

"Thus have we disposed of poor Holmes in the busiest spot on earth, where no one will ever think of looking for him, and we've put him away without even a Christmas box around him. We have buried him for ever in the Strand."

*T*o be fair to Sherlock Holmes, the following generic parody of short-short fiction by the British-Canadian political economist and humorist STEPHEN BUTLER LEACOCK *(1869–1944) merely refers to its protagonist as "the great detective." This wonderfully preposterous little item comes from Leacock's 1916 collection,* Further Foolishness.

An Irreducible Detective Story

STEPHEN LEACOCK

The mystery had now reached its climax. First, the man had been undoubtedly murdered. Second, it was absolutely certain that no conceivable person had done it.

It was therefore time to call in the great detective.

He gave one searching glance at the corpse. In a moment he whipped out a microscope.

"Ha! Ha!" he said, as he picked a hair off the lapel of the dead man's coat. "The mystery is now solved."

He held up the hair.

"Listen," he said, "we have only to find the man who lost this hair and the criminal is in our hands."

The inexorable chain of logic was complete.

The detective set himself to the search.

For four days and nights he moved, unobserved, through the streets of New York scanning closely every face he passed, looking for a man who had lost a hair.

On the fifth day he discovered a man, disguised as a tourist, his head enveloped in a steamer cap that reached below his ears.

The man was about to go on board the *Gloritania*.

The detective followed him on board.

"Arrest him!" he said, and then drawing himself to his full height, he brandished aloft the hair.

"This is his," said the great detective. "It proves his guilt."

"Remove his hat," said the ship's captain sternly.

They did so.

The man was entirely bald.

"Ha!" said the great detective, without a moment of hesitation. "He has committed not *one* murder but about a million."

"The Adventures of Shamrock Jolnes" is one of two wicked lampoons of Sherlock Holmes in Sixes and Sevens, a 1911 collection of prose by William Sydney Porter (1862–1910), better known as O . HENRY, one of America's most popular writers of twist-ending short fiction, including "The Cop and the Anthem," "The Clarion Call," "The Last Leaf," "The Ransom of Red Chief" and "The Gift of the Magi."

The Adventures of Shamrock Jolnes

O . HENRY

I am so fortunate as to count Shamrock Jolnes, the great New York detective, among my muster of friends. Jolnes is what is called the "inside man" of the city detective force. He is an expert in the use of the typewriter, and it is his duty, whenever there is a "murder mystery" to be solved, to sit at a desk telephone at Headquarters and take down the messages of "cranks" who phone in their confessions to having committed the crime.

But on certain "off" days when confessions are coming in slowly and three or four newspapers have run to earth as many different guilty persons, Jolnes will knock about the town with me, exhibiting, to my great delight and instruction, his marvelous powers of observation and deduction.

The other day I dropped in at Headquarters and found the great detective gazing thoughtfully at a string that was tied tightly around his little finger.

"Good morning, Whatsup," he said, without turning his head. "I'm glad to notice that you've had your house fitted up with electric lights at last."

"Will you please tell me," I said, in surprise, "how you knew that? I am sure that I never mentioned the fact to anyone, and the wiring was a rush order not completed until this morning."

"Nothing easier," said Jolnes, genially. "As you came in I caught the odor of the cigar you are smoking. I know an expensive cigar; and I know that not more than three men in New York can afford to smoke cigars and pay gas bills too at the present time. That was an easy one. But I am working just now on a little problem of my own."

"Why have you that string on your finger?" I asked.

"That's the problem," said Jolnes. "My wife tied that on this morning to remind me of something I was to send up to the house. Sit down, Whatsup, and excuse me for a few moments."

The distinguished detective went to a wall telephone, and stood with the receiver to his ear for probably ten minutes.

"Were you listening to a confession?" I asked, when he had returned to his chair.

"Perhaps," said Jolnes, with a smile, "it might be called something of the sort. To be frank with you, Whatsup, I've cut out the dope. I've been increasing the quantity for so long that morphine doesn't have much effect on me any more. I've got to have something more powerful. That telephone I just went to is connected with a room in the Waldorf where there's an author's reading in progress. Now, to get at the solution of this string."

After five minutes of silent pondering, Jolnes looked at me, with a smile, and nodded his head.

"Wonderful man!" I exclaimed. "Already?"

"It is quite simple," he said, holding up his finger. "You see that knot? That is to prevent my forgetting. It is, therefore, a forget-me-knot. A forget-me-not is a flower. It was a sack of flour that I was to send home!"

"Beautiful!" I could not help crying out in admiration.

"Suppose we go out for a ramble," suggested Jolnes.

"There is only one case of importance on hand just now. Old man McCarty, one hundred and four years old, died from eating too many bananas. The evidence points so strongly to the Mafia that the police have surrounded the Second Avenue Katzenjammer Gambrinus Club No. 2, and the capture of the assassin is only the matter of a few hours. The detective force has not yet been called on for assistance."

Jolnes and I went out and up the street toward the corner, where we were to catch a surface car.

Halfway up the block we met Rheingelder, an acquaintance of ours, who held a City Hall position.

"Good morning, Rheingelder," said Jolnes, halting. "Nice breakfast that was you had this morning."

Always on the lookout for the detective's remarkable feats of deduction, I saw Jolnes's eyes flash for an instant upon a long yellow splash on the shirt bosom and a smaller one upon the chin of Rheingelder—both undoubtedly made by the yolk of an egg.

"Oh, dot is some of your detectiveness," said Rheingelder, shaking all over with a smile. "Vell, I pet you trinks und cigars all round dot you cannot tell vot I haf eaten for breakfast."

"Done," said Jolnes. "Sausage, pumpernickel and coffee."

Rheingelder admitted the correctness of the surmise and paid the bet. When we had proceeded on our way I said to Jolnes:

"I thought you looked at the egg spilled on his chin and shirt front."

"I did," said Jolnes. "That is where I began my deduction. Rheingelder is a very economical, saving man. Yesterday eggs dropped in the market to twenty-eight cents per dozen. Today they are quoted at forty-two.
Rheingelder ate eggs yesterday, and today he went back to his usual fare. A
little thing like this isn't anything, Whatsup; it belongs to the primary arithmetic class."

When we boarded the streetcar we found the seats all occupied—prin-
cipally by ladies. Jolnes and I stood on the rear platform.

About the middle of the car there sat an elderly man with a short gray
beard, who looked to be the typical well-dressed New Yorker. At successive
corners other ladies climbed aboard, and soon three or four of them were
standing over the man, clinging to straps and glaring meaningly at the man
who occupied the coveted seat. But he resolutely retained his place.

"We New Yorkers," I remarked to Jolnes, "have about lost our manners, as far as the exercise of them in public goes."

"Perhaps so," said Jolnes, lightly, "but the man you evidently refer to
happens to be a very chivalrous and courteous gentleman from Old Virginia.
He is spending a few days in New York with his wife and two daughters, and
he leaves for the South tonight."

"You know him, then?" I said, in amazement.

"I never saw him before we stepped on the car," declared the detective, smilingly.

"By the gold tooth of the Witch of Endor," I cried, "if you can con-
strue all that from his appearance you are dealing in nothing else than black
art."

"The habit of observation—nothing more," said Jolnes. "If the old
gentleman gets off the car before we do, I think I can demonstrate to you the
accuracy of my deduction."

Three blocks farther along the gentleman rose to leave the car. Jolnes
addressed him at the door:

"Pardon me, sir, but are you not Colonel Hunter, of Norfolk, Virginia?"

"No, suh," was the extremely courteous answer. "My name, suh, is
Ellison—Major Winfield R. Ellison, from Fairfax County, in the same state.
I know a good many people, suh, in Norfolk—the Goodriches, the Tollivers,
and the Crabtrees, suh, but I never had the pleasure of meeting yo' friend
Colonel Hunter. I am happy to say, suh, that I am going back to Virginia
tonight, after having spent a week in yo' city with my wife and three daughters. I shall be in Norfolk in about ten days, and if you will give me yo' name,
suh, I will take pleasure in looking up Colonel Hunter and telling him that
you inquired after him, suh."

"Thank you," said Jolnes. "Tell him that Reynolds sent his regards, if you will be so kind."

I glanced at the great New York detective and saw that a look of intense chagrin had come upon his clear-cut features. Failure in the slightest point always galled Shamrock Jolnes.

"Did you say your *three* daughters?" he asked of the Virginia gentleman.

"Yes, suh, my three daughters, all as fine girls as there are in Fairfax County," was the answer.

With that Major Ellison stopped the car and began to descend the step. Shamrock Jolnes clutched his arm.

"One moment, sir—" he begged, in an urbane voice in which I alone detected the anxiety—"am I not right in believing that one of the young ladies is an *adopted* daughter?"

"You are, suh," admitted the major, from the ground, "but how the devil you knew it, suh, is mo' than I can tell."

"And mo' than I can tell, too," I said, as the car went on.

Jolnes was restored to his calm, observant serenity by having wrested victory from his apparent failure; so after we got off the car he invited me into a café, promising to reveal the process of his latest wonderful feat.

"In the first place," he began after we were comfortably seated, "I knew the gentleman was no New Yorker because he was flushed and uneasy and restless on account of the ladies that were standing, although he did not rise and give them his seat. I decided from his appearance that he was a Southerner rather than a Westerner.

"Next I began to figure out his reason for not relinquishing his seat to a lady when he evidently felt strongly, but not overpoweringly, impelled to do so. I very quickly decided upon that. I noticed that one of his eyes had received a severe jab in one corner, which was red and inflamed, and that all over his face were tiny round marks about the size of the end of an uncut lead pencil. Also upon both of his patent-leather shoes were a number of deep imprints shaped like ovals cut off square at one end.

"Now, there is only one district in New York City where a man is bound to receive scars and wounds and indentations of that sort—and that is along the sidewalks of Twenty-third Street and a portion of Sixth Avenue south of there. I knew from the imprints of trampling French heels on his feet and the marks of countless jabs in the face from umbrellas and parasols carried by women in the shopping district that he had been in conflict with the Amazonian troops. And as he was a man of intelligent appearance, I knew he would not have braved such dangers unless he had been dragged thither by his own womenfolk. Therefore, when he got on the car his anger at the treatment he had received was sufficient to make him keep his seat in spite of his traditions of Southern chivalry."

"That is all very well," I said, "but why did you insist upon daughters—and especially two daughters? Why couldn't a wife alone have taken him shopping?"

"There had to be daughters," said Jolnes, calmly. "If he had only a wife, and she near his own age, he could have bluffed her into going alone. If he had a young wife she would prefer to go alone. So there you are."

"I'll admit that," I said; "but, now, why two daughters? And how, in the name of all the prophets, did you guess that one was adopted when he told you he had three?"

"Don't say guess," said Jolnes, with a touch of pride in his air; "there is no such word in the lexicon of ratiocination. In Major Ellison's buttonhole there was a carnation and a rosebud backed by a geranium leaf. No woman ever combined a carnation and a rosebud into a boutonnière. Close your eyes, Whatsup, and give the logic of your imagination a chance. Cannot you see the lovely Adele fastening the carnation to the lapel so that Papa may be gay upon the street? And then the romping Edith May dancing up with sisterly jealousy to add her rosebud to the adornment?"

"And then," I cried, beginning to feel enthusiasm, "when he declared that he had three daughters—"

"I could see," said Jolnes, "one in the background who added no flower; and I knew that she must be—"

"Adopted!" I broke in. "I give you every credit; but how did you know he was leaving for the South tonight?"

"In his breast pocket," said the great detective, "something large and oval made a protuberance. Good liquor is scarce on trains, and it is a long journey from New York to Fairfax County."

"Again I must bow to you," I said. "And tell me this, so that my last shred of doubt will be cleared away; why did you decide that he was from Virginia?"

"It was very faint, I admit," answered Shamrock Jolnes, "but no trained observer could have failed to detect the odor of mint in the car."

The Stolen Cigar Case

BRET HARTE

I found Hemlock Jones in the old Brook Street lodgings, musing before the fire. With the freedom of an old friend I at once threw myself in my usual familiar attitude at his feet, and gently caressed his boot. I was induced to do this for two reasons: one, that it enabled me to get a good look at his bent, concentrated face, and the other, that it seemed to indicate my reverence for his superhuman insight. So absorbed was he even then, in tracking some mysterious clue, that he did not seem to notice me. But therein I was wrong—as I always was in my attempt to understand that powerful intellect.

"It is raining," he said, without lifting his head.

"You have been out, then?" I said quickly.

"No. But I see that your umbrella is wet, and that your overcoat has drops of water on it."

I sat aghast at his penetration. After a pause he said carelessly, as if dismissing the subject: "Besides, I hear the rain on the window. Listen."

I listened. I could scarcely credit my ears, but there was the soft pattering of drops on the panes. It was evident there was no deceiving this man!

"Have you been busy lately?" I asked, changing the subject. "What new problem—given up by Scotland Yard as inscrutable—has occupied that gigantic intellect?"

He drew back his foot slightly, and seemed to hesitate ere he returned it to its original position. Then he answered wearily: "Mere trifles—nothing to speak of. The Prince Kupoli has been here to get my advice regarding the disappearance of certain rubies from the Kremlin; the Rajah of Pootibad, after vainly beheading his entire bodyguard, has been obliged to seek my assistance to recover a jeweled sword. The Grand Duchess of Pretzel-Brauntswig is desirous of discovering where her husband was on the night of February 14; and last night—" he lowered his voice slightly—"a lodger in this very house, meeting me on the stairs, wanted to know why they didn't answer his bell."

I could not help smiling—until I saw a frown gathering on his inscrutable forehead.

"Pray remember," he said coldly, "that it was through just such an apparently trivial question that I found out Why Paul Ferroll Killed His Wife, and What Happened to Jones!"

I became dumb at once. He paused for a moment, and then suddenly changing back to his usual pitiless, analytical style, he said: "When I say these are trifles, they are so in comparison to an affair that is now before me. A crime has been committed—and, singularly enough, against myself. You start," he said. "You wonder who would have dared to attempt it. So did I; nevertheless, it has been done. *I have been robbed!*"

"You robbed! You, Hemlock Jones, the Terror of Peculators!" I gasped in amazement, arising and gripping the table as I faced him.

"Yes! Listen. I would confess it to no other. But *you* who have followed my career, who know my methods; you, for whom I have partly lifted the veil that conceals my plans from ordinary humanity—you, who have for years rapturously accepted my confidences, passionately admired my inductions and inferences, placed yourself at my beck and call, become my slave, groveled at my feet, given up your practice except those few unremunerative and rapidly decreasing patients to whom, in moments of abstraction over *my* problems, you have administered strychnine for quinine and arsenic for Epsom salts; you, who have sacrificed anything and everybody to me—*you* I make my confidant!"

I arose and embraced him warmly, yet he was already so engrossed in thought that at the same moment he mechanically placed his hand upon his watch chain as if to consult the time. "Sit down," he said. "Have a cigar?"

"I have given up cigar smoking," I said.

"Why?" he asked.

I hesitated, and perhaps colored. I had really given it up because, with my diminished practice, it was too expensive. I could afford only a pipe. "I prefer a pipe," I said laughingly. "But tell me of this robbery. What have you lost?"

He arose, and planting himself before the fire with his hands under his coat-tails, looked down upon me reflectively for a moment. "Do you remember the cigar case presented to me by the Turkish ambassador for discovering the missing favorite of the Grand Vizier in the fifth chorus girl at the Hilarity Theater? It was that one. I mean the cigar case. It was incrusted with diamonds.''

"And the largest one had been supplanted by paste," I said.

"Ah," he said, with a reflective smile, "you know that?"

"You told me yourself. I remember considering it a proof of your extraordinary perception. But, by Jove, you don't mean to say you have lost it?"

He was silent for a moment. "No: it has been stolen, it is true, but I shall still find it. And by myself alone! In your profession, my dear fellow, when a member is seriously ill, he does not prescribe for himself, but calls in a brother doctor. Therein we differ. I shall take this matter in my own hands."

"And where could you find better?" I said enthusiastically. "I should say the cigar case is as good as recovered already."

"I shall remind you of that again," he said lightly. "And now, to show you my confidence in your judgment, in spite of my determination to pursue this alone, I am willing to listen to any suggestions from you."

He drew a memorandum book from his pocket and, with a grave smile, took up his pencil.

I could scarcely believe my senses. He, the great Hemlock Jones, accepting suggestions from a humble individual like myself! I kissed his hand reverently, and began in a joyous tone:

"First, I should advertise, offering a reward; I should give the same intimation in handbills, distributed at the 'pubs' and the pastry cooks'. I should next visit the different pawnbrokers; I should give notice at the police station. I should examine the servants. I should thoroughly search the house and my own pockets. I speak relatively," I added, with a laugh. "Of course I mean *your* own."

He gravely made an entry of these details.

"Perhaps," I added, "you have already done this?"

"Perhaps," he returned enigmatically. "Now, my dear friend," he continued, putting the notebook in his pocket and rising, "would you excuse me for a few moments? Make yourself perfectly at home until I return; there may be some things," he added with a sweep of his hand toward his heterogeneously filled shelves, "that may interest you and while away the time. There are pipes and tobacco in that corner."

Then nodding to me with the same inscrutable face he left the room. I was too well accustomed to his methods to think much of his unceremonious withdrawal, and made no doubt he was off to investigate some clue which had suddenly occurred to his active intelligence.

Left to myself I cast a cursory glance over his shelves. There were a number of small glass jars containing earthy substances, labeled PAVEMENT

AND ROAD SWEEPINGS, from the principal thoroughfares and suburbs of London, with the subdirections FOR IDENTIFYING FOOT TRACKS. There were several other jars, labeled FLUFF FROM OMNIBUS AND ROAD-CAR SEATS, COCONUT FIBER AND ROPE STRANDS FROM MATTINGS IN PUBLIC PLACES, CIGARETTE STUMPS AND MATCH ENDS FROM FLOOR OF PALACE THEATRE, ROW A, 1 TO 50. Everywhere were evidences of this wonderful man's system and perspicacity.

I was thus engaged when I heard the slight creaking of a door, and I looked up as a stranger entered. He was a rough-looking man, with a shabby overcoat and a still more disreputable muffler around his throat and the lower part of his face. Considerably annoyed at his intrusion, I turned upon him rather sharply, when, with a mumbled, growling apology for mistaking the room, he shuffled out again and closed the door. I followed him quickly to the landing and saw that he disappeared down the stairs. With my mind full of the robbery, the incident made a singular impression upon me. I knew my friend's habit of hasty absences from his room in his moments of deep inspiration; it was only too probable that, with his powerful intellect and magnificent perceptive genius concentrated on one subject, he should be careless of his own belongings, and no doubt even forget to take the ordinary precaution of locking up his drawers. I tried one or two and found that I was right, although for some reason I was unable to open one to its fullest extent. The handles were sticky, as if someone had opened it with dirty fingers. Knowing Hemlock's fastidious cleanliness, I resolved to inform him of this circumstance, but I forgot it, alas! until—but I am anticipating my story.

His absence was strangely prolonged. I at last seated myself by the fire and, lulled by warmth and the patter of the rain, fell asleep. I may have dreamt, for during my sleep I had a vague semiconsciousness as of hands being softly pressed on my pockets—no doubt induced by the story of the robbery. When I came fully to my senses, I found Hemlock Jones sitting on the other side of the hearth, his deeply concentrated gaze fixed on the fire.

"I found you so comfortably asleep that I could not bear to awaken you," he said, with a smile.

I rubbed my eyes. "And what news?" I asked. "How have you succeeded?"

"Better than I expected," he said, "and I think," he added, tapping his notebook, "I owe much to *you*."

Deeply gratified, I awaited more. But in vain. I ought to have remembered that in his moods Hemlock Jones was reticence itself. I told him simply of the strange intrusion, but he only laughed.

Later, when I arose to go, he looked at me playfully. "If you were a married man," he said, "I would advise you not to go home until you had brushed your sleeve. There are a few short brown sealskin hairs on the inner side of your forearm, just where they would have adhered if your arm had encircled a sealskin coat with some pressure!"

"For once you are at fault," I said triumphantly; "the hair is my own, as you will perceive; I have just had it cut at the barber shop, and no doubt this arm projected beyond the apron."

He frowned slightly, yet, nevertheless, on my turning to go he embraced me warmly—a rare exhibition in that man of ice. He even helped me on with my overcoat and pulled out and smoothed down the flaps of my pockets. He was particular, too, in fitting my arm in my overcoat sleeve, shaking the sleeve down from the armhole to the cuff with his deft fingers. "Come again soon!" he said, clapping me on the back.

"At any and all times," I said enthusiastically; "I only ask ten minutes twice a day to eat a crust at my office, and four hours' sleep at night, and the rest of my time is devoted to you always, as you know."

"It is indeed," he said, with his impenetrable smile.

Nevertheless, I did not find him at home when I next called. One afternoon, when nearing my own home, I met him in one of his favorite disguises—a long blue swallow-tailed coat, striped cotton trousers, large turn-over collar, blacked face, and white hat, carrying a tambourine. Of course to others the disguise was perfect, although it was known to myself, and I passed him—according to an old understanding between us—without the slightest recognition, trusting to a later explanation. At another time, as I was making a professional visit to the wife of a publican at the East End, I saw him, in the disguise of a broken-down artisan, looking into the window of an adjacent pawnshop. I was delighted to see that he was evidently following my suggestions, and in my joy I ventured to tip him a wink; it was abstractedly returned.

Two days later I received a note appointing a meeting at his lodgings that night. That meeting, alas! was the one memorable occurrence of my life, and the last meeting I ever had with Hemlock Jones! I will try to set it down calmly, though my pulses still throb with the recollection of it.

I found him standing before the fire, with that look upon his face which I had seen only once or twice—a look which I may call an absolute concatenation of inductive and deductive ratiocination—from which all that was human, tender, or sympathetic was absolutely discharged. He was simply an icy algebraic symbol!

After I had entered he locked the doors, fastened the window, and even placed a chair before the chimney. As I watched these significant precautions with absorbing interest, he suddenly drew a revolver and, presenting it to my temple, said in low, icy tones:

"Hand over that cigar case!"

Even in my bewilderment my reply was truthful, spontaneous, and involuntary. "I haven't got it," I said.

He smiled bitterly, and threw down his revolver. "I expected that reply! Then let me now confront you with something more awful, more deadly, more relentless and convincing than that mere lethal weapon—the damning inductive and deductive proofs of your guilt!" He drew from his pocket a roll of paper and a notebook.

"But surely," I gasped, "you are joking! You could not believe—"

"Silence! Sit down!"

I obeyed.

"You have condemned yourself," he went on pitilessly. "Condemned yourself on my processes—processes familiar to you, applauded by you, accepted by you for years! We will go back to the time when you first saw the cigar case. Your expressions," he said in cold, deliberate tones, consulting his paper, "were, 'How beautiful! I wish it were mine.' This was your first step in crime—and my first indication. From 'I *wish* it were mine' to 'I *will* have it mine' and the mere detail, '*How can* I make it mine?' the advance was obvious. Silence! But as in my methods it was necessary that there should be an overwhelming inducement to the crime, that unholy admiration of yours for the mere trinket itself was not enough. You are a smoker of cigars."

"But," I burst out passionately, "I told you I had given up smoking cigars."

"Fool!" he said coldly. "That is the *second* time you have committed yourself. Of course you told me! What more natural than for you to blazon forth that prepared and unsolicited statement to *prevent* accusation. Yet, as I said before, even that wretched attempt to cover up your tracks was not enough. I still had to find that overwhelming, impelling motive necessary to affect a man like you. That motive I found in the strongest of all impulses—love, I suppose you would call it—" he added bitterly—"that night you called! You had brought the most conclusive proofs of it on your sleeve."

"But—" I almost screamed.

"Silence!" he thundered. "I know what you would say. You would say that even if you had embraced some Young Person in a sealskin coat, what had that to do with the robbery? Let me tell you, then, that that sealskin coat represented the quality and character of your fatal entanglement! You bartered your honor for it—that stolen cigar case was the purchaser of the sealskin coat!

"Silence! Having thoroughly established your motive, I now proceed to the commission of the crime itself. Ordinary people would have begun with that—with an attempt to discover the whereabouts of the missing object. These are not *my* methods."

So overpowering was his penetration that, although I knew myself innocent, I licked my lips with avidity to hear the further details of this lucid exposition of my crime.

"You committed that theft the night I showed you the cigar case, and after I had carelessly thrown it in that drawer. You were sitting in that chair, and I had arisen to take something from that shelf. In that instant you secured your booty without rising. Silence! Do you remember when I helped you on with your overcoat the other night? I was particular about fitting your arm in. While doing so I measured your arm with a spring tape measure, from the shoulder to the cuff. A later visit to your tailor confirmed that measurement. It proved to be *the exact distance between your chair and that drawer!*" I sat stunned.

"The rest are mere corroborative details! You were again tampering with the drawer when I discovered you doing so! Do not start! The stranger that blundered into the room with a muffler on—was myself! More, I had placed a little soap on the drawer handles when I purposely left you alone. The soap was on your hand when I shook it at parting. I softly felt your pockets, when you were asleep, for further developments. I embraced you when you left—that I might feel if you had the cigar case or any other articles hidden on your body. This confirmed me in the belief that you had already disposed of it in the manner and for the purpose I have shown you. As I still believed you capable of remorse and confession, I twice allowed you to see I was on your track: once in the garb of an itinerant Negro minstrel, and the second time as a workman looking in the window of the pawnshop where you pledged your booty.

"But," I burst out, "if you had asked the pawnbroker, you would have seen how unjust—"

"Fool!" he hissed. "Do you suppose I followed any of your suggestions, the suggestions of the thief? On the contrary, they told me what to avoid."

"And I suppose," I said bitterly, "you have not even searched your drawer."

"No," he said calmly.

I was for the first time really vexed. I went to the nearest drawer and pulled it out sharply. It stuck as it had before, leaving a section of the drawer unopened. By working it, however, I discovered that it was impeded by some obstacle that had slipped to the upper part of the drawer, and held it firmly fast. Inserting my hand, I pulled out the impeding object. It was the missing cigar case! I turned to him with a cry of joy.

But I was appalled at his expression. A look of contempt was now added to his acute, penetrating gaze. "I have been mistaken," he said slowly. "I had not allowed for your weakness and cowardice! I thought too highly of you even in your guilt! But I see now why you tampered with that drawer the other night. By some inexplicable means—possibly another theft—you took the cigar case out of pawn and, liked a whipped hound, restored it to me in this feeble, clumsy fashion. You thought to deceive me, Hemlock Jones! More, you thought to destroy my infallibility. Go! I give you your liberty. I shall not summon the three policemen who wait in the adjoining room—but out of my sight forever!"

As I stood once more dazed and petrified, he took me firmly by the ear and led me into the hall, closing the door behind him. This reopened presently, wide enough to permit him to thrust out my hat, overcoat, umbrella, and overshoes, and then closed against me forever!

I never saw him again. I am bound to say, however, that thereafter my business increased, I recovered much of my old practice, and a few of my patients recovered also. I became rich. I had a brougham and a house in the West End. But I often wondered, if, in some lapse of consciousness, I had not really stolen his cigar case!

*W**ith the possible exception of Greenwich Village, New York's West Side probably boasts a higher concentration of resident actors, artists, musicians and writers than anywhere in the country, and one time or another, most of them have probably browsed that biblio-philic Valhalla, the Gryphon Book Shop on Broadway between 80th and 81st Streets. That's where I first met my colleague and* Weird Tales *enthusiast* J O N   W H I T E *, a Brooklyn native who attended the University of California at Berkeley and City College of New York. Jon's articles, poems and book reviews have appeared in* Antiquarian Book-man, Crime Bent, Ellery Queen's Mystery Magazine, Fistula *(which he published),* Heavy Metal, Publishers Weekly *and* Twilight Zone Magazine. *His brotherly ad-vice from Mycroft to Sherlock Holmes is (or ought to be) positively the last word on that Irene Adler business!*

A Letter from Mycroft Holmes

J O N   W H I T E

Dear S.,

It was with the greatest of delight that I received your note, despite its discouraging contents, because, old boy, it's been a damn long time!

Well, now. It is indeed a surprise that you, of all people, could get into such a predicament. I am not too sure that I can handle this problem properly. When, so long ago, you used to come to me with a difficult murder or such, I could advise you with confidence. But this is a bit out of my field. And you, dear brother, are the last person in the world to whom I would have expected this to happen.

In brief, you say this woman from Bohemia, this Irene, is blackmailing you, with compromising photographs, into mar-riage.

Well, now. Is it really such a bad thing at that? According to that Boswell of yours, a rather dim fellow I've always thought, this Irene is quite a prize. And besides, don't you think it's time you settled down?

It's also time, brother, that you grew up in regard to

women. This is your most serious lack, an immature dependence upon the maternal type, such as Mrs. Hudson. (And herein lies my surprise that this Irene can blackmail you at all. I was unaware of the fact that you had ever put yourself into any compromising position, or positions. Your naiveté on such grounds is extraordinary, and seems almost to give the lie to the photographs.)

Further, it is obvious that the woman possesses a genuine fondness for you. She cannot wish to marry you for your money, for you have no wealth. She is willing to go as far as blackmail in order to affiance you. Strange, is it not, that she cannot rely on her own very abundant charms, the same charms that have captured the hearts of half the men in Europe? It is a sad reflection on you, brother.

There is nothing more to say. Marry her! It will do you a world of good.

I suppose you still have many doubts. Drop around the Diogenes Club this evening, and we can have a long talk about it, man to man.

Your loving brother,

Mycroft

RAY RUSSELL's first fiction sale was to Esquire in 1953. Since then, his short stories, poems and articles have appeared in The Midatlantic Review, Odyssey, The Paris Review, Playboy (which he edited for many years), Theology Today, Verbatim and fifteen other magazines, plus over a hundred anthologies; his work has been published in eleven languages. Amongst his seventeen books is the excellent The Case Against Satan, his first novel. His seventh, Absolute Power, was published in 1992. His many honors include an international screenwriting award in 1963; the Sri Chinmoy Poetry Award in 1977; the World Fantasy Life Achievement Award in 1991 and the Horror Writers of America Life Achievement Award in 1993. Ray's Sherlockian spoof comes from the May 1955 issue of Playboy.

The Murder of Conan Doyle

RAY RUSSELL

The other day, a member of our staff slunk into the office smoking a calabash pipe, wearing a deerstalker cap and muttering in nasal tones faintly reminiscent of Basil Rathbone. Since this individual has frequently displayed a marked tendency toward eccentric behavior, we shrugged it all off as the latest manifestation of his twisted though talented mind and went about our usual editorial task of separating paper clips without giving the matter a second thought.

That evening, however, relaxing in front of our television screen with a short beer and a tall blonde, it suddenly became clear as crystal. Our colleague had simply succumbed to the preponderance of ancient Sherlock Holmes films recently available via video and starring the aforementioned Mr. Rathbone. The following night, the situation became clearer still. Relaxing again (this time with a tall beer and a short blonde, for variety), we were privileged to watch Leslie Howard's boy Ronald also portray the Baker Street sleuth. This may strike some sour malcontents as too much of a good thing, but we've always been avid admirers of the Holmes tales and have never been able to get enough of them. The more the merrier, we said, ruffling our sideburns, lighting our calabash, donning our deerstalker and blowing the eraser dust from our typewriter. The beer languished in our glass, the blonde languished on our davenport, and when the creative frenzy had spent itself, both had disappeared. But what cared we? Another urgently needed television script had been given the world! And here, you lucky readers, it is—without the slightest apology to Sir Arthur Conan Doyle:

ESTABLISHING SHOT: *The familiar Baker Street apartment. Dr. Squatson is discovered packing his portmanteau with a heavy heart and several extra collars. A tear falls and stains his tweed pajamas as a stray memory wafts across his mind. He sighs longly.*

SQUATSON: Poor Foames! Never again will the world know a mind to match his!

With a last glance about his old room, he lifts his luggage and prepares to leave. But a sudden knock arrests him.

SQUATSON: Who can this be? Can it be Hemlock Foames? No—impossible! Did I not personally witness his gruesome death by fire, rack, sword and vat at the hands of Professor Goryarty? Did I not see he and that vile maniac tumble together into a cauldron of boiling coffee? Of course I did!

He opens the door, disclosing only kind-hearted Mother Mulrooney, the landlady. She is weeping.

MOTHER MULROONEY: Faith, and is it leavin' me now entirely ye are, Dr. Squatson, ye spalpeen, bedad?

SQUATSON: Alas. These premises are but a source of sorrow to me now, kind-hearted Mother Mulrooney. Forgive me. I must go.

MOTHER MULROONEY *(screaming):* Squatson, you old barrel! Did you really miss me, then?

SQUATSON: I'm afraid I don't quite . . .

MOTHER MULROONEY: You fool! You lovable, bungling, incompetent fool! Are you entirely witless?

SQUATSON: Great Scott! It isn't . . .

MOTHER MULROONEY: It isn't what, you decrepit old quack?

SQUATSON: By George, if it is, I'll . . . I'll . . .

MOTHER MULROONEY: You'll what, you fumbling old abortionist?

SQUATSON: Foames!! Bless my soul, it's Foames!

MOTHER MULROONEY: Well, ra-ther!

Kind-hearted Mother Mulrooney rips away her gray wig, false nose, padded dress and apron. There, naked as a savage, stands the lanky shape of Hemlock Foames.

FOAMES: Get me a robe, old boy. This London weather . . .

SQUATSON *(obeying):* But see here, Foames, you can't possibly be here, you know. You're upsetting everything. Why, da h it all, the report has gone out that you are dead, and by Jove, you *must* be! Come now, old fellow, be reasonable . . .

FOAMES: I am, Squatson, being perfectly reasonable. My appearance is founded upon cold and precise logic. You recall that night in Soho, when Goryarty had me swinging like a pendulum from the rafters?

SQUATSON: Indeed I do.

FOAMES: You remember Goryarty amused himself by putting me through a half-dozen hellish tortures, the last of which was to coat me in a thick layer of bubbling beeswax? You also remember, I'm sure, how I stifled a yawn, cried "This is the last straw!" and fell upon the Professor, tooth and nail. You surely can't forget how we struggled and fell into a cauldron of scalding coffee which was there to keep me awake for further torments.

SQUATSON: Yes, yes . . .

FOAMES: Well, then. My body was saved from the deadly heat of the coffee by its coating of hardened wax! Fundamental, my dear Squatson.
Squatson gasps and stands speechless.

FOAMES: Don't stand there like a monkey with a stick up your nose! Get me some clothes! There's not a moment to be wasted, for London has been shocked by a series of wanton murders, all of which have been perpetrated upon theatrical gentlemen. Quick, Squatson! Cocaine! Opium! Clothes! Our destination is the Thespian Society in Fleet Street where, even now, a party is in progress!
Music and commercial, during which audience adjourns to kitchen for short beer and tall blonde or vice versa. When they return, they find Foames and Squatson living it up over the Thespian Society's punch bowl. Squatson is saying . . .

SQUATSON: Another cup, Foames?

FOAMES: No thank you, Squatson. My brain must be without parallel tonight.

SQUATSON: I say, this place is a veritable gallery of dramatic notables. That's Laddie Badd, draining the punch bowl through a straw.

FOAMES: Who?

SQUATSON: The versatile Hollywood tragedian. His amazing range of portrayals has run the gamut through tough kid crooks, tough kid cops, tough kid priests and tough kid milkmen.

FOAMES *(yawning):* Ah, yes. Laddie Badd. Real name Homer Witherspoon; born 1922 in Akron, Ohio, of unwed parents. Hobbies: archery and lechery. Small freckle on left kneecap. A nonentity. Forget him.

SQUATSON: By Tophet, Foames, I'll outwit that card-index mind of yours yet! Who, for instance, is that bearded gentleman reciting Marlowe in the corner? Eh? Tell me that!

FOAMES: Quentin Drake-Chalmers, Shakespearean actor. Now too fat to play Hamlet, he is planning an abridged *King Lear,* reducing the cast to one. Remember his modern dress *Romeo* eight years ago, when he read all the blank verse as prose and all the prose as blank verse? Exhilarating.

In his youth, he appeared in a neo-Greek tragedy of his own concoction called *Oedipus Meets Electra:* in this fiasco the characters stood completely still throughout, while the scenery moved behind them. He burned incense during intermissions to contribute to the unrealistic illusion and succeeded in asphyxiating half the audience. Also, each character spoke in a different language; all wore costumes of different periods; all were made-up with luminous paint which glowed a dull blue in the blackouts between the thirty-seven scenes. The man is an obvious ham, and therefore an egomaniac. Since most murderers are egomaniacs—rating themselves above the law—this fellow will bear watching. Keep an eye on him.

SQUATSON: I will, by Jove! *(He hiccoughs stoutly and adds . . .)* Foames—

FOAMES: Yes?

SQUATSON: Not to change the subject, and mind you I understand how you survived the blistering coffee, but, tell me, how in blazes did you withstand the lethal effects of that boiling, molten wax?

FOAMES *(snorting):* Good Lord, man, don't bother me with trivia now! That case is closed! Let us live in the present. *(A pause. Then):* Aha!

SQUATSON: What is it?

FOAMES: That lovely creature making so gracious an egress from the ladies' john: might I be mistaken or is that Emily Klodd, stage name Sidonie Brassiere, born 1929 in Wessex of itinerant acrobats?

SQUATSON: It *is* Miss Brassiere.

FOAMES: So. When was the date of my supposed demise, Squatson?

SQUATSON: You died March 10th, old chap.

FOAMES: Hum. As I recall, the London Catarrh of March 10th carried the following headline: "AMAZING DISAPPEARANCE OF PROMINENT ACTRESS. SIDONIE BRASSIERE'S FAILURE TO APPEAR CAUSES WIDESPREAD CONSTERNATION." Squatson! Everything's clear now!

SQUATSON *(drooling senselessly):* Eh?

FOAMES: Suppose a certain arch-fiend, who shall remain nameless, wished to blackmail wealthy but profligate actors on grounds of, shall we say, indiscreet behavior. What would he do?

SQUATSON: Why, disguise himself as Sidonie Brassiere, I suppose, lure them to some boudoir or other . . .

FOAMES: Exactly. But what would happen if these gentlemen went so far as to discover the true sex of their supposed paramour? What would the evil malefactor be forced to do then?

SQUATSON: Why, murder them, naturally!

FOAMES: Naturally. Squatson: it was not Sidonie Brassiere who vanished on March 10th, but a certain arch-fiend, who shall remain nameless, *disguised* as Sidonie Brassiere! And he disappeared from mortal ken to be present at the death of Hemlock Foames!

SQUATSON *(gulping):* You mean Sidonie Brassiere is none other than—

FOAMES: Yes! Professor Goryarty—who shall remain nameless! Come, follow me and we shall unmask him.

With rapid strides, they approach the sultry actress.

FOAMES *(addressing her):* Professor Goryarty, I place you under arrest!

SIDONIE: I *beg* your pardon! My name is Sidonie Brassiere.

FOAMES: You lie in your teeth! But Hemlock Foames shall foil your dissembling!

With one bold gesture, he rips her gown and only garment from her body and dashes it triumphantly to the floor.

FOAMES: Oops. Extremely sorry, old girl. But who, then, is Goryarty?

SQUATSON *(with sudden knowledge):* You are! !

FOAMES *(blinking):* I? You're off your chump, Squatson.

SQUATSON: Not bloody likely! Oh, you look like Hemlock Foames you do, you walk and talk like Hemlock Foames, but by St. George and Merrie England, you're *not* Hemlock Foames!

FOAMES: And why not, pray tell?

SQUATSON: That unpardonable error you just committed—would Hemlock Foames, the greatest mind in all of London, have made such a mistake? Not on your tintype!

Crestfallen, "Foames" whisks off false nose, chin, eyebrows, and five o'clock shadow, standing revealed as Professor Goryarty.

GORYARTY *(sighing):* Ah, well, it was good while it lasted. You have me dead to rights, Dr. Squatson. That dolt, Foames, is tied up in a closet in Soho. He's unharmed.

SQUATSON: Come along, you fiend! And explain one thing, if you will. How did you and Foames escape being parboiled in that steaming kettle of coffee?

GORYARTY: Oh, that: it was really tea.

SQUATSON: Ah. And why all that nonsense about Sidonie Brassiere? Ripping off her dress and all that?

GORYARTY *(regarding Squatson with a slow wink and a leer):* It was worth it, wasn't it, old bean?

SQUATSON: By Christopher, you're right, you rascal!

*O*n *a memorable evening in April, 1948, "The Adventure of the Conk-Singleton Papers" (named after one of Watson's untold cases) was performed at the annual Mystery Writers of America's Edgar Allan Poe Awards Dinner. Clayton Rawson, author of the "Great Merlini" mysteries and later editor of Ellery Queen's Mystery Magazine, played Sherlock Holmes to Lawrence G. Blochman's Watson. The role of the visitor was filled by J OHN D ICKSON C ARR (1905–1977), who himself twice won the "Edgar." Author of a series of mind-boggling "impossible crime" novels featuring one of two detectives, Bencolin or Dr. Fell (including the ultimate "locked room" puzzle, The Three Coffins), as "Carter Dickson" Carr penned a second (to my mind, even better) series starring Henry Merrivale, a comic sleuth loosely modeled on Mycroft Holmes.*

The Adventure of the Conk-Singleton Papers

J OHN D ICKSON C ARR

NARRATOR: Crime marches on! . . . A long, thin silhouette emerges against the gaslight. Here is an unpublished record: "In turning over my notes of some twenty years I cannot find any startling event on New Year's Eve except that which is forever associated with the Conk-Singleton Papers. On New Year's Eve of 1887, it is perhaps unnecessary to state, Mr. Sherlock Holmes did not wear a paper hat and blow squeakers at the Hotel Metropole. Far into the night, while the wind howled round our sitting room in 221B Baker Street, Holmes sat bending over a microscope" . . .

    At Rise: *(Sherlock Holmes at microscope, Watson immersed in a copy of H. Rider Haggard's* King Solomon's Mines*)*

HOLMES: *(After a moment looks up and stares glassily out at audience)* It is spinach, Watson. Unquestionably, it is spinach!

WATSON: Holmes, you amaze me! What new wizardry is this?

HOLMES: *(Rising)* It means a man's life, Watson. The gardener was lying when he said he found Riccoletti's body in the gooseberry bushes. *(He rubs his hands)* I think, perhaps, a note to our friend Lestrade . . .

WATSON: *(Jumps up)* Holmes! Merciful Heaven. I had forgotten!

HOLMES: Forgotten what?

WATSON: A note for you was delivered by hand this morning. You must forgive me. I was attending the funeral of my last patient.

HOLMES: *(Impatiently)* The letter, Watson! The letter! *(Watson takes note from his pocket, hands it to Holmes, who examines postmark, holds letter up to light, then opens with care and reads)* "There will call upon you tonight, at three o'clock in the morning precisely, a gentleman who desires to consult you about a matter of the deepest moment. Be in your chamber at that hour, and do not take it amiss if the visitor wears a mask."

WATSON: This is indeed a mystery. What can it mean?

HOLMES: These are deep waters, Watson. If Porlock had not warned me about the Scarborough emeralds . . . *(Thoughtfully)* Three o'clock . . . *(Clock strikes three. Bong! Bong! Bong! Immediately followed by three loud raps on door in same tempo)*

WATSON: And that, if I mistake not, is our client now.

(Enter visitor dressed in evening clothes but covered with medals—decorations, stars, ribbons, etc.)

VISITOR: Mr. Sherlock Holmes?

HOLMES: I am Mr. Sherlock Holmes. This is my friend and colleague, Dr. Watson.

VISITOR: You will forgive me, Mr. Holmes, if I do not reveal my identity. I also wear plain evening dress so as not to be conspicuous.

HOLMES: *(Coldly)* You would be better served, my Lord, if Your Lordship removed the mask.

VISITOR: *(Staggering back)* You know me then?

HOLMES: Who could fail to know Lord Cosmo Conk-Singleton, third son of the Duke of Folkstone and private secretary to the Prime Minister?

WATSON: You mean—Mr. Gladstone!

VISITOR: *(Finger at side of nose)* Sssh!

HOLMES: *(Same)* Ssssh!

WATSON: *(Same to audience)* Sssssh!

VISITOR: The matter upon which I have come to consult you, Mr. Holmes, is no ordinary one.

HOLMES: It seldom is. Pray be seated.

VISITOR: *(Sits)* It will be not unknown to you, Mr. Holmes, that for some time there has been—shall we say—disagreement between Mr. Gladstone and Her Gracious Majesty, Queen Victoria. I have here a diplomatic communication in Her Majesty's own hand, sent to Mr. Gladstone on December 15, 1886. You are empowered to read it. *(Hands important-looking document to Holmes)*

WATSON: These are deep waters, Holmes.

HOLMES: Her Majesty, I perceive, was not amused.

VISITOR: She was indeed *(hesitates)* somewhat vexed. *(Then suddenly amazed)* But how could you possibly know—

HOLMES: Her Majesty has twice underlined the word "bastard." And she has placed three exclamation points following her instructions as to what Mr. Gladstone should do with the Naval Treaty involving a certain foreign power. Surely our inference is obvious.

WATSON: Excellent!

HOLMES: But very superficial. *(Reading again)* "Even that German sausage, my late husband, could have done better." Hmm! Yes! But how do these diplomatic matters concern me?

VISITOR: Mr. Holmes, the Prime Minister has been poisoned!

WATSON: What?

VISITOR: On December 24th Mr. Gladstone received—apparently as a Christmas present from Queen Victoria—a case of Scotch whiskey.

HOLMES: I see. And did the case indeed contain whiskey?

VISITOR: Whiskey, yes. But each bottle was most unhappily charged with two ounces of prussic acid!

WATSON: Merciful heaven! The man is dead!

VISITOR: No, Dr. Watson, no! *Dei gratia,* he still lives! The strength of the whiskey neutralized the poison.

HOLMES: *(Blandly)* Come, come, this is most disappoi—most interesting. Have you any proof, my Lord, that the Prime Minister drank this particular whiskey?

VISITOR: *(Producing document)* Here is a letter of thanks, in Mr. Gladstone's own hand, written on Christmas Eve. Pray read it aloud.

HOLMES: Will you oblige, Watson?

WATSON: *(Very dignified, clears throat gravely, and reads)* December 24th, 1886. Illustrious Madam: How extremely kind of you to send me this case of whiskey for Christmas! I have never tasted such superb whiskey in my life. The whiskey you have sent me for Christmas is superb. I keep tasting it and how kind of you to sen me thish wondrous whichkey which I keep tasting for Xmas. It really is mosh kind of you to keep sending me this whiskey in cases which I kep tashing for whichmas. Hic! Dock, dickory dock, and kissmus.

VISITOR: Can there be any doubt, Mr. Holmes?

HOLMES: None whatever. Then it is your belief, my Lord, that Queen Victoria herself is the poisoner?

VISITOR: No, Mr. Holmes! *(Horrified)* A thousand times, no! But think of the scandal! It bids fair to rend asunder the fabric of the Empire! You must come down to Sussex and investigate. Will you come?

HOLMES: No, my Lord. I will not.

WATSON: *(Amazed)* Holmes, this is unworthy of you! Why won't you go?

HOLMES: Because this man is not Lord Cosmo Conk-Singleton! *(Sensation. Holmes produces revolver)* Let me present you, Watson, to none other than Professor Moriarty.

WATSON: Professor Moriarty!

HOLMES: Your double disguise as a younger man, my dear Professor, deceived me for perhaps ten seconds. The note from Mr. Gladstone seems quite genuine. But the letter from Her Majesty is a manifest forgery.

WATSON: Forgery, Holmes?

HOLMES: Her language, Watson! Her language!

WATSON: You mean—

HOLMES: Queen Victoria, Watson, would never have written in so slighting a fashion of her late husband, Prince Albert. They intended the letter to lure me to Sussex while the Scarborough emeralds were stolen from Yorkshire, not knowing—*(Holmes produces emeralds from his pocket)*— that Lord Scarborough had already given them to me for safekeeping!

VISITOR: *(In a grating voice)* One day, Mr. Holmes, you will try my patience too far!

(Curtain)

The following never-before-published lunacy comes from the fertile word processor of one of America's most vital humorists (he's definitely alive), DANIEL PINKWATER, who, because he trained dogs professionally, claims it is proper to address him as "Captain" (so what does it hurt?). Author of such inimitable farcical books as Blue Moose, Fat Men from Space, The Frankenbagel Monster, The Hoboken Chicken Emergency, Lizard Music, The Worms of Kukumlima *and the sort-of Holmesian "Snarkout" books (see Appendix II), Capt. Pinkwater is also a familiar national "talk radio" personality. "Journal of a Ghurka Physician" is both a witty wrong-end-of-the-telescope view of that famous Norwegian explorer, Sigerson, and a sly parody of the opening of the first Sherlock Holmes book,* A Study in Scarlet.

Journal of a Ghurka Physician

CAPTAIN DANIEL M. PINKWATER

I travelled for two years, therefore, and amused myself by visiting Lhasa and spending some days with the head Lama. You may have read of the remarkable explorations of a Norwegian named Sigerson, but I am sure that it never occurred to you that you were receiving news of your friend . . .

—SHERLOCK HOLMES
("The Adventure of the Empty House")

PREFACE BY THE EDITOR

The narrative which follows is reprinted from the *Journal of a Ghurka Physician*, by Pangdatsang Gompa, B. Sc., privately printed at Kalimpong, West Bengal in 1926. Gompa, a Nepalese, treated a wide range of subjects, ranging from Tibetan medicine to bee culture in the Himalayas, but the outstanding feature of his work is the sharp characterization of the people he met during the turbulent period of the late nineteenth and early twentieth centuries along the Indo-Tibetan frontier.

Unfortunately, almost none of the persons characterized in Gompa's diaries are of the slightest historical interest, with the exception of Holmbjorn Sigerson, a Norwegian explorer whose activities were recounted in the European press for a time before he dropped back into the obscurity common to all of Gompa's other subjects. Yet there are some features of the man Sigerson which bear scrutiny; research has not resulted in any trace of this explorer before 1891, and in 1894, no trace was left of him. This period is roughly the same as that during which a prominent Englishman was presumed dead.

Whether Sherlock Holmes was a character of fiction or history is the subject of a debate which continues to this day. The editor of these passages takes no part in this dispute, but simply presents the details of an encounter between two remarkable men in a remote part of the world.

Fishkill, New York, 1984

ONE

Being a reprint from the reminiscences of Pangdatsang Gompa, B. Sc., late medical officer of the Royal Ghurka Regiment.

In the year 1890 I took my degree of Bachelor of Science from the Royal Medical College at Delhi. This was not the commencement of my professional status, as I had already qualified in Tibetan medicine, having studied at the Chagpori school of medicine in Lhasa. A native of Nepal, my studies in Tibet were made possible through the good offices of Surkhang Rampa, a high Tibetan official who had dealings with my father.

After completing my studies at Chagpori, I returned to Kathmandu with the intention of opening a dispensary, and was approached by another associate of my father, Singh Nain, a travelling merchant and British correspondent, who offered to arrange for me to study Western medicine in exchange for accepting a commission and serving for only twenty years in the army. Eager to progress in my profession, I accepted the offer, and after three years of study, received my diploma and was commissioned straightaway into a Ghurka regiment.

My army life was characterized by misery and ill-luck. The British officers were the lowest type of men. They addressed me as "Doctor Dinge," and were forever jibing at me and mistreating the brave soldiers. Through the slack and unsoldierly conduct of our officers, our first encounter with hostile forces, a small band of poorly armed brigands, turned into a bloody rout. I myself was wounded in the hip and shoulder, and should not have escaped becoming a captive but for my Sherpa orderly, Lopseng, who threw me over a pack mule and led me to safety.

So it was that I was mustered out of the army, an invalid, with nothing to live upon but the pitiful pension doled out to native soldiers. My father had suffered a reversal of fortune, and an ensuing illness from which he did not recover. I was without family, too unwell to earn my living, and forced to subsist on a beggarly allotment.

I made my way to Darjeeling, where I hoped my knowledge of the languages of bordering Nepal and Tibet would be of some use to me. Darjeeling was, at that time, a teeming crossroads. Traders from India and China, English tea planters and government officials, religious pilgrims, and spies hoping to penetrate the closed border of Tibet made the little city a cosmopolis.

My days of study in Delhi had made me unaccustomed to the native quarter, and my most pressing problem in Darjeeling was that I was residing in rooms I could ill afford. For some days I wandered from place to place, viewing an endless succession of strangers, and wondering why I had ever come to this unfriendly place. I was entertaining such thoughts as I sipped my tea on the veranda of the Queen's Hotel, when I cried out with delight at the sight of a familiar face in the thronging crowd below me. It was Dzasa, a Tibetan monk of low intelligence, whose duty it had been to provide cadavers for dissection to the students at the Chagpori. Dzasa recognized me at the same moment, and a glow illuminated his idiot face.

"Gompa! You are dressed just like an Englishman!"

So delighted was I to perceive a friendly expression in that hostile place that I waved and hallooed to the poor unfortunate, just as though he had been my own brother. It would not have done to invite him to join me on the veranda, so I descended and went with him to some native place, reeking with quaint spices. Over cups of odoriferous Tibetan tea we related our recent experiences.

Dzasa, it seemed, was part of the entourage of some notable lama who had travelled out of Tibet, and was at liberty in Darjeeling, awaiting the pleasure of his master, and residing meantime in a nearby lamasery of his order.

"And what are you doing, Brother?" the half-wit asked.

"Trying to find proper rooms at half the going rate," was my reply.

"You ought to meet the funny European who is staying at our monastery," Dzasa said. "We want to kick him out for smoking all the time, but he refuses to leave until he finds rooms he can afford. Maybe you could share the price."

I had misgivings about a European who would be willing to share rooms with a native, even a doctor, but my situation was truly desperate. I asked Dzasa to take me to the man.

Dzasa conducted me to the lamasery. "This is certainly a funny European," the wretched idolater said. "He makes us all laugh. We would let him stay but for the stinking tobacco." Like any lamasery this one was redolent of a thousand vile odors. I wondered how the smell of anything as innocent as tobacco could affect these stencherd monks. The corridors were dark and slippery with spilled yak butter, which the monks used in their lamps, and imported from Tibet, although coal-oil and candles were available locally at less cost. Dzasa opened a door and we issued into a small tidy room. Sitting in a posture of Buddhist meditation was a European of considerable height and remarkable thinness. He was smoking an enormous pipe. He sprang to his feet and extended a bony hand.

"You have been in Tibet, I perceive," he said, motioning me to a nearby chair. "You had a sister who died in childhood. Medical man. Eastern and Western training, both. Commendable. A Ghurka regiment, was it not? My sympathies on the demise of your father. Was it brain fever? Ah, I thought so. Required a tutor in chemistry during your preparatory studies, did you? I am delighted you have gotten over your enthusiasm for females of that type. And what are you doing by way of treatment for your tinea pedis?" This discourse struck me as highly unusual, however, versed as I was in European civilities, I did not titter as the ignorant monk was doing.

"See? I told you he was funny," Dzasa chortled.

"Gompa, B. Sc.," I said smiling.

"Holmbjorn Sigerson," the stranger said. "Are you by any chance looking for someone to share the price of rooms? I have my eye on a suite in Dhamma Street, a stone's throw from Government House."

Before I could utter a response, I found myself outside in the street with this remarkable European. I noted his hawk-like profile and remarkably piercing gaze, which darted to and fro in the manner of a mongoose or some other rodent.

As we made our way through the crowded streets he continued his unusual remarks. "It was fortunate that you were rescued from the battle in which you received your wounds. Got away on a pack animal, I expect. It is a shame the way the British officers treat the native ones—the troops are another matter, of course. You speak Tibetan, no doubt—that will come in handy. You lost your mother when you were only seven, I see. How sad that she never liked you. When did you study typewriting?"

He went on and on. I politely pretended that he was saying nothing unusual, although it did seem strange that he knew so many things about me.

The rooms were admirably suited to our purposes, decorated entirely in Western style. I communicated to Holmbjorn Sigerson my desire to conclude our bargain upon the spot and take possession of the apartment immediately.

"Aren't you interested in discussing our respective habits and proclivities?" my companion asked. "Wouldn't you like to find out whether I engage in any practices to which you might object before embarking on a career of housekeeping with me?"

"Sir," I replied, "I am a former native officer of the British Army—and your garments tell me all I need to know about you. We are both gentlemen—what possible objections could either of us entertain?"

We made arrangements at once with the landlady, Mrs. Mookerjee, and set about transporting and laying out our respective possessions. I left my hotel and took up residence in the new rooms that very night.

Holmbjorn Sigerson proved an ideal dwelling partner, quiet and regular in his habits, cheerful in conversation, neat and tidy. His predilection for tobacco was matched by my own, and many an evening we spent, each man in a fragrant cloud of his own making. Some business or other kept Sigerson away from the rooms much of the time. I never saw him at the bar of the Queen's Hotel, or any of the places where Europeans gathered, which puzzled me, as he hardly seemed the sort of man who would confine his social activities to the indigenous population. During the first weeks of our tenancy I did little more than walk about the city, seeking what amusement I could find, and biding my time while my health slowly improved. Whenever I encountered Holmbjorn Sigerson in our cheery sitting room he would fix me with a quizzical stare and begin one of his unconventional dissertations.

"You have been in the native market, I perceive. You watched a snake charmer, and gave the fellow a rupee. You paid a call on an acquaintance in the medical profession, another army doctor, most probably in his rooms at the garrison. You lunched alone on curry of prawns, and drank the local beer, although you favor the imported variety. The waiter was a hunchback."

I never knew just how I ought to respond to these unusual sallies on the part of my companion. He seemed to take pleasure in relating the details of my daily life, although they were perfectly commonplace, and of course already known to me. I generally smiled politely and ventured some comment on the weather, or an item in the day's newspapers. At this point Holmbjorn Sigerson would fall silent for a long period and smoke his pipe with a perplexed expression.

Barring a certain awkwardness in conversation, my new companion and I got on quite well. Our routines did not vary with the exception of the introduction of an an elderly personage who came to our rooms to give

Sigerson instruction in playing the sitar or Indian fiddle. I had never found pleasure in the primitive native music, much preferring a waltz or polka, and on those occasions when Sigerson received his tutor, I would retire to my bedroom, leaving the sitting room to their unholy twanging and screeching. The lessons were mercifully short, and music would soon be abandoned in favor of conversation in a language I took to be Norwegian. That Sigerson was an amateur was evident even to my unsympathetic ear, and I was grateful that he never practiced between encounters with his mentor, although this, of course, accounted for his lack of progress. It seemed to me that his musical studies were undertaken merely as a curiosity, something with which to amuse his friends when he returned to Scandinavia, for such I took to be his place of origin, although I was never so forward as to inquire.

"Gompa, have you no curiosity about anything?" my companion asked one morning. His question left me at a loss—previously his remarks had been entirely declaratory, and generally a catalogue of my dreary comings and goings. "I mean to say," Sigerson continued, growing red in the face, "haven't you noticed something strange about me?"

I scrutinized my companion. I was terribly afraid that he was about to reveal something nasty about his character, the knowledge of which would compel me to give up my comfortable rooms. "Strange?" I asked. "I'm afraid I don't know what you mean. Please don't tell me anything which would alter our very satisfactory relationship."

"Gompa!" he shouted, "Are you aware that I have described to you your minutest activities almost every day? Doesn't that strike you as strange?" I felt relief and a tinge of shame at the confession I had half-expected instead of this innocent topic.

"Oh, that! Yes, I have noticed your behavior in that regard, but it is a matter of no consequence. I have travelled here and there in the sub-continent, and have encountered residents of various regions and countries. I know that customs vary, and I have learned tolerance. Please don't think that your conduct has been in any way offensive."

"But how do I do it? Think, man, think! Surely you don't believe that I follow you about on your mindless excursions. Don't you have any desire to know how I gain such information?"

At last I began to understand. "Calm yourself, my dear Sigerson," I said. "You must remember that I am a medical man, and a native of these parts. I have some knowledge of the matter which perturbs you. Darjeeling is located more than seven thousand feet above sea level, which is of small consequence to one whose first breaths were drawn in the Himalayas, but might have a radical effect on the perceptions of one accustomed to lesser altitudes. Moreover, it cannot be denied that there is a greater incidence of clairvoyance among the people of these mountains. In Tibet, I encountered certain mystical lamas who were all but omniscient. Occasionally, a stranger visiting this part of the world finds that something in the atmosphere has caused his psychic powers to awaken."

Sigerson exploded, "Psychic powers! Rot! I am not asking for comfort because I have suddenly become telepathic, and can't understand it—nor am I interested in your cracked-pot theories of the effects of altitude on the human psyche. My observations about your activities are based on minute observations of certain details about your person and behaviour. From observation of these details, I deduce the features of your activity with which I have amazed you. It is all perfectly logical and scientific."

"Remarkable!" I exclaimed.

"Ah!" said Sigerson. "You see the light."

"Do you mean to say," I enquired, "that you have been arriving at your unusual knowledge of my history and activities by a conscious and deliberate exercise of logic?"

"You understand at last," said Sigerson.

"It was not," I continued, "an involuntary psychic event, but instead conclusions arrived at through minute observation and purposeful reasoning?"

"Just so," said Sigerson.

"How amazing!" I cried. "Why didn't you simply ask me? I would have confided in you." I confess I was highly flattered that this strange European had found me worthy of such attention. For the first time, I felt that Sigerson and I were destined to become close friends. I realized in the next moment that I still had much to learn about the moods and tempers of this remarkable man—for at the very moment of our most intimate conversation, he kicked a great hole in his Indian fiddle, and, with an oath, rushed out of the apartment.

Suggested by one of the less familiar sections of Jonathan Swift's Gulliver's Travels, "The Struldbrugg Reaction" is one of the strangest Sherlock Holmes travesties I have ever read. Its author, JOHN SUTHERLAND, an English professor at Colby College, Maine, is a student of Eighteenth Century satire and has published a textbook and articles in professional journals. This story first appeared in the July 1964 edition of The Magazine of Fantasy and Science Fiction.

The Struldbrugg Reaction

JOHN SUTHERLAND

". . . They were the most mortifying Sight I ever beheld; and the Women more horrible than the Men. Besides the usual Deformities in extreme old Age, they acquired an additional Ghastliness in Proportion to their Number of Years, which is not to be described; and among half a Dozen I soon distinguished which was the oldest, although there were not above a Century or two between them.

The Reader will easily believe, that from what I had heard and seen, my keen Appetite for Perpetuity of Life was much abated . . . The King . . . raillied me very pleasantly; wishing I would send a Couple of Struldbruggs to my own Country, to arm our People against the Fear of Death . . ." (from Travels into Several Remote Nations of the World, by Lemuel Gulliver)

Since we have grown so very old, I must confess to a degree of self-indulgence which formerly I might have scorned. Hence there was nothing unusual about my being still asleep at nine o'clock on that fateful morning in August when my manservant, George, shook me so respectfully by the shoulder. Nonetheless, I started wide awake on the instant at the sight of his wide owl-like eyes and downturned solemn mouth. And when through my incipient cataracts I saw at his side Anthony, the faithful servant of my ancient comrade and mentor in scientific detection, Haricot Bones, I knew some fresh adventure must be in the wind. But little did I imagine that Bones' classic skills soon were to be tried in perilous competition with the ruthlessly direct methodology of a late–twentieth century American private investigator.

The rain dashed in hot, sullen streams against the steel-framed windows of my hotel bedroom. From the streets of New York—which seemed as far beneath our luxurious suite as the fleeting dreams of a past century—the roar of automotive traffic rose to astonish me once again with the vulgar, assertive power of the brash new world into which our stubborn bodies had endured.

Surely the world had changed vastly, I mused, since Bones and I had been young men together in our digs on Baker Street. We had not realized then, of course, how very young we were. Nor had we realized in that better, simpler day, as we pursued implacably the archcriminal, Dr. O'Shaunnessy, that finally we should overtake him—and that he would have his revenge. Yet so it came to pass—and a bitter, fiendish revenge it has proved to be!

"Up, Dawson, up! Catch the hour before it flies!"

Painfully I turned my head upon its pillow. Sure enough, there sat Bones, alert in his wheelchair in the center of my bedroom. His hawklike visage and piercing eyes were as commanding at ninety-five (which is all he will confess to) as ever they had been in earlier, happier years. But perhaps, I reflected, he would not agree that those had been happier years. He had not at that time suffered from Dr. O'Shaunnessy's revenge to the extent I had. Moreover, his moods had mellowed with age, and to the best of my knowledge he had not felt need to revert to cocaine for at least thirty years. Of course, there had been some unfortunate experiments with hashish—and now there was mescaline . . .

Again my reflections were interrupted: "Up, Dawson, up! The game is afoot! Anthony will help George to dress you and mount you in your wheelchair." Bones' distinguished features twisted into an arch—although extremely wrinkled—smile. "It is ridiculous that you should lie there mooning over your old friend's petty vices when one fiendish crime has been perpetrated, and another impends!"

"Astonishing!" I exclaimed. "Astonishing!"

"Not at all, Dawson," he replied with evident satisfaction. He oscillated his chair by turning first one wheel and then the other. "You must know by now that to me your thoughts oft are writ plain upon your face, hide them as you will behind the blotches of senile dermatitis." Then the sound of his grim chuckle, like the last stifled shrieks of a hyena choking on chickenfeathers, called most unexpectedly to my mind a queer experience I once had at Bloemfontein, before the relief of Mafeking.

But George and Anthony huddled me into my dressing gown, and the significance of this recollection momentarily eluded me. When George pushed me past Bones enroute to the lavatory, I could not forbear murmuring: "I only meant, my dear Haricot, that it is astonishing in this brave new world to find that so much still depends upon the efforts of such very old gentlemen as ourselves."

"Just so, Dawson, just so," Bones grumbled. I saw him color, and knew that I had scored a touch. But I also knew that his deductions had been correct (as so often before), and I flinched to think of the petty malice of my deception.

Bones wheeled to watch in the mirror as George trimmed the grizzled remnants of my beard. "You are thinking of chickenfeathers," he announced in a high, strained voice.

"Quite right, Haricot," I replied. "But you cannot astonish me with simple tricks of lipreading after all these years. I know my lips move as I keen over my tattered store of memories. However, in this particular case, you can oblige me mightily—if you will be good enough to elucidate further this strange, obsessive image."

"I'm sorry, my dear Dawson, but I cannot," he admitted. "Perhaps if you were to tell me . . . ?"

"I shan't trouble you with the trivial circumstance which brought the uncouth word to my mind and lips just now," I broke in hastily. "However, the image of chickenfeathers is linked indelibly in my recollection with an extraordinary experience I once had when serving as a Surgeon with the Home County Rifles at Bloemfontein . . ." And I went on to tell how, for night after night, I had been unable to sleep because of the groans and sighs of the wounded men and the unearthly, shrieking laughter of prowling hyenas. I had had a touch of fever, and my old wound from the Afghan campaign began again to trouble me. (Soon I was to be invalided home.) One grisly brute of a great dog hyena haunted my fancy like a demon. Sometimes it stole limbs from the pits behind the amputation tents—sometimes it robbed the officers' henroost. We were all near off our heads with the horror of it when, one hot black night, the brute's usual shrieks of laughter suddenly slid down scale to end in the most ghastly wheezing chuckles. Finally even these ceased. We went out next morning to find the huge mangy brute choked to death, a human arm protruding from its slavering mouth as if there were a man inside signalling for help. But when we opened it up, we found its throat and wind-pipe choked only with chickenfeathers.

Gravely, Bones heard me out. "Truly an horrendous vision," he said. "But you should have told me sooner, my dear Dawson, that you found my own innocent chuckling so unpleasant."

"It's not that, my dear Haricot . . ."

"We've campaigned together too long for you to hookwink me, old friend."

"But truly, my dear Haricot," I replied, "no matter what first brought the image to my mind, I have the most unearthly feeling that it has some tremendous occult significance for us now. Perhaps it is intended as a warning against greed."

"Why my scientific Dr. Dawson," Bones said lightly, "I never thought you would yield so grossly to superstition in your old age."

Our servants stowed us in one cab, themselves and our wheelchairs in another. As we swung in convoy through the gaudy canyons of the entertainment district, Bones began to tell me something of our errand.

"I was approached," he said, "by an extremely fat, ancient female person, wearing scarlet trousers, a yellow shirt, and a shining blue-grey wig."

"An entertainer from the music halls?" I hazarded.

"If you had been more observant during the past few weeks, my dear Dawson, you would recognize that I describe a quite conventional American costume."

"Extraordinary!"

"Indeed. Whatever one may think of her taste in dress, this person was old enough to recall some of the much-publicized successes of my middle career. She had seen a notice in the papers that we were visiting in this city. I must confess I was flattered that she should seek me out in her distress."

"Very gratifying, I'm sure," I murmured coldly, stung by his slur on my powers of observation.

"She has a granddaughter," Bones went on, "whom she believes to be in deadly danger. At present we are enroute to call upon that young woman at her place of employment—which, coincidentally, is also the scene of the recent crime. Her employer is a private inquiry agent—of a rather disreputable genre, I was given to understand by the grandparent."

"Why in the world did you agree to take the case?" I asked, thinking of the many distinguished clients we had turned away since Bones' semi-retirement more than a half-century before. But Bones only smiled his inscrutable smile and—after reaching quickly into his waistcoat pocket—began softly to hum a tune from *Pinafore*. These characteristic actions told me that he had disconnected his hearing aid, and I could hope for no more information at that time.

*T*he private inquiry agent's name turned out to be Mickey O'Reilly. His office was on the second floor of a dingy brick building on a sidestreet crowded with taverns and tenements. To the vast amusement of a horde of street urchins, our men had to carry us up the narrow front steps. Fortunately, Bones had provided himself with a pocketful of small native coins, and a few handfuls tossed judiciously into the scrum (by Anthony, at Bones' direction) purchased us respite from their jeers and importunities. (They seemed particularly amused by Bones' old deerstalker, which I must confess seemed unsuitable headgear—both for the city, and for the wet, tropical climate.)

Mammiferous and steatopygous in the extreme, the young woman we sought at once informed us that she had been chosen Miss Yonkers Ballbearing in 1961, and had been runnerup in a beauty contest in Ocean City, New Jersey, in the same year. Bones made some more formal introductions, and I discovered that her name was Rose-Albertine Chandler. Her hair was an extremely bright red, and it seemed to have been trained, like ivy, to grow backward and upward from every side to shape a shining fountain of fire on top of her head.

As she flounced about helping George and Anthony to arrange our chairs, her body vibrated in a manner which might have charmed my susceptible heart a short decade before, when I still was commuting to Zurich for monkey-gland treatments. Her musky perfume, mingled with the scent of powder and perspiration, hung heavy in the air of the grubby little office. When she reseated herself, the flimsy material of her blouse clung in the heat to her damp, half-exposed mammaries. Through some ingenious artifice of her staymaker, the two plump organs protruded at an upward angle from her torso, to confront us like mortars, or howitzers, across the no-man's-land of her typewriting machine. Our servants, I perceived, were deeply moved by her charms.

A short, stout, crophaired person, his face inflamed by dissipation, entered from a back room which appeared to serve both as private office and as bedchamber. The person's rumpled olive-purple suit was of artificial silk, and he wore an olive-purple shirt to match; a smouldering cigar stump protruded from his thick lips, and a half-empty pint of cheap native whiskey depended from his left hand. With a certain negligent grace, Rose-Albertine introduced him to us as her employer, Mickey O'Reilly.

"Call me Mick," he said, and offered Bones a pull at his flask.

As O'Reilly paced the grimy, splintered floor amidst mingled fumes of tobacco and whiskey, sweat and scent, he poured out a passionate tale of blood and slaughter fit to chill the blood of even slightly less experienced investigators than Bones and myself. Hardened campaigner that I am, I must confess I yearned for a nice biscuit and a steadying glass of sherry long before the brutal inquiry agent had finished his strange recital.

"I'm a private eye, see?" said O'Reilly. "And there's lots of mugs would like me rubbed, see? But I had this pal—would give his right arm for me, see? He cooled a couple of hoods, and the rest lay low . . ."

"Yes, yes," said Bones, but his eyes were elsewhere—darting about the floor looking for clues—racing like liberated mongooses back at the snakepits after long dull years of idle luxury. I could see nothing but the dust of ages, but I knew that each splinter scratched from the ancient floor, each blob and dribble of dirt or excrement, had its special message for Haricot's trained senses.

"And there he lay, see?" O'Reilly continued twenty minutes later. Each time O'Reilly said "see," he slapped viciously at the sinister bulge of a shoulder holster under his sleazy purple jacket. "Blood was running out under the door like flood tide in the Hudson River. Old Rose-Alley here took one look and flopped like a gut-shot bitch." His voice trembled, then hardened, and he spoke as if from a larynx of reinforced concrete: "My old Buddy, Cash O'Toole, cashed in at last, see? Shot and cut like he'd gone through the A&P meat-grinder, and I'll get the dirty bastuds 'at did it, if it takes till judgment day, see?"

"Quite right, Mr. O'Reilly, I'm sure," said Haricot smoothly. "You have every reason to be disturbed, but of course you realize that you must not take the law into your own hands."

"Damn the law!" cried O'Reilly. "It's blood I want!" He drew his automatic pistol—I observed that it was a .45 calibre Colt—and emptied its clip. Then he snapped open as ugly a spring stiletto as I have had the displeasure of seeing since the Black Hand chased us through Syracuse in '93. With this he proceeded to incise deep crosses in the soft, blunt noses of two bullets. Then he reloaded, putting the doctored bullets on top where they would be first to enter the chamber.

"Dum-dums," said Haricot calmly. "It was the only way we could stop the Fuzzy-Wuzzys—whatever sentimentalists may claim."

"I want revenge, see?" growled O'Reilly. "I'll blow holes in the bastuds they can stick their own heads through. I'll cut their hearts out and make them eat them!" He hurled his empty flask into a corner where it broke with a sodden crash, then staggered out the door, pistol in one hand, knife in the other.

"Ooh, eech!" said Rose-Albertine suddenly, and flopped forward over her writing machine.

"Fetch the ammonia salts, Anthony," Haricot said. "The wretched female has fainted at a most inconvenient juncture." In response to his command, both our servants lunged eagerly to the relief of the unconscious beauty.

"But where has that brute, O'Reilly, gone?" I asked. "Is it safe to allow him to wander forth armed in his present state of mind?"

"I believe, my dear Dawson, that he has gone to interrogate one Lefty Spaghanini, the leader of the East Side mob. As for your second question—nothing in this ephemeral world is safe. We can but watch and wait."

"But how can you be sure where he is going?"

"A cut on his shoe, and those blobs of clay you see just inside the threshold, told me much. A chance remark I once overheard in a back street in Peoria correlates with their implications, as does some information I received in confidence from our sleeping beauty's grandparent." He waved negligently at the flurry around Rose-Albertine.

"Bones, you astonish me!"

"Elementary, my dear Dawson," he said, then reached gracefully into his waistcoat pocket to switch off his hearing aid. I could but stare in admiration at the high-domed forehead behind which such wonders of ratiocination were so constantly and consistently performed.

*L*ate that afternoon, after Anthony had removed the remnants of our five o'clock tea, I determined to quiz Bones further. He had been busy with mysterious errands for most of the day, while I must confess I had been content to recuperate in the airconditioned survival chamber of our hotel suite after the harrowing expedition of the morning.

"May I ask again, my dear Haricot," I ventured, "why you have decided to involve yourself in such a sordid affair?" (I feared, although I dared not say so, that his affections had been entrapped by the flamboyant grandparent. I knew he was still taking Swiss gland treatments.)

Bones turned his wheelchair to stare out the window. As he began to speak, I watched with admiring fascination the silhouette of his hawklike visage. "You will recall, my dear Dawson," he said, "a certain fateful morning in a Sussex pub, when our tea had a peculiarly acrid flavor?"

"Of course. But that was many years ago—although we still suffer the consequences."

"*Suffer,*" he said, "is your word for it. I await further experience. However, the fiend responsible for the adulteration—I refer, of course, to Dr. O'Shaunnessy—intended without doubt to poison us. In the event, as all the world knows, the new poison he had synthesized combined with an antidote of my own invention to set off what the press has been pleased to call the Struldbrugg Reaction. Now, although our bodies continue to decay at a most distressing rate, our vital spirits continue unimpaired. If we can escape violence, we may live on for many hundreds of years!"

"An appalling prospect," I said bitterly.

"As I said before," he replied, "that is a matter of opinion. We must await the event. But what would you say if I informed you that Mr. Michael O'Reilly, the private agent we visited this morning, and Mr. Cassius O'-Toole, whose mutilated corpse I viewed in the morgue this afternoon, both were descendants of the late unlamented Dr. O'Shaunnessy?"

"Surely you jest, Bones," I protested.

"Not at all, my dear Dawson," he replied. "You will recall that O'Shaunnessy steadfastly refused to divulge the secret of that remarkable poison—refused, in fact, to admit his complicity in its formulation. One reason for my neglect of more public problems in scientific detection has been my unremitting pursuit of every wisp and fragment of evidence which might lead me to that lost formula. Just think, Dawson," he said, swinging his chair to confront me, his hawk's eyes burning with enthusiasm, "think what this may mean for humanity! The secret of eternal life! The fountain of youth!"

"But think of all we have suffered, Haricot," I protested. "One can hardly call this state we endure *youth!*"

"Bagatelle. If we can but keep life in body, all other things will be added unto us. You would be amazed if I told you about some of the feats I have accomplished after my monthly injection in Zurich!" He swung back to the window. "But all this is beside the point. I allowed you to believe this to be a mere pleasure tour, but I led us over here following a lead I received from one of my agents—a little man who keeps a shop in the Tottenham Court Road. From an aged aunt in Eastcheap he got wind of some papers left by Dr. O'Shaunnessy. These papers had been dispatched in secret to American relatives—undoubtedly in an attempt to evade my net. With little to guide me but the names O'Reilly and O'Toole, and some addresses fifty years out of date, I came posthaste to comb the great cities of the New World. Now my search is over—but with O'Toole dead, Mickey O'Reilly is our sole remaining link with the secret of the Struldbrugg Reaction."

"Then your interest in this case is personal, after all. Perhaps Miss Chandler's grandparent was another of the fictions you have invented to amuse me?"

"Not at all, my dear Dawson," Bones assured me solemnly. "Coincidence has always been a favorite guest at my table."

At that moment George entered to announce with suspicious enthusiasm: "Miss Rose-Albertine Chandler." I considered that the servants had competed most improperly that morning in their lust to play Prince Charming to her Sleeping Beauty. However, one must admit that they aroused her with efficiency.

Rose-Albertine flounced in right behind him, her abundant charms steaming from the heat of the outside world. "Did you hear the guy on TV?" she asked breathlessly. "He says Mickey's cooled three guys already, and that he's out for more!"

"What are the police doing?" asked Bones calmly.

"Well, Jeez, they don't know for sure who done it. The guy on TV called it 'Gangland Massacre in East Side A. C.' But, Jeez, your guys told me how you said that old Mick was gunning for Spaghanini—and he was one of them. 'Gruesomely mutilated' the guy said, just like Mick said he'd fix all those bastuds! Jeez—I hope they have some pictures in the *News* tomorrow!"

"Most extraordinary and irregular," said Bones thoughtfully. "While I am not yet prepared to name the killer of Mr. Cassius O'Toole, I am quite sure that Mr. Spaghanini had little or nothing to do with it."

"Yeah," said Rose-Albertine, with a toss of her fountain of blood-red

hair, "that's the way it is with old Mick when he gets mad. It sure don't pay
to fool around with him!"

Furtively I propelled my rubber-tired chair to the window and
switched the fan in the airconditioning unit to high; Rose-Albertine's aura of
sweat, powder, chewing gum, and cheap perfume was almost too much for
my abraded nasal mucosae. "My dear Bones," I said, "this is appalling! Is it
not your duty to release any information you may have right away, before
any more crimes are committed?"

Bones' sharp look cut through me like an edged weapon. "You will
recall the matter of which we were just speaking, which, I believe, should
take priority. Moreover, these people are foreigners who have their own
folkways. We have no right to interfere. I do not know that the police consider any crime to have been committed this afternoon. The dead men were
known criminals, and Mr. O'Reilly, after all, is a licensed investigator. Who
are we to question his methods?"

"But he seeks only private revenge," I protested, "and he is mad!"

"The Americans attach a peculiar virtue to private enterprise," Bones
replied coldly, "and many men are mad."

That evening and all next day Bones kept to himself. He remained in
his bedroom but left the door ajar. I could catch glimpses of him in his
chrome-plated wheelchair. Sometimes he darted about the luxurious chamber like a trout in a forest pool; sometimes he stopped, contemplative in
mid-carpet, for hours at a time. Sometimes he seemed to be immersed in
minute calculations in the small black notebook which he always carried with
him. Sometimes he filled the suite with the piercing strains of his violin, as he
composed wild chords to express his fancy or his vision.

One concession alone would Bones make to our fears—although he
may have made it more for the sake of the garish petitioner who first brought
him into the case. Rose-Albertine remained with us. She spent most of her
time with our men, who readily agreed to find her a place to stay with them
in the servants' quarters. Both George and Anthony boasted stoutly that they
would mount strict guard over her both day and night. No matter how O'-
Toole had met his end—they said—O'Reilly's enemies would find in Rose-
Alley Chandler no easy victim for their spite. I could only hope that they
were correct.

Furtive mouse-like men crept in and out; I recognized them as creatures of the same sort employed by Bones in London to search out information. Rose-Albertine and our two menservants attended to our needs—although with what seemed increasing difficulty. Indeed, our men appeared to
be getting extremely tired—perhaps, I thought, from the nervous strain of
guard duty. I feared, also, that they might be drinking. However, they
emerged at intervals from their quarters to inform us whenever an announcement of another of O'Reilly's killings came over the picture-wireless. "Mad

Mystery Killer Still at Large," and "Terror Reigns in Underworld," are two fragments which stuck in George's memory long enough for him to repeat them to us.

By the middle of the second afternoon, when Bones finally emerged from his bedchamber, the toll of O'Reilly's victims stood at eight. Like a comet Haricot wheeled his gleaming chair across the sitting room to ring for the servants, and when they appeared (Rose-Albertine breathless and dishevelled between them) he gave orders to prepare for a quick trip back to O'Reilly's rooms. "If my calculations are accurate," he said, "this will be the crisis. Dr. Dawson, if you will be so good as to bring your old army revolver? We may have desperate men to deal with!"

I nodded my agreement, and our men leapt to action.

*W*hen our taxis pulled up in front of the sordid edifice which contained O'Reilly's rooms, something indefinably different about the street caught my attention. A parking space appeared at the curb just where needed. When George and Anthony came bustling around with our chairs to help us disembark, no mob of clamoring urchins gathered to make insulting remarks or to demand baksheesh. Finally, when a half-grown lad sidled up to Bones and began to speak in rapid, low tones, as if making a report, I understood. Twice before, in London, had I seen counterparts of this situation: the gang of street arabs who controlled this block, I realized, must be in Bones' pay. Now we were all actors in a deadly puppet drama, for which Bones held many strings. Uneasily, I wondered if he held enough.

"We shall wait by the front steps," Bones informed us, after we had been safely disengaged from the taxi and remounted into our chairs. "I have been informed by my young leftenant that O'Reilly left Zlotnik's Rathskeller just twenty-one minutes ago, and is now imbibing what is known as a 'boilermaker' in Harry's Tavern—an establishment which is only a half-block from us. I have sent him notice to join us here immediately. He has been told that I wish to present him with important evidence concerning the identity of the murderer of his friend O'Toole."

"Jeez," said Rose-Albertine, "you'd better not just be fooling around, old man. I think maybe I'd better get out of here. Mick's liable to start shooting if you cross him up—even just a little bit!"

"Fear not," said Haricot. "Dr. Dawson is armed and ready for any eventuality. We are old campaigners, he and I. Once we were called the tongs of justice, and many a tough nut have we cracked between us! But I shall not 'cross up' your friend, O'Reilly; I shall perform as promised."

"OK," replied Rose-Albertine. "I'll stay. But I know I shouldn't!" She huddled between George and Anthony, both of whom were drooping like fagged runners after a five mile race.

A shrill whistle sounded from down the block. "He's on his way," said Haricot calmly. "And by the way, I should mention that I've also invited a number of persons who, I am told, are leaders in the local underworld. They have evinced considerable interest in O'Reilly's violent activities of the past few days. And they should be arriving fairly soon." He pulled out his watch, listened to be sure it was still ticking, then considered it soberly, as if wondering whether or not it was going to explode.

Rose-Albertine was seated on O'Reilly's steps between our two haggard menservants. I was arranged in my chair on one side the steps, Bones on the other. As representatives of an older, more stable society, we were rather like the symbolically protective lions on either side the steps of the New York Public Library—if I may venture a provincial comparison. However, as we sat thinking of the blood and slaughter which had disgraced the past few days, Anthony and George quite evidently were trying to entice their fair charge to enter the building with them. After some whispered discussion, she agreed. "You guys!" she exclaimed, simpering. "Don't you ever get enough?"

Then a lithe, darkskinned boy darted by like a swallow, pausing in flight only long enough to whisper, "He's here!" Close behind, like a pursuing storm, came O'Reilly himself, his olive-purple suit even more baggy and sweatstained than before, his eyes more bloodshot, and his chin bristling like the back of a hedgehog. No weapons sullied his hands, but his clothes bulged ominously; I felt sure he was armed to the teeth. As he sprang like a rogue panther to confront us, I could feel that he was still raving mad with his blood-lust for revenge.

"Well, you old bastud," he said to Bones, "here I am. What've yuh got to tell me? Spit it out—and it had better be good!"

"The problem," replied Bones, "is really extremely elementary, once one puts aside some of the purely fortuitous circumstantial evidence. I had the pleasure of explicating a similar case in Paris, in 1898, when I was called in for consultation by the Sûreté. About the same time, a German colleague, Herr Professor-Doktor Fluegelbein, very kindly called to my attention a closely related variant which occurred in Hamburg in 1863. Now the minimum necessary . . ."

"Can it!" growled O'Reilly, drawing his pistol with a brutal gesture and waving it under Haricot's nose. "Can it, or I'll blow your ass out of that tin buggy. Now, who done it? Just name a name, and I'll gut-shoot the bastud!"

"My dear O'Reilly," Haricot protested, "you have no idea—I assure you it is not as simple as that."

"Talk!" O'Reilly punched Bones roughly in the chest with the muzzle of his gun.

"There is a toilet-room in the basement of this building," Bones began. (I must confess I had no notion of what he was leading up to.)

"You won't be in no shape to use it, if you don't hurry," said O'Reilly.

"Now this toilet-room is small, dirty, ill-lighted, and extremely smelly," Bones went on calmly. "It contains only the minimum essential plumbing fixture . . ."

"You want I should ram your head in it? Get to the point!"

"Very well," replied Bones, "but whatever happens, don't blame me. Remember that each one of us, ultimately, is responsible for his own fate—that our own past actions determine both our present state and our future fortunes. You are—" he said, looking at O'Reilly's brutal features with evident distaste— "what you have made yourself. Now, if you wish, I suggest that you proceed immediately to this toilet-room, where you may find awaiting you the person you seek."

"Is he laying for me there?" demanded O'Reilly, swinging his gun in a wild arc. "Well, they've laid there before! Sometimes at night they're laying for me all over when I get back from the tavern. But I always shoot the bastuds before they can get me! I gut-shoot them, and watch them crawl and puke and lick blood before they die!" Gun in hand, he bounded up the dirty steps and disappeared into the building. I noted that Rose-Albertine and her two Prince Charmings also had vanished within. I hoped they stayed well out of O'Reilly's way.

"A charming example of primitive paranoia," Bones remarked.

"But as you, yourself, have pointed out," I protested, "his behavior seems to be perfectly acceptable to the natives of this country. Furthermore, what he reports may actually have occurred. Can we classify him as mad, if he suffers from no delusions?"

"Perhaps not. But hark—the problem may solve itself!" A burst of heavy firing resounded from within the building, like thunder, or like distant cannon on a still day.

"I trust he has not attacked the young female in his fury!"

"Rose-Alley? Where is she?" Bones' piercing glances flashed in every direction like sparks from a revolving pinwheel. "Here you," he called to one of the street arabs, "lend a hand! Dr. Dawson and I must be transported in our wheelchairs to the basement of this building. Here now! Quick now!"

Such was the persuasive force of his personality (aided by his purse) that we soon found ourselves propelled through dingy catacombs, enroute to the focal toilet. Behind us like a chorus of the lesser demons crept a cautious semicircle of young ragamuffins. The room was half-filled with dusty cartons and barrels—behind any one of which, I thought, might lurk an enraged gunman. Grimly I clutched my trusty old Webley in my palsied hand. Just ahead a scouting boy turned and tensely waved, then pointed to a series of dark splotches which ran across the concrete floor like oil drippings from a leaky crankcase. "Fresh blood!" he said, simply. The trail emerged from beneath the silent, closed door of the toilet-room.

At my direction, the boy kicked open the door, then leaped to safety. But when I peered within, my gun almost dropped from my trembling hand as I thought for one mad moment, *I have been here before!* The door seemed to open into the crepuscular, pre-dawn glow of the South African plain, and there before me once again lay the corpse of a great dog hyena—. It was choked with chickenfeathers, covered with chickenfeathers—and protruding from its mouth was the grisly remnant of a human arm! My swimming head wavered, and a gagging sound escaped my clenched lips.

"Steady, Dawson, steady!" came the cool voice of Bones from his station at my side. "You and I have seen too much in our day for you to flinch now at the wreckage of such a crude decoy."

Then I saw what tricks my eyes had played upon me. By the dim light I could just make out a scarecrow-like figure—made of a broom, an old jacket, and a couple of bedpillows—which lay broken across the toilet seat. One sleeve of the jacket protruded pathetically upward, insecurely caught on a splinter of broken broomstick. The pillows had burst, and drifting feathers seemed almost to fill the dirty little room.

"What . . . ?" I began, but was cut off by a woman's piercing scream. A cry for help followed the scream, and then the shrill words: "No, Mick! No, no, Mick! Don't shoot! Don't shoot!"

"Here, Rose-Alley!" Haricot's assured tones filled the circumambient ether with new hope, as a gush of pure oxygen may bring life to a drowning man.

Her spike heels clattering like castanets on the concrete floor, her hair dishevelled, her body half unclothed, Rose-Albertine ran toward us from a dark, far corner of the cellar. In close pursuit staggered Mickey O'Reilly, blood dripping from his wounded body, his pistol protruding menacingly from his beefy fist. I tried to bring my old Webley to bear, but my shaking fingers refused their duty.

Twenty ragged boys in a half-circle, with Bones and I in their midst like aged choir-masters, served as audience for the final dramatic scene. Like a queen at bay, Rose-Albertine turned proudly to face her apelike pursuer. She was clad only in a wisp of skirt, and her proud, naked breasts were levelled at O'Reilly's head like the twin muzzles of an elephant rifle. Staggering, O'Reilly pointed his heavy pistol upward from the hip, then pulled the trigger. Only a sharp metallic click greeted our straining ears, as the firing pin struck either a faulty cartridge or an empty chamber. O'Reilly sank to his knees as the blood pouring down his legs formed a pool around him. "You, too, Rose-Alley," he moaned. "I never thought you'd two-time me, you bitch!" His gun cocked again and again as he triggered it convulsively. "I'm all shot out. You've got it made, you bitch! I can't . . . I can't . . ." With these last words, he pitched forward on his face—dead. With a sob, Rose-Albertine sprang forward to throw herself on his bloody corpse.

★   ★   ★

A half hour later, a strangely mixed assemblage foregathered in the late O'Reilly's front office. There were, of course, myself and Bones, Rose-Albertine, and our two menservants (who had emerged sheepishly from behind some barrels with the rest of Rose-Albertine's clothing, after they were assured that all was safe). In addition, five swarthy gentlemen appeared, three of whom were privately introduced to me as the chiefs of some local bands of criminals; the other two, who were very similar in appearance, were publicly introduced as detective-inspectors from the police. Lurking like shadows in the corners of the room were a half-dozen of the street arabs who had proved so brave and so helpful.

Bones wheeled his chair to the center of the room, and before his commanding gaze, all fell silent. "My first clues," he said, "were a few scattered bloodspots and three lumps of clay—all of which had been overlooked by the police. With these to start with, two days of painstaking investigation were necessary to untangle the wily killer's subtle spoor. With expert assistance (he nodded gracefully to the street arabs in the corners), it was not difficult to trace O'Toole's thin trail of blood to the basement toilet, where the discovery of a spent bullet helped to confirm my developing hypothesis. The lads also helped me to trace the provenance of the tiny lumps of clay which I found just this side the office threshold. We matched them, finally, with some mounds of subsoil around a sidewalk excavation right beside Zlotnik's Rathskeller. With this much established, I was ready to restage the circumstances of the crime—and as luck would have it, at the same time to help rude justice thrust her way to the light."

"What . . . ?" I tried to ask, but no one heeded my interruption.

"Gentlemen," Bones went on, his hawk's eyes sweeping the intent assemblage, "as you may by now have surmised, O'Reilly himself shot and killed his best friend, Cassius O'Toole. Returning from his regular nightly tour of the local taverns, O'Reilly, as was his custom, staggered to the basement toilet to relieve himself before attempting the stairs to these rooms. In the dim light, he mistook O'Toole (who was there on a similar errand) for an enemy in ambush, and shot him down. O'Reilly then retired. Due to O'-Reilly's sadistic habit of shooting low, O'Toole survived long enough to crawl upstairs and drag himself into O'Reilly's rooms in search of aid. Awakened from drunken sleep by his friend's cries, O'Reilly rushed into their outer office just in time to watch his friend expire, and—in all innocence—pledge to take a dreadful revenge upon his killer."

"Extraordinary," I murmured.

"Elementary, my dear Dawson," Bones began modestly. "Even the police . . ."

"That's not what I mean," I interjected. "I fear there may be a flaw in your otherwise perfect solution. O'Reilly, you must recall, spoke of Rose-Albertine as having been a witness to the bloody scene here in the outer office . . ."

"No more of that, Dawson," Haricot interrupted in his turn. "While candor compels me to admit that Rose-Alley may indeed have been present, we must recall that we still are gentlemen. We must have a care for the young lady's reputation!"

Hot blood flushed my face as I felt the justice of his rebuke.

After a painful moment of silence, Bones continued: "As I was saying, my dear Dawson, the problem in its essentials was so elementary that even the police might have been able to solve it in time—particularly if they had troubled to read my little monograph on the classification of the subsoils of Manhattan. Of course, the police never seem to be able to make their observations with the minute particularity which is necessary for real success. They are so taken up with their rote-learning of fingerprints; so accustomed to using the crib-notes furnished by underworld informers—that they cannot pass the more subtle tests of true detection."

"Perhaps so," I replied. "But what happened to O'Reilly himself? Did one of these gangster persons here shoot him?"

"No, no!" exclaimed Bones hurriedly. "On the contrary! Ironically enough, O'Reilly achieved his own last, best wish, and took vengeance upon the killer of O'Toole—by shooting himself."

"But how?!"

"My able leftenant," Bones said, nodding toward one of the street arabs, "arranged at my direction the decoy dummy in a corner behind the toilet. When O'Reilly further confirmed my initial hypothesis by firing upon this dummy, his bullets ricocheted from the stone cellar walls to return most justly upon his own body. He was—as, ironically, in a different sense he wished to be—his own judge, jury, and executioner."

As I recalled Haricot's devotion to billiards, I at last understood his cryptic remark about helping "rude justice." "Marvelous!" I murmured, in sincere tribute to his genius.

Hours later, after satisfying some of the curiosity of Haricot's many new admirers, Bones and I relaxed in the drawing room of our hotel suite. Rose-Albertine had gone off to recuperate in her gaudy grandparent's apartment in Yonkers. Our exhausted servants had retired to their quarters to sleep.

"It is curious," I said, "that of all the horrors of the day, by far the worst for me was the sight of that broken, feathercovered dummy sprawled across that sordid toilet seat."

"Just so," said Haricot, to whom I previously had described my sensations in more detail. "Illusion is all. We are such stuff as dreams are made on, and to requite us, our dreams—for better or worse—make us. Our lives are

but spiderwebs of consciousness dangling in the black abyss of illusion—
stretch them as we will with new formulas for immortality. But *apropos*—
what say you now to O'Shaunnessy's revenge?"

"Spiderweb or no," I replied, "life again is amusing, and I now am
grateful to our unloving enemy. You may be pleased to hear that I have
decided to resume my course of treatments in Zurich. But what of the formula you were seeking? Is the Struldbrugg Reaction lost forever to mankind,
now that O'Shaunnessy's last two heirs are dead?"

"Aha," said Bones, "we may discover more about that later. However,
you should be told that Anthony was serving interests beyond those of nature
while engaged in the agreeable pursuit of young Rose-Alley. He was commissioned by me to obtain the key to O'Reilly's desk and inner room. Hidden in the desk, he found for me this paper."

Carefully, from a long manila envelope, Bones drew out a sheet of thin
yellowed paper. Across it, like a record of the migration of a flock of peripatetic partridges, scrabbled the figures and symbols of scores of complex chemical formulae. They were traced with brown ink in a tiny, precise hand; after
more than fifty years I still could recognize the highly individual style of Dr.
O'Shaunnessy.

"We cannot know for some time," Bones went on portentously,
"what my tests of these equations will reveal. My hopes, however, are high."
Nimbly he rolled to the sideboard and poured us each a glass of light sherry.
"Come, let us drink to the future! To the Struldbrugg Reaction! To the
bulldog breed! Never say die!"

Glass held high, I capped his gallant toast: "Let us make Struldbruggs of
all mankind! Never say die!"

New Adventures of Sherlock Holmes

The results of Professor Moriarty's final battle with Sherlock Holmes are well known, but what might have happened had the two enemies squared off over—a chessboard?! FRITZ LEIBER *(1910–1992), author of the thrice-filmed* Conjure Wife, *the* Grey Mouser *series and many other works of science-fantasy, speculates impressively on the outcome. NOTE: Though it is possible to replay the game described in "The Moriarty Gambit," it is not necessary to do so or even to know the rules of chess to appreciate the psychological battle being waged.*

The Moriarty Gambit

FRITZ LEIBER

Mr. Sherlock Holmes delved shoulder-deep in the large tin box wherein he stored the neatly red-taped records of his cases and handed me a tall black boxwood chessman of the pattern named for our midcentury czar of British chess, Howard Staunton.

"Have a care with it, Watson," he said.

I thought I discerned the reason for the warning. The piece was a king and the tiny cross which tops the crown had been broken off and was now tied to the neck of the piece by a length of black thread.

Then my good friend continued, "For it is the sole memento of my first encounter with the mighty Professor Moriarty of detestable memory—an encounter which occurred over the chessboard."

"You astound me, Holmes," I said. "I never dreamed you played chess or had bothered to give the noble game more than a moment's thought. I assumed you spoke your one word on chess in connection with the Amberley affair, when you said that an ability to play it well was one mark of a scheming mind."

My friend smiled at me—a little teasingly, I fancied. "That was Holmes Limited speaking," he said. "Your pardon, dear fellow, but I must say that you often give undue weight to the somewhat prosy remarks of Holmes Limited, while remaining deaf to the inspired utterances of Holmes Unlimited."

"What's this about there being two Sherlock Holmeses?" I demanded. "Now I'm more at sea than ever!"

"Then give me the wheel, Watson, and let me pilot you into harbor. You recall how when we first shared lodgings and you tried to solve the little mystery of my profession, you noted down that my knowledge of literature, philosophy, and astronomy was nil? Likewise my knowledge of history, et cetera, except insofar as it related directly to crime or the current scene?"

"I do," I admitted. "Holmes, I've often been rather embarrassed by those amateurish deductive efforts—"

"Please. You perhaps also recall how, soon after making your astute observation—yes, Watson, it was!—you began to discover that I was well up in all sorts of obscure and even dilettante fields—medieval manuscripts, speculative Continental philosophy, the literature of *Sturm and Drang,* and exotic zoology, to name but a few?"

"That's certainly true," I agreed. "And now that you mention it, I recall being once or twice vaguely bothered by the discrepancy between my two observations. I wondered which was mistaken."

My friend laughed outright. "Good old Watson! Simultaneously seeing and not seeing the two Holmeses! Dear fellow, both your observations were completely accurate. Your failure was in not realizing that they related to two different *personae.*"

"Make it a little clearer," I said shortly, somewhat nettled at his patronage.

"Gladly. Holmes Limited (whom we might also call the Practical Holmes, the Man Inside, or even the Stay-at-Home Holmes) is a shrewd sensible fellow with specific aims in life and sufficient means of achieving them, a good businessman, who knows among other things that a person can only get so much thought-lumber into his mental attic.

"Whereas Holmes Unlimited (Holmes the Adventurer, the Man Outside, the far-ranging Sherlock) is a maddeningly energetic dreamer, a modern Alexander who firmly believes that no mental or physical realm is beyond his conquest, and who knows of a certainty that the more lumber a man puts in his attic, the bigger his attic becomes."

"I begin to discern your meaning," I said. "But then which Holmes is the real Holmes?"

"Neither, my dear chap! Or both! One's as valid as the other. Put it this way: I have discovered that each Holmes is superbly effective if given the proper work to do. So I share out my life's activities between them. Thus far it has proved a capital arrangement!"

I shook my head. "As a medical man I'm not sure I can approve the encouragement of such a large split in the human personality. There are dangers in such subjective legerdemain, Holmes. Moreover, I don't know how Gregson and Lestrade, to name but two, would react to your admission that you are a kind of Jekyll-and-Hyde.''

"I do!'' Holmes caroled. "They'd say they'd suspected it all along and out with a strait jacket. Seriously, dear doctor, it is my belief that most men have such a split in them, though perhaps not yawning as wide, and furthermore that they'll profit most by admitting the fact and giving each *persona* his proper employment—make the Inside Man secretary of the little self-organization and the Outside Man roving correspondent. Or to put it as acutely as I am able, a man has most chance of happiness and success in this world if he makes his Limited Man Treasurer of his concerns and his Unlimited Man President.''

I nodded thoughtfully. "There's wisdom in that, I'll agree; but tell me, Holmes, how did you ever come to play chess—and of all things a game with Professor Moriarty?''

"Not merely play the Royal Game, Watson, but play it so inspiredly— or schemingly, if you will—that a season of first-class competition would have turned me into a recognized master. For that bold opinion I have the sober word of my one-time chess crony, the redoubtable British master Henry Edward Bird. You see, it was Holmes Unlimited who learned chess and he never does things by halves.

"Moreover, my encounter with Moriarty was no offhand game at Simpson's Divan or St. George's or the Mephisto—though for a time I frequented those chessic haunts—but in the first round of the London International Tournament of 1883, although (for a reason which will become clear at the end of my narrative) you would look in vain in the entry list of that competition for a Prof. Moriarty or an S. Vernet. (During my brief chess career I used my grandmother's maiden name.)

"You might assume I would have been entered in the Minor Tournament, improbably called the Vizayanagaram by reason of the Maharajah of that state having contributed £200 to the prize fund. For the Vizayanagaram had a formidable entry list, including von Bardeleben, Gossip, and Izzey Gunsberg, who'd been the player inside the Mephisto automaton.

"But Eddie Bird persuaded me to attempt the Grand Tourney and then browbeat Minchin and Steel (the organizers) into permitting my entry—on his own vouching for my ability and by hammering at the point that they had already allowed the entry of three other comparative unknowns: a J. Mortimer, a Rev. A. B. Skipworth, and a mathematician named Prof. Moriarty.

" 'We'll show them, Sherlock,' Eddie assured me. 'At least we'll show up that conceited mathematician. I lost an offhand game to him at Birmingham. He's insufferable!'

"Even then I knew a little more about Moriarty than Eddie did. I was aware of his two celebrated mathematical papers and also that there was something dubious about the man. I looked forward to observing Moriarty while under the strain of an intellectual competition that allows no secrets of temperament to be kept wholly hid.

"As to showing him up—or any other player in the tournament, for that matter—truthfully, I wasn't quite as confident as Eddie of my ability. But I resolved not to betray my misgivings to Eddie Bird or anyone else. A confident manner can't substitute for brains, but it can catalyze them wonderfully.

"April 23rd, 1883, Watson. The Victoria Hall of the Criterion was electric with the presence of the warring masters and the buzz of the crowd that had gathered to observe and adore them. Zukertort was there, and Steinitz, and Blackburne, and Tchigorin—the four eventual high-scorers in that order—four chessic giants, Watson, four full-foreheaded full-bearded men at the apex of their intellectual powers.

"Zukertort—a neat little Pole with a proud military bearing. He'd been an army doctor like yourself, Watson—served with the Prussians on three campaigns. Expert pistol shot and fencer. Had mastered twelve languages and twice twelve fields of knowledge. Zukertort Unlimited was a fantastic example of the Outside Man given free rein, Watson! He was to win 22 of the first 23 games he played in this tournament to clinch the £300 first prize.

"Steinitz—club-footed, lame, but a giant, Watson, the father of modern chess. A narrower genius than Zukertort's but a deeper and more tenacious one—three years later he was to beat him for the world's championship in a match held in America.

"Tchigorin—handsome, flashing-eyed, with a glare that went right through you. A Russian tiger of chess. A virtuoso to the fingertips, scorning the illumination of theory and books but playing chess nonetheless like a man who could see in the dark. (And all of them, by the by, were outstanding blindfold players.)

"And England's own incomparably brilliant Blackburne. A mild-mannered man, Watson—but on the Continent they called him the Black Death!"

Holmes' eyes were shining. I sensed what his enthusiasm for the game must once have been. Then he said more reflectively, though still aglow, "Watson, I truly believe that any one of those four men might have been a Holmes or a Moriarty—though perhaps Steinitz would have fitted best the Professor's role and Zukertort my own. It was a decade that matured men for masterly, fantastically ambitious, faintly theatric feats of the intellect. Some day, Watson, Holmes Unlimited will write a monograph on chess mastery and enthusiasm as an index to a nation's intellectual vitality and—do not laugh, pray!—the relationship between the number of chess masters in a country and the excellence of its espionage system."

He laughed then and continued, "Back to 1883. As you can imagine, young S. Vernet felt somewhat awed in the presence of these adult prodigies—awed, and most depressed about his own chances. However, his spirits revived somewhat when he discovered that his first-round opponent was to be, by the luck of the draw, Prof. Moriarty. At least, S. Vernet thought, he wouldn't have to face one of the giants at the onset.

"Little did he know! Watson, can you picture Moriarty at the chessboard? That pale high-domed forehead, the curious reptilian sway—why, they were made to overawe a chessic opponent!

"I had white for the first game. Ignoring my outstretched hand, Moriarty shot me one searching contemptuous look from those deep-sunken eyes and then touched the lever that set my clock ticking. London 1883 was the first tournament in which were used chess-clocks, that ingenious, characteristically British invention of T. B. Wilson of Manchester.

"Nettled, I advanced my queen's pawn two squares and Moriarty instantly retorted in kind. I offered the Queen's Gambit and—oh, Watson, if you knew chess and if we had a board and men I could show you the game move for move, for it is engraved on my memory."

"Holmes," I said, standing up, "I have a confession to make. I am something of a chess amateur myself and have a board and men in the bottom of my trunk."

"This is a revelation of unsuspected depths," Holmes said, gazing at me quizzically. "Watson a woodpusher!"

Somewhat stung, I replied, "Not quite a dub. While I was convalescing there from my wounds, I won the championship of the base hospital at Peshawur."

"Deeper and deeper! My dear fellow, why didn't you ever tell me?"

"To be perfectly truthful, Holmes," I said, "I always feared your disapproval. I thought you must scorn chess as a frivolous waste of ratiocinative energy. So when we first roomed at Baker Street, I hid my chessmen—just as I got rid of my bull pup."

"But you should have deduced I was a chess addict, Watson. You knew I reveled in cryptograms, problems, and analysis of all sorts. Moreover, it ought to have occurred to you that no strongly intellectual man who used the anodynes of morphine and cocaine could possibly have failed to try the supreme mental anodyne of chess."

"I can only say that you never gave me the impression of being the sort of man who would even tolerate chess."

Holmes shrugged. "In a way your observation was most accurate, Watson. Holmes Limited detested chess and still does. But for the moment that mean little cost-accounting man is off somewhere. So quick, Watson, out with your chessmen before he comes back, and I will show you my most electric experience in the world of 64 squares!"

Within minutes my chessmen—a small battered Staunton set—were arrayed in proper fighting order on their dingy cream-and-green board. Holmes began to move the pieces with never a hesitation for memory searching, though pausing now and again to comment.

HOLMES	MORIARTY
1. P-Q4	P-Q4
2. P-QB4	

"Offering the Queen's Gambit, as I said, Watson. But the Professor did not take my bait."

I could not resist interrupting to say, "How I wish I'd been there, Holmes! I visualize it as the historic encounter between young Paul Morphy and Adolf Anderssen."

"Not a bad comparison, Watson. Anderssen also was a mathematician—though otherwise an amiable enough man, I gather. But to continue—"

2. . . .	P-K3
3. N-QB3	P-QB4

"He played the Tarrasch Defense, Watson, some time before the move was made popular by Dr. Siegbert Tarrasch—another medical chess master, as I suppose you know. Unquestionably Moriarty was a chess researchist of the first water."

4. PxQP	PxQP

"And now, astoundingly, he offered me in turn the von Hennig-Schara Gambit years before it was introduced in the tournament at Duisburg. In view of these circumstances I prefer to call it the Moriarty Gambit—a designation doubtless the chess world would never accept, but nonetheless the only valid one for me."

5. QxP	N-QB3

"I was of course unable to take his queen's knight with my pawn because it would leave my queen *en prise* to his. I saw I could probably regain the advantage of a pawn by retiring my queen to its original square, but in so doing I would yield the Professor a sharp initiative. I didn't want that, so on an impulse I made a more aggressive move with my queen."

6. Q-QR4	PxP
7. N-KB3	P-Q5
8. N-QN5	B-Q2

"His bishop aimed at my queen in most sinister fashion, but now I saw my opportunity, Watson, to win a pawn and simplify the position."

| 9. QNxQP | B-N5 CH |

"I reached out my hand to interpose my queen's bishop, but just in the nick of time I saw Moriarty's devilish trap. If I interposed and if he then took my knight with his, and I his bishop with my queen, he would win her with a knight check at his QB7. The Professor had undercut me! I made the only move that would avert the catastrophe, though seeing that my king would be desperately harried in consequence."

10. K-Q1	NxN
11. QxB	NxN
12. KPxN	B-R5 CH

"A *double* check, Watson—something few players ever suffer and survive, as I imagine you know. I looked up and saw that the Professor was smiling faintly, while his head had ceased its rhythmic sway as his eyes cruelly fixed on my terribly threatened king.

"Incidentally, Watson, Moriarty and I were moving our pieces and tapping our clocks in rapid-fire fashion. The rate of play in the Major Tournament was 15 moves an hour, but that snail's pace was not for our brightly-lit minds. A few heads turned at other tables. A few spectators moved to watch us."

| 13. K-K2 | Q-Q8 CH |
| 14. K-K3 | |

"My king had escaped by the skin of his royal teeth from Moriarty's marauding queen! But his unguarded situation in the center of the board was desperate. Moriarty played—"

| 14. . . . | 0-0-0 |

"—castling his own king into safety and adding his queen's rook to the heavy pieces concentrating against my monarch. At this point Moriarty said to me quietly and yet harshly, his lip curling, 'I give you six moves more, Mr. Vernet. Seven at the most.' I made no answer. I had just seen a possibility on the board that electrified me. At once I moved—"

15. B-Q2

"Now his queen, so free a moment before, was threatened in turn and could not escape except by taking my rook. Moriarty shot me a strange look, yet his manner was still contemptuous as he quickly played—"

15. . . .	QxR
16. B-QR6	

"And now, having sacrificed one rook, I was offering him the other!"

16. . . .	R-K1 ch
17. K-B4	

"At long last now Moriarty studied the board for several minutes. He saw I would mate in two if he at once captured my rook. Realizing his king must have more air at all costs, he made a counter-sacrifice and then drove off my king before capturing."

17. . . .	R-K5 ch
18. PxR	P-KN4 ch
19. K-N3	QxR

"As he took my second rook, leaving himself still one rook ahead in material, he glared at me defiantly. I surveyed the board and said quietly, 'It is mate in five moves, Professor Moriarty.' And then I did a rather extraordinary thing, Watson—I reached across the table and for a moment lightly laid my right hand on his left shoulder. He drew back with a snarl. We played the next moves rapid fire, for mine left him in each case no alternatives."

20. QxP ch	K-Q1
21. Q-B8 ch	K-K2
22. B-N4 ch	K-B3
23. Q-B5 ch	K-N2
24. QxNP mate	

"And now in this moment of my triumph, the meaning of my shoulder-touch must have become clear to Moriarty. It was an epaulette mate—the black pawns standing to either side of his king, like epaulettes on the shoulders of black royalty, prevented him from moving aside from my queen's fatal check.

"In retrospect I like to think that my shoulder-touch also foreshadowed the day when I hauled off the Napoleon of British crime to British justice.

"But that was in the future. At the time my gesture merely added to the completeness of my chessboard triumph and to Moriarty's chagrin at his defeat.

"He gave me a look, Watson, that went through me like a knife. If ever murder glared from two eyes it was then. His fingers writhed, making claws. It must have cost him a titanic effort not to attempt to strangle me then and there.

"He snatched up his vanquished king and, pressing sideways his thumb with terrible pressure, snapped off the cross on the crown. Then he dropped the fragments on the center of the board, stood up, and glided rapidly from the room.

"I have always thought, Watson, that Moriarty's unique manner of admitting defeat symbolized his renouncing of chess in favor of a deadlier form of competition against his fellow men. Incidentally, Watson, I don't believe he ever connected the S. Vernet who ended his chess career with the S. Holmes who terminated his crime career. Perhaps his dark egotistic mind deliberately forgot Vernet's appearance. From a sort of courtesy I never revealed the connection to him, even atop Reichenbach Falls.

"Meanwhile the first round of London 1883 went on around me. Zukertort was already brewing against Blackburne what is widely recognized as the most celebrated chess combination of all times. The few spectators drifted away from my table, and I sat there gazing at Moriarty's shattered king, my mind furiously active in a new direction.

"I had just perpetrated a notable chessic brilliancy—for a double check countered in three moves by a two-rook sacrifice surely merits that description—yet I felt no elation from it. My imagination was obsessed by the glimpse I had caught of the black depths of murderous malignancy in Moriarty's soul.

"It occurred to me that the study and if need be the nullification of such evil constituted a worthier challenge for a ratiocinative man—a more pressing task in the service of society, if you will—than weaving nets to trap boxwood kings. The Limited and Unlimited Holmeses had a conference then and there, and as a result of it I did one of the few shabby things I've ever been aware of doing in my life, Watson. I pocketed the fragments of Moriarty's king and I walked out of Victoria Hall and never went back or said any word. Eddie Bird never spoke to me again.

"That's why you won't find Moriarty's name or mine in the tournament records. They were expunged for our most unmannerly, un-British retirement from the tourney.

"Yet I am convinced I did the right thing. There are times, Watson, when a man simply must give up chess. As I slowly moved past the boards of the mighty competitors I now would never meet, I noted among the observers a noble-visaged full-bearded man in a white suit far finer than that on the back of any one of the pondering chess masters. It was Baron Ignatz Kolisch, the Austrian grand master of the game who had given it up in order to devote all his mental energies to creating winning combinations on the stock market.

"I pressed past the wise and wealthy baron—who must have had a very sound Inside Man indeed—and quietly left the Criterion."

*J*ON KOONS *has acted on Broadway, in films and TV, and stage manages and directs theatrical, film and video productions. An Atlantic City magician, Mr. Koons owns his own production company, which supplies variety entertainment throughout New Jersey, New York, Pennsylvania and other states. In his spare time (?), he trains and books clowns, which may have led him to wonder how Sherlock Holmes and Dr. Watson would have fared in the world of the Nineteenth Century circus.*

The Adventure of the Missing Countess

JON KOONS

It was a glorious spring day in the year 1889. The air was still brisk, but surprisingly fresh for the city, and the walks and lanes down which I trod were lined with fragrant and colorful rosebay willow and London Pride.

I awoke this morning fully with the intent of escorting my lovely wife, Mary, at her request, to the travelling circus that had made nearby Tunbridge Wells its temporary home, but those plans were laid aside, much to my wife's dismay, by an urgent communication from my friend and associate, Sherlock Holmes. As I walked the accustomed route to 221-B Baker Street, I reflected on some of Holmes' past adventures which started out in this exact same manner. Upon arriving at my destination, Holmes greeted me warmly.

"Ah, Watson, so good of you to come."

"Come, Holmes," I replied, "I have rarely declined an opportunity to accompany you on one of your cases."

"Quite so, but since Mary Morstan made an honest man of you, your availability has been somewhat more limited."

"One of the small disadvantages of married life, I'm afraid."

"A small disadvantage to be sure. Married life agrees with you, old boy."

"Not that I disagree, mind you, but what leads you to that conclusion, Holmes?"

"Elementary, my friend. You have, of late, been more ebullient than ever. Your apparel has been more carefully coordinated, the obvious influence of a woman's keen eye for fashion, and is better tended to, save for the small stain there on your vest . . . kippers, I would say . . . which indicates that you are being well fed. The fact that your ample stature has become even more so by eight or ten pounds would tend to support this conclusion. You are more precisely groomed, your shoes are finely polished and you appear more rested and less tense, an obvious benefit of the sort of companionship that you formerly lacked. Your occasional discourse regarding your wife is always favorable, and the very fact that you have been less available to join me lately clearly indicates that you are enjoying your current situation and reaping the benefits."

"Holmes, you never cease to amaze me."

"Nor I myself, old boy."

"So, what are we on to today?"

"Come, Watson. I'll tell you all I know in the cab."

In the carriage, Holmes explained what he knew of the case.

"Do you know the name Countess Virginia Thorgood Willoughby?"

"As a matter of fact I do. I read an account of the Countess Willoughby recently in the society pages of the *Strand Magazine*. If memory serves, she's a widow who lives alone with her seventeen-year-old daughter. She lost her husband during a visit to America last year, although the particulars of the event elude me."

"Very good, Watson. What else do you recall?"

"She returned with her daughter to London six months ago to leave the incident behind and raise her daughter with a sense of proper British morality, something which, according to the article, the Countess found lacking in America."

"Precisely. She did not wish her young, impressionable daughter, Alexandra, to succumb to the improper influences that she said the Americans seemed to thrive on. Apparently she was a bit too late, as her daughter was already enamored of American ways and was, by all accounts, unhappy with the sudden move back to England. She caused her mother a good deal of embarrassment by making her feelings known at every opportunity, not least of all in public."

"But what does this have to do with us?"

"It seems, Watson old man, that upon arriving home from the opera late last night, Countess Willoughby found her home a shambles and her daughter missing. She has not been seen since approximately five hours before the discovery of the transgression, which is why our destination is their Kensington residence. The Countess immediately sent word to Scotland Yard, which investigated with its usual fervor but aside from finding a concise ransom note, is unable to fathom the meaning of any of the available clues. As has happened more than once, as well you know, Inspector Lestrade sent for my aid, which he will gladly employ and thereafter forget to acknowledge. But no matter, my dear Watson. I have been hungry for a new mystery to occupy my time. I was, of course, dismayed to be called so long after the crime had been discovered, but Lestrade assures me that the scene, and any evidence which might be present, will be left undisturbed until our arrival. So now you know as much as I about this case, save that we are presently going to meet the Countess in the company of her legal advisor and recent social companion, Kent Osgood, whose role in these proceedings has yet to be determined."

"Surely, Holmes, this is a simple case of kidnapping, not worthy of your extraordinary talents."

"Perhaps, Watson," Holmes replied. "Perhaps."

Holmes then fell silent and gazed out the window, his fingers pressed together in a steepled attitude, as was his custom during moments of deep thought. As I looked upon my friend, bedecked in his customary deerstalker cap, cape-backed overcoat and pipe, all of which had become, I daresay largely due to my accounts of his adventures, his trademarks, I pondered my own good fortune not only to be in the presence of greatness, but to be his personal friend and longtime companion as well.

We arrived at the address in Kensington shortly afterwards and were ushered into the house with all due haste by a maid who appeared utterly distraught. She took us directly to the sitting room where Inspector Lestrade, the Countess and Mr. Osgood were waiting. At once we could see the disarray caused by the perpetrators. Furniture had been knocked askew or overturned. Drawers were opened and rummaged through, and all manner of things were strewn about the room.

"*M*r. Holmes," cried the Countess, "I am at my wits' end. You are the only man in all of London who can save my little girl. Please say that you will help me."

"I shall do what I can, madame. Please try to calm yourself so that you may answer some questions for me."

"I will do my best," said the Countess as she grasped the hand of her companion. After some brief introductions, Holmes began his questioning.

"Countess Willoughby, I am told you discovered your daughter missing when you returned from the opera last night . . ."

"Yes, Mr. Holmes, that is so. I blame myself. Had I not been out of the house last night for so frivolous a reason perhaps my little girl would still be here with me now . . ." She began to weep, and Mr. Osgood embraced her.

"Now we've been all through that, Virginia. You are not to blame," said Osgood in a comforting tone.

"Mr. Osgood is quite right. You cannot be held accountable for actions about which you had no prior knowledge. If I may continue? Is it your custom to frequent the opera, or was last evening a special event?"

"If I may, Mr. Holmes," Osgood interjected. "Since Virginia and I have been keeping company these last several months we have made it a weekly ritual to visit the opera, or perhaps a concert. We generally do so on a Friday evening, but this past Friday Virginia was feeling a bit under the weather, so we postponed our weekly entertainment until last night, Tuesday."

"Was anyone else aware of this change of plans?"

"Not to my knowledge. It was the maid's day off. We had invited Alexandra, as we usually do, but she unfortunately declined, as she usually does."

"And at exactly what time did you leave the premises?"

"The opera we saw was *The Magic Flute*, at Royal Albert Hall. It was to begin at eight o'clock. As you are no doubt aware, Albert Hall is not far, so we left here at a quarter past seven, I would say."

"And you returned . . . ?"

"They returned," piped Lestrade, obviously feeling left out, "at exactly seventeen past midnight, according to my report."

"Thank you, Inspector. Your assistance, as always, has been invaluable. Now if you will permit me to inspect the premises, I shall see what clues I can unearth. If you please, Watson."

As we began to scrutinize the room, Inspector Lestrade commented on the lack of available clues, save a knife thrust through a photograph of Alexandra hanging over the mantel. Holmes nodded. I followed my friend to and fro, carefully noting every item that he examined.

I spotted something unusual on the floor near the entrance.

"What do you make of this, Holmes?" I called out. He joined me at the door, stooped down on his knees and pulled his glass from his pocket.

"Good show, Watson. Sawdust!"

"Sawdust? Then perhaps we are looking for someone in the construction trade. Or perhaps woodworking."

"Perhaps, Watson. Come look at this photograph. Young Miss Willoughby is quite an attractive lass, is she not?" She was indeed, I agreed. The hand-tinted photograph showed her long golden hair and lovely, delicate features.

Holmes pulled the knife from the photograph and handed it to me. "What can you tell me about this knife?"

"Well . . ." I studied the knife carefully but could not see what he was getting at. "The handle is worn more on the left side than the right, so . . . our suspect is left-handed?"

"Excellent. Please continue."

"The blade is very dull, which means that it is used by someone who is either neglectful of its poor condition or else who does not require a sharp edge."

"Bravo, Watson. Very astute. There is more, but time is fleeting. Inspector," Holmes said, turning to Lestrade, "I would like to see the ransom note, then I want to inspect the girl's bed chamber."

"Here's the note. No point looking into the bedroom."

"Quite," was all Holmes said. He glanced briefly at the note and then handed it to me. "Please read this aloud, Watson."

"If you ever want to see Alexandra alive again, deliver a sum of one thousand British pounds to the Charing Cross train station on April 29th at noon. Put it in a small bag and leave it at the signal flag at track 9. Go to ticket window five afterwards and Alexandra will be waiting. Come alone. If we see police, I will kill her." As I finished reading, the Countess once again burst into tears.

Holmes asked the maid to direct him to the girl's bedroom, and went off directly, only to return a few moments later.

"I told you it was pointless, Holmes." Inspector Lestrade looked at me with a smug look.

"I have seen all I need to," Holmes replied simply. "I shall contact Watson three days hence and he shall relay my instructions. In the meantime, feel free to tidy up the damage and go about your business. Countess, your daughter is safe, so you needn't fear. Three days, then!" And with that he nodded to the group and was out the door. Both Lestrade and the Countess were obviously bewildered, and looked to me for clarification, which I could not provide.

I quickly followed. "No time to explain, Watson," Holmes stated, as he hailed a cab. "Be at Baker Street in three days." As he climbed into the cab, he turned and said, "And bring your lovely wife Mary with you."

"Holmes . . . ?"

"Time is short, Watson. I've clues and motives to juggle." The cab started off.

Puzzled by Holmes' behavior, I took advantage of my proximity to Kensington Gardens, and strolled through the park pondering the events of the day. Could Holmes have pieced together the clues and unravelled the mystery so quickly? I had, of course, witnessed his uncanny abilities on numerous occasions before, but it seemed he reached some conclusion in an impossibly brief amount of time. Why did he leave so abruptly? What purpose would his three day absence serve? And to what end was my wife's presence requested? Think as I might, I could not decipher his reasoning. Winded from my exertions, I sat upon the steps of the Albert Memorial and watched two badgers frolic through some oxeye daisies, Mary's favorite flower. I knew only one thing for certain. Holmes had been right. I was putting on weight.

*T*hree days later my wife and I arrived at Baker Street. It had been some little time since Mary had been there, but she remembered it well and felt quite comfortable, although no less curious than I about the circumstances. Shortly after our arrival, Mrs. Hudson, the landlady, handed me a wire from Holmes. It instructed me, and Mary, to meet him, at, of all places, R. J. Toby Colossal Travelling Circus in Tunbridge Wells. He entreated us to enjoy the three o'clock show, and then wait afterwards at the Torture King tent on the midway where he would meet us. Mary was delighted to be included in Holmes' adventure, but even more now that it appeared she would get to see the circus after all. We departed immediately for Tunbridge Wells.

*T*he festival was a splendid sight to behold. A great tent, striped in bright red and blue, was the centerpiece to a dizzying display of color and movement. Wonderful carriages, arranged in a half circle, resplendent in their brilliant reds and whites, were trimmed out with yellows and greens and gaudy rococo gold leaf. Some of the carriages bore cages which held magnificent beasts of all types, while others displayed performers' names and promises of wonders to come. While looking closely at a caged lion I discovered, curiously enough, that my inclination to sneeze while in the presence of common house cats was also very much a reality in the presence of these larger rather less amiable cats, a fact which did not please me but apparently amused my wife no end. A carousel hosting painted horses and carriages turned round and round for the amusement of the children, and the sound of calliope music filled the air. Aromas of all types, some pleasant and some not so, assaulted the nose. The midway was quite a sight, sporting tall impressively illustrated banners describing the likes of such oddities as the Incredible Bearded Woman, the Tantalizing Egyptian Snake Charmer, the Amazing Dog-Faced Boy, and the Death-Defying Torture King. I noted the location of the latter's tent for future reference.

*I*n our wanderings I saw no sign of Holmes. Having strolled the grounds of the circus, and after having partaken, at Mary's behest, of some sort of gooey confection made from nuts, bits of dried fruit, chocolate and caramel, much of which I was still trying unobtrusively to pry from my teeth, we headed for the main tent, as it was nearly three. While purchasing our tickets we were met by Countess Willoughby, Mr. Osgood and Inspector Lestrade. I introduced my wife to the gathering, and we took seats near the large wooden ring which served as the stage area. The ring was floored with a generous amount of sawdust, and much to my dismay, I began to sneeze once again.

"*M*r. Watson . . ." began the Countess.

"Doctor, Countess," I corrected her.

"Forgive me. Dr. Watson, I do not understand what we are doing here. Perhaps you can shed some light?"

"I should be delighted to, but I am as much in the dark as you. Sherlock Holmes is the most knowledgeable person I know, but I must confess that I still do not entirely understand all of his methodology. If it is any comfort to you, from what I know of my friend, you shall have your answers, and most likely your daughter, before the day is up."

Lestrade complained, "No good will come of building this lady's hopes up. Scotland Yard has been investigating this case for three days as well, and we have drawn no conclusions. Holmes is good, I'll grant you, but I dare say he's not so good as to deliver this lady's daughter on a silver platter!"

Mr. Osgood agreed. "Yes, Dr. Watson. Suppose you are wrong. I should think that instilling false hope is something you would wish to avoid."

"Mr. Osgood, Inspector Lestrade," said my wife, "I was once a client of Sherlock Holmes. I am confident that he will solve this mystery and return your daughter to you. If anyone can, he can."

"Thank you, my dear," replied the Countess. "You are very kind."

*A*t that moment, the crowd fell silent. The circus was about to begin. Mary took my hand and we settled down to enjoy the show. Neither of us had been to the circus since we were children. The ringmaster, in his jodhpurs, red frock coat and top hat, introduced the acts each and all, and the band played merrily as the performers took their places in the large circular stage area. A lovely young lady led six stallions of varied colors around the ring, and demonstrated her mastery of horsemanship. The tent fairly vibrated with applause. Next, a colorful clown on stilts juggled three lit torches. He tried to blow them out, one by one, but every time he transferred them from hand to hand they relit, one by one, much to Mary's delight. Finally dousing the flames, he walked across the ring, but seemingly unaware of the tightrope which blocked his passage, became entangled in it. His stilts shot out from under him, leaving him dangling from the rope. After many precarious antics he gained the top of the rope and proceeded to walk its length to a small platform. He bowed to the thunderous applause of the crowd, and in doing so fell to the net below, and then ran off. Next came the elephants, followed by some acrobats and then it was again time for the clowns, this time several of them dressed in the costume of a fire brigade. The "fire clowns" ran circles around one another in an attempt to "save" a burning building, bumping into each other, falling down, dusting off, and falling down again. One clown jumped into the crowd, tweaked Mary's nose, pulled my moustache and bolted back into the ring. Mary told me that the clown was very familiar somehow, but I explained that he had been the same stilt-walking clown from earlier in the show. After the clowns had failed to "save" the building, they rapidly retreated from the tent, as the crowd roared with laughter. Several foreign chaps and scantily clad young ladies flew through the air on trapeze, after which a young man, about twentyish, I would say, led a teenaged boy to a door-sized wooden wall and fastened him to it by the arms and legs. The man then stepped back and displayed a set of dangerous looking knives, which he proceeded to throw directly at the boy. Mary held my hand as I caught my breath, and the crowd was silent with fear. He hurled the knives one by one, impaling them in the wooden wall, each time narrowly missing the boy. Only when the boy was completely surrounded by knives was he released and able to take his bows with the young man. Several additional acts followed, including trained dogs, more clown antics, a dancing Russian bear, and an additional display of acrobatics. At the end of the show, Mary and I, along with Countess Willoughby, Mr. Osgood and Inspector Lestrade, headed for the Torture King tent, which I took note of previously.

"How did you enjoy the show?" Mary asked the group as a whole.

"Very amusing," the Countess answered, although it was obvious she was distracted by other concerns. Osgood agreed.

"Well, since you asked," Lestrade said unpleasantly, "I think it was rubbish. All just stuff and nonsense."

We stood silently as a group in front of the designated meeting area, awaiting Holmes' arrival. Numerous patrons, and even many of the performers on their way to the changing tent, passed by, but there was as yet no sign of Holmes. One clown, the featured performer throughout the show, stopped before us to further display his antics. He pulled three colored balls from a pocket and juggled them in a number of different patterns before tossing them high into the air and allowing them to fall directly on his head. His body crunched lower to the ground as each ball hit until he was flat on his back. Mary, Osgood and I applauded. The Countess then turned to me and said, "Dr. Watson. While this is all quite amusing, I am finding it hard to keep my spirits light in the face of our purpose here."

"Quite right," added Osgood, "where is this Sherlock Holmes of yours?"

*J*ust then the clown jumped up and onto his hands, where he stood momentarily. "I seem to have turned myself around. You all look so tall. But if I keep this up I'll lose my head." He righted himself, then placed a pipe between his teeth, from where he retrieved it I could not say, and then blew into the stem, causing a great cloud of ash to erupt into the air. "I say, would you have some tobacco that I can borrow? My pipe has gone empty."

"Well, no actually, I do not," I said.

"Just as well," said the clown, "it would probably smell like an old Persian slipper, anyway."

"As a matter of fact . . . wait a moment. How could you know that?"

"Elementary, my dear Watson."

"Holmes!?"

"Holmes? Sherlock Holmes?" The startled Countess asked.

"What's all this then, Holmes?" Lestrade said.

"Excuse me, but I seem to be a bit confused . . ." Osgood said.

"All your questions will be answered. Please follow me." Holmes started off in the direction of the dressing tent and our party obligingly followed. "Sorry to have taken you all by surprise like this, but it was necessary," he explained. My theatrical inclinations have been a long time without expression. It was good to utilize my talents once again." He stopped outside the tent, and proceeded with his explanation. "While at your home, Countess, I found several clues which led me here. The sawdust on your floor was fouled with soil and animal refuse. Had it been tracked in from a carpentry shoppe or similar establishment it would have been purer." He removed his red rubber nose and yarn fringed bald pate wig. "The knife that impaled your daughter's photograph was not thrust in, but thrown from across the room, as indicated by the angle at which it hit. Furthermore, the knife is a specially balanced one, edged for use in a knife throwing act. The shattered glass from the frame was spread in a pattern that suggested an impact of great force. Had the knife been thrust into the photograph manually, the pattern would have been less remarkable. Finally I detected a faint odor of greasepaint in the room. Someone connected with this circus, the only one within reasonable distance, seemed the logical choice."

"Astounding," I said.

"Simple deductive reasoning, Watson. The culprit, obviously an amateur, overturned and disturbed both furniture and belongings in an effort to simulate a robbery, or perhaps a struggle, but the ruse was unconvincing. Had he sought to rob the house, valuables would have been missing, and furniture left undisturbed. If the purpose of the break-in was a kidnapping, belongings would not have been touched, and had there been an actual struggle, I find it unlikely that large, heavy pieces of furniture would have been overturned while trying to apprehend a small, seventeen year old girl."

"Mr. Holmes," the Countess interposed, "you said at my house that my daughter is safe. How can you be so sure? And where is she?"

"She is here, madame. You have seen her. You all have."

"Here," objected Lestrade. "What do you mean?"

"You'll see soon enough. Please accompany me into the tent."

Once inside, we found ourselves in the company of several performers in varying stages of undress, many in the process of removing make-up. Holmes walked to the center of the room and spoke aloud. "Pardon me, but my friends have joined me so that we may solve a crime." He looked around the room, and his gaze fell upon the young man who had performed the knife throwing act, who suddenly appeared nervous, and began edging his way towards the exit. Holmes nodded to a burly toff, the Man of Steel, from the show, who blocked the young man's passage and said "Aye wouldn' go no-wheres if aye was you," and so he gave up the attempt.

"Now, young Master Errol Smithy, or should I use your real name, Chuck Hanson? I shall make a series of statements, and you will answer yes or no depending on the accuracy. You are personally acquainted with Countess Willoughby's daughter, Alexandra, are you not?"

"Well, I . . . We kind of . . ." Hanson stammered and looked around the room for help, but none was forthcoming.

"Yes or no, Mr. Hanson?"

"Yes."

"You are in love with Alexandra, and have been since you met her in America last year."

"Hey, how could you know that?"

"That qualifies as a yes, wouldn't you say, Watson?"

"Indubitably, Holmes."

"You have, in fact, been lovers, and plotted this kidnapping ruse so that you could be married." Countess Willoughby gasped. Osgood helped her to a seat.

"Look, we knew her mother would never approve of us. I'm just a circus brat from the poor side of the tracks. We planned to get hitched back home, in New Jersey, but when they moved back to England, I had to find a way to be with her. I sold all of my belongings, except my knives, and used all of my savings to book cheap passage to England and then got the job with the circus here. I contacted her as soon as I could and we planned the whole thing."

"Logically, your lack of money would present a problem, and hence the reason for the kidnapping ruse."

"At first we were just going to run off and elope, but I thought of the kidnapping scheme to get some money to make our start in life a little easier. Don't blame Alex. It's all my fault. I just love her so." He flopped down into the nearest chair and laid his head in his hands.

Holmes asked Lestrade for the ransom note. The inspector handed it to him. "This was the most incriminating piece of evidence in unravelling the puzzle. Attend. 'If you ever want to see Alexandra alive again, deliver a sum of one thousand British pounds to the Charing Cross train station on April 29th at noon.' The note refers to 'Alexandra', a familiar use of the name, indicating personal acquaintance. Secondly, the reference to 'British pounds' suggested to me that the "kidnapper" was someone who thinks in terms of a different monetary system. American dollars are unique and standard across that country, whereas the European designation of 'pound notes' as currency are issued by any of several countries. Local residents would not specify the country of origin. Only an American in a foreign country would make such a distinction. Next point," Holmes continued, "the use of 'train station' rather than 'railway station' is American, as is the note's poor grammatical style in general. There are numerous other clues, but they are of no great moment." He handed the note back to Lestrade. "I left the home of the Countess and came immediately to this circus, where I was hired temporarily as a new performer. Over the past three days I have had the opportunity to discover, at leisure, all of the additional information that I required from the company of performers and from young Chuck himself. He is twenty-one years old, from Hackensack, New Jersey, in America, and as you may have observed during his act, is left-handed.

"When the circus arrived in Tunbridge Wells, the closest stop to London on the touring schedule, he and Alexandra waited for an opportunity to carry out their plan. The only time the Countess left the house with any regularity was on Friday, but the circus had late performances those nights. When the Countess rescheduled her outing, it was exactly the turn of luck that they had hoped for. Tuesday is the only day on which the circus has no performances. It was a very fortunate happenstance indeed that the supposed abduction could be carried out without his absence from the circus being noticed."

"All right, Holmes." Lestrade interrupted, a little too loudly. "You've told us how you found him out, and that he had means and motive, but aside from what he says, what evidence do you have that the girl was involved of her own free will?"

"Inspector, your investigation of the Willoughby premises was incomplete. When I investigated Miss Alexandra's bed chamber, I took particular note of the items on, or rather the items missing from, her vanity and wardrobe. Nothing was disturbed to suggest a theft, but small gaps with empty hangers in the wardrobe indicated the removal of a few select pieces of necessary apparel. And no young lady of proper breeding would feel complete without her brush and hand mirror, which were conspicuously missing from the vanity. In addition, only Alexandra knew the exact time that her mother and the maid would be away from the house, and for precisely how long."

"Mr. Holmes, please. My daughter would never do such a thing!"

"I quite agree, Holmes," Osgood added. "Your conjectures are bordering on slanderous. I suggest you prove your theory immediately, if you can, otherwise I shall be forced to advise Countess Willoughby to file suit against you on behalf of her daughter."

"Kent, please!" the Countess chided. "I have no interest in proof or legal suits. I only want my daughter back. Mr. Holmes, you have brought us all the way here to listen to your brilliant deductions, but where is my daughter?"

"Walking through that very tent flap at any moment," Holmes stated calmly. As if on cue, the tent flap pulled back and a lone figure entered the tent.

"Ha!" Lestrade scoffed. "It's just the boy from the knife act." The boy had entered, seeing a crowd of curious faces intently staring at him, and stopped frozen in his tracks. His face went ashen. Tears started to well up in his eyes.

"ALEXANDRA!" The Countess was beside herself.

"Hi, mummy," the girl said sheepishly through her tears.

"Alexandra, indeed!" Holmes said triumphantly. "Hair dyed black and cut in the style of a young lad, dressed as a young lad, but Alexandra, nonetheless. Her boyish figure made it a convincing disguise. I learned her habit to change costume out of sight of the others, but she always returns to the tent so as not to draw attention to her absence."

The Countess embraced her daughter.

"But why, Alexandra? Why?"

"Because I love him, Mother."

"Well now," Lestrade coughed, embarrassed, "seems like Mr. Holmes has done a right good piece of reasoning, after all. But it's all in the hands of the law now. I assume, Countess, that you would like to press charges against this young scalawag?"

"No, Inspector, I would not."

"Virginia, really! As your legal advisor I must advise you to . . ."

"Do be quiet, Kent."

"Mother . . . ?"

"I think we must all sit down and have a long chat," said the Countess. "If you love this boy so much that you staged this elaborate deception, and if he left behind his life in America to follow you here, well . . . we shall all discuss it at length when we get home."

"Oh, Mother," said the girl as she heartily embraced her dam. They walked out of the tent, followed by Hanson and Osgood, who, still cowed, nodded to us with a shrug before departing. Lestrade looked as if about to say something, but simply turned and left.

After the others departed, Sherlock Holmes took a seat and immediately began rubbing some sort of white cream on his face to remove the remains of his clown make-up. He spoke as he cleansed.

"Mrs. Watson, so good of you to come."

"Likewise, Mr. Holmes. But why did you ask me to accompany my husband?"

"Watson mentioned your desire to see the circus, which I so rudely interrupted. Besides, I wanted to see what it was that has been making my old friend appear so happy lately."

"Why, thank you, Mr. Holmes."

"Think nothing of it, madame. Now then, you two must stay on with me for the next show."

"What on earth for?"

"I would like to see it rather than be a part of it just once . . ."

"By the way, Holmes," I asked, "how did you learn the juggling and stilt-walking and such?"

"Simply a matter of balance, coordination and concentration, if one is physically fit. As a young lad I was always fascinated with clowns, so I learned the basics of the craft, thinking I might one day become a circus performer. It seems I've managed to do just that. I was able to learn the intricacies of the skills once I arrived. The routines themselves haven't changed much since I saw the circus as a boy, so I was familiar with them already. So, what do you say? Will you see the next show with me?"

"Mary and I would be delighted to spend an entertaining evening with my closest friend and companion. Can you, by any chance, deduce who that might be, Mr. Sherlock Holmes?"

"I haven't a clue, Watson. I haven't a clue."

While researching The Game Is Afoot, *I examined many scarce, obscure items. One of them was* Sherlock Holmes in Gibraltar, *a forty-nine-page paperback produced by Gibraltar Books Ltd., whose catalog includes books about birds, guns, towers, wildlife and sailing on . . . well, where do you think?* Sherlock Holmes in Gibraltar *by* SAM BENADY *contains two tales. "The Gibraltar Letter" is the better of the pair.*

The Gibraltar Letter

SAM BENADY

*Many of the accounts which I have written about the exploits of my
good friend Mr. Sherlock Holmes were never intended for publication,
especially those involving matters of state and those whose publication
might cause suffering to innocent parties. I have been careful to record
all such cases, however, and have deposited them in my dispatch box in
the vaults of Cox's Bank in Charing Cross. One day, perhaps, when
it is safe to do so, these accounts may be collated and published by some
future historian of scientific detection.*

I first heard the story of the affair of the Gibraltar letter from Holmes some years after it happened. We had been sitting in our chambers in Baker Street one cold winter's evening, pleasantly relaxed after one of Mrs. Hudson's substantial and delicious meals, when I rose reluctantly and went to the mantelpiece to retrieve my pipe.

"Be a good fellow and toss me my tobacco, Watson," said Sherlock Holmes languidly, stretching out an arm.

I reached for the Persian slipper where Holmes habitually kept his shag, and grasped it by the tip. To my surprise, I felt a hard irregular object wedged in the pointed toe.

"Why, there's something here that certainly is not tobacco!" I said, as I probed with my forefinger into the depths of the slipper. Holmes watched with some amusement as I withdrew the mysterious object on the tip of my finger. It was a gold ring, set with a magnificent ruby.

"Really, Holmes," I cried, "I thought that I had become inured to your Bohemian habits, but to use a valuable object like this so carelessly—"

"Ah, but my use of this ring was quite logical," replied my friend with a smile. "It was the only object which I could find which would fit snugly into the toe of the slipper."

"But why—?"

"Because there is a hole in the slipper, through which most of my tobacco is at this moment falling on to the carpet," said Holmes tartly.

A little chagrined, I bent over to pick up the scattered tobacco, remarking, I dare say somewhat peevishly, "A valuable ring like this one should be better guarded."

"On the contrary, it was very safely kept there," replied Holmes. "It has been there since we first met, and you have never noticed it before."

"But how did it come into your possession? A family heirloom, perhaps," I hazarded.

"Indeed not. It was a gift from an august personage, in gratitude for a service which I was able to perform." He gazed at the ceiling and puffed reflectively at his pipe. I waited patiently and after a while he began to recount the story which I have recorded here.

"It happened in '76—some years before your time, Watson. One day I received a note from my brother Mycroft, summoning me to his club. You know the Diogenes Club, that haven for the unsociable, where no talking is permitted save in the Strangers' Room. Mycroft met me there, and motioned me to an armchair.

" 'You have been to Gibraltar before,' he began, eyeing me keenly.

" 'Only very briefly, during the affair of the *Mary Celeste,*' I replied. 'But from your choice of words, I deduce that you wish me to go again.'

" 'Not I, Sherlock, but I have a most urgent request, I might almost say a command, from a certain gracious lady—'

" 'You need say no more,' I interrupted. 'Tell me what I must do.'

" 'Since your knowledge of history, except the history of criminal activity, is sketchy to say the least, you may not be aware that the fortress of Gibraltar was captured from Spain in 1704, and ceded to the British Crown by the Treaty of Utrecht in 1713. Since then Spain has attempted on many occasions to regain the Rock, but has always been foiled by British diplomacy or British valour, and each successive defence of Gibraltar has brought it closer to the heart of the average Englishman, so that now any British Government which proposed to return the place to Spain would be faced with such a public outcry that it would be forced to resign in short order.

" 'In the early days, however, Parliament had less power, and the

Crown had correspondingly more. George I was under constant pressure from his Spanish counterpart Philip V to return Gibraltar to Spain, and indeed some of his own Ministers held that this, in exchange for a treaty, would be to Britain's advantage. In response to these pressures, King George publicly wrote letters to Philip promising to cede back the fortress, but only if the British Parliament should give its approval, which he knew it was most unlikely to do. This did not satisfy the Spanish king, who continued to press with the obstinacy of a weak and ailing man, and in the end our King wrote a secret letter promising that the British Crown would consent to return the Rock to Spain after 150 years, provided only that Spain pressed its claim by presenting this letter within a year of the expiry of this period.

" 'The letter was never delivered to Philip, although rumours of it must have reached the Spanish Court. Before it could be sent, he lost patience with diplomacy and besieged Gibraltar. Instead George sent the letter to the Governor of Gibraltar, the Earl of Portmore, possibly thinking that it might prove to be a useful bargaining counter if the siege went badly for the defenders.

" 'In the event, the Spanish attack failed, but in the chaos of the siege the letter was misplaced and never found. Thought to have been accidentally destroyed, it was almost forgotten and in the aftermath of defeat Philip never dared to renew his demand, and George was no doubt only too glad to forget its existence.'

" 'I take it that the letter has reappeared,' I remarked.

" 'Of course!' snapped Mycroft. 'I would hardly have mentioned it otherwise. The problem is that it has disappeared again, and so has its finder. And he is a Royal Duke—the Duke of C—!' he added with a groan.

"So it was that less than a week later I found myself stepping ashore at Gibraltar on a bright autumn morning from one of Her Majesty's fastest frigates. I was met on the quayside by the Governor's son and aide-de-camp, Robert Napier. He lost no time in explaining what had happened, during the short carriage ride to the Governor's residence, known as the Convent, and while we waited for His Excellency the Governor, Lord Napier of Magdala.

" 'The Duke arrived in Gibraltar in October '75, just over a year ago, and left in the spring of this year with his brother, the Prince of Wales, who was on his way back to England after touring India. A few weeks ago he suddenly returned to Gibraltar unannounced and in secret. Of course my father invited him to stay in the Convent. One evening shortly after his arrival, he retired to his room early, taking down a book of seventeenth century sermons from the book-case in his room to read in bed. Hidden between the pages of this book he found a letter. Quickly realising what it was that he had found, he took it down to the Governor, and read it aloud to us.'

" 'Who was present when it was read out?' I enquired.

" 'His Excellency, myself and my mother only.'

" 'No one else at all?' I persisted.

" 'Oh, there were servants in and out of the room at the time, who might have heard part of it—'

" 'Who were these servants?'

" 'Absolutely trustworthy, Mr. Holmes. You need not seek a traitor among them. Only my father's batman, Barker, who has been with him for many years, and a Gibraltarian maid, Conchita Demaya, who has served the Convent faithfully since she was a girl, could possibly have heard anything.'

" 'Very well. What happened next?'

" 'Before he finished, the Duke appeared to realise how dangerous the document might be. He stopped reading, folded it and placed it in his pocket, saying that he would take it to England on his return, for it was of great historical interest, but that it should be kept safe until then.'

" 'And is it in fact such a dangerous document?' I asked.

" 'Indeed it is, Mr. Holmes,' boomed a new voice, as the imposing figure of Lord Napier of Magdala walked into the room. 'The letter gave an unequivocal promise from the Crown of Great Britain that the sovereignty of Gibraltar would be transferred to Spain on its presentation before the end of the year 1876—this year, Mr. Holmes! Her Majesty would feel morally obliged to honour this undertaking by her ancestor, and this would inevitably bring her into constitutional conflict with her Ministers. Even if the Prime Minister bowed to her wishes, the public anger which the cession of the Rock would arouse would surely cause the fall of the Government and further decrease the Crown's popularity, which is already at a low ebb. And now the Duke has disappeared—and the letter has gone with him!'

" 'Ah, yes, the disappearance of the Duke. Tell me how this happened, your Excellency,' I said.

" 'That evening, the Duke returned to his room, taking the letter with him. On the following day he rode to the Cork Woods in Spain with a groom—' Lord Napier hesitated, looking decidedly uncomfortable.

" 'Come, my lord! I must have all the information in this case, however embarrassing it may be,' said I firmly.

"The Governor's already high colour deepened to purple, and he seemed ready to explode with rage at my temerity. Then he passed his hand over his brow and sat down. When he spoke, he had regained control of himself:

" 'You are young, Mr. Holmes, and you come highly recommended, so I will try to make allowances for your manner. You are right, of course. You must have all the facts at your disposal, even though what I am about to tell you I have not even dared to report to Her Majesty.' Lord Napier hesitated still, and I said helpfully:

" 'You are about to tell me that the Duke left a mistress here, or in

Spain, whom he could not forget when he returned to England, hence his unexpected return.'

" 'Robert! You did not—'

" 'Lord Napier's son quickly shook his head.

" 'It was merely a logical deduction, Lord Napier,' said I reassuringly. 'What other information would you feel justified in concealing from your Monarch? But pray continue with your story. I presume that you do not believe that the Duke has simply eloped with this person.'

" 'No, that is inconceivable. The Duke's sense of duty would forbid it, although I believe that he is very deeply enamoured of the lady, who is a young and beautiful widow named Ana Pedroz. During his previous stay in Gibraltar, he used to visit her regularly after riding with the Royal Calpe Hunt. On this occasion, he rode with his usual groom, Pepe Ansaldo, a Gibraltarian, to the village of Gaucín where this lady lives, in the hills above the Cork Woods, and dined at the "Hostal Inglés" which is a hostelry popular with the officers of the garrison. There the groom remained with the owner, one Pedro Real, who is his distant relative, while the Duke visited Señora Pedroz.

" 'When he did not return on the following morning as arranged, Ansaldo was alarmed and went to the house of the Duke's lover which stands on its own some distance away from the village. There was nobody there, and the house had obviously been ransacked. Do you think that the abductors, whoever they are, could have found the letter? We searched for it high and low in the Duke's bedroom here, and in Señora Pedroz' house, but it was not to be found.'

" 'I think we can assume that the abductors made their attack because they knew of the letter; for mere thieves or *bandoleros* would not have abducted the Duke without demanding a ransom. If this is so, it is quite evident that it cannot have been found, else it would not have been necessary to abduct the Duke and the woman,' I replied. 'They were certainly alive when they were removed, for there would have been no reason to carry away dead bodies, although of course they may not be by now.'

" 'Surely no Spaniard would dare to assassinate an English Royal Duke!' Robert Napier burst out, his voice full of horror.

" 'We must consider every possibility,' I said gravely. 'If the letter and the abduction are connected, and we must assume that they are, who would be most interested in getting their hands on this letter?'

" 'Every Spaniard dreams of regaining Gibraltar for his country,' said Lord Napier heavily, 'and there are many political groups which would see the advantage of having the credit for such an achievement. The young King Alfonso XII is an honourable man, who would probably much prefer not to use a document obtained in such a dastardly way, but if it were offered to him publicly he would be forced to act on it lest the recently restored Bourbon dynasty of Spain be again swept away by popular discontent.'

" 'For the agreement offered in the letter to be valid, it must be presented before the end of this year, that is to say in less than two months,' said I, 'This makes the matter most urgent, for every day that these villains do not have the letter in their hands will make them more impatient, and this may drive them to desperate acts. I must start the investigation immediately.'

"I was shown to the bedroom used by the Duke. As Lord Napier said, it had been thoroughly searched: even the panelling had been removed from the wall. I asked for the book where the letter had been found. It was a volume of Donne's sermons, and it fell open easily at a page which was stained by the imprint of a document which had lain there for many years. Obviously the book had not been read for a century and a half, or the letter would have come to light earlier.

" 'Are you not wasting your time here?' asked Robert Napier curiously. 'Nothing can remain undiscovered in this room, surely. Should we not go to Gaucín and seek traces of the Duke there? He must have carried the letter with him, for he obviously realised its importance. Perhaps he hid it somewhere in the hostelry where he dined, or in his mistress'—in Ana Pedroz' house.'

" 'All in good time. Tell me, did the Duke keep a diary?'

" 'Yes, it is here where we found it, on his bedside table. We examined it closely but there were no recent entries.'

" 'I examined the journal. The last entry was dated several days before the Duke's disappearance. A torn edge showed that the next page had been ripped.

" 'Look at this!' I said.

" 'We noticed that, of course,' said Napier a little impatiently. 'The page was nowhere to be found. We will never know what was written there, if indeed anything was.'

" 'Ah, but you are wrong,' said I triumphantly, holding the diary up at an angle to the midday sun, which was streaming in from the window. 'See, when the Duke wrote he bore down heavily with his pen at times, and this has left an impression on the following page.'

"Napier's eyes lit up, and he came up to my shoulder as we struggled to make out the words impressed on the blank page.

" '. . . Cannot bear to destroy . . . enormous historical importance . . . dangerous in wrong hands . . . must hide it safely . . .' we read with great difficulty. Then the faint marks became illegible except for one word, 'friend'.

" 'My word, but you have a keen eye, Mr. Holmes. He must have destroyed the page on which he wrote in order to leave no clue to the hiding place he chose,' cried Robert Napier in great excitement. 'And now we know where the letter is hidden!'

" 'Do we?'

" 'Of course we do, man. "Friend" can only mean his woman in Spain—he must have hidden the letter in her house. Pray God it has not been found! We must go to Gaucín at once; maybe we can find it—'

" 'I believe that the solution to the mystery lies here,' I said calmly, wandering around the room and examining the paintings on the walls, which were mostly of hunting scenes and of horses. Napier shook his head at me in despair, and I continued: 'Think, Captain Napier, would you describe the woman you love as a "friend"?'

" 'No, I suppose not,' he said reluctantly. 'But who then could he possibly have meant? The Duke has made no other close attachments here. I was perhaps his closest confidant and he certainly did not give me the letter to hide!'

" 'I did not answer, but asked instead: 'Has this room been kept locked since the Duke's disappearance?'

" 'As soon as we returned from the Hunt, we searched the room thoroughly, and it has been locked and guarded since,' said Napier impatiently. 'But surely we should be in Spain searching for the Duke!'

" 'We must be patient. Your men have been searching in Spain for over a week to no avail. We must seek clues here to the Duke's whereabouts. Now, you must arrange to leave the door of the room open, and withdraw the guard; then we will retire to the room across the corridor and await events.'

"That evening we sat in that darkened room, with the door ajar, for several hours. Many of the servants of the Convent passed up and down the corridor, but none of them gave the Duke's room, with its open door, more than a passing glance. The maidservant Conchita passed, and stared curiously into the room; I felt Napier stir at my side, and put out a hand to restrain him as she passed on down the corridor. Then for a long while, the corridor was empty.

"Darkness was falling when a silent figure came furtively along the corridor towards the Duke's room. He stopped, looked from side to side, and then took down a painting from the wall outside the door and carried it into the room.

" 'Why, it is Barker, Father's batman!' whispered Napier in amazement. We crept across the hallway and in the gloom of the room opposite we could see the dim figure of the old soldier as he began to slit the back of the painting with a knife.

"Before he could go any further we were upon him. When he saw us, he made no attempt to defend himself, but dropped the knife and fell on his knees to the floor, burying his head in his hands and crying over and over again:

"'Forgive me, oh, forgive me. I was tempted, and I fell.'

"In response to a call from Napier, servants came and took the weeping man away. I picked up the painting and showed it to my companion. It was the portrait of a noble chestnut stallion, and bore the name of the horse: 'Caesar's Friend'. I slipped my hand into the slit made by Barker's knife and gently pulled out a parchment and read its opening words to Robert Napier and his father, who had joined us:

"'His Majesty King George, King of England and Elector of Hanover, to his most Catholic Majesty King Philip . . .'

"'Mr. Holmes, I congratulate you,' said Lord Napier handsomely, 'But how will this help us to find the Duke?'

"'Barker is the link, my Lord,' I replied. 'We must question him.'

"The interrogation of the unfortunate Barker revealed what I had surmised. He had become addicted to gambling and had lost sums which were beyond his power to pay. His main creditor was a man called Ricoletti, who had indicated to Barker that he would accept payment in the form of little items of information about the Governor and his entourage.

"'How could you do this, Barker!' said Lord Napier fiercely. 'You were once worthy of my trust!'

"The old soldier cringed away from his master. 'Forgive me, my Lord,' he groaned. 'It seemed to be the only means I had of repaying my debts, and at first he was satisfied with trivial gossip, but then he began to demand more, and when I heard the Duke reading the letter I knew that this was the sort of information that Ricoletti wanted—the sort that he could sell to the Spaniards, and I went to him that very evening. How could I know that the devil would dare to kidnap the Duke—?'

"'Enough, Barker,' interrupted Lord Napier sternly. 'You returned to steal the document, did you not? You are still in the pay of the Queen's enemies! Do not pretend remorse now.'

"'He promised that it was the last favour which I would have to do to pay off my debt, and that then I would be free,' said the old soldier desperately. 'I told him that I would not do it, and he replied with a laugh that if I did not find the letter the Duke would die and my part in the matter would be revealed. When we had searched the room I found a half-burnt scrap of paper in the fireplace. I concealed it and examined it later, but all I could read were the words "—sar's friend". I racked my brains over it, but I could make nothing of it, until tonight I remembered the painting outside the Duke's room—'

"'You can help us now, and perhaps mitigate your punishment to some extent,' I said. 'Where can we find Ricoletti?'

" 'I do not know, sir,' said Barker earnestly. 'I believe he is a Gibraltarian, but he lives in Spain, I don't know where, but I do know that he comes to Gibraltar after dark to visit taverns in the hope of picking up scraps of information which he can sell or use for blackmail. But I haven't seen him since the day he threatened me and demanded that I bring him the letter.'

" 'He must have taken fright at the hue and cry after the Duke's disappearance, and gone into hiding,' Lord Napier said wearily. 'We have no way of finding him. Take this man away.'

" 'If Ricoletti originally came from Gibraltar,' said I thoughtfully, as Barker was led away, 'then he must be known to some Gibraltarians. I should like to question the maid Conchita and the Duke's groom. They may have some light to shed on this dark affair.'

"The groom Pepe Ansaldo and the serving maid stood nervously some distance from each other, but the frequent glances they exchanged showed that there was a bond between them. Conspiracy or affection? I wondered. I questioned the groom, a dark-haired, handsome fellow, first, and heard how he had left the Duke as usual near the house of Ana Pedroz. When he had returned as arranged the house was deserted and no trace of the Duke or the woman could be found.

" 'Do you have any idea where your master may be?' I asked him.

"His looked at me straight in the face and answered firmly, 'No, sir; if I had, I would have said so already. The Duke was good to me, and I would do anything to see him and the lady safe.'

"Conchita looked admiringly at him for his bold words, and he flushed slightly and smiled at her reassuringly.

" 'You must realise,' I said, turning to her, 'that as one of the persons who heard about the letter, you are suspected of having given away the secret to the Duke's abductors.'

"Conchita's clear brown eyes looked steadfastly at me, but she made no answer: she had no need to. Ansaldo came swiftly to her side, and taking her hand, said belligerently to me: 'Mr. Holmes, my Conchita had no part in this matter. and neither did I. We are true Gibraltarians; we are British, and we have no love for Spain!'

" 'I say there, Ansaldo!' began Napier, shocked at the groom's boldness, but I motioned him to silence and said to the couple:

" 'I believe that you are both telling me the truth, and I know now that I can rely on your help to find the Duke; tell me now, do you know of a man called Ricoletti?'

"The reaction from both of them showed that they did. 'He is a bad man, sir,' burst forth the maid, and Pepe nodded, adding, 'He was born with a club foot, and this seems to have embittered him, as if he blames the world around him for his infirmity. He was notorious in Gibraltar as a thief and a scoundrel and had to leave before justice caught up with him. He swore then that he would revenge himself on us, the Gibraltarians, for our treatment of him—'

" 'He's married to a Spanish woman, and she's worse than he is!' Conchita interrupted passionately. 'She used to look after babies here in Gibraltar, and several of them died mysteriously. People said that she dosed them with laudanum to keep them quiet, and gave them so much that they died of it! Nothing could be proved, but she and her husband had to leave Gibraltar after that.'

" 'A charming couple!' I remarked. 'Do you know where I can find them, for I am sure that where they are, there the Duke will be too!'

" 'They bought a derelict house in Gaucín,' said Pepe. 'They tried to make it into an inn, perhaps hoping to attract customers away from my cousin Pedro Real, whose hostelry is famous throughout Andalucía, but few travellers had the stomach to stay there more than once. The woman is a slattern, the inn was filthy and the food uneatable, and any customers who braved the bedbugs and the poisonous wine were soon driven away by the surly manners of the Ricolettis. They still live there, I believe, but it's no longer an inn.'

" 'But presumably it is large enough to conceal two prisoners!' I said. Ansaldo nodded, and I continued: 'I must go to Gaucín at once!'

" 'I will go with you! We'll take a well-armed band of officers—' said Robert Napier, but I shook my head firmly.

" 'The last thing we want is a hue and cry which will warn our quarry to flee, perhaps after murdering their prisoners.'

" 'Indeed not, and even were you successful, the news that an armed band of English soldiers had attacked a Spanish village would cause an international scandal which we certainly cannot afford,' stated Lord Napier firmly. 'But even if you are right and the Duke is in the power of this evil man, what can we do to free him, Mr. Holmes?'

" 'These people will not have any accomplices in this affair. They will want to keep their actions secret and also to avoid sharing out any reward they might hope to get. I think that two Spanish peasants arriving quietly in Gaucín at night could seek a night's lodging *chez* Ricoletti and soon find the captives and free them. I will need a companion who can speak fluent Spanish—'

" 'I will go with you, Mr. Holmes,' Pepe burst out. 'I know Gaucín and its people well, and I will do anything to help save the Duke from these fiends.'

"A few hours later Pepe and I were riding along the rough track which led up the mountains towards Gaucín. Although it was November, the weather was warm and dry. We passed by groves of olive trees, and then the track led upwards into the mountains and was lined and in some places almost roofed over by cork oaks and carob trees, the latter heavy with dark brown pods. These soon gave way to pines, and the breeze in our faces took on a chilly bite.

" 'There's Gaucín!' called Pepe, who was riding just ahead.

"I spurred my patient steed until I caught up with him at the top of the rise. The white houses of Gaucín were strung along the next ridge ahead of us, ending with the stark ruined walls of the castle, which was built on the very edge of a sheer rocky precipice that overlooked the valley below. On the horizon in the far distance the faint outline of the Rock of Gibraltar could be seen.

"A few minutes later we were riding up the main and indeed the only street in Gaucín and shortly afterwards we were comfortably ensconced in the parlour of the 'Hostal Inglés' where we were royally entertained by Pepe's cousin, Pedro Real, who was a colourful character with bristling moustachios and a tremendous paunch, and who kept pressing us repeatedly to drink the raw local brandy. Eventually I was able to get him on to the subject of Ricoletti.

" 'Ah, that scoundrel,' he said scornfully, spitting into the roaring log fire in front of us. 'He thought he could take my livelihood from me, with that miserable excuse for an inn that he opened! He failed, of course, but he still sits there dreaming of making his fortune and hatching plots with that harridan of a wife of his.'

" 'Are they there now?' I asked quickly, as he paused for breath.

" 'They must be. I heard him coming up the road late one night, with two heavily laden donkeys—why, it must have been the night the Duke disappeared! Do you think—?'

" 'It seems very likely that the Duke and Señora Pedroz were rendered insensible by this evil couple and are now held somewhere in their house.'

" 'But that cannot be!' Pepe burst out, 'I went there with the *guardia* on the next morning and watched while he searched the place. Not even a mouse could have escaped his eye! The Ricolettis were not there and no captives were hidden there.'

" 'They must be there,' protested Pedro Real. 'I would surely have heard them if they had passed this way, and there is no other way out of Gaucín than the street which passes this house.'

" 'Perhaps a hidden cellar—' I suggested.

" 'Impossible!' stated Pedro Real with finality. 'I remember when that house was built. It sits firmly on the solid rock of the crag, just below the castle. There is no cellar underneath it. You would need gunpowder to blast a hole in that rock and the village would surely have noticed if that fool Ricoletti had tried!' he added with a laugh.

" 'Well, we must go and see this place,' I said.

" 'I will come with you,' said Pedro Real, wheezing slightly as he heaved himself out of his chair.

"A few minutes later, the three of us crept up the unpaved street leading towards the Ricolettis' house. It was pitch dark by now and only a few faint flickering lights from the windows of the houses we passed served to illuminate our way. But no light shone from the Ricolettis' house when we arrived there. It lay there, squat and black, with the greater blackness of the ruined castle looming over it. Pedro Real stood well back as Pepe and I approached in our guise of travelling peasants and knocked at the door. We knocked and knocked again, but there was no answer, and nothing stirred within.

"Pepe and I put our shoulders to the door, but it would not budge. Then Pedro lumbered up and added his considerable weight to our efforts. The wood around the lock splintered and we were inside. Lighting lamps which we had brought with us, we looked around. The house was in disorder but it was the disorder of slatternly neglect rather than signs of a struggle. The only movement was of the cockroaches on the table, attracted by the mouldering remains of food which lay there. There was a general smell of decay but over it all a faint sweetish odour reached my nostrils. It came from a corner of the room we were in, where a dirty cloth lay, with a small bottle by its side.

"Lifting these to my nose, I sniffed cautiously, and then exclaimed: 'Chloroform! That's how they overcame the Duke and the lady. Now we know that they were here; but where can they be now?'

" 'Perhaps they have been spirited away from Gaucín,' Pepe suggested gloomily. 'They may be miles away by now.'

" 'Never!' Pedro Real insisted. 'I've told you, I heard them go up the street that night, but I didn't hear them return, and I miss nothing that passes my house by night or day. They must be here somewhere; there is no other way out of Gaucín.'

" 'If they did not go down the street, they must have gone up it,' I remarked. 'What lies beyond this house?'

" 'Only the castle,' said Pedro Real, 'But it is ruined and uninhabited. No one could live there.'

" 'Nevertheless, since we have eliminated all other possibilities, the castle it must be,' I told them. 'We will go there now.'

" 'We left the house and continued up the street carrying our lanterns and were soon clambering over the loose stones which had fallen away from the crumbling ramparts of the castle. The autumn breeze had stiffened into an icy wind, and rain began to fall. No light was visible within the castle as we passed silently through the gate, and Pepe muttered, 'Surely they can't be in here!'

"I held up my hand for silence and listened. At first I could hear nothing except for the whispering of the wind in the trees and an occasional bark from a restless dog in the village below us. Then I became conscious of the murmuring of voices, which seemed to come from beneath our feet. I threw myself to the ground and pressed my ear to the cold flags, while my two companions gaped, evidently thinking that I had taken leave of my senses, but I was able to satisfy myself that the voices were coming from directly beneath our feet.

" 'What lies below here?' I asked Pedro.

" 'Why, nothing,' he answered in surprise, but then almost immediately added, 'Wait! I remember now; there are some steps leading downwards just beyond this arch in front of us, but for as long as I can remember they have been blocked by stones which must have fallen from the walls many years ago.'

"We hurried through the arch and looked around. There, to the side, was a flight of stairs apparently leading into the bowels of the earth. We stepped over a pile of stones and I cautiously shone my lantern down the stairwell to illuminate our descent. The stairs appeared to have been cleared recently; no doubt this explained the pile of stones at the stairhead. I signalled to my companions and we began to creep down silently. At the foot of the stairs was a wooden door which looked new; Ricoletti had evidently cleared away the rubble secretly and put in this door so that he could use this secret place for his evil purposes. I pushed gently against the door, which swung silently inwards, and drawing a pistol from my belt I stepped into the room.

"For a few seconds none of the occupants was aware of my intrusion, and I was able to look around. The room was barely and meanly furnished with two straw pallets and two chairs. On each of these a prisoner was bound—a pale and defiant young man, who in spite of the bruises and dried blood which covered his face and head was easily recognisable as the Duke, and on the second chair a young black-haired woman lay limply with her eyes closed. A knife was held to her neck by an evil-looking squint-eyed woman who laughed as the point pierced the skin, and a red trickle of blood ran down and began to drip onto the floor. Standing menacingly over the Duke was a villainous looking, heavily built man with a club foot who was saying:

" 'Very well, my little princeling, if we cannot get your secret by starving you or by beating you, perhaps we can find another way to make you sing: Tell me where you have hidden the letter, or my dear wife will cut the lady's throat!'

"The Duke struggled vainly with his bonds, and cried out hoarsely 'No!', but whether this was a further refusal to cooperate, or an appeal to save his Ana, we never found out, for at that moment Ricoletti turned and saw me standing at the door. Growling angrily, he came at me with a lumbering, clumsy rush, but I clapped the muzzle of my pistol to his forehead, and he stopped and stood stock still, trembling with fear and rage.

"The woman turned, her face distorted with hate, and screeched in broken English: 'Let him go, or I keel the girl!'

"I turned to her, and said, more coolly than I actually felt: 'Madam, if another drop of the lady's blood falls to the floor, I will blow your husband's brains out. Drop the knife!'

"Behind that mask of evil some sort of love for her unsavoury spouse must have been hidden, for with a curse she let the knife fall to the ground, and I let out my breath in a sigh of relief. But the exchange had distracted my attention from Ricoletti, who flung me to the ground and leapt for the door. He did not get far, however, for at the foot of the steps he cannoned into Pedro Real's enormous paunch, which almost filled the stairway, and fell back into the room. Pepe Ansaldo stepped forward and struck him sharply on the head with the butt of his pistol and he fell to the ground unconscious, while I recovered my own weapon before Mrs. Ricoletti could reach it. Pepe covered the evil couple with his gun while I freed the Duke and Sra. Pedroz, who was already recovering from her faint.

"Later, after our prisoners had been delivered to the *guardia* of Gaucín, my companions and I sat with the Duke in the parlour of the 'Hostal Inglés', while Pedro's wife tended to Ana Pedroz, who was weak from hunger and ill-treatment, for the Ricolettis had tried to starve their prisoners into submission, before they had tortured the Duke in a vain attempt to force him to tell where he had hidden the letter.

" 'The letter! We must make sure that it has not been found by one of Ricoletti's minions,' said the Duke anxiously, and I hastened to reassure him.

" 'Do not fear, your Royal Highness, it is in Lord Napier's safe in Gibraltar where I placed it after I had discovered it in the place where you had hidden it.'

" 'Mr. Holmes, you are a marvel!' said the Duke. 'I'm sure I left no clue to guide you. How did you find the letter?'

" 'I have my methods, Sir,' I replied.''

" *T*hat was an amazing tale, Holmes!" I remarked when he had finished. "And the most surprising aspect of it is that no whisper of this affair has ever reached the newspapers, either in Spain or in England. Quite apart from the scandal which would have been caused to our Royal family if the Duke's illicit affair had come to light, think of the political implications of that letter—"

"More than one person in Gibraltar must have known of the story," said Sherlock Holmes quietly, "but the people of Gibraltar are above all loyal subjects of the British Crown. They would not dream of embarrassing our Queen by making the matter public, and even less would they consider doing anything which might weaken the links between England and the Rock to which they are so passionately attached."

"I am still curious about one thing," I said pensively. "You did not say what became of Señora Pedroz."

"Ah, Watson, you were always an incurable romantic, and I did not want to disappoint you," said my friend with a laugh. "Ana Pedroz had already told the Duke before they were abducted that she intended to marry an elderly banker from the town of Ronda, who knew of her liaison with the Duke but was prepared to forgive it because of his love for her. She was a practical lady, and realised that there was no future in continuing an affair with a Duke who would never be allowed to marry her, although he did love her, I believe. We took the Duke back with us to Gibraltar, and from there he travelled directly to England, carrying the letter with him. I sometimes wonder what he told his Royal mother about the whole affair. As far as I am aware he never set eyes on the lady again."

". . . a full account of Riculetti of the club foot and his abominable wife."

—SHERLOCK HOLMES
The Musgrave Ritual

*P*rofessional actor, singer and one of New York's most popular improvisational comedians, CAROLE BUGGÉ is an award-winning poet and the author of short stories that have appeared in my anthologies Haunted America, Lovers and Other Monsters and Masterpieces of Terror and the Unknown. In addition to the following superior pastiche, Ms. Buggé recently composed and wrote a new Sherlock Holmes musical.

The Strange Case of the Tongue-Tied Tenor

CAROLE BUGGÉ

The spring of 1890 brought a week of grainy London afternoons which depressed my medical practice as well as my spirits, and so it was on one of those dull grey days that I escaped my dreary surgery and headed for my old digs at 221B Baker Street to pay a visit on my friend Mr. Sherlock Holmes.

Mrs. Hudson greeted me with more than her usual effusiveness, for she had not seen me for some weeks, and the company of her only tenant, while undoubtedly invigorating, was also a trial which she bore with the fierce stoicism of her Scottish ancestors. As we ascended the familiar staircase, she threw her hands up in dismay.

"Oh, Dr. Watson, thank heaven you've come—maybe now he'll eat and sleep like a normal human being for a change!"

If Holmes was neither eating nor sleeping—bodily necessities which he did not always regard as such—it meant either that he was on a case or subject to the influence of the evil drug he turned to in his constant battle against ennui.

As I entered Holmes' sitting room, I saw that he was not alone. Seated on the sofa opposite the door was a stocky, red-faced gentleman with a full head of curly ginger hair and a face which was the likely result of a cross between a cherub and a bulldog. Holmes was sprawled out in his usual chair.

"Ah, Watson—come in; you are just in time to hear a most amusing little problem."

The red-faced man appeared to bristle at Holmes' words.

"My dear Mr. Holmes, forgive me for saying so, but to me there is nothing amusing about it," he said, or rather whispered, for his voice was nothing more than a faint throaty croak.

"Yes, yes, I'm sure—please forgive me," Holmes replied, with more impatience than contrition. "And allow me to introduce my colleague and very good friend, Dr. Watson. Watson, may I present Mr. Gerald Huntley."

"Not *the* Gerald Huntley—"

"The one and same—operatic tenor extraordinaire. Mr. Huntley has come to me on a matter of some distress to a singer of his caliber. Simply put, Watson, he has lost his voice."

Mr. Huntley's face grew redder as Holmes spoke.

"Well, that's terrible, of course, but surely that is a matter for a medical doctor—"

"Ah, but there's more, isn't there, Mr. Huntley?" Holmes said smoothly, with a smile which in the dim light looked almost predatory. The tenor blinked rapidly and shook his red curls, which offset the deepening flush on his face.

"I don't know what you mean, exactly—"

Holmes rose and stood over Huntley, his tall, spare frame looming like a bird of prey over the man.

"Mr. Huntley," he said in a sharp voice, "I am a busy man, and an impatient one, as you have perhaps gathered. I therefore suggest to you that you withhold nothing from me, either now or later, if you have any hope of my taking your case. You will therefore start by telling me why you feel you are in mortal danger and what connection that might have to your current clandestine love affair."

The singer swallowed hard and fell back against the couch. He drew a lace handkerchief from his breast pocket and passed it over his damp brow.

"You are truly everything they said you were, Mr. Holmes, and more," he croaked, making another pass with the handkerchief.

"That's better," said Holmes, settling into his chair again with a satisfied smile, though whether he was referring to the implied cooperation or the compliment I could not say.

"You are correct, sir, in everything that you say, though before I tell you my story I must say I cannot see how you could possibly know—"

"Tut, tut, man, there is nothing so mysterious about it," answered Holmes, though evidently pleased to have scored an impression. Holmes was, in his own way, no less a performer than our tenor, and his most faithful audience—apart from myself—was his steady stream of clients. No magician ever flourished his hat and cape with more relish or flair than Holmes unveiled his deductions to the breathless gasps of his admirers.

"That you are frightened is not hard to deduce. I happened to be looking out the window when you alighted from your cab, and only a criminal or a man who believes his life is threatened looks about furtively the way you did. I do you the honour to suppose you are not the former; I may therefore logically take you to be the latter."

Our illustrious guest hung his head.

"Quite right, I'm afraid, Mr. Holmes."

"As to the woman, there are so many signs I hardly know where to begin. If your fresh manicure and haircut had not alerted me, I could not have helped but notice that your boots, though unaccustomed to frequent polishings, have recently been shined to a glimmer. Your hat"—and here he brandished our guest's bowler—"is scented with one cologne, and yet this morning you put on quite a different, muskier scent. Add this to the baggy appearance of your vest and the fact that you have cinched your pants in an extra loop. When a man changes his perfume, takes extraordinary care over his person, and on top of that loses weight so rapidly that he cannot change his wardrobe quickly enough to keep his clothes from hanging loosely upon him—surely even to the inexperienced eye that bespeaks a recent and consuming infatuation of the most virulent kind."

With that Holmes went to the mantel, where he kept the Persian slipper which contained his shag tobacco. From the pipe rack he selected a long carved cherrywood pipe and stood waiting for our guest to recover his breath. Mr. Huntley looked very sheepish and defeated; at last he spoke.

"I must admit everything you say is true, and that furthermore, everything I have done has been in spite of my better instincts."

Holmes smiled disdainfully. "Affairs of the heart usually manage to override one's better instincts. Pray continue, Mr. Huntley," he said, folding his long frame into his favourite chair.

"There is not much to tell, really," the tenor whispered, and I felt a pang at witnessing the ruin of so great a voice. "I have been engaged to sing Don José in a production of *Carmen;* it is a role I have done many times, of course, but this was the first time I had performed with—her."

"You refer of course to Madame Olga Rayenskavya, the Russian mezzo-soprano."

"Well, yes, but how—?"

"Oh, come, come, Mr. Huntley; a casual perusal of the entertainment section of any number of London dailies would reveal that you are both appearing in *Carmen* in repertory for the next two weeks at the Royal Albert Hall."

"Yes, of course."

"So how did you come to be involved with this—temptress?"

"Enchantress would be more like it," said our guest, rubbing his eyes wearily. "I have neither eaten nor slept more than a few hours since she wrapped her spell around me. It is a sickness, a fever; I am like one of Ulysses' men Circe turned into pigs: it seems all I can do is grunt and grovel at her feet. I am powerless to extricate myself, even though I feel this affair has brought danger upon my head."

"What form has this danger taken?"

"Well, there have been several signs, but last night I stayed somewhat late after the performance; it is my custom to take tea in my dressing room after I sing. When I had finished my tea I remembered I had left my scarf in the wings somewhere; the Royal Albert is very drafty, as you may know, and so I had worn my scarf about my neck right up until my first entrance. It was very dark and quiet, as most everyone had gone home. Nonetheless, I thought I heard footsteps on the catwalk above the stage as I crossed to get my scarf. As I reached the stage left wings I heard a sound directly above me, and if I had not had my wits about me and leapt out of the way, I doubt that I would be sitting here now."

"Out of the way of what?" I asked, caught up in his story.

"A sandbag fell directly upon the spot where I had been standing. I had thought up until that moment that I was imagining everything, but sandbags do not simply fall from the sky for no reason at all. After last night I am convinced that someone is trying to get me out of the way."

"Out of the way of what, I wonder," said Holmes, pulling pensively at his pipe.

"I don't know, but I am convinced there is a connection with this wretched affair."

"The lady in question is married, is she not, to a conductor?" I said, recalling having read something about her engagement in the paper.

Mr. Huntley smiled bitterly. "Oh, yes, and that is not the least of the irony in my situation. Her husband is none other than Sir Terrance Farthingale, the maestro for this production of *Carmen*."

"Hmm, I see," said Holmes, tapping his pipe out into a potted plant on the tea table, a habit Mrs. Hudson hated. "You have pitched your tent rather close to the lion's den."

"I have made a rotten mess of things, if that's what you mean," said our downcast friend with a sigh.

"From what you know of Sir Terrance, do you think he would be capable of—?" I started to say, but Mr. Huntley interrupted me with a gesture.

"Dr. Watson, if I have learned one thing from all of this it is that when it comes to love, a man might be capable of anything at all."

"But what makes you think that losing your voice is somehow connected to all of this?" I inquired.

"Oh, I don't think there's a connection, except maybe that it was brought on by fatigue and worry—"

"Oh, but there I disagree with you, Mr. Huntley," Holmes interrupted. "Quite the contrary: I believe it to be a key to solving the case."

Both of us stared at him. He proceeded to fill and light his pipe before continuing, increasing our anticipation by making us wait for his response. He took a deep draught and exhaled slowly.

"Consider the facts. A man has a liaison with another man's wife. Soon he comes to feel his life is in peril. Shortly after a narrow escape he finds himself unable to perform his chosen profession—in short, he finds himself out of commission, temporarily or otherwise. He is still alive, but harm has undoubtedly been done to him; more importantly, as you yourself stated, Mr. Huntley, he is *out of the way*. So it seems it was not necessary to kill him after all, merely get him out of the way."

"Out of the way of what?" I interjected.

"That is precisely what we must find out, Watson." Holmes laid down his pipe and rose from his chair. "Good day, Mr. Huntley—if I have need of further information I shall be in contact with you."

Mr. Huntley scrambled to his feet rather confusedly, not used to Holmes' characteristically unceremonious treatment.

"We did not discuss the subject of fee—"

"There will be plenty of time for that, Mr. Huntley; I think you will find my fees by no means extravagant," said Holmes, bustling him to the door.

"Well, then, I will take my leave of you—"

"What about Mr. Huntley's safety?" I asked, seeing the anxious expression on his face.

"Oh, I should think Mr. Huntley's safety is for the time being assured; so long as he has no voice, he is certain to remain alive and well. Good day, Mr. Huntley. I shall let you know if there are any developments."

"Thank you, Mr. Holmes. Good day, Dr. Watson."

"Good day."

"Oh, one more question, Mr. Huntley. Who serves you your tea?"

"My dresser, McPearson. He has been with me for years."

"Very well. Thank you—I will be in touch."

After our guest was gone Holmes sprawled out on the couch and intertwined his long fingers behind his head.

"There, you see, Watson: you upbraid me with my refusal to have anything to do with the fairer sex, and yet this is the likely outcome of such an encounter. A man loses his means of livelihood and nearly his life, all for the sake of a woman."

"Oh. Holmes, you're incorrigible. Mr. Huntley has acted indiscreetly, to say the least. To use this as a moral for the entire—" but I stopped when I saw Holmes laughing that peculiar silent laugh of his.

"Ah, Watson, forgive me for taking advantage of your earnestness. Sometimes I cannot help tweaking you to see how you will react."

"I should think you would find the consistency of my responses rather boring by now," I said, feeling somewhat put out.

"Oh, come along, Watson, don't be cross! Let me make it up to you by standing you to the Wellington at Simpson's: I do believe theirs is the best Yorkshire pudding in town."

I am used to accompanying my friend in the testing of his many various hypotheses, but I must say this was one theory I was by no means averse to examining. And so it was that less than half an hour later I found myself seated across from Holmes, confronted by an undeniably agreeable specimen of Wellington's lesser known victory.

"Well, Watson," said my companion after we had finished our cigars and coffee, "what do you say to a little trip 'round to the Royal Albert, to the scene of the crime, as it were?"

"No crime has as yet been committed, Holmes."

"As yet, Watson; but it is only a matter of time."

"What do you expect to find at the Royal Albert?"

"I expect nothing, but I shall know when and if I find it."

The backstage area at the Royal Albert Hall is not usually accessible to the public, but the man guarding the stage door was more impressed by the mention of the name Sherlock Holmes than by the considerable tip offered to him by that august person. In any event, we soon found ourselves in the winding corridors leading to the various dressing rooms. Holmes headed straight for Gerald Huntley's, and upon knocking was greeted by an ancient gentleman of impressive sidewhiskers and rheumatic eyes of a remarkably pale blue hue.

"Ah, Mr. McPearson, isn't it?" said Holmes brightly.

"At your service, Sir. I'm afraid Mr. Huntley isn't in at the moment, Sir," he wheezed in a burr as Scottish as a field of mountain heather.

"Yes, yes, I know," answered Holmes, "we've come on his behalf. I am Mr. Sherlock Holmes, and this is my companion, Dr. Watson."

"Well, I'm glad he finally had the sense to see a doctor," the old man snorted. "I told him something like this would happen if he didn't take better care of himself."

I opened my mouth to explain but a look from Holmes silenced me.

"Yes, well, my colleague here has reason to believe Mr. Huntley may have ingested something—hazardous."

"Hmmp! Not very likely—he hasn't 'ingested' much of anything in the last few weeks!"

"You serve him his tea, do you not?"

"Indeed I do, as I have for the last eight years. That's one thing, at least;

I've never known Mr. Gerald to refuse a good cup of tea, if it's made the way he likes it, and I know just the way he likes it."

"Yes, yes, I'm sure you do," said Holmes, trying unsuccessfully to bury the edge of impatience in his tone. "I wonder if you would grant me a very great favor—"

"If it'll help Mr. Huntley get better, I'd be glad to."

"Would you show me how you make him his tea? I—uh, that is, Dr. Watson here wants to assure that Mr. Huntley's routine remains undisturbed during his—convalescence."

McPearson seemed pleased by Holmes' interest in his tea-making skills. He bent closer and spoke in a conspiratorial whisper.

"Do you know you're the second man who's asked me about my methods in the last week?"

"Oh, really?" Holmes said casually.

"Aye; Mr. Huntley has always said no one could brew a cup quite like myself, and if I do say so—"

"You said another gentleman inquired earlier in the week—?" Holmes interrupted, his tone one of absent-minded disinterest.

"Aye, and a strange one he was at that. I fancy I have a fair eye for a man, and he was a right odd laddie. Said he was a stagehand here, but I can't say as I ever noticed him around. A fellow like that would be hard to miss, too—"

"What was he like?"

"Well, first off he had this yellow hair—it was really more like straw than hair, and so pale that it was almost white—as though he had been scared by something. It weren't the white hair of an old man—he was just a young laddie. And he spoke with a stutter, which was so bad that sometimes I was wantin' to finish the word for him just so's we could get on with it."

As our garrulous Scotsman described his visitor, Holmes' eyes narrowed and his lean face tightened.

"What did you show him?"

"I just showed him how I make the tea—my little 'secret', if you can call it that, is that I put just a wee bit of water in at first and let it steep in that and then add the rest of the water straight from the kettle right at the end. That way it's strong and hot and warms you up, and Mr. Huntley swears the flavor is better, too. I learned the trick off a Norwegian sea captain by the name of Olaf Niels."

Holmes glanced around the dressing room.

"Is that your teapot?" he said, pointing to a stout blue willow pot which looked as though it had seen years of service.

"Aye—they keep the kettle down the hall, so I have to go down there twice to fill the pot."

"And you generally leave the pot unattended while you wait for it to steep?"

"Aye, I've other things to do than hover around waiting for tea leaves. I usually lay out Mr. Huntley's dressing gown and then go back for the tea."

"I see. Do you mind if we have a look at the kettle?"

"No—in fact, if you like, I'll make you gentlemen a cup of tea right now."

Holmes was already out the door, so I answered.

"Thank you, Mr. McPearson; that would be very nice."

We followed Mr. McPearson down narrow hallways to the communal tea area. A few stagehands lingered around a much-used kettle, smoking and playing cards. Ignoring them, Holmes pulled out his magnifying glass and began poking around. McPearson did not comment on this but set about to making the tea. Suddenly Holmes stiffened and a muffled cry escaped his throat.

"Ha! Watson—it is a sloppy workman who leaves behind traces such as this!" With a flourish, he pulled out the small leather pouch he always carried and swept something into it. "Thank you, Mr. McPearson; you've been enormously helpful," he said, pulling me after him toward the exit.

"What about your tea?" McPearson called after us in a hurt voice.

"Another time, perhaps—" I called back as Holmes swept me out the door and into a hansom cab.

"What is it, Holmes?" I said as the cab rattled through the streets. "What did you find there?"

"I'm not certain, Watson, but I may have found what I was looking for. First, however, some experimentation is required."

I had some business to attend to at my neglected surgery, and so agreed to meet Holmes later in the evening.

When I entered the front hallway Mrs. Hudson was there to greet me.

"Oh, Dr. Watson—he'll drive me batty with those experiments of his! See if you can't take his mind off of his work for a while."

"I'll do my best, Mrs. Hudson," I said dubiously, as a bitter odor drifted down the stairs toward us. Rolling her eyes, Mrs. Hudson bustled me into my old sitting room, closing the door behind her with a click.

The lamp by the window lit the room with its yellow glow, and I saw the lean frame of my friend bent over his improvised lab table, sheathed in the green smoke which swirled about his head. His thick black hair, usually impeccably neat, fell in unruly locks over his forehead. At first I thought Holmes had not heard me enter, and was startled to hear him address me without turning to look at me.

"Ah, Watson, your timing is, as usual, impeccable. Come have a look."

I stopped by the door to remove my coat.

"Come, Watson, come—it won't last forever, you know!" His face, in the lingering azure smoke, was pale and taut.

"What is it, Holmes?"

"Poison, Watson—a rare South African curare derivative I had the notion to write a small monograph about once."

I bent over the beaker from which the green smoke emanated. Immediately I began to feel weak and dizzy. Holmes evidently noticed this, because I felt his strong grip on my shoulder.

"Not so close, Watson—not so close! It is a very concentrated tincture. Come, let us get some fresh air."

With that he guided me over to the window, where he opened the shutters wide to let in a breeze. Even the thick air of London was a welcome relief to me after inhaling the stultifying fumes of Holmes' experiment.

"What is the connection, Holmes?"

"Curare, as you may know, acts in part as an agent of paralysis—you may perhaps have heard of its use in certain voodoo rituals to paralyze the victim."

"Yes, I have heard of it, but—"

"This particular derivative, Watson, owes its effectiveness to its ability to localize its effect, thus paralyzing only a single muscle or group of muscles. Administered as a drink—"

"Huntley's vocal cords—paralyzed!"

"Precisely, Watson. Fortunately for Mr. Huntley, the effect will eventually wear off, but someone evidently took great pains to remove him from the picture temporarily."

"But why, Holmes? And who would—?"

"The why is not yet entirely clear to me, Watson. But the who . . ." A shadow passed over my friend's stern face, and I fancied I saw him shudder. He rose and walked to the window, looking out into the night, where a soft rain had started to fall.

"The gentleman described to us by Mr. McPearson is well known to me. His name is Freddie Stockton, and he is an agent of" —here Holmes paused and drew his hand across his brow—"Professor Moriarty."

"Good God, Holmes."

"Yes. These are deeper waters than I at first suspected, Watson, and we must watch our step if we do not wish to find ourselves at the bottom of the river."

"But Holmes, how is Moriarty involved—?"

"That is exactly what I intend to discover. I suggest you disassociate yourself from me for a while, Watson. It will be better if I proceed on my own from now on."

"Don't be ridiculous, Holmes. I wouldn't think of abandoning the chase now."

Holmes suddenly looked very tired and worn. His shoulders drooped and he looked as if he could hardly stand.

"You don't understand, Watson," he said in a weary voice. "Moriarty is no ordinary villain; he has half the criminals of London at his beck and call. And I would never forgive myself if something should happen to you through my carelessness. No, it really would be better if I go on alone from here. I can't put you at risk."

"Holmes, since when have you ever known me to abandon you in times of danger? I beg you not to speak of this again unless you wish to risk seriously insulting me."

Holmes looked at me and then laughed softly.

"Good old Watson, stalwart to the last," he said with an unaccustomed softness in voice. "All right; I admit I did not expect you to budge for a moment, but I had to try—surely you can understand that."

"Yes, I suppose so. Now, what is our next step?"

"To penetrate the web, Watson, that surrounds the spider."

"And how do we do that?"

"We might start by interviewing some of the flies."

And so I soon found myself seated next to my friend in a hansom, revolver in my coat pocket, the thrill of the chase tight in my throat. Holmes sat back in the shadows of the cab, his long fingertips pressed tightly together, hat low over his eyes. If I did not know better I would have said he did not draw a breath during the entire ride, so still he sat.

Finally we arrived at our destination: the heart of London's East End, teeming with vermin of both the animal and human variety. We wound our way through stalls of vegetable sellers and past women selling another kind of ware, until finally we reached a squalid alley. The sign said PLUMMER'S COURT, and although I instinctively shrank back from entering the narrow, dark corridor framed by a brick wall on one side and a shuttered building on the other, Holmes strode forth with such confidence that I was ashamed not to follow him. As we walked along the flagstone pavement I thought I heard scurrying noises at our feet. We stopped at a doorway which to my untrained eye looked boarded up and deserted, but when Holmes rapped three times with his stick there were answering sounds from within. Presently a latch was drawn and the door opened slightly. An unshaven face appeared, and a gruff voice asked, "What is it you want?"

"I want to speak with Mr. Freddie Stockton."

"And who might you be?"

"I am Sherlock Holmes."

The name evidently had an effect, because I could hear muffled voices from within. In response to something said to him, the man at the door opened it wide enough to admit us, closing it quickly after we entered.

The room was dark and smelled of horses—it had evidently until recently been used as a stable. Four men sat around a thick oaken table, smoking cigarettes and drinking. They were a rough-looking lot, none more so than the one with the stiff white-blond hair. He had thick shoulders and a snarling mouth, which curled in disgust when Holmes addressed him.

"So, Mr. Stockton, we meet again. I trust all has gone well for you since you were a guest of Scotland Yard after that unfortunate incident involving the jewelry theft. Pity they did not see it your way, really it is. Still, you seem none the worse for wear."

The surly fellow rose from his chair and put his face close to Holmes'. My hand closed round my revolver as he spoke.

"You got a lotta nerve c-c-comin' here. You—"

"Come, come, Mr. Stockton; there's no need to be uncivil. I just would like you to deliver a message to the Professor from me. If you like I can come back at a more convenient time—"

Stockton's bloodshot eyes narrowed.

"What kinda m-m-message?"

"Simply that I'm on to his game, and that he should be more judicious in his use of poisons. I have a bit of expertise in the various forms of curare, I'm afraid, and I saw through his little charade."

Stockton's already florid face reddened, and it was then I saw the long curved dagger hanging from his belt. Holmes certainly had seen it, and yet he was as cool as always. He turned to leave.

"Oh, and one more thing. He really should send someone a little less—memorable—than yourself on such public errands. Good day, gentlemen."

And before any of the men could intervene, Holmes pulled me along with him and we were out the door. As we hurried back down the narrow street I glanced over my shoulder nervously, but evidently no one had followed us.

"That was awfully risky, Holmes. Why did you do it?"

"To put the fear of God into Moriarty, Watson. The more closely he believes he is being watched, the more likely he is to make a mistake. Besides, I knew we were in no great danger. Moriarty's men do nothing without instructions from him, and if he wanted to abduct us he could do that anytime he wished."

In spite of Holmes' brave words, I could not help feeling we were in danger, and it was with regret that I turned off in the direction of my surgery once we were back in familiar territory. I pleaded with Holmes to take a cab to Baker Street, but he refused, saying the night air would clear his brain. As I watched his tall, spare form recede, I felt a shiver go down my spine, and I almost ran after him.

The next morning my fears were realized when I was awakened before dawn by a telegram from Mrs. Hudson summoning me urgently to Baker Street. I arrived unshaven and barely dressed, so great was my dread. Mrs. Hudson greeted me at the door.

"They brought him in last night, Dr. Watson. I begged him to go to hospital, but he would have none of it."

"What's happened? Where is he?"

"He's upstairs, Dr. Watson. I'd like to get my hands round the villain that did this to him."

I took the stairs two at a time and in an instant was in the sitting room. Holmes was lying on the couch, and standing over him was Dr. Leslie Oakshott, the surgeon who would soon make a name for himself all over London, receiving a knighthood in the process.

"I'm afraid Mr. Holmes has refused a hospital bed, though I still feel it would be better in his condition," said Dr. Oakshott.

I looked down at Holmes. His left shoulder was heavily bandaged, and he was unconscious.

"What happened?"

"A gunshot wound to the chest. Missed the heart by only inches. He lost a lot of blood, Dr. Watson; we nearly lost him."

"Is he—?"

"He has been unconscious for several hours, and needs careful watching. The bullet went clean through but there is always the possibility of infection." Dr. Oakshott glanced at his watch. "I've several appointments awaiting me; I've done what I can, and would be grateful if you—"

"Of course; I'll stay with him as long as necessary. Thank you, Dr. Oakshott."

"Certainly, Dr. Watson. If he awakens you may need some morphine for the pain. Call me at once if he shows any sign of fever."

When Dr. Oakshott had gone, I sat down next to the couch and looked at my friend. His face was pale and drawn, and a dark patch of blood had soaked through the dressing on his shoulder. He who prided himself in his mastery and control lay now before me utterly helpless, and I felt a wave of rage at the fiend Moriarty, who was doubtless behind this assault.

Outside the first cries of the pickle-sellers and fishmongers were breaking through the early morning haze, and I settled back in my chair in a sort of reverie, remembering all the times Holmes and I had dashed out of these very rooms at all hours of the day and night, on the track of some crime or another. I bitterly reproached myself for letting Holmes walk home alone on the previous night, knowing all the while that if I had been with him I would have likely been shot too; still, I could not help feeling angry with myself for abandoning him against my better judgement. My daydreaming was interrupted only by Mrs. Hudson coming and going with tea, and I watched the grey light of morning dissolve into the greenish glow of a misty London afternoon. Sometime in the early evening Holmes stirred and moaned. I knelt beside him.

"Watson," he whispered, his voice very faint. "What time is it? How long have I been out?"

I glanced at the mantel clock.

"It's six o'clock."

"In the evening?" He tried to sit up, but sank back with a groan.

"Yes, Holmes."

He paused, and I could see he was breathing hard from the effort of speaking.

"Holmes, don't try to talk."

"I must, Watson; it is imperative that we move quickly."

"Holmes, you're not moving anywhere."

"Then you must help me, Watson. A life may depend on it."

"Very well. Tell me what to do."

"There is a performance of *Carmen* tonight. When Moriarty had me attacked, he tipped his hand: whatever is going to happen will happen soon, most probably tonight."

"What is going to happen?"

"I have several theories. I will follow the mostly likely first. Kindly get down my volume of *Who's Who*."

I moved to Holmes's bookcase, extracting the weighty volume, taking care not to drop the many slips of paper Holmes had inserted between the pages over the years.

"Hand it to me, please."

I did so reluctantly, for I could see from his white face and compressed lips that the effort of holding the book was causing him considerable pain.

"Holmes, let me—"

"No, Watson—you must send a telegram by runner to the Royal Albert Hall. Immediate reply requested."

"What am I to say?"

"Inquire as to who is singing the role of Don José tonight."

"Is that all?"

"Quite all. Thank you."

I did as was requested of me, and then sat down next to Holmes. The room was quite cool, and yet beads of sweat gathered upon his forehead, and he breathed with difficulty.

"Holmes, I must take your temperature."

"No, Watson! Time is of the essence. Read to me," he said, handing me *Who's Who,* "under the entry Farthingale."

"There are two. Sir Terrance, the conductor, and his brother, Sir Anthony, Member of Parliament—"

"Yes, curious, isn't it?"

"I don't see why—"

"No, no, of course not. Now, Watson, you are somewhat more up on operatic plots than I. Refresh my memory as to the story of *Carmen,* if you would." He settled back on the couch, but the movement caused him to grimace with pain.

"Holmes, at least let me get you some morphine—"

"No, Watson; I need my mind clear. Now, *Carmen,* if you please."

"Well, it's a love triangle of sorts, about a vixen who attracts the attentions of a jealous lover—"

"Don José?"

"Yes. In the end he stabs her outside the bullring—"

"Yes, just as I thought. Now we only await the arrival of our telegram," he said, leaning his head back and closing his eyes. I was grateful that he was resting and tiptoed about, making myself busy by clearing the tea things. Eight o'clock came and went, with still no answer to our telegram. Finally I heard Mrs. Hudson's knock on the door, and she entered with the telegram. No sooner had I taken it from her than I heard Holmes's voice calling me from the couch asking to see it. I handed it to him and he looked at it intently, then before I could speak, suddenly rose from the couch. He staggered, but waved off my offer of assistance and went straight to his crime files, where he kept notes on criminals from around the world. He emerged with the file labelled "Q" and, after rifling through it, evidently found what he was looking for. After studying it intently for some moments, he scribbled something on a piece of paper and thrust it at Mrs. Hudson.

"Have that sent to Inspector Lestrade at Scotland Yard immediately."

"Yes, Mr. Holmes."

Holmes glanced up at the clock.

"Good God, Watson—we must hurry!"

"You're not going anywhere in your condition, Holmes."

Holmes gripped me by the shoulders.

"Watson, there is no time to explain, but believe me when I say that I am all that stands between a murderer and his victim!" He relaxed his grip, and I saw that he was about to faint. I helped him over to the couch.

"I believe I will take you up on the offer of some morphine—not too much, just enough to dull the pain, if you don't mind."

"Very well, Holmes, I'll get my syringe, but I cannot condone this—"

"Watson, I swear to you if there were any other way I would take it, but there isn't. Please believe me."

I injected the morphine and helped him get into his coat, then into a cab, with the assistance of Mrs. Hudson. Holmes told the driver to hurry to the Royal Albert Hall. I wanted to ask Holmes what was up, but the sight of his grim, pale face next to me silenced my questions.

When we arrived at the Royal Albert he led me not to the main entrance but around to the backstage door, where, fortunately for us, the same man stood guard and recognized us. It did not take Holmes long to convince the man to let us in, and soon we were at the heavy red fire door marked Stage Right. Singers in exotic Spanish costumes came and went around us, and Holmes hovered momentarily just outside the door. Then he pushed it open slowly, and I could see the vast stage of the Royal Albert Hall. I followed him into the darkened wings, where a few stagehands stood with their hands in their pockets. It was quite dark, so no one took particular notice of the two cloaked forms who picked their way over coiled ropes and sandbags toward the stage.

Two lone figures stood on a gaudily painted set of a bullring. I recognized the lady as the regal Olga Rayenskavya, but did not recognize the man, who was short and swarthy and had his back to me. They were singing the duet I thought I recognized as the Act Four finale, near the end of the opera. Just then I felt Holmes' grip on my arm. My eyes followed his hand as he pointed toward the stage, and in an instant I saw what he saw: a flash of steel under the bright rainbow lights. Before I could cry out, Holmes had sprung onto the stage and grasped the hand that held the gleaming weapon, holding it aloft and away from its intended target. Immediately cries went up from the house, and then pandemonium broke loose. The orchestra stopped playing, and several members rose from their chairs to better see what was happening on stage. Two stagehands sprang from the wings at Holmes, while the tenor surprised everyone by bolting offstage as fast as he could.

"Stop him!" Holmes cried to his captors. "Stop that man! He is a murderer!"

No one had the presence of mind to follow Holmes' instructions, so when I saw the man approaching me at top speed, I set myself for a good old-fashioned rugby tackle and brought him down heavily upon the floorboards, knocking the wind out of him. It was only when I got up that I realized he still clutched the knife, with its blade of real steel. Fortunately, neither of us had fallen on it, but I picked it up to examine it; it was curved and reminded me of the blade which hung from Freddie Stockton's belt. It was at that moment I saw Inspector Lestrade walking purposefully toward me, flanked by several of London's finest, and I was never so glad to see the good Inspector as at that moment. I handed over my charge, surprised that Lestrade seemed to recognize him, and then hurried onto the stage, where Holmes lay propped up against the set, flushed and panting. Madame Olga knelt beside him, wiping his brow. Removing his overcoat, I saw that his wound had begun to bleed again, and summoned two stagehands to help me carry him outside. Madame Olga followed us, and when we laid Holmes in a cab she stood at the door while I got in.

"Your friend, he has saved my life," she said in a thick Russian accent. "I will never forget this." She lowered her beautiful black eyes. "There are some who would say I am a bad woman, but—I will never forget what he has done."

As the cab drove off I looked back and saw her standing in the light rain which had begun to fall, looking after us. A tall figure which I took to be Sir Terrance came and put his arm around her. I thought to myself that I too would forgive many things for such a woman, just as Sir Terrance undoubtedly had.

By the time we got to Baker Street Holmes had lost consciousness and remained in a delirium for the better part of the night. By the next day he had regained consciousness, but I was master now and would not let him speak, so that in spite of my curiosity it was several days before I heard the whole story.

"You see, Watson," he said as he lay propped up with pillows in front of the fire, "I felt all along that the good professor had no business with our friend Mr. Huntley except to get him out of the way. That is why he sent Mr. Stockton to put curare in his tea, so he could put his understudy Mr. Quintaros in his stead."

"But how did you know Quintaros would try to murder Madame Rayenskaya?"

"I didn't know, Watson; I deduced. The question to answer was why Moriarty needed Huntley out of the way. When I thought to look up Sir Terrance, and saw that he had a brother who is a Member of Parliament, my suspicions were close to being confirmed, and when I saw Mr. Huntley's understudy was to be the notorious South American singer Juan Quintaros, who fled his own country under suspicion of murder—well, if you want to commit a murder, get a murderer, and that is precisely what Moriarty did."

"But I still don't see that connection with Sir Terrance—"

"Consider, Watson. A man's wife is having an affair, and is then murdered during a performance by the substitution of a real knife for a fake one. The understudy who actually commits the crime might be excused for several reasons: he has no reason to kill a woman he does not even know, he is undoubtedly preoccupied with his performance and therefore less likely to notice the substitution of the real knife when he has never seen the fake one. No, Watson, the suspicion falls not on the actual murderer but on the person who substituted the real knife, and that could be anyone. The most likely suspect is of course the jealous husband. Moriarty thought all of this out, of course, and then when all signs point to Sir Terrance, Moriarty pulls the rug out from under his unsuspecting accomplice, sacrifices Quintaros to the jury, and Sir Terrance is left bewildered but very much in Moriarty's debt. And who better to have in your debt than the brother of a Member of Parliament?"

"I see. It was a complicated hand he played, Holmes, and I doubt if anyone else but you could have figured it out."

"Well, Watson, perhaps you are right. But Moriarty played his cards a little too freely, and he forgot that sometimes the joker is wild. And now, Watson, if you will permit me to smoke, I would appreciate it if you would hand me my pipe."

*M*ost of the pastiches in this section are new Sherlock Holmes adventures, but the late *JAMES C. IRALDI, a well-known New York member of the Baker Street Irregulars, chose the honorable alternative of dipping into Dr. Watson's time-battered dispatch box to disclose details of an untold case alluded to in Conan Doyle's "The Adventure of the Missing Three-Quarter." The Problem of the Purple Maculas was published in 1968 in a limited edition by Holmesian specialist Luther Norris.*

The Problem of the Purple Maculas

JAMES C. IRALDI

". . . and there was Henry Staunton, whom I helped to hang."

—*SHERLOCK HOLMES*
The Missing Three-Quarter

It was towards the end of November, 1890, that I had a note from Sherlock Holmes, couched in his usual laconic style.

"Interesting problem at hand. Will expect you before noon. S.H."

Needless to say, I gave my patients a rest and eagerly went to keep the appointment. It was a pouring wet day when I set off, after making hurried arrangements at home, for the familiar address which had been the starting-point of so many of those adventures which were the normal condition of my friend's existence. Even an aching limb, protesting against the damp spell, failed to temper my enthusiasm as I hailed a cab, prepared to assist him in any way my slow methods and natural limitations permitted.

I found Sherlock Holmes seated near the hearth, his brier aglow and a pile of discarded newspapers crumpled on the floor beside him.

"Ah, come in, Watson, come in!" he cried cheerfully. "Draw up the basket-chair to the fire and take the seasonal chill out of your limbs!"

His keen, ever-active eyes scanned me meanwhile in that characteristic introspective fashion of his with which I was well familiar.

"I see Mrs. Watson is indisposed. Nothing serious I hope?"

"No. A slight chill. I've advised a few days in bed," I replied as I seated myself in the chair he had indicated with his pipe. I glanced over at him. "May I ask how you knew? You have not taken to pumping my maid, have you?"

"No, no, my dear Watson," he answered with a hearty chuckle which caused his grave, hawk-like features to relapse into more kindly lines. "Never that! It was a simple deduction, based upon the flour smeared on the underside of your left sleeve."

I raised my arm. It was as he said. A thin film of white still adhered to the fabric in spite of the chafing from my waterproof.

"Your explanation is equally obscure," I said, somewhat testily as I brushed it off. "I have no doubt that the connection between this and my wife's ailment is self-evident to a logical mind. Since I do not possess your gift, and am somewhat slow in my logical faculties . . ."

"Not slow, Watson," he broke in quickly, and quite seriously, "but merely undeveloped in so far as deducing from cause to effect. I have had occasion before to say that you possess faculties which though not sparkling nevertheless serve to illumine the qualities of keener minds. A by no means common gift, and one which I value highly, I assure you."

I shook my head dubiously. "I still fail to . . ."

"You still fail to grasp the connecting link between your sleeve and your wife? Yet the inference is clear. You no doubt had good reason for entering the kitchen this morning?"

I nodded. "Quite true. But how . . . ?"

"You could scarcely have gathered up flour in your dispensary," he cried, with an impatient wave of his arm. "Why does a solid British G.P. enter the culinary domain? To speak to the cook; to arrange for this evening's supper—better still, to suggest a fitting meal for the ailing one. Why did not your wife undertake this typical household task? Because she herself is the bed-ridden one. I shall venture even further and add that in all probability you bid her good-bye simply by poking your head through the bedroom door."

It was quite so. Upon receiving Holmes' message I had hurried to the kitchen to leave instructions with our cook, hastened upstairs to tell my wife and had then flung myself out of the house without a further glance at my clothing.

"As usual," I said, "you have made it all seem absurdly simple. That final inference being based upon the fact that she would assuredly have noticed the sleeve had I presented myself to her before leaving."

"Quite so."

"Since you did not send me that note," I went on, "simply to tell me that I had got flour on my garments, you have, evidently, an enquiry afoot at this time?"

By way of reply, Holmes tossed over an envelope which contained the following message:

Dear Mr. Holmes,
  I have a splendid opportunity for you to utilize your methods in helping us identify the body of a man found yesterday morning in the river. No signs of violence. Thought you might be interested.

               Patterson

"We may have a clear field in which to start our enquiries. The papers have not yet got hold of it. What do you say, Watson? Care to join forces?"

My momentary hesitation, brief as it was, did not fail to catch his eye. He frowned. "Your wife?"

"No, no, Holmes, she will be perfectly all right without me."

"I may have need of a man of medicine."

"Oh, you need have no fears on that score. I shall come and with pleasure, you know that."

"Then why did you hesitate just now when I proposed having you along?"

"I have made no arrangements with my locum tenens . . . In the event that the case be of some duration."

The shadows fled from his brows. He smiled cheerfully. "Oh, in that case, it can easily be arranged. A telegram or two . . ."

And thus it came about that on that rainy November day we set off upon one of our most singular investigations, never dreaming that before it was over, it would become a cause célèbre which would make all England ring.

We made a brief detour to the Wigmore Street Post Office where I sent off a telegram to my wife and another to Dr. Anstruther. Then we proceeded to Scotland Yard.

Inspector Patterson greeted us on our arrival in his customary dour fashion, and without wasting any time went along with us to the chill, dank mortuary wherein unknown derelicts are quartered until disposed of. On a sign from him, an attendant removed the shroud which covered one of the several stark figures lying on rough deal tables in various sections of the room. Revealed to our sober gaze lay the rigid form of a young man in his early twenties, with a clean-shaven face, thick black hair surmounting a high brow, dark eyes now bulging dimly from their sockets, a well-cut nose and full lips twisted in a dreadful grin which revealed even rows of sound teeth.

Here and there the white skin bore scratches and bruises and small irregular patches a deep purple in colour. The contusions and abrasions were most in evidence about the chest and shoulders; while the dark blemishes covered various portions of the trunk and face. That silent and pathetic figure with its blotched and contorted features gave even my professionally tempered nerves a jolt, but they failed to affect my friend's.

"These contusions," he remarked, pointing to the bruised form, "were most probably caused at the time of death, or very shortly afterwards. But those purple marks are most peculiar. Any theory as to their cause, Inspector?"

Patterson stopped in the act of lighting a cigar. "Body was in the water most of the night," he said evasively. "May have got knocked about by the currents and eddies. There are a lot of piles and posts along Chelsea Reach, you know. Cadogan Pier isn't too far away from where the body was found."

"How long has he been dead?"

"The police surgeon says about ten hours before the grappling-irons brought him in. He was found by the river police at about nine yesterday morning, near the new Chelsea Bridge."

"Hum, that would place the time of death between eleven o'clock and midnight on Monday," mused Holmes. Then in a louder voice he asked, "Did the surgeon explain these discolourations?"

"Said they were simply scrapes most likely, caused perhaps by the fall into the river."

"Any indication as to the actual cause of death?"

"Well," said Patterson guardedly, with a slight shrug of his shoulders, "he didn't want to commit himself until after the inquest and autopsy. No water was found in the lungs; but neither have we uncovered any evidence of foul play. So far, the verdict seems to be 'Death by misadventure'."

Holmes glanced towards me. "This is your territory, Doctor. What do you make of it?"

A gleam in his eye, a tensing of his attitude as he had spoken, served to put me on my guard. After another careful examination, I spoke cautiously.

"A sudden fall into cold water from a height," I said, "with the resultant shock and fear, might bring on a heart attack. Especially in a person suffering from a cardiac condition." I pointed to the twisted features. "Such convulsions are sometimes indicative of painful, violent death, which might easily have been caused by heart failure."

"In other words, Watson, the man might have died in sheer panic before having even struck the water?"

"That's it exactly," I replied, pleased that he had accepted my theory without question. "It also explains," I concluded somewhat rashly, "the total absence of water in the lungs."

"But not the purple blemishes," observed Sherlock Holmes very quietly.

"The police surgeon," broke in the Inspector irrascibly at this moment, "didn't consider them to be serious at all, or in any way connected with the man's death. It's a clear case of accidental death caused by a fall into the river. The autopsy may clear up that aspect of it. What we would like to find out before proceeding any further, is the man's identity. There's not a paper or personal identification of any description amongst his things. No one has yet come forward to claim the body. The lists of missing persons have been consulted, but no one answering his description has been reported."

Patterson snorted with exasperation, then turned to look at my friend who had listened with rapt attention to his words.

"Perhaps that's where you can help us, Mr. Holmes," he added. "Your scientific methods might give us a clue to his trade or profession; or some indication as to where he hails from. Any sort of lead which might put us on the track of his relations or his friends."

Holmes's eyes gleamed. A slight colour now tinged his cheek. The problem was a challenge: his analytical methods against the regular police investigation procedure. His present demeanor was that of a master-craftsman who sees his work ready at hand, called in after others less gifted had failed.

He was now standing over the lifeless form, examining it with swift appraising glances. After closely surveying the twisted, mottled features, he turned to the tightly clenched hands, then to the rest of the body. In silence, broken only by his rapid, nervous pacings, we watched his every move so intently that the sound of his voice, high-pitched and querulous, made us all start up in surprise when he asked:

"Where are his clothes, boots?"

Patterson was prepared for this, and a pile of garments was quickly brought forward and spread out on a convenient work-bench. Again we relapsed into silence as my friend, completely oblivious of our presence, quickly yet expertly examined the personal effects of the dead man. He turned out the pockets and scanned the water-matted dross and wool fragments which usually accumulate in the lining. Nothing escaped those keen bright eyes as he concentrated his attention on coat and shirt, then trousers and boots. This completed, he turned again to the Scotland Yard Inspector.

"Was a hat found?"

"No."

"Waterproof or outer coat?"

Patterson shook his head once more. "None."

Holmes pursed his lips, nodded thoughtfully. "I see," he murmured, before directing his attention to the articles found in the pockets.

These were more or less the customary things the average man carries about with him in his everyday life: a bunch of keys, some coins, a pencil and nail file, a comb, a water-soaked billfold which still retained some sodden paper currency, and a large, old-fashioned silver watch.

Holmes picked it up and eyed it intently. Glancing over his shoulder, I could see that it was one of those heavily engraved time-pieces of foreign manufacture, bearing the name of its maker on the enamelled dial. The ornate hands had stopped at exactly three minutes past 2:30. It carried no marks of blows or dents, and had evidently suffered no ill effects other than from immersion.

"This might be suggestive, Watson," he muttered, "most suggestive. Notice that it is quite undamaged. The crystal is still intact." He raised his head. There were traces of repressed excitement in his voice when he asked, "Has this watch been opened, Inspector? Or the hands moved or tampered with?"

"No, sir. That's exactly the way it was when we removed it from the man's waistcoat pocket. We don't consider it of any importance. It may have stopped days before, or the fellow just forgot to wind it."

"You may be right," said Holmes with a slight shrug. "Let us see what else there is . . . Ah! What have we here?"

He was holding up a circular piece of glass-like substance, light brown in colour, of about an inch in thickness. After eyeing it speculatively for some seconds, he snapped off a small fragment and ground it to powder between his strong, lean fingers. These he carried first to his nose, then to his lips. The experiment appeared to satisfy him for I saw him nod to himself, a quick light coming to his eyes. Swiftly he walked back to the body, re-examined the dead man's hands, even to the extent of forcing open the rigid fingers of the left hand. Again he nodded as he gave vent to a grunt of satisfaction. Once more he returned to the work-bench, selected the trousers and submitted them to another rigorous inspection. When he had finished I could see that the light of triumph shone in his eyes as he said, "That is all. There is nothing else to be learned here."

To Patterson he asked, "Have you got a room where we can talk and smoke?"

The Inspector nodded. "This way, gentlemen."

Without another word we filed out of that sombre chamber and followed him up a flight of steps to a small room which, though bare of ornaments and sparsely furnished, nevertheless looked cozy and cheerful by comparison.

It was Inspector Patterson himself who first spoke after we had found chairs and charged our pipes.

"Well, Mr. Holmes," he remarked, "I don't suppose you learned very much from your probings?"

"The body's immersion has naturally robbed me of several suggestive facts, I concede," replied my friend quietly. "However, I can say with assurance that my researches have not been entirely barren."

"Then you did find out something about the man?" cried Patterson, making an effort to conceal his surprise.

"Only that he was a bachelor, inclined to be vain of his personal appearance; did not smoke, and earned a precarious livelihood by playing the 'cello in some fashionable restaurant." Holmes paused, then added slowly, "And was without any doubt the victim of foul play."

Patterson started up, visibly shaken by this unexpected statement. "You mean the man was murdered?"

"I do."

The Scotland Yarder struggled to regain his composure. Naturally stolid and not easily moved, he resented any unexpected revelation which forced him to depart from his usual reserve. A note of irritation was quite noticeable in his voice when he added, "What makes you so certain of this, Mr. Holmes?"

"Those peculiar stains, to begin with," said my friend, "and the odd behavior of the watch, my dear Patterson."

"I don't attach much significance to those stains," said Patterson stubbornly. "If they are important, the medicos will tell us. But what has the watch to do with it?"

"According to the available data," replied Holmes, "the man died around midnight, presumably from a fall into the Thames. Is it likely that the watch should have continued to run, for two and a half hours, after its immersion?"

The Inspector removed the cigar from his lips, surveyed it thoughtfully for a moment, then slowly nodded his large gray head. "I'm beginning to see what you mean, Mr. Holmes. The man could have been dead at least two hours before his watch stopped running."

"Exactly."

"Does it not also give us the exact moment when the body fell into the water?" I put in.

"I should be more inclined to believe that it was hurled into the river!" observed Holmes ominously.

"And we blindly assumed that the difference between the time of death and the time registered by that watch was of no importance!" groaned Patterson. He faced my friend. "Mr. Holmes," he said, "if our investigations later confirm these deductions I shall swear you are a wizard!"

"And you would be wrong, Patterson. My inferences are based upon a series of facts, each one confirming the next. You are astonished by my conclusions because you are unfamiliar with the line of reasoning which I followed to reach them."

"I'll grant you that," said the Inspector. "Tell me. How did you conclude that he was a 'cellist? By his long hair? By the length of his fingers?"

"By no means," replied Holmes, a frosty smile appearing on his lips for a fleeting moment. "I deduced it from the calluses on the fingers of the left hand—the nails of which, by the way, were cut much shorter than those on the right. I also noticed the frayed shirt-cuff which brushes against the body of the instrument when the player is reaching for the higher positions. I was at first inclined towards a violinist, but subsequent examination of the trouser-legs gave me my most corroborative facts."

"In what way?" Patterson's steely gray eyes never left the detective's grave features as he put his question.

"The 'cellist," replied my friend, demonstrating with quick gestures of hands and knees, "holds his instrument between his knees, in this way. Now, at a point just below the knee of the trousers, on the inside of the leg, I noticed a distinct curve worn into the nap of the fabric. Only a violoncello, gentlemen, could make such a mark!"

"Wonderful!" exclaimed the usually imperturbable Patterson. "Incredible!"

"I assure you, Inspector," said Holmes deprecatingly, "that it is quite superficial." Yet I could see that Patterson's sincere praise had pleased him. "Furthermore," he resumed, "upon finding the rosin . . ."

"So that's what it was!" barked the Inspector, slapping his thigh indignantly. "And I thought it was glue!"

"You saw how easily it crumbled between my fingers. Glue—granting the possibility of its having resisted the action of water and retained its hardness—glue would never have done that. The rosin only confirmed my earlier suppositions. It gave me conclusive proof that the man was a string instrumentalist."

"Who was employed in a restaurant, you said," interposed the Inspector. "Why a restaurant? Why couldn't it have been a concert hall? Or a theatre?"

"Because of the floor-wax on the soles of the dead man's boots," replied the detective after a moment's reflection. "There are no waxed floors in music-halls or theatres."

"A dance-hall, then?"

"Have you ever seen a 'cellist playing in a dance-hall, Inspector? Reed and percussion instruments, yes; possibly violins, but violoncellos seldom if ever."

"I don't go to those places, so I wouldn't know," rumbled Patterson, "but I'll take your word for it, Mr. Holmes."

"Then start your enquiries for a missing musician among the better class cafes, where dancing is not only permitted but encouraged. These are not so numerous as you may think."

Patterson finished jotting down in his large notebook before asking my friend how he had deduced that the man was a bachelor.

Sherlock Holmes tapped his pipe against a convenient ash tray. "Did you take note of his stocking?" he asked. "A bachelor is prone to neglect them. But no self-respecting wife would ever permit her musician-husband to appear in public with holes in his footwear, or with buttons missing from shirt and coat. I counted no less than three lacking in both garments."

"Bachelor he was!" agreed the Inspector, duly noting the fact in his notebook. "And vain, too," he added, "if that comb, and the hair oil he used are any indication. No need to tell us how you found out he was not a smoking man, Mr. Holmes. There wasn't a trace of tobacco anywhere on him. No pipe, no loose shreds to indicate he was an habitual user of the weed." He closed his notebook before proceeding. "Now, as I see it—and this is only a tentative theory, mind you—the poor devil was waylaid in some dark street or alley, killed and then thrown into the river after the murderer had removed all identification from his pockets. In the darkness, he overlooked the watch . . ."

"The victim, meanwhile," broke in Sherlock Holmes drily, "obligingly taking off his hat and coat to facilitate the murderer's work?"

"Well, I do admit there are some objections . . ."

"Several, in fact," interrupted the other, with a shake of the head. "It is far more likely that the man was indoors when he met his end. This would account for the missing outer garments as well as the missing personal papers. As for the watch, I do not think it was overlooked."

"You think it was left deliberately?"

"I do. The murderer might have thought to establish some sort of alibi in case the crime was laid at his door. However, it is still too early in the case to start theorizing."

"One more question, Mr. Holmes. What do you think he died of?"

Holmes stopped in the process of refilling his pipe. His shaggy brows corrugated deeply, his thin lips pressed together for a second before replying. "The man died from the effects of an alkaloid, as yet unknown, which was injected into the blood stream. I should like to draw your attention again to those purple blotches, Inspector. They are of the utmost significance." He rose to his feet as he finished his statement.

"Come, Watson," he added. "Back to Baker Street for a pipe or two over this matter. There are several fields of conjecture and speculation opened to us, worth at least half an ounce of shag."

Then turning to the Scotland Yarder he said, "Please keep me informed of further developments, will you, Inspector?"

As we jostled along in a cab through the rain-drenched streets, I refrained from asking my companion the many questions which lay on my tongue. As was his custom, he seldom discussed his cases until he held all his facts well in hand. Musing over the grim scene we had witnessed, I found myself formulating reasons and motives for such a crime. The untouched billfold, the silver watch, clearly indicated that it could not be robbery. Revenge was far more likely, but why so peculiar a means of causing death? Did not the murderer realize that its very strangeness might hold a clue to its solution? Did he actually think that he could cover up his tracks simply by using a strange and unknown poison? A glance around at my friend changed the trend of my thoughts.

Holmes, plunged deep in his waterproof, pipe clenched between his teeth, his long legs stretched out before him, seemed to be dozing all the way to 221B. But I, who knew him better than any other man, knew that he was at work on the problem. Knew that his keen, incisive mind was already balancing alternate theories, fitting the known facts into a clear, concise pattern. We pulled up at last before the door.

"There's a gentleman by the name of Mr. Edward Morrison waiting to see you, Mr. Holmes," cried the page as he admitted us. "Been waiting an 'alf hour, sir."

Holmes gave me a swift meaning look. He disliked overlapping cases, and the thought of another at this time nettled him, I could see. We ascended rapidly.

Our visitor rose as we entered. Holmes immediately apologized for having been delayed, and vanished into his room. I removed my waterproof, trying to appraise the thin young man as I attempted to put him at his ease with a polite phrase or two. Light-haired, he appeared to be in his late twenties. The dark suit he wore seemed to accentuate the paleness of his skin. It was not the pallor of ill health, however, but of those who spend a great deal of their time indoors. He had a pleasant smile, yet the creases of worry were apparent around his light blue eyes. I was about to make some trite reference to the weather when Holmes returned, whipping his old robe about his lank and spare frame, his keen eyes studying him as he introduced himself.

"Tell me, Mr. Morrison," he inquired, after we had taken our seats, "do you not find a wind instrument somewhat wearying to one who is evidently none too robust?"

Holmes seldom overlooked an opportunity to impress his clients with his powers of observation and deduction. He loved to astonish them by a display of his remarkable talents in making swift, analytical studies of their habits, traits or profession. In the present instance, though accustomed to my friend's extraordinary gifts, I confess to sharing Mr. Morrison's astonishment. Our new client could only stare in surprise before asking:

"How on earth did you guess that, Mr. Holmes? No one could have . . ."

Sherlock Holmes stopped him with a gesture. The quick smile of pleasure which had come to his lips vanished, and a frown creased his high forehead.

"Young man," he said sternly, "I never guess! It is destructive to the inferential faculties, and abhorrent to the trained analytical reasoner. I base my inferences upon a chain of reasoning drawn from the appearance of things." He stopped to apply a glowing coal to his pipe before resuming.

"The links in my chain were forged, Mr. Morrison, by noticing your under-lip and your right thumb. On your lip I observed the layer of protective skin left there by the reed; and when we shook hands I distinctly felt the horny ridge on the top knuckle of your thumb."

Turning to me he explained further.

"Such markings are indicative of the clarinet player. Pressure on the lip gives us our first clue; and the callus on the thumb is caused by the weight of the instrument which rests upon it."

His good humour returned as he watched with amused eyes our surprised faces and listened to our ejaculations of praise. He had now made himself quite comfortable in the depths of his favourite easy chair, and was puffing on his brier with contentment and abandon, his legs stretched out towards the blaze.

Musingly he added: "I have of late toyed with the idea of revising my monograph on 'The Influence of a Trade' to include a paragraph on the indelible marks left by musical instruments upon the hands and fingers of their performers. But of course," he put in quickly, "that need not be taken up at this time."

He faced the young man.

"Mr. Morrison, this is my friend and colleague, Dr. Watson. You may feel free to discuss your problem before him. In what way can I be of service to you?"

"By discreetly investigating the present whereabouts of a friend of mine," replied the other, after a slight hesitation, wetting his lips nervously, and exhibiting other signs of discomfort and disquietude.

"Discreetly?" repeated Holmes with a frown.

"There is a woman involved, sir. A married woman."

"But why come to me?" There was no mistaking the acerbity in my friend's tone, a bluntness which clearly spelled dislike for the kind of enquiry that Morrison's reply had evoked. "At present I am extremely occupied and cannot further burden myself with what may only be an illicit love affair. Why do you not go to the police? They are better equipped to undertake such cases."

"The police are not discreet, sir."

Sherlock Holmes stirred angrily in his chair.

"There are many detective agencies in the city who would be only too glad to delve into such unethical affairs. And with a discretion worthy of better things. I should suggest that you see one of them."

But Edward Morrison, with a display of determination which surprised me, refused to accept Holmes' dismissal. Evidently behind that sensitive exterior lay a core of firmness, a will to be heard.

"You must forgive me, Mr. Holmes," he said, "for insisting that you take this case. Perhaps I have not stated it very clearly. It is a delicate matter which, if improperly handled, might bring about the very disclosures I dread." He passed his white, long-fingered hand over his brow, then went on doggedly. "Yet, anxious as I am to avoid a scandal and fearful of committing what may well be an unpardonable breach of loyalty to a friend, I cannot sit idly by without making some effort to discover what has become of him."

"Your loyalty is most commendable, my dear Mr. Morrison," remarked Holmes ironically, "but why are you so anxious to protect the honour of a man who has shown such lack of principle, and disregard for the moral code by which we live?"

Our visitor did not reply. The picture of dejection, he kept his eyes on the worn rug, looking uncomfortable and ill at ease, his head held low.

Holmes turned round in his chair. "Come, come, sir!" he said, his voice strident with irritation. "Would you have me believe that your sole concern is your foolish friend's present circumstances?"

Morrison's voice was contrite when he spoke again. "Forgive me, Mr. Holmes, for trying to withhold a personal matter in the case. You see, I am engaged to marry Miss Geraldine Foote, sister of the missing man. As you have correctly surmised, my concern is less for him than for his family. They are fine people and I would not cause them unnecessary pain for all the world." He paused, then made a gesture of entreaty. "Cannot you see that I dare not go to the police? It would drag the whole disgraceful affair into the public prints!"

"Hum," murmured Holmes, relenting somewhat. "This changes the complexion of things." Then, more briskly, he added, "But I fail to see what can be done to avoid the resulting scandal, should it come out later that this person—what is his name? Foote?—should Foote have run off with another man's wife. Such deplorable behaviour can neither be condoned nor kept secret."

Morrison was about to speak at this point, but a gesture from the detective made him close his lips.

"However, on behalf of his people, I shall look into the matter and endeavour to trace him. But it must be clearly understood that my services will end there: that I shall not stand in the way of any justifiable redress which may be demanded by those whom he has injured." He reached for his notebook.

"Now, Mr. Morrison," he said, his voice still brisk and businesslike, but less harsh, "let me have a few pertinent facts. First, where does your friend live?"

"At 14 Dean Street, Soho."

"With his family?"

"No, sir. He lives alone, in a furnished suite of rooms. His folks live in Dorsetshire. We visit them each year during the Summer holidays."

"Would you know his landlady's name?"

"Yes. I've had occasion to visit him at times. Her name is Mrs. Ferrucci, an Italian . . ."

"Quite so. Could you describe Mr. Foote?"

"Easily. I've known him for many years. He is now twenty-six years of age, is five feet, nine inches in height, and weighs about twelve stone. Has very dark hair, thick and curly, and wears neither beard nor moustaches."

"No scars or other marks of identification?"

"Not to my knowledge, Mr. Holmes." A faint smile hovered around the troubled eyes as our client added: "He is considered quite handsome by most ladies."

"Such a description," commented Holmes drily, "would fit any number of men. How long has he been missing?"

"Since Monday evening, when he was called away . . ."

"Monday evening?" repeated Holmes quickly, a new note, a rising inflection of interest apparent now in his voice. His manner had changed suddenly. Until now listless and disinterested, his attitude assumed intense concentration at this point in the interrogation. He abruptly changed the trend of his questioning and asked:

"Is your friend a musician like yourself, Mr. Morrison?"

"Yes, sir, he is. But I can't understand how you could have known this, Mr. Holmes. I haven't . . ."

"What instrument does he play?" My friend's smooth voice broke in quickly. Although edged with excitement, it was well under control. Yet I could feel the suspense coiled beneath the surface.

"The violoncello. We play in the same orchestra."

Sherlock Holmes sprang to his feet, eyes gleaming, his face now flushed and darkened.

"And I thought it a coincidence, Watson," he exclaimed, his voice shrill, "a coincidence that both should be musicians! I was slow in connecting the two men, palpably slow, but no harm has been done by my lapse."

He turned brusquely toward our startled visitor who had witnessed the sudden metamorphosis of a languid form reclining in a shabby robe in an old armchair, to a veritable ferret in human guise, pacing swiftly back and forth, gesticulating, talking rapidly and asking questions.

"Mr. Morrison, you were saying that on Monday evening—that would be the day before yesterday—your friend was called away. Where did this take place? In the establishment in which you are both employed?"

"Yes, sir."

"And that is?"

"Henri Dumont's Cafe Continental, on Shaftesbury Avenue. We play concert and dance music there, from six until midnight."

"I see. Can you remember under what circumstances this call came for your friend? Please try to recall everything in connection with it. It may well be of the utmost importance."

"It was during the after supper lull. We were having our meal—which the Cafe supplies us, even though not paying us a very generous wage—when one of the dining room staff came to our table with a message for Arnold—for Mr. Foote."

"You have no idea of the contents of that note?"

"None whatever. But I do remember that Arnold seemed quite cut up after reading it."

"Did he leave at once?"

"No, sir. He first went to our orchestra leader, Mr. Orlando. Later, Mr. Orlando told us that Arnold had begged permission to leave, saying that some very urgent business had to be attended to immediately."

"And this permission was granted?"

"Yes, it was, but only after some heated discussion between them. You see, Mr. Holmes, there are only five of us, and each one is indispensable in such a small band. But Arnold swore he would return in time for the later dancing." Morrison stopped, shook his head sadly. "He never did. That was the last time I saw him."

"At what time did all this take place?"

"Around ten thirty, sir."

Holmes absorbed this in silence for a while. When he spoke again, his voice was casual. "Can you remember whether your friend wore his hat and coat when he left?"

Morrison did not answer at once. His brow creased in thought as he struggled with the question. Finally he said: "I did not see him leave. But when we went home that night, his things were no longer there in the usual place."

"It is then safe to assume that he had them on." Holmes rubbed his hands together, a faint grin of satisfaction appearing on his face. It was becoming quite evident to me now, that he had as yet no intentions of telling our visitor the true facts behind Arnold Foote's disappearance. I confess to being unable, at this time, to fathom his reasons for this apparent insensitiveness. Holmes, although cold and unemotional, was neither callous nor cruel. However, I maintained a reserved silence, knowing that my friend's actions, no matter how incomprehensible to the outsider, would later prove to be justified.

Holmes reached over for his notes and a pencil.

"Now, Mr. Morrison," he said, "what can you tell us about the woman in the case?"

"Very little, I fear. Arnold spoke of her frequently to me. His experiences with women have been quite extensive, yet this particular person seems to have fascinated him far more than any of the others."

"This affair, then, is of some duration?"

"Well over a year at least, sir."

"Did you ever have occasion to meet her?"

"No. Although he would ask me to go along with him whenever he wanted to select a gift or token for her, my being an intimate of the family, as it were, made him naturally reticent and secretive where she was concerned."

"Then you cannot give us any information whatsoever with regard to her appearance, her age, height—anything which might help us identify or trace her?"

"All I can tell you, Mr. Holmes, is that she has honey-brown hair, is above medium in height, has very small hands and feet, is inordinately fond of costume jewelry, possesses very stylish clothes, and is two or three years older than Arnold himself. And according to his glowing description, she must be extremely attractive."

"Capital, my dear Mr. Morrison!" exclaimed my friend, sitting bolt upright in his chair, his bushy eyebrows raised in delighted surprise. "You are a model client, gifted with an exceptional memory for detail!"

My expression must have clearly mirrored the astonishment I felt on hearing this description from a man who had declared to have never set eyes upon the woman. But Holmes, chuckling as he caught sight of my face, easily explained it away.

"Mr. Morrison is merely repeating some of the phrases spoken by his friend. As for the other details did not our shrewd young friend here mention having accompanied Arnold Foote on various errands for the purpose of selecting presents for the charmer? He was thus enabled to obtain a fairly accurate picture of the woman's tastes, her height, size of gloves, and general appearance."

Edward Morrison nodded his agreement.

"It may prove to be of assistance to us," went on the detective, "you may be sure."

"Would you know where this person resides, Mr. Morrison?" he asked, becoming serious once more.

"From various chance remarks made by Arnold, at different times, I gathered that she lives somewhere in Chelsea."

"Chelsea?" Holmes' eyes sparkled. "Splendid! Did your friend ever mention her husband?"

"Rarely, sir, and only indirectly. It was a subject which was, of course, quite distasteful to him."

"Now, Mr. Morrison, I want you to think carefully before you answer my next question. It is this: Does Arnold Foote know whether the husband is aware of this illicit relationship?"

Morrison gave a visible start, then he nodded slowly and pensively. "I have good reason for believing that he does," he replied very quietly.

Holmes' shoulders stiffened almost imperceptibly.

"What makes you think so, Mr. Morrison?" he asked.

The young man stared gloomily at the rug as he made his reply. "Arnold has been depressed and worried for some time. No amount of questioning ever elicited any replies, but I could see that there was something weighing on his mind. One night, about a week ago I think, as we walked home, he muttered something about 'skating on very thin ice' or some such phrase. Then—and I recall these words clearly—he said, 'Teddy, I think the old man smells a rat'."

"He did not clarify the statement?" asked Holmes.

"No. At that moment we had reached the corner of Dean Street, where he lives, and there we parted."

"And since then he has made no further reference to the subject?"

"None whatsoever."

The detective relapsed into silence, and for several minutes not a word was exchanged. When he spoke again, it was to ask: "You have nothing further to add which may be of use?"

Morrison shook his head. "I'm afraid not, sir."

Something in my friend's manner as he removed the dottles from his pipe and started to refill it with slow deliberation, warned me that he was about to break the tragic news. I waited for the revelation with a troubled brow.

"Mr. Morrison," he said, "I deeply regret the necessity which has compelled me to withhold the news until now. My next words will shock you, I fear; yet they must be spoken. Your friend, Arnold Foote, is dead."

The thin face of our visitor turned deathly pale as he stared with dazed incomprehension at Holmes' grave features. His haggard eyes looked from one to the other with such pathos and grief that I all but sprang to my feet, expecting him to pitch over in a dead faint. But he rallied instantly, for when he spoke his voice, although low, was firm and controlled.

"Are you certain of this, Mr. Holmes? Quite certain?"

Holmes nodded grimly. "As certain as I am that he met with foul play."

"Murdered?" Morrison's pale lips scarcely moved as he uttered the word.

"Yes, he was murdered," repeated my friend, "and it was to facilitate our investigations that I questioned you prior to revealing the fact that he was dead."

Morrison shuddered without raising his head which he had rested on his hands, and remained silent as the detective went on in a kindly tone: "So you see, my dear Mr. Morrison, your well-intentioned efforts to spare his people unnecessary grief have proved to be of no avail."

The young man raised his drawn face.

"How did he die?" he asked.

"We have good reason for suspecting that he was poisoned," began the detective.

"Then it was she—she must have done it!" he exclaimed, his eyes wild and staring, "I tell you it was she!" Then he stopped, shook his head, muttering, "But why? In heaven's name, why?"

"That is what we are trying to discover," replied Holmes soberly. Then in a firmer tone he continued: "Now, sir, pull yourself together. The law claims forfeit for the life of your friend. You must do your utmost to help bring his murderer to justice."

"You are right, Mr. Holmes. I'm sorry I acted like an old woman. Tell me if there is anything I can do . . ."

"Ah! That is much better," exclaimed Holmes. "You well understand, of course, that it is now a police matter and cannot be kept hidden or suppressed any longer. I advise you to go at once to Scotland Yard and to depose everything you have told us. You may also be asked to testify at the inquest and no doubt be called upon to perform the unpleasant duty of identifying the body."

Edward Morrison rose shakily to his feet. "I shall do as you say, Mr. Holmes." And with a faint nod of his head, he reached for his mackintosh and sadly took his leave.

After our unhappy visitor had departed upon his dismal errand, Holmes continued to smoke on in silence for several minutes. I had been quite shocked by his cold, deliberate lack of consideration, and was actually contemplating a few carefully chosen words of reproach on the subject when, as was often his habit, he broke into my thoughts without preamble.

"I quite agree with you, Watson. It was cruel, yet necessary, believe me. I am not so totally lacking in feeling as to ride roughshod over a sensitive person's susceptibilities without good cause. Yet," he went on, in that dogmatic tone he affected at certain times, "sentimentality has no place in the recesses of an analyst's brain. It interferes with the finely-tempered tools which he uses. It nullifies his best efforts."

I nodded thoughtfully. I was recalling the words spoken by Stamford some years before: 'Not out of malevolence, but simply in a spirit of inquiry.'

"Whatever young Morrison's opinion of his friend's derelictions," he went on broodingly, "he could hardly be expected to return illuminating replies to my questions once his mind had been stunned by the news of Foote's tragic end. The dead influence the living at such moments."

And remembering the young man's reaction, I was forced to agree with his sober explanation. Mollified to some extent, and anxious to change the tone of the discussion, I asked: "Do you believe that the woman caused his death? That she poisoned him?"

Holmes had risen to his feet and was pacing restlessly about, puffing his brier, his hands clenched together behind his back. He shook his head in answer to my question. "No, I do not." He stopped and faced about. "I think I see your point, Watson. You are connecting my remark on the alkaloid used, with Morrison's somewhat hysterical outburst accusing the woman."

I nodded. "It seems fairly conclusive, Holmes, that . . . oh, for any number of reasons, the woman decided to rid herself of her lover, and thereupon poisoned him."

Holmes did not reply at once to my observation, but resumed his nervous pacings, deep in thought, and evidently turning over in his mind the data he had gathered from our recent visitor. Finally he returned to his chair.

"It is often a mistake," he said, "to unload before one has taken on board a sufficient cargo. To theorize before our facts arrive can be misleading. I do not say that your theory is erroneous; poison is the legendary weapon of the female murderer, but that does not imply that the weaker sex retains a monopoly. Had we to contend with a common type—arsenic, antimony, strychnine—any one of a round half dozen in everyday medicinal or commercial use, I should tend to agree with you. But this was no ordinary alkaloid."

Knowing my friend's penchant for seeking the dramatic rather than the prosaic, I ventured a mild remonstrance, suggesting that perhaps something less fanciful might have been used.

His retort was brusque and sharp.

"The symptoms were unmistakable to the trained eye of a toxicologist. They clearly conveyed every indication of a toxic agent which, when injected into the blood stream, causes dark blemishes to appear on the skin. I do not possess all my data yet, Watson, but I shall have them! I must have them," he went on fiercely, "for then I may learn with whom we have to deal."

"Whom do you suspect? The husband?"

"It is still too early to reach conclusions which later discoveries may easily discount; but there is a strong balance of probability which favours such a suspicion."

"Perhaps," I suggested, "in a moment of blind, jealous rage, he might have . . ."

"No, Watson," he interrupted, "whoever killed Foote did so after thought and preparation. This was not a crime committed in an outburst of savage rage, but a carefully premeditated one."

"Nevertheless," I persisted, "a jealous man, certain of his wife's unfaithfulness, might well commit such a crime . . ." I stopped. A new thought struck a chill to my heart. "Holmes!" I exclaimed, "if your suspicions are well-founded, and the husband is the murderer, that woman may be in terrible danger. He may . . ."

"Perhaps he has already done so," broke in Holmes, the same thought no doubt crossing his mind at the same moment. There could be no mistaking the ominous tone in his voice.

"You think she is already dead, then?"

"What else is there to think, man? Foote's death took place most probably late Monday night. This is Wednesday. Why has she not come forward? Why does she choose to remain silent?"

"Perhaps she does not know that her lover is dead."

"It is quite possible," he replied, rising to his feet and starting to remove his robe, "but most unlikely."

"You are going out?"

"Yes, Watson, but I should like you to remain here. I am expecting developments, and with you holding the fort, I feel safe in going off for an hour or so."

"Where are you going, Holmes? To that Cafe-whatever-it-was?"

"The Cafe Continental? No. First I shall drop in at the British Museum. Then I intend to pay a visit to Arnold Foote's housekeeper—what was the name? Ah, yes, Ferrucci. I may uncover a salient fact or two before the hounds from Scotland Yard go baying towards Dean Street."

While speaking he had crossed over to his room, and I waited until he had emerged, buckling the belt of his waterproof, before asking: "What do you hope to find, Holmes?"

"In the Museum: data. In Dean Street: the woman—or at least some clue to her identity." He paused at the door and added reflectively: "Somewhere, in the course of my omnivorous readings, I have chanced upon the slenderest of allusions to a poison which stains the skin of its victims. I must try to find that reference, Watson. A purple blemish . . ." He was still mechanically repeating that phrase as the door closed.

I watched from the window until my friend had vanished inside a cab, then I turned to the early afternoon papers which Holmes' dealer had delivered in the meantime. The first reports of the identification of Arnold Foote's body ("thanks to the perspicacity and astuteness of Inspector Patterson and his able assistants") were appearing for the first time. Speculations were being made as to the cause of death, motives, possible culprits, but nothing new had been unearthed and fresh developments were being awaited with every passing hour. An article in the *Standard,* however, revealed that the earlier verdict of death by misadventure would have to be modified in the light of recent findings, following upon the autopsy, which would no doubt bring in a charge of wilful murder by person or persons unknown. That the case was beginning to loom large in the press was proved by later editions which were brought up after four o'clock. I read them all eagerly, hoping to uncover some fresh details which might aid my friend in his investigations. But they contained merely rehashings of earlier reports and my search was in vain.

I spent another hour browsing through my friend's voluminous year-books and indexed cases, brushing up on earlier cases with an eye to future publication—subject to his approval, of course. I chatted over old times with Mrs. Hudson who, meanwhile, had very thoughtfully provided me with a pot of her excellent tea. It was not until well past five o'clock, when I was already beginning to fret and fume impatiently, that Billy came up with a telegram for me. It was from Holmes:

"View halloo. Meet me at Goldini's at six. S.H."

Holmes' use of hunting terms while on a case was not new to me. This could have but one interpretation; the game was breaking cover. His researches had not been fruitless.

My friend was already seated at the table when I reached the restaurant. My eager enquiries concerning his activities during the afternoon fell on deaf ears. Waving his hand towards a chair, he contented himself by saying briefly: "I've taken the liberty of ordering your dinner—and a bottle of Chianti. Fall to; we shall have time enough to discuss things later on."

I obeyed with alacrity for I was hungry and, I must confess, relieved that I could turn away even for only an hour, from the murky business on hand, to something warm and stimulating.

I have frequently had occasion to remark on one of Holmes' peculiar characteristics which permitted him to completely disconnect his mind from the problem under investigation and turn to that inexhaustible fund of fact and anecdote with which his remarkable memory was stocked. His spirited topics that evening, as I remember, touched upon the stains of old Cremona violins, the field of ancient musical instruments, and thence to the composition of intricate cryptograms over which he occasionally spent some of his leisure time in the British Museum.

The rain had stopped when we emerged, but a chilly damp fog enshrouded the streets as we strolled slowly and silently back to Baker Street. It was nearly eight o'clock when we reached our old quarters, and the light streaming brilliantly through the mist warned us that we had a visitor.

It proved to be Inspector Patterson, and the sight of his bulky, homely figure brought vividly back to mind the tragic affair which had haunted us throughout the day.

"I'm glad to see you have not been waiting long, Inspector," cried Sherlock Holmes cheerfully, as he tossed his damp mackintosh over a chair, and placed his cap on the mantel-piece.

"Your landlady told you?"

Holmes grinned and shook his head.

"I deduced that from the length of your cigar. However," he went on, his face becoming serious, "let us not waste time in banter. Only important business could have brought you out on such a dreary evening. What is it, Inspector? Have you traced the woman? Has another mysterious murder taken place?"

Patterson swayed his head in wonder and puzzlement. "There are times, Mr. Holmes," he said, "when I'm inclined to believe you're a mind reader."

"Then another murder *has* taken place?" he asked, half rising from the chair in which he was about to sit.

Patterson nodded grimly.

"A woman?"

"Aye, sir. A pretty but foolish young woman . . ."

"Whose body," broke in Sherlock Holmes, "is marked by a series of purple maculas, similar to those found on the body of Arnold Foote, late 'cellist?"

"My dear Holmes!" I gasped.

"Told you he was a mind reader," grumbled Patterson.

"Who is this woman?" snapped Holmes quickly, impervious to our remarks. "What is her name?"

"She was known at 134 Oakley Crescent as Mrs. Henry Staunton . . ." began the Inspector.

"And at 14 Dean Street?" My friend's eyes now gleamed with excitement.

"As Mrs. Arnold Foote," replied Patterson, cocking a shrewd eye at him. "I thought we had you there, Mr. Holmes!"

"A child could have followed such a trail, after Morrison's testimony. I suppose Foote's housekeeper identified her?"

"Positively!"

"Then the case is closed," said Holmes, sinking back into his chair with a sigh of disappointment. So far as he was concerned, his work was finished. I could tell by his tone and attitude that all interest in the case had evaporated.

"No, Mr. Holmes, the case is not closed," corrected the Scotland Yarder.

"You have only to arrest the woman's husband. Surely it is obvious that he is your man?" Holmes' voice, dry and brittle, showed annoyance at the other's stubbornness.

"There, I agree with you. In fact, he is being sought for questioning. But still . . ." He stopped, fumbled with his cigar, peering at the austere, grave face of the criminologist with anxious eyes.

"Come, Inspector, out with it!" urged my colleague in a sharp tone. "Is there any point in the case which needs clarifying?"

Patterson chewed and worried his cigar thoughtfully before speaking.

Then he said, evasively: "Those were pretty neat deductions you made this morning, over at the mortuary. Hit the nail right on the head. Morrison corroborated every point you made."

Always susceptible to flattery where his work was concerned, Holmes thawed visibly. Encouraged, the Inspector continued: "You also implied that you know something about that purple stain poison which was used by the murderer. At least, you conveyed as much when you had me take note of the splotches on the skin. Now, frankly, I admit that we're up a tree there. The medicos don't know what it is. And we don't know either. As you well know, you can't convince a British jury . . ."

"Inspector," said Holmes at this moment, speaking as if he had ignored every word uttered by the good Patterson, "have you ever heard of matacalda?"

The Scotland Yarder shook his head without hesitation. "Never."

"Have you, Watson?"

"I can't say that I have," I replied guardedly.

"Well, until this afternoon, neither had I, so you need not be downcast about it." Assuming his best didactic manner, he continued: "Matacalda is a vegetable alkaloid extracted from an unknown plant by certain tribes in the Brazilian jungles. Very little is known about it. I myself only learned its name a few hours ago, although I had found obscure references to it in various books of travel. This much is known, however: it forms an important ingredient in the preparation of blow dart poison. It works swiftly once it enters the body, causing paralysis of the muscles which control the lungs, with death ensuing in a matter of minutes. Now mark this," he went on, emphasizing his next words with his pipe stem. "Victims of matacalda poisoning are invariably marked by deep purple splotches or maculas."

Patterson let out a cloud of smoke as Holmes ended his extraordinary statement. Then he observed:

"Sounds like a tall traveler's tale." But the intent expression on his face belied both his words and his scepticism.

"Nevertheless, that is the agent which destroyed both victims. Tell me, Patterson, have you any indication as to the manner in which it was administered?"

The Inspector glanced through his notebook, then looked up. "In Foote's case, the doctors believe it was injected by means of a thin sharp instrument which pierced the scalp just below the occ . . . occi-something bone." He looked over to me. "What's that, Doctor?"

"The occipital bone," I replied, "at the base of the skull where the spinal column . . ."

"Yes, yes," snapped Holmes testily, "cut the medical frills! The woman, man! What of the woman?"

Whatever feelings of justifiable pride he may have felt at this moment on having his findings confirmed by the medical evidence, his lean, drawn features did not reveal them.

Patterson consulted his notes again.

"Police surgeon cautious about committing himself, but suspects unknown toxic agent of virulent powers, similar to that discovered by postmortem examination of the body of Arnold Foote." He stopped reading, then gloomily shook his head. "But we haven't found out yet how it was done," he concluded woefully.

Sherlock Holmes tensed in his chair.

"What do you mean?" he asked abruptly.

"I mean that, although we know, thanks to you, that some queer poison was used, there isn't a cut or puncture anywhere to show how that poison entered the woman's body!"

Almost at once I sensed an awakening of interest in my colleague's manner. His face had regained the old familiar alertness, his shoulders had stiffened, his eye held the gleam I knew so well. Here, at last, was something worthy of his steel. So far, the case had not called upon the full powers of his analytical genius. The deductions praised so highly by Inspector Patterson were, in his opinion, merely a demonstration of the more superficial aspects of crime detection and identification. They had whetted his appetite without satisfying it. Here, indeed, was a unique situation, and one calculated to appeal to his love of the complex and the seemingly inexplicable.

There was an odd light (I will not say of pleasure!) shining in his eyes as he asked quickly:

"Has the body been removed?"

"No. I thought you might care to look things over, so I gave orders to leave everything in status quo."

"Excellent!"

Holmes was already on his feet when he turned to me. "Well, Watson, one more sortie?" Then he chuckled heartily as he caught a glimpse of my expression.

As we clattered down the stairs I experienced anew that never-failing sense of exhilarating adventure which would sweep over me whenever we set off upon a new phase of one of my confrere's cases. It was the thrilling sensation of moments such as this which urged me to abandon my humdrum, everyday pursuits, and play a willing, secondary role in the dramas in which my friend and colleague invariably performed so brilliant a part.

During our drive through the foggy streets, with the gas lamps flickering eerily over the wet and glistening pavements, Inspector Patterson gave us a brief resume of the events which had transpired that afternoon.

Mrs. Emma Grant, part-time servant of the Stauntons, reporting to work at four P.M., her usual hour, had found the dead body of her mistress on the bedroom floor. The police, whom she had notified at once, impressed by the sight of the dark blemishes which disfigured the body, had promptly called in Scotland Yard. It was quickly ascertained by the investigators that the purple marks were identical to those found on the body of Arnold Foote, and had quite evidently been caused by the same agency. According to the police surgeon, the woman had been dead approximately fifteen hours, or since early morning of this day.

The husband, Henry Staunton, having presumably taken to his heels, a warrant had been issued for his arrest on suspicion of murder. It was further learned from the maid that the Staunton household was not a happy one. The couple were childless. Their frequent and bitter quarrels had alienated the few friends they had, and visitors were rare. The disparity of ages (she being some twenty years his junior) plus his moody nature and a jealous and vindictive character, had no doubt contributed much to the incompatibility which had wrecked their married life. An importer of medicinal herbs, Staunton was often away from home for weeks at a time. According to Mrs. Grant, he had only recently returned from a ten day stay on the Continent; Paris, she believed.

Sherlock Holmes stirred for the first time since we had entered the slow-moving vehicle. He had listened silently and intently to Patterson's succinct summary, with chin sunk low on chest, hands thrust deep in his raincoat pockets, his eyes closed. But at this moment he raised his head.

"Did the maid recall the exact day of his return?"

"Yes, as a matter of fact, she did. It was last Saturday, shortly before eight in the evening. She remembered it clearly because of the dreadful quarrel which broke out soon after his arrival. She also recalled hearing Staunton accusing his wife of infidelity, vilifying her brutally, and making ominous threats. To which Mrs. Staunton had retorted in furious rage, that all was over between them, and that she was leaving him. Thereupon, after having packed some of her more precious things, she had departed, swearing never to return."

"And yet, strangely enough," mused Holmes, "she was found dead in that house. What explanation did the maid offer, regarding her mistress's return?"

"She said Mrs. Staunton might have gone to get some of her clothes."

"She was not certain?"

"No. You see, Mrs. Grant had been told by Mr. Staunton that, since the place would be vacant for several days, she did not need to return until Wednesday—today. He was evidently going off on another of his trips."

"Or clearing the field for his next move, most likely," commented my friend. Then he asked: "Have you attempted to trace his movements since last Saturday?"

"I've put two good men to work on just that angle. The ports are being watched, and a descriptive circular has been issued by the Yard. He won't get far if he's still in England. We did uncover the fact that Mrs. Staunton visited Foote's quarters yesterday afternoon. We learned from the housekeeper that the lady looked terribly pale and ill, and when told that Arnold Foote had not spent the previous night (Monday, that is) in his rooms, she exhibited great distress and left immediately."

"A complex affair," muttered Holmes. "Mrs. Staunton was indubitably leading a double life, taking advantage of her husband's absences to live with her lover."

"That's how we view it," agreed Patterson.

For some minutes the only sounds to break the silence which followed were the crunch of wheels on wet asphalt and the steady clop-clop of the horse's hoofs. Occasionally the gaslight from a passing street lamp would fall on the grave, brooding faces of my companions. Holmes, pale and tense, his lips clamped tightly on the stem of his pipe. Patterson, stoical and calm, his heavy-set features showing no sign of strain or fatigue.

"We must be approaching the Thames!" cried Holmes suddenly. "I am sure I heard a boat whistle just now." He peered out into the foggy darkness for a moment. "Yes, yes, we ought to be there shortly," he exclaimed. "This is Flood Street, and those are the lights of the Embankment."

Holmes' accurate knowledge of London streets was never at fault, for a few minutes later we turned into Oakley Crescent.

No. 134 proved to be an old yet attractive Georgian dwelling, with wrought iron railings enclosing a narrow strip of garden. At the gate stood a stalwart police constable good-naturedly coping with a crowd of loafers staring up at the entrance. He saluted as he caught sight of the Inspector's large bulk, and waved the loiterers aside for us to pass.

I obtained only a shadowy glimpse of the narrow, dusty, panelled antechamber, lit by a gas chandelier, as we followed Patterson up a flight of carpeted steps, with its unpolished rods dully reflecting the light overhead. Then we were in the bedroom, the scene of the tragedy which, exploding in the press on the following morning, was to rock the entire country for weeks. A boyish-faced policeman rose hurriedly to his feet and saluted as we entered.

It was a largish room, tastefully decorated in blue and gold wall trimming, with heavy curtains at the wide windows, chairs in brocade and silks, soft rugs, and a vast gilt-framed mirror placed before a well carved dressing table. But I noticed all this later.

It was the slender, sheet-covered form, lying between the bed and the dressing table, which instantly caught my eye and held it with all the fascination that only swift and mysterious death can evoke. Mrs. Edna Staunton had been a beautiful creature, with clear blue eyes, light brown hair, and exquisitely modeled nose, lips and throat. In spite of the hideous blemishes which now marred her features, she still radiated a faint, perfumed aura of feminine attractiveness which tugged at one's heartstrings.

While I stood shaking my head sadly over the piteous ruin of one of Nature's perfect creations, Holmes, who never wasted a moment in maudlin sentiment, had been giving the room a searching examination. Lens in hand, he carefully scrutinized the various toilet articles which littered the dressing table. Then, on his knees, he meticulously went over the carpet in the immediate vicinity of the body. Like some lank, weird bird of sombre plumage, he hopped about the room, muttering to himself, intent upon his work with all the powers of concentration at his command, completely unaware of those of us who were witnessing this strange spectacle. In silence we watched and waited, while he continued his investigations, impressed by the earnestness he exhibited, and his painstaking exactitude.

Finally he approached the sheeted figure, bent one knee and studied the lurid discolourations with frigid analytical detachment. An exclamation broke suddenly from his lips. A movement of his hand attracted my attention and in an instant I was at his side.

He had parted the soft brown hair and was pointing at the white scalp beneath. The keen, alert expression on his face, the tightening of thin lips and the quiver of nostrils were symptoms I diagnosed with ease.

"What do you think caused that, Watson?" he muttered, his voice hoarse with excitement. Craning my head, I could see to what he had alluded. Directly over the parietal bone, above the right ear, were a series of thin parallel scratches, less than an inch in length.

"What do you think it is, Holmes?" I countered, unable at the moment to account for so slight an abrasion.

"The solution to the mystery," he replied, rising to his feet and brushing the knees of his trousers as he went towards the dressing table.

"The mystery of her death?" I asked, following him.

"No, Watson, the mystery of how the poison was administered!"

I heard an ejaculation from Inspector Patterson and turned in time to see him retrieving the cigar which had toppled from his lax lips as my friend's ringing words fell on his ears.

As we eagerly approached the toilet table, watching Holmes with expectant eyes, he carefully lifted an object from its surface, then whirled round.

"And this," he cried dramatically, holding aloft a silver-mounted tortoise-shell comb, "this is the instrument of death!"

So long as memory serves, I shall never forget his face at that supreme moment of triumph. The colour had mounted to his usually sallow cheeks and his eyes glowed with sheer joy at the homage we paid him with our words of praise, our cries of astonishment. For the moment, the cold analytical reasoner became a human being, eager for admiration and applause. Then the hidden Holmes vanished as swiftly as he had appeared, the incisive reasoning machine returned.

After having scanned the spot on which the comb had lain, he was now intent upon examining the poisoned article itself, studying the long thin teeth through his pocket lens, turning it over with the utmost care.

"A conception worthy of the Borgias!" he cried at last, ill-repressed admiration in his voice. "This innocent-looking comb is deadlier than a cobra reared to strike! The merest scratch is sufficient to cause death."

Holding it out for us to see, but at a safe distance, he added: "Not only have the center teeth been filed to razor sharpness and smeared with poison, but the remaining teeth have been lowered a fraction of an inch. I could distinctly see the marks of the file through my lens!"

"What a devilish device!" I cried, horrified.

"Aye, Watson, devilish and cunning. Who would suspect so terrible a weapon masquerading under the guise of a common, everyday article such as this? With the possible exception of Culverton Smith's little ivory box, I cannot recall in all my experience of murder weapons, another which filled me with such utter loathing."

"What made you suspect a comb in the first place?" asked Patterson, who had hardly uttered a word since entering the room.

"Where the others looked for the obvious, I sought for the unusual. Once having found the scratches on the head, I could scarcely fail to recognize the object that had made them."

Patterson nodded. "Of course," he agreed, his shrewd eyes looking down at the covered body. "Must be a slow-acting poison," he observed as an afterthought. "She had time to replace the thing on the dressing table before collapsing."

"Perhaps the murderer himself did so," I interjected quickly, realizing with a sharp pang that Holmes had apparently failed to account for this most vital point.

But Sherlock Holmes merely shook his head. "No, no, gentlemen, I disagree with you. The poison acts too rapidly for the victim to do what you have implied, Patterson. The thought had already crossed my mind only to be discarded. I have a simpler explanation. You might ask the maidservant, Mrs. Grant, to step in here for a moment."

Inspector Patterson gave the necessary order, and the policeman who had remained on duty left the room at once. A minute or two later he returned with a sturdy, dour-faced woman, faded of feature and with gray-streaked hair.

Holmes greeted her with an encouraging smile. "No need for alarm, Mrs. Grant," he said, "I only wish to ask you a simple question."

The comb, which he had retained in his hand at his side, was suddenly level with the woman's pale, unblinking eyes, the silver mounting twinkling and shining under the gaslight.

"This comb was lying near Mrs. Staunton's body when you entered this room earlier this afternoon. What made you replace it on the table?"

She remained staring at him silently for several seconds, calm and unperturbed. In the hush which followed, I could hear the harsh sounds of a "growler" lumbering by, and the far-off hum of voices from the street. I held my breath, waiting for her to speak. Then the stolid features relaxed, the tightly-pressed lips moved.

"You are a clever man, sir," she said, her voice still retaining traces of a Scottish burr worn thin from disuse. "A very clever man who makes a body remember things she had forgotten."

"What made you remove it?" insisted Holmes.

The heavy shoulders heaved in a helpless shrug.

"Who can say? I was that shocked to see the poor lass lying on the floor. I just had to do something. Ma'am was always so fussy about that comb, never a place she went to without taking it along with her. So . . ."

"So you automatically picked it up and put it back in its place, as a well-trained servant should," concluded Holmes for her, a glint of savage delight shining on his face. "Thank you, Mrs. Grant; your testimony has aided us materially."

"The comb will of course figure in the trial, Inspector," remarked my friend after the maid had left. "I entrust it to you. Remember, a careless movement resulting in the slightest scratch or abrasion will cause a frightful death. So handle it gingerly and advise your men accordingly."

Patterson nodded gravely. "I'll take proper care of it, never fear, Mr. Holmes, and so will my men." Then, shaking his grizzled head from side to side in wonderment, he added: "Wish I knew how you get your results."

"Yes, Holmes," I put in, "how did you discover it was the servant who had replaced the comb?"

"Simply by observing the dust on the dressing table," he replied. "As you can see," he went on, pointing with his finger, "a four day accumulation covers its surface, outlining every article. Upon lifting the comb, however, I could distinctly see that the dust beneath, although scuffed and disturbed, did not show the same clear imprint as the rest of the objects. Hence I deduced that it had only recently been placed there. The police would never have touched it. Who, then, had preceded them? The only person who met all the requirements was Mrs. Grant—the first person to enter the room and find the body."

"Holmes," I said, after a long silence, my voice quivering with emotion, "you have seldom risen to greater heights!"

"Best bit of detecting I've ever witnessed!" was Inspector Patterson's only comment, but it sufficed to bring a glow of pleasure to my friend's ascetic features.

"Well, Patterson," remarked Sherlock Holmes some time later as we were leaving the Staunton House, "there is your case. It is still incomplete, and some obscure details remain to be cleared up, but in the main, I believe you have got enough to hold Henry Staunton for questioning."

"Enough to hang him," said the Inspector grimly, tapping the leather case in which lay the tortoise-shell comb.

RETROSPECTIVE

Three months have gone by. Henry Staunton, the Oakley Crescent murderer, has been tried and convicted of the poisoning of his wife and of her lover, Arnold Foote. The most dramatic trial of the decade ended after four tempestuous weeks of controversy and debate. With the execution of the poisoner early in February, the whole sensational affair that had rocked the country was already in the process of being forgotten in the never-ending swirl and bustle of everyday life.

I had not seen Sherlock Holmes since that eventful evening in November. A hurried note from him which reached me on the 25th informed me that he had been called in by the French Government on a matter of grave importance. I could only conjecture as to what it was, for his terse messages which reached me from time to time, conveyed only that his investigations might be of long duration.

I was, as a consequence, agreeably surprised on a late afternoon in mid-February, to learn through Mycroft Holmes, that my friend was back in town and wished to see me. My practice being quiet, I wasted no time but went to Baker Street the same evening.

As I knocked upon the well-remembered door, the sound of his strident voice made my heart leap with pleasure, and on entering, my eyes dimmed as I caught sight of the lean pale face, the faded bathrobe.

"Ah, Watson!" he exclaimed, "it is good to see you."

His face was thinner, more deeply lined than I ever remembered seeing it. His cheek bones were more prominent, and his thick, black eyebrows stood out against the pallor of his skin. Yet his keen, ever-alert eyes retained their old fire, his voice all of its commanding power and resonance.

He was seated at his desk, his long nervous fingers deftly inserting various papers and documents into a large blue envelope.

"But perhaps I am intruding upon you," I remarked, after having warmly responded to his greeting. "If you are busy . . ."

"No, Watson, only a preliminary weaving of my web. There is nothing more to be done at this stage." He held up the pale blue folder on the surface of which I noticed a large letter 'M'. "My case is almost complete, but I cannot spring into action for several weeks." He rose to his feet, placed the folder into one of the pigeonholes of his desk, then crossed over to his favourite chair by the fireplace.

"You must forgive me," he resumed, as I followed to take my accustomed place across from him, "for not notifying you earlier of my return. My present investigation necessitates the utmost secrecy. No one, save only those I trust implicitly, must know of my presence here in London at this time. I came back in disguise; the only persons with whom I have communicated are my brother and Police Inspector Patterson."

"This investigation, then, is of great importance?"

"So important," he replied very earnestly, "that if I bring it off successfully it will be the crowning achievement of my career."

"I need hardly have to say that I am at your disposal, Holmes. Should you need . . ."

"Rest assured, my dear Watson," he broke in, "that when the time comes I shall most certainly have need of a faithful ally. It is a waiting game that I play, against a formidable foe whose every move must be carefully weighed if I am to land him in the net I am preparing."

I experienced a pang of disappointment which I attempted to conceal. I ought to have known that it was not his nature to send for me just for the pleasure of seeing an old and trusted friend. His proud, self-contained personality and unemotional character made him shun any display of sentiment towards anyone, even his only friend.

"Come, come, Watson," he cried, a mischievous twinkle lurking in his eyes. "What I have to say will amply reward you for any time you may have to spend away from your patients."

"I am always happy to see you, Holmes," I said quietly, the bitterness thawed by the cordiality in his voice, "and to listen to whatever you might have to say. At present, having no serious cases to attend to, I am quite free to help you in any way I can."

"Splendid!" he exclaimed, crossing his thin knees and settling back more comfortably in his seat. "I suppose," he said, after a pause during which he sat thoughtfully puffing his pipe, "I suppose that you are wondering why I have asked you to drop in today?"

"You have a case to go over with me?"

"Right, Watson," he replied, glancing keenly in my direction, his heavy brows drawn low over his eyes, as if expecting a reaction from me. "The Staunton affair."

I started up in my chair in surprise.

"Is not that an unusual departure from your customary methods of work?" I asked, for none knew better than I that, in his clear and orderly mind, each case displaced the last, and present problems invariably blurred all recollections of past ones.

"It is," he agreed, "but there were unusual aspects about the case which prompted me to deviate from my rule."

"But what feature could have induced you to dwell upon the Oakley Crescent Murders at this time, three months after the conclusion of your investigations?"

"The significance of the tortoise-shell comb," he answered gravely, "in connection with the death of Mrs. Edna Staunton."

"I was not aware that there existed any significant aspect in connection with her death," I observed, my mind reverting to the grim scene in the Staunton bedroom. "The poisoned comb, I concede, was an extraordinary method of committing a crime, without precedent, perhaps, in modern criminal annals. But . . ."

"No, no, Watson," he said quickly, "say unusual if you like—even grotesque if you prefer it, but not entirely unprecedented, for there *are* parallels in modern criminology."

"Indeed? I should like to hear some."

"Very well."

A reminiscent light came to his eyes as he resumed after a momentary reflection.

"I might mention, by way of illustration, the Wurlitzer Case at Salzburg, in 1877, in which a poisoned earring was used. The fact that the victim—a woman of means whose wealth was coveted by the murderer—had recently had her ears pierced at his insistence, was chiefly instrumental in bringing the poisoner to justice. Another, differing only in the method of application, is the Selmer Poisoning Case of Brittany, some two years ago. You may recall that a sharpened nail, driven through the sole of the boot, then smeared with a deadly acid, caused the death of its wearer, François Selmer, a rich cattle merchant. His nephew was later convicted of the crime when it was proved that the marks on the leather could only have been made by his own hammer. There are others, less striking perhaps, but these will suffice to bring out the various points of resemblance existing between them."

Holmes paused while he crammed his pipe with fresh shag, then tossed his pouch over to me as he continued.

"The singular circumstance which I alluded to just now concerns the presence of the sharpened comb at the side of Mrs. Staunton's body."

"Then the different theories," I put in, "evolved by the more sensational sheets to explain away that very aspect of the case were all inaccurate?"

"Do you mean those wild and absurd explanations advanced by unimaginative reporters?" he cried impatiently. "That Staunton suffered a mental lapse? That he lost his nerve? That he became careless and overconfident?" He gestured angrily. "Piffle, Watson, sheer piffle! Such implausible solutions outraged every logical faculty I possess! I read them all and found them to be wholly inconsistent with the facts, and with the character of the criminal himself."

He leaned forward in his chair, an intent look on his face as he added: "Because it was the cunning and resourceful manner in which he murdered Arnold Foote and disposed of his body that gave me my first clear insight into the workings of his mind. This, in turn, enabled me to forge the links in my chain of reasoning which led me eventually to true solution."

"How did you bring this about?" I asked.

"By referring to my notes on the case, and the reading of a staggering pile of newspapers which carried a complete day-by-day account of the court proceedings. Having thus gathered in my harvest—and a goodly crop it proved to be!—I surrounded myself one evening with a motley assortment of shag, cushions and hot coffee, and proceeded to thresh it out. It cost me a night's sleep, but at dawn I had my solution to the mystery."

"I should be very glad to hear what it was."

"And you shall, Watson, but all in good time. First, I should like to recapitulate briefly the sequence of events in the murder of Foote. It will serve to refresh your memory and thus enable you to obtain a firmer grip on the essentials."

He snuggled more deeply into his chair, and made certain that his brier was drawing properly before resuming.

"The true facts in the death of the 'cellist came out, as you know, in Henry Staunton's confession made soon after his arrest at Newhaven. This document is of particular interest, for not only did it tell us how the crime was done, but it also served to cast a revealing light upon what was to come.

"Staunton contrived, by a simple yet effective ruse, to entice this none-too-bright musician to his home on Oakley Crescent and there killed him by plunging a steel bodkin impregnated with an alkaloid into the base of his skull. Following a preconceived plan, the murderer then hid the body and calmly went to spend some hours with acquaintances in a near-by cafe."

"One moment, Holmes," I broke in, "there is one aspect of this which has never been clear to me. Where was his wife on this particular evening?"

"Have you forgotten that, following upon a last bitter quarrel, Mrs. Staunton had left him?"

"By Jove!" I exclaimed, "you are quite right! It had completely slipped my mind."

"Yet, it was of enormous importance," he observed. "But to return to Staunton. Having now established some sort of alibi, he returned some time around two A.M. leading a horse and cab which he had coolly appropriated without the owner's knowledge, and used it to carry the body to the river."

"Now that I come to think of it," I interjected, "that cabby never found out the grisly service his cab had rendered a murderer that night."

"Neither did he ever learn that a would-be murderer had been spying his movements, and knew of his habit of spending some time indoors on wet nights," added my friend. "And took full advantage of it later. Doubtless, the bad weather aided him, but his having donned the cabby's own hat and waterproof, which he had flung inside his vehicle—thus effecting a perfect disguise—was a master stroke of daring and of quick thinking, besides demonstrating a swift grasp of opportunity. Barely ten minutes after he had hurled Foote's body over the hand railing of the bridge, the cab was back at its place and no one the wiser."

I gave a reminiscent nod. "Staunton actually bragged about that exploit, I remember."

"And with some justification. The crime had been so cunningly planned, and had been carried out with such careful regard to detail and timing, that not a hitch occurred to mar it. I tell you, Watson, that the police might have been hard put to secure his conviction had he not made that wild, damning admission when he was arrested."

I had not forgotten the incident. Staunton, caught off guard when tendered the customary warning, had hotly denied all responsibility for the death of his wife, while conceding by his denial, implications of guilt for the murder of Arnold Foote.

"Staunton possessed the three most dangerous qualities of the criminal," continued Holmes; "cunning, resourcefulness and daring. And, I might add, used them effectively."

"Then why did he not destroy that infernal comb?" I asked. "Surely self-preservation alone ought to have dictated so obvious a course."

"That, my dear fellow, was one of the very questions I asked myself when reviewing the case. How could a man of Staunton's calibre have overlooked so incriminating a piece of evidence? What had impelled this crafty schemer to make use of that strange and terrible matacalda twice in rapid succession—an obvious and fatal blunder?"

Holmes stopped to knock out the cold ashes from his pipe. Then he refilled it slowly, deep in thought, his brows drawn low, his eyes half closed.

"I could not reconcile these two facts," he resumed, "with Staunton's crafty and ingenious mind. Twist and turn them as I might, they refused to fit into an otherwise orderly pattern." He frowned. "Something was wrong, Watson. Instinctively I felt that somewhere in my chain of reasoning lay a defective link. By a process of elimination I succeeded in discovering my error. It lay in having until now gone along on the assumption that, having killed Arnold Foote, Staunton, of necessity, had also murdered his wife. But, I reasoned, if he had indeed committed both crimes, was it conceivable that he should bungle the second after having so cunningly covered up his tracks in the first? It was illogical, hence inadmissible.

"Confronted with this misconception, I began to cast about for an alternative theory, one which, while retaining the known facts, would enable me to reach a totally different conclusion. In view of the lapse of time, this could no longer be reached by the ordinary methods of observation and confirmation; only analytical deductions from these facts could give me the correct interpretation of them. Feverishly I began to go over my notes, sensing that somewhere among them was the answer I sought."

"You were successful?" I asked quickly.

"Beyond expectation," he replied, then relapsed once more into a deep thoughtful silence, his arms propped up on his knees, holding his pipe between his hands, contemplating the glowing sea-coals.

"Were I the ideal reasoner you so often have made me out to be," he began, after a long interval of silence, "I should have quickly perceived the significance underlying the Staunton maid's replies to my questions as to why she had replaced the comb."

"But what possible connection could there be between her replies and the solution to the death of Mrs. Staunton?"

"Do you recall her words?" he asked, countering my question with one of his own.

"Vaguely," I answered. "Was it not something about the 'poor lass lying dead on the floor'?"

"Good old Watson!" he said, with a dry chuckle.

"Well, she also referred to her mistress's fondness for that particular comb, and to the fact—and this is noteworthy—that she always took it with her wherever she went. We know that Mrs. Staunton, following the last quarrel with her husband, had packed a few things and had then fled from the house."

"Swearing never to return," I put in, as some of the details returned to me.

"Quite so. Now, at such moments of stress, a woman's instinct is to carry away her most cherished and useful possessions, is it not?"

"You mean . . ." I began.

"I am prepared to stake my reputation on it," he put in, anticipating my question, "that when she left Oakley Crescent, the tortoise-shell comb was in her possession!"

I stared at him in blank surprise. "But if that is the case, how could Staunton have poisoned it?"

"Since he did not have access to the comb at any time during the three days which preceded her death, it was utterly impossible for him to have done so," he replied quietly.

"Really, Holmes," I cried, lifting my hands in a helpless gesture, "I am now more confused than ever. Would it not be better if you revealed the steps you took to unravel this intricate puzzle? How did you eventually solve it?"

"Simply by applying my oft-repeated formula. Having eliminated the impossible—that is, Staunton's complicity in the death of his wife—I had now to contend with whatever remained, however improbable, in order to arrive at the truth. No sooner had I reached this conclusion than the facts began to arrange themselves in their proper order. The old conceptions had perforce to give way to the new. Viewed thus from an entirely different angle, the true elements in the case now assumed their rightful perspective. The answer, of course, lay with the poisoned comb. Its very presence at the side of Mrs. Staunton's body finally suggested the true, the only possible solution."

"I make some claim to belated credit," he went on, "for remembering Mrs. Grant's words in connection with the poisoned instrument. But the truth is that I was woefully lacking in the mixture of imagination and exact knowledge which you are so fond of depicting. I also claim extenuating circumstances—for what man can cope with the warped mind of a vindictive woman, consumed by a hatred beyond description and a terrible sense of loss?"

I drew a deep breath. "Holmes," I begged, "who poisoned the comb? Who brought it back to the house?"

"Is it not obvious that it was—that it could only have been—Mrs. Staunton herself?"

"Good heavens!" I exclaimed aghast, staring wildly at his set features, my mind in a turmoil. "Do you mean to say that she . . . she actually committed suicide in that terrible fashion?"

"The facts speak for themselves, Watson. No other interpretation is possible."

"But why on earth could she not have gone to the police?" I asked, more calmly, now that the first shock had passed. "If she suspected, or knew, that her husband had murdered her lover, why could she not have brought the matter to their attention by less involved means? Why not a direct accusation?"

"And have the facts of her adulterous relationship aired in open court, to be later blazoned upon every newspaper in the kingdom?" he inquired sardonically. "Really, Watson," he went on, shaking his head in a puzzled manner, "I never quite get your limitations. Do you still fail to grasp the fact that her suicide, as you call it—that her self-murder, rather—was purely incidental to her scheme of revenge? That by purposely using the same poison—thereby attracting the attention of the police—she sent to the scaffold the man who had destroyed her lover?"

"Then Staunton's reiterated denials of all complicity in her death were justified?" I said, musingly.

"Entirely so," he replied. "Yet who believed him? Did not counsel for the prosecution stress the fact that Staunton, by insisting that his wife had committed suicide, hoped to escape the extreme penalty? It was futile effort, for without any doubt her violent death swayed the jury when they rendered their verdict."

"I wonder how she learned about the poison and its fearful properties?" I said, after a spell of silence. "Any theories, Holmes?"

He moved his head dubiously. "There, my dear Watson, we trespass into the field of surmise and conjecture. A wife has her own methods of finding out her husband's secrets. An unguarded word, a threat from him, perhaps even a boast as to the manner in which he had removed his young rival—any of these may have given her an inkling of the truth. The fact that she made use of it with such telling effect amply proves that she was fully aware of its potentialities. We shall have to be content with that."

"It was a fearful revenge, Holmes," I said, breaking into the long silence which followed his last words. "Yet, somehow, I cannot find it in my heart to condemn her too bitterly."

"And I," said my friend, reaching out for his pouch, "find that for the third time in my career, I have been beaten by a woman. Yet I cannot say that I shall ever begrudge Mrs. Staunton her triumph!"

*R*OBERTA *R*OGOW *wrote this cleverly titled, carefully researched adventure (see Appendix I) especially for* The Game Is Afoot. *A New Jersey children's librarian, she compiled* Futurespeak: A Fan's Guide to the Language of Science Fiction *(Paragon, 1991) and contributes fiction to the* Merovingen Nights *anthologies and to small press periodicals.*

Our American Cousins

ROBERTA ROGOW

It was a glorious morning in June of 1905 when I paid an early morning visit to my friend, Sherlock Holmes. The English weather had turned unaccountably mild, with not a cloud in the sky to mar its vivid blue. The very sparrows chirped with more vigor. And yet, my friend was wrapped in one of his darkest moods.

I found him standing by the window, smoking his old pipe, contemplating the crowds thronging Baker Street.

In vain I pleaded with him to join me in a stroll through the streets and parks of London. I expostulated on the benefits of fresh air on the lungs.

"The late Queen, God rest her blessed soul, was taken for rides in the fresh air almost to the end of her life," I told him, waving away the smoke that wreathed his brow.

"Fresh air? To what end?" Holmes said gloomily. "To join the mob below us? I have noted three horseless carriages pass in the last half-hour. I begin to wonder if I did well by returning from the Continent to set up my practice again. My best days are over, Watson. There are no more interesting cases left for me."

I waved my morning *Times* at him. "Nonsense, Holmes! You must not permit yourself this apathy. We are living in an age of miracles! Here, in the newspaper, are accounts that would be considered unbelievable only a few years ago. A flying machine has been tested by the Frenchman Bleriot! A cure for malaria has been discovered! The American President has actually brought the Russian and Japanese War to a standstill, and is playing host to a peace conference at his summer home!"

Holmes was not to be brought out of his despondency. "Americans are all very well in their place, which is their own country. Now, thanks to Mr. Thomas Cook and his ilk, they are able to travel to our shores, where they congregate in public places and comment, loudly, on our customs and manners. Unfortunately, thanks in part to your chronicles of our work together, they regard this address as one of those public places, and persist in staring at my window as if it were some sort of raree-show. For instance, the young couple across the road are Americans. They are of good family, but not wealthy themselves. They are recently married. She was educated in England, but he is unfamiliar with our ways. He has recently come down from one of their more prestigious universities, but until they come to consult me, I will not be able to tell for certain if it is Harvard or Yale."

I drew near enough to the window to follow his gaze. Across the busy road were a tall young man and woman, holding an animated discussion. All I could see of them were the tops of their hats, in his case a rakish straw boater, in hers, a tower of tulle and artificial flowers.

"How can you be so sure they are Americans, and whether they are here to consult you?" I asked.

"That they are Americans is obvious by the cut of his suit and most particularly his hat, which is the style favored by young men in their last year at Harvard or Yale University. Their dress is fashionable, but not expensive, and their shoes have been mended, indicating a turn for economy. The young woman is, very properly, wearing gloves, but the young man is not, and his wedding-ring is noticeably bright. He fidgets with it, as if unused to its presence, from which I can deduce they have not been married long. As for their familiarity with English customs, when they crossed the road, he looked to the left to check the oncoming traffic, while she looked to the right. Americans habitually keep to the right-hand side of the road."

"Of course. And how do you know they are not mere curiosity-seekers?"

Holmes smiled. "When the young man points forcibly at this window and expostulates with his wife, one may deduce a morning call." A knock on the door downstairs gave Holmes the satisfaction of being, as always, right.

Mrs. Hudson appeared to announce: "Mr. and Mrs. Franklin Delano Roosevelt, to see Mr. Holmes."

"Without an appointment?" I said.

"Show them in, Mrs. Hudson," Holmes said grandly. "I'm surprised at you, Watson. Such an avid follower of current events should recognize the name of the President of the United States!"

"But . . ." I sputtered.

Holmes indulged himself in a smile. "Of course this is not the famous Rough Rider himself," he said.

Mr. and Mrs. Roosevelt were, indeed, nothing like the stout, mustachioed American President in appearance. Both were quite young. Mr. Roosevelt was strikingly handsome, with clean-cut features, an aquiline nose and chiseled jaw, a ready smile and blue eyes, with an air of impetuous vitality, dressed in a cream-colored suit and tattersall waistcoat, topped with that infamous straw boater. Mrs. Roosevelt was much more reserved in manner. When she raised her head to speak (in a soft, high voice), I could see that she was what the Americans call "plain", with fine, fair hair bundled under that immense hat, clear blue eyes, and a mouthful of protruding teeth. She was dressed in a pale peach-colored summer frock trimmed with cream-colored lace. She followed her husband into the room and sat down on one of the chairs near the table by the window, with her hands folded over her parasol.

Mr. Roosevelt bounded forward to shake Holmes by the hand. "Thank you for seeing us, Sir," he said. "I know you usually insist on an appointment, but you see, we're on our honeymoon, and we only have a little time in London before we move on to Paris and Venice."

Holmes shot a triumphant glance at me and indicated two chairs for his guests. "Your name is not unknown, Mr. Roosevelt," he said.

Mrs. Roosevelt spoke from her place near the window. "We cannot get out of the shadow of my Uncle Ted," she said ruefully, in a high and tremulous voice. "Franklin, I really feel we are imposing on Mr. Holmes . . ."

"Now, Babs," her husband expostulated. "We've been over this twice. I'm sure there's more to this than meets the eye."

"Since I have no idea what is wrong," Holmes interrupted them, "I must request enlightenment. What brings the relations of the American leader to my door?"

Mrs. Roosevelt clenched her hands tighter. "A letter is missing," she said.

Holmes raised his eyebrows. "A compromising letter?"

Mr. Roosevelt shook his head. "A perfectly ordinary family letter from Cousin Theodore. It came in last night's mail. It must have chased us clear across the Atlantic, for we only arrived the day before yesterday, and we were planning to leave London for Paris the day after tomorrow."

Mrs. Roosevelt took up the tale. "We received the letter last night, when we went up to our rooms to dress for dinner. I glanced over the letter, meaning to answer it when we got back, so as to mail it this morning. However, when I went to look for it in my writing-case, it was gone!"

Holmes puffed on his pipe. "Interesting. I take it you have already searched for this letter?"

Mrs. Roosevelt colored. "I am not in the habit of leaving my personal correspondence about, Mr. Holmes. I know I placed the letter into my writing-case before we went to dinner. It was most certainly not there when I returned. It is quite trivial, of course; far too inconsequential to summon the police . . ." Her voice trailed off, and she looked at her young husband. He took up the chorus.

"I can't make sense of it, Mr. Holmes. Autograph-hounds are always looking for Cousin Theodore's signature, and he's always 'Dee-lighted!' to oblige them. But a personal letter? Not a likely thing to lift, is it?"

"Indeed." Holmes frowned. "Can you recall the contents of the letter?"

Mrs. Roosevelt shrugged slightly. "Family gossip, no more. My cousin Alice has been before a magistrate again . . ."

"What?" I uttered. Here was a juicy cause for scandal, surely?

Mr. Roosevelt dismissed it with a laugh, "For driving her roadster 40 miles an hour while smoking cigarettes. Hardly a cause for blackmail."

Holmes agreed. "The escapades of Miss Alice Roosevelt have been noted in the public press, Watson. One cannot blackmail someone whose guilty secrets are already known. Continue, Mrs. Roosevelt. What else was in the letter?"

Mrs. Roosevelt frowned. "My Aunt Edith is worried about the coming peace conference at Sagamore Hill."

Holmes leaned forward eagerly. Mr. Roosevelt continued: "It seems that the Russians have brought such a large suite that she is in despair as to where to house them all, and some of her servants refuse to wait on the Japanese."

Holmes leaned back in his chair, disappointed. "Nothing particularly useful there, either. Servant problems are worrisome, but not especially embarrassing, except to the householder, eh, Watson?"

Mrs. Roosevelt ignored this comment and continued her recollection. "And Uncle Ted is very enthusiastic about the progress of the digging of the canal across the Isthmus of Panama. He is even thinking of paying a visit to the Canal Zone himself, perhaps next year . . ."

"That, of course is not for publication," Mr. Roosevelt said. "There will be a certain outcry when Cousin Theodore announces his decision to go to Panama. The President of the United States *never* leaves the country while in office. Of course, Cousin Theodore has done a number of things that the President of the United States has never done before, so one more will make little difference. But you do see the implications, Mr. Holmes."

Holmes nodded. "Yes, I do. The activities of the President are of interest to a number of people, not all of whom wish him well. As I recall, his predecessor suffered a fatal accident."

Mrs. Roosevelt gasped. "Oh, dear! Do you think some horrid anarchist would use the information in this letter . . . Oh, no!"

Mr. Roosevelt stood behind her and patted her shoulder. "Don't worry, Babs, Mr. Holmes will find the letter. Won't you, Mr. Holmes?" He turned that brilliant smile on my friend, who matched it with one of his own.

"I shall certainly do my best to solve this little problem, Mr. Roosevelt," he said. "Where are you staying while you are in London?"

"We're at Brown's Hotel," Mr. Roosevelt said. "Once they saw the magic Name they insisted on giving us the Royal Suite."

"It's far too large for us," Mrs. Roosevelt twittered. "It takes up most of the floor. I understand the other suite is being made ready for a visit from the Archbishop of York. I should very much like to meet him."

"Yes, Babs," her husband interrupted. "Now, Mr. Holmes, I've already thought about this affair. The hall porter swears no one came onto our floor while we were out, and Brown's isn't the sort of place where strangers wander in off the street."

Holmes regarded the young pair with cool eyes. "Quite right," he said. "May I ask your plans for the rest of the day?"

"I was going to visit my old school," Mrs. Roosevelt said. "I spent several years at Allenwood, near London. Alas, my dear old mistress is no longer with us, but I thought Franklin and I could see the grounds . . ."

"I have to see Barclays' Bank about some more money," Mr. Roosevelt said. "You go on without me, Babs."

She said nothing, but bowed her head meekly.

"I will make some inquiries, and we can meet at Brown's Hotel for tea, at four o'clock this afternoon," Holmes said. "I will undoubtedly have more information for you then."

Mrs. Roosevelt rose from her chair, and Holmes escorted the couple to the door.

"By the by, Mr. Roosevelt," he asked, as an afterthought, "when did you leave Harvard?"

The young man grinned. "That's good, Mr. Holmes! I'm not exactly out of school yet. I've got a few final exams to make up. But it was Harvard, all right! How did you know?"

Holmes tapped the straw hat, which was still in Mr. Roosevelt's hand. "You can almost always tell where a man is from by his hat," he said. "I shall see you both at Brown's."

Having shown Mr. and Mrs. Roosevelt out, he turned to me with a wink. "Well, Watson, what do you make of this Purloined Letter?"

"On the face of it, it seems a trivial matter," I said, as Holmes divested himself of his dressing-gown and shrugged into his coat. "A personal letter, from a gentleman to his niece who is on her honeymoon, discussing family matters which would, under any other circumstances, be of no interest to anyone else. I do not see why anyone would want to take it."

"Unless, as young Mr. Roosevelt suspects, the information that the peripatetic President has decided to inspect the work at Panama gets into the hands of assassins. I believe, Watson, that the best place to begin is at Brown's Hotel."

*B*rown's is a discreet hotel, a resting-place for travelling clergy, military men, and gentry and their families, run along the lines of a well-appointed town house from which the host has, for some inexplicable reason, absented himself. We were greeted by the manager, a most genteel person in proper morning dress, who wrung his hands at the thought of one of his guests being imposed upon to the extent of having personal correspondence removed.

"This is a most respectable establishment," he insisted. "Is it not, Mrs. Dawson?"

Mrs. Dawson, the housekeeper, a majestic female of overwhelming dignity, agreed. "Nothing like this has ever happened at Brown's," she insisted. "We keep strict order here. Only our guests are permitted past the first storey. Our servants are of the highest character. They have all come to us with excellent references."

"Undoubtedly," I said, to mollify the outraged woman.

"None of my girls would dream of removing anything from a guest's room that was not clearly meant to be removed," she insisted. "They'd be let go at once . . . without a character!"

"And Mr. and Mrs. Roosevelt's servants?" Holmes asked.

Mrs. Dawson looked, if anything, more affronted. "They do not travel with servants," she said. "Mr. Brown was quite taken aback when they arrived, quite alone, without even so much as a maid for Mrs. Roosevelt."

Holmes raised an eyebrow at this revelation. I privately wondered who, if anyone, did up Mrs. Roosevelt's buttons and stays, which, as I recalled from my own married days, could be a tedious task.

Holmes's voice broke into my domestic reverie. "I should like to see the rooms used by Mr. and Mrs. Roosevelt," Holmes requested. The housekeeper led us up a flight of stairs to a large suite, consisting of two bed-rooms, a sitting-room, and a private bath. Holmes glanced at both bed-rooms, noting that one seemed to be strewn with male attire, while the other was much tidier. Steamer-trunks were laid out in both rooms.

Holmes went over the room with his lens. The furnishings were comfortable rather than opulent, of cherry-wood and mahogany, with a round table in the middle of the sitting-room flanked by a pair of arm-chairs, an upholstered sofa along one wall, and a well-appointed cherry-wood desk between the two windows facing the street. Light was provided by an electric chandelier, the sole accommodation to the Twentieth Century. Holmes carefully went over the desk, which had been furnished with writing paper, pens, blotting-paper and ink. Holmes inspected the writing-materials closely and nodded. He opened the center drawer of the desk and pointed out the marbled-paper writing-case.

"Not locked away, Watson. Quite easy for anyone to get into . . . provided one knew where to look. Now, we'll see the chambermaid."

Mrs. Dawson at once insisted on being present when the girl was questioned. "If that minx has been up to some deviltry, out she goes!" she threatened.

The chambermaid, a pert-looking Cockney miss, whose uptilted nose was well-spattered with freckles, arrived with one of her cohorts, somewhat breathless from having been summoned from the kitchen, where she had been having her luncheon. Mrs. Dawson, the housekeeper, glared at her.

"Now Betty, these gentlemen want to know about that letter you took from Mrs. Roosevelt's desk," the housekeeper stated.

The maid began to expostulate with us at once. "I never took nothing," she said shrilly. "Who's giving me a bad character?"

"The letter is missing," Holmes said. "It was not left on the desk, nor is any other personal item in plain sight. No one could have come into this room between the time the letter was received and the time it was found missing but yourself. Ergo, Miss Betty, I think you had better come clean, and tell us exactly who put you up to it!"

"And then you can pack up your things and get out!" Mrs. Dawson added.

Holmes advanced upon the girl, who shrank back, convincingly.

From the corridor outside the room came a sudden flurry of expostulation. "Mrs. Roosevelt, you can't go in there!"

The high-pitched voice of our morning visitor came clearly through the door. "And why, pray, may I not enter my own rooms?"

Holmes and I looked up to see Mrs. Roosevelt descending upon us. Her former diffidence had been replaced by outraged indignation. "Mr. Holmes! There is no need to browbeat the young woman!"

Holmes took a deep breath. "Mrs. Roosevelt," he said, in a more moderate tone. "It is obvious that this girl removed your letter from its place. I cannot believe she did it of her own accord."

"Nor can I," Mrs. Roosevelt said, striding into the room. "But there is an old saying about flies and honey, is there not?" She led Betty to the sofa and indicated that the girl should sit beside her, much to Mrs. Dawson's disgust and Holmes's astonishment.

"Now, my dear," Mrs. Roosevelt said, patting the girl's work-worn hand. "Mr. Holmes did not mean to upset you. I'm sure you had a very good reason for wanting a look at a letter from Mr. Roosevelt of America."

Betty began to snivel. "Oh, ma'am, I never meant no harm! It was my young man, you see. He's ever so interested in the people what comes to Brown's. I told 'im as 'ow you and your Mister was related to the American President, which Mrs. Dawson says is like the Prime Minister, and 'e said as 'e wished 'e could see somethink from Mr. Roosevelt. So I nipped up 'ere and took the letter, and I swear, ma'am, I meant no 'arm! I was going to put it back, but old Mrs. Emory rang, and with one thing and another . . ." She sniffed pathetically. I exchanged speaking glances with Holmes. Mrs. Roosevelt appeared to be taken in by this blatant attempt to play on her sympathies.

"Do you enjoy your work here?" Mrs. Roosevelt asked, apparently with genuine concern.

"Oh, yes, ma'am. Most of our people are very nice and respectable. Not flashy, like what they gets at the Ritz or the Savoy, and no goings-on, like what they has at the Cavendish, but real quality. County, is what Mrs. Dawson calls 'em. They always gives me a nice present when they leaves."

"I hope Mr. Roosevelt and I are a credit to the establishment," Mrs. Roosevelt said, entirely without irony.

"Oh, yes, ma'am. I see now that I was wrong to take the letter."

"It is a family matter," Mrs. Roosevelt said, leaning forward confidentially. "The letter was from my uncle, and he would be most displeased if I didn't answer it."

Betty nodded, a red-brown curl escaping from under her cap. "I had an auntie the same way. I told Lucy, what does for the third floor, to put the letter back into my things when Diego was done with it. It should be there right now."

"We shall accompany you," Holmes said.

"I should like to see where the servants live," Mrs. Roosevelt announced, sending Mrs. Dawson into near apoplexy. "I have worked among the Poor," she added, as she followed me up the winding back-stairs to the servants' dormitories. "Working conditions for servants are truly deplorable. Something should be done about them."

Mrs. Dawson insisted on accompanying Holmes, Mrs. Roosevelt, Betty and myself to the top of the house, where the chambermaids were housed in a barren barracks of a room. Mrs. Roosevelt shook her head at the primitive sanitary accommodations. Holmes was more interested in the pathetic possessions that Betty had accumulated, which she kept in a small chest at the foot of her bed.

"I see your young man is a world-traveller," he said, thumbing a packet of garish picture-postal cards. "Stoker on a freighter. Is he in port?"

"How did you know?" Betty asked, round-eyed. "Stoker, he is, going to go for his certificate as soon as ever he can. See the nice things he sent me?" She displayed a hideous ivory elephant and a necklace made of palm-nuts and brightly-colored seeds.

Mrs. Roosevelt smiled faintly at these trinkets. "Where is the letter?" she asked anxiously.

"Lucy said she put it here," Betty said, diving into her box. She looked up blankly. "It's gone! She said she put it back, but Diego must have took it with him when I went to see after Mrs. Emory!" She burst into tears.

Mrs. Dawson was down upon the girl like a hawk. "Seeing young men is quite against the rules!" she hissed.

"It was only for a minute, Mrs. Dawson, and I didn't see him, he saw me!" Betty whined. "All he did was come into the kitchen, to ask if I could see him off tonight. I was going to ask you if I could, after supper?"

Mrs. Dawson began to draw herself up for some terrific denunciation. Mrs. Roosevelt interrupted. "I am sure Mrs. Dawson would have been willing to let you see your young man off, Betty, but you should not have taken it upon yourself to do so. As for my letter, that was very bad of you. Curiosity aside, you must never read other people's correspondence. However, I am convinced that you are not to blame for this incident. You must love your Diego very much, to risk your employment for him."

Betty nodded. "Oh, ma'am, 'e's so romantic! And so 'andsome!"

Mrs. Roosevelt smiled, understandingly. "Then you are no worse than many women, who will do anything for their men. I think you should get back to your work now."

Betty glanced at the housekeeper. Mrs. Dawson looked thunderous.

"I would be most distressed if the girl were to lose her position on our account," Mrs. Roosevelt said gently.

"It better not happen again," Mrs. Dawson growled.

Betty's regard for Mrs. Roosevelt now approached the worshipful. Holmes frowned and began to pace, difficult though it was in that crowded room.

"Mrs. Roosevelt," he said finally. "You have been of great assistance. Thanks to you, I can now proceed with my inquiries elsewhere. Watson, will you escort Mrs. Roosevelt to her own rooms? We shall meet for tea, in the lounge, at four o'clock this afternoon. I should have more information for you then." Holmes whirled out of the room, leaving me to mollify Mrs. Dawson, while Mrs. Roosevelt gave Betty a "nice present" which was, I suspected, quite generous.

Tea at Brown's is a ritual not to be missed. It is not served in the dining-room, but in the lounge, which is fitted up like a drawing-room in a town house, with chairs of many sizes set beside small tables on which soft-footed waiters may deposit sandwiches, cakes, and, of course, tea, while American, German, and French tourists sigh and say how very English it all is.

Nothing will convince them that the average Englishman does not indulge in such ample fare every day.

Mrs. Roosevelt and I sat, enthroned in roomy armchairs, with tea and cakes before us, waiting for Holmes, when Mr. Roosevelt breezed in and snatched a handful of cucumber sandwiches off the nearest tray, to the scandalized horror of the waiter.

"I've had an excellent day, Babs. Got two fine prints and a Marryat First Edition. Mamma will have to fit the prints onto a wall, somehow, when she does my bedroom. How was your school?"

Mrs. Roosevelt flushed. "I had forgotten, Franklin, it is their holiday. The school was closed, so I had to return early. Mr. Holmes was questioning the chambermaid. She did take the letter, just as you thought, but she seems to have lost it."

Mr. Roosevelt made an impatient noise. "Babs, this won't do! We leave for France day after tomorrow, and we can't go off without warning Cousin Theodore that someone is after him. I wanted to look at some more bookstores, too . . . what's that?"

Our repast was interrupted by a disturbance in the foyer. The concessionaire, a stout man with a military air, was endeavoring to remove what can best be described as an Elderly Naval Person, a stooping old man in a much-stained pea-jacket and bell-bottom trousers, with a mane of white hair streaming out from under a seaman's cap, from the lounge. A strong aroma of gin followed the old sailor as he invaded the lounge, loudly insisting on seeing me!

"I tell you, you can't go in there! That's for guests," the concessionaire shouted.

"And I tells you, you lubber, that I've a good mind to report you! I'm here a-purpose to see Dr. Watson, with a message from Mr. Sherlock Holmes!"

"I'm Dr. Watson," I said. "What's this about a message?"

"Mr. Sherlock 'Olmes says that you're to meet 'im where I'm ter show yer, this very night," said the old sailor, who looked and smelled much the worse for drink.

Mr. Roosevelt looked at his wife. "This must be about that letter," he said. "Dr. Watson, I'm going with you. Babs, you'll have to go to the dinner party without me."

Mrs. Roosevelt looked stricken. "I . . . I can't!" she barely whispered. I could hardly believe this was the same woman who had faced down the dragon of a housekeeper not two hours before. "I don't know any of these people! What shall I say?"

"Oh, tell them all about Cousin Alice," Mr. Roosevelt said breezily. "That's all they want to know anyway. You'll do all right, Babs, if you'll just forget this silly shyness of yours."

Mrs. Roosevelt gulped slightly. "Yes, Franklin," she said meekly. I wondered at the callousness of the young man, who let his inexperienced bride face the perils of a London dinner-party alone. I have known several men of my own age who have admitted they would rather face Afghan fire than attend such a function without a helpmate.

"Wait for me, Dr. Watson. Here, old boy, have some of these; you look as if you need them!" Mr. Roosevelt delivered a plate of cucumber sandwiches into the old man's hands, and hurried his wife up the stairs, leaving me to deal with the concessionaire. I led the old man into the hall, where he sat down on the wooden bench provided for waiting servants and wolfed down the sandwiches. I looked carefully at his garb as he munched his sandwiches. Surely I had seen that stained jacket before, in the wardrobe where Holmes kept his disguises? I decided to say nothing. If my old friend wished to hide his identity from his client, he undoubtedly had a good reason for doing so.

Some twenty minutes later, Mr. Roosevelt reappeared, having traded his cream-colored suit for a disreputable-looking hacking-jacket worn over a gray-brown knitted jersey. Corduroy trousers completed this ensemble.

"Come along, Doctor," he said, with an infectious laugh. "Let's see where our sea-going friend takes us."

"Do be careful, Franklin," pleaded his wife, from her position on the landing.

He waved gaily. "Don't worry about me, Babs. Just think of the look on Cousin Theodore's face when I cap one of his stories with this one!"

He bounded out of the hotel into the streets, followed by the old salt and myself.

The June sun was giving way to drifting wisps of fog as the elderly sailor led us by circuitous ways through the slums of Whitechapel to the riverfront. There he stopped to catch his breath beneath a lantern illuminating a tavern sign.

"Which ship is it, Mr. Holmes?" Mr. Roosevelt asked, suddenly.

The bent figure before me straightened up. The grimy seaman's cap came off, and with it, the mane of white hair. It was, indeed, my old friend, as I suspected.

"How did you penetrate my disguise?" Holmes asked, not at all happy to be unmasked.

Mr. Roosevelt smiled apologetically. "I've had a little experience with amateur theatricals at Harvard, and I know greasepaint when I smell it. When I got close to you, I caught a whiff of it, although you did a good job covering it with that cheap gin. I know you're in the habit of disguising yourself, and I couldn't think why an old sailor would put make-up on his face . . . I guess it was, um, elementary?"

"I see," Holmes said, ruefully. "I thought I was losing my touch. To tell the truth, Mr. Roosevelt, I didn't expect you to join us on this expedition."

"You may be glad of my help before the night's over, Mr. Holmes," the American said seriously. "I'm not much of a shot with a pistol, but if you're going to the waterfront, you may need a boatman, and I can certainly help you there. I've been on the water since I was a boy, and I can handle almost anything that floats." This was said without bragging, a simple statement of fact.

Holmes nodded briefly. "Very well. We're going to that tavern over there. Leave the talking to me." He donned his disguise once more. Mr. Roosevelt took a soft cap from his jacket pocket and pulled it on, tilting it over one eye so that he looked a very tough customer. I followed, wondering what any of the denizens of the neighborhood would make of a respectable sort like myself in this insalubrious place. If asked, I decided, I could always fall back on my profession. One could summon a doctor anywhere, and he would probably come!

The tavern in question was adorned with the sign of LA PALOMA. Inside, the air was heavy with cheap cigar-smoke and stank of rum. Holmes and Roosevelt spoke to the barman, while I remained in the shadows, trying to hear what was being said.

"I was right," Holmes said, with satisfaction. "And so were you, Mr. Roosevelt. Your boatman's skills are going to be needed tonight. The game's afoot!"

He led us through the twisting alleys to a tumble-down house, in the shadow of London Bridge. We could smell the effluvium of the river, and hear its rush almost at our feet.

Holmes pounded on the door of the house.

"*Que pasa?*" A slatternly woman put her head out the first-story window.

"*Donde esté Diego Mendez?*" Holmes shouted.

"I don' know no body call' Mendez," the landlady yelled back, slamming the window.

"There he goes!" Roosevelt pointed to a figure bolting from an alley.

"Mendez! Stop! We know all!" Holmes shouted. "*Alto!*"

The man stopped and turned. "*Al diablo, Yanquí!*" he shouted. Then he turned and redoubled his efforts to reach the bridge, which would lead him to the shipyards across the river. We pounded after him, splashing through unnamed and unidentifiable muck.

"He's headed for the bridge!" Roosevelt shouted.

"For his ship," Holmes amended. "The *Simon Bolivar* out of Cartagena. It sails with the tide. We must stop him before it leaves!"

We could see the ship, outlined in black against the red-orange of the setting sun, at the docks across the river. Mendez had reached the riverbank and cast about for a way to reach his ship. There were several boatman's wherries pulled up on the banks. He quickly launched one, and began to row.

Roosevelt and Holmes commandeered another boat. I helped shove it into the turbulent Thames and held on for dear life as Roosevelt took the oars.

The currents of the river seemed to seize the tiny boat even as we struck into the water. Mendez, if that was him, was in difficulty from the moment that he dipped his oars, whereas Mr. Roosevelt cleverly kept the boat on course.

Holmes leaned over the side of our dangerously rocking boat. "It's no use, Mendez! We know your plot! The President will be on guard!" he shouted.

As we watched with horrified eyes, the current pulled the oars from the rower's hands. He hung on to the boat with both hands. Roosevelt bent his back, putting every ounce of his skill into maneuvering the craft through this unknown watercourse. The current had the other boat well in its grip, and was reluctant to let it go. Try as he might, young Mr. Roosevelt could not quite reach the other boat.

We were, by this time, in the very middle of the river, where the current shoots through the arches of London Bridge. Mendez shrieked as his boat spun out of control. Roosevelt's face was set and I could see the tautness of his arms as he held us steady.

Then Mendez gave a great cry, and I echoed it as his wherry was pulled inexorably toward the bridge. With a despairing shout, he fell overboard.

Roosevelt struggled with the oars, but could not reach the drowning man. Holmes sat down and said, "Better get us back to shore, Mr. Roosevelt. And then, I think, we could all use a stiff drink."

Mr. Roosevelt rowed back to the bank, where the rightful owners of the wherries stood, furious that they had been taken without permission. It was only after Holmes and I had promised to repay the boatman for the loss of his livelihood that we could get back to Civilization, i.e., London Bridge and a hansom that would take us to Baker Street.

Nearly an hour later, Holmes was himself again. The stage-paint was off his face, and young Mr. Roosevelt and I were well-fortified with stiff brandy-and-sodas.

"Explanations, please, Mr. Holmes," Mr. Roosevelt demanded. "I follow as far as the waterfront. My Cousin Theodore's planned trip to Panama must be the key, but where does this Mendez come in?"

Holmes made himself comfortable in his own chair and began to fill his pipe. "In the chambermaid's room I saw picture postal-cards bearing stamps from Colombia. As I recall, the Isthmus of Panama was once considered Colombian territory. I deduced, therefore, that someone of Colombian connections might well be interested in knowing of the whereabouts of your illustrious cousin, and particularly if he intended to come to Panama . . . and *when!*"

"And what led you to Mendez?"

"His first name was on the postal-cards, of course. He had left a thumb-print on one of them, which indicated a stoker or oiler, not a sailor. The chambermaid told us that the man's ship was sailing tonight. I made the rounds of the waterfront taverns that cater to South American sailors. Diego Mendez was the only Colombian stoker at large. He had been at the tavern La Paloma this afternoon, but by the time we got there, he had obviously returned to his lodgings to get his belongings."

Roosevelt sighed. "Very clever, Mr. Holmes. I'm only sorry the man died."

Holmes shrugged. "He was a rash and foolish man, Mr. Roosevelt. He acted impulsively, no doubt, when he heard that you and your wife were staying at Brown's Hotel. There is no telling what he might have done besides launching an attack on your illustrious relation."

"Oh, I doubt that it would have succeeded," Roosevelt said, with a grin. "It's going to take more than one assassin to remove Cousin Theodore from the scene. By the way . . . where is the letter?"

It was Holmes' turn to sigh. "The letter will undoubtedly be retrieved on the body of the late Diego Mendez. He would not trust such a potentially dangerous item to his seabag, but would carry it on his person. I do not think it will be legible, however."

"Then I can tell Eleanor that her uncle's secret is safe?"

"Until he decides to reveal it himself," Holmes said. "Good night, Mr. Roosevelt. I suggest you do not tell your wife all of our adventures. There is no need to worry her."

Mr. Roosevelt laughed heartily. "Oh, it takes a lot more than a boating accident to worry Eleanor. Good Lord! Look at the time! I might be able to get into my evening kit and get to that dinner party!"

He clattered down the stairs, and we could hear him hailing a cab in the street.

"Better stay the night, Watson," Holmes told me kindly. "You look all in."

So it was that I was still in Baker Street the next morning when Mr. and Mrs. Roosevelt called once more on Sherlock Holmes.

"We're just back from the Morgue," Mr. Roosevelt told us, after the usual pleasantries had been gone through. "The body of a seaman, Diego Mendez, was washed up early this morning. They found a letter on it, carefully wrapped in oiled cloth, with Cousin Theodore's signature on it, and sent for us to identify the body. Naturally, I said we'd never seen the fellow before. We explained that the letter was taken from our room, probably by some autograph-hunter, and we had no idea how it came to be in the possession of Mr. Mendez."

"There really was no need to get the poor chambermaid into any more difficulties," Mrs. Roosevelt said. "And that wretched man has already paid for his deed. I suppose it would have been impossible to charge him with anything tangible . . ." She turned to Holmes. "Franklin told me how brave you were, Mr. Holmes," Mrs. Roosevelt said. "And Dr. Watson, thank you for your kindness." She fumbled in her reticule. "I am aware that you usually accept a fee, or an honorarium . . ."

Holmes waved her away grandly. "The opportunity to be of assistance to so great a statesman as Mr. Theodore Roosevelt is payment enough," he said. "However, I would consider it an honor if I could add this letter to my collection of memorabilia from notable clients."

"Of course, Mr. Holmes," Mrs. Roosevelt said sweetly. She handed him the letter, still wrapped in its cloth. He took it with great ceremony and placed it next to the picture of the King of Bohemia on the mantel.

"Babs," her husband warned, "we still have to pack, and the boat train leaves early tomorrow morning."

"Yes, Franklin. Good-bye, Mr. Holmes."

Holmes stared thoughtfully down at them as they hailed their cab in Baker Street.

"An interesting pair," I commented. "He has a good deal of American energy, and she is genuinely interested in helping the Poor. One wonders what will become of them."

Holmes shrugged and turned away from the window. "She is, indeed, philanthropic, but is easily cowed by her husband. I suppose she will devote herself to her children and Good Works. As for Mr. Roosevelt, he is quite intelligent, and could make something of himself if he applied himself, but a young man who permits his mother to decorate his home, and marries before he is firmly established is far too flighty to succeed in the rough-and-tumble of America. No, Watson, I doubt that we will ever hear of either of them again."

Pieces Problematical

ARTHUR CONAN DOYLE *(1859–1930) wrote two breakfast-table scenes, "How Watson Learned the Trick" and "The Field Bazaar," that are customarily omitted from "complete" editions of the Sherlock Holmes tales. Holmesians tend to dismiss them as parodies by Dr. Watson's "literary agent," but I have always regarded them as privileged behind-the-scenes glimpses of Baker Street on occasions when no crucial case was pending and therefore, as happens in the best of friendships, the companions were oh-so-slightly getting on each other's nerves. Doyle wrote "The Field Bazaar" to help his alma mater, Edinburgh University, enlarge its cricket ground. The vignette was printed in the school magazine,* The Student, *on November 20, 1896.*

The Field Bazaar

ARTHUR CONAN DOYLE

"I should certainly do it," said Sherlock Holmes.

I started at the interruption, for my companion had been eating his breakfast with his attention entirely centred upon the paper which was propped up by the coffee pot. Now I looked across at him to find his eyes fastened upon me with the half-amused, half-questioning expression which he usually assumed when he felt that he had made an intellectual point.

"Do what?" I asked.

He smiled as he took his slipper from the mantelpiece and drew from it enough shag tobacco to fill the old clay pipe with which he invariably rounded off his breakfast.

"A most characteristic question of yours, Watson," said he. "You will not, I am sure, be offended if I say that any reputation for sharpness which I may possess has been entirely gained by the admirable foil which you have made for me. Have I not heard of debutantes who have insisted upon plainness in their chaperones? There is a certain analogy."

Our long companionship in the Baker Street rooms had left us on those easy terms of intimacy when much may be said without offence. And yet I acknowledge that I was nettled at his remark.

"I may be very obtuse," said I, "but I confess that I am unable to see how you have managed to know that I was . . . I was . . ."

"Asked to help in the Edinburgh University Bazaar."

"Precisely. The letter has only just come to hand, and I have not spoken to you since."

"In spite of that," said Holmes, leaning back in his chair and putting his finger tips together, "I would even venture to suggest that the object of the bazaar is to enlarge the University cricket field."

I looked at him in such bewilderment that he vibrated with silent laughter.

"The fact is, my dear Watson, that you are an excellent subject," said he. "You are never *blasé*. You respond instantly to any external stimulus. Your mental processes may be slow but they are never obscure, and I found during breakfast that you were easier reading than the leader in the *Times* in front of me."

"I should be glad to know how you arrived at your conclusions," said I.

"I fear that my good nature in giving explanations has seriously compromised my reputation," said Holmes. "But in this case the train of reasoning is based upon such obvious facts that no credit can be claimed for it. You entered the room with a thoughtful expression, the expression of a man who is debating some point in his mind. In your hand you held a solitary letter. Now last night you retired in the best of spirits, so it was clear that it was this letter in your hand which had caused the change in you."

"This is obvious."

"It is all obvious when it is explained to you. I naturally asked myself what the letter could contain which might have this effect upon you. As you walked you held the flap side of the envelope towards me, and I saw upon it the same shield-shaped device which I have observed upon your old college cricket cap. It was clear, then, that the request came from Edinburgh University—or from some club connected with the University. When you reached the table you laid down the letter beside your plate with the address uppermost, and you walked over to look at the framed photograph upon the left of the mantelpiece."

It amazed me to see the accuracy with which he had observed my movements. "What next?" I asked.

"I began by glancing at the address, and I could tell, even at the distance of six feet, that it was an unofficial communication. This I gathered from the use of the word 'Doctor' upon the address, to which, as a Bachelor of Medicine, you have no legal claim. I knew that University officials are pedantic in their correct use of titles, and I was thus enabled to say with certainty that your letter was unofficial. When on your return to the table you turned over your letter and allowed me to perceive that the enclosure was a printed one, the idea of a bazaar first occurred to me. I had already weighed the possibility of its being a political communication, but this seemed improbable in the present stagnant condition of politics.

"When you returned to the table, your face still retained its expression and it was evident that your examination of the photograph had not changed the current of your thoughts. In that case it must itself bear upon the subject in question. I turned my attention to the photograph, therefore, and saw at once that it consisted of yourself as a member of the Edinburgh University Eleven, with the pavilion and cricket-field in the background. My small experience of cricket clubs has taught me that next to churches and cavalry ensigns they are the most debt-laden things upon earth. When upon your return to the table I saw you take out your pencil and draw lines upon the envelope, I was convinced that you were endeavouring to realize some projected improvement which was to be brought about by a bazaar. Your face still showed some indecision, so that I was able to break in upon you with my advice that you should assist in so good an object."

I could not help smiling at the extreme simplicity of his explanation.

"Of course, it was as easy as possible," said I.

My remark appeared to nettle him.

"I may add," said he, "that the particular help which you have been asked to give was that you should write in their album, and that you have already made up your mind that the present incident will be the subject of your article."

"But how—!" I cried.

"It is as easy as possible," said he, "and I leave its solution to your own ingenuity. In the meantime," he added, raising his paper, "you will excuse me if I return to this very interesting article upon the trees of Cremona, and the exact reasons for their pre-eminence in the manufacture of violins. It is one of those small outlying problems to which I am sometimes tempted to direct my attention."

*S*herlock's reading public heaved a sigh of relief on learning that their hero survived Reichenbach Falls, but soon Dr. Watson revealed news nearly as dreadful: the great sleuth had retired to become a Sussex beekeeper on "a small farm upon the Downs, five miles from Eastbourne . . ." It was inevitable that the press would seek out The Great Man in his (sudden) retirement. Such a case was chronicled by PERCIVAL MASON STONE, who wrote numerous Holmesian essays.

Sussex Interview

P. M. STONE

"Come, come, Mr. Holmes," I countered in a final desperate effort to ward off a curt dismissal. "After all, you must admit, you owe it to posterity that these base insinuations, aimed to discountenance your former exploits, should be checked. Again," I added, gathering courage as I observed that the venerable detective had reseated himself by the fire, "this matter of dates in the Watson chronology. A fine mess he has made of them it seems and a brief statement from you might close an interminable controversy."

"Quite true, young man, quite true," came the slow response, as Sherlock Holmes relighted his pipe and gazed reflectively across the low fender into the fire. I exulted with relief that I had in some manner touched a responsive chord and waited eagerly for his final pronouncement upon my singular quest.

It had been, indeed, a momentous day. Brett, my chief, had finally assented to what he termed a preposterous mission, and I had set forth that morning at 10 o'clock from Victoria, determined that before nightfall I would secure for my paper an interview with Sherlock Holmes. I had, through devious influential channels at Scotland Yard, finally ascertained his address; and upon arrival at Crown Lydgate, just beyond Amberley, a brisk three mile walk across the downs by way of a well-defined drover's path had brought me at length to my goal.

The spot selected by the renowned detective for his retirement was one of remote seclusion. Situated far from the teeming centre of his several crime investigations, the remodeled Tudor farm-house rested in a hollow of the Sussex downs; a winding private roadway was visible westward leading towards Chichester, and in the foreground, at the summit of the slope, stood a small latticed pavilion which afforded a magnificent view of the distant sea.

Upon arrival at a stone gate-house which marked the termination of my upland course I was admitted to the precincts of Faraway by an aged retainer of dour countenance who had evidently been apprized of my coming. Telford at the Yard held, I knew, intermittent communication with Holmes and the Inspector had promised to telephone a brief message by way of introduction.

On being ushered into the spacious library of the house, a few moments later, I was at once impressed with its close resemblance to the picture so familiar to all students of the Baker Street menage. A large oval table, littered with an accumulation of books, manuscript paper and other writing material, occupied the centre of the room; at one side of the wide hearth stood a huge oaken settle, and through the open doorway at my right I caught sight of what was evidently a laboratory, for the shelves revealed rows of bottles and chemical apparatus, while the presence of a small, brick-coated blast furnace indicated that Holmes had not entirely renounced his fond proclivity for research.

A moment later Sherlock Holmes rose from his high-backed arm chair at the farther side of the table and extended to me a cordial welcome. Time had, in fact, touched him with a gentle hand. His spare figure, tall and with the slight stoop at the shoulders, revealed to the unprofessional eye no indication of declining vigor, and a glance at the pile of manuscript gave evidence of those astonishing intellectual forces which had brought him to the pinnacle of a distinguished career.

Within the range of my vision I presently detected one or two other reminders of the London lodgings in Baker Street, long familiar to me through a close study of the Watson chronicles. In a corner of the settle by the fireside stood the worn violin case; the Persian slipper, once the favored receptacle for Holmes' tobacco (one wonders to what use its mate was ever destined), was fastened to the wall close by the bell rope, and carelessly thrown over the end of a long couch I noted a blue dressing gown which had probably been worn by the detective during the early morning hours of work upon his manuscript.

"Great Heavens," I observed, inwardly, "can this be the same garment about which such heated controversy has been waged? And, if such be the case, where is the equally famous mouse-colored gown that figured so prominently in the adventure of *The Empty House?* But, after all," I reflected, "Mrs. Hudson may have held one in reserve, for her lodger was notoriously careless when engaged with his chemical experiments."

A modern touch was added to the room's equipment by the presence of a tall, steel filing cabinet placed in the deep window alcove. This contained, I surmised, a complete card reference pertaining to his innumerable investigations.

Of the familiar morocco case and the syringe which once drew Watson's indignant protests, there was no sign whatever. Long since, no doubt, the detective had renounced this avenue of escape from physical exhaustion, and a solution of 7 per cent. cocaine held for him no further allurements.

It was easily observed that I had interrupted him at some laborious task; possibly, I judged from the array of papers and note-books before him, his long awaited compendium of Crime and Detection. He evinced, however, no irritability at being for the moment turned aside from this monumental task and, asking me to be seated, gave a tug at the long bell rope which hung at one side of the fire-place. An elderly woman responded presently and my host requested that sherry and biscuits be brought in, since luncheon was not to be served until an hour later.

"Mrs. Hudson is, I regret to say, no longer in service here," Holmes remarked a moment later, noting my inquiring glance as the door closed behind the housekeeper's retreating figure. "Martha did in fact come to my assistance shortly after my retirement, but a year or more ago I pensioned her off and the good woman is now residing with a niece in Cumberland. A loyal, devoted supporter she was, indeed," he added with feeling, "and it required the disposition of a saint to cope with the irregular course of my existence in Baker Street.

"But, I note," he continued, after seating himself opposite me near the fire-side and subjecting me to a rather searching glance, "that you came down by way of Crown Lydgate and followed the lower drover's track across the downs. Also," he added, smiling, "you showed good judgment in choosing the left hand corner of the compartment on your journey, for the vista is far more enjoyable and you probably caught sight of the ruined castle on the ridge as you passed through Amberley."

"Yes," I responded with enthusiasm, "and it appears a delightful, inviting region to a city man, I assure you. But how——?"

"Elemen—that is to say, quite simple, Mr. Godfrey," he answered with a smile. "One's mind photographs these trifles after long practice, and my own experience has perhaps extended beyond the apprenticeship stage."

"Even so," I interrupted, "how did——?"

"It is certain that you approached Faraway along the drover's path from Crown Lydgate, for I can see strong evidence of the chalky soil upon your upturned shoe. Had you come down by way of Ferriby Junction—an equally attractive route—and then followed the main highway to my western entrance, the turf path leading in from the gate would have very quickly removed such traces.

"As for the other matter," he resumed, aware that he held my fixed attention, "perhaps I am upon less solid ground, but a strong suspicion of grey dust upon the left elbow of your dark suit tells me that you rested it upon the window sill of the railway carriage."

"Ah! Mr. Holmes," I retorted quickly, "but perhaps I seated myself back to the engine, in which case—"

"Hardly possible, young man," came the ready response as Sherlock Holmes extended to me a glass of sherry and indicated the biscuit box within reach on the table. "You see, I am familiar with these trains and the ten o'clock from Victoria is sparsely patronized. Never have I found difficulty securing a smoking compartment to myself for the journey down—or at the most with two companions. And it would only be natural for you to seat yourself facing the course of your journey. Finally, once leaving the terminal, I believe the sun reflection would strongly favor such a choice."

"Correct you are, sir," I replied, laughing, "and I wonder that Doctor Watson ever caught you napping."

"Poor Watson," Holmes responded. "I badgered him continually, but he always took it in good nature. You will be interested to learn that he is resting at a nursing home in Kensington. That Jezail bullet wound at Maiwand in 1880, you know, brought him a chronic disorder of the leg—"

"You mean the left shoulder?" I interjected, suddenly.

"That's so, young man," the detective replied, directing at me another sharp glance as he refilled his pipe and settled back more comfortably in his chair. "I observe that you are aware of Watson's amazing inconsistencies. First, it's a shoulder, then a leg; and I often wonder," he added with a chuckle, "if he received a cranial fracture during the same engagement."

It was at this juncture of our interview that I barely escaped dismissal for I now—all too abruptly—approached the delicate topic of conflicting dates in the Watson records and their challenge to all devoted students of the saga.

Holmes stiffened at once as I reminded him of the protracted controversies waged over the chronology of his exploits; his long, tapering fingers drummed on the table and I surmised that my injudicious remarks had aroused in him unpleasant recollections.

My appeal to reason, however, quickly mollified him, for he presently suggested another glass of sherry. We moved closer to the fireside, where I reclined against the cushioned settle and my host turned upon me an enquiring, more conciliatory glance.

"Dates—dates—dates," he exclaimed vehemently. "One might add, a fig for dates. And, after all, Watson, poor chap, had some excuse; his practice and the urgent demands of my investigations gave him little time for an accurate, chronological record of events."

"That is so, Mr. Holmes," I agreed. "You will understand, sir, that none among the vast throng of your admirers desires to intrude upon your privacy at this late stage; it is merely that we seek elucidation upon certain phases of your professional work and early training."

"That will come in due season, Mr. Godfrey," Holmes responded slowly as he stooped to throw a fresh log on the glowing embers of the fire. "I might add that these critical surveys have not always brought me vexation or dismay at Watson's inaccuracies. Some of them are amusing and highly ingenious.

"For instance," he resumed, after a moment of reflection, "that episode of my college career which featured Trevor and his damnable pup. The fact is, he smuggled the animal inside the gates after nightfall—a certain porter at the lodge could amplify my brief statement—and in consequence Trevor was given a rare old dust-up, I assure you, by the authorities.

"My own college career ran full circle, so to speak, and I took up residence in Montague Street during the year 1876. That is a long time ago, young man, and criminal investigation has undergone vast changes during that period. My own methods are now, perhaps, antiquated, though I have upon certain occasions been sought by Yard officials who are kindly disposed to look upon me as one keeping abreast of the times."

"I can well understand that, sir," I interposed. "But," I added, "to return for a moment, with your permission, to the moot question of dates in Doctor Watson's records. Are you willing to present a brief statement that might serve to clear away some of the inconsistencies that have provoked discussion?"

"Willing enough," Sherlock Holmes responded readily, a smile stealing across his thin, smoothly shaven features. "But I do believe our critics, even though they employ ingenious methods which indicate exhaustive research, lay undue stress upon what are, after all, inconsequential matters of detail.

"I assure you," he continued, "that all the cases so ably recorded by my confrère will bear the most rigid scrutiny so far as my own participation in their solution is concerned; but both Watson and myself were grossly delinquent in the matter of chronological memoranda. Again, I have never, alas, been awarded medals in the art of calligraphy and the doctor did not at all times consult me while engaged in his laborious deciphering of my hurried notes.

"Watson is determined," the detective concluded, "to present an extended reply to these persevering investigators of our adventures; but I have counseled him against precipitate action, and, furthermore, I wish first to consult an old diary that is lodged in a battered tin box at Cox's bank."

At this point announcement was made by Holmes' housekeeper that luncheon was served, and presently we repaired to a small, oak-raftered dining room which immediately adjoined the library on the west. Through the wide casement windows one caught an inviting view of the rolling downs, along the upper ridge of which a flock of sheep were sharply outlined against the crystal blue skyline. Closer at hand my eye followed the course of a turf path winding down to the western entrance of Faraway, and strung overhead I observed the telephone wire which served as almost his only means of communication with the outside world.

During the following three quarters of an hour Holmes proved himself an extremely courteous and genial host. My fears concerning a possible reluctance on his part to answer my queries, had been dispelled by the warmth of his manner, and cautiously now I broached one or two topics which would, I hoped, bring me some astonishing revelation.

Concerning the period of his wanderings in Central Asia, following the Reichenbach affair, he had little to say. "I appreciate," he agreed, "that my own published records covering this pilgrimage are both sketchy and tantalizing. Some day, however, the complete document may be released; as a matter of fact I have long since approved of such a course, but my brother Mycroft's executors up to now have been unable to find all the note-books that were left, you recall, in his custody. I believe that my report on the geology of Central Tibet may hold more than casual interest for certain among our learned societies.

"You realize," he continued, "that the preparation of this monograph will draw heavily upon my time and energy; furthermore, both Watson and the local medico, who have my health in charge, caution me to devote only a few hours each day to such labors."

"Let us hope, sir, that many years of rest and enjoyment remain for you," I interjected. "And many of us are equally hopeful that you and Doctor Watson may offer us at least one more volume devoted to certain unrecorded cases that were mentioned in the earlier chronicles. Many conjectures have been advanced concerning them and the precise nature of your own participation."

"Such an event may eventually materialize," Sherlock Holmes responded, smiling, "and I trust you may feel no disappointment at the results." As he spoke we rose to return once more to our former seats by the library fireside, and within a moment or two the housekeeper brought in the coffee urn which she placed, together with cups and saucers, upon a low smoking stand.

"Am I overpresumptuous, Mr. Holmes," I inquired, "if I ask you for further details concerning this work?"

"Not at all; there is no secret about it, I assure you. During the past year I have spent a portion of each day compiling additional episodes of my professional career from my own note-books and those other records so carefully preserved by Watson. The doctor, let me add, took no active part in some of these adventures; consequently, although he has consented to write a foreword of explanation, the main task of editing falls upon me. And I hope," he added with humorous severity, "that the dates, in all instances, may stand beyond suspicion."

In reply to my further queries, the detective informed me that it was first intended to delay publication of the volume until after his decease, but continued pressure from a London publisher had finally brought permission to announce it for the forthcoming year.

"It is practically ready now," he confessed, as he refilled his pipe and extended a long arm towards the match box on the smoking stand. "You will understand, however, that my other venture—the compendium of Crime and Detection—has consumed a vast amount of energy, and I could not allow less important matters to interrupt my progress on the major work. I have now arrived midway in the final volume and, please God, I may be spared to bring it to completion."

"Naturally one is extremely interested," I hazarded, "to learn just which cases you have selected from that famous tin box at Cox's bank."

"The book will record only six more of my early cases," Holmes readily responded. "They are cases of supreme interest and importance, I assure you; and it is only because of my dilatory methods that these episodes were not entrusted to Watson's editorship years ago.

"First of all I deal at some length with the Arnsworth Castle affair, in Derbyshire, in 1888. Then follows an account of my experiences with the Camberwell poisoning gang; the singular affair of the aluminium crutch which, by the way, appears to have stirred up some amusing conjectures; the Tankerville Club scandal which involved among others a high cabinet official; the long drawn out chase across Yorkshire in pursuit of the Tarleton murderers; and, finally, a case of unusual importance which I shall refer to as the affair of the Bermondsey Dwarf."

At this point in his statement Sherlock Holmes paused and gazed for a moment or two into the fire. "That case," he resumed at length, "introduced to me the most malevolent figures ever to cross my path, with the possible exceptions of Professor Moriarty and Doctor Grimesby Roylott. You will be amazed at the account I have presented of human depravity. It forms a fitting conclusion to the volume, for in certain respects my resources were taxed as in no other instance, and the case possesses also a singular pathological interest.

"I am going up to town tomorrow to visit Watson," the detective concluded, briskly rising to knock the ashes from his pipe. "His birthday comes along shortly and I must secure somewhere a pound or two of the abominable shag tobacco which he favors as of yore. But on second thought," he added with a chuckle, "perhaps I would confer a favor upon posterity if I were to present him with a bound volume of almanacks covering the active period of our associations together."

A glance at my watch now informed me that I should give immediate thought to my return journey, and I crossed the room to reclaim my hat and stick from the couch where I had deposited them upon my arrival. There were, to be sure, many matters which I had not touched upon: the confusion of dates in the chronicle of the Red-Headed League; Mycroft's final illness; further particulars concerning Mrs. Hudson's affairs; and more comprehensive details relative to Holmes's apprenticeship in the art of detection at the time he resided in Montague Street. But time did not permit a continuation of the interview; and, furthermore, I surmised from a glance or two which he had directed towards the table, that he was anxious to resume work upon his famous *magnum opus*.

There was, nevertheless, one inquiry which I was determined to pursue. As I stood at the threshold and assisted Sherlock Holmes with his topcoat—for he had announced his intention to accompany me to the gate—I exclaimed, "Oh! a final question, sir. There have been many queer statements made, as you know, about Professor Moriarty. Some of your critics have dared to advance the theory that he never existed; others have suggested that he escaped death at the Reichenbach and later returned to London, where he resumed his nefarious operations."

The detective gazed at me long and silently, and for a moment I suspected that I would carry away with me no fresh enlightenment. Then he turned suddenly, crossed to the window alcove, and swung open the heavy door of a small safe which I had previously noted beyond the filing cabinet. From an upper compartment he withdrew an object wrapped in tissue paper, and this he handed to me.

"My one and only souvenir of Moriarty as he is generally known," Sherlock Holmes remarked slowly, "and you are the only individual—with the exception of Watson—who has ever inspected it."

I removed the wrapping and examined curiously a short fragment of heavy watch chain, from the centre portion of which was suspended a gold medal, measuring in diameter about one and one half inches. One side bore the inscription, *St. Andrews 1869,* and on the other side I read the words, *Jasper Mariott—Highest Award Of Merit,* and then the single word *Mathematics* in slightly larger lettering beneath.

"I picked this up from the pathway immediately after the struggle at the Reichenbach," Sherlock Holmes said gravely as I handed the memento back to him. "Upon my return to England, three years or more later, I took occasion to journey northward and eventually unearthed a number of revealing facts pertaining to Mariott's student days and subsequent career.

"You will recall, of course, that he was forced to resign the chair of mathematics at one of our smaller universities, where he had established himself quickly in the highest educational circles and issued several monographs based on exhaustive scientific research. I shall not dwell upon the circumstances of his dismissal, but merely repeat that they led to his later adoption of the name Moriarty and his spectacular rise to a commanding position in the London underworld of that day."

"The legend persists, Mr. Holmes," I interrupted, "that Moriarty was alive at the time of the European war, and that even now no definite news of his death ever has been recorded."

"Nonsense, sheer nonsense," the detective replied, with some indication of annoyance. "You may take my word for it that his influence has long since been removed from the world. Moriarty—Mariott—call him by any name you desire—lies at the foot of the Reichenbach Fall, and no mumbo-jumbo of modern science or sorcery can bring him back to life again."

Warm sunlight flooded the landscape as we followed a gravel pathway up the slope towards the pavilion which I had observed that morning. A glance towards my right afforded me a view of the southerly exposed garden area where the elderly retainer, who had admitted me to the precincts of Faraway, was engaged in trimming a hedge. Beyond him I caught sight of a stone sun-dial, and arranged along the farther border of the enclosure were a number of conical bee hives.

Presently we stood together at the summit of the ridge and gazed across the tremendous rolling expanse of the downs, upon which racing shadows were cast from a small cluster of billowing white clouds. Sheep were grazing a quarter of a mile away; a heavy tractor was toiling upward along one of the winding roads below us; and westward I observed the square tower of a parish church just beyond the main highway.

"This is my world," Holmes said with deep emotion, after a long silence during which I had been captivated by the full sweep of a magnificent prospect extending to the distant sea.

"Elemental," I responded, somewhat dreamily, as I mentally compared the glorious scene before me with the more familiar urban environment of my daily duties.

"That will do, young man," said the detective sharply, "and you had better step along if you plan to catch the 4:12 from Crown Lydgate. Just keep to the lower path after you pass the water tower on the first ridge—it will save you a quarter hour."

Chagrined at having offended my distinguished host at this final stage of a long-sought interview, I glanced at my watch and extended a hand in farewell. But as Sherlock Holmes turned to descend the slope toward his cottage I thought I heard a subdued chuckle; and then there came to me unmistakably—though I doubt they were intended for my ears—the words, "Elemental, indeed!"

This excerpt "From the Diary of Sherlock Holmes," felicitous in tone but parodistic in content, first appeared on November 23, 1911, in the British periodical, Eye-Witness, and was reprinted the following June in Boston's The Living Age before inclusion in Lost Diaries *(Duckworth & Co., London 1913) by* M A U R I C E   B A R I N G *(1874–1945), who was educated at Cambridge and wrote some fifty volumes of biography, criticism, fiction, plays, poetry and translations. Baring is credited with introducing the works of Anton Chekhov to Western literature.*

From the Diary of Sherlock Holmes

M A U R I C E   B A R I N G

Baker Street, January 1.—Starting a diary in order to jot down a few useful incidents which will be of no use to Watson. Watson very often fails to see that an unsuccessful case is more interesting from a professional point of view than a successful case. He means well.

January 6.—Watson has gone to Brighton for a few days, for change of air. This morning quite an interesting little incident happened which I note as a useful example of how sometimes people who have no powers of deduction nevertheless stumble on the truth for the wrong reason. (This never happens to Watson, *fortunately*.) Lestrade called from Scotland Yard with reference to the theft of a diamond and ruby ring from Lady Dorothy Smith's wedding presents. The facts of the case were briefly these: On Thursday evening such of the presents as were jewels had been brought down from Lady Dorothy's bedroom to the drawing-room to be shown to an admiring group of friends. The ring was amongst them. After they had been shown, the jewels were taken upstairs once more and locked in the safe. The next morning the ring was missing. Lestrade, after investigating the matter, came to the conclusion that the ring had not been stolen, but had either been dropped in the draw-ing-room, or replaced in one of the other cases; but since he had searched the room and the remaining cases, his theory so far received no support. I accom-panied him to Eaton Square to the residence of Lady Middlesex, Lady Doro-thy's mother.

While we were engaged in searching the drawing-room, Lestrade uttered a cry of triumph and produced the ring from the lining of the armchair. I told him he might enjoy the triumph, but that the matter was not quite so simple as he seemed to think. A glance at the ring had shown me not only that the stones were false, but that the false ring had been made in a hurry. To deduce the name of its maker was of course child's play. Lestrade or any pupil of Scotland Yard would have taken for granted it was the same jeweller who had made the real ring. I asked for the bridegroom's present, and in a short time I was interviewing the jeweller who had provided it. As I thought, he had made a ring, with imitation stones (made of the dust of real stones), a week ago, for a young lady. She had given no name and had fetched and paid for it herself. I deduced the obvious fact that Lady Dorothy had lost the real ring, her uncle's gift, and, not daring to say so, had had an imitation ring made. I returned to the house, where I found Lestrade, who had called to make arrangements for watching the presents during their exhibition.

I asked for Lady Dorothy, who at once said to me:

"The ring was found yesterday by Mr. Lestrade."

"I know," I answered, "but which ring?"

She could not repress a slight twitch of the eyelids as she said: "There was only one ring."

I told her of my discovery and of my investigations.

"This is a very odd coincidence, Mr. Holmes," she said. "Some one else must have ordered an imitation. But you shall examine my ring for yourself." Whereupon she fetched the ring, and I saw it was no imitation. She had of course in the meantime found the real ring.

But to my intense annoyance she took it to Lestrade and said to him:

"Isn't this the ring you found yesterday, Mr. Lestrade?"

Lestrade examined it and said, "Of course it is absolutely identical in every respect."

"And do you think it is an imitation?" asked this most provoking young lady.

"Certainly not," said Lestrade, and turning to me he added: "Ah! Holmes, that is where theory leads one. At the Yard we go in for facts."

I could say nothing; but as I said good-bye to Lady Dorothy, I congratulated her on having found the real ring. The incident, although it proved the correctness of my reasoning, was vexing as it gave that ignorant blunderer an opportunity of crowing over me.

January 10.—A man called just as Watson and I were having breakfast. He didn't give his name. He asked me if I knew who he was. I said, "Beyond seeing that you are unmarried, that you have travelled up this morning from Sussex, that you have served in the French Army, that you write for reviews, and are especially interested in the battles of the Middle Ages, that you give lectures, that you are a Roman Catholic, and that you have once been to Japan, I don't know who you are."

The man replied that he *was* unmarried, but that he lived in Manchester, that he had never been to Sussex or Japan, that he had never written a line in his life, that he had never served in any army save the English Territorial force, that so far from being a Roman Catholic he was a Freemason, and that he was by trade an electrical engineer—I suspected him of lying; and I asked him why his boots were covered with the clayey and chalk mixture peculiar to Horsham; why his boots were French Army service boots, elastic-sided, and bought probably at Valmy; why the second half of a return ticket from Southwater was emerging from his ticket-pocket; why he wore the medal of St. Anthony on his watch-chain; why he smoked Caporal cigarettes; why the proofs of an article on the Battle of Eylau were protruding from his breast-pocket, together with a copy of the *Tablet;* why he carried in his hand a parcel which, owing to the untidy way in which it had been made (an untidiness which, in harmony with the rest of his clothes, showed that he could not be married) revealed the fact that it contained photographic magic lantern slides; and why he was tattooed on the left wrist with a Japanese fish.

"The reason I have come to consult you will explain some of these things," he answered.

"I was staying last night at the Windsor Hotel, and this morning when I woke up I found an entirely different set of clothes from my own. I called the waiter and pointed this out, but neither the waiter nor any of the other servants, after making full enquiries, were able to account for the change. None of the other occupants of the hotel had complained of anything being wrong with their own clothes.

"Two gentlemen had gone out early from the hotel at 7:30. One of them had left for good, the other was expected to return.

"All the belongings I am wearing, including this parcel, which contains slides, belong to someone else.

"My own things contained nothing valuable, and consisted of clothes and boots very similar to these; my coat was also stuffed with papers. As to the tattoo, it was done at a Turkish bath by a shampooer, who learnt the trick in the Navy."

The case did not present any features of the slightest interest. I merely advised the man to return to the hotel and await the real owner of the clothes, who was evidently the man who had gone out at 7:30.

This is a case of my reasoning being, with one partial exception, perfectly correct. Everything I had deduced would no doubt have fitted the real owner of the clothes.

Watson asked rather irrelevantly why I had not noticed that the clothes were not the man's own clothes.

A stupid question, as the clothes were reach-me-downs which fitted him as well as such clothes ever do fit, and he was probably of the same build as their rightful owner.

January 12.—Found a carbuncle of unusual size in the plum-pudding. Suspected the makings of an interesting case. But luckily, before I had stated any hypothesis to Watson—who was greatly excited—Mrs. Turner came in and noticed it and said her naughty nephew Bill had been at his tricks again, and that the red stone had come from a Christmas tree. Of course, I had not examined the stone with my lens.

ZaSu Pitts *(1898–1963) was a film and TV actress whose dramatic work in two of Erich von Stroheim's silent movie classics,* Greed *(1924) and* The Wedding March *(1928), were overshadowed by memorable comic turns in numerous films, including "two-reelers" with Thelma Todd; the 1934 version of* Mrs. Wiggs of the Cabbage Patch, *costarring with W. C. Fields; Miss Preen in an early TV broadcast of* The Man Who Came to Dinner *and (her last film) 1963's* It's a Mad Mad Mad Mad World. *On March 14, 1947, at a meeting of a Detroit branch of the Baker Street Irregulars, Ms. Pitts assumed the role of Sherlock Holmes's landlady. Her transcribed remarks, "Mrs. Hudson Speaks," appeared later that year in* The Baker Street Journal.

Mrs. Hudson Speaks

ZaSu Pitts

ANNOUNCER: It is my pleasure to present Mrs. Martha Hudson. Mrs. Hudson.

MRS. HUDSON: How do you do, dear gentlemen? This is the first time I've ever spoken to a club of American gentlemen and I'm a very old woman and a wee bit nervous. Of course, in the old days, we used to have Americans in the house. But that's a weary time ago and here on the South Downs we haven't seen an American, except soldier-Americans, in years and years. So you'll forgive me, I'm sure, if I'm nervous. Deary me, I'm all a-flutter.

I suppose you want to hear about Mr. Holmes. Well, gentlemen, I'm happy to say that he's very well indeed. Of course, he isn't as young as he once was; but who is? I always say. He suffers cruel from rheumatism, poor dear, and I tell you it just goes to my heart to see him sitting there, sometimes, with his rug over his poor knees and that faraway look in his eyes that I've learned to know so well. But age comes to us all; and we have a deal to be thankful for.

Of course he can't take the interest in his bees that he used to take. We're both over ninety, did you know that? But, naturally, you did. Mr. Hopkins tells me that you American gentlemen know about everything that used to happen in the old days in Baker Street; so of course you know how old we are. Deary me, Mr. Hopkins is getting on, too. It seems just like yesterday when he used to come to the old house, and him hardly thirty, and ask advice of Mr. Holmes; and I'm bound to say he always got it and good advice it was.

We see Mr. Hopkins every month or so and he always brings us news. He's been retired for a long time now, as maybe you've heard. But he's got the O.B.E., has Mr. Hopkins, and I'm told there's even some talk of making him a knight. Wouldn't that be a fine thing! If he gets it, wouldn't I like to see that jealous little Mr. Lestrade or big, fat Mr. Jones! Dear, dear, and they're both of them dead and gone these 20 years; and sons of their name with great, big positions at Scotland Yard! I do hope the King does something handsome for Mr. Hopkins before it's too late: for he'll be 82 years old this very blessed year. But I'm sure I'd never be able to call him "Sir Stanley."

Now, I know something you're all wondering. And I'm going to answer a question you all want to ask. Mr. Hopkins told us how you argue and write books about us all. So I'm sure you'd like to ask me about "Mrs. Turner."

Well, gentlemen, everybody thinks that was mysterious and it wasn't a bit. There was never any landlady but me at 221B; and my name has been the same, ever since I went to church with Mr. Hudson. But, deary me, a body has to take a holiday, once in a way. That's all there was to it. I was in Brighton for a breath of air and Jennie Turner, who was the widow of my cousin Jack Turner, took care of things for a fortnight. She was devoted to Mr. Holmes and he paid her a compliment by pretending that she was the landlady, while I was gone. Mr. Hopkins says that you American gentlemen—and some gentlemen in England too—have all sorts of notions about that "Mrs. Turner" business. Well, that's the straight truth of it and I'm happy to settle it for you.

You'll never dream who came to see us, the other day. I didn't recognize him, of course. I didn't know who in the world it was, when that grey-haired man knocked on the door and gave me his card and asked to see Mr. Holmes.

It was one of Mr. Holmes's good days, I'm thankful to say, and he was up and about and he'd even been drinking a gin-and-tonic that I'd made up for him. I wish you could have seen his old eyes light up, when that grey-haired man walked into the sitting-room and held out his hand. "Well, well, well," he cried out, in exactly his old voice, "I'll wager you're making more than a shilling-a-day in these times."

If you'll believe me, gentlemen, it was that very scamp of a Wiggins, as ever was! They sat and talked for hours and such a Cockney that Wiggins is, for all his gold watch-chain! He's an ironmonger in the Commercial Road and he's very well-to-do, but he did get pretty badly blitzed, back in 1940. I gave them tea and some cakes I'd made with the last of my sugar and that Wiggins said, "What, no curried chicken?" The sauce of him! As if I'd serve curried chicken at five-o'clock tea! But, just the same, it was fine to see him, for old times' sake. Well do I mind how he used to tramp his dirty feet over my clean stair-carpet in Baker Street; him and his precious ragamuffins!

Now of course you'll want to know of Dr. Watson. Poor, poor Dr. Watson! He's a very old man, of course, and we can't expect him to be up-and-coming like he used to be. But he's been in a nursing home, these past two years, and I'm afraid he'll never come out of it. It's a lovely place down in Devon and the head-doctor is a man named Stamford. I think his father was a doctor, too, and used to be some sort of friend, long ago, of both Mr. Holmes and our doctor. This Stamford writes Mr. Holmes every month and reports on the doctor's health. But I'm bound to say he hasn't been very encouraging in a long, long time and something tells me we'll never hear his cheery voice again.

Mrs. Watson passed away, almost 20 years ago, the poor darling. And what's all this I hear, gentlemen, about your wondering if the doctor was married twice, or even three times? Let me tell you, there was never any Mrs. Watson but one, and she was always sweet Miss Mary to her old Martha Hudson, that she was.

Oh yes, I know that the doctor spoke about his "sad bereavement," away back in 1894. That was the time when Mr. Holmes said that work is the best antidote to sorrow; and a truer word was never spoken. But didn't you know, gentlemen, that the doctor and Miss Mary had a baby boy, while Mr. Holmes was away gallivanting to the ends of the earth; and that the poor little mite died just before his first birthday? And what do you suppose was the precious child's name? Why, Sherlock Holmes Watson, to be sure. What else could it be? I ought to know; for I was the blessed baby's sponsor in baptism, at St. Mary Abbots Church in Kensington.

You see, gentlemen, the doctor was never a one for talking about himself and his own affairs; and, even in his best years, he was the most forgetful mortal that ever breathed. It just broke his heart—and Miss Mary's, too—when that darling baby died. So, of course, he never said a word about it in any of his stories.

But you may take old Martha Hudson's word that there was never any lady in the doctor's heart but one; and I call it a sin and a shame for anybody to suggest that her place was ever taken by another! He was never the same, after she died. And, to tell the truth, Mr. Holmes was worse cut up by it than I've ever seen him in 60 years. She used to come down here to see us, every single Wednesday of the year. And there's a picture of the little lamb, right on Mr. Holmes's desk at this moment.

Well, is there anything else you'd like to have me tell you? Oh, deary me, I nearly forgot. Mr. Hopkins said that some of you think that my Hudson was that wicked convict that acted so bad to old squire Trevor, when Mr. Holmes was in college. Well, that isn't so at all. I never saw that bad Hudson and I certainly never wanted to. A convict indeed! My Hudson was a respectable tradesman, I'd have you know, in a very small way in Peckham, and he died when I was barely 25 years old. But he was a saving sort and he left me a little property. So, with never a chick or child of my own and a little money in the postal-bank, I cast about and, after a while, I took the house in Baker Street and put up a card for lodgers. And, one winter's day, Mr. Holmes and the doctor came to the door and they let my first-floor sitting-room and my two bedrooms and you know the rest.

I hope I haven't wearied you with this long story, gentlemen. But Mr. Hopkins told me that you'd be interested in anything about the dear, old days. So he arranged for me to come to Eastbourne, and speak into one of these microphones; and I suppose everything I've said will come out, just as I spoke it.

Good-bye, gentlemen. You're all friends of mine, because you all love Mr. Holmes. And I hope you'll not forget old Martha Hudson.

Twenty-five years after his death, A N T H O N Y B O U C H E R (1911–1968) is still one of America's most important genre critics-editors. He wrote mystery and science fiction reviews for two New York newspapers and cofounded and edited "The Magazine of Fantasy and Science Fiction," where his introductions virtually amounted to an ongoing college-level course in genre literature. Boucher, whose real name was William Anthony Parker White, himself wrote excellent science-fantasy and mystery fiction, such as The Compleat Werewolf, Rocket to the Morgue, Nine Times Nine *and* The Case of the Seven Sneezes. *He penned a few Sherlockian spoofs, including* The Case of the Baker Street Irregulars *(see Appendix II) and the next embarrassingly plausible "adventure."*

The Adventure of the Bogle-Wolf

A N T H O N Y   B O U C H E R

It was on a chill January afternoon in 1889 that I sat before the fire in my Paddington home, thoroughly exhausted from some hours of such strenuous activity as I had not known since our pursuit of the Andaman Islander on the Thames. I did not stir when I heard the bell, not recalling until its fifth clang that among the other vexations of this day was the fact that it was the maid's afternoon out. Charging my pipe load of Arcadia mixture to revive my flagging spirits, I reluctantly answered the summons.

It was with a mixture of joy and apprehension that I beheld upon the step the familiar figure of my friend Sherlock Holmes. Pleased though I was to see him, I nevertheless feared that he might find me, in my present condition, regrettably slow in responding to the challenge of whatever game might be afoot. But Holmes seemed as inactively disposed as I, inclined to do nothing, after our exchange of greetings, but follow me back to the fire, sink into the chair on the opposite side, and companionably stoke up his villainous black clay.

"London has grown dull," Holmes complained as I performed the expected rites with the tantalus and gasogene which had been his wedding present to us. "And dullness, my dear Watson, is the only insufferable malady.

It is over two months since my pretended illness, which so deeply concerned you, enabled Inspector Morton to arrest that devil, Mr. Culverton Smith: and in all that time not a single problem of interest has come my way. Oh, the newspapers devoted some space, of course, to that wretched affair of the Taliaferro opals; but a four-year old child could have seen that the thief must be an albino Lascar." He broke off and regarded me with some concern. "My dear fellow, you aren't ill, are you?"

"The January chill," I hastened to explain. "Here; this will take the edge off it for both of us."

"Ennui . . ." Holmes murmured. "The French, Watson, have certain invaluable words. Consider, too, their use of our own word, *spleen* . . . One needs my grandmother's language to describe my state at the moment. The concretely expressed gratitude of the reigning family of Holland would in itself be sufficient to maintain my modest needs for years to come; but my mind needs a case. I must sharpen my teeth, Watson, on whatever bone I can find.

"This afternoon," he continued after a pause and a sip, "I called by at the Diogenes Club, but Mycroft was engaged on a mission of such secrecy that its nature might not be hinted even to me. I needed a mere five minutes to determine, from the ash beside Mycroft's habitual chair and the smudge of violet ink on the clerk's left forefinger, this his errand concerned a certain highly placed young gallant whose activities it would be wiser for me to ignore. Then I came to you, my old friend, in the hope that your practice— ever growing, I trust?—might have produced some little problem of a teasing, if petty, sort."

"No problem," I said wearily, and added, "from my practice."

"If I cannot find stimulating distraction somewhere . . ." His normally incisive voice trailed off, and the thumb of his right hand made the significant gesture of depressing a hypodermic syringe.

"In God's name, Holmes!" I cried. "You would not return to that?"

He sat in silence for a moment, smoking and smiling. Then he asked casually, "Polar or grizzly?"

"Polar," I responded automatically, and then leapt to my feet. "Holmes," I exclaimed, "this is too much! That you should want some stimulating distraction, as you call it, I can understand; but that you should invade the privacy of your friends, spying on them in their domestic moments like the pettiest enquiry agent—"

His welcome laugh and a gesture of his long thin hand interrupted my indignation. "Watson, Watson," he lamented, shaking his head. "Will you never learn that I practice neither black magic nor sneaking skulduggery? When I find a healthy young man in a state of complete exhaustion, dust on his hands and on the knees of his trousers, his rug awry and the furniture misplaced, and when moreover he winces at my casual allusion to a four-year-old child, it is obvious that he has been spending the afternoon entertaining an infant, and at least in part by imitating animals on all fours. To one who knows your character as I do, Watson, it is equally obvious that the child would find you most acceptable in the role of a bear. It remained only to ask, 'Polar or grizzly?'—though in view of your predilection for tales of Arctic adventure, that answer, too, should have been obvious. I regret that I seem to be losing my touch."

"Now—" I began.

"I know," he interrupted me with some acerbity. "Now it is all perfectly simple—once I have explained it. To see the answer before it is explained—that, I might point out, is the desideratum. However, I might go on to deduce that the child belongs to a friend of your wife's (since I recall no couples with children in your own acquaintance), and that your wife and the child's mother have gone out together. Probably, in view of the day and the hour, to a matinee. Quite possibly, in view of the season, to a pantomime—which might perhaps indicate an older child in the family, taken to the theatre while this one, too young for public appearance, is left with the friend's obliging husband."

"Holmes," I exclaimed, "King James the First should have known you before he wrote his studies on witchcraft."

"Tush, Watson," my friend protested. "That was the merest guesswork. But there is no guesswork in concluding from the faint cries which I detect from the upper story that the young man in question has awakened from his nap and demands attention."

"This," I announced to Holmes when I had done my clumsy best to freshen the child after his nap, "is Master Elias Whitney."

"Ah? A namesake, no doubt, of the late Principal of the Theological College of St. George's?"

"His nephew," I replied, marvelling as always at this man who had at his fingertips every fact of English life. "His mother, Kate, is a dear friend of Mary's. His father . . ." But professional reticence caused me to say no more of his poor father, little dreaming how the perverse proclivity which at that time caused me so much concern as a medical man was later to lead me into the adventure which I have chronicled elsewhere as *The Man with the Twisted Lip*.

"Ah there, young feller," Holmes said genially.

Young Elias gravely contemplated the piercing eyes, the hawklike features, the firmly sensitive lips of my friend, and delivered his verdict. "Funny man," he said.

I could not repress a smile, nor a lively sense of anticipation as I watched to see what species of animal Holmes would be obliged to portray for the young gentleman's entertainment. But I was disappointed in my expectations as young Elias disregarded the temptations of the rug which had been the Arctic Circle, settled himself on the hassock by the fire, and demanded, "Tell story."

Holmes' eyes twinkled. "He's found your weak spot, Watson, my lad—a confirmed story teller, in and out of school. Well, if he must have animals, tell him of our experiences at Baskerville Hall."

I was about to protest as to the suitability for young ears of that gruesome narrative when the boy himself said, "No. Tell story about bogle-bear."

"He's come to the right shop," Holmes observed. "Your Scottish ancestry, my dear fellow, must team with stories of bogles."

"He means," I explained patiently, "a polar bear, such as I had the honor of portraying. No, Elias, I'm sorry, but I don't know any stories about polar bears. But I can recall that in my own childhood I was always partial to stories about wolves. Would one of those interest you?"

"Bogle-wolf?" Elias suggested.

"I am not positive on the subject, but I strongly doubt that there is such a beast as a polar wolf. This wolf is simply an ordinary wolf, such as one may encounter, at least in fairy tales, upon any corner. It lived in a deep dark forest—"

"Corners in forest?" Elias asked with interest.

Holmes had refilled his glass from the tantalus and settled back in the chair. "Pray continue, Watson," he urged. "I find fairy tales particularly suitable for you, in view of the romantic touches in your narratives of my own adventures. I am eager to see you at work."

"No," I answered Elias. "There were no corners in the forest, only a long winding pathway which led from one cottage to another. Now in the first cottage there lived a little girl called Red Riding Hood—"

"Know 'bout Riding Good," Elias said.

I felt somewhat rebuffed. "Would you prefer another story, then?"

"No. Like Riding Good. Tell 'bout Riding Good."

"The public," Holmes observed, "always prefers a story which it already knows."

I told about "Riding Good." Since the story may perhaps be familiar to the reader from his own nursery days, I shall here omit the details of the narrative, which I told in full as it was often related to us by our old Nannie in those happy sunlit days when Harry and I were children. I told of the first meeting with the wolf, of the wolf's nefarious practices upon grandmother, of Red Riding Hood's horrible interview with the disguised wolf, of her gradual realization of her great peril, and of the final intrusion of the gallant woodcutter (whom I described, I confess, with certain of the more outstanding physical traits of my friend) and his destruction of the wolf and restoration of grandmother—a detail, I am given to understand, frequently omitted from modern versions.

I was flattered by the rapt attention of young Elias, and I was not only flattered but puzzled by the equally rapt attention of Sherlock Holmes. As I progressed with my narrative, his eyes lit up, he followed my every word, and soon, after an automatic reach for the absent Persian slipper, extracted his pouch, loaded the clay, and surrounded himself with those poisonous clouds which I had come to associate with the final stages of a problem.

When I had concluded, he sprang to his feet and took several eager paces about the room. "That's done it, Watson!" he exclaimed, and there was the old life in his voice. "Elias!" He pointed a long forefinger at the child, who visibly quailed before it. "Do you want to know the *truth* about Red Riding Hood?"

"Know troof 'bout Riding Good?" the child repeated numbly.

"What dolts men can be!" Holmes ejaculated to himself. "To repeat that story for generations and never perceive its meaning! And yet in the very words of this child there was a hint of truth. *Bogle-wolf* . . . Surely you must see it, Watson?"

"See what?" I stammered.

"There are two essential points. Fix your mind on them, Watson. First, Red Riding Hood noticed the wolfishness of 'grandmother' only gradually—almost feature by feature. Second, after the wolf was killed, there was grandmother."

"But my dear Holmes—"

"You still do not understand? Then listen!" His eyes sparkled. "It was, indeed, a bogle-wolf: it was a *werewolf,* a wolf which is only the lupine shape of a malevolent and anthropophagous human being. And that human being was . . . *Grandmother!*

"It is perfectly clear. Red Riding Hood did not look up at once and see that the form in bed was a wolf. No; little by little, she noticed the appearance of wolfish characteristics. It is obvious that she was watching the werewolf change from human being to wolf.

"And when the wolf was killed, there was grandmother. Not springing alive from the stomach—that is palpably a later rationalization, impossible even by the standards of the fairy tale. But there was grandmother, lying on the floor, stretched out by the blow of the woodman's axe—for the werewolf, when slain, always resumes its human form."

"Holmes," I gasped, "you are right. That must be the truth. So simple and yet so startling. And after all these centuries, you alone—"

With a lightning motion of his lithe body, Holmes whirled on young Elias. "Now, young feller, you know. Tell your mother that while she was attending the pantomime, you, my lad, have been the first boy in the world to learn the truth about Red Riding Hood!"

The boy sat silent for a moment, gazing at the man before him. Then his mouth parted and his eyes screwed up. He was still silent for what seemed like minutes, but at last an anguished wail came from that horribly distorted countenance. In all the adventures which I have shared with my friend Sherlock Holmes, I have never heard a scream of such pure and undiluted rage, agony and frustration.

So loud was the scream that we did not hear the key in the front door. Our first warning of the ladies' return was the whirlwind entrance of Kate Whitney, who dashed to the hassock, seized her agonized offspring in her arms, and vainly tried to still his screams.

My wife, entering with the still panto-rapt young Isa, turned on me furiously. "James!" she cried, loudly enough to be heard even over those wails. "What *have* you been doing to that child?"

"James," Sherlock Holmes observed. "A pet name, no doubt? And to think that I should have known you for so long, my dear fellow, without troubling to discover that your middle initial must stand for Hamish."★

Mary turned to face him. "Mr. Holmes," she said, with ominous politeness. Her eyes took in the disordered rug, the rearranged furniture, the lowered level of the tantalus.

Kate Whitney's voice kept repeating, "What did the mans do to ums?" At last Master Elias controlled his hysteria sufficiently to point a damning finger at Sherlock Holmes.

"Bad man!" he said accusingly. "Bad man spoil Riding Good. Spoil it all up!" And he resumed his vociferous vocalizations.

I spoke as loudly and as calmly as I could. I said, "About that little matter of the Vatican Vaccination Scandal, old man. Don't you think we could talk it over in the consulting room?"

The glare in Mary's eyes softened a little. Close to my ear she whispered, "Another commission?" and I mumbled "The usual percentage." She relaxed, and even let me take the tantalus with us.

"There," said Sherlock Holmes later, "you have the typical instance for the public's reaction to truth. You must never expect the scientific attitude from the popular mind, which always prefers the accepted falsehood to the unfamiliar truth. I have been contemplating a small monograph upon such delusory traditions; I am sure, for example, that since your friend Doyle wrote his legend about what he terms the *Marie Celeste,* the correct name *Mary Celeste* will fall into complete disuse. And yet we must try where we may to restore truth, and scorn the public hostility. *Populus me sibilat . . .*"

". . . *at nummi,*" I paraphrased glumly, recalling my unfortunate half-promise to Mary, *"desunt in arca . . ."*

★The Scottish equivalent of James.—MK

*S*herlock Holmes in Oz?! This startling-charming pastiche was published in 1971 by The International Wizard of Oz Club in the first issue of its magazine, Oziana. RUTH BERMAN has written poetry in Weird Tales and other periodicals, as well as "a few dozen stories in assorted magazines and anthologies," including Amazing, Analog, Isaac Asimov's SF Magazine, The Magazine of Fantasy and Science Fiction, Shadows and Jessica Amanda Salmonson's Tales by Moonlight. Ms. Berman has published numerous Holmesian tales and articles. NOTE: Though it is not necessary to know L. Frank Baum's Oz books to enjoy this pastiche, a few useful details are provided in Appendix I.

Sherlock Holmes in Oz

RUTH BERMAN

"**B**ut," said Dorothy, "why can't you find it in the Magic Picture?"

Ozma shook her head. "The pearl's own magic works against it."

Inga fidgeted, hooking his feet around the legs of the chair and unhooking them again. "My parents won't like it if I've lost one of the talismans." He jumped up and began pacing the Throne Room, half hoping, against all logic, to find the missing gem on the floor. It was certainly not in the Banquet Hall.

"But it wasn't *your* fault, Inga," Dorothy argued.

"I should have watched—" he began.

"I have an idea!" the Scarecrow interrupted.

The Wizard put down the heavy volume he was consulting, *Magic Gems: An Illustrated Guide with Notes and Pedigrees,* keeping one finger inside the Pingaree section, and beetled his brows at the Scarecrow. He had been up all night, trying one spell after another to locate the pearl, and all he had found was a box of ruby hairpins belonging to Glinda the Good, the Soldier with the Green Whiskers' second-best, pearl-backed hairbrush, and Ojo the Lucky's favorite agate marble. He had run out of spells to try.

They all leaned expectantly toward the straw man.

"Sherlock Holmes," he said, and stopped, as if that was enough.

"I don't understand," said Ozma.

"The greatest of all detectives," said the Scarecrow. "Why not hire him?"

Inga looked blank. Ozma and the Wizard looked thoughtful. Dorothy looked puzzled. "When I lived in Kansas," she said, "I once read a story called 'A Study in Scarlet' about a detective named Sherlock Holmes. But he was just a character in a book. He wasn't real."

"But you were in the Great Outside World then, my dear," said Ozma. "Here in Oz we should be able to manage it—at least, I hope so! Wizard—?"

The little man was counting out spells on his fingers. He took hold of the fingers of his left hand and shook them gently. "I think we can do it, Ozma. Of course, there's time-synchronization, and universe-parallelogistics, and—"

Dorothy winced at the long words. "But you can do it, Wiz?" she asked doubtfully.

"Yes," said the Wizard, smiling. He shoved his hands in his pockets, and tilted the chair back. It slid and almost tipped on the smooth floor. The Wizard waved his feet wildly, and brought the chair back down with a thump. "I think," he added. He stood up. "Let's meet again after lunch. I need to work on this."

After lunch (the Wizard had his sent into his laboratory on a tray), they reassembled, and found the Wizard carefully laying out strips of old calendars and strips of pages of Sherlock Holmes stories (magically photographed from a copy of *The Complete Sherlock Holmes*—the Wizard did not like to tear up real books) in a large bowl of shining lapis lazuli. On top of these he added some red powder, some yellow powder, a pipe, an oddly shaped cap, and a pinch of grey fog. He snapped his fingers, and a spark fell into the bowl. The Scarecrow moved back, so as to keep his flammable self well away from the fire, but the others leaned forward in fascination. The contents of the bowl took fire, and a warm, tobacco-smelling odor crept through the room. The Wizard took a deep sniff, sat perfectly still with his nose still crinkled, and then nodded. "Ready," he said.

Ozma put her hands to the Magic Belt she wore and whispered a few words.

The flame in the bowl flashed up towards the ceiling, and went out.

Two men appeared in the room, a tall, lean, sharp-boned man in a tweed suit, and a shorter, rounder man, in a frock coat like the Wizard's.

"Good heavens!" said the second man, turning in a circle and staring at the emerald-studded walls, the throne cut from a single slab of malachite, and the peculiar occupants of the room: a stuffed dummy, a boy dressed in doublet and hose, pacing back and forth with his eyes fixed on the ground, a pretty girl and a startlingly beautiful girl, a little older, both wearing crowns, and one blessedly ordinary-looking man. "Sir, what is this?" he said to the last.

The tall man, without moving his body, turned his head once to the right, once to the left, and then said, "May I help you, Ma'am?" to Ozma. The two questions came simultaneously, and neither was heard clearly.

The Scarecrow, breaking out of the wonder that had held the Ozites silent, stepped forward and said, "Mr. Sherlock Holmes? Dr. Watson?"

There was another brief silence. Even Holmes was momentarily daunted by the sight of a dummy, crackling with the straw that stuffed it, which could move and speak and hold out a hand to shake. However, Holmes recovered, and shook the hand. "You have the advantage of us, sir."

"Oh, I'm sorry. I'm the Scarecrow." The Scarecrow flung out his hand to point at the others, putting himself off balance in doing so. He swayed, but Holmes caught his shoulder. "Thank you." He pointed again, more cautiously. "Her Majesty, Princess Ozma of Oz, Princess Dorothy Gale, our guest, Prince Inga of Pingaree, and the Wizard of Oz."

Watson stared again, first at the live Scarecrow, and then at the dark-haired girl called "Her Majesty." Manners, he reflected, were manners, especially with ladies present. He bowed to Ozma.

Holmes looked once more around the chamber, and then followed Watson's move and bowed to Ozma. "You wished my help in recovering a lost gem, Ma'am?" he said.

"Why, yes," she said. "But how—"

"His Highness is clearly in search of some small object, although his manner suggests that he does not expect to find it—"

"That's right," said Inga, staring up in wonder at the tall detective.

"—and I observe a book on the subject of rare gems by your chair . . . Mr. Wizard," he said. "You know our names, and you do not seem surprised to see us here—" Holmes paused, and glanced at the live Scarecrow. "—I must admit I am at a loss as to how we come to be here—but I conclude that we are here by your intention." He nodded at Inga and the Wizard's book, and stopped.

"I see," said Ozma. "You came by magic. And will you help us?"

"Yes, Ma'am," said Holmes, glancing again at the Scarecrow. "It should prove a most instructive case." He drew a chair into the group and sat down.

"We don't use money in Oz," said Ozma. "You do in England, don't you?"

"Yes," said Holmes, a little startled.

"Perhaps you will accept some of our emeralds in payment, then."

Holmes glanced at the great stones inset in the walls. "One will be more than I should accept," he said drily.

"But magic!" protested Watson. "There's no such thing."

"Not in England," the Wizard said. "But there is here."

Holmes smiled. " 'When you have eliminated the impossible, whatever remains, no matter how improbable, must be true'," he quoted himself. "But, as my cousin says, 'Discard the impossible; then, if nothing remains, some part of the impossible must be possible.' It is impossible that we should be here. Yet here we are."

Watson looked doubtfully at the Scarecrow, then shrugged and pulled up a chair. He drew a prescription-pad and a pencil out of his pockets and began scribbling notes.

"Now, if you will tell me all the circumstances regarding the gem, Ma'am?" said Holmes.

"Inga's parents gave a talisman to me to mark the friendship between our two countries," she said. "They call it the Rainbow Pearl, because it shines of itself in all the colors of the rainbow. It has the power to turn waters aside—to bring rain that falls where it is not needed over to parched lands, or to drive a river into other channels. Inga presented it to me at a banquet last night. There is a long table at the end of the Banquet Hall. We placed it there, so that all could admire it."

"Guarded?" said Holmes.

"No—we have very little crime in Oz, Mr. Holmes. Besides, there were so many people in the room looking at it . . . Once we heard someone banging at the main door to the hall, but when Jellia Jamb went to look, there was no one there. I suppose we were all looking at that door then, and someone could have taken the pearl at that moment. At any rate, it was a few minutes after that when Jellia—she loves pretty things—went to look at the pearl and found it gone. We searched for it for hours, but without success."

"Is Miss Jamb trustworthy?" asked Holmes.

"Jellia! She's been at the palace longer than I have myself!" exclaimed Ozma.

"Jellia's always been completely trustworthy," added the Wizard.

Holmes rose. "I should like to examine the Banquet Hall, Ma'am."

"Of course. We've left it just as it was last night."

"I'd be glad to show you the way," the Scarecrow volunteered.

"Thank you."

Watson stuffed his writing materials back into his pocket, and the two men followed the Scarecrow out the back door of the Throne Room into the private little room behind it, and from there into a narrow corridor which led to the Banquet Hall.

Holmes asked the Scarecrow to tell him, so far as he could remember, who had sat where. He was surprised when the Scarecrow was able to name the occupant of every chair.

"It's my famous brains," the Scarecrow explained. "The Wizard himself gave them to me, and they're very sharp. Although," he added wistfully, "they don't seem to be very useful in detection."

"With training, you could most probably learn. You already have memory and observation."

The Scarecrow, feeling immensely flattered, went on with his list.

While the straw man spoke, Holmes paced methodically up and down the hall, covering every square inch.

After completing the list, the Scarecrow swung himself up on the table, next to where Watson had seated himself, and watched in fascination as Holmes criss-crossed the room.

"Interesting," the detective observed some minutes later, after examining the long table.

"What?" The Scarecrow hopped off the table, and he and Watson came to look over the detective's shoulder.

"A potted cactus plant," said Holmes, pointing at the far end of the sideboard. "And here—an empty saucer, somewhat stained with soil and the ring of a flowerpot."

"Ruggedo!" gasped the Scarecrow.

"I beg your pardon, sir?"

"That cactus used to be Wutz, an evil wizard. He and Ruggedo, the Nome King, tried to conquer Oz. But they were transformed into cacti—a powerful spell that not even Ozma or the Wizard would be able to break. And the Ruggedo-cactus stood right here!"

"Was it here last night?"

The Scarecrow wrinkled his forehead so deeply that he even squeezed his eyes shut in concentration. "I don't remember," he said at last. "I spent most of the time talking to friends—I don't eat, you know—"

Holmes blinked, then nodded, accepting the information as a peculiarity consistent with what he had observed of this strange country, and filed the datum away in his mind.

The Scarecrow continued, "—and then all our thoughts were so set on looking for the pearl, I don't think anyone would have noticed the cactus or if it was gone."

Holmes nodded. "Had this Ruggedo friends who would want to help him escape?"

The Scarecrow shrugged. "Some of the Nomes, perhaps. Or a being that meant to hurt Oz and wanted his help." He tapped at his forehead, feeling an idea on the way. "Nomes love jewels," he said excitedly, "and Ruggedo loves jewels most of all. If someone disenchanted him last night, I'm sure he stole the pearl!"

"Who would have the ability to disenchant him?"

"No one that I know. But you'd have to ask Wiz, or Ozma."

"How far did you search the palace?" asked Holmes.

The Scarecrow was a little taken aback at the sudden change of subject, but after a moment he answered, "This room, the main corridor, and all the rooms fronting it. There didn't seem to be time for anyone who could have taken it to get further than that. We have porters at the doors to guide people—the palace is so large, I'm afraid visitors get lost in it—and they didn't see anyone. Of course, there are the windows. We haven't searched the grounds entirely, yet. We wanted to wait till nightfall before going on with the search, because the light from the pearl would make it so conspicuous."

Holmes walked out into the main corridor, and paused to examine the entrance. There was a little debris collected just outside, where people had rushed out in search of the thief: a tumbler with a stain of evaporated Ozade spreading out on the floor beneath it, a length of thread with an iron nail tied to each end, someone's left shoe, and a tall, pointed hat with bells on it. Holmes went to the nearest window and peered out. He beheld a pleasant expanse of turf and garden. Inga, Princess Dorothy, and some other children were playing tag. Beyond them was a wall curving around the palace. "Does that extend completely around the building?" he asked, pointing at the wall.

"Yes. There are plenty of gates, of course, but Ozma has asked people not to leave until we've had a chance to search for the pearl some more. A few people have come in since then, but no one's gone out."

Holmes drew out his pipe and tobacco pouch and began tamping leaf into the bowl of the pipe.

The Scarecrow shrank back against the opposite wall.

"Forgive me," said Holmes, hastily taking the pipe out of his mouth. He opened the pouch, held the pipe over it, hesitated, then closed the pouch. "Forgive me," he repeated apologetically, "but I find tobacco an aid to concentration. And I can assure you that I shall be most careful with the fire."

"That's all right," said the Scarecrow, more cheerfully than he felt. He waited till Holmes had lit the pipe and blown out and crushed the match before coming closer.

Holmes, deep in thought, wandered back into the Banquet Hall, trailing clouds of blue smoke.

"Difficult problem, eh, Holmes?" commented Watson. "Not much like the blue carbuncle, is it?"

"The pearl is no problem, Watson," said Holmes irritably. "It's the thief that worries me. You do want to catch the thief?" he added, turning to the Scarecrow.

"Why . . . why . . . yes. But—you don't mean you already know where the pearl is?"

"I know how to find it." Puffing away like a steam locomotive, Holmes wandered on out the back door, and back the way they had come.

Inside the Throne Room they found business in session. As Ozma had said, there was little crime in Oz, but where there are people with their own minds, there will be disputes. The usual process in Ozite quarrels was to go to one of the rulers for arbitration. There were not many cases for Ozma's court to go through that day, because people who entered the palace grounds would not be able to leave until the pearl was found or the search abandoned. There were enough disputants willing to accept the potential delay to give Ozma an hour's work that day, however.

When Holmes entered, Ozma was hearing a dispute between a Hopper and a Horner. As was usual with those two peoples, the problem sounded simple and wasn't. The Horner had made an ill-timed joke, and the Hopper had taken offense. The one had to be persuaded to apologize, and the other had to be convinced that no real insult had been intended in the first place. Both were stubborn.

When the quarrel was finally cajoled into a reconciliation, Ozma turned her attention to the detective. "Yes, Mr. Holmes?"

"I want you to make an announcement, Ma'am," he said. "Say that the pearl is found. Spread the news over the entire palace."

"But—" she began. She stopped and inspected his face. He clearly did not mean that he actually had the pearl. It was a trick of some kind. And if it failed, the disappointment would make matters worse than before. But he looked confident, and Dr. Watson looked puzzled but confident of his friend. She decided to trust Holmes's confidence, backed as it was by Watson's. She jumped off the throne, and ran out of the room, glad of the chance to move again after sitting still so long. She flung open a window in the corridor. "Dorothy! Inga!" she called. "It's found! Tell everyone!"

The court recorder ran out with the message, too, and in a few minutes there was a crowd of curious Ozites gathered in the room, eager for explanation. ("'Curious' in more ways than one!" said Watson to himself, gazing at a live sawhorse, a man with a pumpkin instead of a head, a dummy like the Scarecrow only female and dressed in bright patchwork, a short, fat, copper man, a tall, thin, tin man, and a variety of beasts, as well as a few ordinary individuals.)

When the room began to be crowded, Holmes stepped up on the platform which supported Ozma's throne, and called, "Silence, please."

The chatter of the crowd died away.

"Will someone close the door?" he called.

The Patchwork Girl turned a cartwheel against it, knocking it shut.

There was silence. Holmes glanced over the assemblage, taking in the assorted figures. "I must thank you," he said, "for providing me with a most . . . unusual case. The discovery that the laws of logic hold even when those of science do not is, although not surprising to the abstract reasoner, nonetheless gratifying. To be sure, where evidence indicates the mode of operation to be, considered by itself, non-magical, the deductive process becomes simpler.''

The crowd shuffled uneasily. Holmes's remarks, however abstractly reasonable, did not seem to be going anywhere.

Suddenly there came a violent knocking at the door.

"Who's there?'' called Holmes.

The Pumpkinhead pulled it open, and a lion and a tiger bounded out into the corridor to see. "No one!'' they roared, and Watson opened his eyes wide at hearing animals talk. Even Holmes looked startled.

Half a minute more passed. People milled forward and backward in the Throne Room, bored and puzzled.

"Aha!'' cried Holmes, leaping in back of the throne.

Hubbub broke out as each being asked his or her neighbor, "What's happening?''

Ozma rose and hushed them.

Holmes reappeared from behind the throne, bearing a kicking, scratching, biting Nome in his arms.

"Kaliko!'' a dozen or more voices exclaimed in unison.

The Nome tried to reach Holmes's knee with one more kick, and subsided.

"Put him down, Mr. Holmes,'' said Ozma.

"Yes, Ma'am.'' Holmes stood close to the Nome, ready to grab him, if necessary, but Kaliko crossed his arms over his chest and stood still.

"Kaliko, what is this?'' Ozma asked gently.

"I hate being king! I hate it!'' he exclaimed.

"I don't understand.''

"I used to be a *good* Nome,'' Kaliko complained, "as Nomes go. But now it's 'King, we need more iron', 'King, we're running out of rubies', 'King, I don't feel like digging today.' No one ever asks me if I want to give orders today!'' He stamped his foot once, and went on more calmly, "My old master, Ruggedo, was a bad Nome, but he wasn't a bad king. I came to steal him home.''

"But he's been turned into a cactus,'' said Ozma.

"I know,'' said Kaliko dolefully, "but I thought our magicians could try their luck at breaking the spell. You never can tell—they might succeed. Or the Hearer may be able to hear his thoughts, and he could rule through the Hearer.''

"I see. And the pearl?''

"Well, I was stealing Ruggedo anyway, and there it was, begging for a Nome to cherish it. Only Nomes *really* understand gems.''

"Where did you hide it?''

"Won't tell.'' Kaliko sat down and sulked.

"That's not necessary, Ma'am. He's already shown us." Holmes dropped back behind the throne again and fumbled at the back corner of the platform's risers. He came up again, holding a large and, by now, somewhat battered cactus in a flowerpot. He rooted about in the dirt and pulled out something that glowed in his hand. He opened his hand, and a flood of color shone sparkling in the room. "Let me introduce to you the famous Rainbow Pearl!" he cried.

There was a hushed murmur of wonder from the crowd, except for Watson, who bit back a laugh, recognizing Holmes's incorrigible love of drama. He wondered if Holmes even realized that he was echoing himself.

"Mr. Holmes, this is marvelous!" exclaimed Ozma.

"Elementary, Ma'am," he answered.

Watson repressed an indulgent smile. He could tell when Holmes was proud of himself, but Holmes invariably tried to play down his own achievements. "How did you know the pearl was there?" he asked, to force his friend to enjoy the victory.

"By the scanty trail of soil which dropped out of the pot's drainhole," Holmes said. "I knew the cactus must be somewhere in this room, but the trail did not last long enough to show precisely where. The pearl was stolen at night; the thief could scarcely hope to escape with it then, while the whole palace was roused and searching. I must admit," he said regretfully, "I did not realize the cactus was the primary objective in the crime. I supposed that the thief grabbed the pot because it would be easy to stuff the pearl down inside the loose earth to prevent its light from betraying him. A few nights later, when the search was less intense, he could escape unseen."

"That's right," admitted Kaliko sadly. "When people started shouting that the pearl was found, I was afraid it might be a bluff, but I had to check. If it wasn't a bluff," he added defiantly, "I was going to steal it back while you were all watching the front door. But you were waiting for me at the back," he told Holmes, with a sigh.

"How did you make the noise?" asked Ozma.

"A knocker," said Holmes promptly. "A boyish prank—a device with a nail set to fall rattling against a door or window. The prankster is safe, being far enough away to run out of sight—or around to a back entrance—before he can be found."

Holmes handed the pearl to Ozma, and the Ozites burst into cheers. Holmes, looking embarrassed, bowed to them.

"What about Ruggedo?" said Kaliko stubbornly, over the cheering.

Ozma hesitated, then said slowly, "I can't see what harm it would do—and I suppose Ruggedo would rather be at home than in exile, even in the shape of a cactus plant." She glanced at the Scarecrow for advice. The straw man nodded. Ozma touched her Magic Belt and murmured a few words. The Nome and the cactus vanished.

Holmes blinked. "Don't you find life in a magic country . . . unsettling, Ma'am?"

"Not when you're used to it," she said laughing. "Can I persuade you and Dr. Watson to stay to dinner?"

"We have our own responsibilities in our world—" he began.

"We'll return you to the second when you left, in any case."

"You are most kind."

The Scarecrow volunteered to show the two guests around the palace, if they felt like exploring, until dinnertime. Ozma heard him saying eagerly, as the three left the room, "Tell me, how do you train yourself to be a detective?"

She laughed, and then carefully surveyed the crowd, already diminishing rapidly. There was no one there seeking the ruler's aid. She was free. She rose, stepped down, strolled casually over to Inga, and touched his shoulder. "You're it," she said, and ran out of the room, down the corridor, and out into the garden . . . The Rainbow Pearl threw bright lights over the flowers, and spread the sunlight in sparkles on the grass.

CRAIG SHAW GARDNER *writes both horror and hilarious fantasy, including a series of Arabian Nights spoofs and the rib-tickling "Ebenezum" and "Wuntvor" novels, but when he told me he planned to submit a story that introduced Sherlock Holmes to the guys-and-dolls world of Damon Runyon, I thought he was biting off too big a piece of cheesecake . . . but being one smart operator, he consulted Mindy's, with results that have turned out quite nicely-nicely, thank you!*

The Sinister Cheesecake

CRAIG SHAW GARDNER

It is about seven in the evening on the finest of June days on Broadway, which many citizens, myself included, believe is the finest of streets in the finest of cities, and I am standing there not doing much of anything except perhaps perusing the many fine dolls that happen to be passing my way, when suddenly my attention is distracted by this old geezer, who despite being rather on the aged and feeble side, has the kind of voice that would do any geezer proud.

He is shouting and waving and pointing at this one particular doll on this fine evening, saying things like "Stop her!" and "She mustn't get away!" and "The future of the League of Nations may be at stake!" The doll, and a very fine doll she is, with blonde hair that curls most vigorously and a figure that could receive positive comments from someone even older than the geezer currently following her, is shaking her head, and smiling most sadly, but beautifully, as if this geezer who is following her is clearly off his nut, and no doubt the coppers will be taking him away at any minute as soon as they get done with their more important tasks, say looking the other way at one of Nathan Detroit's informal gatherings, or perhaps eating donuts down at Sid's Donut Emporium.

Now, there are a number of other citizens residing upon the steps around me, for this particular corner of Broadway has developed a reputation for being a particularly fine vantage point for that occupation in which we had been currently employed, and while this particular doll is the sort that might make our whole evening's employment worthwhile, all this shouting could put the kibosh on the entire deal. So it is that a certain citizen, known hereabouts as Hard-Luck Harvey Hossengriff, took a step forward to get a better look at this situation.

"Excuse me, sir," said Hard-Luck, who always has a habit of getting right to the point before the situation gets any worse. "Are you, perhaps, bothering this doll?"

"Bothering her?" the geezer sneers back at Hard-Luck, which is usually not a good idea, for what Harvey Hossengriff lacks in luck he makes up for with a wicked right uppercut. However, Hard-Luck restrains himself from an immediate demonstration of his talents, perhaps because as the old man speaks it becomes evident from his choice of words that he is not from around here, and thus might be cut a little slack before things are explained to him and he is taught a lesson he will never forget.

"I'm afraid I have to do more than bother her!" the geezer goes on. "While she may seem like an innocent young woman, this Miss Hilda Von Arpel is in league with a group of spies who could bring this country to its knees!"

Well, this is another matter entirely. So it goes that Hard-Luck decides completely against teaching this geezer a lesson he will never forget, at least for the moment, and says instead, "Excuse me, but you have made the most serious of accusations against this here doll, and, at the very least, we should give this Judy a chance to defend herself."

With that, Hard-Luck turns to this Miss Hilda Von Arpel with a slight bow and a wave of his hand, for while he doesn't have any luck, he certainly has manners, and further, since the old geezer has called this doll "miss," Hard-Luck is already thinking in terms of marriage, another area in which luck has so far escaped him.

Unfortunately, his most gracious and impressive gesture will not lead towards marriage or much of anything else, for the doll no longer stands in Hard-Luck's vicinity. Indeed, the doll has taken a powder, and has vanished as quickly as a friendly game after Officer O'Clanrahan's police whistle.

This leads the old geezer to shout in a most vociferous manner. "Aha!" he shouted. And "That proves it!" And "She'll never get away with it now!" And this is followed by other exclamations of the same general sort at such a length that Hard-Luck considers giving the old geezer a wicked right upper-cut anyway, until Easy Frank the Loan Shark steps between Hard-Luck and his target and asks what was now upon the minds of many of the other citizens.

"Excuse me, sir," Easy Frank interrupts. "The doll has scrammed. This is a fact that anybody with two eyes in his head can plainly see. What, then, might you mean by all this talk of aha and proving and getting away?"

At this, the geezer rubs at his hawklike nose and looks most keenly at

Easy Frank. "Quite right. I was carried away by the chase." He begins to pace back and forth most vigorously, giving the surrounding citizens the notion that, even though he was a geezer, he has a lot of spunk, and perhaps could return a wicked right uppercut or two himself.

The geezer stops and stares with great purpose at Hard-Luck Harvey Hossengriff. "It's the problem with keeping bees! You lose your edge."

The surrounding citizens, quite taken by the force of this fellow's statement, all nod their heads as if they understand exactly what the geezer was discussing.

"How do I explain myself?" the geezer ruminates. He glances quickly at the surrounding citizens. "I gather that a number of you do, how do you put it, 'play the horses'?"

Now the surrounding citizens cannot deny this statement, for the only way most of them would not play the horses would be for want of sufficient scratch. But a number of those in the crowd might want to know exactly why the geezer would want to know such a fact.

"Playing the horses can be a most lucrative endeavor," Easy Frank therefore says, "which is besides most times quite legal and completely above-board."

"Oh, it is not for me to make a judgement on the nature of the game," the geezer replies. "Believe me, I have done a thing or two in my time that was, shall we say, not quite within the law."

Well, a statement of this type immediately endears the geezer to any number of the surrounding citizens, many of whom could make similar pronouncements without breaking a sweat. So it is that all around begin to listen even more closely to what the geezer has to say.

"I was instead, only making an observation. I know for a fact that certain individuals have visited race tracks hereabouts!" And with that, he turns to a former boxer, now called Cauliflower for obvious reasons, and states, "You, sir, have recently been to Saratoga!"

At this, Cauliflower gasps, and states that he most certainly has, just the day before, although he wished he hadn't, for while he was in Saratoga he has dropped a bundle.

"How, sir, could you know such a thing?" Easy Frank demands.

"Quite elementary, really," the geezer replies, "for he has a certain type of red clay on his shoes that one only finds in Upstate New York, specifically in Saratoga!" And with that, the old fellow continues around the circle, and describes those tracks which a number of the other citizens have visited, including many in the greater New York area and even a couple in New Jersey. Then does the geezer turn back to Easy Frank and say "But you, good sir, have not been to a track in quite some time!"

At this, Easy Frank and all around him are astonished, for it is well known in these parts that as a youth Frank did nothing but lose on horses, and only came into his own bankroll after he restricted his financial activities to loaning money to other citizens so that they could lose for themselves.

"Child's play, really," the geezer replies to the many remarks of astonishment. "I did a study upon the issue on my voyage to America. I pride myself upon keeping up to date on such specifics as these."

"May I ask," Easy Frank replied quickly, "what the name of a fellow who knows such specifics might be?"

"Ah," the geezer answers back, "I had half-expected you to guess. I, good sirs, am Sherlock Holmes!"

And the geezer says this in a great voice, with his right arm lifted toward the heavens, as if we were to be in some way impressed. Of course, none of the citizens standing around could see this, because when many of those same citizens sport monikers like Harry the Horse, Nicely Nicely Johnson, The Lemon Drop Kid, and, indeed, Hard-Luck Harvey Hossengriff, a name like Sherlock Holmes is in no way special, and, frankly, could actually use a little work.

But I cannot forget certain statements this Mr. Sherlock Holmes had made earlier, before all the racetracks and such, so I steps forward and says, "But you have said some very serious things about this Miss Hilda Von Arpel. You mentioned such matters as the League of Nations and bringing this country to its knees." And, as I says this, a number of the citizens nodded their heads as if these were very serious matters indeed. For a country which allows one to freely play the horses at any number of tracks in the greater New York area, and to just as freely peruse dolls on a warm June evening, is a very great country indeed.

"Do you remember that this Miss Hilda Von Arpel had a mole, just here?" And with that, the geezer presses a finger to his cheek.

Well, a number of the citizens nod their heads in agreement, for, while there was much to admire in all parts of this particular doll, still, after her blonde curls and attractive form and wonderful smile and perhaps four or five other outstanding features, most of those around this circle had managed to notice that mole, especially since it was in the vicinity of an extremely tantalizing dimple.

"Well, Miss Von Arpel has no mole!" Sherlock Holmes insists. "That was a miniaturized dot, filled with secret code of the utmost urgency." He fixes us all then with a keenness of gaze usually seen only in certain parole officers and the nuns over at Saint Stephen's parish school. "And she is about to pass it on to certain foreign nationals who do not have our best interests at heart."

This seems most unbelievable to most of the citizens gathered around here. Still, this geezer has already displayed a remarkable knowledge of race track mud, the sort of fact that many citizens might find extremely useful under the right circumstances, so many here are willing to give him the benefit of the doubt.

I decide it is my turn to ask the question: "What could the doll hide in a dot that would be of interest to these foreign national guys?"

With this, Sherlock Holmes looks carefully from side to side, as if to assure himself that only the dozen or so citizens gathered round would hear. "The exact nature of the information dot not only would transmit sounds but visual images, smells, tastes, and tactile impressions! And that is only the beginning!"

Now, we all agree that he doesn't need to say any more, since such a thing would be of great interest to any citizen, foreign or not. So it was clear that this Miss Hilda Von Arpel had to be stopped, and further that we would give this Mr. Sherlock Holmes a hand in doing this, during which time the geezer might tell us a bit more of what he knew about race tracks.

So we were all smiles and hearty handshakes, with the possible exception of Hard-Luck, who still could not see beyond the Miss on the beginning of Miss Hilda Von Arpel's name.

"So tell us, Mr. Sherlock Holmes," I further inquire, "what assistance we may be able to give you?"

"I have had previous encounters with our Miss Von Arpel. She will pass the information that she has in public, the more public the better." He hit us again with that gaze that made you want to confess something just to make it go away. "So, quickly, where is the most public place around here?"

At that, the citizens all volunteer the various high points of the neighborhood, including the Hot Box, a local nightclub of some repute. But Sherlock Holmes says that a lady who walked unescorted into such an establishment would no doubt draw attention. He makes the same objection to such long-standing institutions as Good Time Charley Bernstein's joint. So what are we left with, I says, but Mindy's, the restaurant where everybody meets and eats for blocks around.

"Aha!" Mr. Sherlock Holmes exclaims in that way he has. "Mindy's! Precisely." And he further tells me to lead the way. Which I do.

But the rest of the citizens who accompany us, for what might happen next promises to be even more interesting than perusing dolls, ask what they can do.

"I think we will make the crowd in Mindy's a little more crowded," replies Mr. Sherlock Holmes. "Should we surround her, she will not be able to pass the secret along to anyone."

Well, everyone shows great enthusiasm for this plan, so we get to Mindy's in no time at all. And, amazingly enough, there, in one corner, at a table all by herself, sits Miss Hilda Von Arpel.

"Aha!" goes Mr. Sherlock Holmes, and there is a great deal of wonderment all around, although, if one can determine what race track one has visited just by looking at one's shoes, finding a doll in a restaurant should be no trouble at all. In fact, only one of the citizens in our particular crowd seems less than enthusiastic about our meeting, and this citizen is none other than Hard-Luck Harvey Hossengriff.

"I cannot see as how such a doll as this can do the terrible thing you have spoken of," Hard-Luck therefore announces to the crowd. "I will go over and speak to this doll directly."

And, so-saying, Hard-Luck makes a beeline across Mindy's straight to Miss Hilda Von Arpel's table.

Now, a couple of the other citizens make to restrain Hard-Luck from this rash course of action, but Mr. Sherlock Holmes says that no, this fits right in with our plans. And he further nods at the door behind us, for who should walk in but three fellows who are obviously not from around here, and even more so than Mr. Sherlock Holmes. For these three gentlemen all sport full, dark beards, and further they all wear heavy coats more suited to December than June. And all around see that they eyeball Miss Hilda Von Arpel, and the doll is eyeballing them in return.

"Why, look," Mr. Sherlock Holmes says to all around, as if he has lived around the corner from Mindy's for all of his life, "but here enter some strangers to our fair city."

Now Cauliflower picks up on this right away, for, while his nose and ears have taken on interesting new shapes, there is very little wrong with his brain. "Hey!" he says. "Let's welcome these gentlemen! I think these strangers would be greatly benefited if we were to show them some sights!"

And with that, Cauliflower and a dozen of his closest friends escort the three newcomers out of Mindy's for some very active sightseeing.

This leaves only Mr. Sherlock Holmes, Easy Frank and myself left of the original group of citizens. But Mr. Holmes nods to both of us as if this was what he was planning all along, and marches straight over to the table now occupied not just by Miss Hilda Von Arpel, but by Hard-Luck Harvey as well.

"Oh!" Miss Von Arpel exclaims as the three of us approach the table. "Harvey, you have defended me before. You may have to do so again!"

"I will do anything you wish, dearest," Harvey says with the sort of smitten smile a guy can only get for a doll, "for the sake of our future happiness."

"Then again," Miss Hilda Von Arpel replies with a smile, "perhaps we should simply ignore these ruffians. Harvey, please finish your cheesecake."

Hard-Luck obligingly takes a large bite, then continues to smile at the Judy of his dreams.

"Give yourself up, Miss Von Arpel," Sherlock Holmes demands. "We have apprehended your friends. Now there is nowhere for the miniature dot to go."

"What miniature dot?" Harvey demands between mouthfuls of his dessert. "Do you see a beauty mark anywhere on this beautiful doll?"

And, indeed, the beauty mark that used to be prominently displayed on Miss Hilda Von Arpel's round and pink cheek is no longer in evidence!

"Are you enjoying your cheesecake?" is Mr. Holmes' only reply.

"It is excellent," Hard-Luck replies as he chews. "Mindy's cheesecake is decidedly the best made in the whole of this half of the city."

Sherlock Holmes nods at this, as if he had expected that answer all along. "I have done a study of cheesecakes since I have come to this country, including eighteen major and twenty-four minor types of said delicacy, and you are no doubt correct."

Hard-Luck nods in agreement as he continues his repast.

"It is a shame," Mr. Holmes continues most casually, "about the burn mark upon the crust."

It is then I sees exactly in which direction this geezer is driving. "Burn mark?" I yell. "Mindy's cheesecakes are prepared just so! They are never burned!"

At this, the doll begins to look most uncomfortable.

"Exactly!" Mr. Sherlock Holmes adds as he gives me the most encouraging smile. He nods to Hard-Luck, who is staring most fixedly at the round black spot upon the graham crackers at cheesecake's end. "Miss Hilda Von Arpel was planning for you to swallow the microscopic dot!"

"Swallow?" Hard-Luck replies, as if such a thing was the last thought on his mind.

"You must excuse me, dear Harvey," Miss Hilda Von Arpel interjects, "but I feel I must powder my nose."

However, Easy Frank and myself are both in a position to see that Miss Von Arpel can do no powdering whatsoever, so she is forced to stay put.

"Then, of course," Sherlock Holmes continues to Hard-Luck, "she would retrieve it, by any means necessary."

"Retrieve? By any means necessary?" Hard-Luck puts down his fork in a way that suggests he may never eat cheesecake again. He then looks at Miss Hilda Von Arpel in a way that suggests the courtship may be over.

"If you continue to make such accusations," Miss Von Arpel demands, "I will be forced to go to the authorities!"

"Ah, Miss Von Arpel," Sherlock Holmes replies with the kind of smile you see on cats right after they have lunched on parakeet, "I do believe the authorities have already arrived."

And with that he looks straight at Hard-Luck. "You are working for Mr. Hoover, are you not, Mr. Hossengriff?"

It is Hard-Luck's turn to look uncomfortable. "Um," he says. And "You see—" Until he finally gives up and asks "How did you know? We are a brand new organization. We get very little publicity. Well, there is that business in Chicago—" Here, Hard-Luck Harvey Hossengriff pauses, still greatly confused.

"I have certain connections both here and abroad," Mr. Holmes replies most casually. "Let us just say that I have my methods. If you would kindly place handcuffs upon the suspect?"

And with this Hard-Luck pulls a pair of cuffs from his pocket and snaps them quickly around Miss Von Arpel's delicate and pale wrists. Then does this fellow, who apparently was a copper all along, but a right guy for all of that, in that he never ran in a single one of the local citizens, rise from his seat and leads Miss Hilda Von Arpel from the restaurant. And Sherlock Holmes takes the remains of the cheesecake and inserts it into a jar he had somewhere about his person.

"Disaster has been averted," he announces to Easy Frank and myself, "and the information on this miniature dot will be returned to its rightful owner. But I could not have done it without your assistance."

"Any good citizen would have done the same," Easy Frank agrees most heartily.

"You are one clever fellow, Mr. Sherlock Holmes," is my response. "I have half a mind to write this whole adventure up for posterity."

But at this the geezer only nods again, as if this was one more thing he was expecting all along.

*C*ompared to sending Sherlock Holmes to Oz, it may not seem so radical to involve him in the topsy-turvy world of Gilbert and Sullivan operettas. According to the Library of Congress, CRIGHTON SELLARS was the pen name of Irma Peixotto Sellars. Author of Contrary Winds (Doubleday, New York, 1948), Ms. Sellars frequently contributed pieces to The Baker Street Journal. (See Appendix I for an afterword about the Gilbert and Sullivan operetta alluded to in this story).

The Dilemma of the Distressed Savoyard

CRIGHTON SELLARS

It was November twenty-seventh in the year 1885, a raw, cold morning with fog wreathing so thickly through Baker Street that we could not see the houses across from us—not even Camden House, directly opposite, which was standing vacant and which had somehow got the reputation of being haunted. It was that morning that Sherlock Holmes chose to surprise me by serving up, in the butter dish, a criminal relic which I have mentioned once before. Before I lifted the lid from the dish, he informed me, with much relish, that it was indeed a criminal relic I was about to survey, which I thought very bad taste indeed, but was much mollified when I disclosed the contents and perceived that nothing but a sprig of parsley reposed on top of the butter.

"A relic?" I asked, puzzled, holding up the parsley.

"Yes," he agreed, "or practically a replica of it. It is what was supposed to be the clue to the multiple murders occurring in the Abernetty family circle."

"And why does it appear this morning, pray?"

"Because, as it happens, I have never given you any details concerning it, and this is such an ideal day to stay indoors and talk. I was almost too cold to sleep last night and tried to warm myself by going over in my mind the various incidents of the Abernetty case, which took place in such excessively warm weather that I was hopeful I might feel a bit more comfortable. But that sort of mental suggestion is not efficacious, Watson, and all it did was amuse me afresh."

Just then there was a knock at the door and Mrs. Hudson brought in a card on the small gold salver studded with emeralds, which had been presented to Holmes by the reigning house of Saxe-Hesseburg as a slight reward for his services in a very delicate business indeed.

"Mr. Alexander Wellington Johns, 5 Hans Place," read Holmes.

"He said, sir," explained Mrs. Hudson, "that he hoped he was not disturbing you by coming too early, realizing that the artistic temperament likes to sleep late."

"Well, Mrs. Hudson, tell him that I am at breakfast and hope that he will be good enough to join me and Doctor Watson at our meal. There's more ham, eggs and toast in the kitchen, I presume?"

"Indeed yes, sir, they shall be up immediately, with another pot of coffee; almost as soon as the gentleman himself."

"I am interested to see Mr. Johns," Holmes confessed, when our good landlady had withdrawn. "I fancy he must have some association with literary or theatrical worlds, and he most evidently has money."

I knew that he wished me to ask him why he said this, but I also could deduce these facts from his message, his address and the style of his card. Before I had decided whether or not to indulge Holmes in the questions for which he was angling, our visitor had entered the room. He was rather a small man with dreamy blue eyes, white side-whiskers, a little, round, bald head and pointed, faunlike ears. He was well and expensively dressed, though his clothes were of slightly old-fashioned cut. In one hand he held a white beaver hat and in the other a gold-handled umbrella. He had tiny feet, in thin leather pumps (he must have come in a cab, for they were dry and immaculate) and as he came into the room, lightly, almost dancing, he gave the effect of a twinkling, almost Puckish motion, that was irresistibly graceful and merry. We smiled at him involuntarily, for he was a cheerful thing to see on a grey day.

"Mr. Holmes? Doctor Watson? I am delighted to be allowed to breakfast with you," said he, putting down his hat and umbrella, divesting himself of his great-coat in a flash, and dancing forward to the table to shake hands with us. "I cannot tell you what a load is off my mind since I have decided to ask your help in resolving my dilemma. I lay awake all night pondering, but the moment the solution of my trouble occurred to me, I rose and came here instantly."

"Sit down, Mr. Johns," said Holmes, waving him to a chair. "Ah! Here is our excellent Mrs. Hudson with more breakfast. Watson, will you help our guest? I perceive, sir, that you are hungry."

"And so would you be, Mr. Holmes, had you been cudgelling your brains all night, trying to find a suitable plot for a very special client."

"I don't doubt it, sir. But if, as you say, you have already arrived at a solution, why come to me at all?"

"Because that was my solution. To give it up and come to you for an amusingly criminal, yet fantastically gory sort of thing that I need. You see, it seemed to me, Mr. Holmes, that you were the very man to help me. If you will allow me to devote myself to this excellent ham and egg, I shall soon be strong enough to explain everything. Dear me! Such a surprise! Coffee for breakfast! How American."

"Yes," said Holmes. "I seldom drink tea. The coffee habit is one that I got from the days I spent in America, and Watson has learned to enjoy it with me."

"I am glad to hear it," said Mr. Johns. "It shows a mind entirely emancipated from the English groove, and that is just what I am looking for."

When we had all finished our hearty breakfast Mr. Johns joined us with his pipe in front of the glowing fire, and for a moment we sat in satiated silence before Holmes said, "I perceive, sir, that you are a writer, a musician, a *bon vivant* and an admirer of Gilbert and Sullivan."

"Yes, I am all of those things, sir; which I imagine you deduce from the ink on my spatulate fingers and the wine-list and Savoy programme protruding from my great-coat pockets; and so taking all those things together, perhaps you know the reason why I have come here." He puffed away at his little pipe with such an utterly impish expression on his face, that I thought instantly of Pan and another sort of pipe.

As I might have expected, Sherlock Holmes was not disconcerted for an instant. "Naturally I know," he said. "You are a man who has thought himself very clever, up to now; but you are now tangled up in a sort of Gilbertian plot which involves, or is supposed to involve, some crime, so you come to me to resolve your difficulties."

"Perfect!" said the little man, applauding delicately. "You are a sorcerer, Mr. Holmes, even though you live at 221B Baker Street instead of 70 St. Mary Axe. Do you recall Mr. Gilbert's John Wellington Wells? He was partly named after me, though altered slightly to make a more euphonious metre for singing. However, that will come into my story in due course."

"Pray continue," said Holmes, and waving toward the Persian slipper added, "And re-fill your pipe."

"Thank you, but I prefer my Strephon Mixture, if you don't mind. And now you shall hear everything in detail. You must know, gentlemen, that in me you see the sole plot-source and inspiration-monger for every English writer of the present day, with the single exception of yourself, Doctor Watson; for you, by confining yourself to reporting the remarkable cases solved by your friend Mr. Holmes, need no other inspiration."

We bowed and Mr. Johns smiled, put his tongue in his cheek and somehow managed to continue. "I can assure you, gentlemen, that it keeps me continually busy to supply my authors with different variants of the same plots, or judicious mixtures of several at once. You may not believe it, but there are only a very few plots—not more than a dozen at most. Let me see—" He told them off on his fingers. "The frustrated lovers, with feuding families; the child lost in infancy, or the heir disguised, who can turn out to be whomsoever the plot most needs; the underdog, of either sex, who comes out on top and wins whatever the prize happens to be—this of course includes the younger son and daughter of the fairytales, viz, Cinderella; the marriage of ill-assorted persons; the lucky charm, happening or machinations of a god from the machine that enable *anyone* to do *anything*; the deserving poor who become rich; the undeserving rich who become poor; the two's-company-three's-a-crowd plot; the villain apprehended; the villain foiled; the happy ending; the unhappy ending; the mistaken identity, including babes mixed about at birth—"

"That's more than twelve," I said, as he seemed to be sailing on without hesitation. "You said there were only twelve and no more."

"So I did," he acknowledged, "but I made the mistake of letting some variants slip in, possibly because I slept little last night. All these basic plots, you know, can be treated in any manner one wishes; as comedy, tragedy, sober reality, or fantasy, and their combined variety works out to infinity. You may be interested to know that among other illustrious clients (including of course all English playwrights) I have the honour to be retained by Mr. William Schwenck Gilbert of the famous duo of Gilbert and Sullivan, whose current opera is the present popular passion of London. Mr. Gilbert comes to me for all his plots, and around these ideas that I supply, he writes his matchless fantasy, satire and smoothly graceful verse for the lines, lyrics and choruses. Needless to say, I am one of his greatest admirers and seldom miss a performance of his operas, and though I have the highest respect for Mr. Sullivan and his beautiful and melodious music, which I am always playing on my piano, yet I have always had a small bone to pick with him, for until this very last opera, *The Mikado,* Mr. Sullivan has been most outspoken about the fact that he did not like Mr. Gilbert's plots—which of course, are really mine—and had been very emphatic in his objections. That was the real reason of their late quarrel—and of course it was my fault. I felt so badly about it that I surpassed myself on the *Mikado* plot, using the disguised heir motif and combining it with a supposed-crime plot, that was so like the adventure of the Honourable Fitzherbert at Upper Tooting—only he really had a body that might belong to anyone till its head was found—that when the present crisis confronted me, I decided to come here for help. Mr. Holmes, my predicament is this: *The Mikado* has run a long time, and Mr. Gilbert wishes to get ready the scheme for his next opera. I have submitted several ideas that I thought were suitable—the children mixed in infancy, the love-spell or charm, the marriage of Titania and Bottom the Weaver, or its equivalent—all of them have been repudiated by Mr. Sullivan, who says that they are nothing but a re-hash of *Pinafore, The Sorcerer* and *Iolanthe,* and the public will accuse him and Mr. Gilbert of repetition! Mr. Gilbert is much upset, for he wants a plot very soon, or their reputations will be gone."

"Why is there such a hurry?"

"There isn't really; for *The Mikado* can run many months yet, but Mr. Gilbert always wants to have everything finished away ahead of time—so different from Mr. Sullivan, who is always in a great rush at the last minute." The little man got up and began to skip about, light as a dandelion puff. "Excuse me," he said, "but I always dance a little after meals. It helps digestion."

He skipped over to the window and peered out into the fog. "What is that?" he gasped, pointing.

We both joined him. "What is what?"

"In the window of the house opposite. It looks like a man in evening dress carrying a large gun; but I cannot believe my eyes."

"You have seen the premonition, then," said Sherlock Holmes, drawing the curtain and lighting another gas-jet. "It is a rare privilege."

"But evening dress *and a gun,*" said Mr. Johns, following us back to the fire. *"Impossible!* To wear evening dress for a hunting costume is as bad as shooting a fox. It's not done!"

"There is a legend," said Holmes, "that the man was not satisfied with the crimes he committed on earth, so his ghost came back to commit more, his ambition being one crime a day. He wears the costume in which he died, having been run over by a hansom cab while on his way to the Savoy Opera."

"Who told you all this?" asked little Mr. Johns, skipping back to his chair.

"Frankly, I invented it all," said Holmes laughing, as we all sat down again. "All that you could possibly have seen was swirling fog, that may have suggested the picture you described."

"But your invention, Mr. Holmes, is remarkable. One crime a day is an intriguing idea—and of course the reason I came here was to ask you to suggest a criminal plot, something quite brutal, gory and terrible, that Mr. Gilbert could clothe with his famous wit and fantasy, to make it acclaimed by all as a gentle gem. However came you to invent a ghost returning to perform one crime a day?"

"I fear that I am not as inventive as you imagine, Mr. Johns. Just before you arrived, I was recalling a case of mine in which such a condition existed for four successive days; so it wasn't a great idea to have a vindictive fog-wraith wish to go on like that forever."

"You have started a very interesting train of thought, Mr. Holmes. I wonder if you would be good enough to tell me the story of your case."

"It may turn out to be a long story, Mr. Johns."

"And so it should be, for a full evening's entertainment; and I wish you to know that if I submit it, or a variant of it, to Mr. Gilbert to use, you shall have full remuneration. Do not be afraid to tell all, thinking that I could not use a tale of the utmost violence and villainy; for the worse it is, the more fun can Mr. Gilbert get out of it."

"Very well, sir," said Holmes, "I will tell you the details of the infamous series of murders in the Abernetty family, as related to me by Mrs. Abernetty, and about which Watson and I happened to be speaking just before you arrived."

"I am all ears, Mr. Holmes," said Mr. Johns, taking out his notebook.

"Then I shall begin in a moment, Mr. Johns," said Holmes, "but first, Watson, will you be good enough to put the butter dish down here on the hearth? I wish to demonstrate something about the parsley."

"We have already had parsley in the Bab Ballads," said our client, "and Mr. Sullivan will again say that Mr. Gilbert is repeating himself."

"You will not find it so, I assure you," said Holmes smiling, "even though that parsley was also associated with a murder. You will understand when you hear my story, and you may omit the parsley if you wish.

"Some years ago, before I had met Watson and we came here to live in Baker Street, I was on a walking trip in the Chiltern Hills, and one morning, when in the heart of them, some twelve or fifteen miles from Dunstable, I became so charmed with the beauty of the hilly country, that I decided that if I could find a remote farm, I would like to stay there for a day or two. It was not long before I came to a homestead, secluded and far from other habitation, that just suited my fancy, so I entered a shady lane and rapped at the front door of a large, thatched house that looked comfortable and picturesque. At first there was no answer, so I knocked again, with a curious knocker of green bronze that seemed very ancient.

"'Come in,' called a woman's voice, so cultured and gentle that I was much surprised. I went into the hall and the voice spoke again, 'In here,' said its owner.

"I went into a large dining room with a fine, beamed ceiling and there sat a surprisingly handsome, blonde, middle-aged lady by the side of the breakfast table, which, though it was quite half-past ten o'clock, was yet uncleared.

"'Are you the police?' she asked.

"At this I was mildly astonished, but I replied, 'No, Madam. I am Sherlock Holmes, the consulting detective, on a walking tour; and I came to see if I might stay here a few days—but of course if you—'

"'Oh, if you are not the police,' she interrupted, 'you will be quite welcome. It will be delightful to have you. We see so few people, alas! And a detective too; exactly what I was wanting. Sit down, sir, and have a cup of tea. It's cold, but it can't be heated up, because the servant won't hear me call, I fear. You are a good listener, I hope, for I have been sitting here for a long time, wishing that some one would come by, to hear my story of what has been happening here at High Table Farm, and to advise me about sending for the police.'

"This seemed to me such a strange speech that I thought perhaps some recent and terrible happening had made the lady incoherent, but as the situation held promise of interest, I sat down and thanked her for her invitation, saying that I should be very glad to hear her story. As for the tea being cold, I said it did not greatly matter on such a hot day.

" 'Yes, it is hot, is it not?' said she and got up to look at a thermometer on the wall by the buffet. 'It is exactly eighty-five degrees Fahrenheit, and at no time since I came in here, at half past eight, has it been less than eighty degrees. It is now exactly twenty minutes to eleven o'clock.' She sat down again at the table and continued, 'Help yourself to toast, sir. It is buttered, so pray do not disturb the butter in the dish yonder, for it is very significant. Very significant indeed, at such a temperature; just as it was yesterday and the day before, and the day before that. You know how hot *they* were!'

"I thought she was more than slightly fey, perhaps indeed from the heat, for it was an excessively warm day, and so I helped myself to some of the buttered toast and some flabby scrambled eggs and begged her to tell the whole story.

" 'I shall be delighted, sir.' Wearing a long, pale green peignoir of some fine gauzy stuff trimmed with exquisite lace, she sat opposite me and politely handing me some gooseberry jam, began her story. 'I am Mrs. Margaret Abernetty, wife, or perhaps I should say, widow, of Professor Despard Abernetty of St. Glasborough University. He is, as you know, the eminent Scottish Archaeologist and authority on Roman relics in the remains of vitrified forts. It was because he had heard of a particularly fine and well-preserved one on the hill there, belonging to this farm, that he engaged it for the summer vacation, with special permission from the owner to excavate. We have been here a month now, Despard and I and our two sons, Robin and Richard, with only one servant, Rose, whom I obtained from the village workhouse. Since that time not a soul from the outside world has one of us seen, until you came, Mr. Holmes, and not a day up to last Sunday passed without my husband and the boys making highly interesting discoveries in the Roman fort. Every night they came back from it, loaded with all sorts of relics they had dug up. Down beyond those trees there,' she pointed through the open window, 'there is a gardener's cottage, now uninhabited, in which every day the excavated treasures are deposited for safekeeping.'

"I thought that she was certainly overcoming her initial incoherence and making very clear statements, when she suddenly said, 'I do not wish to go down there, Mr. Holmes, for everyone in that cottage is dead—all four of them.'

" 'I thought you said no one lived there.'

" 'No one does. I am referring to my husband, the two boys and Rose.'

" 'What! Pray explain yourself.'

" 'So I shall. Since Monday, sir, there has been one crime a day on this farm. Oh, Mr. Holmes, it is horrible! I had no idea of such consequences or I would never have invoked the curse; but it came true and I alone am left! This is Thursday, is it not?' I nodded, quite stupefied by her story, and she went on, 'Only Thursday! And I have lived through years of distraction! I shall tell you about it and you may judge.'

" 'It all started last Saturday afternoon when my oldest boy Robin informed me just before dinner that they had made a most remarkable find and that his father had just taken it to the gardener's house. "What is it?" I asked. "A cestus," said he. Now I have not been among classicists and students of ancient Rome so long for nothing, and I knew the moment he spoke, that the cestus was the girdle of Venus, which, worn by any woman, would make every man in the world fall in love with her.'

" 'Pardon me, Mrs. Abernetty,' I said, 'that would be *The* Cestus. Your son said *a* cestus, which is a very different thing.'

" 'Oh no indeed,' said she. 'It was indeed the Venus's girdle, for I have seen its effects. Let me tell you, that suddenly before my eyes, all those three men, my husband, Robin and Richard fell instantly in love with Rose, the workhouse foundling, the instant that she took it in her hand.'

" 'How could that happen?'

" 'Very easily indeed. They had gone down after dinner to look at it again—it is so light now in the long evenings. I crept after them to see what they were going to do with it, for I thought I would like to have it, and when I looked in the window, there they were, showing it to Rose, who should have been home, washing up from dinner; but I could not catch a glimpse of it because they were all crowding around her.

" 'May I take it in my hand?" asks she; "Certainly," says Despard, and must have given it to her, for that instant they all three fell in love with her.'

" 'How do you know that, Mrs. Abernetty?' I asked.

" 'How does any woman ever know?' she returned. 'By the look in their eyes, of course. I was furious, of course, and cried out a curse on them, little thinking that it would come true so quickly.'

" 'What was the curse?'

" 'That all of them would die before the next week-end. Of course on Sunday it was impossible to commit a crime, but no sooner had the Monday come when Robin, inflamed with jealousy for the love of Rose, killed his father, there in the gardener's cottage, just after breakfast. Next morning after breakfast—that was Tuesday—my Richard killed Robin, for the same reason and at the same time. On Wednesday, the wretched Rose killed Richard, because it was Robin whom she loved and she wanted revenge. But she made a great mistake; next morning she revisited the scene of her crime (they always do) and I followed her and killed her with the cestus. That was something it was good for, for all my trouble came on its account and on hers. That brings us, Mr. Holmes, to two hours ago, and since then I have just been sitting here.'

"My brain was stunned with this bizarre recital, which sounded like the ravings of a madwoman; and I did not know what to say for a moment. Then I found myself asking, 'How were you able to kill her with the cestus? Did you strangle her?'

" 'Of course not. How could I have done so? I put it around my hand and hit her at the base of the brain—the medulla oblongata is most vulnerable to such a blow. She died instantly. That is why she could not come to warm the tea.' 'Naturally,' I found myself saying. 'Can you describe this cestus with which you killed Rose, Mrs. Abernetty?'

" 'I think so. It was made of some rather decayed strips of leather, weighted with iron or lead and wound about itself so as to go over the fingers of the right hand down to the knuckles, and make a very nasty fist with which to be struck. There were other straps to be criss-crossed around the wrist and arm, but I let them dangle, as I was in a hurry.'

" 'Then most positively, Mrs. Abernetty, what your husband found in the fort was the weighted cestus of a Roman gladiator and not at all what you supposed. Indeed, the Cestus of Venus was entirely mythical and could not possibly have had actual existence.'

" 'I must contradict you, sir, for though I admit that the cestus, with which everyone was killed, may have belonged to some ancient gladiator of one of the legions stationed somewhere about here, near Icneild Way and Watling Street, yet I myself saw the thing put the spell of love on all my men, for that worthless workhouse brat. Yet stay; perhaps that may be the solution. They may be one and the same, as you say the girdle is entirely mythical.' "

Mr. Johns chuckled. "You picked the right story to tell me, Mr. Holmes. The lady seems to have spoken in exactly the manner that most intrigues Mr. Gilbert. It must have been a rather bewildering situation in real life."

"I must confess that I did not know exactly what to make of it, and wondered what my duty was. If the woman was mad, as she seemed to be, what was she doing sitting alone in an apparently deserted farm house, near old Roman ruins in the Chiltern Hills? Perhaps indeed some crime, or crimes, had been committed and terror had unhinged her brain. It occurred to me that I had better investigate the gardener's house. As I rose, the clock struck eleven and Mrs. Abernetty said, 'Where are you going?'

" 'To the gardener's house. To investigate these crimes. The corpses cannot be left there.'

" 'Can they not? It would be so much more convenient. Why bother?'

" 'Nevertheless, I am going down there.'

" 'Well then, do not blame me if you do not come back, but join them there in death. But if you insist on going, now that you are up, will you be good enough to hand me those callipers and the architect's scale from the mantel shelf?'

" 'What are you going to do with them?' I asked, as I handed them to her.

" 'Measure the time that you are gone by the depth that this sprig of parsley sinks into the butter. By long experimentation I have found that when the temperature is eighty-five degrees, as it is now, the parsley sinks one eighty-ninth of an inch every seven and five-eighths minutes. The scale is of course different at different temperatures, and in this way I am enabled to tell lapse of time without looking at the sun or at a clock. I may as well tell you before you go off to die, that I am as famous for my mathematical calculations as my husband is, or was, for his Roman excavations. Are you determined to go?' "

" 'Yes, if you will promise to stay here till I return.'

" 'Oh I shouldn't think of venturing out in the sun on such a hot day.'

" 'I shan't be long,' I said, as I left her, to go out and down toward the clump of trees where she had pointed. 'I'm afraid you will,' she sighed, as she bent to make use of the callipers.

There was indeed a small cottage on the far side of the clump of trees. It was ominously silent as I cautiously approached an open side window, but once there, I found myself looking into a small room fitted up as a study with a desk in the middle and books and various relics of Roman times ranged on shelves about the walls. As I stood there, the door of the room opened and a man of about forty years of age, with spectacles and a brown beard, came in. He carried a spade in one hand and a basket in the other, and though he was dressed roughly, was most evidently a gentleman.

" 'Hullo!' he exclaimed, as he caught sight of my head and shoulders at the casement, 'Who the devil are you?'

" 'I am Sherlock Holmes, the consulting detective, at your service, sir.'

" 'I don't know that I shall need them; detecting services, I mean, but your presence here is rather surprising. What brings you?'

" 'I was given to understand by Mrs. Abernetty'—I began.

" 'Oh,' he said, putting down the shovel and basket. 'Come around to the door, sir, and I'll let you in. I am Professor Abernetty.'

" 'Yes,' he said some time later, as we sat in the little study where I had been giving him the explanation of why I had come to the cottage, 'my poor wife is undergoing her annual midsummer madness. Poor mad Margaret, that is how excessive heat always affects her. At any other time of the year she is as sane as you or I, and indeed is a brilliant mathematician, but great heat seems to go to her brain; and while she never gets violent, she indulges in the wildest flights of fantasy. That is why we always come to some remote farm during the holidays, so that I can hide her failing from our friends. If it is cool tomorrow, she will be herself again—and a very fine woman she is, I can tell you.'

"Two stalwart youths came striding in eagerly, one of them carrying something very carefully. 'My sons, Robin and Richard,' said Abernetty. 'This is Mr. Sherlock Holmes, who is on a walking trip.'

" 'I am glad to meet you, Mr. Holmes,' said the elder. 'Are you interested in Roman relics? I have just found some more leaden strips, Father, that evidently weighted a gladiator's cestus, though not a scrap of the leather is preserved, as in the one we found yesterday.'

"Before I could answer him, a bell rang loudly from the direction of the house.

" 'Dinner!' they all cried enthusiastically, and Richard said, 'I hope Rose made the chicken fricassé that she promised us. Won't you join us at our meal, Mr. Holmes? Rose is an excellent cook.'

" 'I am sure she is, but,' I said, fibbing, but feeling that I could not face Mrs. Abernetty again, 'I am sorry that I am due at Dunstable this afternoon and must be on my way.'—And that, Mr. Johns, is one of the most fantastic adventures that ever happened to me, and I hope you can make something out of it for Mr. Gilbert."

"It is certainly in his line," said Mr. Johns smiling "and I am greatly obliged to you for relating it. He should make something very engaging out of it, in his inimitable fashion. Of course we can't use the girdle of Venus motif, for Mr. Sullivan will object, and rightly, that it is only the love-spell idea over again; but the fantasy of one crime a day turning out to be imaginary crimes that are no crimes, is just in our line—and perhaps that ghost of yours might be linked up, in some fashion, besides some of the other unique ideas. You have a pretty fancy, Mr. Holmes. If I may say so, your imagination might have done as well had you been an author, as it serves you in solving crimes."

"Thank you," smiled Holmes, "but I believe I do more good in the world in my present profession."

"But the parsley?" I asked. "What was the significance of it?"

"Why nothing at all. Look at it there on the hearth, Watson, just as a small practical demonstration of how deranged the poor woman was. You see plainly that in spite of the warmth of the fire, the parsley has not sunk into the butter at all, and on the contrary, the pat has melted and spread out from the bottom, while the parsley proudly rides atop. It somehow symbolizes to me the madness and absurdity of my whole adventure; and if ever,

Watson, you hear me say to you that a case reminds me of that of the Aber-netty family, by the significance of the depth to which the parsley had sunk into the butter, you may know that I consider it very fantastic indeed."

"I am sure Mr. Gilbert will be charmed with it," said Mr. Johns, get-ting up and executing a satisfied little *pas seul*. "He loves horror with a happy ending."

"Ah!" said Sherlock Holmes, "if that could only be true somewhere else than in the brain of Mrs. Abernetty, or the plot of a Savoy opera!"

*P*astiches exist in which Sherlock Holmes confronts an enemy who makes Professor Moriarty seem downright wholesome by comparison: Bram Stoker's noble Transylvanian vampire Dracula. But though supernatural terror is my favorite form of genre literature, I generally balk at its introduction into ratiocinative fiction, except as a misdirective ruse. Yet when the prolific fantasy writer *DARRELL SCHWEITZER*, who edits Weird Tales magazine, submitted the following oil-and-water mixture, I perceived that he not only succeeded in capturing Dr. Watson's style, but remained absolutely true to the quintessential rationalism that Conan Doyle bestowed upon his sleuth. So, with some trepidation, I offer "The Adventure of the Death-Fetch." Aficionados, you have been duly warned . . .

The Adventure of the Death-Fetch

DARRELL SCHWEITZER

In retrospect, the most amazing thing is that Watson confided the story to me at all. I was nobody, a nineteen-year-old college student from America visiting English relatives during Christmas break. I just happened to be in the house when the old doctor came to call. He had been a friend of my grandfather long before I was born, and was still on the closest terms with my several aunts; and of course he was *the* Doctor John Watson, who could have commanded the immediate and rapt attention of any audience he chose.

So, why did he tell me and only me? Why not, at least, my aunts? I think it was precisely because I was no one of any consequence or particular credibility and would soon be returning to school far away. He was like the servant of King Midas in the fairy tale, who can no longer bear the secret that the king has ass's ears. He has to "get it off his chest," as we Americans say. The point is not being believed, or recording the truth, but release from the sheer act of telling. The luckless courtier, fearing for his life, finally has to dig a hole in the swamp, stick his head in it, and whisper the secret. Not that it did him much good, for the wind in the rattling reeds endlessly repeated what he had said.

There being no swamp conveniently at hand for Dr. Watson, I would have to do.

The old gentleman must have been nearly eighty at the time. I remember him as stout, but not quite obese, nearly bald, with a generous white moustache. He often sat smoking by the remains of our fire long after the rest of the household had gone to bed. I imagined that he was reminiscing over a lifetime of wonderful adventures. Well, maybe.

I was up late, too, that particular night, on my way into the kitchen for some tea after struggling with a wretched attempt at a novel. I chanced through the parlor. Doctor Watson stirred slightly where he sat.

"Oh, Doctor. I'm sorry. I didn't know you were still there."

He waved me to the empty chair opposite him. I sat without a further word, completely in awe of the great man.

I swallowed hard and stared at the floor for perhaps five minutes, jerking my head up once, startled, when the burnt log in the fireplace settled, throwing off sparks. I could hear occasional automobiles passing by in the street outside.

Dr. Watson's pipe had gone out and he set it aside. He folded his age-spotted hands in his lap, cleared his throat, and leaned forward.

He had my absolute attention. I knew that he was about to *tell a story*. My heart almost stopped.

"I am sure you know there were some cases of Sherlock Holmes which never worked out, and thus went unrecorded."

I lost what little composure I had and blurted, "Yes, yes, Doctor. You mention them from time to time. Like the one about the man and the umbrella—"

He raised a hand to silence me. "Not like that, boy. Some I never found the time to write up, and I inserted those allusions as reminders to myself; but others were *deliberately suppressed,* and never committed to paper at all, because Holmes expressly forbade it. One in particular—"

At least I didn't say anything as stupid as, *"Then why are you telling me?"* No, I had the good sense to sit absolutely motionless and silent, and just listen.

*I*t was about this same season *(Watson began)* in the year 1900, a few days after Christmas if I recall correctly—I cannot be certain of such facts without my notebooks, and in any case the incident of which I speak was never entered into them—but I am certain it was a bright and brisk winter day, with new-fallen snow on the sidewalks, but no sense of festivity in the air. Instead, the city seemed to have reached a profound calm, a time to rest and tidy up and go on with one's regular business.

Holmes remarked how somehow, in defiance of all logic, it appeared that the calendar revealed patterns of criminality.

"Possibly the superstitions are true," I mused, "and lunatics really *are* driven by the moon."

"There may be scattered facts buried in the morass of superstition, Watson," said he, "if only science has the patience to ferret them out—"

We had now come, conversing as we walked, to the corner of Baker Street and Marylebone Road, having been abroad on some business or other—damn that I don't have my notes with me—when this train of thought was suddenly interrupted by an attractive, well-dressed young woman who rushed up and grasped Holmes by the arm.

"Mr. Sherlock Holmes? You *are* Mr. Sherlock Holmes, are you not?"

Holmes gently eased her hand off him. "I am indeed, Miss—"

"Oh! Thank God! My father said that no one else could possibly save him!"

To my amazement and considerable irritation, Holmes began walking briskly, leaving the poor girl to trail after us like a common beggar. I'd often had words with him in private about these lapses of the expected courtesy, but now I could only follow along, somewhat flustered. Meanwhile the young lady—whose age I would have guessed at a few years short of twenty—breathlessly related a completely disjointed tale about a mysterious curse, approaching danger, and quite a bit else I couldn't make head or tail out of.

At the doorstep of 221, Holmes turned on her sharply.

"And now Miss—I'm afraid I did not catch your name."

"Thurston. My name is Abigail Thurston."

"Any relation to Sir Humphrey Thurston, the noted explorer of Southeast Asia?"

"He is my father, as I've already told you—"

"I am not sure you've told me much of anything—yet!" Holmes turned to go inside. Miss Thurston's features revealed a completely understandable admixture of disappointment, grief, and quite possibly—and I couldn't have blamed her—rage.

"Holmes!" I said. "Please!"

"And now Miss Abigail Thurston, as I have no other business this morning, I shall be glad to admit you." As she, then I, followed him up the stairs, he continued, "You must pardon my abrupt manner, but it has its uses."

When I had shown her to a chair and rung Mrs. Hudson for some tea, Holmes explained further, "My primary purpose has been to startle you into *sense,* Miss Thurston. A story told all in a jumble is like a brook plunging over a precipice—very pretty, but, alas, babbling. Now that the initial rush of excitement is past, perhaps now you can tell me, calmly and succinctly, why you have come to see me. I enjoin you to leave out none of the facts, however trivial they may seem to you. Describe the events *exactly,* in the order that they occurred, filling in such background as may be necessary to illuminate the entire tale.''

She breathed deeply, then began in measured tones. "I am indeed the daughter of the explorer, Sir Humphrey Thurston. You are perhaps familiar with his discoveries of lost cities in the jungles of Indo-China. His books are intended for a limited, scholarly audience, but there have been numerous articles about him in the popular magazines—''

"Suffice it to say that I am familiar with your father and his admirable contributions to science. Do go on.''

"My mother died when I was quite small, Mr. Holmes, and my father spent so much time abroad that he was almost a stranger to me. I was raised by relatives, under the supervision of a series of governesses. All this while Father seemed more a guardian angel than a parent, someone always looking out for my welfare, concerned and benevolent, but invisible. Oh, there were letters and gifts in the post, but he remained *outside* my actual life. Each time he came, we had to become acquainted all over again. Such is the difference in a child's life between six and eight and twelve. *I* had changed profoundly, while he was always the same, brave, mysterious, inevitably sunburnt from long years in the jungles and deserts; home for a short time to rest, write his reports, and perhaps give a few lectures before setting forth again in the quest of knowledge. So things have continued. This past month he has returned again, after an absence of three years, to discover his little girl become a *woman,* and again a stranger. He has promised to remain this time until I am married and secure in a home of my own—''

"Then it should be a happy occasion for you,'' said Holmes, smiling to reassure her, the corners of his mouth twitching to betray impatience. The smile vanished. "But I perceive it is not. Please get to the point, then. *Why* have you come rushing to Baker Street on a winter's day when you would surely be much more comfortable in a warm house in the company of your much-travelled sire?''

She paused, looking alarmed once more, glancing to me first as if for reassurance. I could only smile and nod, wordlessly bidding her to continue.

"The first few days of his visit were indeed happy, Mr. Holmes, but very suddenly, a shadow came over him. For a week and more, he seemed distracted and brooding. Then five days ago he withdrew into his study, refusing to venture out for any reason. He is afraid, deathly afraid!''

"Of what, pray tell?''

"I cannot discern the central fear, exactly, only its broader effects. Certainly he has become morbidly afraid of his own reflection. He will not allow a mirror to be brought anywhere near him. He even shaves with his eyes closed, by touch alone, rather than risk seeing himself."

"This *is* extraordinary," I said.

"But surely," said Holmes, "this sort of mania is more in Doctor Watson's line than mine, work for a medical man of a specialized sort, not a detective."

"Oh no, Sir! My father is completely sane. I am certain of that. But I am equally certain that he is not telling me everything, perhaps in an attempt to spare me some horror—for it must be a horror that makes so bold an adventurer cringe behind a locked door with a loaded elephant gun across his knees!"

I leaned forward and spoke to her in my most soothing medical manner. "I am sure, Miss Thurston, that your father has a very good reason for acting as he does, and that, indeed, his chief object is to protect you."

"Yes," said Holmes. "I am certain it is."

"His very words were, 'Summon Sherlock Holmes, girl, or I shall not live out the week!' So here I am. Please come and see him, Mr. Holmes, *at once!*"

Holmes shot to his feet. "Watson! How foolish of us to have even removed our hats and coats. Come!" He took our guest by the hand and helped her up. "As I said, Miss Thurston, I have no other business this morning."

*I*t was but a short cab ride to the Thurston residence, in the most fashionable part of west London. We rode in silence, crowded together, the girl in the middle, Holmes deep in thought. Unconsciously almost, Miss Thurston took my hand for reassurance. I held her firmly, but gently.

It was admittedly an intriguing problem: what, if not a sudden mania, could cause so brave a man as Sir Humphrey Thurston to be paralyzed with fear at the sight of his own reflection?

As we neared the house, the girl suddenly struggled to stand up in the still moving cab.

"Father!"

She pointed. I had only a glimpse of a tall, muscular man on the further streetcorner, and noted the tan coat and top hat, white gloves, and silver-tipped stick. He turned at the sound of Miss Thurston's cry, revealing a grey-bearded face, dark eyes, and a broad, high forehead, then moved speedily away in long strides, not quite running. Abruptly, he vanished down a side street.

Holmes pounded on the ceiling of the cab for the driver to stop and we three scrambled out, I attending to Miss Thurston and the driver while

Holmes set off at a furious run, only to return moments later, breathing hard, having lost all trace of Sir Humphrey.

"I don't know what explanation I can offer," said Miss Thurston. "Perhaps my father's difficulty, mania or whatever it is, has passed, and I have wasted your time."

Holmes nodded to me.

"Mental disease is not my specialty," I said, "but from what medical papers I've read, and from the talk of my colleagues, I do not think it likely that so powerful a delusion would go away so quickly. It makes no sense."

"Indeed, it does not," said Holmes. "One moment, the man behaves as if he is faced with mortal danger. The next, he is out for a stroll as if nothing had happened, but he flees the approach of his beloved daughter and vanishes with, I must confess, remarkable speed and agility."

"What do we do now, Mr. Holmes?"

"If you would, admit us to his chamber. Perhaps he left some clue."

"Yes, yes. I should have thought of that. Pray forgive me—"

"Do not trouble yourself, Miss Thurston. Only lead the way."

She unlocked the door herself. Although it was a fine, large house, there were no servants in evidence. I helped her off with her coat and hung it for her in a closet off to one side. As we ascended the front stairs, she hastily explained that another of her father's inexplicable behaviors was to give leave to the entire staff until—she supposed—the crisis had passed.

"Oh, I do fear that it *is* a mania, Mr. Holmes."

I was beginning to fear as much myself, but had scarcely a moment to consider the possibility when a voice thundered from above, "Abigail! Is that you?"

Miss Thurston looked to Holmes, then to me with an expression of utmost bewilderment and fright. I think she all but fainted at that moment. I made ready to catch her lest she tumble back down the stairs.

Again came the voice, from somewhere off to the left of the top of the stairs. "Abigail! If that's you, speak up, girl! If it's Hawkins, you damned blackguard, I have my gun ready and am fully prepared to shoot!"

Holmes shouted in reply, "Sir Humphrey, it is Sherlock Holmes and his colleague Dr. Watson. We have been admitted by your daughter, who is here with us."

"Abigail?"

"Yes, Father, it is I. I've brought them as you asked."

Heavy footsteps crossed the floor upstairs. A door opened with a click of the lock being undone.

"Thank God, then . . ."

Holmes, Miss Thurston, and I were admitted into Sir Humphrey's study. I was astounded to confront the *same man* we had seen on the street. The broad shoulders, bearded face, high forehead, dark eyes, and athletic gait were unmistakable. But now he wasn't dressed for the outdoors. He wore a dressing gown and slippers. An elephant gun lay across the chair where he had obviously been sitting moments before. On the table by his right hand were a bottle and glass of brandy, a notebook, a pen and an uncapped ink jar.

"Thank God you are here, Mr. Holmes," he said. "Doubtless my daughter has told you of my distress and seeming madness. If anyone on Earth may convince me that I am *not* mad, it is you, Mr. Holmes. I can trust no one else to uncover the fiendish devices by which I have been made to see the impossible."

We all sat. Thurston offered Holmes and me glasses of brandy. Holmes waved his aside. I accepted out of politeness, but after a single sip placed it on the table beside me.

Sir Humphrey seemed about ready to speak, when Holmes interrupted.

"First, a question. Have you been, for any reason, outside of the house this morning?"

Thurston looked startled. "Certainly not. I have not been out of this *room* for five days—" He paused, as if uncertain of how to proceed.

It was Holmes's turn to be astonished, but only I, who knew him well, could detect the subtle change in his manner and expression. To the others he must have seemed, as before, calm and attentive, purely analytical.

The silence went on for a minute or two. Now that I had a chance to examine our surroundings, the room proved to be exactly what I expected, a cluttered assembly of mementoes and books, a large bronze Buddha seated on a teakwood stand, strangely demonic Asian masks hanging on the walls amid framed citations and photographs. In a place of honor behind his writing desk hung a portrait of a beautiful woman whose features resembled those of Abigail Thurston but were somewhat older. This I took to be her mother.

"Do go on, Sir Humphrey," said Holmes, "and tell us what has taken place during these five days in which you have never once left this room."

"You'll probably think I am out of my mind, Mr. Holmes. Indeed, I think so myself, whenever I am unable to convince myself that I am beguiled by some devilish trickery. For the life of me, I cannot figure out how it is done."

"How what is done, Sir Humphrey?"

"Mr. Holmes, do you know what I mean when I say I have seen my *death-fetch?*"

Abigail Thurston let out a cry, then covered her mouth with her hand.

Holmes seemed unperturbed. "In the superstitions of many races, a man who is about to die may encounter his spirit-likeness. The German term is *doppelgänger,* meaning double-walker. Certainly such an apparition is held to be a portent of the direst sort, and to be *touched* by this figure means instantaneous death. You haven't been touched by it then, have you, Sir Humphrey?"

Thurston's face reddened. "If you mean to mock me, Mr. Holmes, then my faith in you is misplaced."

"I do not mock. Nor do I deal in phantoms. My practice stands firmly flat-footed upon the ground. No ghosts need apply. Therefore I must agree with your conclusion, even before I have examined the evidence, that you are the victim of trickery of some kind. But first, describe to me what you *think* you have seen."

"*Myself*, Mr. Holmes. My daughter has surely mentioned my sudden aversion to mirrors."

"Don't we all see ourselves in mirrors?"

"I saw myself *twice.*"

"Twice?"

"Five mornings ago, I stood before the mirror shaving, when a second image appeared in the glass, as if an *exact duplicate of myself* were looking over my shoulder. I whirled about, razor in hand, and confronted *myself* as surely if I gazed into a second mirror, only the face of this *other* was contorted with the most venomous hatred, Mr. Holmes, the most absolute malevolence I have ever beheld. The lips were about to form an utterance which I somehow *knew* would mean my immediate death.

"So I slashed frantically with my razor. I felt the blade pass through only the air, but the figure vanished, like a burst soap bubble."

"And it did not harm you in any way," said Holmes, "any more than a soap bubble—or some projected illusion of light and shadow."

"Oh no, Mr. Holmes, this was no magic-lantern show. It was a fully three-dimensional image. Each time I saw it, it was as real to my eyes as you and Dr. Watson appear now."

"You saw it, then, more than once?"

"Three times, Mr. Holmes, until I had the sense to remove all mirrors and reflective surfaces from the room. That is how it *gets in*. I am certain of that."

"And I am certain, Sir Humphrey, that *you* are certain of far more than you have told me. Unless you give me *all* of the facts, I cannot help you, however much your daughter may entreat me. Who, for instance, is the 'blackguard Hawkins' you took us for on the stairs?"

Thurston refilled his glass and took a long draught of brandy, then settled back. "Yes, you are right, of course, Mr. Holmes. I shall have to tell you and Dr. Watson everything." He turned to his daughter. "But you, my dear, perhaps should not hear what we have to say."

"Father, I think I am old enough."

"It is not a pretty story."

★ ★ ★

"My early years were wild," Sir Humphrey began. "I was no paragon of scientific respectability at twenty-one, but little more than a common criminal. I have never before admitted that I was dismissed from the Indian Army under extremely disreputable circumstances and only escaped court martial because a sympathetic officer allowed me time to flee, change my name, and disappear. The offense involved the pillage of a native temple, and the officer's sympathy had been purchased with some of the loot.

"And so, under another name, I wandered the East. I had no means by which to return to England, nor had I any desire to present myself to friends and family as a failure and a disgrace. Once in a very great while I dispatched a letter filled with fanciful, if artfully vague, tales of confidential adventures in government service.

"In the course of my travels I picked up several languages and a profound education in the ways of the world's wickedness. I fell in with the roughest possible company, and was myself more often than not on the wrong side of the law. In the gold fields of Australia there was a certain dispute and a man died of it, and once more I had to vanish. In Shanghai I worked as an agent for a wealthy mandarin, whose true activities, when they became known to the Chinese authorities, caused his head to be pickled in brine.

"But the blackest depths were in Rangoon, for there I met Wendall Hawkins. He was a vile rogue, Mr. Holmes, even among such company as I found him. Murderer, thief, pirate, and more—I am sure. He was a huge, powerful man with an enormous, dark beard, who used to jokingly boast— though I think he half believed it—that he was the reincarnation of Edward Teach, the notorious buccaneer commonly known as Blackbeard.

"Reckless as I was, my normal instinct would have been to avoid such a man as I would a live cobra, but he had something which fascinated me: an idol six inches in height, of a hideous, bat-winged dog, carven of the finest milky green jade, stylized in a manner which resembled the Chinese but wasn't. Its eyes were purest sapphires.

"Mr. Holmes, I was more than just a thieving lout in those days. Already the direction of my life's work was clear to me—though I had yet to learn its manner—for if ever I suffered from a true mania, it was the craving to penetrate the deepest secrets of the mysterious Orient. Oh, I wanted riches, yes, but more than that I hoped to come back to England famous, like some Burton or Livingston or Speke, having brought the light of European science to the darkest and most forbidden corners of the globe.

"I knew what this idol was, even before Wendall Hawkins told me. It was an artifact of the Chan-Tzo people who inhabit the Plateau of Leng in central Asia, in that unmapped and unexplored region northwest of Tibet, where theoretically the Chinese and Russian empires adjoin, but in fact no civilized person has ever set foot—for all the ravings of Madame Blavatsky contain much nonsense about the place. The very name, Chan-Tzo, is often mistranslated as 'Corpse-Eaters,' and so occultists whisper fearfully of the hideous rites of the 'Corpse-Eating Cult of Leng.' In truth necrophagy is the least of Leng's horrors. The Chan-Tzo are 'Vomiters of Souls' . . . but I am far ahead of myself.

"Hawkins had the idol and he had a map—which had been acquired, he darkly hinted, at the cost of several lives—written in an obscure Burmese dialect. He needed me to translate. That was why he had come to me. Otherwise he would share his treasure-hunt with as few as possible—for that was what it was to be. We would journey to Leng armed to the teeth, slaughter any natives who stood in our way, and return to civilization rich men. I tried to console my conscience with the belief that I, at least, would be travelling as much for knowledge as for wealth, and that through my efforts this find could be of scientific value.

"Hawkins and ten others had pooled funds to buy a steam launch, which we christened, to suit our leader's fancy, the *Queen Anne's Revenge*. Once we had secured sufficient ammunition and supplies, we slipped up the Irrawaddy by night and journeyed deep into the interior, beyond the reach of any colonial authorities, ultimately anchoring at Putao near the Chinese border and continuing overland.

"I don't have to tell you that the trip was a disaster. Supplies went bad or disappeared. We all had fevers. What native guides we could hire or seize at gunpoint misled us, then got away. I alone could read the damned map, but it was cryptic, even if you could make out the script. Much of the time I merely guessed and tried to find our way by the stars.

"Many times I was certain that none of us would get back alive. The first to die was the crazy American, something-or-other Jones, a lunatic who carried a bullwhip and fancied himself an archaeologist. We found Jones in his tent, bloated to half again normal size, his face eaten away by foot-long jungle leeches.

"One by one the others perished, from accidents, from disease that might have been poisoning. Gutzman, the South African, caught a dart in the neck one night. Van Eysen, the Dutchman, tried to make off with most of our remaining food and clean water. Hawkins shot him in the back, then killed the Malay when he protested, and the Lascar on general principles. Another Englishman, Gunn, got his throat cut merely so that there would be one mouth less to feed.

"Since I alone could read the map—or pretended to—I was certain Hawkins needed me alive. In the end, there were only the two of us, ragged and emaciated wretches staggering on in a timeless delirium of pain and dread. It was nothing less than a living death.

"At last we emerged from the jungle and climbed onto the windswept tableland of central Asia. Still the journey seemed endless. I had no idea of where we were going anymore, for all I made a show of consulting the map over and over so that Hawkins would not kill me. Each night I dreamed of the black and forbidding Plateau of Leng, which was revealed to me in a series of visions, its ruins and artificial caverns of shocking antiquity, perhaps older even than mankind itself, as were the immemorial blasphemies of the Chan-Tzo.

"What Hawkins dreamed, I cannot say. His speech had ceased to be coherent, except on the point of threatening me should I waver from our purpose. I knew he was insane then, and that I would die with him, likewise insane, unless I could somehow escape his company.

"I was past thinking clearly. How fortunate, then, that my plan was simplicity itself—almost the bare truth rather than some contrived stratagem.

"I fell to the ground and refused to rise, no matter how much Hawkins screamed that he would blow my brains out with his pistol. I said I was dying, that his pistol would be a mercy. *He* would offer me no mercy. I was counting on that. Instead, he forced me to translate the map for him and make notes as best I could. There was nothing to write with but a thorn and my own blood, but I wrote, and when he was satisfied, he laughed, folded the map into his pocket, took *all* our remaining supplies, and left me to my fate on the trackless, endless plain.

"And so we parted. I hoped I had sent him to Hell, deliberately mixing up the directions so he'd end up only the Devil knew where. He, of course, assumed I would be vulture's meat before another day or two.

"But I did not die. Mad with fever and privation, my mind filled with fantastic and horrible hallucinations, I wandered for what might have been days or even weeks, until, by the kindness of providence alone, I stumbled into the camp of some nomads, who, seeing that I was a white man, bore me on camel-back into the Chinese province of Sinkiang and there turned me over to a trader, who brought me to a missionary.

"This proved to be my salvation, both physical and otherwise. I married the missionary's daughter, Abigail's mother, and largely through the influence of her family I later found a place on a much more respectable Anglo-French expedition to Angkor. That was the true beginning of my scientific career. Still the mysteries of the East haunted me, but my cravings were directed into proper channels until I achieved the renown I have today."

★   ★   ★

At this point Sir Humphrey paused. The only sound was the slow ticking of a great clock in some other room. Abigail Thurston's face was white from the shock of what she had heard. She scarcely seemed to breathe. Holmes sat very still, his chin held in his hand, staring into space.

I was the one who broke the silence.

"Surely, Sir Humphrey, there is more to the story than that. I don't see how your luckless expedition or whatever fate the rascal Hawkins must have met has anything to do with the here and now."

Thurston's reaction was explosive.

"Damn it, man! It has *everything* to do with my predicament and what may well be my inevitable fate. But . . . you are right. There is more to tell. After many years of roving the world, giving lectures, publishing books, after I was knighted by the Queen—after my past life seemed a bad dream from which I had finally awakened—I thought I was safe. But it was not to be. *This past fortnight I began to receive communications from the fiend Hawkins!*"

"Communications?" said Holmes. "How so?"

"There. On the desk."

Holmes reached over and opened an ornately carven, lacquered box, removing a sheaf of papers. He glanced at them briefly and gave them to me.

"What do you make of them, Watson?"

"I cannot read the writing. The paper is an Oriental rice-paper. The penmanship shows the author to be under considerable mental strain, perhaps intoxicated. Notice the frequent scratchings and blottings. Beyond that, I can make out nothing."

Sir Humphrey spoke. "The language is an archaic—some would say degenerate—form of Burmese, the script a kind of code used by criminals in the Far East. Between these two elements, I am perhaps the only *living* man who can read what is written here, for Wendall Hawkins *is not alive,* if his words are to be believed."

"Surely if he is dead," said Holmes, "your troubles are at an end."

"No, Mr. Holmes, they are not, for all of these letters were written *after* Hawkins's death—long after it. It seems that he *reached* the Plateau of Leng, which I saw only in visions. There the almost sub-human priests of the Chan-Tzo murdered him after what might have been *years* of indescribable tortures, then brought him back into a kind of half-life as an animate corpse at their command, hideously disfigured, the skin flayed from his face, his heart ripped out, the cavity in his chest filled with inextinguishable fire. He is implacable now, driven both by the will of his masters and his own rage for revenge against me, whom he blames for his unending agony. He knows all the secrets of the Chan-Tzo priests, and the conjuring of death-fetches is easily within his power."

"He says all *that* in these letters?" I asked.

"That and more, Dr. Watson, and if it is true, I am defenseless. My only hope is that Mr. Holmes and yourself can prove me to be *deluded,* the victim of a *hoax* perpetrated by the vile Hawkins who has no doubt returned, but returned, I still dare to hope, as no more than a mortal villain. If you can do this, I certainly have the means to reward you handsomely for your services."

"My services are charged on a fixed scale," said Holmes, "but let us not concern ourselves with the monetary details now. I shall indeed collar this Hawkins for you and unmask his devices—which I am sure would make the tricks of our English spirit mediums child's play in comparison—but they are devices none the less. For what else can they be?"

"Mr. Holmes, I will be forever in your debt."

"We shall watch and wait until Hawkins is forced to show his hand. But first, I think Dr. Watson should escort Miss Abigail to a safer place, my own rooms, which I shall not be needing until this affair is concluded." When Thurston's daughter made to protest, Holmes turned to her and said, "You have been a heroine, but now that the battle is actually joined, I think it best that you remove yourself from the field. Will you go with Dr. Watson?"

"Whatever you say, Mr. Holmes."

"Splendid. Now I must busy myself examining the house inside and out, to discover any way our enemy might use to gain entrance."

Thurston picked up the elephant gun and laid it across his lap, then began idly polishing the barrel with a cloth.

"I've survived five days like this. I think I shall be safe here behind the locked door for a little while longer yet. Your plan makes excellent sense, Mr. Holmes."

We left Sir Humphrey alone in the room. As Holmes and I escorted Miss Thurston down the stairs, the detective asked me, "Well, Watson, what do you think?"

"A unique case, Holmes. One worthy of your talents."

"About Sir Humphrey. What about him?"

"I judge him to be of fundamentally sound mind, but what superstitious fears he may harbor are being played upon by the murderous Hawkins, who sounds himself to be completely mad."

"Mad or not, he shall have to manifest himself in a decidedly *material* form before long, at which point he will be susceptible to capture by mundane means."

"One thing doesn't fit, Holmes. Who, or what, did we see upon our arrival here? Sir Humphrey hadn't been out of the room."

"An imposter, possibly a trained actor in league with Hawkins. I agree that all the pieces of the puzzle are not yet in place. But have patience. You know my methods."

"I am so glad that you and Dr. Watson will help Father," Miss Thurston said softly as we reached the base of the stairs. "You are sent from Heaven, both of you."

Holmes smiled indulgently. "Not from nearly so far, but we shall do what we can."

Alas, we could do but little. As we stood there at the base of the stairs and I helped Miss Thurston on with her coat, she turned and chanced to look back up the stairs. Suddenly she screamed.

"Good God!" I exclaimed.

Near the top of the stairs was a figure who appeared to be Sir Humphrey, but dressed for the outside, in coat and top hat, as we had seen him before. He *could not* have gotten past us.

"You! Stop!" Holmes was already in pursuit, bounding up the steps three at a time.

The figure moved so swiftly the eye could hardly follow, and soft-footedly. I heard only Holmes's boots pounding on the wooden stairs. Then there came a cry from within the study. Sir Humphrey shouted something in a foreign language, his tone that of abject terror, his words broken off in a gurgling scream. The elephant gun went off with a thunderous roar.

I left Miss Thurston and hurried up after Holmes. By the time I reached the study door, which was blown apart from the inside as if a cannonball had gone through it, Holmes was inside.

He rushed out again, his eyes wild, his face bloodless, and he saw Miss Abigail Thurston coming up behind me.

"For the love of God, Watson! Don't let her in!"

"Father!" she screamed. "Oh, you must let me pass!"

For all she struggled, I held her fast.

"Watson! Do not let her through no matter what happens! It is just . . . too horrible!"

I think that was the only time I ever saw Sherlock Holmes truly shocked, at a loss for words.

I forced Miss Thurston back down the stairs despite her vehement protests, holding on to her until the police arrived, which they did shortly, summoned by the neighbors who had heard the screams and the shot. Only after she had been conveyed away in a police wagon, accompanied by a patrolman, was I able to examine the body of Sir Humphrey Thurston, who was indeed murdered, as I had feared.

Though still seated in his chair, he had been mutilated hideously, almost beyond recognition.

His throat was cut from ear to ear. That was enough to have killed him. But the flesh had been almost entirely torn away from his face, and a strange series of symbols, like the ones I had seen in the letters, had been carved in the bare bone of his forehead. The crown of his skull had been smashed in by some blunt instrument, and—it revolted me to discover—most of his brain was gone.

The final detail was the worst, for it had been deliberately designed to mock us. The still smoking elephant gun lay across his lap, and, carefully placed so that it would be *reflected in the mirrored surface of the polished gun barrel,* was a small jade idol with emerald eyes, a stylized figure of a bat-winged dog.

"Yes, Holmes," I said, "it is entirely too horrible."

Dr Watson stopped telling the story, and I, the nineteen-year-old American college student, could only gape at him open-mouthed, like some imbecile, trying not to reach the attractively obvious conclusion that the good doctor's mind had gone soft after so many years. It was a terrible thing, just to entertain such a notion. I almost wept.

I would have remained there forever, frozen where I sat, wordless, had not Dr. Watson gone on.

"It was a case which I could not record, which Holmes *ordered* me to suppress on pain of the dissolution of our friendship. It just didn't work out."

"Wh-what do you mean, didn't work out?"

"I mean exactly that. The affair concluded too quickly and ended in abject failure. We accomplished nothing. He would have no more of the matter, the specifics, as he acidly phrased it, being left to the 'official imagination,' which, sure enough, concluded the murder to be the work of a madman or madmen, perhaps directed by a sinister Oriental cult, a new Thuggee. But even the police could not account for the powerful stench of *decay* which lingered in the explorer's study even long after the body had been removed, as if something long dead had invaded, done its worst, and departed as inexplicably as it had come.

"Enormous pressure was brought to bear to prevent any accurate reportage in the newspapers, to prevent panic. I think those instructions came from the very highest level. Sir Humphrey's obituary, ironically, listed the cause of his demise as an Asiatic fever. I signed the death certificate to that effect.

"My own conclusions were profoundly disturbing. The mystery could not be resolved. What we—even Miss Thurston—had witnessed were not merely unlikely, but *impossible.*

" 'I *reject* the impossible,' said Holmes vehemently. 'as a matter of policy. Such things *cannot be*—'

" 'You and I and the girl saw, Holmes. They *are.*'

" 'No, Watson! No! The irrational has *no place* in detective work. We must confine ourselves to the tangible and physical, carefully building upon meticulous reason, or else the whole edifice of my life's work crumbles into dust. Against the supernatural, I am helpless, my methods of no use. My methods *have* been useful in the past, don't you think? And so they shall be in the future, but we must remain within certain bounds, and so preserve them.' "

*A*gain I, the college boy, was left speechless.

"Holmes made me swear an oath—and I swore it—never to write up this case—and I never wrote it—"

Had he, in a sense at least, broken his oath by telling me? I dared not ask. Was there some urgency now, of which he had lately become aware?

"I wanted to tell someone," was all he said. "I thought I should."

King Midas. Ass's ears. Who will believe the wind in the reeds?

I merely know that a week after I returned to school in America I received a telegram saying that Dr. Watson had died peacefully of heart failure, sitting in that very chair by the fire. A week later a parcel arrived with a note from one of my aunts, expressing some bewilderment that he had wanted me to have the contents.

It was the idol of the bat-winged dog.

Fecundity and literary excellence sometimes go hand in hand, but few contemporary writers can compare with the staggering fictional output of E D W A R D D . H O C H , *past president of the Mystery Writers of America. To date, every issue of* Ellery Queen's Mystery Magazine *since May 1973 has contained at least one Hoch story, and that is just one of many periodicals and anthologies to publish him. When asked how many pieces bear his byline, he shrugs and says, "More than I can count." The number (somewhere around seven hundred) includes such popular series as the borderline-fantasy Simon Ark mysteries, the Jeffrey Rand cryptography puzzles and the wildly inventive thefts of Nick Velvet, a thief who only steals valueless objects. "The Theft of the Persian Slipper" is one of the latter tales.*

The Theft of the Persian Slipper

E D W A R D D . H O C H

"Nick Velvet?"

The man who greeted him at the airport in Rome was dressed like Hollywood's idea of an American gangster. He'd been reading a copy of an English-language newspaper published daily in Italy, and he folded this under his arm as Nick approached. Obviously he knew he had the right man.

"That's me," Nick agreed. "Where's your boss?"

"He doesn't meet people at airports. I'll take you to his hotel."

They drove through the crowded Roman streets to a fancy hotel just a bit too Americanized with its plush decor and vague bustle. "I'll bet the boss loves it here," Nick said. "Just like New York."

The man ignored him and motioned toward the elevator. A few minutes later they were entering the suite of Joe Bonoto. "Velvet. Pleasure to meet you."

Nick shook the wrinkled hand. Joe Bonoto was older than he'd expected, an aged man living on memories of the past. Deported from the United States, he ruled a band of faithful followers in the hills of Sicily. To call them Mafia or even bandits was inaccurate. They were dedicated to no cause greater than the welfare of Joe Bonoto.

"I've come a long way," Nick told him.

"But your roots are here. In the old country."

"My roots are in the old Italian section of Greenwich Village. That's as far back as they go."

Joe Bonoto signaled for drinks. "You'll find the trip worthwhile. We want you to steal something."

"That's my business," Nick said, and indeed it was. Nick Velvet stole the unusual, the bizarre, the valueless. Never money or jewelry or objets d'art. "What is it?"

Joe Bonoto smiled. The surface of his face crinkled like a relief map. "A relic of Sherlock Holmes."

"Sherlock Holmes?"

The smile broadened. "There is a new ski resort in Meiringen, Switzerland, overlooking Reichenbach Falls. Naturally it has a Sherlock Holmes room, in honor of the place where Holmes and Moriarty fought to the death. Are you by any chance a Sherlockian, Velvet?"

"I read all of Conan Doyle's stories in my youth, but I haven't looked at them in years. I guess I can't be called a Sherlockian. Just what is this relic you want stolen?"

"Holmes's Persian slipper—the one in which he kept his pipe tobacco. It hangs near the fireplace in the Holmes room they have at Meiringen."

"There are other rooms like that," Nick pointed out. "I've read about one in London, and another somewhere in Switzerland. I'm sure they all have Persian slippers on display. What makes this one so valuable?"

Bonoto spread his hands. "It is not valuable, Mr. Velvet! You do not steal valuable objects, do you?"

"Correct. But you brought me over from New York and you're willing to pay my fee of $20,000. It must be worth that much to you."

"For Sherlockians it has a sentimental value."

"Why not steal it yourself?"

"My men are too well-known to the police. You can catch a plane to New York and never be seen here again."

"All right," Nick agreed. He'd stolen stranger things in his time, with even less explanation. Besides, Switzerland might be a nice place to visit at this time of year.

His first sight of Reichenbach Falls was a breathtaking one, and he wished that Gloria had been there to see it too. A thin stream of white water dropped down from some unseen spot among the trees, hit an outcropping of rock, and changed into a broad cone of foam and mist. He'd expected something like Niagara, but this was utterly different—a fearful, coal-black abyss as sinister now as it had been the day Doctor Watson described it.

Nick remembered the story of Holmes and Moriarty at the falls, and he could well understand the desire of a new ski resort to cash in on the legend.

In truth, the resort was some distance from the falls proper, on a hill that faced in the opposite direction. It was still too warm for skiing, and Nick had the place virtually to himself when he checked in.

"Here to see the falls?" a sandy-haired Englishman asked him in the lobby.

"Among other things. I drove up from Italy. Name's Nick Velvet."

"Mine's Cottonwood. Felix Cottonwood. I travel in tobacco."

"Tobacco?"

"My firm supplies tobacco products to many resorts in this area. I come around in the autumn and the spring to take orders."

Nick glanced around the lobby. "I understand they have a Sherlock Holmes room here."

"Right this way. It's a prime tourist attraction."

Cottonwood led him down a short passage to a cluttered sitting room fenced off by a low railing. Here indeed was the famous room at 221B Baker Street, with its bust of Holmes by the window, its bullet-pocked "V.R." on the wall, and—yes—its Persian slipper hanging by the fireplace.

"It seems complete in every detail," Nick said. "I'm surprised that souvenir hunters don't hop the railing and make off with things."

"There's an alarm system," Cottonwood answered casually. "But there's never any trouble like that. Sherlockians are content to come and look. Rooms like this are all they have that's new and exciting, unless someday someone comes up with Watson's fabled dispatch-box of unpublished cases."

They returned to the lobby and Nick excused himself to go to his room. He decided to wait till the following day before attempting to steal the slipper. The thing was too easy, too certain.

And the very simplicity of the assignment is what gave him doubts.

He spent the following day touring the area and getting to know the other off-season guests at the ski resort. He found time after lunch to take another look at the Sherlock Holmes room, this time noting especially the electric-eye alarms that criss-crossed the reconstruction of 221B Baker Street.

That night, when activity had settled down to a table of late drinkers in the resort's rustic bar, Nick made his move. He leaped quickly over the railing and carefully avoided the first of the electric-eye beams, using a misty aerosol spray that pinpointed their path without setting off the alarms. It was a trick he'd learned from a recent film, which proved an occasional Saturday night at the movies with Gloria need not be a total waste.

He crossed the second beam and reached out for the curved Persian slipper on its hook by the fireplace. He wondered if it really was filled with tobacco or if there might be something far more valuable inside—something to tempt a man like Joe Bonoto.

In a moment he would know.

"Hold it right there," a woman's voice said suddenly from behind him. "I have a gun pointed at the back of your neck."

He turned slowly, keeping his hands in sight, and saw that she was only a girl, surely still in her early twenties. She had a tiny automatic pointed at him, but it only added to her beauty—in a way that moviemakers had discovered long ago. She was dark, probably French, but her English had been learned in Britain if he was any judge of accents.

"I'm Nick Velvet," he said with a smile. "Who are you?"

Even against a gun he was more at ease with a beautiful girl than with a goon like Bonoto, and perhaps she sensed this. "My name is Annette—don't move—Annette DuFrois. I followed you here from Rome."

He silently cursed himself. It wasn't like him to travel all that distance without spotting a tail, especially a girl as pretty as Annette DuFrois. "What do you want?" he asked her, feeling just a bit foolish.

"To talk, right now. Come out of the room very carefully, without tripping the alarms. If any bells ring, I'll shoot you."

"But—" He glanced back fondly at Holmes's Persian slipper, then decided it might be safer where it was for the present.

He negotiated the light beams with ease on the return trip, then walked ahead of the girl to the side exit. There was a moment when he might have disarmed her with ease, but he was curious now about her reason for following him. He decided to listen before he acted.

"Which way?" he asked when they were outside.

"Straight ahead. I have a car parked down the road."

"Is that it?" he asked, reaching a low-slung white sports car parked among the weeds.

For answer she poked his ribs with the gun. "Inside. The door's unlocked."

Nick bent almost double to fit under the low roof, and the girl followed him into the front seat. He felt the gun nudge him again. "All right, we're here. Now what is all this?"

"You're working for Joe Bonoto," she said. "I saw you at his hotel."

Nick didn't answer at once. A car passed them on the road and its headlights flickered for an instant on her face. "You have lovely eyes, Miss DuFrois."

She raised the gun an inch, otherwise ignoring his remark. "He hired you to steal something from that Sherlock Holmes exhibit, didn't he?"

"Does that concern you?"

"Joe Bonoto concerns me. A long time ago he caused the death of my brother."

The girl was much too young for anything to have happened to her brother too long ago, but Nick said, "Tell me about it."

"There's not much to tell. Richard was running with a bad crowd. He had a job as a courier for Joe Bonoto, and he was paid off in narcotics. Richard became hooked on heroin and died in Paris of an overdose." She stared off into space for a moment, as if remembering it. "I was twelve years old at the time, and I couldn't understand what was happening to him. I was with him when he died."

"That's a reason for you to risk your neck going up against Joe Bonoto?"

"It's reason enough for me. Somebody has to keep the Joe Bonotos of this world from taking over."

Nick wondered if he had ever been that young and idealistic. "You're too pretty to be a philosopher, especially a dead philosopher."

"Are you threatening me?"

"Joe Bonoto will threaten you, if you get in his way."

"I have the gun, remember. You'll do what I say."

"And what's that?"

"Where are you to meet Bonoto after you steal this thing?"

"I'm not. I'll pass it to one of his men." That wasn't strictly true, but he wasn't about to set up his client for a bullet before he'd been paid.

The subterfuge didn't work. Annette raised the gun another few inches, until it was pointed at Nick's chin. "Joe Bonoto doesn't work that way. He never did. He doesn't trust anyone, including you. He'll be close by, ready to show himself and collect the loot personally."

He knew she spoke the truth. "You want to kill him, don't you? I suppose you figure gunning him down up here in Switzerland is a lot easier than shooting up his hotel in Rome or his villa in Sicily."

"Perhaps."

"Well, you won't get any help from me."

"Then I suppose I'll have to shoot you," she said calmly.

"I suppose you will. I've got no great love for Joe Bonoto, but he is paying me. I'm not about to lure him into a trap."

Annette DuFrois smiled. "I'm not asking you to do that. If I kill you now, and hide your body, he'd show up here sooner or later—just to find out what happened to you."

Nick weighed the possibilities and decided it was time to move. They'd talked long enough. He measured the distance between them and decided he could easily reach her before she could fire a shot. There was always an instant's hesitation when an amateur was faced with the need to kill. And that instant was all he needed.

Nick moved.

He was almost on her when the gun exploded in his face, spraying his eyes and face with a stinging cloud of chemical Mace. He'd made one miscalculation—she hadn't planned to shoot him at all.

"You fool," she said, and brought the pistol down on his helpless head.

He woke to awareness slowly, and his first conscious thought was the realization that he was face down in damp grass that tickled his nose. Then he felt something kick him in the ribs and he rolled over. It was just beginning to get light, and he could make out the gangster type who'd met him at the Rome airport. The man was standing over him with a gun, and Joe Bonoto himself hovered in the background, half sitting in the front seat of his car with one hand on the open door.

"Get up, punk," the gangster type growled.

Nick staggered to his feet, still rubbing eyes that felt like burning coals. That damned girl, she'd dumped him from the car and left him by the side of the road!

"We waited for your call," Bonoto said quietly. "When we didn't hear anything we came looking for you. We checked the ski resort and then we spotted you out here."

"I had an accident," Nick mumbled.

"Yeah."

"Besides, I wasn't supposed to call till morning."

Joe Bonoto leaned down. "It was lonely waiting for you. I kept remembering I paid you half your fee already. What happened?"

"A car sideswiped me." His vision was clear at last and he had only a slight headache from the blow of Annette's gun.

"Where is the slipper?"

"Still back at the resort. I didn't have a chance to lift it yet."

"We pay you twenty thousand dollars so we can come up here and get it ourselves?"

"I'll get it," Nick assured them, but Bonoto had made his point. He was on the scene now, and Nick's only payment was likely to come from the barrel of a gun. "Just stay out of sight so you won't be recognized." Or shot, he might have added, remembering Annette.

"Can you get the slipper now, this morning?"

It was still early, and Nick knew the other resort guests wouldn't yet be prowling about. "I can try. Give me a half hour, then drive up the side road and I'll meet you there."

Joe Bonoto nodded. "No tricks."

Nick quickly realized that Annette had driven him some distance from the resort before dumping him out of the car. By the time he walked back, the sun was over the rim of the mountains, but except for a few employees there was still little sign of movement about the place. His car was where he'd left it, and there was no evidence that Annette had returned.

Once more he hurried down the corridor to the Sherlock Holmes room. All was as he remembered it, except for one thing.

The Persian slipper was gone from its hook beside the fireplace.

Nick glanced at his watch. He had twenty minutes before it would be time to meet Bonoto—twenty minutes to explain the slipper's disappearance. Had Annette returned to steal it? He hadn't mentioned what object he was after, but she might have guessed. Or been after it herself from the beginning.

On the other hand, Bonoto might have stolen it and simply saved himself twenty grand.

Nick let his eyes roam over the other objects before him in the Holmes room, but nothing else seemed to have changed. Only the slipper was missing. Someone—Bonoto or Annette or someone else—had negotiated the electric-eye beams and got away with it.

Nick went to the door of the resort and looked down the road. The car belonging to Bonoto had drawn nearer—it was parked just off the road under some trees. Watching it, he was aware of the utter silence of the morning. Only the distant roar of the waterfall—always present and therefore unnoticed—reached his ears.

It was almost as if the spirit of Sherlock Holmes himself had entered the resort and taken down the familiar Persian slipper to fill his calabash pipe.

He went back up to his room to get the gun from his suitcase. Joe Bonoto was not the most stable man on earth, and Nick wanted to be armed when he told him the slipper was missing. Downstairs now there was more activity, as some of the guests had appeared for breakfast. He waved to Felix Cottonwood and a few of the others he'd got to know. Then he went outside and started down the road to Bonoto's waiting car.

The first thing he saw was Bonoto's gunman, sprawled in the weeds to the right of the car. There was little blood, because the dry earth had soaked it up quickly.

Nick drew a deep breath and looked inside the car.

Joe Bonoto was slumped behind a windshield punctured by three spiderwebbed holes. He was an old man, and he hadn't even moved fast enough to die on his feet.

Nick walked away fast without touching anything. His first impulse was to drive to the nearest large airport and book a flight back to New York. The entire assignment had been a bust—the slipper was gone, his client was dead, and the police would surely be looking for him before long.

But then he remembered Annette DuFrois.

Just maybe something could be salvaged from this after all.

It took him till midafternoon to locate her, and long before that some morning strollers came upon the bodies of Bonoto and his bodyguard. Local police cars converged on the scene, with police from more distant points arriving as word of the murdered man's identity became known.

Nick made himself scarce while employees and guests were being questioned, and concentrated on finding Annette. It was her low white sports car that finally revealed her, when he spotted it parked at an inn on one of the winding country roads to the south. He pulled up behind it and slouched down in his seat, waiting.

Presently she appeared, wearing a trim yellow pants suit and carrying a shoulder bag that no doubt held her gun. Nick waited until she had one hand on the door handle and then jumped from his car. Startled, she tried for her purse, but he grabbed it and held it tight. "No more Mace in the face, please."

"How did you find me?"

"It took patience."

"Have you decided to help?"

"You don't need any help. Bonoto and his bodyguard are both dead, back at the resort."

The color drained from her face. "You think I did it?"

"You're a likely suspect. And someone else might have heard you threatening him. The police will surely be looking for your car if somebody remembers seeing it around the place last night."

She gazed into his face. "You're not lying to me? Bonoto is really dead?"

"He's really dead. Isn't it time we talked about your position in all this?"

"I didn't kill him."

"I know that," Nick said.

"You do?" She seemed surprised. "How?"

"It was very quiet just before they were killed—an early morning sort of quiet. At least four shots were fired, one for the bodyguard and three through the car windshield at Bonoto. Yet I heard nothing. That can only mean the killer used a silencer. And a silenced gun isn't the weapon of a woman who announces her intentions in advance, a woman bent on avenging a dead brother. You have a tiny gun that fires Mace, and you probably have one just as tiny for bullets. Bonoto was killed by a professional, someone using a large-caliber silenced weapon."

"Who?"

"Does it matter to you?"

"No, I suppose not. But I'm curious."

"I came to steal something for Bonoto, as you know."

"From the Sherlock Holmes exhibit?"

He nodded. "Someone beat me to it. I think that someone must also be the killer. He might have been escaping from the resort when he encountered Bonoto and was recognized."

"What is it that's so valuable?"

"The Persian slipper in which Holmes was said to have kept his tobacco."

"But—"

"Tobacco." He repeated the word slowly, and suddenly he remembered the unusual occupation of Mr. Felix Cottonwood.

Annette was at his side as they sped back up the hill to the resort. He left her car behind because it was too easily identified, and he didn't want the police stopping them now.

"But why would Cottonwood want the slipper?" she asked. "And why would he want to kill Bonoto?"

"That's what I intend to find out."

The police were still very much in evidence when they returned, and a Swiss officer stopped Nick's car at the entrance to the parking lot, allowing it to pass only after they'd identified themselves as guests. He looked first for Cottonwood in the bar, but the sandy-haired Englishman was nowhere in sight.

"He may have skipped already," Nick said, heading for the front desk. But as he was about to ask the clerk, he saw Felix Cottonwood emerge from an elevator.

"Well, it's Mr. Velvet, isn't it? And I don't believe I know the young lady."

Nick didn't bother with introductions. "It's important I talk with you, Cottonwood. I know about the slipper."

"Slipper?"

"The Sherlockian slipper you stole from the Holmes display."

"Now really, Velvet, I think you're going too far. I am a salesman, not a thief."

"And what is it you sell?"

"I told you—tobacco products."

Nick glanced around the lobby, then pointed toward a secluded corner. "Let's go talk."

"If you must talk I prefer the open air. The police around here are quite unnerving."

Nick motioned Annette to wait for him and followed the Englishman outside. Now in the warmth of the afternoon sun there was a grandeur about the place that defied any attempt at description. As they walked together down the path toward Reichenbach Falls, he knew exactly the emotions Arthur Conan Doyle must have felt on seeing this place.

"This should be private enough," Nick said as they strolled.

Felix Cottonwood smiled. "Oh, yes. Even electronic listening devices would be helpless against the roar of those falls."

"Then suppose you tell me about the tobacco business. And especially about the tobacco in the toe of that Persian slipper. I suspect it's hash or hemp at the very least."

Cottonwood allowed himself a chuckle of mirth. "My good man, even if I dealt in drugs, which I do not, the toe of a slipper would hold barely enough for a dozen cigarettes."

They were closer to the falls now, and Nick could feel the spray on his face. Underfoot, the blackish soil was soft with moisture. "But you did steal the slipper, didn't you?"

"Be careful," the Englishman said. "This path is treacherous."

"Didn't you?" Nick repeated.

"Did I?"

"Your mind runs to electronic listening devices, and probably to silenced pistols as well. Why did you kill Bonoto?"

Cottonwood sighed. "You're an exasperating man, Velvet. You chose the right criminal for the wrong reason. Yes, I killed Bonoto and his gunman, but it had nothing to do with narcotics—or even with tobacco, for that matter. It was only the slipper we were after, and what it contained."

"Which is—?"

Felix Cottonwood drew himself up, becoming for a moment the very model of a British gentleman. "There exists—and has always existed—one item of Sherlockiana more valuable than any other, and more elusive. Today, with the worldwide revival of interest in Holmes, it is not an exaggeration to say this one object could be worth a million dollars."

"Yet it's small enough to be hidden in the toe of a Persian slipper?"

"Quite correct. There was no time to dig it free from the tobacco, so I removed the entire slipper from the room. It is, however, this object that I sought, that I pursued across half of Europe. At last an aged scholar told me where he'd hidden it—but unfortunately he also told others. Bonoto was planning to move in on the Sherlock Holmes business in exactly the manner that the American mob has moved into the distribution of pornography. This I could not allow. He hired you to keep his name out of it, but when I saw him there this morning I knew the truth. And I shot him."

"You're very frank," Nick said.

Felix Cottonwood smiled and turned on the narrow path. There was a mist of spray clinging to his face and eyebrows, and in his right hand he held a silenced pistol. "I'm sorry, Velvet. I was only frank because it didn't matter. I have to kill you, too."

Nick saw death only seconds away as he lunged at the Englishman, then heard the gentle cough of the weapon's discharge. The shot went wild, and he gripped Cottonwood's wrist, forcing the gun into the air. It was no good yelling for the police—the roar of the falls muffled every sound.

They struggled for a moment and then Nick felt his feet sliding on the damp ground. He saw the edge of the chasm looming close.

He felt himself falling.

And then somehow he was clinging to a low bush at the edge of the path, and Felix Cottonwood was tumbling over him, tumbling and screaming into the black depths below.

Nick got unsteadily to his feet and tried to peer into the gorge, but there was nothing to see except the rising mists.

Cottonwood's pistol lay at the edge of the path where it had fallen. Nick picked it up and threw it into the abyss after its owner.

Annette DuFrois was waiting back at the resort. "What happened?" she asked.

"Nothing much. He's gone away."

"And the slipper?"

"It must be in his room. I'm going after it." There was no longer any buyer for the prize, and Nick had no idea what he'd do with it, but he hated unfinished assignments. He had to know what was hidden in the tobacco in that toe.

Finding Cottonwood's room number and opening the door took only a few minutes. Locating the slipper in its hiding place proved to be a bit more difficult. Going through the books and belongings in his suitcase, Nick wondered if he had been a bad man at all—or only a good man with an obsession.

The Persian slipper yielded itself at last, stuffed down inside a bulky climbing boot. Working to empty out the tobacco, Nick could already feel something small and hard in the toe.

Something metallic, with a tiny tag attached.

It was what Bonoto and Cottonwood had died for.

It was the key to a dispatch-box, in the bank of Cox & Company at Charing Cross.

I read somewhere that the reason Charles Dickens's A Christmas Carol *is a perennial favorite is not because of its vivid pictorialism, nor even its ethical "message," but because poor old Scrooge is given an eleventh-hour chance to redeem himself. All well and good, but to paraphrase Shakespeare, is there rain enough in the sweet heavens to whitewash the brilliant but wicked mathematician who nearly put an end to Sherlock Holmes's career? R O B E R T B L O C H, a past president of the Mystery Writers of America and author of* Psycho *and "Yours Truly, Jack the Ripper," seems to think so. This amusing nonpareil was published in 1953 by* The Baker Street Journal. *(For comments, plus late-breaking news concerning Professor Moriarty, see Appendix I).*

The Dynamics of an Asteroid

R O B E R T B L O C H

Honestly, some of the patients you get are a scream. Positively a scream!

Not that I'd want any other kind of work—where else can you make up to twenty dollars a day, and all you do, really, is sort of play nursemaid for a couple of hours? Compared to a hospital or working in some G. P.'s office, it's nothing at all. But the *types* you run into!

Take this last one I had—I didn't tell you about him, did I? He was a hundred years old.

One hundred years *old! Can you imagine?* No, I'm pretty sure of it, the way he talked and all. And to hear him tell it, up to three months ago he was dressing and feeding himself and handling everything in the house out of his wheelchair. Of course, he ordered what he needed over the phone and the hotel sent it right up, meals and everything. But think of that—one hundred years old and all alone in a wheelchair, and he did everything himself!

Of course, you might guess it just to look at him. He'd been some kind of professor of arithmetic or mathematics, whatever they call it, but that was when he was young. Imagine, sixty years ago or so! And then he was in this accident and his left side was paralyzed and he went into a wheelchair. Sixty years, that's a long time to live in a wheelchair. Doctor Cooper, he was handling the case, just stopping in once a week, he said it was amazing.

But the old boy was tough, I got to say that for him. Just one look at him was enough to let you know. Of course when I was put on the case he was in bed already, but sitting up. And when he sat up you couldn't tell he was paralyzed at first. He had a big bald head and a bulgy forehead and his eyes were sunk way back, like they sometimes get. But he wasn't shriveled or even very wrinkled.

He'd stick that head out and his face would move from side to side but all the while those little eyes would stare at you to make sure you were listening. He talked a lot. Talked and wrote. He was forever having me mail stuff for him. A lot of it went abroad to foreigners in colleges over there—professors, I guess. And people in the government over here, and fellas like this Einstein.

That's what I wanted to tell you about—he wrote to Einstein! Did you ever hear of such a thing in all your life?

At first he didn't talk about what he was doing, at least not very much. But he kept getting weaker and weaker and along about the last month he couldn't write. And of course it was hard for him to sleep. Doctor Cooper was all for giving him hypos but he wouldn't take them. Not him! He was tough.

But some nights he'd call me in—I slept in the other room on the couch—and he liked for me to read to him. He got all kinds of crazy-sounding magazines; scientific ones, I guess. And some of them were in German and French and I-don't-know-what-all. Of course I couldn't read those, and when I tried to read the regular English ones he got mad because of course I didn't know all those two-dollar words.

So mostly he had me read the papers. And that's where the crazy part started.

Take like the crime news. You know, there's been a lot of killings lately, all these G. I. murderers and that. And I'd get to reading about them and all of a sudden he'd be laughing.

At first it bothered me. I thought he was just plain *se*-nile. The way they get sometimes, you know.

But once, about two weeks before he died, he was listening to me read about one of those crime syndicates; I mean where they all gang up and plot like blackmail extortions and things.

And he gave this chuckle of his and he said, "Strange, isn't it, Miss Hawes?"

So I said, "What's strange?"

And he said, "To think that it's still going on. It takes one back, Miss Hawes. It takes one back."

I said, "You mean they used to have gangs like this when you were—" I stopped real quick, because I'd almost said, "alive."

And the funny thing happened, because he finished the sentence for me and *he* said, "alive?" Then he laughed again. "Yes, they had gangs when I was alive, and master criminals and workers behind the scenes. I was one myself, although you may find that hard to believe. Just as it may be hard for you to believe that I died over sixty years ago."

Then I knew for sure he was getting *se*-nile. And it must have showed on my face.

"Perhaps you might be interested in my story," he said. And of course I said, "Yes," even though I wasn't. To tell you the truth I kept right on reading the paper all the while he was talking, but I wish now I'd listened a little more because some of it was real wild.

So he kept on rambling about how it was when he was a young man in college or university or wherever, and he was studying all this fancy mathematics stuff, and then he got out and he couldn't get a job. I guess he finally got to teaching for a sort of a small private school and then he was a tutor, like, for rich kids over in England.

And he wrote some books but nobody paid any attention because he was ahead of his time, whatever that means.

Well, to make a long story short, I gather he wanted to get married and his girl turned him down for a richer fella, and he just went all to pieces. That's how he became a criminal, to hear him tell it.

And, to hear him tell it, he was a real big-shot. He was like one of those super-criminals you hear about; never did anything himself but just gave advice. He would plan things for the rest to do and get a commission.

He said he had a logical mind and because of all that studying he did, he knew just how to organize things. Pretty soon he was working for gangs all over Europe, too, and he made a fortune. That part of it I can believe, because even now he was living in this big hotel suite and he hadn't worked for over sixty years, being in a wheelchair and all.

But all the while he told me this he kept working in names and dates and places that didn't make any sense to me, and I just couldn't be expected to pay too much attention.

Finally he saw I wasn't listening and he shut up. That suited me, except that I wondered what he'd meant about him dying, like he said.

A couple of nights later that came up again. I was reading about some doctors out west, keeping somebody alive massaging the heart during an operation—you know. They did it over at Sinai a few months ago, didn't they?

Anyhow, he said, "Doctors! Call themselves medical authorities and they don't know the first thing about life. If I'd listened to them, I'd be dead and buried these sixty-odd years past."

Well, it just happened that I was pretty tired, and I guess I must have dozed off right in the middle of what he was saying. But I remember him starting out with this story about how he got tangled up with the police and some detective was out to get him, only he got him first. After they had a big fight somewhere, I forget the name, he was left for dead. Only he wasn't dead, he was just paralyzed.

This was over in Europe someplace, and he decided to stay there when he got patched up. He had plenty of money put away in a dozen different banks, and nobody was looking for him; being crippled up, he was glad to get out.

Besides, this detective was supposed to be dead and he was wanted for killing him if he ever showed up. So it was a good idea to retire. After that he just moved around from place to place all over Europe. Once he thought he'd go back home, but the funniest thing happened, to hear him tell it—the man he was supposed to have killed wasn't dead after all, but still alive. And if he went back it would start all over again.

So he stayed dead, as far as anyone knew. I guess he came over to this country from where he lived in Germany, when the Nazis got started there.

"It's a strange experience, being dead for so many years," he said. "But I see I'm boring you, Miss Hawes . . ."

That's when I knew I must have dozed off. I apologized all over the place, but he just chuckled. Didn't bother him a bit.

No, that's not all. Wait a minute, there's one thing more I want to tell you about. That's this crazy business about the asteroid. You know what an asteroid is? Neither do I. Some kind of a planet, I guess—only he wasn't even talking about a real one, but just a fake one. Called it a man-made sat-something. Oh yes, a satellite, that was it. A man-made satellite.

It was the newspaper that started him off. Remember, last week, when they ran this story about how at last the government is going to build a space-platform for launching rockets to the moon? Did you *ever* hear anything so crazy in all your life? But I guess they're going to do it.

Well, I was reading him this story—he was pretty weak, you know, and Doctor Cooper said it wouldn't be long—and I was just reading along, when all at once I noticed he was sitting up. He hadn't sat up for nearly a week, and he wasn't eating very much or anything any more, but here he was, sitting up straight. And he said, "Would you mind reading that over again, Miss Hawes? Slowly, please?" He was always very polite like that, I will say that for him.

So I read it over, and he began to chuckle again, and he got the funniest look on his face. It wasn't exactly a smile, but you know, like that. His cheeks were all sunk in the way they get before the end, but for a minute I'd swear he looked positively young again.

"I knew it!" he said. "I knew they'd do it! That's the news I've been waiting for."

Then he began to talk a blue streak. I said, "Please, you know Doctor Cooper said you mustn't exert yourself. You must rest."

And he said, "I'll have a long time for resting now. And in peace, I trust." And he kept right on talking.

Now I don't know how much of this he was making up, because it sounds so utterly ridiculous, but of course he *did* send those letters out and he'd get answers, too. They all knew him, all these scientists.

But the way he told it, after the time he fell and nearly died, he decided to reform. He wanted to do something for the world, I guess, and he got to studying his mathematics again. He said he'd written this book with the crazy title—I remember that part all right—it was called *The Dynamics of an Asteroid*. And it was about these space-platforms.

"Yes, that's right, Miss Hawes," he told me. "Over sixty years ago. No wonder nobody took it seriously; I was ahead of my time. And I spent years of pioneering work, simply trying to get a hearing from the proper authorities in the field. Bit by bit, I managed."

The point is, I guess he kept working out these theories of his and writing to scientists and feeding them ideas, like this Einstein and a whole lot of others. He didn't want any credit, just so long as they would work on his notions. And after a long time, they did. He said he had this idea for building a space-platform or an artificial whatchamacallit all these years, and he pounded away and pounded away and even sent diagrams.

In Germany he made experimental models or whatever they do and donated them to universities and the government—but he never let them use his name. All he wanted was to do some good for humanity.

"It was the least I could do to atone, Miss Hawes," he said. "I wanted, in my small way, to help man reach the stars. And now, I see, the work has borne fruit. What more reward could I ask?"

Of course I knew enough to humor him, it was the least I could do for the poor old fella, the way he was. So I told him how wonderful I thought it was and how he ought to be getting *his* name in the newspapers, too, along with these other big-shot scientists.

"That can never be," he said. "And it no longer matters. My name will live only as a symbol of infamy." Whatever *that* is.

Well, I don't know how we ended up, but it was the same night, quite late, that the crisis came. I'd been sleeping on the sofa in the other room when I heard him sort of gasping and I went into the bedroom quick and took one look and then called Doctor Cooper.

By the time he got there, though, it was all over. It wasn't what you call a painful death. He just got delirious and then went right off with just a short coma. Heart gave out, Doctor Cooper said.

But for a few minutes, there, while he was delirious, he came out with some of the most awful stuff. It was as if he was another person—probably the way he'd been when he was a criminal back in the 'nineties or whenever, if he'd told me the truth.

He kept cursing away at somebody or other; this detective fella, I guess. He wasn't so much mad at the fella as he was jealous because the detective was famous and he wasn't. You see, like I told you before, he was supposed to have killed him only he revived and got away. And now the poor old guy acted as though he was right there in the room—and did he swear!

Then he started to wrestle with him; you know how it is when they go out of their head. Only I figured it out that he thought he was back fighting with him at the time when he was left for dead.

They were fighting on some cliff, and there was a waterfall or something—this was in Germany or the Alps or around there, I guess—and this detective was using jiu-jitsu and he threw the old guy off into the water and he hit his head and bounced and swam away. But the detective didn't notice because he was climbing up the cliff himself in order not to leave any footprints, so people would think he was dead. Oh, it doesn't make any sense, but that's the way it came out.

Then, just before the coma, he was sitting up in bed after all this wrestling around, and I was trying to hold him down. But he didn't even know I was in the room, you see—he just saw the detective.

And he said, "Keep your glory! Keep your cheap notoriety, and your fame! I'll die unhonoured, unmourned and unsung, but in the end I triumph. My deeds will bring men to the stars! One thing you must admit—there's nothing elementary about *my* deductions!"

Real crazy stuff, I tell you!

And then he went off into the coma and died. Just like that. But can you imagine, such a mixed-up business?

I wonder how much of it was really true? I mean, about him being a master-criminal and reforming and then helping scientists invent these space-platforms. I never heard of that book, *The Dynamics of an Asteroid,* or whatever.

Maybe I'll look it up sometime. I wish I knew the name of that detective he hated so much; that would help.

But I've got *his* name, anyway. Irish. Moriarity, I think it was—Professor Moriarity.

What better way to close The Game Is Afoot *than with a gracious vignette by the man who to millions of Americans was, is and always will be Sherlock Holmes?* B A S I L R A T H B O N E *(1892–1967), son of a South African mining engineer, portrayed Holmes in fourteen films and hundreds of times on radio. His many other excellent screen perform-ances include Tybalt in* Romeo and Juliet, *Mr. Murdstone in* David Copperfield, *Greta Garbo's husband in* Anna Karenina *and a splendid assortment of sometimes seri-ous, sometimes comic swashbuckling "heavies" in films like* The Adventures of Robin Hood, Captain Blood *and Danny Kaye's* The Court Jester. *Rathbone, who often starred on Broadway, returned to New York in 1953 to reprise Sherlock Holmes in a short-lived play by his wife, Ouida (see Appendix II). "Daydream," which first appeared in* The Baker Street Journal *(October 1947), is ostensibly told by a Scotland Yard Inspector, but to me it is a Pirandellian meeting between Sherlock and Holmes, as the author slyly suggests when the narrator seems to hear "my own voice as if it had been someone else's."*

"Daydream"

B A S I L   R A T H B O N E

I had always loved the county of Sussex. It held for me some of the happiest memories of my life—my early childhood. Early in June I had slipped down, for a few days' much-needed rest to the little village of Heathfield, to dream again of the past and to try and shut out, for a brief period at least, both the present and the future.

A soft spring had ushered in a temperate summer. I walked a great deal, reread Galsworthy's *Forsyte Saga,* and slept with merciful regularity and con-tentment.

The last afternoon of my holiday I was walking back across the gentle countryside to my lodgings in Heathfield, when I was rudely stung by a bee. Startled, I grabbed a handful of soft earth and applied it to the sting; an old fashioned remedy I had learned as a child. Suddenly I became aware that the air about me was swarming with bees. I stood motionless and waited.

It was then that I noticed the small house with a thatched roof and a well-kept garden, with beehives at one end, that Mrs. Messenger, my land-lady, had so often mentioned. Mrs. Messenger was large, comfortable and ageless. She rented me a room "with board." She also loved to chat, which she did with a ceaseless rhythm reminiscent of a light sea breaking on a sandy beach. It was not unpleasant so long as one made no effort to retaliate.

Apparently "he" had come to live in the thatched cottage many years ago. At first his visits were infrequent. But, as time passed, he came more often and stayed longer. He called the place his bee farm. As he bothered no one, no one bothered him, which is both an old English custom and a good one. Now, in 1946, he had become almost a legend. He had been "some-one" once, and Mrs. Messenger's father was sure he came from London and was either a doctor or a lawyer or both.

I saw him now, on this late Summer afternoon, seated in his garden, a rug over his knees; reading a book. In spite of his great age he wore no reading glasses; and though he made no movement there was a curious sense of animation in his apparently inanimate body. He had the majestic beauty of a very old tree: his features were sharp, emphasizing a particularly prominent nose. The veins in his hands ran clear blue, like swollen mountain streams, and the transparency of his skin had a shell-like quality.

He was smoking a meerschaum pipe with obvious relish. Suddenly he looked up and our eyes met. It embarrassed me to have been caught staring at him.

"Won't you come in?" he called in a surprisingly firm voice.

"Thank you, sir," I replied, "but I have no right to impose on your privacy."

"If it were an imposition I should not have invited you," he replied.

As I opened the little white wicker gate and went in, I felt his eyes searching me.

"Pull up a chair and sit down."

He gave me another quick glance of penetrating comprehension. As I reached for the chair and sat down I had an odd feeling that I was dreaming.

"I'm sorry to see that you have been stung by one of my bees."

Self-consciously I wiped the patch of dirt from my face and smiled: the smile was intended to say that it didn't matter.

"You must forgive the little fellow," he continued; "he's paid for it with his life."

"It seems unfair that he should have had to," I said, hearing my own voice as if it had been some one else's.

"No," mused the old man, "it's a law of nature. 'God moves in a mysterious way His wonders to perform.' "

A thrush began to sing in a hedge near by. The incident—for an inci-dent it had become—was strangely tempered with magic. I felt excited.

"May I order you some tea?"

"Thank you, no," I declined.

"I used to be a prolific coffee drinker myself. I have always found tea an insipid substitute by comparison."

A faint smile hovered about the corners of his mouth.

"Do you live here?" he continued.

"No, sir, I'm on a short holiday."

"Do you come here often?"

"As often as I can. I love Sussex. I was born near here."

"Really!" This time the smile reached up and touched his eyes. "It's a comforting little corner of the earth, isn't it, especially in times like these?"

"Have you lived here all through the war, sir?" I asked.

"Yes." The smile disappeared. Slowly he pulled an old Webley revolver from under the rug which covered his knees. "If 'they' had come, six of them would not have lived to tell the story . . . I learned to use this thing many years ago. I have never missed my man."

He cradled the gun in his hand, and left me momentarily for that world which to each of us is his own; that little world in which we are born and in which we die, alone. He replaced the gun on his knees and looked at me. There was quite a pause before I had the courage to ask, "Were you in the first World War, sir?"

"Indirectly—and you?"

"I'm an Inspector at Scotland Yard."

"I thought so!" Once again he looked at me with penetrating comprehension and smiled.

At that moment the book in his lap fell to the ground. I reached down, picked it up, and handed it back to him.

"Thank you." He made a sound that closely resembled a chuckle. "And how are things at the Yard these days?"

"Modern science and equipment have done much to help us," I said.

"Yessss." His hand went to a pocket and brought forth an old magnifying glass. "When I was a young man they used things like this. Modern inventions have proved to be great time savers, but they have dulled our natural instincts and made us lazy, most of us at least—press a button here, or pull a lever there, and it all happens, hey presto!" He looked annoyed and a little tired.

"You may be right, sir. But there's no middle course; we either go forward or back."

He put the magnifying glass and revolver back into two voluminous pockets of an old sports jacket, with leather patches at the elbows. Then he took a deep breath and released it in a long-drawn-out sigh.

"I've followed your career very closely, Inspector. The Yard is fortunate in your services."

"That's kind of you, sir."

"Not at all . . . you see, I knew your father quite well at one time."

"You knew my father!" The words stumbled out.

"Yesss. He was a brilliant man, your father. He interested me deeply. His mind was balanced precariously on that thin line between sanity and insanity. Is he still living?"

"No, sir; he died in 1936."

The old man nodded his head reflectively. "These fellows with their newfangled ideas would have found him intensely interesting subject matter. What do you call them? psycho . . . psychoanalysts!"

"Psychoanalysis can be very helpful if used intelligently, don't you think, sir?"

"No, I don't," he snapped back. "It's a lot of rubbish—PSYCHO-ANALYSIS!" He spat out the word contemptuously. "It's nothing more than a simple process of deduction by elimination."

We talked of crime and its different ways of detection, both past and present; its motives, and society's responsibility for conditions that foster the criminal, until a cool breeze crossed the garden with its silent warning of the day's departure.

He rose slowly to a full six feet and held out his hand. "I must go in now. It's been pleasant talking with you."

"I am deeply indebted to you, sir." I wanted to say so much more, but felt oddly constrained. He held out the book in his hand.

"Do you know these stories?"

I glanced at the title: *The Adventures of Sherlock Holmes.*

"They are often overdramatized; but they make good reading." Once again the smile crept up from the corners of his mouth, and this time danced in his eyes.

I acknowledged an intimate acquaintance with all the works to which he referred, and he seemed greatly pleased by my references to "The Master." He accompanied me slowly to the little white wicker gate and, on the way, we spoke briefly of S. C. Roberts, and Christopher Morley and Vincent Starrett.

"The adventures as written by our dear friend Dr. Watson mean a great deal to me at my time of life," he reflected, retaining my hand and shaking it slowly like a pump handle. "As someone once said, 'Remembrance is the only sure immortality we can know.'"

On my return, Mrs. Messenger greeted me with a cup of tea and an urgent telegram from Scotland Yard, requesting my immediate return. I didn't speak to her of my visit to "him." I was afraid she might consider me as childish as the youngsters in Heathfield who still believed "he" was the great Sherlock Holmes.

Which they did, until they reached an age when he was dismissed, together with Santa Claus, Tinkerbell, and all other worthwhile people who, for a brief and beautiful period, are more real than reality itself.

Appendix I
Miscellaneous Notes

THE ADVENTURE OF THE TWO COLLABORATORS (PP. 41–43)

Richard D'Oyly Carte, one of London's shrewdest theatrical producers, teamed up James Barrie and Arthur Conan Doyle to write *Jane Annie; or, The Good Conduct Prize,* "A new and original English Comic Opera" with music by Ernest Ford. The show opened at the Savoy Theatre on May 13, 1893, and ran approximately two months. It was one of the worst failures in the history of the D'Oyly Carte Opera Company.

Ever a champion of literary underdogs, I used to think that *Jane Annie* could not be all that bad. Barrie was, after all, one of England's finest dramatists, and Doyle was no theatrical novice, either. But I eventually succeeded in tracking down and purchasing a rare copy of the libretto and regret to report that *Jane Annie* richly deserved its fate. Except for a few moments that feebly echo Gilbert and Sullivan, it is unbearably cloying. Here, for instance, is part of a song that Bab, "a bad girl," sings early in the first act:

> Bright-eyed Bab I used to be,
>   Now these eyes are lead;
> Languor has come over me,
>   Hangs my little head.
> Now my figure—once like this—
>   Droops like autumn berry;
> Pity me, my secret is,
>   Me is sleepy very!

THE MYSTERY OF PINKHAM'S DIAMOND STUD (PP. 44–49)

The first parody of Sherlock Holmes by John Kendrick Bangs occurs in *The Pursuit of the Houseboat* (Harper and Brothers, New York, 1897). An earlier book, *A Houseboat on the Styx,* chronicles the adventures in Hades of a company of "Associated Shades" that includes Boswell and Sam Johnson, Caesar and Napoleon, Confucius and Solomon, Noah, Nero, Walter Raleigh, Socrates, Shakespeare and others. At the end of the story, the houseboat is hijacked, but in the sequential "Pursuit" the humorist—unaware that Sherlock Holmes didn't really die at Reichenbach Falls—brings the allegedly deceased sleuth to Hades to solve the mystery.

"The Mystery of Pinkham's Diamond Stud," included in this collection, is the tenth chapter of *The Dreamers: A Club,* one of two Bangs books published in 1899 by Harper. The other, *The Enchanted Typewriter,* also features Holmes in the ninth chapter.

Seven years later in 1906, Bangs cross-pollinated Sherlock with Raffles, the popular gentleman thief whose exploits were chronicled by E. W. Hornung (Arthur Conan Doyle's brother-in-law!), and produced *R. Holmes & Co.,* the escapades of Raffles Holmes, supposedly Sherlock's son and the grandson of Raffles.

Holmes's final appearance in a Bangs book is "A Pragmatic Enigma," the fourth story in *Potted Fiction* (Doubleday, Page, New York, 1908), but the humorist also wrote "Shylock Homes: His Posthumous Memoirs," a syndicated series of ten episodes printed in American newspapers in 1903.

THE ENCHANTED GARDEN (PP. 123–44)

Henry FitzGerald Heard wrote three Mr. Mycroft novels, *A Taste for Honey, Reply Paid,* which begins with a code that the author solves "un-Conanically" via spirit medium,★ and *The Notched Hairpin,* as well as two short stories, "Mr. Montalba, Obsequist" and "The Enchanted Garden" (in this volume), published, respectively, in the September 1945 and March 1949 issues of *Ellery Queen's Mystery Magazine.*

SHERLOCK HOLMES AND THE DROOD MYSTERY (PP. 155–62)

Andrew Lang's "At the Sign of the Ship" predates Edmund Pearson's Drood solution by eight years, having appeared in the September 1905 issue of *Longman's Magazine.* In the December 1924 *Munsey's Magazine,* Harry B. Smith wrote one of the longer analyses, "Sherlock Holmes Solves the Mystery of Edwin Drood." There are at least five other attempts: "Sherlock Holmes and the Edwin Drood Mystery" by Nathan L. Bengis (*The Baker Street Journal,* January 1955); the 1964 Danish study, *Sherlock Holmes løser Edwin Drood Gaaden* by Henry Lauritzen; "The Master Would Easily Have Solved *The Mystery of Edwin Drood"* by Colin Prestige (*Sherlock Holmes Journal,* Winter 1968); the same author's "Sherlock Holmes and Edwin Drood" (*The Baker*

★Though Arthur Conan Doyle was a spiritualist who devoted his last Professor Challenger novel to the study of occultism, his artistic judgment wisely steered him away from introducing supernatural events into the Sherlock Holmes tales, except as "red herrings."

Street Journal, September 1968) and *The Disappearance of Edwin Drood* by Peter Rowland (Constable & Company Ltd., Great Britain, 1991).

Pearson's assay is a good Holmes pastiche, though it fails to unriddle the Drood case, yet not so disastrously as Rowland's novel. Though Rowland is a "Boz" scholar, his "solution" ignores the vital Edwin Drood plot clues that Charles Dickens communicated to business associates and relatives, and ends his story with a supernatural episode wholly incompatible to the character of Sherlock Holmes.*

The ultimate solution to *The Mystery of Edwin Drood* has yet to be published. To date, the most accurate I have seen (not involving Sherlock Holmes) is Charles Forsyte's *The Decoding of Edwin Drood* (Charles Scribners Sons, New York, 1980).

Our American Cousins (pp. 388–402)

Roberta Rogow based her pastiche upon a number of historical facts, described by the author as follows:

"1. Franklin and Eleanor Roosevelt were married on March 17, 1905, so Uncle Ted could give away the bride, then march in the St. Patrick's Day Parade. Franklin then finished law school and Eleanor lived in an apartment hotel. They took their belated honeymoon in June. Their first stop was London, where they spent five days. They stayed at Brown's Hotel and were given the royal suite, to Eleanor's dismay—it was far more than their budget allowed. From there they went to Paris, Venice and Switzerland.

"2. Theodore Roosevelt spent the summer of 1905 cajoling Russian and Japanese representatives into a peace treaty, which ended the Russo-Japanese War. The treaty was signed at Portsmouth, New Hampshire, in August—but 'Aunt Edith's' qualms might have applied to other visiting dignitaries as well as to ambassadors. For his efforts in working out the peace treaty, Theodore Roosevelt was awarded the Nobel Peace Prize.

"3. Theodore Roosevelt visited Panama in 1906, but considered the trip as early as 1905, when the digging commenced in earnest.

"4. In 1912, during his third-party run for the presidency, Theodore Roosevelt *was* the target of an attempted assassination. The bullet was deflected by the bulky text of a speech he had in his coat.

---

*At the Cloisterham churchyard, Holmes confronts a ghostly double that he later explains he anticipated might show up. A similar "haunt" materializes in Darrell Schweitzer's "The Adventure of the Death-Fetch," elsewhere in this volume, but in that tale, Holmes, ever the rationalist, behaves *in character*. (See preceding note.)

"5. Concerning Alice Roosevelt (later Longworth) and her scandalous behavior, Theodore Roosevelt once said, "I can run the country or control
Alice, I cannot do both!""

"6. As for Franklin and Eleanor, in spite of a devastating bout of polio that
left his legs permanently disabled, he went on to a distinguished career
that culminated in twelve years (1932–1945) as President of the United
States, while Eleanor continued to champion liberal causes, both before
and after Franklin's death, serving as United States Representative to the
United Nations . . . thus proving that Sherlock Holmes was not *always*
right.""

An interesting sidelight: Franklin Roosevelt was an honorary member
of the Baker Street Irregulars. From 1942 to 1945, he exchanged several
letters about Sherlock Holmes with Irregulars Christopher Morley, Edgar W.
Smith and Belden Wigglesworth.

Sherlock Holmes in Oz (pp. 431–40)

Those whose knowledge of Oz is limited to the 1939 Metro-Goldwyn-
Mayer film will not be acquainted with Princess Ozma, rightful ruler of the
territories of the Gillikins, Munchkins, Quadlings and Winkies which, taken
with the Emerald City, comprise the land of Oz. Attended by her faithful
friend Jellia Jamb, Ozma holds a court that includes several members of royalty (not all of them human), but the best known—and loved—is surely Princess Dorothy, who very sensibly gave up Kansas for a (noplacelike) home
with her Uncle Henry and Aunt Em in Oz. The Wizard also eventually
returned and, with the help of Glinda, the Good Witch of the South *(yes!)*, at
last learned how to work real magic.

There is a great deal of magical equipment in Ozma's royal palace. The
magic picture is a super–TV screen that can show what anyone is doing
anytime and anywhere (shades of Big Brother?), while Ozma's magic belt is a
powerful sorcerous tool capable of changing people and things into whatever
the wearer wishes.

The magic belt once belonged to Ruggedo, peppery king of the gob-
lin-like Nomes. Replaced on the throne by his former servant, Kaliko, the
exiled Ruggedo repeatedly tried to conquer Oz and was ultimately transformed into a flower pot.

The Dilemma of the Distressed Savoyard (pp. 449–60)

This sprightly story appeared in the October 1946 issue of *The Baker Street
Journal,* which accurately states that the tale links Holmes's "Abernetty case"

with the plot of Gilbert and Sullivan's spoof of theatrical "mellerdrammer," *Ruddigore*. But a footnote in the BSJ claims that "in the biography *Sir Arthur Sullivan His Life, Letters and Diaries,* by Herbert Sullivan and Newman Flower, two paragraphs, on pages 203 and 204, . . . bear significantly upon Doctor Watson's account of how this highly pleasing plot came to be conceived."

This is misleading and incorrect. In both the original and revised editions of Sullivan-Flower, page 203 discusses the infamous "carpet quarrel"; page 204 is devoted to Sullivan's opera, *Ivanhoe.* The "official" biography *W. S. Gilbert His Life and Letters* by Sidney Dark and Rowland Grey states that *Ruddigore* was derived from *Ages Ago,* a sketch written years earlier for London producer Thomas German Reed.

Ages Ago is important for another reason. At one of its rehearsals in November, 1869, William S. Gilbert was first introduced to Arthur Sullivan, a meeting that was certainly noted by the producer. Two years later, German Reed commissioned them to write *Thespis,* the first of their fourteen collaborative operettas.

THE DYNAMICS OF AN ASTEROID (PP. 488–93)

Robert Bloch's story stems from a passage in "The Final Problem" in which Sherlock Holmes describes Moriarty as "a man of good birth and excellent education, endowed by Nature with a phenomenal mathematical faculty. At the age of twenty-one he wrote a treatise upon the Binomial Theorem, which has had a European vogue. On the strength of it, he won the Mathematical Chair at one of our smaller universities, and had, to all appearance, a most brilliant career before him. But the man had hereditary tendencies of the most diabolical kind."

The title is derived from *The Valley of Fear.* Speaking to Watson about Moriarty's mathematical abilities, Holmes says, "Is he not the celebrated author of *The Dynamics of an Asteroid*—a book which ascends to such rarefied heights of pure mathematics that it is said there was no man in the scientific press capable of criticizing it?"

During the summer of 1993, the American Astronomical Society claimed that detailed literary analysis proved that Moriarty was based on Simon Newcomb, a Nineteenth-Century American astronomer who wrote about asteroid dynamics, the binomial theorem and, like his fictional counterpart, was thoroughly conversant with "the obliquity of the ecliptic." Newcomb also predicted that nothing heavier than air could ever fly, which, according to Bloch, is where Moriarty outdid him.

Appendix II
Holmesiography

It has been claimed that Sherlock Holmes is the most popular fictional character ever created. I'm not sure this is true; Dracula, Scrooge and—well—Mickey Mouse spring to mind, while in terms of impact on Western thought and literature, I suspect one must also include Don Juan, Don Quixote, Faust, Hamlet and Zarathustra (and how about an honorable mention and a bottle of sack for Falstaff?).

But it is probably no exaggeration to state that more has been written about Sherlock Holmes than any other imaginary person. *The World Bibliography of Sherlock Holmes and Dr. Watson* (see below) lists 6,221 items, and that tally is far from complete.

The following catalog consists of a checklist of books, films and related material that I think worth examining. When I have reservations, as I do about some items, please understand they are my wholly idiosyncratic personal opinions.*

PARODIES

The Case of the Baker Street Irregulars by Anthony Boucher is an amusing novel about the murder of a writer whose frequent badmouthing of Sherlock Holmes prompts prominent members of the Baker Street Irregulars club to protest when a film studio hires him to write the screenplay of "The Adventure of the Speckled Band." The puzzling plot includes several Canonical pastiches, as well as a splendid tip concerning the preparation of fondue. (Chapter 19)

---

*Therefore, the popular BBC-TV series is not included. I regard Jeremy Brett's interpretation of Sherlock Holmes as an outrage and an abomination.

★ ★ ★

Copper Beeches by Arthur H. Lewis tells what happens when the Philadelphia branch of the Baker Street Irregulars gets caught up in a quarrel that escalates into murder. The story begins deceptively straight-faced but, little by little, turns into a broadfooted spoof of literary aficionados in general and Holmesians in particular, with telling sideswipes at Philly's social pretensions.

The Incredible Shlock Holmes and *The Memoirs of Shlock Holmes* by Robert L. Fish are two generous collections of clever Sherlock Holmes parodies.

The Misadventures of Sherlock Holmes, edited by Ellery Queen, is a long out-of-print selection of thirty-four Holmes parodies (nine of which appear in *The Game Is Afoot*). There is an encouraging rumor that a specialty publisher may soon reissue this book.

The Private Life of Sherlock Holmes (no relationship to the Vincent Starrett item below) by Michael and Mollie Hardwick is a novelization of the Billy Wilder film of the same name. At the time of its release, critics and Holmesians decried the movie for implying that Holmes and Watson had a homosexual relationship, but in the novel, this amusing episode is inoffensive, and perfectly motivated. After this comparatively brief sequence comes a longer, exciting quasi-science-fictional adventure involving Mycroft Holmes and . . . the Loch Ness monster! (I tried watching the film itself recently on TV, but two gaffes in the first few minutes irritated me enough to switch it off. First, the exterior of Mrs. Hudson's apartment building displays the address as 221*B,* an error so common [see Introduction] that I might have tolerated it, had it not come so soon after the opening scene in which a pair of hands removes Dr. Watson's journal from the bank safety deposit box it is traditionally stored in. Someone then blows the dust off . . . but if it was being kept in a safety deposit box, *where in tarnation did the dust come from?*)

Sherlock Jr. is a wonderful and cinematically seminal featurette in which, according to film critic Leonard Maltin, its director and star Buster Keaton "reached his technical and artistic pinnacle" in "five reels of unadulterated joy which has undoubtedly influenced countless filmmakers . . ." Its Holmesian connection is chiefly titular, but why quibble?

★ ★ ★

The Snarkout Boys and the Avocado of Death by Daniel Pinkwater is a preposterously funny mystery (sort of)/science-fantasy (I guess) novel about the Snarkout Boys (one of whom is a girl) and their wild adventures battling the villainous Wallace Nussbaum with the aid of one Osgood Sigerson and Ormond Sacker (and if you don't know who they are, ask any Holmesian). The adventure continues in an even more outrageous sequel, *The Snarkout Boys and the Baconburg Horror,* a werewolf tale (sort of, but not really).

They Might Be Giants by James Goldman is a treasure of a film starring George C. Scott as a New York lawyer who thinks he is Sherlock Holmes, and Joanne Woodward as a psychiatrist who just happens to be named Dr. Watson. The amusing, romantic plot grows steadily more surrealistic, culminating in a dark and deeply moving final confrontation with "Professor Moriarty." (Book collectors, note: though extremely difficult to find, the screenplay *was* published in paperback.)

Without a Clue is a slight, but pleasant film comedy which dares to suggest that Sherlock Holmes was the wholly fictional creation of Dr. Watson, whose success as sole author of the tales forces him to hire an actor to "become" Holmes. The wacky consequences are expertly performed by Michael Caine as Holmes and Ben Kingsley as Watson.

Pastiches

Though this section consists of new Sherlock Holmes adventures and free adaptations, I would feel remiss if I did not mention two superior film adaptations of *The Hound of the Baskervilles:* the 1939 American version starring Basil Rathbone and Nigel Bruce and the 1959 British "Hound." Though both unfortunately end disappointingly (how can filmmakers ignore Conan Doyle's harrowing and highly visual climax in which the titular hound bounds out of the fog with its eyes and hackles aglow with hellish light?), the UK version boasts an excellent Holmes and Watson, Peter Cushing and Andre Morrell, respectively, and the Hollywood version is remarkably faithful to the book. Thus, on his initial appearance, Nigel Bruce's Dr. Watson is as competent and resourceful as the Conan Doyle original.

A Study in Terror by Ellery Queen is the best of several novels to pit Sherlock Holmes against Jack the Ripper. Detective Ellery Queen discovers an unpublished manuscript of Watson's that tells about Holmes investigating and allegedly failing to solve the infamous Whitechapel murders, but in a brilliant finale, Ellery not only vindicates Sherlock Holmes, but also solves the case himself.

A Study in Terror, the 1965 British film starring John Neville and Donald Houston as Holmes and Watson, is a good cinematic version of the Ellery Queen novel noted above, though it unfortunately dispenses with the book's clever story-within-a-story plot.

A Taste for Honey by H. F. Heard introduces an elderly beekeeper felicitously named Mr. Mycroft, who solves an obvious, yet deliciously grisly murder mystery with the aid of Sydney Silchester, perhaps the most irritating amanuensis in all detective fiction. Silchester's wholly intentional obtuseness paves the way for a memorable finale in which Mr. Mycroft at last reveals his true identity.

Baker Street, a Broadway musical with book by Jerome Coopersmith and music and lyrics by Marian Grudeff and Raymond Jessel, was described by one critic as a mélange "with a gay disregard for characters, places and time," but in spite of saddling Sherlock Holmes with a completely unconvincing passion for Irene Adler, the recorded performance has many entertaining moments, most of them attributable to the "Rathbonean" crispness of Fritz Weaver's Holmes.

The Exploits of Sherlock Holmes is a collection of twelve short stories by an American master of mystery construction, John Dickson Carr, in collaboration with Adrian Conan Doyle (Arthur's son). The series is uneven, possibly because Carr fell ill and had no hand in writing half the tales. Still, the characters of Holmes and Watson have an authentic "feel" and a few stories are as good as some of the original adventures. One, "The Adventure of the Black Baronet," was televised in May, 1953, starring Basil Rathbone. Watson was ably played by Martyn Green, newly arrived in America after a long career as London's leading interpreter of Gilbert and Sullivan comedy leads.*

---

*Nigel Bruce was still alive, but reportedly too ill to reprise the role of Watson. He died in October, 1953, two days before Rathbone opened (and quickly closed) on Broadway in his wife's script, *Sherlock Holmes.*

★ ★ ★

The Final Adventures of Sherlock Holmes, "collected by" Peter Haining, is an assortment of apocrypha, incunabula and nonfictional sidelights and insights that, despite its cynically misleading title, will appeal to Holmesian scholars and completists.

The Incredible Umbrella is a trio of humorous science-fantasy tales that I wrote in the late 1970s; the second and third novellas are Sherlock Holmes pastiches. The middle adventure, which was first runner-up in the 1978 British Fantasy Awards, is based on the same Watsonian "tale-not-yet-told" as one of *The Exploits of Sherlock Holmes* cited above . . . which makes for an amusing Holmesian dilemma, since both versions were authorized by the Conan Doyle Estate.

Murder by Decree is an interesting, but ultimately unsatisfying 1979 Canadian-British motion picture. As in *A Study in Terror* (a superior film cited above), Sherlock Holmes tracks down Jack the Ripper, only to be thwarted by a high-level governmental cover-up. The film boasts a fine cast, though the usually excellent Christopher Plummer wears too much heart on his sleeve to make for a convincing Sherlock Holmes. James Mason, however, is the definitive Watson: a John Bullish old campaigner superficially reminiscent of Nigel Bruce, but fitter in mind and body. His argument with Holmes concerning the proper ingestion of peas is not to be missed!

The New Adventures of Sherlock Holmes by Anthony Boucher and Denis Green is a charming series of recordings of the 1940s radio broadcasts starring Basil Rathbone and Nigel Bruce. As narrator, Watson is smarter on radio than in the movies, which must have pleased Bruce, who disliked turning Doyle's personable doctor into a dimwit.

The Painful Predicament of Sherlock Holmes is a one-act play by William Gillette, the first actor Arthur Conan Doyle sanctioned to portray Holmes. Gillette devoted much of his career to playing the detective in his own four-act melodrama, *Sherlock Holmes,* revived some years ago on Broadway in a production that featured Alan Sues, of Rowan and Martin's "Laugh-In," as Moriarty. Later produced on cable TV with Frank Langella as a surprisingly effective Sherlock Holmes, the full-length play is claptrap that culminates in a sticky romantic entanglement for Holmes, and not even with Irene Adler.

On the other hand, "The Painful Predicament," which my readers theatre ensemble, The Open Book, recently produced in New York, is a comical, but plausible Holmesian adventure that still "plays" well.

*S*herlock Holmes is an unpublished play written for Basil Rathbone by his wife, Ouida. It opened on Broadway on October 10, 1953, just two days after the death of Nigel Bruce. Though New York critics were not kind to it, its producer, Bill Doll, loaned me his copy of the script, and I found it considerably superior to William Gillette's *Sherlock Holmes* (see above). As I write this, I am eagerly awaiting a copy in the mail from Peter Blau, a prominent Washington, D. C., Holmesian scholar, in hopes that I might anthologize it in a future collection.

*T*he Science-Fictional Sherlock Holmes, privately printed in 1960, is a slim volume of eight stories, most of them well-written, all conceptually fascinating. The authors include Poul Anderson, August Derleth, Gordon R. Dickson, John J. McGuire, H. Beam Piper, Mack Reynolds and my personal favorite, Anthony Boucher, who not only contributed two short stories, but also wrote the book's introduction.

*S*herlock Holmes Through Time and Space, is a larger, more accessible anthology on similar lines to *The Science-Fictional Sherlock Holmes,* noted above. Edited by Isaac Asimov, Martin Harry Greenberg and Charles Waugh, it contains fifteen stories, one of them by Isaac Asimov, who also wrote the introduction. The first tale is authentic Sherlock Holmes, Conan Doyle's "The Adventure of the Devil's Foot," a borderline science-fantasy tale which might have influenced Leo Perutz's 1930 masterpiece, *The Master of the Day of Judgment.*

*T*he Ordeal of Beryl Stapleton, "An Excerpt from the Papers of John H. Watson, M. D., Edited by J. C. Charles," is a bizarre bit of Holmesian bondage (!). In this "excised passage" from *The Hound of the Baskervilles,* Beryl Stapleton, who has been found lashed to a post in Merripit House, is revealed to have been stripped and whipped by the villain. Sending Holmes out, Watson violates patient confidentiality by describing her wounds and how he treats them. Pallid as bondage, this brief manuscript is a well-done, but pointless pastiche.

★　★　★

The Scarlet Claw (1944) is one of the best of the fourteen Sherlock Holmes films starring Basil Rathbone and Nigel Bruce. Holmes buffs who dislike some of the later films because they were "modernized" ought to take another look; time has transmuted the World War II adventures into period pieces. I am particularly fond of *Sherlock Holmes and the Secret Weapon* (1942) because of its brief foray into horror as Moriarty tries to murder Holmes by slowly draining the blood from his body. The moving final scene from *Sherlock Holmes and the Voice of Terror* (1942) is lifted straight from Conan Doyle's "His Last Bow," and *The House of Fear* (1945) deserves honorable mention because Dr. Watson actually solves the mystery before Holmes does!

The West End Horror by Nicholas Meyer is yet another Holmes vs. Jack the Ripper contest, but an entertaining one that features well-researched, convincingly realized "cameo" appearances by famous Victorians like Gilbert and Sullivan, Bram Stoker, etc. This was Meyer's second Holmes pastiche, following the popular, but flabby *The Seven Percent Solution*. (To my mind, Meyer's film adaption of his own book is far more satisfactory. The cinematic "Solution" is better constructed, has an excellent cast and a marvelously risqué song by Stephen Sondheim.) *The Canary Trainer,* Meyer's third Holmes adventure, was about to be released as *The Game Is Afoot* was going to press.

Young Sherlock Holmes is a 1985 film about Holmes and Watson as boys. Despite a disastrously ill-advised "Indiana Jones-ish" climax, this un-Canonical adventure has a great deal of charm and an especially satisfying final revelation *after the end credits are done.*

PONDERINGS

The Annotated Sherlock Holmes is William S. Baring-Gould's gigantic collection of all the Sherlock Holmes novels and short stories arranged in probable chronological order with a generous number of prefatory essays, as well as textual notes, bibliophilic data and illustrations. Clarkson Potter, who originally published it, told me Baring-Gould worked at least ten years on this massive, indispensable labor of love.

A Compendium of Canonical Weaponry, compiled by Bruce Dettman and Michael Bedford, is one of the best Holmesian "chapbooks" that Luther

Norris, of Culver City, California, published in a limited edition of only 300 copies.

The History of Sherlock Holmes in Stage, Films, T.V. & Radio Since 1899 is a sixty-six-page magazine published in 1975 by E-GO Enterprises Inc., of Sherman Oaks, California. This scarce item contains a generous assortment of photo-articles about theatrical Holmes manifestations, with the Rathbone-Bruce series given the lion's share of the space, but a few literary topics are included, as well, probably because Luther Norris (see above item) was one of the magazine's contributors.

In the Footsteps of Sherlock Holmes and The London of Sherlock Holmes by Michael Harrison are treasure troves of contemporaneous geographical and sociological detail that helps the reader follow Sherlock Holmes's footsteps, figuratively and literally.

The Life of Sir Arthur Conan Doyle by John Dickson Carr is the estate-authorized "official life" of the creator of Sherlock Holmes. In the words of the Holmesian scholar Vincent Starrett, it is "a superb performance; magnificent reading from first to last."

The Private Life of Sherlock Holmes (no relationship to the Michael and Mollie Hardwick novel above) is a cornerstone collection of essays by Vincent Starrett, one of the first important members of the Baker Street Irregulars society. Starrett also edited *221B*, published by Biblo and Tannen, an anthology of interesting articles by "various hands," including illustrator Frederic Dorr Steele.

Profile by Gaslight, edited by Edgar W. Smith, is a splendid volume of essays about Sherlock Holmes, Watson, "The Baker Street Scene" and the Baker Street Irregulars (the society, that is). Its table of contents is an impressive roster of literary figures, including (in part) Stephen Vincent Benet, Heywood Broun, Anthony Boucher, Carolyn Wells, Howard Haycraft, Christopher Morley, Fletcher Pratt, Dorothy Sayers, Vincent Starrett, Rex Stout (his wickedly funny essay, "Watson Was a Woman"), Louis Untermeyer and Alexander Woollcott.

★ ★ ★

The Sherlock Holmes Companion by Michael and Mollie Hardwick is a vital reference work consisting of essays, quotations, synopses of all 60 Holmes plots, plus a Who's Who of more than 200 major characters.

Sherlock Holmes, Rare-Book Collector by Madeleine B. Stern is a fine monograph, published in 1953 by the Bibliographical Society of America, that speculates on the contents of Holmes's personal library.

Sherlock Holmes in America is an endlessly fascinating compilation by Bill Blackbeard of Sherlockian advertisements, burlesques, comic strips, cartoons, illustrations and other ephemera and memorabilia drawn from American newspapers, periodicals and other sources.

Sherlock Holmes in Portrait and Profile boasts an historic assortment of Holmesian photos and art work, with excellent commentary by Walter Klinefelter and an introduction by Vincent Starrett.

Sherlock Holmes of Baker Street is William S. Baring-Gould's eminently readable biography of The Great Detective. Holmesian scholars have disagreed with various of Baring-Gould's conclusions, but most of this "official" life story has a ring of truth, though Rex Stout never verified (or denied) the rumor that Nero Wolfe, America's greatest private detective, is the offspring of Sherlock Holmes and . . . (who else?) Irene Adler!

The World Bibliography of Sherlock Holmes and Dr. Watson by Ronald Burt De Waal is an encyclopedic catalog of classified and annotated materials relating to every conceivable aspect of Sherlock Holmes and Dr. Watson: a must-have for every Baker Street enthusiast.

Farewell, Sherlock! Farewell, Watson, too.
First to last, you've been loyal and true.
   Of the human totality
   Who've lived in reality
There've been none quite as real as you.

—ISAAC ASIMOV